THE POSTAL SERVICE
GUIDE TO U.S. STAMPS

THE POSTAL SERVICE
GUIDE TO U.S. STAMPS

29th Edition
Updated Stamp Values

HarperResource
An Imprint of HarperCollins Publishers

HarperCollins books may be purchased for educational, business, or sales
promotional use. For information please write: Special Markets Department,
HarperCollins Publishers Inc., 10 East 53rd Street, New York, NY 10022.

Printed in the United States of America.

Library of Congress Cataloging-in-Publication Data has been applied for.

ISBN 0-06-095856-1

02 03 04 05 06 ❖/QWT 10 9 8 7 6 5 4 3 2 1

Table of Contents

COAST-TO-COAST COLLECTING

Seeing the Country Through Stamps

This year, the Greetings From America stamp pane shows just how fascinating stamp collecting can be. Did you know that it's the first pane of 50 stamps in 10 years? Or that the designs evoke retro "large-letter" postcards used to advertise cities, states, and tourist attractions? Stamp collectors know—because they keep an eye out not only for distinctive stamps but also for the diverse American landmarks that appear on them. Issuances such as Greetings From America suggest the richness of the American scene, with its many extraordinary icons, monuments, and natural wonders. You never know what will turn up on a stamp, and that's all part of the fun.

Stamp collecting can be a lifelong hobby. It's fun and educational for all ages, and it's easy to start without a big investment. Read on to find out how to start or build your very own collection.

What is philately?

The word *philately (fi-latt'-eh-lee)* means the study of stamps and other postal materials. Stamp collectors are sometimes called philatelists.

How do I start collecting stamps?

It's easy. You can start by simply saving stamps from letters, packages, and postcards. Ask your friends and family to save stamps from their mail.

Neighborhood businesses that get a lot of mail—banks, stores, travel agencies, and others—might save their envelopes for you, too.

Or, start your collection by choosing one or two favorite subjects. Then, collect stamps that fit your theme—art, history, sports, transportation, science, animals, and others—whatever you choose! This is called topical or thematic stamp collecting. See the stamps pictured in these feature articles for ideas to get you started on a space theme!

Will it cost me a lot to start a collection?

No! Start with used stamps and a few inexpensive accessories (such as a small album and a package of stamp hinges), and you can have a great time on a limited budget. Remember to put stamps, albums, and hinges on your birthday and holiday wish lists, too!

What kinds of stamps are there?

There are a number of different types of stamps. Their purposes can be described as commemorative, definitive, or special; their formats can be in sheets, booklets, or coils. And all of these now exist with conventional adhesive (the "lick-and-stick" gum) or self-adhesive (the "no-lick, peel-and-stick" type).

Definitive stamps (also called "regular issues") are the most common type of postage stamp. They feature everything from statesmen to animals and from the American flag to historic vehicles. They tend to be fairly small (generally less than an inch square), with denominations (the face value printed on the stamp) from one cent to many dollars. They are printed in large quantities, often more than once, and tend to be available for several years.

Commemorative stamps are usually larger and more colorful than definitives. They are printed in smaller quantities and typically are printed only once. They remain on sale for a limited period of time, generally about a year; many post offices carry them for only a few months. They are issued for specific rates, most often the prime letter rate. They honor, or commemorate, important people, events, or subjects, all of which reflect some aspect of American culture.

Special stamps supplement the regular issues and tend to be more commemorative in appearance (larger and more colorful), while meeting specific needs. They may be reprinted, but tend to remain on sale for only the life of the specific rate for which they are issued. These include Christmas and Love stamps, Holiday Celebration stamps, international rate stamps (previously known as airmail stamps), Priority Mail, and Express Mail stamps.

Sheet stamps are printed as large press sheets, then trimmed into smaller units called panes, most of which measure less than eight by ten inches. Panes generally contain twenty stamps, but may contain up to a hundred or as few as one stamp; smaller commemorative panes, with fewer than ten stamps, are often called souvenir sheets, depending on their purpose. Individual stamps tend to have perfs (perforations) or die-cut edges (generally with a wavy pattern) on all sides.

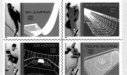

36 U.S.C. Sec. 220506. Official Licensed Product of the United States Olympic Committee.

Booklet stamps are designed to be folded into a convenient unit. Booklets generally contain twenty stamps and may contain separate panes of stamps in a small folder or may be issued in a flat unit designed to be folded into a booklet by the customer. Most individual booklet stamps have at least one straight edge (no perfs or die-cuts) and sometimes two adjacent straight edges.

Coil stamps are issued in rolls. Customers often buy them in rolls of a hundred stamps; business mailers can buy them in rolls of up to ten thousand stamps. Individual coil stamps usually have two straight edges on opposite sides.

How do I remove stamps from envelopes?

If you wish, you can save whole envelopes with stamps on them and store them anywhere—from shoe boxes to special albums. These are called "covers." Collecting entire envelopes reflects a specialty called "postal history." It's a good idea to save the whole envelope if there's something special about the address or return address (famous places or people for example), or the postmark (a date or location of some historic significance). See also the information below on collectible "first day covers" later in this article.

If you want to remove stamps from envelopes, it pays to be careful. The best way to remove stamps from envelopes is to soak them. Here's how:

1. Tear or cut off the upper right-hand corner of the envelope, leaving enough margin around the stamps to ensure they aren't damaged.
2. Place it, stamp side down, in a small pan of warm (not hot) water. If the stamp is affixed to a piece of colored envelope, use colder water; it may take longer, but any dyes from the paper are less likely to run and discolor the stamp. After a few minutes, the stamp should sink to the bottom. Remove the envelope piece from the water as soon as the stamp is off.
3. Wait a few more minutes for any remaining gum to dislodge from the stamp. The newer self-adhesive gums tend to take a bit longer.
4. Lift the stamp out. If you use your fingers, be sure your hands are clean, since oil from your skin can hasten discoloration of the stamps over time. Tongs—a good stamp-collecting tool like tweezers—can be used to minimize contact. Wet stamps are delicate and should be handled carefully.

5. Place the stamp between two paper towels and put a heavy object, such as a book, on top. This will keep the stamp from curling as it dries. Leave the stamp there overnight.
6. If the stamp shows signs of remaining adhesive, even after lengthy soaking, dry it face down on a single paper towel with nothing touching the back. If necessary, it can be flattened after it's dried; otherwise, it may stick to surfaces when drying.

How do I collect first day covers?

The fastest way to get a first day cover is to buy the stamp yourself (it will usually go on sale the day after the first day of issue), attach it to your own envelope (or cover), and send it to the first day post office for cancellation. You can submit up to fifty envelopes, up to thirty days after the stamp's issue date. Here's how:

1. Write your address in the lower right-hand corner of each first day envelope, at least 5/8 inch from the bottom. Leave plenty of room for the stamp(s) and cancellation. Use a peel-off label if you prefer.

2. Insert a piece of cardboard (about as thick as a postcard) into each envelope. You can tuck the flap in or seal the envelope.

3. Affix your stamp(s) to your first day envelope(s).

4. Put your first day envelope(s) inside another, larger envelope and mail it to "Customer-Affixed Envelopes" in care of the postmaster of the first day city. Your envelopes will be canceled and returned.

Or, you can purchase a plain envelope with the stamp(s) already affixed and canceled. These are now sold directly by mail order through the U.S. Postal Service.

36 u.s.c. sec. 220506.
Official Licensed Product of the
United States Olympic Committee.

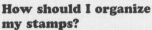

How should I organize my stamps?

However you want to, of course—it's your collection. But be sure to protect them so they don't get damaged or lost. You can attach your stamps to loose-leaf paper and put them in a three-ring binder. Or, arrange them in a more formal album, which you can buy in stores or by mail order.

What kinds of stamp albums can I buy?

Some stamp albums feature specific categories with pictures of the stamps that should appear on each page. You may want to select one with loose-leaf pages so you can add pages as your collection grows. Personal computers can help you design your own pages, featuring your collection in a totally personalized manner.

Software programs can help you with stamp-album pages, and common page-design programs can help you customize any design.

A *stock book* is an album with plastic or paper pockets on each page. There are no pictures of stamps, so you can organize the stock book in any way. These books are especially useful for holding duplicate stamps, stamps for trading, and stamps that you've saved but haven't yet had time to put in the album containing your permanent collection.

How do I put a stamp in the album?

It's best to use a stamp hinge—a small strip of thin material (often glassine) with gum on one side. Unlike tape or glue (which should *never* be used), hinges let you peel the stamp off the page without damaging it. Hinges come either folded or unfolded. Here's how to use a folded hinge:

1. Lightly moisten about three fourths of the short end of the hinge, leaving the area nearest the fold unmoistened. Press the hinge to the back of the stamp, placing the fold about 1/8 inch from the top of the stamp; that way, it can't be seen once the stamp is mounted in the album.

2. Lightly moisten most of the long end of the hinge (again, leaving the area closest to the fold unmoistened), position the stamp where you want it in the album, and press down to secure it.
3. Using tongs, gently lift the stamp from the bottom to make sure it's not stuck to the page.

If you have an unfolded hinge, simply fold it about one-third the length (gummed side out), giving you short and long ends, and proceed as above.

Instead of a hinge, you can insert the entire stamp into a mount—a small, clear plastic sleeve. Mounts are more expensive than hinges, but they protect stamps from air, dirt, and moisture. Hinges are fine for used stamps (stamps without adhesive that you've removed from mail), but mounts offer better protection for mint stamps (new stamps with adhesive, such as those you buy from the post office).

Is there anything else I need?

Here's a list of other materials and accessories you may find helpful:

Glassine envelopes are made of a special thin, see-through paper that protects stamps from grease and air. You can use them to keep stamps until you put them in your album.

A *stamp catalog* is a reference book with illustrations to help you identify stamps (like this book). It also lists the values of used and unused (mint) stamps.

A *magnifying glass* (or *loupe*) helps you examine stamps by making them appear larger. Sometimes it's important to examine certain details of stamps more closely.

A *perforation gauge* measures perforations along the edges of stamps. Sometimes the size and number of perfs are needed to identify stamps. The same principle can be used to measure the distance between peaks or ridges on newer die-cut self-adhesive stamps, with wavy die cuts that simulate perforations.

A *watermark tray* (and *watermark fluid*) help make watermarks on stamps more visible. A watermark is a design or pattern that is pressed into some stamp paper during manufacturing. This equipment is necessary only with stamps—mostly older stamps—with watermarks that help to identify them.

| Superb | Very Fine | Fine | Good |

How can I tell what a stamp is worth?

Ask yourself two questions: "How rare is it?" and "What condition is it in?" The price listed in a stamp catalog gives you some idea of how rare it is. However, the stamp may sell at more or less than the catalog price, depending on its condition. Catalog prices and condition are discussed further below.

Always try to find stamps in the best possible condition.

How should I judge the condition of a stamp?

Stamp dealers put stamps into categories according to their condition. Look at the pictured examples to see the differences among categories. A stamp in mint condition is the same as when purchased from the post office. An unused stamp has no cancellation but may not have any gum on the back. Mint stamps are usually worth more than unused stamps. Hinge marks on mint stamps can reduce value, which is why the use of stamp mounts is recommended for mint stamps.

You can begin to judge the condition of a stamp by examining the front of it. Are the colors bright or faded? Is the stamp clean, dirty, or stained? Is the stamp torn or creased? Torn stamps are not considered "collectible," but you may want to keep an example as a space filler until you get a better copy.

Are all the perforations intact? Has the stamp been canceled? A stamp with a light cancellation is in better condition than one with heavy marks across it.

Is the stamp design centered on the paper, crooked, or off to one side? In the examples pictured, this centering can range from "superb" (perfectly centered on the stamp) to "good" (the design on at least one side is marred somewhat by the perfs). Anything

| Light Cancel– Very Fine | Medium Cancel–Fine | Heavy Cancel |

less would be graded "fair" or "poor" and, like torn copies, should be saved only as space fillers. Centering varies widely on older stamps; modern production techniques make it unlikely that copies with less than "fine" centering could be found.

Now look at the back of the stamp. Is there a thin spot in the paper? If so, it may have been caused by careless removal from a hinge or envelope.

The values listed in this book are for used and unused stamps in "very fine" condition that may have been hinged.

Where else can I find stamps?

Check the classified ads in philatelic newspapers and magazines at your local library. Some are listed under "periodicals" in this book (see page 542), and most will send you a free sample copy on request. There also are a number of stamp-related sites on the Internet, which can be accessed through most search programs and services.

What other stamp materials can I collect?

Postal stationery products are popular among some collectors. These have the stamp design printed and/or embossed (with an impressed or raised image) directly on them.

Stamped envelopes were first issued in the United States in 1853. More than five hundred million of them are printed each year.

Stamped cards (also called *postal cards*) were first issued in 1873. The first U.S. multicolored commemorative stamped cards were released in 1956. Several different stamped card designs are issued each year.

Aerogrammes (also called *air letters*) are designed to be letters and envelopes all in one. They are specially stamped, marked for folding, and gummed for sealing.

Other philatelic collectibles include:

Plate numbers (including *plate blocks*) appear on or adjacent to stamps. These are most common on sheet stamps. Plate blocks are the group of stamps (usually four) which have the printing plate numbers in the adjoining selvage—or margin (usually in the corner of the pane). On coils, these numbers appear in the margins of the stamps themselves, and collectors may save a *plate number strip* of three or five stamps with the number on the center stamp. On booklets, the plate numbers usually appear on the booklet "tab" by which the panes are affixed to the booklet cover.

Booklet panes are panes of stamps affixed in, or as part of, a thin folder to form a booklet. With self-adhesive stamps, a newer convertible booklet format has been created, so that the stamps, liner, and booklet are all one unit. Usually, collectors of booklet panes save the entire pane or the entire booklet.

Marginal blocks (including **copyright blocks**) feature marginal inscriptions other than the plate numbers. The most common is the copyright block, which features the copyright symbol ©, copyright date, and U.S. Postal Service information. All U.S. stamp designs since 1978 are copyrighted.

First day covers (FDCs) are envelopes bearing new stamps that are postmarked on the first day of sale. For each new postal issue, the U.S. Postal Service generally selects one location, usually related to the stamp subject, as the place for the first day dedication ceremony and the first day postmark. See page 10 for information on how to collect these covers.

First day ceremony programs are given to persons who attend first day ceremonies. They contain a list of participants, information on the stamp subject, and the actual stamp attached and postmarked.

Are there any stamp groups I can join?

Yes! Stamp clubs can be a great source for new stamps and stamp collecting advice. These clubs often meet at schools, libraries, and community centers. Ask your local postmaster or librarian for the locations of stamp clubs in your area and other contact information (including Internet sites, in some cases).

Greetings From America

Celebrating a Nation on the Move

From the halls of the United States Military Academy to the sand and surf at Waikiki Beach in Hawaii, the 2002 commemorative stamps offer a grand tour of the best of America. With this year's Greeting From America stamp pane, we pay homage to a few of the places and things that make each state unique. Join the U.S. Postal Service as it goes on the road with the 2002 stamp program.

Greetings From America is a bold tapestry of colors and graphics. Illustrator Lonnie Busch combined iconic images of parks, harbors, skylines, and a variety of other notable vistas and views with scenes depicting flora, fauna, and natural wonders. The back of each stamp lists the year the state was admitted to the Union, the state flower, and the state tree. Reminiscent of retro "large letter" postcards, these lively stamps will inspire you to learn more about each state. Send your own special greeting from each state you explore.

James VanDerZee 1886–1983

With this year's striking Masters of American Photography stamp pane, the U.S. Postal Service honors developments in the art of photography while showing us our world from unexpected angles. The pane includes stunning images from across the country—from a view of Massaponax Church in Virginia during the Civil War to a monumental 1867 photograph of Cape Horn on the Columbia River in Oregon. Or, if you prefer, explore the

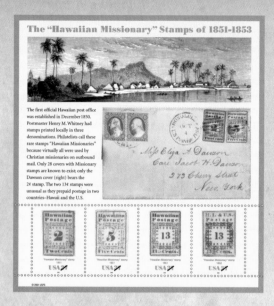

The "Hawaiian Missionary" Stamps of 1851-1853

The first official Hawaiian post office was established in December 1850. Postmaster Henry M. Whitney had stamps printed locally in three denominations. Philatelists call these rare stamps "Hawaiian Missionaries" because virtually all were used by Christian missionaries on outbound mail. Only 28 covers with Missionary stamps are known to exist; only the Dawson cover (right) bears the 2¢ stamp. The two 13¢ stamps were unusual as they prepaid postage in two countries—Hawaii and the U.S.

© 2001 USPS

New York City of André Kertész or Garry Winogrand, whose photographs allow us to see our world in a wholly new and exciting way.

Travel, like photography, often alters our perspective. One distinctly Hawaiian landmark, Diamond Head, actually appears on three new stamp issuances this year. On the Hawaiian Missionaries Souvenir Sheet, an 1862 engraving of Diamond Head offers a hint of what life was like in the former Kingdom of Hawaii. On the Duke Kahanamoku stamp, the background is dominated by Diamond Head, a point of reference for the countless surfers who have ridden the waves at Waikiki Beach. And on the Greetings From Hawaii stamp, Diamond Head shows its natural beauty in a view that visitors and locals alike have long enjoyed.

The 2002 stamps also take us to the Longleaf Pine Forest. Although greatly reduced in size, the longleaf pine forest still occupies parts of its natural range in the coastal plains from southeastern Virginia to eastern Texas. The fourth in the

LONGLEAF PINE FOREST

FOURTH IN A SERIES

NATURE OF AMERICA

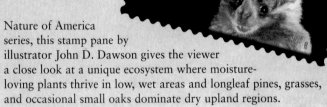

Nature of America
series, this stamp pane by
illustrator John D. Dawson gives the viewer
a close look at a unique ecosystem where moisture-
loving plants thrive in low, wet areas and longleaf pines, grasses,
and occasional small oaks dominate dry upland regions.

Let this year's fascinating American Bats stamps inspire you
to visit Austin, Texas, where 1.5 million bats roost beneath the
Congress Avenue Bridge. Of approximately 950 bat species in the
world, 45 are found in North America, where they help balance
populations of night-flying insects, including the mosquitoes in
our own backyards and other pests that cost farmers billions of
dollars annually. Bats also disperse seeds from fruits, and they
are vital to the pollination of desert plants in the American
Southwest. From mid-March to early November, the Austin bats
take to the evening sky in dark, swirling columns. Without a
doubt, their nightly appearance is one of the country's most
fascinating displays of nature in an urban setting.

If you're intrigued by this year's American Treasures
stamp featuring the artwork of John James Audubon, you may
wish to journey to Key West, Florida. At
what is now the Audubon House and
Tropical Gardens, the artist himself is
believed to have drawn a number of
local species for his renowned *Birds of
America*. Today you can even join an
art class surrounded by splendid
tropical foliage. Record your own
impressions of the American landscape
in wild colors, and keep an eye out for
the area's many extraordinary birds.

Over the years, the U.S. Postal
Service has issued a wide range of
stamps that celebrate the richness
of our heritage. Throughout the
pages of this book you'll find brief
vignettes on many of the places that
have appeared on U.S. stamps—greetings, if you
will, from America. Enjoy your travels through our nation's
history; just don't forget to write.

Winter Sports

Mentoring a Child

Black Heritage:
Langston Hughes

Happy Birthday

Winter Sports #3552-3555

The U.S. Postal Service recognizes the competitive drive of athletes who take part in winter sports by issuing a pane of stamps depicting figure skating, ice hockey, snowboarding, and ski jumping. Each of the four Winter Sports stamps combines a photograph of an individual competitor with a graphic treatment of the corresponding sports arena or apparatus.

Date of Issue: January 8, 2002
Place of Issue: Park City, UT
Art Director: Phil Jordan

Designer: Jager Di Paola Kemp
Printing: Gravure

Mentoring a Child #3556

Mentors—dedicated volunteers who offer friendship, guidance, and support to youth—can fill a need for positive adult role models. Goals and effects of mentoring include greater self-confidence; improved relationships with peers and adults; better school attendance and academic performance; increased interest in setting goals and preparing for careers; and a reduction in substance abuse and violent behavior. With this stamp, the U.S. Postal Service continues its tradition of raising public awareness of social issues.

Date of Issue: January 10, 2002
Place of Issue: Annapolis, MD
Art Director: Derry Noyes

Designer: Lance Hidy
Printing: Gravure

Black Heritage: Langston Hughes #3557

With this 25th stamp in the Black Heritage series, the U.S. Postal Service honors writer Langston Hughes on the centennial of his birth. Although he considered himself a poet first, he wrote in many literary genres, from short stories to drama. His innovative poetry combined jazz, blues, and the black vernacular with the traditions of poetry in English. Admired in his own time, Hughes is now considered one of the most important American writers of the 20th century.

Date of Issue: February 1, 2002
Place of Issue: New York, NY
Designer: Richard Sheaff

Photographer: Henri
Cartier-Bresson
Printing: Offset, Microprint

Happy Birthday #3558

With vibrant colors and a shower of confetti, this new Happy Birthday stamp makes it easy to add a festive touch to birthday cards and packages. Like the two previous Happy Birthday stamps, which were issued in Special Occasions booklets in 1987 and 1988, the 2002 stamp recognizes the tradition of sending special birthday greetings to family and friends.

Date of Issue: February 8, 2002
Place of Issue: Riverside, CA
Art Director: Terrence W. McCaffrey

Designer: Harry Zelenko
Printing: Gravure

Lunar New Year: Year of the Horse   #3559

This stamp, tenth in the award-winning Lunar New Year series of twelve stamps designed by Clarence Lee, colorfully combines a paper-cut design of a horse with grass-style calligraphy. People born in the Year of the Horse are said to enjoy being in the spotlight. Often in need of reassurance, they are hardworking, honest, independent and sociable. The Year of the Horse begins Feb. 12, 2002 and ends Jan. 31, 2003.

Date of Issue: February 11, 2002   Designer: Clarence Lee
Place of Issue: New York, NY   Printing: Offset/Microprint
Art Director: Terrence W. McCaffrey   "USPS"

United States Military Academy

The United States Military Academy, located at West Point on the Hudson River in New York State, prepares graduates for careers as officers in the U.S. Army and lifetimes of service to the nation. Featuring the West Point coat of arms, this stamp recognizes the bicentennial of the academy.

Date of Issue: March 16, 2002   Photographer: Ted Spiegel
Place of Issue: West Point, NY   Printing: Gravure
Designer: Derry Noyes

Greetings From America

Inspired by the retro "large letter" postcards that were used to adver-tise cities, states, or tourist attractions, artist Lonnie Busch combined flora and fauna with local points of interest into colorful collages that celebrate the unique character of each state. Text on the back of each stamp lists that state's bird, flower, tree, capital, and date of entry into the Union. Greetings From America is the first pane of 50 stamps to be issued in ten years.

Date of Issue: April 4, 2002   Illustrator: Lonnie Busch
Place of Issue: New York, NY   Printing: Gravure
Designer: Richard Sheaff

**Lunar New Year:
Year of the Horse**

United States Military Academy

Greetings From America

Nature of America: Longleaf Pine Forest

Irving Berlin

**American Treasures:
John James Audubon**

Love

Love

Nature of America: Longleaf Pine Forest

The longleaf pine forest occupies parts of the coastal plains from southeastern Virginia to eastern Texas. This stamp pane—fourth in an educational series designed to promote appreciation of North America's major plant and animal communities—takes us to the heart of a longleaf pine forest with artwork by John D. Dawson. The prior issuances in the Nature of America series were Sonoran Desert (1999), Pacific Coast Rain Forest (2000), and Great Plains Prairie (2001).

Date of Issue: April 26, 2002   Illustrator: John D. Dawson
Place of Issue: Tallahassee, FL   Printing: Gravure
Designer: Ethel Kessler

Irving Berlin

An accomplished songwriter, Irving Berlin helped change the direction of American popular music with more than 1,000 songs. Many of them became standards that are still favorites today. The stamp depicts a 1932 photograph of Irving Berlin by Edward Steichen that is superimposed over Berlin's handwritten score of "God Bless America." His signature from that score appears at the bottom of the stamp.

Date of Issue: September 2002   Designer: Greg Berger
Place of Issue: New York, NY   Printing: Gravure
Art Director: Ethel Kessler

American Treasures: John James Audubon

John James Audubon's vividly colored and exquisitely rendered portrait of two tanager species—"Louisiana Tanager" and "Scarlet Tanager"— appears on this second issuance in the American Treasures series. Inaugurated in 2001 with the Amish Quilts stamp pane, the series is intended to showcase beautiful works of American fine art and crafts. John James Audubon (1785-1851) was a self-taught artist and naturalist whose magnum opus, *Birds of America,* has been described as "the finest pictorial ornithological book ever produced."

Date of Issue: June 27, 2002   Designer: Derry Noyes
Place of Issue: Santa Clara, CA   Printing: Gravure

Love

The U.S. Postal Service issues two colorful new Love stamps with stylized block letters and a heart-design "V" spelling the word "LOVE."

Date of Issue: August 16, 2002   Designer: Michael Osborne
Place of Issue: Atlantic City, NJ   Printing: Offset
Art Director: Ethel Kessler

Masters of American Photography

This pane of 20 stamps honors some of our country's most important and influential photographers with a visual sampling of the art form, from its initial stage through the late 20th century. Included are stunning examples of portrait, documentary, landscape, still life, cityscape, and fine art photography. Many of the major themes and events in U.S. history—immigration, the Great Depression, World War II—are captured in these compelling images.

Date of Issue: June 13, 2002   Designer: Derry Noyes
Place of Issue: San Diego, CA   Printing: Gravure

Harry Houdini

This stamp honors Harry Houdini, America's most famous escape artist and magician. Houdini served as president of the Society of American Magicians from 1917 until his death in 1926; this stamp issuance coincides with the 100th anniversary of the society. The portrait on the stamp, which depicts a confident, self-assured man at the height of his career, was taken from a 1911 lithographed poster.

Date of Issue: July 3, 2002   Designer: Richard Sheaff
Place of Issue: New York, NY   Printing: Offset

Andy Warhol

In 2002 the U.S. Postal Service continues its celebration of the fine arts by paying tribute to Andy Warhol, a leading figure in the pop art movement and one of the most influential artists of his time. Warhol's career also included ventures in design, photography, film, television, writing, and publishing. The stamp art features Andy Warhol's *Self-Portrait,* 1964. Based on a photo-booth photograph, the image—silkscreen ink and synthetic polymer paint on canvas—is one of several versions in varying colors.

Date of Issue: August 9, 2002   Designer: Richard Sheaff
Place of Issue: Pittsburgh, PA   Printing: Gravure

Teddy Bears

Four lovable, cuddly teddy bears are featured on the Teddy Bears pane of twenty stamps. All four teddy bears were manufactured in the United States. The Ideal bear dates from circa 1905, the Bruin bear from circa 1907, and the Gund bear from circa 1948. The unlabeled "stick" bear dates from the 1920s. President Theodore Roosevelt's name became forever linked with the stuffed bears that were all the rage in the U.S. during the first decade of the 20th century. Teddy bears remain enormously popular today, and enthusiasts—known in the teddy bear world as arctophiles—pay top dollar for collectibles.

Date of Issue: August 15, 2002   Designer: Margaret Bauer
Place of Issue: Atlantic City, NJ   Printing: Gravure
Art Director: Derry Noyes

Masters of American Photography

Harry Houdini

Andy Warhol

Teddy Bears

**Literary Arts:
Ogden Nash**

Duke Kahanamoku

Neuter or Spay

Women in Journalism

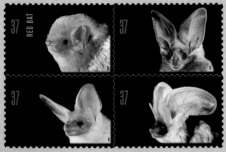

American Bats

Literary Arts: Ogden Nash

The 18th stamp in the Literary Arts series honors poet Ogden Nash on the centennial of his birth. A gentle satirist, Nash poked fun at human foibles in poetry that expressed his wry wit and demonstrated his playfulness with language. Invented words, puns, creative misspellings, and unexpected rhymes made his verse humorous and memorable.

Date of Issue: August 19, 2002
Place of Issue: Baltimore, MD
Designer: Carl T. Herrman
Illustrator: Michael J. Deas
Printing: Gravure

Duke Kahanamoku

Hawaiian swimmer and surfer Duke Kahanamoku was renowned not only for his athletic prowess but also for his grace and good sportsmanship. Kahanamoku is widely considered to be the father of international surfing, and for much of his life he served as a living symbol of hospitality and goodwill to the rest of the world.

Date of Issue: August 24, 2002
Place of Issue: Honolulu, HI
Designer: Carl T. Herrman
Illustrator: Michael J. Deas
Printing: Gravure

Neuter or Spay

Animal shelters and veterinarians throughout the country urge pet owners to combat the problem of animal overpopulation by neutering or spaying their dogs and cats. The U.S. Postal Service raises awareness of this important issue with these stamps featuring a neutered puppy and a spayed kitten.

Date of Issue: September 20, 2002
Place of Issue: Denver, CO
Designer: Derry Noyes
Photographer: Sally Andersen-Bruce
Printing: Gravure

Women in Journalism

Nellie Bly, Ida M. Tarbell, Marguerite Higgins, and Ethel L. Payne made their contributions to journalism at different times, but they were all trailblazers in a field dominated by men. Their work in investigative journalism, war correspondence, and political reporting won awards, brought them fame, and opened doors for later women journalists.

Date of Issue: September 14, 2002
Place of Issue: Fort Worth, TX
Art Director: Howard E. Paine
Designer: Fred Otnes
Printing: Gravure

American Bats

Bats have long been feared and misunderstood, but they are actually beneficial to humans and essential to nature's balance. North American bats consume farm and forest pests, pollinate flowers, and carry seeds to new locations. This stamp pane features striking photographs of four bats whose ranges include the continental United States.

Date of Issue: September 13, 2002
Place of Issue: Austin, TX
Designer: Phil Jordan
Photographer: Merlin D. Tuttle
Printing: Gravure

Legends of Hollywood: Cary Grant

Cary Grant (1904-1986) appears on this year's Legends of Hollywood stamp. A debonair leading man, Grant brought wit and sophistication to his roles in more than 70 movies, including romantic comedies such as *The Philadelphia Story* (1940) and suspenseful thrillers such as *North by Northwest* (1959).

Date of Issue: September 10, 2002   Illustrator: Michael J. Deas
Place of Issue: Los Angeles, CA   Printing: Gravure
Designer: Carl T. Herrman

Christmas: Gossaert

The 2002 Christmas design is a detail of Jan Gossaert's oil-on-panel painting *Madonna and Child*, circa 1520, from The Art Institute of Chicago. Gossaert (circa 1478 to 1532) was a Netherlandish artist credited with being one of the first to bring the innovations of the Italian Renaissance to northern Europe.

Date of Issue: October 10, 2002   Designer: Richard Sheaff
Place of Issue: Chicago, IL   Printing: Offset

Holiday: Snowmen

The U.S. Postal Service's 2002 Holiday issuance features photographs of four whimsical snowmen figures. Popular in folklore, literature, and song, snowmen have come to symbolize the joy and magic of the holiday season and often evoke fond childhood memories of playing in the snow.

Date of Issue: October 2002   Photographer: Sally Andersen-
Place of Issue: TBD   Bruce
Designer: Derry Noyes   Printing: Gravure

Hawaiian Missionaries

This souvenir sheet reproduces examples of Hawaii's first four postage stamps, which were issued in three denominations: 2 cents, 5 cents, and 13 cents. They are called Hawaiian Missionaries by philatelists because most of them were used on correspondence mailed by Christian missionaries from Hawaii to their families, friends, and business associates. These rare stamps are now considered among the world's foremost philatelic items.

Date of Issue: October 24, 2002   Designer: Richard Sheaff
Place of Issue: New York, NY   Printing: Offset/Intaglio

Cary Grant

**Christmas:
Gossaert**

Holiday: Snowmen

The "Hawaiian Missionary" Stamps of 1851-1853

The first official Hawaiian post office was established in December 1850. Postmaster Henry M. Whitney had stamps printed locally in three denominations. Philatelists call these rare stamps "Hawaiian Missionaries" because virtually all were used by Christian missionaries on outbound mail. Only 28 covers with Missionary stamps are known to exist; only the Dawson cover (right) bears the 2¢ stamp. The two 13¢ stamps were unusual as they prepaid postage in two countries–Hawaii and the U.S.

© 2001 USPS

Hawaiian Missionaries

Antique Toys

Edna Ferber

U.S. Flag

Graphic Star

**Carlsbad Caverns National Park
Stamped Card**

Ribbon Star Envelope

Antique Toys

These stamps feature four antique American toy vehicles from the Strong Museum in Rochester, New York. Made primarily of cast iron, the toys were manufactured between 1880 and 1925.

Date of Issue: July 26, 2002
Place of Issue: Rochester, NY
Designer: Derry Noyes

Photographer: Sally Andersen-Bruce
Printing: Gravure

Edna Ferber

The fourth issuance in the Distinguished Americans series honors Pulitzer Prize-winning novelist Edna Ferber (1885-1968).

Date of Issue: July 29, 2002
Place of Issue: Appleton, WI
Designer: Richard Sheaff

Illustrator: Mark Summers
Printing: Offset

U.S. Flag

The stars and stripes of the U.S. flag are featured on this definitive stamp, which was issued in booklets of 10, 18, and 20.

Date of Issue: June 7, 2002
Place of Issue: Washington, DC

Designer: Terrence W. McCaffrey
Printing: Offset, Gravure

Graphic Star

This 3-cent stamp features a red, white, and blue graphic star.

Date of Issue: June 7, 2002
Place of Issue: Washington, DC

Designer: Phil Jordan
Printing: Gravure

Carlsbad Caverns National Park Stamped Card

Featured on this stamped card is an artistic rendering of Carlsbad Cavern in New Mexico.

Date of Issue: June 7, 2002
Place of Issue: Carlsbad, NM
Designer: Carl T. Herrman

Illustrator: Tom Engeman
Printing: FLEX

Ribbon Star Envelope

Depicted on this First-Class stamped envelope is a white star formed by five red-white-and-blue ribbons.

Date of Issue: June 7, 2002
Place of Issue: Washington, DC

Designer: Terrence W. McCaffrey
Printing: Offset

$13.65 U.S. Capitol

The U.S. Capitol, an enduring symbol of American democracy, is the subject of this Express Mail stamp.

Date of Issue: July 2002
Place of Issue: Washington, DC
Designer: Derry Noyes

Photographer: Robert C. Shafer
Printing: Offset

$3.85 Thomas Jefferson Memorial

The Postal Service recognizes the beauty of the Thomas Jefferson Memorial (shown here at twilight) on this Priority Mail stamp.

Date of Issue: July 2002
Place of Issue: Washington, DC
Designer: Derry Noyes

Photographer: Carol Highsmith
Printing: Offset

American Toleware

This 5-cent stamp features an artist's rendering of a toleware coffeepot from the Winterthur Museum in Delaware.

Date of Issue: May 31, 2002
Place of Issue: McLean, VA
Designer: Derry Noyes

Illustrator: Lou Nolan
Printing: Gravure

Heroes of 2001

In honor of the American heroes who responded to the terrorist attacks of September 11, 2001, the Postal Service issues a semipostal that offers the public another way to provide assistance to the families of emergency relief personnel who died or were permanently disabled in the line of duty.

Date of Issue: June 7, 2002
Place of Issue: New York, NY
Designer: Derry Noyes

Photographer: Thomas E. Franklin
Printing: Offset

Coverlet Eagle

This First-Class second ounce letter-rate stamp features an artistic rendering of an eagle, a detail from a coverlet woven by Harry Tyler circa 1853.

Date of Issue: July 12, 2002
Place of Issue: Oak Brook, IL

Designer: Richard Sheaff
Printing: Offset

$13.65 U.S. Capitol

$3.85 Thomas Jefferson Memorial

American Toleware

Heroes of 2001

Coverlet Eagle

Explanation of Catalog Prices

The United States Postal Service sells only the commemoratives and special issues released during the past few years. Current postal stationery and regular issues remain on sale for longer periods of time. Prices in this book are called "catalog prices" by stamp collectors. Collectors use catalog prices as guidelines when buying or trading stamps. **It is important to remember the prices are simply guidelines to the stamp values. Stamp condition is very important in determining the actual value of a stamp.**

Prices are Estimated
Listed prices are estimates of how much you can expect to pay for a stamp from a dealer. **A 20-cent minimum valuation has been established that represents a fair-market price to have a dealer locate and provide a single stamp to a customer. Dealers may charge less per stamp to provide a group of such stamps, and may charge less for such a single stamp. Similarly, a $1.00 minimum has been established for First Day Covers (FDCs).** If you sell a stamp to a dealer, he or she may offer you much less than the catalog price. Dealers pay based on their interest in owning a particular stamp. If they already have a full supply, they may only buy additional stamps at a low price.

Condition Affects Value
The catalog prices are given for unused (mint) stamps and used (canceled) stamps that have been hinged and are in "very fine" condition. Stamps in "superb" condition that have never been hinged may cost more than the listed price. Stamps in less than "fine" condition may cost less.

The prices for used stamps are based on a light cancellation; a heavy cancellation lessens a stamp's value. Canceled stamps may be worth more than uncanceled stamps. This happens if the cancellation is of a special type or for a significant date. Therefore, it is important to study an envelope before removing a stamp and discarding its "cover." Additional information about and examples of stamp conditions can be found in the Introduction to this book.

Sample Listing

				Un	U	PB/LP/PNC	#	FDC	Q(M)
3069	32¢	Georgia O'Keefe	05/23/96	.65	.20	2.75	(4)	1.25	156

Scott Catalog Number (bold type indicates stamp is pictured)

Description

Denomination

Date of Issue

Unused Catalog Price

Used Catalog Price

Plate Block Price, Line Pair Price or **Plate Number** Coil Price

Number of **stamps** in Plate Block, Line Pair or Plate Number Coil

First Day Cover Price

Quantity Issued in **Millions** (where known)

3069

Understanding the Listings

▨ Prices in **regular type** for single unused and used stamps are taken from the *Scott 2001 Specialized Catalogue of U.S. Stamps & Covers,* whose editors have based these prices on **actual retail values** as they found them in the marketplace. The Scott numbering system for stamps is used in this book. Prices quoted for unused and used stamps are for "very fine" condition, except where "very fine" is not available.

▨ Stamp values in *italic* generally refer to items difficult to value accurately.

▨ A dash (—) in a value column means the item is known to exist but information is insufficient for establishing a value.

▨ The stamp listings contain a number of additions designated "*a,*" "*b,*" "*c,*" etc. These represent recognized variations of stamps as well as errors. These listings are as complete as space permits.

Occasionally, a new stamp or major variation may be inserted by the catalog editors into a series or sequence where it was not originally anticipated. These additions are identified by capital letters "*A,*" "*B*" and so forth. For example, a new stamp which logically belonged between 1044 and 1045 is designated 1044A, even though it is entirely different from 1044. The insertion was preferable to a complete renumbering of the series.

▨ Prices for Plate Blocks, First Day Covers, American Commemorative Panels and Souvenir Pages are taken from *Scott 2001 Specialized Catalogue of U.S. Stamps & Covers.*

Sample Variation Listing

			Un	U	PB/LP/PNC	#	FDC	Q(M)
2281	25¢ Honeybee	09/02/88	.45	.20	3.00	(3)	1.25	
a	Imperf. pair		*45.00*					
b	Black omitted		*65.00*					
d	Pair, imperf. between		*1,000.00*					

Scott Catalog Number (bold type indicates stamp is pictured)

Description

Denomination

Date of Issue

Unused Catalog Price

Used Catalog Price

Plate Block Price, Line Pair Price or **Plate Number Coil Price**

Number of stamps in Plate Block, Line Pair or Plate Number Coil

First Day Cover Price

Quantity Issued in **Millions** (where known)

2281

Commemorative and Definitive Stamps

1847-1875

1

2

3

4

5

11

12

14

17

	Issues of 1847	Un	U
	Thin, Bluish Wove Paper,		
	July 1, Imperf., Unwmkd.		
1	5¢ Benjamin Franklin	6,000.00	600.00
a	5¢ dark brown	6,500	6.25
b	5¢ orange brown	7,500.00	850.00
c	5¢ red orange	12,500.00	5,500.00
	Pen cancel		300.00
	Double transfer of top and		
	bottom frame lines		750.00
	Double transfer of top, bottom and		
	left frame lines and numerals		3,000.00
2	10¢ George		
	Washington	27,500.00	1,400.00
	Pen cancel		750.00
	Vertical line through second "F"		
	of "OFFICE"	—	1,900.00
	With "stick pin" in tie, or		
	with "harelip"	—	1,900.00
	Double transfer in lower		
	right "X," or of left and		
	bottom frame lines	—	2,000.00
	Double transfer in		
	"POST OFFICE"	—	2,500.00
	Issues of 1875, Reproductions		
	of 1 and 2, Bluish Paper, Without Gum		
3	5¢ Franklin	800.00	—
4	10¢ Washington	1,000.00	—

5¢. On the originals, the left side of the white shirt frill touches the oval on a level with the top of the "F" of "Five." On the reproductions, it touches the oval about on a level with the top of the figure "5."

10¢. On the originals, line of coat points to "T" of TEN and right line of coat points between "T" and "S" of CENTS.

On the reproductions left, line of coat points to right tip of "X" and right line of coat points to center of "S" of CENTS.

On the reproductions, the eyes have a sleepy look, the line of the mouth is straighter, and in the curl of hair near the left cheek is a strong black dot, while the originals have only a faint one.

	Issues of 1851-57, Imperf.		
5	1¢ Franklin, type I	175,000.00	45,000.00
5A	1¢ blue, type Ib	14,000.00	6,000.00
	#6-9: Franklin (5), 1851		
6	1¢ blue, type Ia	35,000.00	10,000.00
7	1¢ blue, type II	1,100.00	160.00
	Cracked plate	1,350.00	375.00
8	1¢ blue, type III	11,500.00	2,750.00
8A	1¢ blue, type IIIa	4,250.00	1,000.00
9	1¢ blue, type IV	750.00	125.00
	Triple transfer,		
	one inverted	900.00	175.00

	Issues of 1851-57	Un	U
	#10-11, 25-26a all had plates on which at		
	least four outer frame lines (and usually much		
	more) were recut, adding to their value.		
10	3¢ orange brown		
	Washington, type I (11)	3,000.00	100.00
	3¢ copper brown	3,500.00	200.00
	On part-India paper	—	500.00
11	3¢ Washington, type I	240.00	10.00
	3¢ deep claret	325.00	18.00
	Double transfer,		
	"GENTS" for "CENTS"	375.00	50.00
12	5¢ Jefferson, type I	17,500.00	1,100.00
13	10¢ green Washington,		
	type I (14)	14,000.00	800.00
14	10¢ green, type II	4,000.00	225.00
15	10¢ Washington, type III	4,000.00	225.00
16	10¢ green, type IV (14)	25,000.00	1,600.00
17	12¢ Washington	5,000.00	325.00
	Issues of 1857-61, Perf. 15.5		
	(Issued in 1857 except #18, 27, 28A, 29,		
	30, 30A, 35, 36b, 37, 38, 39)		
	#18-24: Franklin (5)		
18	1¢ blue, type I	1,800.00	600.00
19	1¢ blue, type Ia	21,000.00	6,250.00
20	1¢ blue, type II	1,000.00	250.00
21	1¢ blue, type III	12,000.00	2,000.00
22	1¢ blue, type IIIa	1,900.00	475.00
23	1¢ blue, type IV	8,000.00	700.00
24	1¢ blue, type V	175.00	40.00
	"Curl" on shoulder	240.00	67.50
	"Earring" below ear	350.00	95.00
	Long double		
	"curl" in hair	300.00	80.00
b	Laid paper	—	
	#25-26a: Washington (11)		
25	3¢ rose, type I	2,250.00	85.00
	Major cracked plate	3,750.00	550.00
26	3¢ dull red, type II	75.00	7.00
	3¢ brownish carmine	140.00	17.50
	3¢ claret	170.00	22.50
	Left or right frame		
	line double	110.00	17.50
	Cracked plate	750.00	250.00
26a	3¢ dull red, type IIa	225.00	55.00
	Double transfer	325.00	125.00
	Left frame line double	—	150.00

5
Bust of Benjamin Franklin.

Detail of **#7, 20** Type II

Lower scrollwork incomplete (lacks little balls and lower plume ornaments). Side ornaments are complete.

Detail of **#9, 23** Type IV

Similar to Type II, but outer lines recut top, bottom or both.

Detail of **#5, 18, 40** Type I

Has curved, unbroken lines outside labels. Scrollwork is substantially complete at top, forms little balls at bottom.

Detail of **#8, 21** Type III

Outer lines broken in the middle. Side ornaments are substantially complete.

Detail of **#8A, 22** Type IIIa

Outer lines broken top or bottom but not both.

Detail of **#24** Type V

Similar to Type III of 1851-57 but with side ornaments partly cut away.

Detail of **#6, 19** Type Ia

Same as Type I at bottom but top ornaments and outer line partly cut away. Lower scrollwork is complete.

Detail of **#5a** Type Ib

Lower scrollwork is incomplete, the little balls are not so clear.

3¢ Washington Types I-IIa, Series 1851-1857, 1857-1861, 1875

10
Bust of George Washington

Detail of **#10, 11, 25, 41**
Type I
There is an outer frame line at top and bottom.

Detail of **#26**
Type II
The outer frame line has been removed at top and bottom. The side frame lines were recut so as to be continuous from the top to the bottom of the plate.

Detail of **#26a**
Type IIa
The side frame lines extended only to the bottom of the stamp design.

5¢ Jefferson Types I-II, Series 1851-1857, 1857-1861

12
Portrait of
Thomas Jefferson

Detail of **#12, 27-29**
Type I
There are projections on all four sides.

Detail of **#30-30a**
Type II
The projections at top and bottom are partly cut away.

10¢ Washington Types I-IV, Series 1851-1857, 1857-1861, 1875

15
Portrait of
George Washington

Detail of **#13, 31, 43**
Type I
The "shells" at the lower corners are practically complete. The outer line below the label is very nearly complete. The outer lines are broken above the middle of the top label and the "X" in each upper corner.

Detail of **#14, 32**
Type II
The design is complete at the top. The outer line at the bottom is broken in the middle. The shells are partly cut away.

Detail of **#15, 33**
Type III
The outer lines are broken above the top label and the "X" numerals. The outer line at the bottom and the shells are partly cut away, as in Type II.

Detail of **#16, 34** Type IV
The outer lines have been recut at top or bottom or both. Types I, II, III and IV have complete ornaments at the sides of the stamps and three pearls at each outer edge of the bottom panel.

Detail of
#35
Type V
(Two typical examples.)
Side ornaments slightly cut away. Outer lines complete at top except over right "X." Outer lines complete at bottom and shells nearly so.

Issues of 1857-61		Un	U
Perf. 15.5			
#27-29: Jefferson (12)			
27	5¢ brick red, type I	25,000.00	1,300.00
28	5¢ red brown, type I	4,500.00	750.00
b	5¢ brt. red brn., type I	4,750.00	950.00
28A	5¢ Indian red, type I	30,000.00	3,000.00
29	5¢ brown, type I	2,250.00	350.00
	Defective transfer	—	—
30	5¢ orange brown, type II	1,150.00	1,100.00
30A	5¢ brown, type II (30)	1,900.00	275.00
b	Printed on both sides	4,400.00	4,650.00
#31-35: Washington (15)			
31	10¢ green, type I	16,500.00	850.00
32	10¢ green, type II	5,000.00	275.00
33	10¢ green, type III	5,000.00	275.00
	"Curl" on forehead or in left "X"		350.00
34	10¢ green, type IV	32,500.00	2,250.00
35	10¢ green, type V	275.00	65.00
	Small "curl" on forehead	325.00	77.50
	"Curl" in "e" or "t" of "Cents"	350.00	90.00
	Plate I Outer frame lines complete		
36	12¢ blk. Washington (17), plate I	1,300.00	250.00
	Triple transfer	1,600.00	
36b	12¢ black, plate III	750.00	180.00
	Vertical line through rosette	925.00	260.00
37	24¢ gray lilac	1,600.00	350.00
a	24¢ gray	1,600.00	350.00
38	30¢ orange Franklin	1,800.00	450.00
	Recut at bottom	2,100.00	575.00
39	90¢ blue Washington	2,750.00	6,500.00
	Double transfer at top or bottom	2,900.00	—
	Pen cancel		2,000.00

Note: Beware of forged cancellations of #39. Genuine cancellations are rare

Issues of 1875		Un	U
Government Reprints, White Paper			
Without Gum, Perf. 12			
40	1¢ bright blue Franklin (5)	625.00	
41	3¢ scarlet Wash. (11)	3,000.00	
42	5¢ orange brown Jefferson (30)	1,200.00	
43	10¢ blue green Washington (14)	2,750.00	
44	12¢ greenish black Washington (17)	3,250.00	
45	24¢ blackish violet Washington (37)	3,250.00	
46	30¢ yellow orange Franklin (38)	3,250.00	
47	90¢ deep blue Washington (39)	4,500.00	
48-54	Not assigned		
Issue of 1861, Thin,			
Semi-Transparent Paper			

#55-62 are no longer considered postage stamps. Many experts consider them to be essays and/or trial color proofs.

| 62B | 10¢ dark green Washington (58) | 6,750.00 | 950.00 |

30   37

38   39

40

62B

63 **64** **65** **67**

68 **69** **70** **71**

72 **73** **77**

Details

Issues of 1861-62, 1861-66, 1867 and 1875

Detail of **#63, 86, 92**

There is a dash in 63, 86 and 92 added under the tip of the ornament at the right of the numeral in upper left corner.

Detail of **#67, 75, 80, 95**

There is a leaf in 67, 75, 80 and 95 added to the foliated ornaments at each corner.

Detail of **#69, 85E, 90, 97**

In 69, 85E, 90 and 97, ovals and scrolls have been added at the corners.

Detail of **#64-66, 74, 79, 82-83, 85, 85C, 88, 94**

In 64-66, 74, 79, 82-83, 85, 85C, 88 and 94, ornaments at corners have been enlarged and end in a small ball.

Detail of **#68, 85D, 89, 96**

There is an outer line in 68, 85D, 89 and 96 cut below the stars and an outer line added to the ornaments above them.

Detail of **#72, 101**

In 72 and 101, parallel lines form an angle above the ribbon containing "U.S. Postage"; between these lines a row of dashes has been added, along with a point of color to the apex of the lower line.

	Issues of 1861-62	Un	U
	Perf. 12		
63	1¢ blue Franklin	325.00	32.50
	Double transfer	—	45.00
	Dot in "U"	350.00	37.50
a	1¢ ultramarine	750.00	275.00
b	1¢ dark blue	550.00	90.00
c	Laid paper	—	—
d	Vert. pair,		
	imperf. horizontally		—
e	Printed on both sides	—	2,500.00
64	3¢ pink Washington	7,500.00	750.00
a	3¢ pigeon blood pink	17,500.00	3,500.00
b	3¢ rose pink	550.00	150.00
65	3¢ rose Washington	130.00	2.50
	Cracked plate	—	—
	Double transfer	150.00	5.50
b	Laid paper	—	—
d	Vertical pair,		
	imperf. horizontally	3,500.00	750.00
e	Printed on both sides	3,250.00	2,750.00
f	Double impression		6,000.00
66	3¢ lake Washington is considered		
	a Trial Color Proof		
67	5¢ buff Jefferson	20,000.00	800.00
68	10¢ yellow green		
	Washington	750.00	50.00
	10¢ deep yellow green		
	on thin paper	900.00	60.00
	Double transfer	825.00	55.00
a	10¢ dark green	800.00	52.50
b	Vert. pair,		
	imperf. horizontally		3,500.00
69	12¢ blk. Washington	1,250.00	90.00
	12¢ intense black	1,300.00	105.00
	Double transfer of top		
	or bottom frame line	1,350.00	120.00
	Double transfer of top		
	and bottom frame lines	1,400.00	125.00
70	24¢ red lilac		
	Washington	2,000.00	175.00
	Scratch under "A"		
	of "POSTAGE"		—
a	24¢ brown lilac	1,600.00	130.00
b	24¢ steel blue	8,000.00	650.00
c	24¢ violet	9,500.00	1,250.00
d	24¢ grayish lilac	3,250.00	1,250.00
71	30¢ orange Franklin	1,600.00	160.00
a	Printed on both sides		—
72	90¢ bl. Washington	2,750.00	425.00
a	90¢ pale blue	2,500.00	425.00
b	90¢ dark blue	3,000.00	525.00
	Issues of 1861-66		
73	2¢ blk. Andrew Jackson	350.00	50.00
	Double transfer	400.00	55.00
	Major double transfer of top		
	left corner and "POSTAGE"		12,500.00
	Cracked plate	—	—

	Issues of 1861-66	Un	U
	Perf. 12		
	#74 3¢ scarlet Washington was not regularly		
	issued and is considered a Trial Color Proof.		
75	5¢ red brown		
	Jefferson (67)	4,500.00	450.00
76	5¢ brown Jefferson (67)	1,200.00	110.00
a	5¢ dark brown	1,350.00	160.00
	Double transfer of top		
	or bottom frame line	1,300.00	125.00
77	15¢ blk. Lincoln	1,750.00	150.00
	Double transfer	1,850.00	160.00
78	24¢ lilac Washington (70)	1,200.00	100.00
a	24¢ grayish lilac	1,200.00	100.00
b	24¢ gray	1,200.00	100.00
c	24¢ blackish violet	30,000.00	2,250.00
d	Printed on both sides		3,500.00
	Grills on U.S. Stamps		
	Between 1867 and 1870, postage stamps		
	were embossed with pyramid-shaped grills		
	that absorbed cancellation ink to prevent		
	reuse of canceled stamps.		
	Issues of 1867, With Grills		
	Grills A, B and with C: Points Up		
	A. Grill Covers Entire Stamp		
79	3¢ rose Washington (56)	5,000.00	1,100.00
b	Printed on both sides		—
80	5¢ brown Jefferson (57)	—	130,000.00
a	5¢ dark brown		130,000.00
81	30¢ orange Franklin (61)		60,000.00
	B. Grill about 18 x 15mm		
82	3¢ rose Washington (56)		175,000.00
	C. Grill about 13 x 16mm		
83	3¢ rose Washington (56)	5,000.00	950.00
	Double grill	6,250.00	2,250.00
	Grills, D, Z, E, F with Points Down		
	D. Grill about 12 x 14mm		
84	2¢ black Jackson (73)	15,000.00	3,000.00
85	3¢ rose Washington (56)	6,000.00	950.00
	Split grill		1,050.00
	Z. Grill about 11 x 14mm		
85A	1¢ blue Franklin (55)		935,000.00
85B	2¢ black Jackson (73)	7,000.00	1,100.00
	Double transfer	7,500.00	1,150.00
85C	3¢ rose Washington (56)	12,500.00	3,250.00
	Double grill	14,000.00	
85D	10¢ grn. Washington (58)		90,000.00
85E	12¢ blk. Washington (59)	11,000.00	1,500.00
	Double transfer		
	of top frame line		1,600.00
85F	15¢ black Lincoln (77)		220,000.00
	E. Grill about 11 x 13mm		
86	1¢ blue Franklin (55)	2,750.00	450.00
a	1¢ dull blue	2,750.00	425.00
	Double grill	—	575.00
	Split grill	2,850.00	500.00

Issues of 1867	Un	U
With Grills, Perf. 12		
87 2¢ black Jackson (73)	1,400.00	140.00
2¢ intense black	1,500.00	180.00
Double grill	—	—
Double transfer	1,500.00	155.00
88 3¢ rose Washington (65)	800.00	22.50
a 3¢ lake red	875.00	25.00
Double grill	—	—
Very thin paper	825.00	25.00
89 10¢ grn. Washington (68)	5,000.00	300.00
Double grill	6,400.00	500.00
90 12¢ blk. Washington (69)	4,500.00	350.00
Double transfer of top		
or bottom frame line	4,900.00	425.00
91 15¢ black Lincoln (77)	8,750.00	625.00
Double grill	—	950.00
F. Grill about 9 x 13mm		
92 1¢ blue Franklin (63)	1,000.00	200.00
Double transfer	1,050.00	240.00
Double grill	—	370.00
93 2¢ black Jackson (73)	475.00	47.50
Double grill	—	180.00
Very thin paper	525.00	55.00
94 3¢ red Washington (65)	360.00	7.50
a 3¢ rose	360.00	7.50
Double grill	—	
End roller grill		350.00
Quadruple split grill	650.00	130.00
c Vertical pair,		
imperf. horizontally	*1,100.00*	
d Printed on both sides	*2,250.00*	
95 5¢ brown Jefferson (67)	3,000.00	750.00
a 5¢ black brown	3,250.00	950.00
96 10¢ yellow green		
Washington (68)	2,500.00	200.00
a 10¢ dark green	2,500.00	200.00
Double transfer	—	—
Quadruple split grill		625.00
97 12¢ blk. Washington (69)	2,800.00	225.00
Double transfer of top		
or bottom frame line	3,100.00	240.00
Triple grill		—
98 15¢ black Lincoln (77)	3,250.00	300.00
Double transfer of		
upper right corner	—	—
Double grill	—	450.00
Quadruple split grill	4,000.00	625.00
99 24¢ gray lilac		
Washington (70)	5,500.00	850.00
100 30¢ orange Franklin (71)	5,500.00	700.00
Double grill	7,250.00	1,500.00
101 90¢ bl. Washington (72)	10,000.00	1,400.00
Double grill	*14,000.00*	

Issues of 1875	Un	U
Reissue of 1861-1866 Issues,		
Without Grill, Perf. 12		
102 1¢ blue Franklin (63)	*750.00*	*1,100.00*
103 2¢ black Jackson (73)	*3,250.00*	*5,000.00*
104 3¢ brown red		
Washington (65)	*3,500.00*	*5,750.00*
105 5¢ brown Jefferson (67)	*2,750.00*	*2,900.00*
106 10¢ grn. Washington (68)	*3,000.00*	*12,500.00*
107 12¢ blk. Washington (69)	*4,250.00*	*6,000.00*
108 15¢ black Lincoln (77)	*4,250.00*	*9,000.00*
109 24¢ deep violet		
Washington (70)	*5,000.00*	*9,000.00*
110 30¢ brownish orange		
Franklin (71)	*5,000.00*	*12,500.00*
111 90¢ bl. Washington (72)	*6,250.00*	*50,000.00*
Issues of 1869, With Grill,		
Hardware Paper		
G. Grill about 9.5 x 9mm		
112 1¢ buff Franklin	*750.00*	*160.00*
Double grill	*1,175.00*	*340.00*
b Without grill	*4,250.00*	
113 2¢ br. Post Horse and		
Rider	700.00	75.00
Split grill	850.00	100.00
Double transfer		95.00
114 3¢ Locomotive	300.00	20.00
Triple grill	—	—
Sextuple grill	—	*3,250.00*
Gray paper	—	95.00
a Without grill	1,100.00	
d Double impression		*3,500.00*
115 6¢ Washington	2,750.00	210.00
Quadruple split grill	—	825.00
116 10¢ Shield and Eagle	2,000.00	140.00
End roller grill	—	—
117 12¢ *S.S. Adriatic*	2,250.00	150.00
Split grill	2,700.00	165.00
118 15¢ Landing of Columbus,		
type I	7,500.00	650.00
119 15¢ type II (118)	3,250.00	250.00
b Center inverted	*275,000.00*	*18,000.00*
c Center double, one inverted		*35,000.00*
120 24¢ Declaration of		
Independence	7,000.00	750.00
b Center inverted	*275,000.00*	*19,000.00*
121 30¢ Shield, Eagle		
and Flags	7,000.00	550.00
Double grill	—	1,100.00
b Flags inverted	*210,000.00*	*65,000.00*
122 90¢ Lincoln	9,250.00	2,400.00
Split grill	—	—
Issues of 1875, Reissue of 1869 Issue,		
Without Grill, Hard White Paper, Perf. 12		
123 1¢ buff (112)	500.00	325.00
124 2¢ brown (113)	700.00	475.00
125 3¢ blue (114)	*5,250.00*	*15,000.00*
126 6¢ blue (115)	1,600.00	1,700.00

112

113

114

115

116

117

118

120

121

122

Details

15¢ Landing of Columbus, Types I-III, Series 1869-1875

Detail of **#118** Type I

Picture unframed.

Detail of **#119** Type II

Picture framed.

#129 Type III

Same as Type I but without fringe of brown shading lines around central vignette.

134

135

136

137

138

139

140

141

142

143

144

156

157

158

Details

Detail of #**134, 145**

Detail of #**135, 146**

Detail of #**136, 147**

Detail of #**156, 167, 182, 192**

1¢. In the pearl at the left of the numeral "1" there is a small crescent.

Detail of #**157, 168, 178, 180, 183, 193**

2¢. Under the scroll at the left of "U.S." there is a small diagonal line. This mark seldom shows clearly.

Detail of #**158, 169, 184, 194**

3¢. The under part of the upper tail of the left ribbon is heavily shaded.

Issues of 1875	Un	U
127	10¢ yellow (116)	2,100.00	1,750.00
128	12¢ green (117)	2,750.00	2,750.00
129	15¢ brown and blue, type III (118)	2,000.00	1,000.00
a	Imperf. horizontally	3,500.00	7,000
130	24¢ grn. & violet (120)	2,250.00	1,400.00
131	30¢ bl. & carmine (121)	3,000.00	2,500.00
132	90¢ car. & black (122)	5,000.00	5,500.00

Issue of 1880, Reissue of 1869, Soft Porous Paper

		Un	U
133	1¢ buff (112)	325.00	200.00
a	1¢ brown orange, issued without gum	240.00	175.00

Issues of 1870-71
With Grill, White Wove Paper, No Secret Marks
H. Grill about 10 x 12mm

		Un	U
134	1¢ Franklin	2,000.00	140.00
	End roller grill		650.00
135	2¢ Jackson	1,200.00	70.00
136	3¢ Washington	725.00	19.00
	Cracked plate	—	90.00
137	6¢ Lincoln	4,250.00	525.00
	Double grill	—	900.00
138	7¢ Edwin M. Stanton	3,000.00	425.00
139	10¢ Jefferson	4,750.00	650.00
140	12¢ Henry Clay	21,000.00	3,000.00
141	15¢ Daniel Webster	5,500.00	1,200.00
142	24¢ Gen. Winfield Scott	—	6,500.00
143	30¢ Alexander Hamilton	14,000.00	2,400.00
144	90¢ Commodore Perry	13,500.00	1,600.00
	Split grill		1,650.00

Issues of 1870-71	Un	U
Without Grill, White Wove Paper, No Secret Marks		
145	1¢ ultra. Franklin (134)	475.00	15.00
146	2¢ red brn. Jackson (135)	325.00	9.00
147	3¢ grn. Washington (136)	300.00	1.50
148	6¢ carmine Lincoln (137)	675.00	25.00
	6¢ violet carmine	700.00	30.00
149	7¢ verm. Stanton (138)	850.00	90.00
150	10¢ brown Jefferson (139)	725.00	20.00
151	12¢ dull violet Clay (140)	1,750.00	160.00
152	15¢ brt. or. Webster (141)	1,900.00	160.00
153	24¢ purple Scott (142)	1,500.00	140.00
154	30¢ black Hamilton (143)	5,000.00	190.00
155	90¢ carmine Perry (144)	4,000.00	300.00

Issues of 1873, Without Grill, White Wove Paper, Thin to Thick, Secret Marks

		Un	U
156	1¢ ultra. Franklin	225.00	3.75
	Paper with silk fibers	—	25.00
f	Imperf. pair	—	550.00
157	2¢ br. Jackson	375.00	17.50
	Double paper	500.00	35.00
c	With grill	1,850.00	750.00
158	3¢ gr. Washington	130.00	.50
	olive green	375.00	15.00
	Cracked plate	—	32.50

Abraham Lincoln House
Springfield, Illinois

Springfield, Illinois—the "city Lincoln loved"— was home to Abraham Lincoln for 24 years. He came to the Illinois capital in 1837 while serving as a state representative, and he remained there to practice law when his legislative term ended in 1841.

Three years later, Lincoln the lawyer was also a husband, father, and new homeowner. In 1844, he bought the first and only home he ever owned, giving Dr. Charles Dresser $1,200 and property worth $300 for a two-story frame house at 413 South Eighth Street; Dr. Dresser was the Episcopal minister who had officiated at the wedding of Lincoln and Mary Todd. The couple and their sons lived in the house until 1861, when Lincoln became the 16th President of the United States and moved his family to Washington, D.C.

Now known as the Lincoln Home National Historic Site, the old family residence has been carefully restored and contains many original furnishings. ■

Issues of 1873		Un	U
Without Grill, White Wove Paper, Thin to Thick, Secret Marks			
159	6¢ dull pk. Lincoln	425.00	17.50
b	With grill	1,800.00	
160	7¢ or. verm. Stanton	1,100.00	80.00
	Ribbed paper	—	95.00
161	10¢ br. Jefferson	700.00	18.00
162	12¢ bl. vio. Clay	1,800.00	95.00
163	15¢ yel. or. Webster	2,100.00	110.00
a	With grill	5,250.00	
164	24¢ pur. Scott	—	
165	30¢ gray blk. Hamilton	2,500.00	100.00
166	90¢ rose carm. Perry	2,750.00	250.00
Issues of 1875, Special Printing, Hard, White Wove Paper, Without Gum, Secret Marks			
	Although perforated, these stamps were usually cut apart with scissors. As a result, the perforations are often much mutilated and the design is frequently damaged.		
167	1¢ ultra. Franklin (156)	10,500.00	
168	2¢ dk. br. Jackson (157)	4,750.00	
169	3¢ blue green Washington (158)	12,500.00	—
170	6¢ dull rose Lincoln (159)	11,500.00	
171	7¢ reddish vermilion Stanton (160)	2,850.00	
172	10¢ pale brown Jefferson (161)	11,500.00	
173	12¢ dark vio. Clay (162)	4,250.00	

Issues of 1875		Un	U
174	15¢ bright orange Webster (163)	11,500.00	
175	24¢ dull pur. Scott (142)	2,900.00	5,000.00
176	30¢ greenish black Hamilton (143)	8,500.00	
177	90¢ vio. car. Perry (144)	10,500.00	
Regular Issue, Yellowish Wove Paper			
178	2¢ verm. Jackson (157)	400.00	10.00
c	With grill	750.00	
179	5¢ Zachary Taylor, June	550.00	20.00
	Cracked plate	—	170.00
	Double paper	625.00	
	Paper with silk fibers		32.50
c	With grill	3,000.00	
Special Printing, Hard, White Wove Paper, Without Gum			
180	2¢ carmine vermilion Jackson (157)	30,000.00	
181	5¢ br. bl. Taylor (179)	50,000.00	
Issues of 1879, Soft, Porous Paper, Thin to Thick, Perf. 12			
182	1¢ dark ultramarine Franklin (156)	300.00	3.50
183	2¢ verm. Jackson (157)	130.00	3.00
a	Double impression	—	—

Jefferson Memorial

Using the Pantheon of ancient Rome as his model, American architect John Russell Pope (1874-1937) designed the classically beautiful Jefferson Memorial in Washington, D.C. The domed, circular structure was dedicated in 1943, two hundred years after the birth of Thomas Jefferson, the third President of the United States.

Marble from Vermont adorns the memorial's outside walls; white Georgia marble lines the interior. Inside, beneath the dome, a 6-foot-high pedestal of Minnesota marble supports a 5-ton, 19-foot-tall bronze statue of Jefferson by Washington-born sculptor Rudulph Evans. The surrounding walls are inscribed with selections from Jefferson's writings, including these immortal words: "I have sworn upon the altar of God eternal hostility against every form of tyranny over the mind of man."

The Postal Service featured the Jefferson Memorial on stamps issued in 1966 and 1973. The earlier stamp, a Beautification of America issue, depicted the memorial during Washington's glorious cherry blossom season. ■

159

160

161

162

163

179

Details

Detail of **#137, 148**

Detail of **#138, 149**

Detail of **#139, 150, 187**

Detail of **#159, 170, 186, 195**

6¢. The first four vertical lines of the shading in the lower part of the left ribbon have been strengthened.

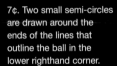

Detail of **#160, 171, 196**

7¢. Two small semi-circles are drawn around the ends of the lines that outline the ball in the lower righthand corner.

Detail of **#161, 172, 188, 197**

10¢. There is a small semi-circle in the scroll at the right end of the upper label.

Detail of **#140, 151**

Detail of **#141, 152**

Detail of **#143, 154, 165, 176**

Detail of **#162, 173, 198**

12¢. The balls of the figure "2" are crescent-shaped.

Detail of **#163, 174, 189, 199**

15¢. In the lower part of the triangle in the upper left corner two lines have been made heavier, forming a "V." This mark can be found on some of the Continental and American (1879) printings, but not all stamps show it.

Detail of **#190**

30¢. In the "S" of "CENTS," the vertical spike across the middle section of the letter has been broadened.

205

206

207

208

209

210

211

212

219

220

221

222

223

224

225

226

227

228

229

Details

Issues of 1881-82, Re-engravings of 1873 Designs

Detail of **#206**

1¢. Upper vertical lines have been deepened, creating a solid effect in parts of background. Upper arabesques shaded.

Detail of **#207**

3¢. Shading at sides of central oval is half its previous width A short horizontal dash has been cut below the "TS" of "CENTS."

Detail of **#208**

6¢. Has three vertical lines instead of four between the edge of the panel and the outside of the stamp.

Detail of **#209**

10¢. Has four vertical lines instead of five between left side of oval and edge of the shield. Horizontal lines in lower part of background strengthened.

Issues of 1879	Un	U
184 3¢ grn. Washington (158)	100.00	.60
Double transfer	—	—
Short transfer	—	6.00
185 5¢ blue Taylor (179)	500.00	12.00
186 6¢ pink Lincoln (159)	950.00	20.00
187 10¢ brown Jefferson		
(139) (no secret mark)	2,250.00	25.00
188 10¢ brown Jefferson		
(161) (with secret mark)	1,750.00	25.00
black brown	1,900.00	37.50
Double transfer		45.00
189 15¢ red or. Webster (163)	350.00	22.50
190 30¢ full blk. Hamilton (143)	1,100.00	55.00
191 90¢ carmine Perry (144)	2,250.00	275.00
Issues of 1880, Special Printing,		
Soft Porous Paper, Without Gum, Perf. 12		
192 1¢ dark ultramarine		
Franklin (156)	25,000.00	
193 2¢ blk. br. Jackson (157)	10,000.00	
194 3¢ blue green		
Washington (158)	32,500.00	
195 6¢ dull rose		
Lincoln (159)	17,000.00	
196 7¢ scarlet vermilion		
Stanton (160)	3,500.00	
197 10¢ deep brown		
Jefferson (161)	17,000.00	
198 12¢ blk. pur. Clay (162)	5,000.00	
199 15¢ or. Webster (163)	17,000.00	
200 24¢ dk. vio. Scott (142)	5,000.00	
201 30¢ greenish black		
Hamilton (143)	12,500.00	
202 90¢ dull carmine		
Perry (144)	14,000.00	
203 2¢ scarlet vermilion		
Jackson (157)	26,000.00	
204 5¢ dp. bl. Taylor (179)	45,000.00	
Issues of 1882, Perf. 12		
205 5¢ Garfield, Apr. 10	275.00	8.00
Special Printing, Soft Porous		
Paper, Without Gum, Perf. 12		
205C 5¢ gray brown		
Garfield (205)	28,500.00	
Issues of 1881-82, Designs		
of 1873 Re-engraved		
206 1¢ Franklin, Aug. 1881	80.00	.90
Double transfer	105.00	6.00
207 3¢ Washington,		
July 16, 1881	80.00	.55
Double transfer	—	12.00
Cracked plate	—	
208 6¢ Lincoln, June 1882	525.00	80.00
a 6¢ deep brown red	475.00	110.00
209 10¢ Jefferson, Apr. 1882	160.00	6.00
10¢ pur. or. olive brown	175.00	6.50
b 10¢ black brown	800.00	47.50

Issues of 1883	Un	U
210 2¢ Washington, Oct. 1	50.00	.60
Double transfer	55.00	2.25
211 4¢ Jackson, Oct. 1	275.00	17.50
Cracked plate	—	
Special Printing, Soft Porous Paper, Perf. 12		
211B 2¢ pale red brown		
Washington (210)	500.00	—
c Horizontal pair,		
imperf. between	2,000.00	
211D 4¢ deep blue green		
Jackson (211) no gum	27,500.00	
Issues of 1887, Perf. 12		
212 1¢ Franklin, June	110.00	1.75
Double transfer	—	
213 2¢ green Washington		
(210), Sept. 10	50.00	.40
Double transfer	—	3.25
b Printed on both sides	—	
214 3¢ vermilion Washington		
(207), Oct. 3	80.00	60.00
Issues of 1888, Perf. 12		
215 4¢ carmine		
Jackson (211), Nov.	225.00	20.00
216 5¢ indigo		
Garfield (205), Feb.	240.00	14.00
217 30¢ orange brown		
Hamilton (165), Jan.	450.00	110.00
218 90¢ pur. Perry (166),		
Feb.	1,300.00	250.00
Issues of 1890-93, Perf. 12		
219 1¢ Franklin, Feb. 22, 1890	27.50	.50
Double transfer	—	—
219D 2¢ lake Washington		
(220), Feb. 22, 1890	250.00	1.00
Double transfer	—	—
220 2¢ Washington, 1890	22.50	.45
Double transfer	—	3.25
a Cap on left "2"	100.00	2.50
c Cap on both "2s"	475.00	20.00
221 3¢ Jackson, Feb. 22, 1890	80.00	7.50
222 4¢ Lincoln, June 2, 1890	90.00	2.75
Double transfer	105.00	—
223 5¢ Grant, June 2, 1890	80.00	2.75
Double transfer	100.00	3.25
224 6¢ Garfield, Feb. 22, 1890	85.00	20.00
225 8¢ Sherman, Mar. 21, 1893	60.00	13.00
226 10¢ Webster,		
Feb. 22, 1890	190.00	3.50
Double transfer	—	—
227 15¢ Clay, Feb. 22, 1890	250.00	20.00
Double transfer	—	—
Triple transfer	—	
228 30¢ Jefferson,		
Feb. 22, 1890	375.00	30.00
Double transfer	—	—
229 90¢ Perry, Feb. 22, 1890	550.00	125.00
Short transfer at bottom	—	—

Issues of 1893			Un	U	PB	#	FDC	Q(M)
Columbian Exposition Issue, Printed by The American Bank Note Co., Perf. 12								
230	1¢ Columbus in Sight of Land	01/02/93	22.50	40	310.00	(6)	*4,000.00*	449
	Double transfer		27.50	.75				
	Cracked plate		90.00					
231	2¢ Landing of Columbus	01/02/93	21.00	.25	250.00	(6)	*3,500.00*	1,464
	Double transfer		26.00	.30				
	Triple transfer		62.50	—				
	Quadruple transfer		95.00					
	Broken hat on third figure left of Columbus		65.00	.35				
	Broken frame line		22.50	.30				
	Recut frame lines		22.50	—				
	Cracked plate		87.50					
232	3¢ *Santa Maria*, Flagship	01/02/93	60.00	15.00	725.00	(6)	*6,000.00*	12
	Double transfer		80.00	—				
233	4¢ ultramarine, Fleet	01/02/93	87.50	7.50	1,050.00	(6)	*9,500.00*	19
a	4¢ blue (error)		*19,000.00*	*15,000.00*	*87,500.00*	(4)		
	Double transfer		125.00	—				
234	5¢ Columbus Soliciting Aid from Queen Isabella	01/02/93	95.00	8.00	1,400.00	(6)	*16,000*	35
	Double transfer		145.00	—				
235	6¢ Columbus Welcomed at Barcelona	01/02/93	85.00	22.50			*20,000.00*	5
a	6¢ red violet		85.00	22.50	1,175.00	(6)		
	Double transfer		110.00	30.00				
236	8¢ Columbus Restored to Favor	03/93	75.00	11.00	825.00	(6)		11
	Double transfer		87.50	—				
237	10¢ Columbus Presenting Natives	01/02/93	140.00	8.00	3,350.00	(6)	*7,500.00*	17
	Double transfer		180.00	12.50				
	Triple transfer		—					
238	15¢ Columbus Announcing His Discovery	01/02/93	240.00	65.00	*3,750.00*	(6)		2
	Double transfer		—	—				
239	30¢ Columbus at La Rábida	01/02/93	300.00	85.00	*8,500.00*	(6)		0.6
240	50¢ Recall of Columbus	01/02/93	600.00	160.00	*14,000.00*	(6)		0.2
	Double transfer		—	—				
	Triple transfer		—	—				
241	$1 Queen Isabella Pledging Her Jewels	01/02/93	1,400.00	650.00	*47,500.00*	(6)		0.05
	Double transfer		—	—				
242	$2 Columbus in Chains	01/02/93	1,450.00	600.00	*67,500.00*	(6)	*52,500.00*	0.05
243	$3 Columbus Describing His Third Voyage	01/02/93	2,250.00	1,000.00				0.03
a	$3 olive green		2,250.00	1,000.00	*85,000.00*	(6)		
244	$4 Queen Isabella and Columbus	01/02/93	3,000.00	1,350.00				0.03
a	$4 rose carmine		3,000.00	1,350.00	*250,000.00*	(6)		
245	$5 Portrait of Columbus	01/02/93	3,500.00	1,600.00	*190,000.00*	(6)		0.03

230

231

232

233

234

235

236

237

238

239

240

241

242

243

244

245

246

248

253

254

255

256

257

258

259

Details

2¢ Washington Types I-III, Series 1894-98

Triangle of **#248-50, 265** Type I

Horizontal lines of uniform thickness run across the triangle.

Triangle of **#251, 266** Type II

Horizontal lines cross the triangle, but are thinner within than without.

Triangle of **#252, 267, 279B-279Be** Type III

The horizontal lines do not cross the double frame lines of the triangle.

Issues of 1894		Un	U	PB	#
Unwmkd., Perf. 12					

Bureau Issues Starting in 1894 and continuing until 1979, the Bureau of Engraving and Printing in Washington produced all U.S. postage stamps except #909-21, 1335, 1355, 1410-18 and 1789. Beginning in 1979, security printers in addition to the Bureau of Engraving and Printing started producing postage stamps under contract with the U.S. Postal Service.

#	Description		Un	U	PB	#
246	1¢ Franklin	10/94	32.50	4.50	400.00	(6)
	Double transfer		40.00	5.50		
247	1¢ blue Franklin (246)	11/94	67.50	2.25	800.00	(6)
	Double transfer		—	3.75		
248	2¢ pink Washington, type I	10/94	27.50	3.25	275.00	(6)
	Double transfer		—	—		
249	2¢ carmine lake, type I (248)	10/94	145.00	3.00	1,750.00	(6)
	Double transfer		—	3.50		
250	2¢ carmine, type I (248)		30.00	1.20		
a	2¢ rose		30.00	2.25		
b	2¢ scarlet		30.00	.45	350.00	(6)
	Double transfer		—	3.25		
c	Vertical pair, imperf. horizontally		3,000.00			
d	Horizontal pair, imperf. between		2,000.00			
251	2¢ carmine, type II (248)		275.00	6.00	3,000.00	(6)
252	2¢ carmine, type III (248)		120.00	6.00		
a	2¢ scarlet		120.00	6.00	1,650.00	(6)
b	Horizontal pair, imperf. vertically		1,500.00			
c	Horizontal pair, imperf. between		1,750.00			
253	3¢ Jackson	09/94	105.00	9.00	1,250.00	(6)
254	4¢ Lincoln	09/94	135.00	4.25	1,750.00	(6)
255	5¢ Grant	09/94	100.00	6.00	1,150.00	(6)
	Worn plate, diagonal lines missing in oval background		100.00	4.50		
	Double transfer		125.00	6.50		
c	Vertical pair, imperf. horiz.		2,250.00			
256	6¢ Garfield	07/94	150.00	22.50	2,650.00	(6)
a	Vertical pair, imperf. horizontally		1,500.00		13,000.00	(6)
257	8¢ Sherman	03/94	140.00	16.00	1,750.00	(6)
258	10¢ Webster	09/94	250.00	11.00	2,850.00	(6)
	Double transfer		290.00	12.50		
259	15¢ Clay	10/94	300.00	55.00	4,500.00	(6)

	Issues of 1894		Un	U	PB	#
260	50¢ Jefferson	11/94	475.00	120.00	*9,000.00*	(6)
261	$1 Perry, type I	11/94	1,000.00	350.00	*17,000.00*	(6)
261A	$1 black Perry, type II (261)	11/94	2,300.00	700.00	*26,500.00*	(6)
262	$2 James Madison	12/94	3,100.00	1,100.00	*40,000.00*	(6)
263	$5 John Marshall	12/94	4,500.00	2,250.00	*21,000.00*	(3)
	Issues of 1895, Wmkd. (191), Perf. 12					
264	1¢ blue Franklin (246)	04/95	6.50	.30	210.00	(6)
265	2¢ carmine Washington,					
	type I (248)	05/95	30.00	1.50	375.00	(6)
	Double transfer		45.00	5.00		
266	2¢ carmine, type II (248)		30.00	3.25	410.00	(6)
267	2¢ carmine, type III (248)		5.50	.25	175.00	(6)
268	3¢ purple Jackson (253)	10/95	37.50	1.25	650.00	(6)
	Double transfer		45.00	3.00		
269	4¢ dark brown Lincoln (254)	06/95	40.00	1.75	700.00	(6)
	Double transfer		45.00	3.25		
270	5¢ chocolate Grant (255)	06/11/95	37.50	2.10	600.00	(6)
	Double transfer		45.00	3.50		
	Worn plate, diagonal lines					
	missing in oval background		40.00	2.75		
271	6¢ dull brown Garfield (256)	08/95	95.00	4.75	2,250.00	(6)
	Very thin paper		105.00	5.00		
a	Wmkd. USIR		9,000.00	5,000.00		
272	8¢ violet brown Sherman (257)	07/95	65.00	1.40	850.00	(6)
	Double transfer		80.00	3.00		
a	Wmkd. USIR		*3,250.00*	600.00	*12,500.00*	(3)
273	10¢ dark green Webster (258)	06/95	95.00	1.60	1,600.00	(6)
	Double transfer		120.00	3.60		
274	15¢ dark blue Clay (259)	09/95	225.00	10.00	3,250.00	(6)
275	50¢ orange Jefferson (260)	11/95	300.00	22.50	5,750.00	(6)
a	50¢ red orange		325.00	27.50	5,750.00	(6)
276	$1 black Perry, type I (261)	08/95	650.00	80.00	*13,500.00*	(6)
276A	$1 black Perry, type II (261)	08/95	1,300.00	175.00	*24,000.00*	(6)
277	$2 bright blue Madison (262)	08/95	1,100.00	350.00		
a	$2 dark blue		1,100.00	350.00	*20,000.00*	(6)
278	$5 dark green Marshall (263)	08/95	2,400.00	500.00	*72,500.00*	(6)

260

261

262

263

277

Watermark 191
Double-line
"USPS" in
capital letters;
detail at right.

Details

$1 Perry, Types I-II, Series 1894

Detail of **#261, 276**
Type I

The circles enclosing
$1 are broken.

Detail of **#261A, 276A**
Type I

The circles enclosing
$1 are complete.

	Issues of 1898-1900		Un	U	PB	#	FDC	Q(M)
	Wmkd. (191), Perf. 12							
279	1¢ deep grn. Franklin (246)	01/98	9.00	.30	175.00	(6)		
	Double transfer		12.00	.90				
279B	2¢ red Washington, type III (248)	01/98	9.00	.30	200.00	(6)		
c	2¢ rose carmine, type III		250.00	75.00	2,750.00	(6)		
d	2¢ orange red, type III		10.00	.35	210.00	(6)		
e	Booklet pane of 6	04/16/00	425.00	425.00				
f	2¢ carmine, type IV		10.00	.30	210.00	(6)		
g	2¢ pink, type IV		11.00	.45	230.00	(6)		
h	2¢ vermillion, type IV		10.00	.30	210.00	(6)		
i	2¢ brown orange, type IV		*100.00*	*6.00*	*400.00*	(3)		
280	4¢ rose brn. Lincoln (254)	10/98	30.00	1.00				
a	4¢ lilac brown		30.00	1.00				
b	4¢ orange brown		30.00	1.00	600.00	(6)		
	Extra frame line at top		50.00	4.25				
281	5¢ dark blue Grant (255)	03/98	35.00	.85	600.00	(6)		
	Double transfer		45.00	2.10				
	Worn plate, diagonal lines missing in oval background		40.00	1.00				
282	6¢ lake Garfield (256)	12/98	45.00	2.75	800.00	(6)		
	Double transfer		57.50	3.75				
a	6¢ purple lake		60.00	4.00	1,000.00	(6)		
282C	10¢ brown Webster (258), type I	11/98	180.00	2.75	2,250.00	(6)		
	Double transfer		200.00	4.50				
283	10¢ orange brown Webster (258), type II		110.00	2.25	1,600.00	(6)		
284	15¢ olive grn. Clay (259)	11/98	150.00	8.25	2,000.00	(6)		
	Issues of 1898, Trans-Mississippi Exposition Issue							
285	1¢ Jacques Marquette on the Mississippi	06/17/98	30.00	6.25	300.00	(6)	*12,500.00*	71
	Double transfer		40.00	7.50				
286	2¢ Farming in the West	06/17/98	27.50	1.60	275.00	(6)	*9,500.00*	160
	Double transfer		42.50	2.50				
	Worn plate		30.00	1.90				
287	4¢ Indian Hunting Buffalo	06/17/98	150.00	24.00	1,400.00	(6)	*27,500.00*	5
288	5¢ John Charles Frémont on the Rocky Mountains	06/17/98	140.00	21.00	1,300.00	(6)	*17,500.00*	8
289	8¢ Troops Guarding Wagon Train	06/17/98	180.00	42.50	2,750.00	(6)	*20,000*	3
a	Vertical pair, imperf. horizontally		*19,000.00*		*75,000.00*	(4)		
290	10¢ Hardships of Emigration	06/17/98	180.00	27.50	3,000.00	(6)	*27,500.00*	5
291	50¢ Western Mining Prospector	06/17/98	650.00	190.00	*25,000*	(6)	*30,000.00*	0.5
292	$1 Western Cattle in Storm	06/17/98	1,250.00	550.00	*50,000.00*	(6)	—	0.06
293	$2 Mississippi River Bridge	06/17/98	2,100.00	1,000.00	*150,000.00*	(6)		0.06

282C

285

286

287

288

289

290

291

292

293

Details

10¢ Webster Types I-II, Series 1898

Detail of **#282C**
Type I

The tips of the foliate ornaments do not impinge on the white curved line below "TEN CENTS."

Detail of **#283**
Type II

The tips of the ornaments break the curved line below the "E" of "TEN" and the "T" of "CENTS."

294

295

296

297

298

299

300

301

302

303

304

305

306

307

308

309

310

311

312

313

Issues of 1901-1903			Un	U	PB	#	FDC	Q(M)
Issues of 1901, Pan-American Exposition Issue, Perf. 12								
294	1¢ Fast Lake Navigation	05/01/01	18.00	3.00	225.00	(6)	*4,500.00*	91
a	Center inverted		*10,000.00*	*8,500.00*	*75,000.00*	(4)		
295	2¢ Empire State Express	05/01/01	17.50	1.00	225.00	(6)	*2,750.00*	210
a	Center inverted		*42,500.00*	*17,500.00*	*375,000.00*	(4)		
296	4¢ Electric Automobile	05/01/01	82.50	15.00	2,100.00	(6)		6
a	Center inverted		*22,500.00*		*140,000.00*	(4)		
297	5¢ Bridge at Niagara Falls	05/01/01	95.00	14.00	2,250.00	(6)	*15,000.00*	7
298	8¢ Canal Locks at Sault Ste. Marie	05/01/01	120.00	50.00	*4,000.00*	(6)		5
299	10¢ Fast Ocean Navigation	05/01/01	170.00	25.00	7,000.00	(6)		5
	Wmkd. (191), Perf. 12 (All issued in 1903 except #300b, 306, 308)							
300	1¢ Franklin	02/03	12.00	.20	200.00	(6)		
	Double transfer		17.50	1.00				
	Worn plate		13.00	.30				
	Cracked plate		14.00	.30				
b	Booklet pane of 6	03/06/07	600.00	2,750.00				
301	2¢ Washington	01/17/03	16.00	.20	240.00	(6)	*2,750.00*	
	Double transfer		27.50	1.00				
	Cracked plate		—	1.00				
c	Booklet pane of 6	01/24/03	500.00	2,250.00				
302	3¢ Jackson	02/03	55.00	2.75	725.00	(6)		
	Double transfer		77.50	3.75				
	Cracked plate		—	—				
303	4¢ Grant	02/03	60.00	1.25	750.00	(6)		
	Double transfer		77.50	2.75				
304	5¢ Lincoln	01/03	60.00	1.50	750.00	(6)		
305	6¢ Garfield	02/03	72.50	2.50	875.00	(6)		
	6¢ brownish lake		72.50	2.50				
	Double transfer		77.50	3.50				
306	8¢ Martha Washington	12/02	45.00	2.00	675.00	(6)		
	8¢ lavender		55.00	2.75				
307	10¢ Daniel Webster	02/03	70.00	1.40	1,000.00	(6)		
308	13¢ Benjamin Harrison	11/18/02	50.00	7.50	625.00	(6)		
309	15¢ Henry Clay	05/27/03	170.00	4.75	3,000.00	(6)		
	Double transfer		210.00	9.00				
310	50¢ Jefferson	03/23/03	475.00	22.50	*7,000.00*	(6)		
311	$1 David G. Farragut	06/05/03	775.00	55.00	*18,000.00*	(6)		
312	$2 Madison	06/05/03	1,250.00	190.00	*32,500.00*	(6)		
313	$5 Marshall	06/05/03	3,000.00	750.00	*110,000.00*	(6)		

For listings of #312 and 313 with perf. 10, see #479 and 480.

	Issues of 1906-08		Un	U	PB/LP	#	FDC	Q(M)
	Imperf. (All issued in 1908 except #314)							
314	1¢ bl. grn. Franklin (300)	10/02/06	18.00	15.00	170.00	(6)		
314A	4¢ brown Grant (303)	04/08	*40,000.00*	*35,000.00*				
	#314A was issued imperforated, but all copies were privately perforated at the sides.							
315	5¢ blue Lincoln (304)	05/12/08	260.00	*600.00*	2,750.00	(6)		
	Coil Stamps, Perf. 12 Horizontally							
316	1¢ bl. grn. pair Franklin (300)	02/18/08	*105,000*	—	175,000.00	(2)		
317	5¢ blue pair Lincoln (304)	02/24/08	*12,500.00*	—	*28,000.00*	(2)		
	Coil Stamp, Perf. 12 Vertically							
318	1¢ bl. grn. pair Franklin (300)	07/31/08	11,000.00	—	*17,000.00*	(2)		
	Issues of 1903, Perf. 12							
319	2¢ Washington	11/12/03	6.00	.20	100.00	(6)		
a	2¢ lake, type I		—	—				
b	2¢ carmine rose, type I		8.00	.35	140.00	(6)		
c	2¢ scarlet, type I		6.00	.25	95.00	(6)		
d	Vertical pair, imperf. horizontally		*6,000.00*					
e	Vertical pair, imperf. between		*1,250.00*					
f	2¢ lake, type II		8.00	.25	240.00	(6)		
g	Booklet pane of 6, carmine, type I	12/03/03	120.00	*225.00*				
h	Booklet pane of 6, carmine, type II		290.00					
i	2¢ carmine, type II		27.50	*50.00*				
j	2¢ carmine rose, type II		20.00	.75	500.00	(6)		
k	2¢ scarlet, type II		18.00	.45	500.00	(6)		
m	Booklet pane of 6, lake		—					
n	Booklet pane of 6, carmine rose		180.00	*300.00*				
p	Booklet pane of 6, scarlet		170.00	*275.00*				
q	Booklet pane of 6, lake		210.00	*450.00*				
	Issues of 1906, Washington (319), Imperf.							
320	2¢ carmine	10/02/06	18.00	12.00	200.00	(6)		
	Double transfer		25.00	16.00				
a	2¢ lake, die II		50.00	40.00	725.00	(6)		
b	2¢ scarlet		18.00	12.50	200.00	(6)		
c	2¢ carmine rose, type I		55.00	40.00				
d	2¢ carmine, type II		—					
	Issues of 1908, Coil Stamp (319), Perf. 12 Horizontally							
321	2¢ carmine pair, type I	02/18/08	*125,000.00*		—			
	Coil Stamp, Perf. 12 Vertically							
322	2¢ carmine pair, type II	07/31/08	11,000.00	—	*14,000.00*	(2)		
	Issues of 1904, Louisiana Purchase Exposition Issue, Perf. 12							
323	1¢ Robert R. Livingston	04/30/04	30.00	4.00	275.00	(6)	*6,000.00*	80
	Diagonal line through left "1"		50.00	11.00				
324	2¢ Thomas Jefferson	04/30/04	27.50	1.50	275.00	(6)	*4,750.00*	193
325	3¢ James Monroe	04/30/04	90.00	30.00	950.00	(6)	*5,000.00*	5
326	5¢ William McKinley	04/30/04	95.00	25.00	1,000.00	(6)	*22,500.00*	7
327	10¢ Map of Louisiana Purchase	04/30/04	180.00	30.00	2,250.00	(6)	*24,000.00*	4
	Issues of 1907, Jamestown Exposition Issue, Wmkd. (191), Perf. 12							
328	1¢ Captain John Smith	04/26/07	30.00	4.00	275.00	(6)	*6,000.00*	78
	Double transfer		35.00	5.00				
329	2¢ Founding of Jamestown, 1607	04/26/07	35.00	3.50	375.00	(6)	*9,000.00*	149
330	5¢ Pocahontas	04/26/07	135.00	27.50	2,600.00	(6)		

319

323

324

325

326

327

328

329

330

Details

2¢ Washington Die I-II, Series 1903

Detail of #319a, 319b, 319g Die I

Detail of #319c, 319f, 319h, 319i Die II

1908-1909

331 **332** **333** **334**

335 **336** **337** **338**

339 **340** **341** **342**

Details

3¢ Washington Types I-IV, Series 1908-1919

Detail of **#333, 345, 359, 376, 389, 394, 426, 445, 456, 464, 483, 493, 501-01b**
Type I

Top line of toga rope is weak and rope shading lines are thin. Fifth line from left is missing. Line between lips is thin.

Detail of **#529**
Type I

Top row of toga rope is strong but fifth shading line is missing as in Type I. Toga button center shading line consists of two dashes, central dot. "P," "O" of "POSTAGE" are separated by line of color.

Detail of **#530, 535**
Type IV

Top rope shading lines are complete. Second, fourth toga button shading lines are broken in middle, third line is continuous with dot in center. "P," "O" of "POSTAGE" are joined.

	Issues of 1908-09		Un	U	PB/LP	#
	Wmkd. (191) Perf. 12 (All issued in 1908 except #336, 338-42, 345-47)					
331	1¢ Franklin	12/08	7.25	.20	77.50	(6)
	Double transfer		9.50	.60		
a	Booklet pane of 6	12/02/08	160.00	*140.00*		
332	2¢ Washington	11/08	6.75	.20	70.00	(6)
	Double transfer		12.50	—		
	Cracked plate		—	—		
a	Booklet pane of 6	11/16/08	135.00	*125.00*		
333	3¢ Washington, type I	12/08	35.00	2.50	350.00	(6)
a	"China Clay" paper		*1,000.00*		9,000.00	(6)
334	4¢ Washington	12/08	42.50	1.00	425.00	(6)
	Double transfer		55.00	—		
a	"China Clay" paper		*1,300.00*			
335	5¢ Washington	12/08	52.50	2.00	525.00	(6)
a	"China Clay" paper		*1,000.00*			
336	6¢ Washington	01/09	65.00	5.00	750.00	(6)
a	"China Clay" paper		*750.00*			
337	8¢ Washington	12/08	50.00	2.50	500.00	(6)
	Double transfer		57.50	—		
a	"China Clay" paper		*1,000.00*			
338	10¢ Washington	01/09	70.00	1.40	800.00	(6)
a	"China Clay" paper		*1,000.00*			
339	13¢ Washington	01/09	42.50	19.00	500.00	(6)
	Line through "TAG" of "POSTAGE"		70.00	—		
a	"China Clay" paper		*1,000.00*			
340	15¢ Washington	01/09	70.00	5.50	650.00	(6)
a	"China Clay" paper		*1,000.00*			
341	50¢ Washington	01/13/09	350.00	20.00	*7,000.00*	(6)
342	$1 Washington	01/29/09	525.00	90.00	*16,000.00*	(6)
	Imperf.					
343	1¢ green Franklin (331)	12/08	5.00	4.50	47.50	(6)
	Double transfer		11.00	7.00		
344	2¢ carmine Washington (332)	12/10/08	6.00	3.00	77.50	(6)
	Double transfer		12.50	4.00		
	Foreign entry, design of 1¢		*1,250.00*	—		
	#345-47: Washington (333-35)					
345	3¢ deep violet, type I	1809	11.50	20.00	155.00	(6)
	Double transfer		22.50	—		
346	4¢ orange brown	02/25/09	19.00	22.50	175.00	(6)
	Double transfer		37.50	—		
347	5¢ blue	02/25/09	36.00	35.00	290.00	(6)
	Cracked plate		—			
	Issues of 1908-10, Coil Stamps, Perf. 12 Horizontally					
	#350-51, 354-56: Washington (Designs of 334-35, 338)					
348	1¢ green Franklin (331)	12/29/08	37.50	22.50	290.00	(2)
349	2¢ carmine Washington (332)	01/09	80.00	12.50	550.00	(2)
	Foreign entry, design of 1¢		—	*1,750.00*		
350	4¢ orange brown	08/15/10	170.00	120.00	1,250.00	(2)
351	5¢ blue	01/09	180.00	160.00	1,250.00	(2)
	Issues of 1909, Coil Stamps, Perf. 12 Vertically					
352	1¢ green Franklin (331)	01/09	95.00	47.50	750.00	(2)
	Double transfer		—	—		

	Issues of 1909		Un	U	PB/LP	#	FDC	Q(M)
	Coil Stamps, Perf. 12 Vertically							
353	2¢ carmine Washington (332)	01/12/09	95.00	12.50	750.00	(2)		
354	4¢ orange brown	02/23/09	220.00	85.00	1,500.00	(2)		
355	5¢ blue	02/23/09	230.00	120.00	1,500.00	(2)		
356	10¢ yellow	01/07/09	2,500.00	1,250.00	11,000.00	(2)		
	Bluish Paper, Perf. 12, #359-66: Washington (Designs of 333-40)							
357	1¢ green Franklin (331)	02/16/09	90.00	100.00	1,000.00	(6)		
358	2¢ carmine Washington (332)	02/16/09	85.00	*100.00*	975.00	(6)		
	Double transfer		—					
359	3¢ deep violet, type I	1909	2,000.00	*2,500.00*	*22,500.00*	(6)		
360	4¢ orange brown	1909	*24,000.00*		*110,000.00*	(4)		
361	5¢ blue	1909	5,000.00	*12,500.00*	*60,000.00*	(6)		
362	6¢ red orange	1909	1,500.00	*5,000.00*	*16,000.00*	(6)		
363	8¢ olive green	1909	*26,000.00*		*115,000.00*	(3)		
364	10¢ yellow	1909	1,800.00	*4,500.00*	*32,500.00*	(6)		
365	13¢ blue green	1909	3,000.00	*2,500.00*	*30,000.00*	(6)		
366	15¢ pale ultramarine	1909	1,450.00	*9,000.00*	*11,000.00*	(6)		
	Lincoln Memorial Issue, Wmkd. (191)							
367	2¢ Bust of Abraham Lincoln	02/12/09	5.50	1.75	150.00	(6)	500.00	148
	Double transfer		7.50	2.50				
	Imperf.							
368	2¢ carmine (367)	02/12/09	21.00	20.00	180.00	(6)	*12,500.00*	1
	Double transfer		42.50	27.50				
	Bluish Paper							
369	2¢ carmine (367)	02/09	210.00	260.00	2,900.00	(6)		0.6
	Alaska-Yukon Pacific Exposition Issue							
370	2¢ Willam H. Seward	06/01/09	8.75	2.00	220.00	(6)	*3,000.00*	153
	Double transfer		10.50	4.50				
	Imperf.							
371	2¢ carmine (370)	06/09	24.00	22.50	220.00	(6)		0.5
	Double transfer		37.50	27.50				
	Hudson-Fulton Celebration Issue, Wmkd. (191)							
372	2¢ *Half Moon & Clermont*	09/25/09	12.50	4.50	290.00	(6)	750.00	73
	Double transfer		15.00	4.75				
	Imperf.							
373	2¢ carmine (372)	09/25/09	27.50	25.00	240.00	(6)	7,000.00	0.2
	Double transfer		42.50	30.00				
	Issues of 1910-11, Wmkd. (190) #376-82: Washington (Designs of 333-38, 340)							
374	1¢ green Franklin (331)	11/23/10	6.75	.20	77.50	(6)		
	Double transfer		13.50	—				
	Cracked plate		—	—				
a	Booklet pane of 6	10/07/10	175.00	*125.00*				
375	2¢ carmine Washington (332)	11/23/10	6.75	.20	85.00	(6)		
	Cracked plate		—	—				
	Double transfer		11.50	—				
	Foreign entry, design of 1¢		—	*1,000.00*				
a	Booklet pane of 6	11/30/10	95.00	*95.00*				
b	2¢ lake		*525.00*					
376	3¢ deep violet, type I	01/16/11	20.00	1.50	210.00	(6)		

367

370

372

USPS

Watermark 190
Single-line
"USPS"
in capital letters;
detail at right.

397

398

399

400

	Issues of 1911		Un	U	PB/LP	#	FDC	Q(M)
	Wmkd. (190), Perf. 12							
377	4¢ brown	01/20/11	32.50	.50	280.00	(6)		
	Double transfer		—	—				
378	5¢ blue	01/25/11	32.50	.50	325.00	(6)		
	Double transfer		—	—				
379	6¢ red orange	01/25/11	37.50	.70	500.00	(6)		
380	8¢ olive green	02/08/11	115.00	12.50	1,075.00	(6)		
381	10¢ yellow	01/24/11	105.00	3.75	1,125.00	(6)		
382	15¢ pale ultramarine	03/01/11	275.00	15.00	2,400.00	(6)		
	Issues of 1910, Imperf.							
383	1¢ green Franklin (331)	12/10	2.50	2.00	45.00	(6)		
	Double transfer		6.50	—				
384	2¢ carmine Washington (332)	12/10	4.00	2.50	130.00	(6)		
	Foreign entry, design of 1¢		—					
	Double transfer		7.50	—				
	Rosette plate, crack on head		*150.00*	—				
	Issues of 1910, Coil Stamps, Perf. 12 Horizontally							
385	1¢ green Franklin (331)	11/01/10	40.00	17.50	475.00	(2)		
386	2¢ carmine Washington (332)	11/01/10	70.00	22.50	850.00	(2)		
	Issues of 1910-1911, Coil Stamps, Wmkd. (190), Perf. 12 Vertically							
387	1¢ green Franklin (331)	11/01/10	160.00	55.00	675.00	(2)		
388	2¢ carmine Washington							
	(332)	11/01/10	900.00	*375.00*	*7,000.00*	(2)		
389	3¢ deep violet Washington,							
	type I (333)	01/24/11	*57,500.00*	*11,500.00*	*125,000.00*	(2)		
	Issues of 1910-1913, Coil Stamps, Perf. 8.5 Horizontally							
390	1¢ green Franklin (331)	12/12/10	5.00	*6.50*	37.50	(2)		
	Double transfer		—	—				
391	2¢ carmine Washington							
	(332)	12/23/10	40.00	14.00	260.00	(2)		
	Coil Stamps, Perf. 8.5 Vertically #394-96: Washington (Designs of 333-35)							
392	1¢ green Franklin (331)	12/12/10	25.00	22.50	190.00	(2)		
	Double transfer		—	—				
393	2¢ carmine Washington							
	(332)	12/16/10	47.50	8.50	300.00	(2)		
394	3¢ deep violet, type I	09/18/11	57.50	52.50	400.00	(2)		
395	4¢ brown	04/15/12	57.50	47.50	400.00	(2)		
396	5¢ blue	03/13	57.50	47.50	400.00	(2)		
	Issues of 1913, Panama Pacific Exposition Issue, Wmkd. (190), Perf. 12							
397	1¢ Vasco Nunez de Balboa	01/01/13	16.50	1.50	175.00	(6)	*5,000.00*	167*
	Double transfer		21.00	2.50				
398	2¢ Pedro Miguel Locks,							
	Panama Canal	01/13	21.00	.50	275.00	(6)		251*
	Double transfer		40.00	2.00				
a	2¢ carmine lake		*1,000.00*					
399	5¢ Golden Gate	01/01/13	75.00	9.50	1,900.00	(6)	*21,000.00*	14*
400	10¢ Discovery of							
	San Francisco Bay	01/01/13	135.00	20.00	2,350.00	(6)	10,000.00	8*
400A	10¢ orange (400)	08/13	210.00	16.00	*11,500.00*	(6)		
	*Includes perf. 10 printing quantities.							

1912-1915

	Issues of 1914-15		Un	U	PB/LP	#
	Perf. 10					
401	1¢ green (397)	12/14	25.00	5.50	340.00	(6)
402	2¢ carmine (398)	01/15	75.00	1.50	1,950.00	(6)
403	5¢ blue (399)	02/15	175.00	15.00	4,000.00	(6)
404	10¢ irabge (400)	07/15	925.00	62.50	*12,500.00*	(6)
	Issues of 1912-14, Wmkd. (190), Perf. 12					
405	1¢ green	02/12	6.75	.20	95.00	(6)
	Cracked plate		14.50	—		
	Double transfer		8.00	—		
a	Vertical pair, imperf. horizontally		*900.00*	—		
b	Booklet pane of 6	02/08/12	60.00	*50.00*		
406	2¢ carmine, type I	02/12	6.75	.20	105.00	(6)
	Double transfer		9.00	—		
a	Booklet pane of 6	02/08/12	60.00	*60.00*		
b	Double impression		—			
c	2¢ lake		*500.00*	—		
407	7¢ black	04/14	80.00	11.00	1,200.00	(6)
	Imperf. #408-13: Washington (Designs of 405-6)					
408	1¢ green	03/12	1.10	.55	18.00	(6)
	Double transfer		2.40	1.00		
	Cracked plate		—	—		
409	2¢ carmine, type I	02/12	1.30	.60	35.00	(6)
	Cracked plate		14.00	—		
	Coil Stamps, Perf. 8.5 Horizontally					
410	1¢ green	03/12	6.00	4.00	30.00	(2)
	Double transfer		—	—		
411	2¢ carmine, type I	03/12	10.00	3.75	55.00	(2)
	Double transfer		12.50	—		
	Coil Stamps, Perf. 8.5 Vertically					
412	1¢ green	03/18/12	25.00	5.50	120.00	(2)
413	2¢ carmine, type I	03/12	50.00	1.10	280.00	(2)
	Double transfer		52.50	—		
	Perf. 12					
414	8¢ Franklin	02/12	45.00	1.25	475.00	(6)
415	9¢ Franklin	04/14	55.00	12.50	650.00	(6)
416	10¢ Franklin	01/12	45.00	.40	500.00	(6)

405   406   407   414   415   416

Details

2¢ Washington, Types I-VII, Series 1912-21

Detail of **#406-06a, 411, 413, 425-25e, 442, 444, 449, 453, 461, 463-63a, 482, 499-99f** Type I

One shading line in first curve of ribbon above left "2" and one in second curve of ribbon above right "2." Toga button has only a faint outline. Top line of toga rope, from button to front of the throat, is very faint. Shading lines of face end in the front of the ear, with little or no joining, to form lock of hair.

Detail of **#482a, 500** Type Ia

Similar to Type I but all lines are shorter.

Detail of **#454, 487, 491, 539** Type II

Shading lines in ribbons as in Type I. Toga button, rope and rope shading lines are heavy. Shading lines of face at lock of hair end in strong vertical curved line.

Detail of **#450, 455, 488, 492, 540, 546** Type III

Two lines of shading in curves of ribbons.

Detail of **#526, 532** Type IV

Top line of toga rope is broken. Toga button shading lines form "DID." Line of color in left "2" is very thin and usually broken.

Detail of **#527, 533** Type V

Top line of toga rope is complete. Toga button has five verticle shading lines. Line of color in left "2" is very thin and usually broken. Nose shading dots are as shown.

Detail of **#528, 534** Type Va

Same as Type V except third row from bottom of nose shading dots has four dots instead of six. Overall height of design is 1/3mm shorter than Type V.

Detail of **#528A, 534A** Type VI

Generally same as Type V except line of color in left "2" is very heavy.

Detail of **#528B, 534B** Type VII

Line of color in left "2" is continuous, clearly defined and heavier than in Type V or Va but not as heavy as Type VI. An additional vertical row of dots has been added to upper lip. Numerous additional dots appear in hair at top of head.

417

418

419

420

421

423

434

After 1915 (from 1916 to date),
all postage stamps, except #519 and 832b,
are on unwatermarked paper.

	Issues of 1912-14		Un	U	PB	#
417	12¢ Franklin	04/14	50.00	4.25	625.00	(6)
	Double transfer		55.00	—		
	Triple transfer		72.50	—		
418	15¢ Franklin	02/12	85.00	3.50	850.00	(6)
	Double transfer		—	—		
419	20¢ Franklin	04/14	200.00	15.00	1,950.00	(6)
420	30¢ Franklin	04/14	125.00	15.00	1,450.00	(6)
421	50¢ Franklin	08/14	425.00	17.50	10,00.00	(6)
	Wmkd. (191)					
422	50¢ Franklin (421)	02/12/12	250.00	15.00	4,750.00	(6)
423	$1 Franklin	02/12/12	525.00	60.00	12,000.00	(6)
	Double transfer		550.00			
	Issues of 1914-15, Wmkd. (190), Perf. 10 #424-30: Wash. (Designs of 405-06, 333-36, 407)					
424	1¢ green	09/05/14	2.50	.20	42.50	(6)
	Cracked plate		—	—		
	Double transfer		4.75	—		
	Experimental precancel, New Orleans			—		
a	Perf. 12 x 10		2750.00	3,000.00		
b	Perf. 10 x 12			3,000.00		
c	Vertical pair, imperf. horizontally		1,750.00	1,250.00		
d	Booklet pane of 6		5.25	3.25		
e	As "d", imperf.		1,600.00			
425	2¢ rose red, type I	09/05/14	2.30	.20	27.50	(6)
	Cracked plate		9.50	—		
	Double transfer		—	—		
c	Perf. 10 x 12			—		
d	Perf. 12 x 10		10,000.00	4,500.00		
e	Booklet pane of 6	01/06/14	17.50	15.00		
426	3¢ deep violet, type I	09/18/14	14.00	1.25	175.00	(6)
427	4¢ brown	09/07/14	35.00	.50	475.00	(6)
	Double transfer		45.00	—		
428	5¢ blue	09/14/14	35.00	.50	390.00	(6)
a	Perf. 12 x 10			7,000.00		
429	6¢ red orange	09/28/14	50.00	1.40	525.00	(6)
430	7¢ black	09/10/14	90.00	4.00	950.00	(6)
	#431-33, 435, 437-40: Franklin (414-21, 423)					
431	8¢ pale olive green	09/26/14	36.00	1.50	550.00	(6)
	Double impression		—			
432	9¢ salmon red	10/06/14	50.00	7.50	700.00	(6)
433	10¢ orange yellow	09/09/14	47.50	.40	825.00	(6)
434	11¢ Franklin	08/11/15	25.00	7.50	240.00	(6)
435	12¢ claret brown	09/10/14	27.50	4.00	290.00	(6)
	Double transfer		35.00	—		
	Triple transfer		40.00	—		
a	12¢ copper red		30.00	4.00	325.00	(6)
436	Not assigned					
437	15¢ gray	09/16/14	135.00	7.25	1,125.00	(6)
438	20¢ ultramarine	09/19/14	220.00	4.00	3,250.00	(6)
439	30¢ orange red	09/19/14	260.00	16.00	4,100.00	(6)
440	50¢ violet	12/10/15	575.00	16.00	15,000.00	(6)

	Issues of 1914		Un	U	PB/LP	#
	Coil Stamps, Perf. 10 Horizontally #441-59: Wash.					
	(Designs of 405-06, 333-35; Flat Press, 18.5-19 x 22mm)					
441	1¢ green	11/14/14	1.00	1.00	7.75	(2)
442	2¢ carmine, type I	07/22/14	10.00	6.00	60.00	(2)
	Coil Stamps, Perf. 10 Vertically					
443	1¢ green	05/29/14	25.00	5.00	155.00	(2)
444	2¢ carmine, type I	04/25/14	40.00	1.50	290.00	(2)
445	3¢ violet, type I	12/18/14	225.00	125.00	1,300.00	(2)
446	4¢ brown	10/02/14	125.00	42.50	750.00	(2)
447	5¢ blue	07/30/14	45.00	27.50	260.00	(2)
	Issues of 1915-16, Coil Stamps, Perf. 10 Horizontally					
	(Rotary Press, Designs 18.5-19 x 22.5mm)					
448	1¢ green	12/12/15	6.00	3.25	40.00	(2)
449	2¢ red, type I	12/05/15	2,600.00	500.00	*15,000*	(2)
450	2¢ carmine, type III	02/16	10.00	3.00	77.50	(2)
451	Not assigned					
	Issues of 1914-16, Coil Stamps, Perf. 10 Vertically (Rotary Press, Designs 19.5 20 x 22mm)					
452	1¢ green	11/11/14	10.00	2.00	75.00	(2)
453	2¢ carmine rose, type I	07/03/14	150.00	4.25	725.00	(2)
	Cracked plate		—	—		
454	2¢ red, type II	06/15	82.50	10.00	425.00	(2)
455	2¢ carmine, type III	12/15	8.50	1.00	50.00	(2)
456	3¢ violet, type I	02/02/16	240.00	90.00	1,250.00	(2)
457	4¢ brown	02/18/16	25.00	17.50	150.00	(2)
	Cracked plate		35.00	—		
458	5¢ blue	03/09/16	30.00	17.50	180.00	(2)
	Issue of 1914, Horizontal Coil Stamp, Imperf.					
459	2¢ carmine, type I	06/30/14	240.00	*1,100.00*	1,050.00	(2)
	Issues of 1915, Wmkd. (191), Perf. 10					
460	$1 violet black Franklin (423)	02/08/15	850.00	100.00	*12,000.00*	(6)
	Double transfer		900.00	—		
	Perf. 11					
461	2¢ pale carmine red Washington					
	(406), type I	06/17/15	150.00	*275.00*	1,450.00	(6)
	Privately perforated copies of #409 have been made to resemble 461.					
	Issues of 1916-17, Unwmkd., Perf. 10 #462-69: Wash. (Designs of 405-06, 333-36, 407)					
462	1¢ green	09/27/16	7.00	.35	160.00	(6)
	Experimental precancel, Springfield, MA,					
	or New Orleans, LA			10.00		
a	Booklet pane of 6	10/15/16	9.50	*5.00*		
463	2¢ carmine, type I	09/25/16	4.50	.25	130.00	(6)
	Experimental precancel, Springfield, MA			22.50		
	Double transfer		6.50	—		
a	Booklet pane of 6	10/08/16	95.00	*65.00*		
464	3¢ violet, type I	11/11/16	75.00	14.00	1,350.00	(6)
	Double transfer in "CENTS"		*90.00*	—		
465	4¢ orange brown	10/07/16	45.00	1.80	650.00	(6)
466	5¢ blue	10/17/16	75.00	1.80	950.00	(6)
	Experimental precancel, Springfield, MA			175.00		
467	5¢ carmine (error in plate of 2¢)		550.00	*700.00*		
468	6¢ red orange	10/10/16	95.00	7.50	1,350.00	(6)
	Experimental precancel, Springfield, MA			175.00		
469	7¢ black	10/10/16	130.00	12.50	1,350.00	(6)
	Experimental precancel, Springfield, MA			175.00		

	Issues of 1916-17		Un	U	PB/LP	#	FDC
	#470-78: Franklin (Designs of 414-16, 434, 417-21, 423)						
470	8¢ olive green	11/13/16	60.00	6.00	600.00	(6)	
	Experimental precancel, Springfield, MA			165.00			
471	9¢ salmon red	11/16/16	60.00	16.00	750.00	(6)	
472	10¢ orange yellow	10/17/16	110.00	1.40	1,350.00	(6)	
473	11¢ dark green	11/16/16	40.00	17.50	360.00	(6)	
	Experimental precancel, Springfield, MA			575.00			
474	12¢ claret brown	10/10/16	55.00	5.50	625.00	(6)	
	Double transfer		65.00	6.50			
	Triple transfer		77.50	9.50			
475	15¢ gray	11/16/16	200.00	12.50	3,000.00	(6)	
476	20¢ light ultramarine	12/05/16	250.00	14.00	3,600.00	(6)	
476A	30¢ orange red		3,750.00	—	40,000	(6)	
477	50¢ light violet	03/02/17	1,100.00	65.00	57,500.00	(6)	
478	$1 violet black	12/22/16	800.00	19.00	13,000.00	(6)	
	Double transfer		825.00	25.00			
479	$2 dark blue Madison (312)	03/22/17	290.00	40.00	4,000.00	(6)	
480	$5 light green Marshall (313)	03/22/17	240.00	40.00	2,900.00	(6)	
	Issues of 1916-17, Imperf.						
	#481-96: Washington (Designs of 405-06, 333-35)						
481	1¢ green	11/16	1.00	.55	13.00	(6)	
	Double transfer		2.50	1.25			
482	2¢ carmine, type I	12/08/16	1.40	1.25	22.50	(6)	
482A	2¢ deep rose, type Ia			20,000.00			
483	3¢ violet, type I	10/13/17	13.00	7.50	115.00	(6)	
	Double transfer		17.50	—			
484	3¢ violet, type II		10.00	5.00	87.50	(6)	
	Double transfer		12.50	—			
485	5¢ carmine (error in plate of 2¢)	03/17	10,500.00		130.00	(6)	
	Issues of 1916-22, Coil Stamps, Perf. 10 Horizontally						
486	1¢ green	01/18	.90	.25	4.75	(2)	
	Double transfer		2.25	—			
487	2¢ carmine, type II	11/15/16	13.50	3.00	105.00	(2)	
488	2¢ carmine, type III	1919	2.50	1.75	15.00	(2)	
	Cracked plate		12.00	7.50			
489	3¢ violet, type I	10/10/17	5.00	1.50	32.50	(2)	
	Coil Stamps, Perf. 10 Vertically						
490	1¢ green	11/17/16	.55	.25	3.50	(2)	
	Cracked plate (horizontal)		7.50	—			
	Cracked plate (vertical) retouched		9.00	—			
	Rosette crack		60.00	—			
491	2¢ carmine, type II	11/17/16	2,200.00	750.00	12,000.00	(2)	
492	2¢ carmine, type III		9.50	.25	55.00	(2)	
493	3¢ violet, type I	07/23/17	16.00	3.00	110.00	(2)	
494	3¢ violet, type II	02/04/18	10.00	1.00	75.00	(2)	
495	4¢ orange brown	04/15/17	10.00	4.00	75.00	(2)	
	Cracked plate		25.00	—			
496	5¢ blue	01/15/19	3.50	1.00	30.00	(2)	
497	10¢ orange yellow						
	Franklin (416)	01/31/22	20.00	10.50	140.00	(2)	4,500.00

	Issues of 1917-19		Un	U	PB	#
	Perf. 11, #498-507: Washington (Designs of 405-06, 333-36, 407)					
498	1¢ green	03/17	.35	.25	16.50	(6)
	Cracked plate		7.50	—		
a	Vertical pair, imperf. horizontally		200.00			
b	Horizontal pair, imperf. between		150.00			
c	Vertical pair, imperf. between		450.00			
d	Double impression		175.00	750.00		
e	Booklet pane of 6	04/06/17	2.50	1.00		
f	Booklet pane of 30	09/17	1,000.00			
g	Perf. 10 top or bottom		5,000.00	—		
499	2¢ rose, type I	03/17	.35	.25	16.50	(6)
	Double transfer		6.00	—		
a	Vertical pair, imperf. horizontally		175.00			
b	Horizontal pair, imperf. vertically		450.00	225.00		
c	Vertical pair, imperf. between		650.00	225.00		
e	Booklet pane of 6	03/31/17	4.00	1.25		
f	Booklet pane of 30	09/17	28,000.00			
g	Double impression		175.00	—		
500	2¢ deep rose, type Ia		275.00	225.00	2,100.00	(6)
	Pair, types I and Ia		1,275.00			
501	3¢ light violet, type I	03/17	11.00	.25	125.00	(6)
b	Booklet pane of 6	10/17/17	75.00	50.00		
c	Vertical pair, imperf. horizontally, type I		450.00			
d	Double impression		2,500.00	2,500.00		
502	3¢ dark violet, type II		14.00	.40	140.00	(6)
b	Booklet pane of 6	02/28/18	60.00	50.00		
c	Vertical pair, imperf. horizontally		350.00	—		
d	Double impression		500.00			
e	Perf. 10, top or bottom		—	6,000.00		
503	4¢ brown	03/17	10.00	.25	130.00	(6)
504	5¢ blue	03/17	9.00	.25	125.00	(6)
	Double transfer		11.00			
505	5¢ rose (error in plate of 2¢)		350.00	500.00		
506	6¢ red orange	03/17	12.50	.25	170.00	(6
507	7¢ black	03/17	27.50	1.10	250.00	(6)
	#508-12, 514-18: Franklin (Designs of 414-16, 434, 417-21, 423)					
508	8¢ olive bister	03/17	12.00	.50	170.00	(6)
b	Vertical pair, imperf. between		—	—		
c	Perf. 10 top or bottom			3,250.00		
509	9¢ salmon red	03/17	14.00	1.75	140.00	(6)
510	10¢ orange yellow	03/17	17.00	.20	180.00	(6)
511	11¢ light green	05/17	9.00	2.50	125.00	(6)
	Double transfer		12.50	3.25		
512	12¢ claret brown	05/17	9.00	.35	125.00	(6)
a	12¢ brown carmine		9.50	.40		
b	Perf. 10, top or bottom		—	3,250.00		
513	13¢ apple green	01/10/19	11.00	6.00	125.00	(6)
	13¢ deep apple green		12.50	6.50		
514	15¢ gray	05/17	37.50	1.00	550.00	(6)
515	20¢ light ultramarine	05/17	47.50	.25	600.00	(6)
	20¢ deep ultramarine		50.00	.25		
b	Vertical pair, imperf. between		1,500.00			
c	Double impression		1,250.00			
d	Perf. 10 at top or bottom		—	10,000.00		
516	30¢ orange red	05/17	37.50	1.00	600.00	(6)
a	Perf. 10 top or bottom		5,000.00	—		

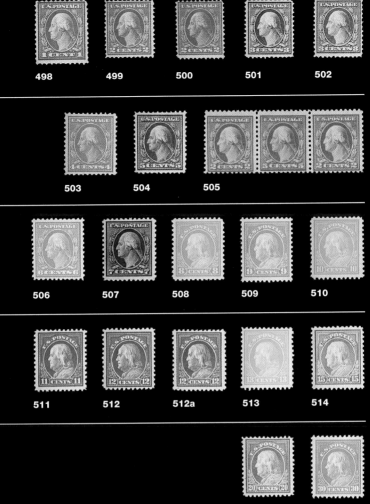

498 499 500 501 502

503 504 505

506 507 508 509 510

511 512 512a 513 514

515 516

Read about the newest issues in the "2001 Issues—New U.S. Postage Stamps" section.

517

523

524

Issues of 1917		Un	U	PB	#	FDC	Q(M)
Wmkd. (191), Perf. 11							
517	50¢ red violet	05/17	67.50	.50	1,600.00	(6)		
b	Vertical pair, imperf. between							
	and at bottom		—	7,000.00				
c	Perf. 10, top or bottom			10,000.00				
518	$1 violet brown	05/17	52.50	1.50	1,300.00	(6)		
b	$1 deep brown		1,800.00	1,050.00				
519	2¢ carm. Washington (332)	10/10/17	400.00	1,100.00	2,700.00	(6)		
	Privately perforated copies of #344 have been made to resemble #519.							
520-22	Not assigned							
	Issues of 1918, Unwmkd.							
523	$2 Franklin	08/19/18	600.00	230.00	12,000.00	(8)		
524	$5 Franklin	08/19/18	210.00	35.00	4,000.00	(8)		
	Issues of 1918-20 #525-35: Washington (Designs of 405-06, 333)							
525	1¢ gray green	12/18	2.50	.50	22.50	(6)		
	1¢ Emerald		3.50	1.00				
a	1¢ dark green		3.25	1.00				
c	Horizontal pair, imperf. between		100.00					
d	Double impression		35.00	30.00				
526	2¢ carmine, type IV	03/06/20	27.50	3.50	240.00	(6)	800.00	
	Gash on forehead		40.00	—				
	Malformed "2" at left		37.50	6.00				
527	2¢ carmine, type V	03/20/20	20.00	1.00	165.00	(6)		
	Line through "2" and "EN"		30.00	—				
a	Double impression		60.00	10.00				
b	Vertical pair, imperf. horizontally		600.00					
c	Horizontal pair, imperf. vertically		1,000.00					
528	2¢ carmine, type Va	05/04/20	9.50	.25	82.50	(6)		
c	Double impression		27.50					
g	Vertical pair, imperf. between		3,500.00					
528A	2¢ carmine, type VI	06/24/20	52.50	1.50	425.00	(6)		
d	Double impression		160.00					
f	Vertical pair, imperf. horizontally		—					
h	Vertical pair, imperf. between		1,000.00					
528B	2¢ carmine, type VII	11/03/20	22.50	.35	175.00	(6)		
	Retouched on cheek		400.00	—				
e	Double impression		70.00					
529	3¢ violet, type III	03/18	3.25	.25	57.50	(6)		
a	Double impression		40.00	—				
b	Printed on both sides		1,500.00					
530	3¢ purple, type IV		1.60	.20	17.50	(6)		
	"Blister" under "U.S."		4.50	—				
	Recut under "U.S."		4.50	—				
a	Double impression		25.00	7.00	—			
b	Printed on both sides		250.00					
	Imperf.							
531	1¢ green	01/19	9.50	8.00	85.00	(6)		
532	2¢ carmine rose, type IV	03/20	40.00	27.50	325.00	(6)		
533	2¢ carmine, type V	05/04/20	120.00	80.00	1,100.00	(6)		
534	2¢ carmine, type Va	05/25/20	11.00	6.50	105.00	(6)		
534A	2¢ carmine, type VI	07/26/20	45.00	22.50	375.00	(6)		
534B	2¢ carmine, type VII	12/02/20	2,100.00	1,250.00	17,000.00	(6)		
535	3¢ violet, type IV	1918	9.00	5.00	75.00	(6)		
a	Double impression		100.00	—				
	Issues of 1919, Perf. 12.5							
536	1¢ gray green							
	Washington (405)	08/15/19	22.50	20.00	200.00	(6)		
a	Horizontal pair, imperf. vertically		800.00					

	Issues of 1919		Un	U	PB	#	FDC	Q(M)
	Perf. 11							
537	3¢ Allied Victory	03/03/19	9.00	3.25	105.00	(6)	*750.00*	100
	Double transfer		—	—				
a	deep red violet		*1,400.00*	*2,000.00*	10,000.00	(6)		
b	light reddish violet		9.00	3.00	105.00	(6)		
c	red violet		50.00	12.00				
	Issues of 1919, George Washington, Unwmkd., Perf. 11 x 10							
538	1¢ green	06/19	11.00	8.50	110.00	(4)		
	Double transfer		17.50	—				
a	Vertical pair, imperf. horizontally		50.00	*100.00*	900.00	(4)		
539	2¢ carmine rose, type II		2,750.00	*4,750.00*	*15,000.00*	(4)		
540	2¢ carmine rose, type III	06/14/19	13.00	8.50	105.00	(4)		
	Double transfer		22.50	—				
a	Vertical pair, imperf. horizontally		50.00	*100.00*	1,000.00	(4)		
b	Horizontal pair, imperf. vertically		*1,250.00*					
541	3¢ violet, type II	06/19	45.00	30.00	360.00	(4)		
	Issue of 1920, Perf. 10 x 11							
542	1¢ green	05/26/20	14.00	1.10	165.00	(6)	*1,750.00*	
	Issues of 1921, Perf. 10							
543	1¢ green	05/21	.50	.25	14.00	(4)		
	Double transfer			—				
	Triple transfer		—	—				
a	Horizontal pair, imperf. between		*1,750.00*					
	Issue of 1922, Perf. 11							
544	1¢ green		*15,000.00*	3,250.00				
	Issues of 1921							
545	1¢ green	05/21	190.00	175.00	1,100.00	(4)		
546	2¢ carmine rose, type III	05/21	125.00	*160.00*	775.00	(4)		
	Recut in hair		140.00	*185.00*				
a	Perf. 10 at left		*6,500.00*					
	Issue of 1920							
547	$2 Franklin	11/01/20	180.00	40.00	4,000.00	(8)		
	Pilgrim Tercentenary Issue							
548	1¢ The *Mayflower*	12/21/20	4.50	2.25	45.00	(6)	*900.00*	138
	Double transfer		—	—				
549	2¢ Landing of the Pilgrims	12/21/20	6.50	1.60	65.00	(6)	*700.00*	196
550	5¢ Signing of the Compact	12/21/20	42.50	12.50	450.00	(6)	—	11
	Issues of 1922-1925 (See also #581-91, 594-606, 622-23, 631-42, 658-79, 684-87, 692-701, 723)							
551	½¢ Nathan Hale	04/04/25	.20	.20	5.75	(6)	17.50	(4)
	"Cap" on fraction bar		.75	.20				
552	1¢ Franklin	01/17/23	1.50	.20	22.50	(6)	25.00	(2)
	Double transfer		3.50	—				
a	Booklet pane of 6	08/11/23	6.00	*2.00*				
553	1½¢ Warren G. Harding	03/19/25	2.60	.20	27.50	(6)	30.00	(2)
554	2¢ Washington	01/15/23	1.40	.20	20.00	(6)	37.50	
	Double transfer		2.50	.80				
a	Horizontal pair, imperf. vertically		300.00					
b	Vertical pair, imperf. horizontally		*4,000.00*					
c	Booklet pane of 6	02/10/23	6.75	*2.00*				
d	Perf. 10 at top or bottom		—	*4,000.00*				
555	3¢ Lincoln	02/12/23	18.00	1.00	160.00	(6)	35.00	
556	4¢ Martha Washington	01/15/23	19.00	.25	160.00	(6)	60.00	
a	Vertical pair, imperf. horizontally		*10,500.00*					
b	Perf. 10, top or bottom		*2,500.00*	*10,000.00*				
557	5¢ Theodore Roosevelt	10/27/22	19.00	.20	190.00	(6)	*125.00*	
a	Imperf., pair		*1,500.00*					
b	Horizontal pair, imperf. vertically		—					
c	Perf. 10, top or bottom		—	*4,000.00*				

537

547

548

549

550

551

552

553

554

555

556

557

558

559

560

561

562

563

564

565

566

567

568

569

570

571

572

573

Issues of 1922-1923		Un	U	PB	#	FDC
Perf. 11						
558 6¢ Garfield	11/20/22	35.00	.85	400.00	(6)	225.00
Double transfer		55.00	2.00			
Same, recut		55.00	2.00			
559 7¢ McKinley	05/01/23	9.25	.55	70.00	(6)	175.00
Double transfer		—	—			
560 8¢ Grant	05/01/23	50.00	.60	575.00	(6)	175.00
Double transfer		—	—			
561 9¢ Jefferson	01/15/23	14.00	1.10	160.00	(6)	175.00
Double transfer		—	—			
562 10¢ Monroe	01/15/23	18.00	.20	200.00	(6)	175.00
a Vertical pair, imperf. horizontally		1,750.00				
b Imperf., pair		1,500.00				
c Perf. 10 at top or bottom			4,000.00			
563 11¢ Rutherford B. Hayes	10/04/22	1.40	.40	27.50	(6)	600.00
d Imperf., pair			17,500.00			
564 12¢ Grover Cleveland	03/20/23	6.00	.20	72.50	(6)	175.00
a Horizontal pair, imperf. vertically		1,750.00				
565 14¢ American Indian	05/01/23	4.00	.75	47.50	(6)	400.00
Double transfer		—	—			
566 15¢ Statue of Liberty	11/11/22	23.00	.20	275.00	(6)	550.00
567 20¢ Golden Gate	05/01/23	22.00	.20	250.00	(6)	500.00
a Horizontal pair, imperf. vertically		1,500.00				
568 25¢ Niagara Falls	11/11/22	18.00	.45	240.00	(6)	650.00
b Vertical pair, imperf. horizontally		1,750.00				
c Perf. 10 at one side		5,000.00				
569 30¢ Buffalo	03/20/23	32.50	.35	230.00	(6)	850.00
Double transfer		55.00	—			
570 50¢ Arlington Amphitheater	11/11/22	55.00	.20	600.00	(6)	1,250.00
571 $1 Lincoln Memorial	02/12/23	45.00	.45	300.00	(6)	7,000.00
Double transfer		90.00	1.50			
572 $2 U.S. Capitol	03/20/23	90.00	9.00	675.00	(6)	15,000.00
573 $5 Head of Freedom,						
Capitol Dome	03/20/23	150.00	15.00	1,900.00	(8)	25,000.00
a Carmine lake and dark blue		200.00	16.00	2,400.00	(8)	
574 Not assigned						
Issues of 1923-1925, Imperf.						
575 1¢ green Franklin (552)	03/20/23	7.25	5.00	70.00	(6)	
576 1½¢ yel. brn. Harding (553)	04/04/25	1.50	1.50	20.00	(6)	45.00
577 2¢ carmine Washington (554)		1.60	1.25	25.00	(6)	
Issues of 1923, Perf. 11 x 10						
578 1¢ green Franklin (552)	1923	100.00	160.00	800.00	(4)	
579 2¢ carmine Washington (554)	1923	90.00	140.00	600.00	(4)	
Recut in eye		110.00	150.00			
Issues of 1923-1926, Perf. 10 (See also #551-73, 622-23, 631-42, 658-79, 684-87, 692-701, 723)						
580 Not assigned						
581 1¢ green Franklin (552)	04/21/23	11.00	.65	120.00	(4)	6,000.00
582 1½¢ brn. Harding (553)	03/19/25	5.50	.60	45.00	(4)	40.00
Pair with full horiz. gutter between		160.00				
583 2¢ carm. Wash. (554)	04/14/24	3.00	.25	32.50	(4)	
a Booklet pane of 6	08/27/26	90.00	50.00			1,500.00
584 3¢ violet Lincoln (555)	08/01/25	32.50	2.25	260.00	(4)	55.00
585 4¢ yellow brown Martha						
Washington (556)	03/25	19.00	.45	230.00	(4)	55.00
586 5¢ blue T. Roosevelt (557)	12/24	19.00	.25	225.00	(4)	57.50
587 6¢ red orange Garfield (558)	03/25	9.25	.35	95.00	(4)	60.00
588 7¢ black McKinley (559)	05/29/26	13.50	5.50	115.00	(4)	70.00

1923-1929

	Issues of 1925-1926		Un	U	PB/LP	#	FDC	Q(M)
	Perf. 11 x 10							
589	8¢ olive grn. Grant (560)	05/29/26	30.00	3.50	240.00	(4)	72.50	
590	9¢ rose Jefferson (561)	05/29/26	6.00	2.25	50.00	(4)	72.50	
591	10¢ orange Monroe (562)	06/08/25	72.50	.25	475.00	(4)	95.00	
592-93	Not assigned							
	Issues of 1923, Perf. 11							
594	1¢ green Franklin (552), design 19.75 x 22.25mm	1923	*18,000.00*	6,000.00				
595	2¢ carmine Washington (554), design 19.75 x 22.25mm	1923	300.00	*325.00*	2,100.00	(4)		
596	1¢ green Franklin (552), design 19.25 x 22.5mm	1923		*70,000.00*				
	Issues of 1923-1929, Coil Stamps, Perf. 10 Vertically							
597	1¢ green Franklin (552)	07/18/23	.30	.20	2.25	(2)	*600.00*	
	Gripper cracks or double transfer		2.60	1.00				
598	1½¢ brown Harding (553)	03/19/25	1.00	.20	*4.75*	(2)	60.00	
599	2¢ carmine Washington (554), type I	01/23	.40	.20	2.30	(2)	*1,500.00*	
	Double transfer		1.90	1.00				
	Gripper cracks		2.30	2.00				
599A	2¢ carmine Washington (554), type II	03/29	125.00	11.00	675.00	(2)		
600	3¢ violet Lincoln (555)	05/10/24	7.25	.20	25.00	(2)	80.00	
601	4¢ yellow brown M. Washington (556)	08/05/23	4.50	.35	30.00	(2)		
602	5¢ dark blue T. Roosevelt (557)	03/05/24	1.75	.20	10.00	(2)	85.00	
603	10¢ orange Monroe (562)	12/01/24	4.00	.20	26.50	(2)	100.00	
	Coil Stamps, Perf. 10 Horizontally							
604	1¢ yel. grn. Franklin (552)	07/19/24	.35	.20	3.75	(2)	90.00	
605	1½¢ yel. brn. Harding (553)	05/09/25	.35	.20	3.50	(2)	70.00	
606	2¢ carmine Washington (554)	12/31/23	.35	.20	2.60	(2)	125.00	
607-09	Not assigned							
	Issues of 1923, Harding Memorial Issue, Perf. 11							
610	2¢ blk. Warren Gamaliel Harding	09/01/23	.65	.20	20.00	(6)	30.00	1,459
	Double transfer		1.75	.50				
a	Horizontal pair, imperf. vertically		*2,000.00*					
	Imperf.							
611	2¢ blk. Harding (610)	11/15/23	6.25	4.00	75.00	(6)	90.00	0.8
	Perf. 10							
612	2¢ blk. Harding (610)	09/12/23	17.50	1.75	300.00	(4)	100.00	100
	Perf. 11							
613	2¢ black Harding (610)	1923		*27,500.00*				
	Issues of 1924, Huguenot-Walloon Tercentary Issue, May 1							
614	1¢ Ship *Nieu Nederland*	01/05/24	2.75	3.25	40.00	(6)	40.00	51
615	2¢ Walloons' Landing at Fort Orange (Albany)	01/05/24	5.50	2.25	55.00	(6)	55.00	78
	Double transfer		12.00	3.50				
616	5¢ Huguenot Monument to Jan Ribault at Duval County, Florida	01/05/24	22.50	13.00	225.00	(6)	80.00	6

599   610

614   615   616

Details

2¢ Washington, Types I-II, Series 1923-29

Detail of **#599, 634**
Type I

No heavy hair lines at top
center of head.

Detail of **#599A, 634A**
Type II

Three heavy hair lines at
top center of head.

617

618

619

620

621

622

623

627

628

629

630

	Issues of 1925		Un	U	PB	#	FDC	Q(M)
	Lexington-Concord Issue, Perf. 11							
617	1¢ Washington at Cambridge	04/04/25	2.50	2.50	40.00	(6)	35.00	16
618	2¢ "The Birth of Liberty,"							
	by Henry Sandham	04/04/25	5.00	4.00	55.00	(6)	37.50	27
619	5¢ "The Minute Man,"							
	by Daniel Chester French	04/04/25	20.00	13.00	200.00	(6)	85.00	5
	Line over head		42.50	19.00				
	Norse-American Issue							
620	2¢ Sloop *Restaurationen*	05/18/25	4.00	3.00	180.00	(8)	25.00	9
621	5¢ Viking Ship	05/18/25	15.00	10.50	525.00	(8)	40.00	2
	Issues of 1925-1926 (See also #551-79, 581-91, 594-606, 631-42, 658-79, 684-87, 692-701, 723)							
622	13¢ Benjamin Harrison	01/11/26	13.50	.45	145.00	(6)	22.50	
623	17¢ Woodrow Wilson	12/28/25	15.00	.25	160.00	(6)	27.50	
624-26	Not assigned							
	Issues of 1926							
627	2¢ Independence							
	Sesquicentennial Exposition	05/10/26	3.25	.50	35.00	(6)	10.00	308
628	5¢ John Ericsson Memorial	05/29/26	6.50	3.25	75.00	(6)	30.00	20
629	2¢ Alexander Hamilton's Battery	10/18/26	2.25	1.70	35.00	(6)	6.25	41
a	Vertical pair, imperf. between		—					
	International Philatelic Exhibition Souvenir Sheet							
630	2¢ Battle of White Plains,							
	sheet of 25 with selvage							
	inscription (629)	10/18/26	375.00	450.00			1,500.00	0.1
	Dot over first "S" of "States"		400.00	475.00				
	Imperf. (See also #551-79, 581-91, 594-606, 622-23, 658-79, 684-87, 692-701, 723)							
631	1½¢ yellow brown							
	Harding (553)	08/27/26	1.90	1.70	62.50	(4)	35.00	
	Issues of 1926-1934, Perf. 11 x 10.5 (See also #551-73, 575-79, 581-91, 594-606, 622-23,							
	631-42, 684-87, 692-701, 723)							
632	1¢ green Franklin (552)	06/10/27	.20	.20	2.00	(4)	45.00	
	Pair with full vertical gutter between		150.00	—				
	Cracked plate		—	—				
a	Booklet pane of 6	11/02/27	5.50	2.25			3,250.00	
b	Vertical pair, imperf. between		2,500.00	125.00				
c	Horizontal pair, imperf. between		7,500.00					
633	1½¢ yellow brown							
	Harding (553)	05/17/27	1.90	.20	62.50	(4)	45.00	
634	2¢ carmine Washington							
	(554), type I	12/10/26	.20	.20	2.10	(4)	47.50	
	Pair with full vertical gutter between		200.00					
b	2¢ carmine lake, type I		—	—	—	(4)		
c	Horizontal pair, imperf. between		7,000.00					
d	Booklet pane of 6	02/25/27	1.75	1.10				
634A	2¢ carmine Washington							
	(554), type II	12/28/27	350.00	13.50	2,000.00	(4)		
	Pair with full vertical or							
	horizontal gutter between		1,000.00	—				
635	3¢ violet Lincoln (555)	02/03/27	.40	.20	13.50	(4)	47.50	
a	3¢ bright violet Lincoln	02/07/34	.20	.20	5.50	(4)	25.00	
	Gripper cracks		3.25	2.00				
636	4¢ yellow brown Martha							
	Washington (556)	05/17/27	2.10	.20	72.50	(4)	50.00	
	Pair with full vertical gutter between		200.00					
637	5¢ dark blue Theodore							
	Roosevelt (557)	03/24/27	2.10	.20	13.00	(4)	50.00	
	Pair with full vertical gutter between		275.00					

	Issues of 1927-1931		Un	U	PB/LB	#	FDC	Q(M)
	Perf. 11 x 10.5							
638	6¢ red orange Garfield (558)	07/27/27	2.10	.20	13.00	(4)	57.50	
	Pair with full vert. gutter between		200.00					
639	7¢ black McKinley (559)	03/24/27	2.10	.20	13.00	(4)	57.50	
a	Vertical pair, imperf.							
	between		275.00	85.00				
640	8¢ olive green Grant (560)	06/10/27	2.10	.20	13.00	(4)	62.50	
641	9¢ orange red Jefferson (561)	1931	2.10	.20	13.00	(4)	72.50	
642	10¢ orange Monroe (562)	02/03/27	3.50	.20	20.00	(4)	90.00	
	Double transfer		—	—				
	Perf. 11							
643	2¢ Vermont Sesquicentennial	08/03/27	1.40	.80	37.50	(6)	6.00	40
644	2¢ Burgoyne at Saratoga	08/03/27	3.50	2.10	32.50	(6)	12.50	26
	Issues of 1928							
645	2¢ Valley Forge	05/26/28	1.05	.40	25.00	(6)	4.00	101
	Perf. 11 x 10.5							
646	2¢ Battle of Monmouth/							
	Molly Pitcher	10/20/28	1.10	1.10	35.00	(4)	15.00	10
	Wide spacing, vertical pair		50.00	—				
	Hawaii Sesquicentennial Issue							
647	2¢ Washington (554)	08/13/28	5.00	4.50	135.00	(4)	15.00	6
	Wide spacing, vertical pair		100.00					
648	5¢ Theodore Roosevelt (557)	08/13/28	14.50	13.50	260.00	(4)	22.50	1
	Aeronautics Conference Issue, Perf. 11							
649	2¢ Wright Airplane	12/12/28	1.25	.80	10.00	(6)	7.00	51
650	5¢ Globe and Airplane	12/12/28	5.25	3.25	50.00	(6)	10.00	10
	Plate flaw "prairie dog"		27.50	12.50				
	Issues of 1929							
651	2¢ George Rogers Clark	02/25/29	.65	.50	10.00	(6)	6.00	17
	Double transfer		4.25	2.25				
652	Not assigned							
	Perf. 11 x 10.5							
653	½¢ olive brown							
	Nathan Hale (551)	5/25/29	.20	.20	1.50	(4)	27.50	
	Electric Light's Golden Jubilee Issue, Perf. 11							
654	2¢ Thomas Edison's First Lamp	06/05/29	.70	.70	22.50	(6)	10.00	32
	Perf. 11 x 10.5							
655	2¢ carmine rose (654)	06/11/29	.65	.20	35.00	(4)	80.00	210
	Coil Stamp, Perf. 10 Vertically							
656	2¢ carmine rose (654)	06/11/29	14.00	1.75	75.00	(2)	90.00	133
	Perf. 11							
657	2¢ Sullivan Expedition	06/17/29	.70	.60	22.50	(6)	4.00	51
a	2¢ lake		475.00	—				

643

644

645

646

647

648

649

650

651

654

657

658

669

680

681

682

683

684

685

Issues of 1929		Un	U	PB/LP	#	FDC	Q(M)
#658-68 overprinted "Kans.," Perf. 11 x 10.5							
(See also #551-73, 575-79, 581-91, 594-606, 622-23, 631-42, 684-87, 692-701, 723)							
658	1¢ Franklin 05/01/29	2.50	2.00	35.00	(4)	50.00	13
a	Vertical pair, one without overprint	325.00					
659	1½¢ brown Harding (553) 05/01/29	4.00	2.90	50.00	(4)	52.50	8
	Wide spacing, pair	70.00					
660	2¢ carmine Washington (554) 05/01/29	4.50	1.10	47.50	(4)	52.50	87
661	3¢ violet Lincoln (555) 05/01/29	22.50	15.00	210.00	(4)	60.00	3
662	4¢ yellow brown Martha						
	Washington (556) 05/01/29	22.50	9.00	210.00	(4)	62.50	2
663	5¢ deep blue T. Roosevelt (557) 05/01/29	14.00	9.75	150.00	(4)	80.00	3
664	6¢ red orange Garfield (558) 05/01/29	32.50	18.00	450.00	(4)	90.00	1
665	7¢ black McKinley (559) 05/01/29	30.00	27.50	500.00	(4)	100.00	1
666	8¢ olive green Grant (560) 05/01/29	110.00	75.00	775.00	(4)	125.00	2
667	9¢ light rose Jefferson (561) 05/01/29	16.00	11.25	225.00	(4)	140.00	1
668	10¢ orange yel. Monroe (562) 05/01/29	25.00	12.00	350.00	(4)	175.00	3
	#669-79 overprinted "Nebr."						
669	1¢ Franklin 05/01/29	4.00	2.25	50.00	(4)	50.00	8
a	Vertical pair, one without overprint	—					
670	1½¢ brown Harding (553) 05/01/29	3.75	2.50	52.50	(4)	50.00	9
671	2¢ carmine Washington (554) 05/01/29	3.75	1.30	42.50	(4)	55.00	73
672	3¢ violet Lincoln (555) 05/01/29	15.00	12.00	165.00	(4)	65.00	2
673	4¢ yellow brown Martha						
	Washington (556) 05/01/29	22.50	15.00	250.00	(4)	75.00	2
	Wide spacing, pair	120.00					
674	5¢ deep blue T. Roosevelt (557) 05/01/29	20.00	15.00	275.00	(4)	75.00	2
675	6¢ red orange Garfield (558) 05/01/29	47.50	24.00	525.00	(4)	100.00	1
676	7¢ black McKinley (559) 05/01/29	27.50	18.00	300.00	(4)	100.00	0.8
677	8¢ olive green Grant (560) 05/01/29	37.50	25.00	400.00	(4)	125.00	1
678	9¢ light rose Jefferson (561) 05/01/29	42.50	27.50	525.00	(4)	140.00	0.5
679	10¢ orange yel. Monroe (562) 05/01/29	135.00	22.50	950.00	(4)	175.00	2
	Warning: Excellent forgeries of the Kansas and Nebraska overprints exist.						
	Perf. 11						
680	2¢ Battle of Fallen Timbers 09/14/29	.80	.80	22.50	(6)	3.50	29
681	2¢ Ohio River Canalization 10/19/29	.70	.65	15.00	(6)	3.50	33
	Issues of 1930						
682	2¢ Mass. Bay Colony 04/08/30	.60	.50	22.50	(6)	3.50	74
683	2¢ Gov. Joseph West and						
	Chief Shadoo, a Kiowa 04/10/30	1.20	1.20	40.00	(6)	3.50	25
	Perf. 11 x 10.5						
684	1½¢ Warren G. Harding 12/01/30	.35	.20	1.75	(4)	4.50	
	Pair with full horizontal gutter between	175.00					
	Pair with full vertical gutter between	—					
685	4¢ William H. Taft 06/04/30	.90	.20	13.50	(4)	6.00	
	Gouge on right "4"	2.10	.60				
	Recut right "4"	2.10	.65				
	Pair with full horizontal gutter between	—					
	Coil Stamps, Perf. 10 Vertically						
686	1½¢ brn. Harding (684) 12/01/30	1.80	.20	6.50	(2)	5.00	
687	4¢ brown Taft (685) 09/18/30	3.25	.45	13.00	(2)	20.00	

1930-1932

	Issues of 1930		Un	U	PB	#	FDC	Q(M)
	Perf. 11							
688	2¢ Battle of Braddock's Field	07/09/30	1.00	.85	30.00	(6)	4.00	26
689	2¢ Gen. von Steuben	09/17/30	.55	.55	20.00	(6)	4.00	66
a	Imperf., pair		2,750.00		12,500.00	(6)		
	Issues of 1931							
690	2¢ General Pulaski	01/16/31	.30	.20	9.50	(6)	4.00	97
691	Not assigned							
	Perf. 11 x 10.5 (See also #551-73, 575-79, 581-91, 594-606, 622-23, 631-42, 658-79, 684-87, 723)							
692	11¢ light bl. Hayes (563)	09/04/31	2.60	.20	13.50	(4)	100.00	
	Retouched forehead		20.00	1.00				
693	12¢ brown violet Cleveland (564)	08/25/31	5.50	.20	25.00	(4)	100.00	
694	13¢ yellow green Harrison (622)	09/04/31	2.00	.20	13.50	(4)	100.00	
695	14¢ dark blue American Indian (565)	09/08/31	3.75	.25	26.00	(4)	100.00	
696	15¢ gray Statue of Liberty (566)	08/27/31	8.00	.20	37.50	(4)	125.00	
	Perf. 10.5 x 11							
697	17¢ black Wilson (623)	07/25/31	4.50	.20	31.50	(4)	2,750.00	
698	20¢ carmine rose Golden Gate (567)	09/08/31	8.25	.20	37.50	(4)	325.00	
	Double transfer		20.00	—				
699	25¢ blue green Niagara Falls (568)	07/25/31	8.50	.20	45.00	(4)	2,000.00	
700	30¢ brown Buffalo (569)	09/08/31	16.00	.20	67.50	(4)	300.00	
	Cracked plate		26.00	.85				
701	50¢ lilac Arlington Amphitheater (570)	09/04/31	37.50	.20	180.00	(4)	425.00	
	Perf. 11							
702	2¢ "The Greatest Mother"	05/21/31	.25	.20	1.90	(4)	3.00	99
a	Red cross omitted		40,000.00					
703	2¢ Yorktown	10/19/31	.40	.25	2.25	(4)	3.50	25
a	2¢ lake and black		4.50	.75				
b	2¢ dark lake and black		425.00		2,250.00	(4)		
c	Pair, imperf. vertically		5,000.00		—	(6)		
	Issues of 1932, Washington Bicentennial Issue, Perf. 11 x 10.5							
704	½¢ Portrait by Charles W. Peale	01/01/32	.20	.20	5.75	(4)	5.00 (4)	88
	Broken circle		.75	.20				
705	1¢ Bust by Jean Antoine Houdon	01/01/32	.20	.20	4.25	(4)	4.00 (2)	1,266
706	1½¢ Portrait by Charles W. Peale	01/01/32	.40	.20	14.50	(4)	4.00 (2)	305
707	2¢ Portrait by Gilbert Stuart	01/01/32	.20	.20	1.50	(4)	4.00	4,222
	Gripper cracks		1.75	.65				
708	3¢ Portrait by Charles W. Peale	01/01/32	.55	.20	16.50	(4)	4.00	456
709	4¢ Portrait by Charles P. Polk	01/01/32	.25	.20	5.50	(4)	4.00	151
	Broken bottom frame line		1.50	.50				
710	5¢ Portrait by Charles W. Peale	01/01/32	1.60	.20	16.50	(4)	4.00	171
	Cracked plate		5.25	1.10				
711	6¢ Portrait by John Trumbull	01/01/32	3.25	.20	50.00	(4)	4.00	112
712	7¢ Portrait by John Trumbull	01/01/32	.25	.20	9.00	(4)	4.00	83
713	8¢ Portrait by Charles B.J.F. Saint Memin	01/01/32	2.75	.50	50.00	(4)	4.50	97
	Pair, full vert. gutter between		—					
714	9¢ Portrait by W. Williams	01/01/32	2.40	.20	32.50	(4)	4.50	76
715	10¢ Portrait by Gilbert Stuart	01/01/32	10.00	.20	85.00	(4)	4.50	147

688   689   690

702   703

704   705   706

707   708   709

710   711   712

713   714   715

716

717

718

719

720

724

725

726

727

728

729

730

731

732

733

734

	Issues of 1932		Un	U	PB/LP	#	FDC	Q(M)
	Olympic Winter Games Issue, Perf. 11							
716	2¢ Ski Jumper	01/25/32	.40	.20	10.00	(6)	6.00	51
	Recut		3.50	1.50				
	Colored "snowball"		25.00	5.00				
	Perf. 11 x 10.5							
717	2¢ Arbor Day	04/22/32	.20	.20	6.00	(4)	4.00	100
	Olympic Summer Games Issue, Perf. 11 x 10.5							
718	3¢ Runner at Starting Mark	06/15/32	1.40	.20	11.50	(4)	6.00	168
	Gripper cracks		4.25	.75				
719	5¢ Myron's Discobolus	06/15/32	2.20	.20	20.00	(4)	8.00	53
	Gripper cracks		4.25	1.00				
720	3¢ Washington	06/16/32	.20	.20	1.30	(4)	7.50	
	Pair with full vertical or horizontal gutter between		200.00					
	Recut lines on face		2.00	.75				
b	Booklet pane of 6	07/25/32	37.50	7.50			100.00	
c	Vertical pair, imperf. between		1,250.00	1,250.00				
	Coil Stamp, Perf. 10 Vertically							
721	3¢ deep violet (720)	06/24/32	2.75	.20	10.00	(2)	15.00	
	Recut lines around eyes		—	—				
	Coil Stamp, Perf. 10 Horizontally							
722	3¢ deep violet (720)	10/12/32	1.50	.35	6.25	(2)	15.00	
	Coil Stamp, Perf. 10 Vertically (See also #551-73, 575-79, 581-91, 594-606, 622-23, 631-42, 684-87, 692-701)							
723	6¢ deep orange Garfield (558)	08/18/32	11.00	.30	60.00	(2)	15.00	
	Perf. 11							
724	3¢ William Penn	10/24/32	.30	.20	8.00	(6)	3.25	49
a	Vertical pair, imperf. horizontally		—					
725	3¢ Daniel Webster	10/24/32	.30	.25	16.50	(6)	3.25	49
	Issues of 1933							
726	3¢ Georgia Settlement	02/12/33	.30	.20	10.00	(6)	3.25	61
	Perf. 10.5 x 11							
727	3¢ Peace of 1783	04/19/33	.20	.20	3.75	(4)	3.50	73
	Century of Progress Issue							
728	1¢ Restoration of Fort Dearborn	05/25/33	.20	.20	1.90	(4)	3.00 (3)	348
	Gripper cracks		2.00	—				
729	3¢ Federal Building at Chicago	05/25/33	.20	.20	2.25	(4)	3.00	480
	American Philatelic Society Issue Souvenir Sheets, Without Gum, Imperf.							
730	1¢ sheet of 25 (728)	08/25/33	27.50	27.50			100.00	0.4
a	Single stamp from sheet		.75	.45			3.25 (3)	11
731	3¢ sheet of 25 (729)	08/25/33	25.00	25.00			100.00	0.4
a	Single stamp from sheet		.65	.45			3.25	11
	Perf. 10.5 x 11							
732	3¢ National Recovery Act	08/15/33	.20	.20	1.50	(4)	3.25	1,978
	Gripper cracks		1.50	—				
	Recut at right		2.00					
	Perf. 11							
733	3¢ Byrd Antarctic Expedition II	10/09/33	.50	.50	13.00	(6)	10.00	5
	Double transfer		2.75	1.00				
734	5¢ General Tadeusz Kosciuszko	10/13/33	.55	.25	27.50	(6)	4.50	45
a	Horizontal pair, imperf. vertically		2,250.00		25,000.00	(8)		

Issues of 1934		Un	U	PB	#	FDC	Q(M)
National Stamp Exhibition Issue Souvenir Sheet, Without Gum, Imperf.							
735	3¢ Byrd sheet of 6 (733)	02/10/34	12.50	10.00			40.00	0.8
a	Single stamp from sheet		2.00	1.65			5.00	4
	Perf. 11							
736	3¢ Maryland Tercentenary	03/23/34	.20	.20	6.00	(6)	1.60	46
	Double transfer		—	—				
	Mothers of America Issue, Perf. 11 x 10.5							
737	3¢ Portrait of his Mother,							
	by James A. McNeill Whistler	05/02/34	.20	.20	.95	(4)	1.60	193
	Perf. 11							
738	3¢ deep violet (737)	05/02/34	.20	.20	4.25	(6)	1.60	15
739	3¢ Wisconsin Tercentenary	07/07/34	.20	.20	2.90	(6)	1.10	64
a	Vert. pair, imperf. horizontally		350.00					
b	Horiz. pair, imperf. vertically		500.00		2,000.00	(6)		
	National Parks Issue, Unwmkd.							
740	1¢ El Capitan, Yosemite							
	(California)	07/16/34	.20	.20	1.00	(6)	2.25	84
	Recut		1.50	.50				
a	Vertical pair, imperf.							
	horizontally, with gum		500.00					
741	2¢ Grand Canyon (Arizona)	07/24/34	.20	.20	1.25	(6)	2.25	74v
	Double transfer		1.25	—				
a	Vertical pair, imperf.							
	horizontally, with gum		500.00					
b	Horizontal pair, imperf.							
	vertically, with gum		600.00					
742	3¢ Mt. Rainier, and Mirror Lake,							
	(Washington)	08/03/34	.20	.20	1.75	(6)	2.50	95
a	Vertical pair, imperf.							
	horizontally, with gum		475.00					
743	4¢ Cliff Palace, Mesa Verde							
	(Colorado)	09/25/34	.35	.40	7.00	(6)	2.25	19
a	Vertical pair, imperf.							
	horizontally, with gum		875.00					
744	5¢ Old Faithful, Yellowstone							
	(Wyoming)	07/30/34	.70	.65	8.75	(6)	2.25	30
a	Horizontal pair, imperf.							
	vertically, with gum		550.00					
745	6¢ Crater Lake (Oregon)	09/05/34	1.10	.85	15.00	(6)	3.00	16
746	7¢ Great Head, Acadia							
	Park (Maine)	10/02/34	.60	.75	10.00	(6)	3.00	15
a	Horizontal pair, imperf.							
	vertically, with gum		875.00					
747	8¢ Great White Throne,							
	Zion Park (Utah)	09/18/34	1.60	1.50	15.00	(6)	3.25	15
748	9¢ Glacier National Park							
	(Montana)	08/27/34	1.50	.65	15.00	(6)	3.50	17
749	10¢ Great Smoky Mountains							
	(North Carolina)	10/08/34	3.00	1.25	22.50	(6)	6.00	18
	American Philatelic Society Issue Souvenir Sheet, Imperf.							
750	3¢ sheet of 6 (742)	08/28/34	30.00	27.50			40.00	0.5
a	Single stamp from sheet		3.50	3.25			3.25	3
	Trans-Mississippi Philatelic Exposition Issue Souvenir Sheet							
751	1¢ sheet of 6 (740)	10/10/34	12.50	12.50			35.00	0.7
a	Single stamp from sheet		1.40	1.60			3.25 (3)	4

735

736

737

739

740

741

742

744

743

745

746

747

748

749

750

751

Examples of Special Printing Position Blocks

Gutter Block 752

Centerline Block 754

Line Block 756

Arrow Block 763

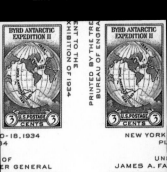

Cross-Gutter Block 768

	Issues of 1935		Un	U	PB	#	FDC	Q(M)
	Special Printing (#752-71), Without Gum, Perf. 10.5 x 11							
752	3¢ violet Peace of 1783 (727)	03/15/35	.20	.20	20.00	(4)	5.00	3
	Perf. 11							
753	3¢ blue Byrd Expedition II (733)	03/15/35	.50	.45	17.50	(6)	6.00	2
	Imperf.							
754	3¢ dp. vio. Whistler's Mother							
	(737)	03/15/35	.60	.60	16.00	(6)	6.00	2
755	3¢ deep violet Wisconsin (739)	03/15/35	.60	.60	16.00	(6)	6.00	2
756	1¢ green Yosemite (740)	03/15/35	.20	.20	5.00	(6)	6.00	3
757	2¢ red Grand Canyon (741)	03/15/35	.25	.25	5.75	(6)	6.00	3
	Double transfer		—					
758	3¢ deep violet Mt. Rainier (742)	03/15/35	.50	.45	14.00	(6)	6.00	2
759	4¢ brown Mesa Verde (743)	03/15/35	.95	.95	20.00	(6)	6.50	2
760	5¢ blue Yellowstone (744)	03/15/35	1.50	1.30	25.00	(6)	6.50	2
	Double transfer		—					
761	6¢ dark blue Crater Lake (745)	03/15/35	2.40	2.10	35.00	(6)	6.50	2
762	7¢ black Acadia (746)	03/15/35	1.50	1.40	30.00	(6)	6.50	2
	Double transfer		—					
763	8¢ sage green Zion (747)	03/15/35	1.60	1.50	37.50	(6)	7.50	2
764	9¢ red orange Glacier (748)	03/15/35	1.90	1.65	42.50	(6)	7.50	2
765	10¢ gray black Smoky Mts. (749)	03/15/35	3.75	3.25	50.00	(6)	7.50	2
766	1¢ yellow grn. (728), pane of 25	03/15/35	25.00	25.00			250.00	0.1
a	Single stamp from pane		.70	.40			5.50 (3)	2
767	3¢ violet (729), pane of 25	03/15/35	23.50	23.50			250.00	0.09
a	Single stamp from pane		.60	.40			5.50	2
768	3¢ dark blue (733), pane of 6	03/15/35	20.00	15.00			250.00	0.3
a	Single stamp from pane		2.80	2.40			6.50	2
769	1¢ green (740), pane of 6	03/15/35	12.50	11.00			250.00	0.3
a	Single stamp from pane		1.85	1.80			4.00	2
770	3¢ deep violet (742), pane of 6	03/15/35	30.00	24.00			250.00	0.2
a	Single stamp from pane		3.25	3.10			5.00	1
771	16¢ dark blue Great Seal of U.S.	03/15/35	2.40	2.25	50.00	(6)	12.50	1
	For perforate variety, see #CE2.							

A number of position pieces can be collected from the panes or sheets of the 1935 Special Printing issues, including horizontal and vertical gutter (#752, 766-70) or line (#753-65, 771) blocks of four (HG/L and VG/L), arrow-and-guideline blocks of four (AGL) and crossed-gutter or centerline blocks of four (CG/L). Pairs sell for half the price of blocks of four. Arrow-and-guideline blocks are top or bottom only.

	HG/L	VG/L	AGL	CG/L		HG/L	VG/L	AGL	CG/L
752	11.50	19.00		50.00	762	8.50	7.50	8.25	14.00
753	4.50	50.00	52.50	57.50	763	7.50	9.50	11.00	17.50
754	3.50	2.80	3.00	7.25	764	10.00	9.00	10.50	22.50
755	3.50	2.80	3.00	7.25	765	18.00	21.00	24.00	30.00
756	.90	1.10	1.25	3.00	766	11.00	14.00		15.00
757	1.40	1.10	1.25	3.50	767	10.50	13.50		15.00
758	2.80	2.50	2.75	5.25	768	15.00	18.00		20.00
759	5.50	4.50	4.75	8.50	769	12.00	18.00		15.00
760	7.00	8.50	9.00	15.00	770	25.00	22.00		30.00
761	13.00	11.00	12.50	20.00	771	13.00	11.00	12.50	60.00

	Issues of 1935		Un	U	PB	#	FD	Q(M)
	Perf. 11 x 10.5							
	Beginning with #772, unused values are for never-hinged stamps.							
772	3¢ Connecticut Tercentenary	04/26/35	.20	.20	1.40	(4)	10.00	71
	Defect in cent design		1.00	.25				
773	3¢ California Pacific							
	International Expo	05/29/35	.20	.20	1.25	(4)	10.00	101
	Pair with full vertical gutter between		—					
	Perf. 11							
774	3¢ Boulder Dam	09/30/35	.20	.20	1.65	(6)	10.00	74
	Perf. 11 x 10.5							
775	3¢ Michigan Centenary	11/01/35	.20	.20	1.25	(4)	10.00	76
	Issues of 1936							
776	3¢ Republic of Texas	03/02/36	.20	.20	1.10	(4)	17.50	124
	Perf. 10.5 x 11							
777	3¢ Rhode Island Tercentenary	05/04/36	.20	.20	1.10	(4)	9.00	67
	Pair with full gutter between		200.00					
	Third International Philatelic Exhibition Issue Souvenir Sheet, Imperf.							
778	Sheet of 4 different stamps							
	(#772, 773, 775 and 776)	05/09/36	1.75	1.75			13.00	3
a-d	Single stamp from sheet		.40	.30				3
779-81	Not assigned							
	Perf. 11 x 10.5							
782	3¢ Arkansas Statehood	06/15/36	.20	.20	1.10	(4)	9.00	73
783	3¢ Oregon Territory	07/14/36	.20	.20	1.10	(4)	8.50	74
	Double transfer		1.00	.50				
784	3¢ Susan B. Anthony	08/26/36	.20	.20	.75	(4)	9.00	270
	Period missing after "B"		.75	.25				

Greetings From Arkansas

From the eastern lowlands to the western uplands, Arkansas offers a host of opportunities for outdoor enthusiasts. Camping, canoeing, and fishing are popular throughout the state, which boasts more than 9,000 miles of rivers and streams, two mountain ranges, several major lakes, and nearly three million acres of national forest. A stroll through diamond fields in Crater of Diamonds State Park might even lead to riches; visitors get to keep any precious stones they dig up.

One of the oldest parks in the United States, Hot Springs National Park protects 47 thermal springs and a collection of bathhouses unmatched in North America. In the 1920s, thousands of years after Native Americans first happened upon this lovely spot, the popularity of the springs soared as wealthy health-seekers from around the world came to be pampered amid the marble, stained-glass, polished brass splendor of Bathhouse Row.

A man-made treasure from an earlier age stands in Little Rock: Begun in 1833, the Old State House is among the South's most beautiful antebellum structures. ■

772

773

774

775

776

777

778

782

783

784

785

786

787

788

789

790

791

792

793

794

795

796

798

799

800

801

802

Issues of 1936-1937		Un	U	PB	#	FDC	Q(M)
Army Issue, Perf. 11 x 10.5							
785	1¢ George Washington, Nathanael Greene and Mount Vernon	.20	.20	.85	(4)	6.00	105
	Pair with full vertical gutter between	—					
786	2¢ Andrew Jackson, Winfield Scott and The Hermitage 01/15/37	.20	.20	.85	(4)	6.00	94
787	3¢ Generals Sherman, Grant and Sheridan 02/18/37	.20	.20	1.10	(4)	6.00	88
788	4¢ Generals Robert E. Lee and "Stonewall" Jackson and Stratford Hall 03/23/37	.30	.20	8.00	(4)	6.00	36
789	5¢ U.S. Military Academy at West Point 05/26/37	.60	.20	8.50	(4)	6.00	37
	Navy Issue						
790	1¢ John Paul Jones, John Barry, *Bon Homme Richard* and *Lexington* 12/15/36	.20	.20	.85	(4)	6.00	105
791	2¢ Stephen Decatur, Thomas MacDonough and *Saratoga* 01/15/37	.20	.20	.75	(4)	6.00	92
792	3¢ David G. Farragut and David D. Porter, *Hartford* and *Powhatan* 02/18/37	.20	.20	1.00	(4)	6.00	93
793	4¢ Admirals William T. Sampson, George Dewey and Winfield S. Schley 03/23/37	.30	.20	8.50	(4)	6.00	35
794	5¢ Seal of U.S. Naval Academy and Naval Cadets 05/26/37	.60	.20	8.50	(4)	6.00	37
	Issues of 1937						
795	3¢ Northwest Territory Ordinance 07/13/37	.20	.20	1.10	(4)	7.00	85
	Perf. 11						
796	5¢ Virginia Dare and Parents 08/18/37	.20	.20	6.50	(6)	9.00	25
	Society of Philatelic Americans Issue Souvenir Sheet, Imperf.						
797	10¢ blue green (749) 08/26/37	.60	.40			8.00	5
	Perf. 11 x 10.5						
798	3¢ Constitution Sesquicentennial 09/17/37	.20	.20	1.00	(4)	8.00	100
	Territorial Issues, Perf. 10.5 x 11						
799	3¢ Hawaii 10/18/37	.20	.20	1.25	(4)	8.00	78
	Perf. 11 x 10.5						
800	3¢ Alaska 11/12/37	.20	.20	1.25	(4)	8.00	77
	Pair with full gutter between	—					
801	3¢ Puerto Rico 11/25/37	.20	.20	1.25	(4)	8.00	81
802	3¢ Virgin Islands 12/15/37	.20	.20	1.25	(4)	8.00	76
	Pair with full vertical gutter between	275.00					

Issues of 1938-39		Un	U	PB	#	FDC
Presidential Issue, Perf. 11 x 10.5 (#804b, 806b, 807a issued in 1939, 832b in 1951, 832c in 1954, rest in 1938; see also 839-51)						
803	½¢ Benjamin Franklin 05/19/38	.20	.20	.40	(4)	3.00
804	1¢ George Washington 04/25/38	.20	.20	.25	(4)	3.00
	Pair with full vertical gutter between	160.00	—			
b	Booklet pane of 6 01/27/39	2.00	.35			
805	1½¢ Martha Washington 05/05/38	.20	.20	.20	(4)	3.00
	Pair with full horizontal gutter between	175.00				
b	Horizontal pair, imperf. between	160.00	30.00			
806	2¢ John Adams 06/03/38	.20	.20	.30	(4)	3.00
	Recut at top of head	3.00	1.50			
b	Booklet pane of 6 01/27/39	4.75	.85			15.00
807	3¢ Thomas Jefferson 06/16/38	.20	.20	.25	(4)	3.00
a	Booklet pane of 6 01/27/39	8.50	1.25			17.50
b	Horizontal pair, imperf. between	1,250.00	—			
c	Imperf., pair	2,500.00				
808	4¢ James Madison 07/01/38	.75	.20	3.50	(4)	3.00
809	4½¢ The White House 07/11/38	.20	.20	1.50	(4)	3.00
810	5¢ James Monroe 07/21/38	.20	.20	1.00	(4)	3.00
811	6¢ John Quincy Adams 07/28/38	.20	.20	1.00	(4)	3.00
812	7¢ Andrew Jackson 08/04/38	.25	.20	1.25	(4)	3.00
813	8¢ Martin Van Buren 08/11/38	.30	.20	1.40	(4)	3.00
814	9¢ William H. Harrison 08/18/38	.30	.20	1.40	(4)	3.00
	Pair with full vertical gutter between	—				
815	10¢ John Tyler 09/02/38	.25	.20	1.25	(4)	3.00
816	11¢ James K. Polk 09/08/38	.65	.20	3.00	(4)	3.50
817	12¢ Zachary Taylor 09/14/38	.90	.20	4.00	(4)	3.50
818	13¢ Millard Fillmore 09/22/38	1.25	.20	6.50	(4)	3.50
819	14¢ Franklin Pierce 10/06/38	.90	.20	4.50	(4)	3.50
820	15¢ James Buchanan 10/13/38	.40	.20	1.90	(4)	3.50
821	16¢ Abraham Lincoln 10/20/38	.90	.25	5.00	(4)	5.00
822	17¢ Andrew Johnson 10/27/38	.85	.20	4.50	(4)	5.00
823	18¢ Ulysses S. Grant 11/03/38	1.75	.20	8.75	(4)	5.00
824	19¢ Rutherford B. Hayes 11/10/38	1.25	.35	6.25	(4)	5.00
825	20¢ James A. Garfield 11/10/38	.70	.20	3.50	(4)	5.00
826	21¢ Chester A. Arthur 11/22/38	1.25	.20	7.00	(4)	5.50
827	22¢ Grover Cleveland 11/22/38	1.00	.40	9.50	(4)	5.50
828	24¢ Benjamin Harrison 12/02/38	3.50	.20	17.00	(4)	5.50
829	25¢ William McKinley 12/02/38	.60	.20	3.00	(4)	6.25
830	30¢ Theodore Roosevelt 12/08/38	3.50	.20	16.00	(4)	7.75
831	50¢ William Howard Taft 12/08/38	5.50	.20	24.00	(4)	10.00

803 804 805 806 807

808 809 810 811 812

813 814 815 816 817

818 819 820 821 822

823 824 825 826 827

828 829 830 831

1938-1939

832

833

834

835

836

837

838

852

853

854

855

856

857

858

	Issues of 1938-54		Un	U	PB/LP	#	FDC	Q(M)
	Perf. 11							
832	$1 Woodrow Wilson	08/29/38	7.00	.20	32.50	(4)	50.00	
a	Vertical pair, imperf. horizontally		1,600.00					
b	Watermarked "USIR" (1951)		225.00	65.00	—	(4)		
c	$1 red violet and black	08/31/54	6.00	.20	30.00	(4)	25.00	
d	As "c," vert. pair, imperf. horiz.		1,250.00					
e	Vertical pair, imperf. between		2,750.00					
f	As "c," vert. pair, imperf. between		7,000.00					
833	$2 Warren G. Harding	09/29/38	20.00	3.75	95.00	(4)	100.00	
834	$5 Calvin Coolidge	11/17/38	95.00	3.00	425.00	(4)	150.00	
a	$5 red, brown and black		3,250.00	7,000.00				
	Issues of 1938, Perf. 11 x 10.5							
835	3¢ Constitution Ratification	06/21/38	.25	.20	3.50	(4)	9.00	73
	Perf. 11							
836	3¢ Swedish-Finnish Tercentenary	06/27/38	.20	.20	2.50	(6)	9.00	59
	Perf. 11 x 10.5							
837	3¢ Northwest Territory	07/15/38	.20	.20	7.50	(4)	9.00	66
838	3¢ Iowa Territorial Centennial	08/24/38	.20	.20	5.00	(4)	9.00	47
	Pair with full vertical gutter between		—					
	Issues of 1938-39, Coil Stamps, Perf. 10 Vertically							
839	1¢ green Washington (804)	01/20/39	.30	.20	1.40	(2)	4.75	
840	1½¢ bister brn.							
	Martha Washington (805)	01/20/39	.30	.20	1.50	(2)	4.75	
841	2¢ rose carmine							
	John Adams (806)	01/20/39	.40	.20	1.75	(2)	4.75	
842	3¢ deep violet Jefferson (807)	01/20/39	.50	.20	2.00	(2)	4.75	
	Gripper cracks		—					
	Thin, translucent paper		2.50	—				
843	4¢ red violet Madison (808)	01/20/39	8.00	.40	27.50	(2)	5.00	
844	4½¢ dark gray							
	White House (809)	01/20/38	.70	.40	5.00	(2)	5.00	
845	5¢ bright blue Monroe (810)	01/20/39	5.00	.35	27.50	(2)	5.00	
846	6¢ red orange							
	John Quincy Adams (811)	01/20/39	1.10	.20	7.50	(2)	6.50	
847	10¢ brown red Tyler (815)	01/20/39	11.00	.50	42.50	(2)	9.00	
	Coil Stamps, Perf. 10 Horizontally							
848	1¢ green Washington (804)	01/27/39	.85	.20	2.75	(2)	5.00	
849	1½¢ bister brn.							
	Martha Washington (805)	01/27/39	1.25	.30	4.50	(2)	5.00	
850	2¢ rose carmine							
	John Adams (806)	01/27/39	2.50	.40	6.50	(2)	5.00	
851	3¢ deep violet Jefferson (807)	01/27/39	2.25	.35	6.25	(2)	5.50	
	Perf. 10.5 x 11							
852	3¢ Golden Gate Exposition	02/18/39	.20	.20	1.25	(4)	6.00	114
853	3¢ New York World's Fair	04/01/39	.20	.20	1.75	(4)	12.50	102
	Perf. 11							
854	3¢ Washington's Inauguration	04/30/39	.40	.20	3.50	(6)	6.00	73
	Perf. 11 x 10.5							
855	3¢ Baseball	06/12/39	1.75	.20	7.50	(4)	35.00	81
	Perf. 11							
856	3¢ Panama Canal	08/15/39	.25	.20	3.00	(6)	6.50	68
	Perf. 10.5 x 11							
857	3¢ Printing	09/25/39	.20	.20	1.00	(4)	5.00	71
	Perf. 11 x 10.5							
858	3¢ 50th Anniversary of Statehood (Montana, North Dakota, South Dakota, Washington)	11/02/39	.20	.20	1.10	(4)	5.00	67

1940

Issues of 1940		Un	U	PB	#	FDC	Q(M)
Famous Americans Issue, Perf. 10.5 x 11							
Authors							
859	1¢ Washington Irving	01/29/40	.20	.20	.95	(4)	3.00	56
860	2¢ James Fenimore Cooper	01/29/40	.20	.20	.95	(4)	2.00	53
861	3¢ Ralph Waldo Emerson	02/05/40	.20	.20	1.25	(4)	2.00	53
862	5¢ Louisa May Alcott	02/05/40	.30	.20	8.25	(4)	3.00	22
863	10¢ Samuel L. Clemens (Mark Twain)	02/13/40	1.65	1.20	32.50	(4)	4.50	13
Poets							
864	1¢ Henry W. Longfellow	02/16/40	.20	.20	1.75	(4)	2.00	52
865	2¢ John Greenleaf Whittier	02/16/40	.20	.20	1.75	(4)	2.00	52
866	3¢ James Russell Lowell	02/20/40	.20	.20	2.25	(4)	2.00	52
867	5¢ Walt Whitman	02/20/40	.35	.20	9.00	(4)	4.00	22
868	10¢ James Whitcomb Riley	02/24/40	1.75	1.25	30.00	(4)	6.00	12
Educators							
869	1¢ Horace Mann	03/14/40	.20	.20	1.90	(4)	2.00	52
870	2¢ Mark Hopkins	03/14/40	.20	.20	1.25	(4)	2.00	52
871	3¢ Charles W. Eliot	03/28/40	.20	.20	2.25	(4)	2.00	52
872	5¢ Frances E. Willard	03/28/40	.40	.20	9.00	(4)	4.00	21
873	10¢ Booker T. Washington	04/07/40	1.25	1.10	25.00	(4)	6.50	14
Scientists							
874	1¢ John James Audubon	04/08/40	.20	.20	.95	(4)	2.00	59
875	2¢ Dr. Crawford W. Long	04/08/40	.20	.20	.95	(4)	2.00	58
876	3¢ Luther Burbank	04/17/40	.20	.20	1.10	(4)	2.00	58
877	5¢ Dr. Walter Reed	04/17/40	.25	.20	5.00	(4)	3.00	24
878	10¢ Jane Addams	04/26/40	1.10	.85	16.00	(4)	5.00	15
Composers							
879	1¢ Stephen Collins Foster	05/03/40	.20	.20	1.00	(4)	2.00	57
880	2¢ John Philip Sousa	05/03/40	.20	.20	1.00	(4)	2.00	58
881	3¢ Victor Herbert	05/13/40	.20	.20	1.10	(4)	2.00	56
882	5¢ Edward A. MacDowell	05/13/40	.40	.20	9.25	(4)	3.00	21
883	10¢ Ethelbert Nevin	06/10/40	3.75	1.35	32.50	(4)	5.00	13
Artists							
884	1¢ Gilbert Charles Stuart	09/05/40	.20	.20	1.00	(4)	2.00	54
885	2¢ James A. McNeill Whistler	09/05/40	.20	.20	.95	(4)	2.00	54
886	3¢ Augustus Saint-Gaudens	09/16/40	.20	.20	1.00	(4)	2.00	55
887	5¢ Daniel Chester French	09/16/40	.50	.20	8.00	(4)	3.00	22
888	10¢ Frederic Remington	09/30/40	1.75	1.25	20.00	(4)	5.00	14
Inventors							
889	1¢ Eli Whitney	10/07/40	.20	.20	1.90	(4)	2.00	48
890	2¢ Samuel F.B. Morse	10/07/40	.20	.20	1.10	(4)	2.00	53
891	3¢ Cyrus Hall McCormick	10/14/40	.25	.20	1.75	(4)	2.00	54
892	5¢ Elias Howe	10/14/40	1.10	.30	12.50	(4)	3.00	20
893	10¢ Alexander Graham Bell	10/28/40	11.00	2.00	65.00	(4)	7.50	14

859 860 861 862 863

864 865 866 867 868

869 870 871 872 873

874 875 876 877 878

879 880 881 882 883

884 885 886 887 888

889 890 891 892 893

894

895

896

897

898

899

900

901

902

903

904

905

906

907

908

	Issues of 1940		Un	U	PB	#	FDC	Q(M)
894	3¢ Pony Express	04/03/40	.25	.20	2.75	(4)	6.00	46
	Perf. 10.5 x 11							
895	3¢ Pan American Union	04/14/40	.20	.20	2.75	(4)	4.50	48
	Perf. 11 x 10.5							
896	3¢ Idaho Statehood	07/03/40	.20	.20	1.75	(4)	4.50	51
	Perf. 10.5 x 11							
897	3¢ Wyoming Statehood	07/10/40	.20	.20	1.50	(4)	4.50	50
	Perf. 11 x 10.5							
898	3¢ Coronado Expedition	09/07/40	.20	.20	1.50	(4)	4.50	61
	National Defense Issue							
899	1¢ Statue of Liberty	10/16/40	.20	.20	.45	(4)	4.25	
	Cracked plate		3.00					
	Gripper cracks		3.00					
a	Vertical pair, imperf. between		650.00	—				
b	Horizontal pair, imperf. between		35.00	—				
	Pair with full vertical gutter between		200.00					
900	2¢ 90mm Antiaircraft Gun	10/16/40	.20	.20	.45	(4)	4.25	
a	Horizontal pair, imperf. between		40.00	—				
	Pair with full vertical gutter between		275.00					
901	3¢ Torch of Enlightenment	10/16/40	.20	.20	.60	(4)	4.25	
a	Horizontal pair, imperf. between		27.50	—				
	Pair with full vertical gutter between		—					
	Perf. 10.5 x 11							
902	3¢ Thirteenth Amendment	10/20/40	.20	.20	3.00	(4)	7.50	44
	Issue of 1941, Perf. 11 x 10.5							
903	3¢ Vermont Statehood	03/04/41	.20	.20	1.75	(4)	7.00	55
	Issues of 1942							
904	3¢ Kentucky Statehood	06/01/42	.20	.20	1.10	(4)	4.00	64
905	3¢ Win the War	07/04/42	.20	.20	.40	(4)	3.75	
	Pair with full vertical or horizontal gutter between		175.00					
b	3¢ purple		—	—				
906	5¢ Chinese Resistance	07/07/42	.85	.20	9.00	(4)	6.00	21
	Issues of 1943							
907	2¢ Allied Nations	01/14/43	.20	.20	.30	(4)	3.50	1,700
	Pair with full vertical or horizontal gutter between		225.00					
908	1¢ Four Freedoms	02/12/43	.20	.20	.60	(4)	3.50	1,200

Greetings From Vermont

In 1791, Vermont became the 14th state, joining the 13 original Colonies in the new United States of America. The state's name derives from its major, north-south mountain range, whose heavily forested peaks were *les monts verts,* "the green mountains," to early French explorers.

In summer, the Green Mountains truly live up to their name, while in autumn, shades of gold and crimson appear on the forested slopes, as do busloads of tourists who travel from across the nation to admire the brilliant foliage. A blanket of deep snow covers the ground in winter and turns the mountains into a paradise for cross-country and downhill skiers. As spring approaches, sap begins rising in the millions of sugar maples tapped by farmers to make maple syrup—one of the state's most popular products.

Vermont is also celebrated for its apples, honey, dairy products, Christmas trees, and lumber; maple trees are favorites of furniture makers. ■

Issues of 1943-1944		Un	U	PB	#	FDC	Q(M)
Overrun Countries Issue, Perf. 12							
909	5¢ Poland	06/22/43	.20	.20	4.25*	(4)	7.50	20
910	5¢ Czechoslovakia	07/12/43	.20	.20	2.75*	(4)	4.00	20
911	5¢ Norway	07/27/43	.20	.20	1.30*	(4)	4.00	20
912	5¢ Luxembourg	08/10/43	.20	.20	1.20*	(4)	4.00	20
913	5¢ Netherlands	08/24/43	.20	.20	1.20*	(4)	4.00	20
914	5¢ Belgium	09/14/43	.20	.20	1.10*	(4)	4.00	20
915	5¢ France	09/28/43	.20	.20	1.25*	(4)	4.00	20
916	5¢ Greece	10/12/43	.35	.25	10.00*	(4)	4.00	15
917	5¢ Yugoslavia	10/26/43	.25	.20	4.25*	(4)	4.00	15
918	5¢ Albania	11/09/43	.20	.20	4.25*	(4)	4.00	15
919	5¢ Austria	11/23/43	.20	.20	3.50*	(4)	4.00	15
920	5¢ Denmark	12/07/43	.20	.20	5.25*	(4)	4.00	15
921	5¢ Korea	11/02/44	.20	.20	4.50*	(4)	5.00	15
	"KORPA" plate flaw		17.50	12.50				
*Instead of plate numbers, the selvage is inscribed with the name of the country.								
Issues of 1944, Perf. 11 x 10.5								
922	3¢ Transcontinental Railroad	05/10/44	.20	.20	1.40	(4)	6.00	61
923	3¢ Steamship	05/22/44	.20	.20	1.25	(4)	4.00	61
924	3¢ Telegraph	05/24/44	.20	.20	.90	(4)	3.50	61
925	3¢ Philippine	09/27/44	.20	.20	1.10	(4)	3.50	50
926	3¢ Motion Pictures	10/31/44	.20	.20	.90	(4)	4.00	53

Acadia National Park

Encompassing more than 46,000 scenic acres along the coast of Maine, Acadia National Park has long been a haven for plants, animals, and people. Native Americans were living here at least 5,000 years ago, enjoying the natural bounty of the woodlands and coastal waters. In 1604, an expedition led by French explorer Samuel de Champlain landed on Mount Desert Island, and the decades that followed brought French, then British and American settlers. In the mid-19th century, Thomas Cole, Frederic Church, and other painters of the Hudson River School put the glories of the region on canvas and made Mount Desert and its environs a highly sought-after destination. By the turn of the 20th century, the scenic shores, lakes, woods, and mountains had become playgrounds for society's elite, including George B. Dorr, a conservationist who would devote more than 40 years of his life to preserving the landscape. Dorr's tireless efforts led to the creation of Sieur de Monts National Monument in 1916 and Lafayette National Park in 1919; ten years later, Lafayette was renamed Acadia National Park. ■

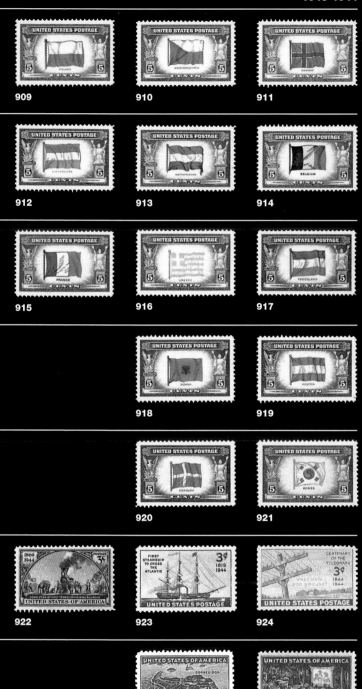

909

910

911

912

913

914

915

916

917

918

919

920

921

922

923

924

925

926

927

928

929

930

931

932

933

934

935

936

937

938

939

940

941

942

943

944

945

946

947

	Issues of 1945, Perf. 11 x 10.5		Un	U	PB	#	FDC	Q(M)
927	3¢ Florida Statehood	03/03/45	.20	.20	.50	(4)	4.50	62
928	5¢ United Nations Conference	04/25/45	.20	.20	.45	(4)	5.00	76
	Perf. 10.5 x 11							
929	3¢ Iwo Jima (Marines)	07/11/45	.20	.20	.40	(4)	10.00	137
	Issues of 1945-46, Franklin D. Roosevelt Issue, Perf. 11 x 10.5							
930	1¢ Roosevelt and Hyde Park							
	Residence	07/26/45	.20	.20	.20	(4)	3.50	128
931	2¢ Roosevelt and "The Little White House"							
	at Warm Springs, Ga.	08/24/45	.20	.20	.35	(4)	3.50	67
932	3¢ Roosevelt and White House	06/27/45	.20	.20	.35	(4)	3.50	134
933	5¢ Roosevelt, Map of Western							
	Hemisphere and Four Freedoms	01/30/46	.20	.20	.45	(4)	3.50	76
934	3¢ Army, Sept. 28	09/28/45	.20	.20	.40	(4)	6.00	128
935	3¢ Navy	10/27/45	.20	.20	.40	(4)	6.00	136
936	3¢ Coast Guard	11/10/45	.20	.20	.40	(4)	6.00	112
937	3¢ Alfred E. Smith	11/26/45	.20	.20	.40	(4)	2.50	309
	Pair with full vertical gutter between	—						
938	3¢ Texas Statehood	12/29/45	.20	.20	.40	(4)	4.00	171
	Issues of 1946							
939	3¢ Merchant Marine	02/26/46	.20	.20	.40	(4)	5.00	136
940	3¢ Veterans of World War II	05/09/46	.20	.20	.40	(4)	4.00	260
941	3¢ Tennessee Statehood	06/01/46	.20	.20	.35	(4)	1.50	132
942	3¢ Iowa Statehood	08/03/46	.20	.20	.30	(4)	1.50	132
943	3¢ Smithsonian Institution	08/10/46	.20	.20	.35	(4)	1.50	139
944	3¢ Kearny Expedition	10/16/46	.20	.20	.30	(4)	1.50	115
	Issues of 1947, Perf. 10.5 x 11							
945	3¢ Thomas A. Edison	02/11/47	.20	.20	.35	(4)	3.00	157
	Perf. 11 x 10.5							
946	3¢ Joseph Pulitzer	04/10/47	.20	.20	.35	(4)	1.50	120
947	3¢ Postage Stamps Centenary	05/17/47	.20	.20	.30	(4)	1.50	127

Tennessee Valley Authority

Most of Tennessee and parts of Virginia, North Carolina, Georgia, Alabama, Kentucky, and Mississippi rely on electrical power generated by the Tennessee Valley Authority (TVA). This federal corporation dates from the Great Depression of the 1930s, when President Franklin D. Roosevelt envisioned an innovative way to manage the resources of the Tennessee River Valley. He asked Congress to establish an entity having both the power of government and the flexibility of private enterprise, and in 1933 the TVA was born.

Over the years, the TVA has built 49 dams, 29 hydroelectric plants, 11 coal-burning plants, five combustion turbine plants, three nuclear plants, and one pumped-storage plant. Its power system now supplies relatively low-cost, reliable power to eight million people in an 80,000-square-mile area. The TVA also works to ensure water quality, conserve fisheries, minimize flooding, and provide opportunities for recreation. Through direct and indirect measures, such as economic development assistance, the TVA has also helped generate hundreds of thousands of jobs in the region. ■

Issues of 1947		Un	U	PB	#	FDC	Q(M)
Centenary International Philatelic Exhibition Issue Souvenir Sheet, Imperf.							
948	Souvenir sheet of 2						
	stamps (#1-2) 05/19/47	.55	.45			2.00	10
a	5¢ single stamp from sheet	.20	.20				
b	10¢ single stamp from sheet	.25	.25				
	Perf. 11 x 10.5						
949	3¢ Doctors 06/09/47	.20	.20	.30	(4)	2.50	133
950	3¢ Utah Settlement 07/24/47	.20	.20	.30	(4)	1.00	132
951	3¢ U.S. Frigate *Constitution* 10/21/47	.20	.20	.30	(4)	6.00	131
	Perf. 10.5 x 11						
952	3¢ Everglades National Park 12/05/47	.20	.20	.30	(4)	1.00	122
	Issues of 1948						
953	3¢ Dr. G.W. Carver 01/05/48	.20	.20	.35	(4)	1.00	122
	Perf. 11 x 10.5						
954	3¢ California Gold 01/24/48	.20	.20	.30	(4)	1.00	131
955	3¢ Mississippi Territory 04/07/48	.20	.20	.30	(4)	1.00	123
956	3¢ Four Chaplains 05/28/48	.20	.20	.40	(4)	3.00	122
957	3¢ Wisconsin Statehood 05/29/48	.20	.20	.35	(4)	1.00	115
958	5¢ Swedish Pioneer 06/04/48	.20	.20	.45	(4)	1.00	64
959	3¢ Progress of Women 07/19/48	.20	.20	.30	(4)	1.00	118
	Perf. 10.5 x 11						
960	3¢ William Allen White 07/31/48	.20	.20	.40	(4)	1.00	78
	Perf. 11 x 10.5						
961	3¢ U.S.-Canada Friendship 08/02/48	.20	.20	.30	(4)	1.00	113
962	3¢ Francis Scott Key 08/09/48	.20	.20	.35	(4)	1.00	121
963	3¢ Salute to Youth 08/11/48	.20	.20	.30	(4)	1.00	78
964	3¢ Oregon Territory 08/14/48	.20	.20	.35	(4)	1.00	52
	Perf. 10.5 x 11						
965	3¢ Harlan F. Stone 08/25/48	.20	.20	.60	(4)	1.00	54
966	3¢ Palomar Observatory 08/30/48	.20	.20	.95	(4)	2.00	61
a	Vertical pair, imperf. between	550.00					
	Perf. 11 x 10.5						
967	3¢ Clara Barton 09/07/48	.20	.20	.30	(4)	3.00	58

Greetings From Mississippi

Mississippi, the "Magnolia State," gets its name from the great river flowing along its western border with Arkansas and Louisiana. Located in the Deep South, Mississippi enjoys relatively mild winters but endures warm and humid summers, a fact of life that has long favored agricultural pursuits. In antebellum times, the benign climate and rich soils allowed vast plantations with hundreds of slaves to grow "king" cotton, which was then shipped on paddle wheelers to textile mills outside the state. Today, a heritage corridor near the Mississippi River includes several plantation homes, as well as Civil War battlefields that played enormous roles in bringing an end to the plantation era.

Agriculture remains a major part of the Mississippi economy. But nowadays, important contributors also include manufacturers of furniture, textiles, and transportation equipment, and producers of pond-raised catfish; 70 percent of the world's catfish supply comes from Mississippi.

Famous Mississippians include Elvis Presley, born in Tupelo, and author William Faulkner, who hailed from New Albany. ■

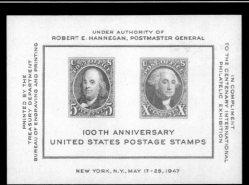

948

949

950

951

952

953

954

955

956

957

958

959

960

961

962

963

964

965

966

967

968

969

970

972

973

971

975

976

977

974

979

980

981

978

983

984

982

986

987

988

985

	Issues of 1948		Un	U	PB	#	FDC	Q(M)
968	3¢ Poultry Industry	09/09/48	.20	.20	.40	(4)	1.50	53
	Perf. 10.5 x 11							
969	3¢ Gold Star Mothers	09/21/48	.20	.20	.40	(4)	1.00	77
	Perf. 11 x 10.5							
970	3¢ Fort Kearny	09/22/48	.20	.20	.40	(4)	1.00	58
971	3¢ Volunteer Firemen	10/04/48	.20	.20	.50	(4)	7.00	56
972	3¢ Indian Centennial	10/15/48	.20	.20	.40	(4)	1.00	58
973	3¢ Rough Riders	10/27/48	.20	.20	.40	(4)	1.00	54
974	3¢ Juliette Gordon Low	10/29/48	.20	.20	.40	(4)	3.00	64
	Perf. 10.5 x 11							
975	3¢ Will Rogers	11/04/48	.20	.20	.40	(4)	1.50	67
976	3¢ Fort Bliss	11/05/48	.20	.20	1.10	(4)	2.00	65
	Perf. 11 x 10.5							
977	3¢ Moina Michael	11/09/48	.20	.20	.40	(4)	1.00	64
978	3¢ Gettysburg Address	11/19/48	.20	.20	.45	(4)	1.00	63
	Perf. 10.5 x 11							
979	3¢ American Turners	11/20/48	.20	.20	.30	(4)	1.00	62
980	3¢ Joel Chandler Harris	12/09/48	.20	.20	.55	(4)	1.25	57
	Issues of 1949, Perf. 11 x 10.5							
981	3¢ Minnesota Territory	03/03/49	.20	.20	.30	(4)	1.00	99
982	3¢ Washington and Lee							
	University	04/12/49	.20	.20	.30	(4)	1.00	105
983	3¢ Puerto Rico Election	04/27/49	.20	.20	.30	(4)	1.00	109
984	3¢ Annapolis Tercentenary	05/23/49	.20	.20	.30	(4)	1.00	107
985	3¢ Grand Army of the Republic	08/29/49	.20	.20	.30	(4)	1.00	117
	Perf. 10.5 x 11							
986	3¢ Edgar Allan Poe	10/07/49	.20	.20	.45	(4)	1.50	123
	Thin outer frame line at top,							
	inner frame line missing		6.00					
	Issues of 1950, Perf. 11 x 10.5							
987	3¢ American Bankers	01/03/50	.20	.20	.35	(4)	2.00	131
	Perf. 10.5 x 11							
988	3¢ Samuel Gompers	01/27/50	.20	.20	.30	(4)	1.00	128

Greetings From Maryland

Known as "great shellfish bay" to Algonquin peoples, the Chesapeake Bay divides Maryland into two parts—the Eastern and Western Shores—and for generations, people have sailed out from both shores to tap the bounty of the bay. Today, local watermen continue to make their livings harvesting oysters, mussels, clams, and crabs that end up as shellfish feasts in area restaurants and residences.

Located on the Eastern Shore are small towns, farms, wildlife refuges, and Ocean City, a major resort area. On the Western Shore are more towns and farms, plus two of Maryland's most important cities. Annapolis, the state capital, includes numerous 18th-century structures and is home to the United States Naval Academy; Baltimore, the largest city, is a major port—and Babe Ruth's birthplace.

In 1952, Maryland spanned its great bay with a 4.3-mile-long bridge. Even earlier, it reached across another great natural barrier when the National Road, Baltimore and Ohio Railroad, and Chesapeake and Ohio Canal linked Maryland to lands west of the Appalachians. ∎

	Issues of 1950		Un	U	PB	#	FDC	Q(M)
	National Capital Sesquicentennial Issue, Perf. 10.5 x 11, 11 x 10.5							
989	3¢ Statue of Freedom on Capitol Dome	04/20/50	.20	.20	.30	(4)	1.00	132
990	3¢ Executive Mansion	06/12/50	.20	.20	.40	(4)	1.00	130
991	3¢ Supreme Court	08/02/50	.20	.20	.30	(4)	1.00	131
992	3¢ U.S. Capitol	11/22/50	.20	.20	.40	(4)	1.00	130
	Gripper cracks		1.00	.50				
	Perf. 11 x 10.5							
993	3¢ Railroad Engineers	04/29/50	.20	.20	.35	(4)	1.50	122
994	3¢ Kansas City, MO	06/03/50	.20	.20	.30	(4)	1.00	122
995	3¢ Boy Scouts	06/30/50	.20	.20	.35	(4)	5.00	132
996	3¢ Indiana Territory	07/04/50	.20	.20	.30	(4)	1.00	122
997	3¢ California Statehood	09/09/50	.20	.20	.30	(4)	1.00	121
	Issues of 1951							
998	3¢ United Confederate Veterans	05/30/51	.20	.20	.30	(4)	1.00	119
999	3¢ Nevada Settlement	07/14/51	.20	.20	.30	(4)	1.00	112
1000	3¢ Landing of Cadillac	07/24/51	.20	.20	.30	(4)	1.00	114
1001	3¢ Colorado Statehood	08/01/51	.20	.20	.30	(4)	1.00	114
1002	3¢ American Chemical Society	09/04/51	.20	.20	.35	(4)	2.00	117
1003	3¢ Battle of Brooklyn	12/10/51	.20	.20	.30	(4)	1.00	116
	Issues of 1952							
1004	3¢ Betsy Ross	01/02/52	.20	.20	.35	(4)	1.00	116
1005	3¢ 4-H Club	01/15/52	.20	.20	.30	(4)	1.00	116
1006	3¢ B&O Railroad	02/28/52	.20	.20	.40	(4)	1.75	113
1007	3¢ American Automobile Association	03/04/52	.20	.20	.30	(4)	1.00	117

Greetings From Nevada

The "Silver State" of Nevada welcomes 30 million visitors a year—and that's just in Las Vegas, in the southern part of the state. City of glitzy casinos, fancy hotels, and round-the-clock entertainment, Las Vegas owes almost all of its economic success to legalized gambling and associated activities.

Gambling is also big business in Reno and the Lake Tahoe area, on the California border. But the thick forests, snowcapped mountains, and deep blue lake waters draw thousands of outdoor enthusiasts as well. This region is vastly different from the rest of Nevada, which is mostly flat, dry, uninhabited, and owned by the United States government; 85 percent of the state is federal property.

Mormons founded Nevada's first town, now called Genoa, near Lake Tahoe in 1849. Ten years later, Virginia City grew up overnight when prospectors struck it rich by finding the fabulous Comstock Lode. Mining remains a major industry in the state. ■

989

990

991

992

993

994

995

996

997

998

999

1000

1001

1002

1003

1004

1005

1006

1007

1008

1009

1010

1011

1012

1013

1014

1015

1016

1017

1018

1019

1020

1021

1022

1023

1024

1025

1026

1027

1028

1029

	Issues of 1952		Un	U	PB	#	FDC	Q(M)
1008	3¢ NATO	04/04/52	.20	.20	.30	(4)	1.00	2,900
1009	3¢ Grand Coulee Dam	05/15/52	.20	.20	.30	(4)	1.00	115
1010	3¢ Arrival of Lafayette	06/13/52	.20	.20	.40	(4)	1.00	113
	Perf. 10.5 x 11							
1011	3¢ Mt. Rushmore Memorial	08/11/52	.20	.20	.35	(4)	1.00	116
	Perf. 11 x 10.5							
1012	3¢ Engineering	09/06/52	.20	.20	.30	(4)	1.00	114
1013	3¢ Service Women	09/11/52	.20	.20	.30	(4)	1.25	124
1014	3¢ Gutenberg Bible	09/30/52	.20	.20	.30	(4)	1.00	116
1015	3¢ Newspaper Boys	10/04/52	.20	.20	.30	(4)	1.00	115
1016	3¢ International Red Cross	11/21/52	.20	.20	.30	(4)	1.50	136
	Issues of 1953							
1017	3¢ National Guard	02/23/53	.20	.20	.30	(4)	1.00	115
1018	3¢ Ohio Statehood	03/02/53	.20	.20	.35	(4)	1.00	119
1019	3¢ Washington Territory	03/02/53	.20	.20	.30	(4)	1.00	114
1020	3¢ Louisiana Purchase	04/30/53	.20	.20	.30	(4)	1.00	114
1021	5¢ Opening of Japan	07/14/53	.20	.20	.65	(4)	1.00	89
1022	3¢ American Bar Association	08/24/53	.20	.20	.30	(4)	5.00	115
1023	3¢ Sagamore Hill	09/14/53	.20	.20	.35	(4)	1.00	116
1024	3¢ Future Farmers	10/13/53	.20	.20	.30	(4)	1.00	115
1025	3¢ Trucking Industry	10/27/53	.20	.20	.30	(4)	1.00	124
1026	3¢ General George S. Patton, Jr.	11/11/53	.20	.20	.40	(4)	4.00	115
1027	3¢ New York City	11/20/53	.20	.20	.35	(4)	1.00	116
1028	3¢ Gadsden Purchase	12/30/53	.20	.20	.30	(4)	1.00	116
	Issue of 1954							
1029	3¢ Columbia University	01/04/54	.20	.20	.30	(4)	1.00	119

Mount Rushmore

Hundreds of thousands of people travel to the Black Hills of southwestern South Dakota every year, looking for the "shrine of democracy" carved into the side of Mount Rushmore. As visitors make their way along the scenic Iron Mountain Road, they glimpse several colossal heads, each about 60 feet in height, with granite eyes gazing toward the horizon. This monumental work by sculptor Gutzon Borglum honors four United States Presidents—George Washington, Thomas Jefferson, Theodore Roosevelt, and Abraham Lincoln—and is the centerpiece of Mount Rushmore National Memorial.

Using dynamite and pneumatic hammers, Borglum began carving the gigantic likenesses in 1927. He died in 1941, and his son Lincoln finished the masterpiece that same year. In 1998, the National Park Service completed a 56-million-dollar redevelopment program at the site, which includes a visitor orientation center, dining facilities, a theater-and-museum complex, a gift shop, and a bookstore; the memorial also features a must-see nightly illumination of the faces. ■

	Issues of 1954-1967		Un	U	PB	#	FDC
	Liberty Issue, Perf. 11 x 10.5						
1030	½¢ Benjamin Franklin	10/20/55	.20	.20	.25	(4)	1.00
1031	1¢ George Washington	03/56	.20	.20	.20	(4)	
	Pair with full vertical or						
	horizontal gutter between		150.00				
b	Wet printing		.20	.20	.20	(4)	1.00
	Perf. 10.5 x 11						
1031A	1¼¢ Palace of the Governors	06/17/60	.20	.20	.45	(4)	1.00
1032	1½¢ Mt. Vernon	02/22/56	.20	.20	1.75	(4)	1.00
	Perf. 11 x 10.5						
1033	2¢ Thomas Jefferson	09/15/54	.20	.20	.25	(4)	1.00
	Pair with full vertical or						
	horizontal gutter between		—				
1034	2½¢ Bunker Hill Monument and						
	Massachusetts Flag	06/17/59	.20	.20	.50	(4)	1.00
1035	3¢ Statue of Liberty	06/24/54	.20	.20	.25	(4)	
a	Booklet pane of 6	06/30/54	4.00	.90			5.00
b	Tagged	07/06/66	.25	.25	5.00	(4)	15.00
c	Imperf., pair		2,000.00				
d	Horizontal pair, imperf. between		—				
e	Wet printing	06/24/54	.20	.20	.30	(4)	1.00
f	As "a," untagged		5.00	1.10			
g	As "a," vertical imperf. between		5,000.00				
1036	4¢ Abraham Lincoln	11/19/54	.20	.20	.35	(4)	
a	Booklet pane of 6	07/31/58	2.75	.80			4.00
b	Tagged	11/02/63	.60	.40	7.50	(4)	50.00
	Perf. 10.5 x 11						
1037	4½¢ The Hermitage	03/16/59	.20	.20	.65	(4)	1.00
	Perf. 11 x 10.5						
1038	5¢ James Monroe	12/02/54	.20	.20	.45	(4)	1.00
	Pair with full vertical gutter between		200.00				
1039	6¢ Theodore Roosevelt	11/18/55	.25	.20	1.25	(4)	
a	Wet printing	11/18/55	.40	.20	1.80	(4)	1.00
1040	7¢ Woodrow Wilson	01/10/56	.20	.20	1.00	(4)	1.00
	Perf. 11						
1041	8¢ Statue of Liberty	04/09/54	.25	.20	2.25	(4)	1.00
a	Carmine double impression		650.00				
1042	8¢ Statue of Liberty, redrawn	03/22/58	.20	.20	.90	(4)	1.00
	Perf. 11 x 10.5						
1042A	8¢ Gen. John J. Pershing	11/17/61	.20	.20	.90	(4)	1.00
	Perf. 10.5 x 11						
1043	9¢ The Alamo	06/14/56	.30	.20	1.30	(4)	1.50
1044	10¢ Independence Hall	07/04/56	.30	.20	1.30	(4)	1.00
d	Tagged	07/06/66	2.00	1.00	35.00	(4)	15.00
	Perf. 11						
1044A	11¢ Statue of Liberty	06/15/61	.30	.20	1.25	(4)	1.00
c	Tagged	01/11/67	2.00	1.60	35.00	(4)	22.50

1030

1031

1031A

1032

1033

1034

1035

1036

1037

1038

1039

1040

1041

1042

1042A

1043

1044

1044A

1045

1046

1047

1048

1049

1050

1051

1052

1053

	Issues of 1955-68		Un	U	PB/LP	#	FDC
	Perf. 11 x 10.5						
1045	12¢ Benjamin Harrison	06/06/59	.35	.20	1.50	(4)	1.00
a	Tagged	1968	.35	.20	4.00	(4)	25.00
1046	15¢ John Jay	12/12/58	.60	.20	3.00	(4)	1.00
a	Tagged	07/06/66	1.10	.35	12.50	(4)	20.00
	Perf. 10.5 x 11						
1047	20¢ Monticello	04/13/56	.40	.20	1.75	(4)	1.25
	Perf. 11 x 10.5						
1048	25¢ Paul Revere	04/18/58	1.10	.20	4.75	(4)	1.25
1049	30¢ Robert E. Lee	09/21/55	.70	.20	3.50	(4)	
a	Wet printing	09/21/55	1.10	.20	5.00	(4)	2.00
1050	40¢ John Marshall	04/58	1.50	.20	7.50	(4)	
a	Wet printing	09/24/55	2.25	.25	12.50	(4)	2.00
1051	50¢ Susan B. Anthony	04/58	1.50	.20	6.75	(4)	
a	Wet printing	08/25/55	1.75	.20	10.00	(4)	6.00
1052	$1 Patrick Henry	10/58	4.50	.20	19.00	(4)	
a	Wet printing	10/07/55	5.25	.20	22.50	(4)	10.00
	Perf. 11						
1053	$5 Alexander Hamilton	03/19/56	70.00	6.75	300.00	(4)	65.00
	Issues of 1954-80, Coil Stamps, Perf. 10 Vertically						
1054	1¢ dark green Washington (1031)	08/57	.20	.20	1.00	(2)	
b	Imperf., pair		2,500.00	—			
c	Wet printing	10/08/54	.35	.20	1.75	(2)	1.00
	Coil Stamp, Perf. 10 Horizontally						
1054A	1¼¢ turquoise Palace of the Governors (1031A)	06/17/60	.20	.20	2.25	(2)	1.00
	Coil Stamps, Perf. 10 Vertically						
1055	2¢ rose carmine Jefferson (1033)	05/57	.20	.20	.75	(2)	
a	Tagged	05/06/68	.20	.20	.75	(2)	11.00
b	Imperf., pair (Bureau precanceled)			550.00			
c	As "a," imperf., pair		575.00				
d	Wet printing	10/22/54	.40	.20	3.50	(2)	1.00
1056	2½¢ gray blue Bunker Hill (1034)	09/09/59	.25	.25	3.50	(2)	2.00
1057	3¢ deep violet Statue of Liberty (1035)	10/56	.20	.20	.55	(2)	
a	Imperf., pair		1,750.00	—	2,750.00	(2)	
b	Tagged	06/26/67	1.00	.50	25.00	(2)	
c	Wet printing	07/20/54	.30	.20	2.00	(2)	1.00
1058	4¢ red violet Lincoln (1036)	07/31/58	.20	.20	2.00	(2)	1.00
a	Imperf., pair		120.00	120.00	200.00	(2)	
b	Wet printing (Bureau precanceled)		27.50	.50	375.00	(2)	
	Coil Stamp, Perf. 10 Horizontally						
1059	4½¢ blue green The Hermitage (1037)	05/01/59	1.50	1.20	14.00	(2)	1.75
	Coil Stamp, Perf. 10 Vertically						
1059A	25¢ green Revere (1048)	02/25/65	.50	.30	2.00	(2)	1.25
b	Tagged	04/03/73	.65	.20	3.00	(2)	14.00
	Dull finish gum	1980	.65		3.00	(2)	
c	Imperf., pair		55.00		100.00	(2)	

	Issues of 1954		Un	U	PB	#	FDC	Q(M)
	Perf. 11 x 10.5							
1060	3¢ Nebraska Territory	05/07/54	.20	.20	.30	(4)	1.00	116
1061	3¢ Kansas Territory	05/31/54	.20	.20	.30	(4)	1.00	114
	Perf. 10.5 x 11							
1062	3¢ George Eastman	07/12/54	.20	.20	.30	(4)	1.00	128
	Perf. 11 x 10.5							
1063	3¢ Lewis and Clark Expedition	07/28/54	.20	.20	.35	(4)	1.00	116
	Issues of 1955, Perf. 10.5 x 11							
1064	3¢ Pennsylvania Academy of the Fine Arts	01/15/55	.20	.20	.35	(4)	1.00	116
	Perf. 11 x 10.5							
1065	3¢ Land-Grant Colleges	02/12/55	.20	.20	.30	4)	1.00	120
1066	8¢ Rotary International	02/23/55	.20	.20	.95	(4)	3.00	54
1067	3¢ Armed Forces Reserve	05/21/55	.20	.20	.30	(4)	1.00	176
	Perf. 10.5 x 11							
1068	3¢ New Hampshire	06/21/55	.20	.20	.40	(4)	1.00	126
	Perf. 11 x 10.5							
1069	3¢ Soo Locks	06/28/55	.20	.20	.30	(4)	1.00	122
1070	3¢ Atoms for Peace	07/28/55	.20	.20	.35	(4)	1.00	134
1071	3¢ Fort Ticonderoga	09/18/55	.20	.20	.30	(4)	1.00	119
	Perf. 10.5 x 11							
1072	3¢ Andrew W. Mellon	12/20/55	.20	.20	.35	(4)	1.00	112

Greetings From Nebraska

For centuries, people on the Great Plains have searched the horizon for Chimney Rock. This familiar landmark, standing 325 feet tall from base to tip, rises near the North Platte River in western Nebraska. It was a beacon of sorts for Native Americans, early explorers, and fur traders, and it became the most famous landmark on the Oregon Trail for 19th-century pioneers. Today, motorists on Nebraska Highway 92 can't miss it as they approach Chimney Rock National Historic Site.

Much has changed since Nebraska became a United States territory in 1854. After the Homestead Act of 1862 promised free land to settlers, farmers came in droves. They would transform what many called the "Great American Desert" into a breadbasket for the nation and the world. More than 90 percent of the land is now made up of farms and cattle ranches, and much of the industry in the state is associated with agriculture. ■

1060

1061

1062

1063

1064

1065

1066

1067

1068

1069

1070

1071

1072

1956

1073

1074

1075

1076

1077

1078

1079

1080

1081

1082

1083

1084

1085

	Issues of 1956		Un	U	PB	#	FDC	Q(M)
1073	3¢ Benjamin Franklin	01/17/56	.20	.20	.35	(4)	1.00	129
	Perf. 11 x 10.5							
1074	3¢ Booker T. Washington	04/05/56	.20	.20	.30	(4)	1.25	121
	Fifth International Philatelic Exhibition Issues Souvenir Sheet, Imperf.							
1075	Statue of Liberty Sheet of 2 stamps							
	(1035, 1041)	04/28/56	2.00	2.00			5.00	3
a	3¢ (1035), single stamp from sheet		.80	.80				
b	8¢ (1041), single stamp from sheet		1.00	1.00				
	Perf. 11 x 10.5							
1076	3¢ New York Coliseum and							
	Columbus Monument	04/30/56	.20	.20	.30	(4)	1.00	120
	Wildlife Conservation Issue							
1077	3¢ Wild Turkey	05/05/56	.20	.20	.35	(4)	1.50	123
1078	3¢ Pronghorn Antelope	06/22/56	.20	.20	.35	(4)	1.50	123
1079	3¢ King Salmon	11/09/56	.20	.20	.35	(4)	1.50	109
	Perf. 10.5 x 11							
1080	3¢ Pure Food and Drug Laws	06/27/56	.20	.20	.30	(4)	1.00	113
	Perf. 11 x 10.5							
1081	3¢ Wheatland	08/05/56	.20	.20	.30	(4)	1.00	125
	Perf. 10.5 x 11							
1082	3¢ Labor Day	09/03/56	.20	.20	.30	(4)	1.00	118
	Perf. 11 x 10.5							
1083	3¢ Nassau Hall	09/22/56	.20	.20	.30	(4)	1.00	122
	Perf. 10.5 x 11							
1084	3¢ Devils Tower	09/24/56	.20	.20	.30	(4)	1.00	118
	Pair with full horizontal gutter between		—					
	Perf. 11 x 10.5							
1085	3¢ Children's Stamp	12/15/56	.20	.20	.30	(4)	1.00	101

Devils Tower National Monument

Resembling a gigantic tree stump rooted in the plains of northeastern Wyoming, Devils Tower has long been the stuff of legend. One Native American tale says children escaped a bear by scrambling atop a stump that lifted them into the sky; later—depending on which ending storytellers choose to use—the children climbed back down with ropes of wildflowers or rose into the heavens and became stars.

Scientists explain this geological curiosity another way. They say the nearly vertical, 865-foot-tall walls of Devils Tower began forming 60 million years ago, when hot magma rose through sedimentary rock layers or entered the neck of an ancient volcano. The magma cooled beneath the surface, contracted, and fractured into columns described by some tale-tellers as scratches made by bear claws. Over time, the Belle Fourche River wore away surface rocks and exposed the volcanic mass.

A U.S. Army colonel gave the formation its official name in the 19th century, and on September 24, 1906, President Theodore Roosevelt made Devils Tower the first national monument. ■

1957-1958

	Issues of 1957		Un	U	PB	#	FDC	Q(M)
1086	3¢ Alexander Hamilton	01/11/57	.20	.20	.30	(4)	1.00	115
	Perf. 10.5 x 11							
1087	3¢ Polio	01/15/57	.20	.20	.30	(4)	1.50	187
	Perf. 11 x 10.5							
1088	3¢ Coast and Geodetic Survey	02/11/57	.20	.20	.30	(4)	1.00	115
1089	3¢ American Institute of Architects	02/23/57	.20	.20	.30	(4)	1.25	107
	Perf. 10.5 x 11							
1090	3¢ Steel Industry	05/22/57	.20	.20	.30	(4)	1.00	112
	Perf. 11 x 10.5							
1091	3¢ International Naval Review-Jamestown Festival	06/10/57	.20	.20	.30	(4)	1.00	118
1092	3¢ Oklahoma Statehood	06/14/57	.20	.20	.35	(4)	1.00	102
1093	3¢ School Teachers	07/01/57	.20	.20	.35	(4)	2.00	102
	Perf. 11							
1094	4¢ Flag	07/04/57	.20	.20	.35	(4)	1.00	84
	Perf. 10.5 x 11							
1095	3¢ Shipbuilding	08/15/57	.20	.20	.30	(4)	1.00	126
	Champion of Liberty Issue, Perf. 11							
1096	8¢ Bust of Ramon Magsaysay on Medal	08/31/57	.20	.20	.85	(4)	1.00	39
	Plate block of 4, ultramarine # omitted		—					
	Perf. 10.5 x 11							
1097	3¢ Marquis de Lafayette	09/06/57	.20	.20	.30	(4)	1.00	123
	Perf. 11							
1098	3¢ Wildlife Conservation	11/22/57	.20	.20	.35	(4)	1.00	174
	Perf. 10.5 x 11							
1099	3¢ Religious Freedom	12/27/57	.20	.20	.30	(4)	1.00	114
	Issues of 1958							
1100	3¢ Gardening-Horticulture	03/15/58	.20	.20	.30	(4)	1.00	123
1101-03	Not assigned							
	Perf. 11 x 10.5							
1104	3¢ Brussels Universal and International Exhibition	04/17/58	.20	.20	.30	(4)	1.00	114
1105	3¢ James Monroe	04/28/58	.20	.20	.30	(4)	1.00	120
1106	3¢ Minnesota Statehood	05/11/58	.20	.20	.30	(4)	1.00	121
	Perf. 11							
1107	3¢ International Geophysical Year	05/31/58	.20	.20	.35	(4)	1.00	126
	Perf. 11 x 10.5							
1108	3¢ Gunston Hall	06/12/58	.20	.20	.30	(4)	1.00	108

Greetings From Oklahoma

Wichita, Apache, and Quapaw populated the land when Spanish explorers, in 1541, rode into what is now Oklahoma. As more Europeans and their descendants spread across the Americas, other tribes arrived, including the Cherokee, Chickasaw, Choctaw, Creek, and Seminole, having walked the long "Trail of Tears." These "Five Civilized Tribes" quickly established schools, businesses, and farms on lands then known as Indian Territory.

In the 1880s, the federal government let white settlers move here, and in 1889, a great land run began. Some homesteaders staked claims "sooner" than they should have; hence the "Sooner State" nickname. Statehood finally arrived in 1907, but in the 1930s, many Oklahomans packed up and left after drought and dust storms ravaged their farms. In time, cattle ranching, wheat farming, and the oil industry helped turn the economy around. ■

1086

1087

1088

1089

1091

1090

1092

1093

1094

1095

1096

1097

1098

1099

1100

1104

1105

1106

1107

1108

1109

1110

1111

1112

1113

1114

1115

1116

1117

1118

1119

1120

1121

1122

1123

1124

1125

1126

1127

1128

1129

1130

1131

Issues of 1958		Un	U	PB	#	FDC	Q(M)
Perf. 10.5 x 11							
1109 3¢ Mackinac Bridge	06/25/58	.20	.20	.30	(4)	1.00	107
Champion of Liberty Issue							
1110 4¢ Bust of Simon Bolivar on							
Medal	07/24/58	.20	.20	.35	(4)	1.00	115
Perf. 11							
1111 8¢ Bust of Bolivar on Medal	07/24/58	.20	.20	1.25	(4)	1.00	39
Plate block of four, ocher # only		—					
Perf. 11 x 10.5							
1112 4¢ Atlantic Cable	08/15/58	.20	.20	.35	(4)	1.00	114
Issues of 1958-1959, Abraham Lincoln Sesquicentennial Issue, Perf. 10.5 x 11							
1113 1¢ Portrait by George Healy	02/12/59	.20	.20	.20	(4)	1.25	120
1114 3¢ Sculptured Head by							
Gutzon Borglum	02/27/59	.20	.20	.40	(4)	1.25	91
Perf. 11 x 10.5							
1115 4¢ Lincoln and Stephen Douglas							
Debating, by Joseph							
Boggs Beale	08/27/58	.20	.20	.40	(4)	1.25	114
1116 4¢ Statue in Lincoln Memorial							
by Daniel Chester French	05/30/59	.20	.20	.40	(4)	1.25	126
Champion of Liberty Issue, Perf. 10.5 x 11							
1117 4¢ Bust of Lajos Kossuth on							
Medal	09/19/58	.20	.20	.30	(4)	1.00	120
Perf. 11							
1118 8¢ Bust of Kossuth on Medal	09/19/58	.20	.20	1.10	(4)	1.00	44
Perf. 10.5 x 11							
1119 4¢ Freedom of the Press	09/22/58	.20	.20	.30	(4)	1.00	118
Perf. 11 x 10.5							
1120 4¢ Overland Mail	10/10/58	.20	.20	.30	(4)	1.00	125
Perf. 10.5 x 11							
1121 4¢ Noah Webster	10/16/58	.20	.20	.35	(4)	1.00	114
Perf. 11							
1122 4¢ Forest Conservation	10/27/58	.20	.20	.30	(4)	1.00	156
Perf. 11 x 10.5							
1123 4¢ Fort Duquesne	11/25/58	.20	.20	.35	(4)	1.00	124
Issues of 1959							
1124 4¢ Oregon Statehood	02/14/59	.20	.20	.30	(4)	1.00	120
Champion of Liberty Issue, Perf. 10.5 x 11							
1125 4¢ Bust of José de San Martin							
on Medal	02/25/59	.20	.20	.30	(4)	1.00	133
a Horizontal pair, imperf. between		1,500.00					
Perf. 11							
1126 8¢ Bust of San Martin							
on Medal	02/25/59	.20	.20	.90	(4)	1.25	45
Perf. 10.5 x 11							
1127 4¢ NATO	04/01/59	.20	.20	.30	(4)	1.25	122
Perf. 11 x 10.5							
1128 4¢ Arctic Explorations	04/06/59	.20	.20	.40	(4)	1.00	131
1129 8¢ World Peace Through							
World Trade	04/20/59	.20	.20	.85	(4)	1.00	47
1130 4¢ Silver Centennial	06/08/59	.20	.20	.30	(4)	1.00	123
Perf. 11							
1131 4¢ St. Lawrence Seaway	06/26/59	.20	.20	.35	(4)	1.25	126
Pair with full horizontal gutter between		—					

	Issues of 1959		Un	U	PB	#	FDC	Q(M)
1132	4¢ 49-Star Flag	07/04/59	.20	.20	.40	(4)	1.00	209
1133	4¢ Soil Conservation	08/26/59	.20	.20	.35	(4)	1.00	121
	Perf. 10.5 x 11							
1134	4¢ Petroleum Industry	08/27/59	.20	.20	.40	(4)	1.25	116
	Perf. 11 x 10.5							
1135	4¢ Dental Health	09/14/59	.20	.20	.40	(4)	3.00	118
	Champion of Liberty Issue, Perf. 10.5 x 11							
1136	4¢ Bust of Ernst Reuter on							
	Medal	09/29/59	.20	.20	.30	(4)	1.00	112
	Perf. 11							
1137	8¢ Bust of Reuter on Medal	09/29/59	.20	.20	.90	(4)	1.00	43
	Perf. 10.5 x 11							
1138	4¢ Dr. Ephraim McDowell	12/03/59	.20	.20	.40	(4)	1.50	115
a	Vertical pair, imperf. between		450.00					
b	Vertical pair, imperf. horizontally		350.00					
	Issues of 1960-61, American Credo Issue, Perf. 11							
1139	4¢ Quotation from Washington's							
	Farewell Address	01/20/60	.20	.20	.40	(4)	1.25	126
1140	4¢ Benjamin Franklin Quotation	03/31/60	.20	.20	.40	(4)	1.25	125
1141	4¢ Thomas Jefferson Quotation	05/18/60	.20	.20	.45	(4)	1.25	115
1142	4¢ Francis Scott Key Quotation	09/14/60	.20	.20	.45	(4)	1.25	122
1143	4¢ Abraham Lincoln Quotation	11/19/60	.20	.20	.50	(4)	1.25	121
	Pair with full horizontal gutter between		—					
1144	4¢ Patrick Henry Quotation	01/11/61	.20	.20	.50	(4)	1.25	113
	Issues of 1960							
1145	4¢ Boy Scouts	02/08/60	.20	.20	.40	(4)	4.00	139
	Olympic Winter Games Issue, Perf. 10.5 x 11							
1146	4¢ Olympic Rings and							
	Snowflake	02/18/60	.20	.20	.40	(4)	1.00	124
	Champion of Liberty Issue							
1147	4¢ Bust of Thomas Masaryk on							
	Medal	03/07/60	.20	.20	.30	(4)	1.00	114
a	Vertical pair, imperf. between		3,250.00					
	Perf. 11							
1148	8¢ Bust of Masaryk on Medal	03/07/60	.20	.20	.95	(4)	1.00	44
a	Horizontal pair, imperf. between		—					
	Perf. 11 x 10.5							
1149	4¢ World Refugee Year	04/07/60	.20	.20	.30	(4)	1.00	113
	Perf. 11							
1150	4¢ Water Conservation	04/18/60	.20	.20	.35	(4)	1.00	122
	Perf. 10.5 x 11							
1151	4¢ SEATO	05/31/60	.20	.20	.35	(4)	1.00	115
a	Vertical pair, imperf. between		160.00					

1132

1133

1134

1135

1136

1137

1138

1139

1140

1141

1142

1143

1144

1145

1146

1147

1148

1149

1150

1151

1152

1153

1154

1155

1156

1157

1158

1159

1160

1161

1162

1163

1164

1165

1166

1167

1168

1169

1170

1171

1172

1173

Issues of 1960		Un	U	PB	#	FDC	Q(M)
Perf. 11 x 10.5							
1152 4¢ American Woman	06/02/60	.20	.20	.30	(4)	1.25	111
Perf. 11							
1153 4¢ 50-Star Flag	07/04/60	.20	.20	.30	(4)	1.00	153
Perf. 11 x 10.5							
1154 4¢ Pony Express	07/19/60	.20	.20	.40	(4)	1.50	120
Perf. 10.5 x 11							
1155 4¢ Employ the Handicapped	08/28/60	.20	.20	.30	(4)	1.00	118
1156 4¢ 5th World Forestry Congress	08/29/60	.20	.20	.30	(4)	1.00	118
Perf. 11							
1157 4¢ Mexican Independence	09/16/60	.20	.20	.30	(4)	1.00	112
1158 4¢ U.S.-Japan Treaty	09/28/60	.20	.20	.30	(4)	1.00	125
Champion of Liberty Issue, Paderewski, Perf. 10.5 x 11							
1159 4¢ Bust of Ignacy Jan Paderewski on Medal	10/08/60	.20	.20	.30	(4)	1.00	120
Perf. 11							
1160 8¢ Bust of Paderewski on Medal	10/08/60	.20	.20	.90	(4)	1.00	43
Perf. 10.5 x 11							
1161 4¢ Sen. Robert A. Taft Memorial	10/10/60	.20	.20	.35	(4)	1.00	107
Perf. 11 x 10.5							
1162 4¢ Wheels of Freedom	10/15/60	.20	.20	.30	(4)	1.00	110
Perf. 11							
1163 4¢ Boys' Clubs of America	10/18/60	.20	.20	.30	(4)	1.00	124
1164 4¢ First Automated Post Office	10/20/60	.20	.20	.30	(4)	1.00	124
Champion of Liberty Issue, Perf. 10.5 x 11							
1165 4¢ Bust of Gustaf Mannerheim on Medal	10/26/60	.20	.20	.30	(4)	1.00	125
Perf. 11							
1166 8¢ Bust of Mannerheim on Medal	10/26/60	.20	.20	.80	(4)	1.00	42
1167 4¢ Camp Fire Girls	11/01/60	.20	.20	.40	(4)	1.00	116
Champion of Liberty Issue, Perf. 10.5 x 11							
1168 4¢ Bust of Giusseppe Garibaldi on Medal	11/02/60	.20	.20	.30	(4)	1.00	126
Perf. 11							
1169 8¢ Bust of Garibaldi on Medal	11/02/60	.20	.20	.85	(4)	1.00	43
Perf. 10.5 x 11							
1170 4¢ Sen. Walter F. George Memorial	11/05/60	.20	.20	.35	(4)	1.00	124
1171 4¢ Andrew Carnegie	11/25/60	.20	.20	.35	(4)	1.00	120
1172 4¢ John Foster Dulles Memorial	12/06/60	.20	.20	.35	(4)	1.00	117
Perf. 11 x 10.5							
1173 4¢ Echo I-Communications for Peace	12/15/60	.20	.20	.65	(4)	2.50	124

Issues of 1961		Un	U	PB	#	FDC	Q(M)
Champion of Liberty Issue, Perf. 10.5 x 11							
1174	4¢ Bust of Gandhi on Medal	01/26/61	.20	.20	.30	(4)	1.00	113
Perf. 11							
1175	8¢ Bust of Gandhi on Medal	01/26/61	.20	.20	1.00	(4)	1.00	42
1176	4¢ Range Conservation	02/02/61	.20	.20	.40	(4)	1.00	111
Perf. 10.5 x 11							
1177	4¢ Horace Greeley	02/03/61	.20	.20	.30	(4)	1.00	99
Issues of 1961-65, Civil War Centennial Issue, Perf. 11 x 10.5							
1178	4¢ Fort Sumter	04/12/61	.20	.20	.85	(4)	3.00	101
1179	4¢ Shiloh	04/07/62	.20	.20	.75	(4)	3.00	125
Perf. 11							
1180	5¢ Gettysburg	07/01/63	.20	.20	.85	(4)	3.00	80
1181	5¢ The Wilderness	05/05/64	.20	.20	.60	(4)	3.00	125
1182	5¢ Appomattox	04/09/65	.25	.25	1.20	(4)	3.00	113
a	Horizontal pair, imperf. vertically	4,500.00						
1183	4¢ Kansas Statehood	05/10/61	.20	.20	.35	(4)	1.00	106
Perf. 11 x 10.5							
1184	4¢ Sen. George W. Norris	07/11/61	.20	.20	.35	(4)	1.00	111
1185	4¢ Naval Aviation	08/20/61	.20	.20	.35	(4)	1.00	117
	Pair with full vertical gutter between	150.00						
Perf. 10.5 x 11							
1186	4¢ Workmen's Compensation	09/04/61	.20	.20	.35	(4)	1.00	121
	With plate # inverted				.60	(4)		
Perf. 11							
1187	4¢ Frederic Remington	10/04/61	.20	.20	.40	(4)	1.25	112
Perf. 10.5 x 11							
1188	4¢ Republic of China	10/10/61	.20	.20	.45	(4)	4.00	111
1189	4¢ Naismith-Basketball	11/06/61	.20	.20	.50	(4)	6.00	109
Perf. 11							
1190	4¢ Nursing	12/28/61	.20	.20	.50	(4)	8.50	145
Issues of 1962							
1191	4¢ New Mexico Statehood	01/06/62	.20	.20	.30	(4)	1.50	113
1192	4¢ Arizona Statehood	02/14/62	.20	.20	.30	(4)	1.50	122
1193	4¢ Project Mercury	02/20/62	.20	.20	.35	(4)	3.00	289
1194	4¢ Malaria Eradication	03/30/62	.20	.20	.30	(4)	1.00	120
Perf. 10.5 x 11							
1195	4¢ Charles Evans Hughes	04/11/62	.20	.20	.30	(4)	1.00	125

Greetings From Kansas

Kansas, the geographic heart of the nation, sits at the center of the contiguous United States. It gets its name from the Kansa, a Native American group who lived here when millions of bison still roamed the Great Plains.

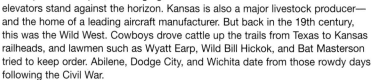

Today, wheat grows in abundance on the wide-open landscapes, and huge grain elevators stand against the horizon. Kansas is also a major livestock producer— and the home of a leading aircraft manufacturer. But back in the 19th century, this was the Wild West. Cowboys drove cattle up the trails from Texas to Kansas railheads, and lawmen such as Wyatt Earp, Wild Bill Hickok, and Bat Masterson tried to keep order. Abilene, Dodge City, and Wichita date from those rowdy days following the Civil War.

Nicknamed the "Sunflower State," Kansas boasts several notable natural features, including 4,039-foot Mount Sunflower, the highest point in the state. Monument Rocks, near Scott City, are 10,000-year-old legacies of Ice Age glaciers. And the Flint Hills region, in east-central Kansas, contains the most extensive unplowed tract of prairie in the country. ∎

1174 **1175** **1176** **1177**

1178 **1179** **1180**

1181 **1182** **1183**

1184 **1185** **1186** **1187**

1188 **1189** **1190** **1191**

1192 **1193** **1194** **1195**

1196

1197

1198

1199

1200

1201

1202

1203

1204

1205

1206

1207

1208

1209

1213

1230

1231

1232

1233

1234

Issues of 1962		Un	U	PB/LP	#	FDC	Q(M)
Perf. 11							
1196 4¢ Seattle World's Fair	04/25/62	.20	.20	.30	(4)	1.00	147
1197 4¢ Louisiana Statehood	04/30/62	.20	.20	.30	(4)	1.00	119
Perf. 11 x 10.5							
1198 4¢ Homestead Act	05/20/62	.20	.20	.30	(4)	1.00	123
1199 4¢ Girl Scout Jubilee	07/24/62	.20	.20	.30	(4)	4.50	127
Pair with full vertical gutter between		250.00					
1200 4¢ Sen. Brien McMahon	07/28/62	.20	.20	.35	(4)	1.00	131
1201 4¢ Apprenticeship	08/31/62	.20	.20	.30	(4)	1.00	120
Perf. 11							
1202 4¢ Sam Rayburn	09/16/62	.20	.20	.30	(4)	1.00	121
1203 4¢ Dag Hammarskjold	10/23/62	.20	.20	.30	(4)	1.00	121
1204 4¢ black, brown and yellow (yellow inverted), Dag Hammarskjold, special printing	11/16/62	.20	.20	1.10	(4)	5.00	40
Christmas Issue							
1205 4¢ Wreath and Candles	11/01/62	.20	.20	.30	(4)	1.10	862
1206 4¢ Higher Education	11/14/62	.20	.20	.35	(4)	1.50	120
1207 4¢ Winslow Homer	12/15/62	.20	.20	.45	(4)	1.50	118
a Horizontal pair, imperf. between		6,750.00					
Issues of 1963-66							
1208 5¢ Flag over White House	01/09/63	.20	.20	.40	(4)	1.00	
Pair with full horizontal gutter between		—					
a Tagged	08/25/66	.20	.20	2.00	(4)	25.00	
b Horizontal pair, imperf. between		1,500.00					
Issues of 1962-66, Perf. 11 x 10.5							
1209 1¢ Andrew Jackson	03/22/63	.20	.20	.20	(4)	1.00	
Pair with full vertical gutter between		—					
a Tagged	07/06/66	.20	.20	.40	(4)	25.00	
1210-12 Not assigned							
1213 5¢ George Washington	11/23/62	.20	.20	.40	(4)	1.00	
a Booklet pane of 5 + label		3.00	1.75			4.00	
b Tagged	10/28/63	.50	.20	4.50	(4)	25.00	
c As "a," tagged	10/28/63	2.00	1.50			100.00	
1214-24 Not assigned							
Coil Stamps, Perf. 10 Vertically							
1225 1¢ green Jackson (1209)	05/31/63	.20	.20	2.25	(2)	1.00	
a Tagged	07/06/66	.20	.20	.75	(2)	15.00	
1226-28 Not assigned							
1229 5¢ dark blue gray Washington (1213)	11/23/62	1.25	.20	4.00	(2)	1.00	
a Tagged	10/28/63	1.40	.20	6.50	(2)	25.00	
b Imperf., pair		450.00		1,250.00	(2)		
Issues of 1963, Perf. 11							
1230 5¢ Carolina Charter	04/06/63	.20	.20	.40	(4)	1.00	130
1231 5¢ Food for Peace-Freedom from Hunger	06/04/63	.20	.20	.40	(4)	1.00	136
1232 5¢ West Virginia Statehood	06/20/63	.20	.20	.40	(4)	1.00	138
1233 5¢ Emancipation Proclamation	08/16/63	.20	.20	.40	(4)	1.50	132
1234 5¢ Alliance for Progress	08/17/63	.20	.20	.40	(4)	1.00	136

	Issues of 1963		Un	U	PB	#	FDC	Q(M)
1235	5¢ Cordell Hull	10/05/63	.20	.20	.45	(4)	1.00	131
	Perf. 11 x 10.5							
1236	5¢ Eleanor Roosevelt	10/11/63	.20	.20	.45	(4)	1.00	133
	Perf. 11							
1237	5¢ The Sciences	10/14/63	.20	.20	.40	(4)	1.25	130
1238	5¢ City Mail Delivery	10/26/63	.20	.20	.50	(4)	1.25	128
a	Tagged omitted		7.50					
1239	5¢ International Red Cross	10/29/63	.20	.20	.40	(4)	1.50	119
	Christmas Issue							
1240	5¢ National Christmas							
	Tree and White House	11/01/63	.20	.20	.40	(4)	1.25	1,300
	Pair with full horizontal gutter between		—					
a	Tagged	11/02/63	.65	.50	5.00	(4)	60.00	
1241	5¢ John James Audubon,							
	(See also #C71)	12/07/63	.20	.20	.45	(4)	1.25	175
	Issues of 1964, Perf. 10.5 x 11							
1242	5¢ Sam Houston	01/10/64	.20	.20	.45	(4)	1.00	126
	Perf. 11							
1243	5¢ Charles M. Russell	03/19/64	.20	.20	.40	(4)	1.25	128
	Perf. 11 x 10.5							
1244	5¢ New York World's Fair	04/22/64	.20	.20	.45	(4)	1.50	146
	Perf. 11							
1245	5¢ John Muir	04/29/64	.20	.20	.45	(4)	1.00	120
	Perf. 11 x 10.5							
1246	5¢ President John Fitzgerald							
	Kennedy Memorial	05/29/64	.20	.20	.60	(4)	2.25	512
	Perf. 10.5 x 11							
1247	5¢ New Jersey Settlement	06/15/64	.20	.20	.45	(4)	1.00	124
	Perf. 11							
1248	5¢ Nevada Statehood	07/22/64	.20	.20	.40	(4)	1.00	123
1249	5¢ Register and Vote	08/01/64	.20	.20	.45	(4)	1.00	453
	Perf. 10.5 x 11							
1250	5¢ Shakespeare	08/14/64	.20	.20	.40	(4)	1.50	123
1251	5¢ Doctors William and							
	Charles Mayo	09/11/64	.20	.20	.60	(4)	3.50	123
	Perf. 11							
1252	5¢ American Music	10/15/64	.20	.20	.40	(4)	1.50	127
a	Blue omitted		1,000.00					
1253	5¢ Homemakers	10/26/64	.20	.20	.40	(4)	1.00	121

Greetings From New Jersey

Delaware Indians, Dutch and Swedish settlers, and finally English colonists called New Jersey home in the 1600s. Over the ensuing centuries, New Jersey would become the most densely populated state in the nation, with almost all of its population now residing in urban areas, especially near New York City, in the northeast, and Philadelphia, in the west. And yet, New Jersey calls itself the "Garden State"—for good reason: Farms and forestlands still make up 60 percent of the land. "Jersey Fresh" fruits and vegetables grow in abundance in the central and southwestern sections of the state; a 1.1-million-acre forested area known as the Pine Barrens stretches across the southeast.

Except for its northernmost region, New Jersey is surrounded by water. On the west, the Delaware River is where George Washington made a historic winter crossing during the Revolutionary War. On the east, the Atlantic shore offers miles and miles of beaches and several popular resort areas. ■

1236

1237

1235

1239

1240

1238

1241

1243

1244

1242

1245

1246

1247

1248

1249

1252

1253

1250

1251

1254 1255

1259

1258

1260

1256 1257 1257b

1261

1262 1263 1264

1265 1266

1267 1268

1270

1272

1269

1271

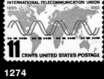

1274

1276

1273

1275

	Issues of 1964		Un	U	PB	#	FDC	Q(M)
	Christmas Issue, Perf. 11							
1254	5¢ Holly	11/09/64	.25	.20			1.00	352
a	Tagged		.60	.50				
1255	5¢ Mistletoe	11/09/64	.25	.20			1.00	352
a	Tagged		.60	.50				
1256	5¢ Poinsettia	11/09/64	.25	.20			1.00	352
a	Tagged		.60	.50				
1257	5¢ Sprig of Conifer	11/09/64	.25	.20			1.00	352
a	Tagged		.60	.50				
b	Block of four, #1254-57		1.00	1.00	1.10	(4)	3.00	
c	As "b," tagged		2.50	2.25			57.50	
	Perf. 10.5 x 11							
1258	5¢ Verrazano-Narrows Bridge	11/21/64	.20	.20	.45	(4)	1.00	120
	Perf. 11							
1259	5¢ Fine Arts	12/02/64	.20	.20	.40	(4)	1.00	126
	Perf. 10.5 x 11							
1260	5¢ Amateur Radio	12/15/64	.20	.20	.50	(4)	1.75	122
	Issues of 1965, Perf. 11							
1261	5¢ Battle of New Orleans	01/08/65	.20	.20	.40	(4)	1.00	116
1262	5¢ Physical Fitness-Sokol	02/15/65	.20	.20	.50	(4)	1.25	115
1263	5¢ Crusade Against Cancer	04/01/65	.20	.20	.40	(4)	2.00	120
	Perf. 10.5 x 11							
1264	5¢ Winston Churchill Memorial	05/13/65	.20	.20	.40	(4)	1.75	125
	Perf. 11							
1265	5¢ Magna Carta	06/15/65	.20	.20	.40	(4)	1.00	120
	Corner block of four, black PB# omitted		—					
1266	5¢ International Cooperation							
	Year-United Nations	06/26/65	.20	.20	.40	(4)	1.00	115
1267	5¢ Salvation Army	07/02/65	.20	.20	.40	(4)	1.75	116
	Perf. 10.5 x 11							
1268	5¢ Dante Alighieri	07/17/65	.20	.20	.40	(4)	1.00	115
1269	5¢ President Herbert Hoover							
	Memorial	08/10/65	.20	.20	.45	(4)	1.00	115
	Perf. 11							
1270	5¢ Robert Fulton	08/19/65	.20	.20	.40	(4)	1.00	116
1271	5¢ Florida Settlement	08/28/65	.20	.20	.45	(4)	1.00	117
a	Yellow omitted		350.00					
1272	5¢ Traffic Safety	09/03/65	.20	.20	.45	(4)	1.00	114
1273	5¢ John Singleton Copley	09/17/65	.20	.20	.50	(4)	1.00	115
1274	11¢ International							
	Telecommunication Union		.35	.20	2.75	(4)	1.10	27
1275	5¢ Adlai E. Stevenson Memorial	10/23/65	.20	.20	.40	(4)	1.00	128
	Christmas Issue							
1276	5¢ Angel with Trumpet							
	(1840 Weather Vane)	11/02/65	.20	.20	.40	(4)	1.00	1,140
a	Tagged	11/15/65	.75	.25	5.50	(4)	42.50	
1277	Not assigned							

Issues of 1965-1978		Un	U	PB	#	FDC
Prominent Americans Issue, Perf. 11 x 10.5, 10.5 x 11 (See also #1299, 1303-05C)						
1278 1¢ Thomas Jefferson	01/12/68	.20	.20	.20	(4)	1.00
a Booklet pane of 8	01/12/68	1.00	.50			2.50
b Bklt. pane of 4 + 2 labels	05/10/71	.80	.30			12.50
c Untagged (Bureau precanceled)			.20			
d Tagging omitted		3.50	—			
1279 1¼¢ Albert Gallatin	01/30/67	.20	.20	6.00	(4)	1.00
1280 2¢ Frank Lloyd Wright	06/08/66	.20	.20	.25	(4)	1.00
Pair with full vertical gutter between		—				
a Booklet pane of 5 + label	01/08/68	1.25	.60			3.50
b Untagged (Bureau precanceled)			.20			
c Booklet pane of 6	05/07/71	1.00	.50			15.00
d Tagging omitted		3.50	—			
1281 3¢ Francis Parkman	09/16/67	.20	.20	.25	(4)	1.00
a Untagged (Bureau precanceled)			.20			
b Tagging omitted		4.50	—			
1282 4¢ Abraham Lincoln	11/19/65	.20	.20	.40	(4)	1.25
a Tagged	12/01/65	.20	.20	.55	(4)	25.00
Pair with full horizontal gutter between		—				
1283 5¢ George Washington	02/22/66	.20	.20	.50	(4)	1.00
a Tagged	02/23/66	.20	.20	.60	(4)	75.00
1283B 5¢ redrawn	11/17/67	.20	.20	.50	(4)	1.00
Dull finish gum		.20		1.40	(4)	
d Untagged (Bureau precanceled)			.20			
1284 6¢ Franklin D. Roosevelt	01/29/66	.20	.20	.60	(4)	1.00
a Tagged	12/29/66	.20	.20	.80	(4)	30.00
b Booklet pane of 8	12/28/67	1.50	.75			2.75
c Booklet pane of 5 + label	01/09/68	1.50	.75			100.00
1285 8¢ Albert Einstein	03/14/66	.20	.20	.85	(4)	2.00
a Tagged	07/06/66	.20	.20	.85	(4)	25.00
1286 10¢ Andrew Jackson	03/15/67	.20	.20	1.00	(4)	1.00
b Untagged (Bureau precanceled)			.20			
1286A 12¢ Henry Ford	07/30/68	.25	.20	1.00	(4)	1.50
c Untagged (Bureau precanceled)			.25			
1287 13¢ John F. Kennedy	05/29/67	.30	.20	1.50	(4)	2.00
a Untagged (Bureau precanceled)			.35			
b Tagging omitted		12.50	—			
1288 15¢ Oliver Wendell Holmes	03/08/68	.30	.20	1.25	(4)	1.00
a Untagged (Bureau precanceled)			.30			
d Type II		.55	.20	8.00	(4)	
f As "d", tagging omitted		5.00	—			
Booklet Stamp, Perf. 10						
1288B 15¢ magenta, tagged						
(1288), Single from booklet		.35	.20			1.00
c Booklet pane of 8	06/14/78	2.80	1.75			3.00
e As "c," vert. imperf. between		—				
Perf. 11 x 10.5, 10.5 x 11						
1289 20¢ George C. Marshall	10/24/67	.40	.20	1.75	(4)	1.10
a Tagged	04/03/73	.40	.20	1.75	(4)	25.00
1290 25¢ Frederick Douglass	02/14/67	.55	.20	2.25	(4)	1.75
a Tagged	04/03/73	.45	.20	2.00	(4)	27.50
b Magenta		25.00	—	150.00		
1291 30¢ John Dewey	10/21/68	.65	.20	2.90	(4)	1.75
a Tagged	04/03/73	.50	.20	2.25	(4)	27.50
1292 40¢ Thomas Paine	01/29/68	.80	.20	3.25	(4)	1.75
a Tagged	04/03/73	.65	.20	2.75	(4)	27.50
1293 50¢ Lucy Stone	08/13/68	1.00	.20	4.25	(4)	2.50
a Tagged	04/03/73	.80	.20	3.50	(4)	30.00

1278   1279

1281

1280   1282

1283   1283B

1284   1285   1286   1286A

1287   1288   1289   1290

1291

1292   1293

1294

1295

1305

1306

1307

1308

1309

1310

1311

1312

1313

1314

	Issues of 1966-1973		Un	U	PB/LP	#	FDC	Q(M)
	Perf. 11 x 10.5, 10.5 x 11							
1294	$1 Eugene O'Neill	10/16/67	2.25	.20	10.00	(4)	6.00	
a	Tagged	04/03/73	1.65	.20	6.75	(4)	35.00	
1295	$5 John Bassett Moore	12/03/66	9.50	2.25	40.00	(4)	40.00	
a	Tagged	04/03/73	8.00	2.00	32.50	(4)	80.00	
1296	Not assigned							
	Issues of 1967-1975, Coil Stamps, Perf. 10 Horizontally							
1297	3¢ violet Parkman (1281)	11/04/75	.20	.20	.45	(2)	1.00	
a	Imperf., pair		30.00		55.00	(2)		
b	Untagged (Bureau precanceled)			.20				
c	As "b," imperf., pair			6.00	25.00	(2)		
1298	6¢ Franklin D. Roosevelt (1284)	12/28/67	.20	.20	1.25	(2)	1.00	
a	Imperf., pair			2,250.00				
b	Tagging omitted			3.00				
	Issues of 1966-1981, Coil Stamps, Perf. 10 Vertically (See also #1279-96)							
1299	1¢ green Jefferson (1278)	01/12/68	.20	.20	.25	(2)	1.00	
a	Untagged (Bureau precanceled)			.20				
b	Imperf., pair		30.00	—	60.00	(2)		
1300-02	Not assigned							
1303	4¢ blk. Lincoln (1282)	05/28/66	.20	.20	.75	(2)	1.00	
a	Untagged (Bureau precanceled)			.20				
b	Imperf., pair		900.00		2,000.00	(2)		
1304	5¢ bl. Washington (1283)	09/08/66	.20	.20	.40	(2)	1.00	
a	Untagged (Bureau precanceled)			.20				
b	Imperf., pair		175.00		400.00	(2)		
e	As "a," imperf. pair			400.00	900.00	(2)		
1304C	5¢ redrawn (1283B)	1981	.20	.20	1.25	(2)		
d	Imperf., pair		800.00					
1305	6¢ gray brown Roosevelt	02/28/68	.20	.20	.55	(2)	1.00	
a	Imperf., pair		75.00		130.00	(2)		
b	Untagged (Bureau precanceled)			.20				
1305E	15¢ magenta, Type I (1288)	06/14/78	.25	.20	1.25	(2)	1.00	
	Dull finish gum		.60		2.00	(2)		
f	Untagged (Bureau precanceled)			.30				
g	Imperf., pair		30.00		75.00	(2)		
h	Pair, imperf. between		200.00		550.00	(2)		
i	Type II, dull gum		.35	.20	2.50	(2)		
j	Type II, dull gum, imperf., pair		90.00		300.00	(2)		
1305C	$1 dull purple Eugene O'Neill (1294)	01/12/73	2.00	.40	5.75	(2)	4.00	
d	Imperf., pair		2,250.00		4,000.00	(2)		
	Issues of 1966, Perf. 11							
1306	5¢ Migratory Bird Treaty	03/16/66	.20	.20	.40	(4)	2.00	117
1307	5¢ Humane Treatment of Animals	04/09/66	.20	.20	.40	(4)	1.25	117
1308	5¢ Indiana Statehood	04/16/66	.20	.20	.40	(4)	1.00	124
1309	5¢ American Circus	05/02/66	.20	.20	.50	(4)	2.00	131
	Sixth International Philatelic Exhibition Issue							
1310	5¢ Stamped Cover	05/21/66	.20	.20	.40	(4)	1.00	122
	Souvenir Sheet, Imperf.							
1311	5¢ Stamped Cover (1310) and Washington, D.C., Scene	05/23/66	.20	.20			1.10	15
	Perf. 11							
1312	5¢ The Bill of Rights	07/01/66	.20	.20	.45	(4)	1.00	114
	Perf. 10.5 x 11							
1313	5¢ Poland's Millennium	07/30/66	.20	.20	.45	(4)	1.00	128
	Perf. 11							
1314	5¢ National Park Service	08/25/66	.20	.20	.45	(4)	1.00	120
a	Tagged	08/26/66	.30	.25	2.00	(4)	30.00	

1966-1967

	Issues of 1966		Un	U	PB	#	FDC	Q(M)
1315	5¢ Marine Corps Reserve	08/29/66	.20	.20	.45	(4)	1.50	125
a	Tagged		.30	.20	2.00	(4)	30.00	
b	Black and bister omitted		16,000.00					
1316	5¢ General Federation of							
	Women's Clubs	09/12/66	.20	.20	.45	(4)	1.00	115
a	Tagged	09/13/66	.30	.20	2.00	(4)	30.00	
	American Folklore Issue							
1317	5¢ Johnny Appleseed and							
	Apple	09/24/66	.20	.20	.45	(4)	1.50	124
a	Tagged	09/26/66	.30	.20	2.00	(4)	30.00	
1318	5¢ Beautification of America	10/05/66	.20	.20	.45	(4)	1.00	128
a	Tagged		.30	.20	2.00	(4)	30.00	
1319	5¢ Great River Road	10/21/66	.20	.20	.45	(4)	1.00	128
a	Tagged	10/22/66	.30	.20	2.00	(4)	30.00	
1320	5¢ Savings Bond-Servicemen	10/26/66	.20	.20	.45	(4)	1.00	116
a	Tagged	10/27/66	.30	.20	1.75	(4)	30.00	
b	Red, dark bl. and blk. omitted		5,000.00					
c	Dark blue omitted		12,000.00					
	Christmas Issue							
1321	5¢ Madonna and Child,							
	by Hans Memling	11/01/66	.20	.20	.40	(4)	1.00	1,174
a	Tagged	11/02/66	.30	.20	1.50	(4)	30.00	
1322	5¢ Mary Cassatt	11/17/66	.20	.20	.60	(4)	1.00	114
a	Tagged		.30	.25	1.75	(4)	30.00	
	Issues of 1967							
1323	5¢ National Grange	04/17/67	.20	.20	.40	(4)	1.00	121
a	Tagging omitted		6.00	—				
1324	5¢ Canada Centenary	05/25/67	.20	.20	.40	(4)	1.00	132
a	Tagging omitted		6.00	—				
1325	5¢ Erie Canal	07/04/67	.20	.20	.40	(4)	1.00	119
a	Tagging omitted		11.00	—				
1326	5¢ Search for Peace	07/05/67	.20	.20	.40	(4)	1.00	122
a	Tagging omitted		5.00	—				
1327	5¢ Henry David Thoreau	07/12/67	.20	.20	.45	(4)	1.00	112
1328	5¢ Nebraska Statehood	07/29/67	.20	.20	.40	(4)	1.00	117
a	Tagging omitted		7.50	—				
1329	5¢ Voice of America	08/01/67	.20	.20	.40	(4)	1.00	112
a	Tagging omitted		15.00	—				
	American Folklore Issue							
1330	5¢ Davy Crockett	08/17/67	.20	.20	.45	(4)	1.10	114
a	Vertical pair, imperf. between		6,000.00					
b	Green omitted		—					
c	Black and green omitted							
e	Tagging omitted		6.00	—				
	Accomplishments in Space Issue							
1331	5¢ Space-Walking Astronaut	09/29/67	.50	.20			3.00	60
b	Tagging omitted		15.00	—				
1332	5¢ Gemini 4 Capsule							
	and Earth	09/29/67	.50	.20	2.75	(4)	3.00	60
a	Tagging omitted		15.00	—				
b	Pair, #1331-1332		1.10	1.25				
c	As "b", Tagging omitted		40.00	—				
1333	5¢ Urban Planning	10/02/67	.20	.20	.50	(4)	1.00	111
1334	5¢ Finland Independence	10/06/67	.20	.20	.50	(4)	1.00	111

1315

1316

1317

1318

1319

1320

1321

1322

1323

1324

1325

1326

1327

1328

1329

1330

1331   1332   1332b

1333

1334

1335

1336

1345

1346

1347

1348

1349

1350

1351

1352

1353

1354

1354a

1337

1338

1339

1340

1341

1342

1343

1344

	Issues of 1967		Un	U	PB	#	FDC	Q(M)
	Perf. 12							
1335	5¢ Thomas Eakins	11/02/67	.20	.20	.50	(4)	1.00	114
	Christmas Issue, Perf. 11							
1336	5¢ Madonna and Child,							
	by Hans Memling	11/06/67	.20	.20	.40	(4)	1.00	1,209
a	Tagging omitted		5.00	—				
1337	5¢ Mississippi Statehood	12/11/67	.20	.20	.50	(4)	1.00	113
a	Tagging omitted		6.00	—				
	Issues of 1968-1971							
1338	6¢ Flag over White House							
	(design 19 x 22mm)	01/24/68	.20	.20	.45	(4)	1.00	
k	Vertical pair, imperf. between		550.00					
m	Tagging omitted		4.00	—				
	Coil Stamp, Perf. 10 Vertically							
1338A	6¢ dk bl, rd and grn (1338)	05/30/69	.20	.20	.30	(2)	1.00	
b	Imperf., pair		500.00					
q	Tagging omitted		8.50	—				
	Perf. 11 x 10.5							
1338D	6¢ dark blue, red and green							
	(1338, design 18.25 x 21mm)	08/07/70	.20	.20	2.60	(20)	1.00	
e	Horizontal pair, imperf. between		175.00					
n	Tagging omitted		5.00	—				
1338F	8¢ dk bl, rd and slt grn (1338)	05/10/71	.20	.20	3.00	(20)	1.00	
i	Imperf., vertical pair		45.00					
j	Horizontal pair, imperf. between		55.00					
o	Tagging omitted		6.50	—				
	Coil Stamp, Perf. 10 Vertically							
1338G	8¢ dk bl, rd and slt grn (1338)	05/10/71	.20	.20	.40	(2)	1.00	
h	Imperf., pair		55.00					
r	Tagging omitted		6.00	—				
	Issues of 1968, Perf. 11							
1339	6¢ Illinois Statehood	02/12/68	.20	.20	.50	(4)	1.00	141
1340	6¢ HemisFair '68	03/30/68	.20	.20	.50	(4)	1.00	144
a	White omitted		1,300.00					
1341	$1 Airlift	04/04/68	2.25	1.25	10.00	(4)	7.00	
	Pair with full horizontal gutter between			—				
1342	6¢ Support Our Youth-Elks	05/01/68	.20	.20	.50	(4)	1.00	147
a	Tagging omitted		7.50	—				
1343	6¢ Law and Order	05/17/68	.20	.20	.50	(4)	2.00	130
1344	6¢ Register and Vote	06/27/68	.20	.20	.50	(4)	1.00	159
	Historic Flag Issue							
1345	6¢ Ft. Moultrie Flag, 1776	07/04/68	.40	.25			3.00	23
1346	6¢ Ft. McHenry (U.S.)							
	Flag, 1795-1818	07/04/68	.30	.25			3.00	23
1347	6¢ Washington's							
	Cruisers Flag, 1775	07/04/68	.25	.25			3.00	23
1348	6¢ Bennington Flag, 1777	07/04/68	.25	.25			3.00	23
1349	6¢ Rhode Island Flag, 1775	07/04/68	.25	.25			3.00	23
1350	6¢ First Stars and							
	Stripes, 1777	07/04/68	.25	.25			3.00	23
1351	6¢ Bunker Hill Flag, 1775	07/04/68	.25	.25			3.00	23
1352	6¢ Grand Union Flag, 1776	07/04/68	.25	.25			3.00	23
1353	6¢ Philadelphia Light Horse							
	Flag, 1775	07/04/68	.25	.25			3.00	23
1354	6¢ First Navy Jack, 1775	07/04/68	.25	.25			3.00	23
a	Strip of 10, #1345-54		2.75	2.75	6.50	(20)	17.50	

	Issues of 1968		Un	U	PB	#	FDC	Q(M)
	Perf. 12							
1355	6¢ Walt Disney	09/11/68	.20	.20	1.25	(4)	15.00	153
a	Ocher omitted		600.00	—				
b	Vertical pair, imperf. horizontally		700.00					
c	Imperf., pair		675.00					
d	Black omitted		2,000.00					
e	Horizontal pair, imperf. between		4,750.00					
f	Blue omitted		2,250.00					
g	Tagging omitted		15.00	—				
	Perf. 11							
1356	6¢ Father Marquette	09/20/68	.20	.20	.50	(4)	1.00	133
	American Folklore Issue							
1357	6¢ Pennsylvania Rifle, Powder Horn, Tomahawk, Pipe and Knife	09/26/68	.20	.20	.50	(4)	1.10	130
1358	6¢ Arkansas River Navigation	10/01/68	.20	.20	.50	(4)	1.00	132
1359	6¢ Leif Erikson	10/09/68	.20	.20	.50	(4)	1.00	129
	Perf. 11 x 10.5							
1360	6¢ Cherokee Strip	10/15/68	.20	.20	.60	(4)	1.00	125
a	Tagging omitted		6.00	—				
	Perf. 11							
1361	6¢ John Trumbull	10/18/68	.20	.20	.60	(4)	1.10	128
1362	6¢ Waterfowl Conservation	10/24/68	.20	.20	.65	(4)	1.50	142
a	Vertical pair, imperf. between		550.00					
b	Red and dark blue omitted		900.00					
	Christmas Issue							
1363	6¢ Angel Gabriel, from "The Annunciation," by Jan Van Eyck	11/01/68	.20	.20	2.00	(10)	1.00	1,411
a	Untagged	11/02/68	.20	.20	2.00	(10)	10.00	
b	Imperf., pair (tagged)		225.00					
c	Light yellow omitted		65.00					
d	Imperf., pair (untagged)		300.00					
1364	6¢ American Indian	11/04/68	.20	.20	.70	(4)	1.50	125
	Issues of 1969, Beautification of America Issue							
1365	6¢ Capitol, Azaleas and Tulips	01/16/69	.30	.20			1.00	48
1366	6¢ Washington Monument, Potomac River and Daffodils	01/16/69	.30	.20			1.00	48
1367	6¢ Poppies and Lupines along Highway	01/16/69	.30	.20			1.00	48
1368	6¢ Blooming Crabapple Trees Lining Avenue	01/16/69	.30	.20			1.00	48
a	Block of 4, #1365-68		1.25	1.75	1.40	(4)	4.00	
1369	6¢ American Legion	03/15/69	.20	.20	.45	(4)	1.00	149
	American Folklore Issue							
1370	6¢ "July Fourth" by Grandma Moses	05/01/69	.20	.20	.50	(4)	1.10	139
a	Horizontal pair, imperf. between		225.00					
b	Black and Prussian blue omitted		850.00					
c	Tagging omitted		7.50	—				
1371	6¢ Apollo 8	05/05/69	.20	.20	.65	(4)	2.75	187
1372	6¢ W.C. Handy	05/17/69	.20	.20	.45	(4)	1.25	126
a	Tagging omitted		7.50	—				
1373	6¢ California Settlement	07/16/69	.20	.20	.45	(4)	1.00	144
1374	6¢ John Wesley Powell	08/01/69	.20	.20	.45	(4)	1.00	136
a	Tagging omitted		7.50	—				
1375	6¢ Alabama Statehood	08/02/69	.20	.20	.45	(4)	1.00	151

1355

1356

1357

1358

1359

1360

1361

1362

1365 1366

1367 1368 1368a

1363

1364

1369

1370

1371

1372

1373

1374

1375

159

378   **1379**   **1379a**

1380

381   **1382**

1383

384

384 Precancel

1385

1386

387   **1388**

1391

Issues of 1969			Un	U	PB	#	FDC	Q(M)
Botanical Congress Issue, Perf. 11								
1376	6¢ Douglas Fir (Northwest)	08/23/69	.40	.20			1.50	40
1377	6¢ Lady's Slipper (Northeast)	08/23/69	.40	.20			1.50	40
1378	6¢ Ocotillo (Southwest)	08/23/69	.40	.20			1.50	40
1379	6¢ Franklinia (Southeast)	08/23/69	.40	.20			1.50	40
a	Block of 4, #1376-79		1.75	2.25	1.90	(4)	5.00	
	Perf. 10.5 x 11							
1380	6¢ Dartmouth College Case	09/22/69	.20	.20	.50	(4)	1.00	130
	Perf. 11							
1381	6¢ Professional Baseball	09/24/69	.65	.20	3.00	(4)	12.00	131
a	Black omitted		1,100.00					
1382	6¢ Intercollegiate Football	09/26/69	.20	.20	.85	(4)	6.50	139
1383	6¢ Dwight D. Eisenhower	10/14/69	.20	.20	.50	(4)	1.00	151
	Christmas Issue, Perf. 11 x 10.5							
1384	6¢ Winter Sunday in Norway, Maine	11/03/69	.20	.20	1.40	(10)	1.00	1,710
	Precanceled		.50	.20				
b	Imperf., pair		1,000.00					
c	Light green omitted		22.50					
d	Light green and yellow omitted		1,000.00	—				
e	Yellow omitted		2,250.00					
f	Tagging omitted		5.00	—				
	Precanceled versions issued on an experimental basis in four cities whose names appear on the stamps: Atlanta, GA; Baltimore, MD; Memphis, TN; and New Haven, CT.							
	Perf. 11							
1385	6¢ Hope for the Crippled	11/20/69	.20	.20	.50	(4)	1.00	128
1386	6¢ William M. Harnett	12/03/69	.20	.20	.55	(4)	1.00	146
	Issues of 1970, Natural History Issue							
1387	6¢ American Bald Eagle	05/06/70	.20	.20			1.50	50
1388	6¢ African Elephant Herd	05/06/70	.20	.20			1.50	50
1389	6¢ Tlingit Chief in Haida Ceremonial Canoe	05/06/70	.20	.20			1.50	50
1390	6¢ Brontosaurus, Stegosaurus and Allosaurus from Jurassic Period	05/06/70	.20	.20			1.50	50
a	Block of 4, #1387-90		.55	.60	.70	(4)	4.00	
1391	6¢ Maine Statehood	07/09/70	.20	.20	.50	(4)	1.25	172
	Perf. 11 x 10.5							
1392	6¢ Wildlife Conservation	07/20/70	.20	.20	.50	(4)	1.00	142

Greetings From Maine

Dirigo—I lead—is the state motto of Maine, easternmost state in the Union and first to greet the dawn of each new day. Along the rocky, tree-lined coast, lighthouses stand sentinel for countless pleasure boats and commercial craft, and hundreds of bays and inlets serve as gateways to historic forts, bustling ports, and quaint seaside villages. Offshore, rich harvests of shellfish, especially lobster, have made Maine famous for seafood.

Inland lie classic New England towns and rolling farmland. Here are potato fields, apple orchards, and blueberry bushes. There are also forested uplands inhabited by deer and moose, and scenic lakes paddled by loons. With more than half a million acres set aside in state and national parks, Maine holds a wealth of natural and recreational resources enjoyed by residents and tourists alike. Hiking, fishing, climbing, canoeing, and cross-country skiing are popular activities, as is leaf-gazing when forests blaze with color every autumn. ■

	Issues of 1970-1974		Un	U	PB/LP	#	FDC	Q(M)
1393	6¢ Dwight D. Eisenhower	08/06/70	.20	.20	.50	(4)	1.00	
a	Booklet pane of 8		1.50	.65			3.00	
b	Booklet pane of 5 + label		1.50	.65			1.50	
c	Untagged (Bureau precanceled)			.20				
	Perf. 10.5 x 11							
1393D	7¢ Benjamin Franklin	10/20/72	.20	.20	.60	(4)	1.00	
e	Untagged (Bureau precanceled)			.20				
f	Tagging omitted		4.00	—				
	Perf. 11							
1394	8¢ Eisenhower	05/10/71	.20	.20	.60	(4)	1.00	
	Pair with full vertical gutter between		—					
a	Tagging omitted		4.00	—				
	Perf. 11 x 10.5							
1395	8¢ deep claret Eisenhower							
	1394), Single from booklet		.20	.20			1.00	
a	Booklet pane of 8	05/10/71	1.80	1.25			2.50	
b	Booklet pane of 6	05/10/71	1.25	.90			2.50	
c	Booklet pane of 4 + 2							
	labels	01/28/72	1.65	.80			2.25	
d	Booklet pane of 7 +							
	label	01/28/72	1.90	1.00			2.25	
1396	8¢ U.S. Postal Service	07/01/71	.20	.20	2.00	(12)	1.00	
1397	14¢ Fiorello H. LaGuardia	04/24/72	.25	.20	1.15	(4)	1.00	
a	Untagged (Bureau precanceled)			.25				
1398	16¢ Ernie Pyle	05/07/71	.30	.20	1.25	(4)	1.50	
a	Untagged (Bureau precanceled)			.35				
1399	18¢ Dr. Elizabeth Blackwell	01/23/74	.35	.20	1.50	(4)	1.25	
1400	21¢ Amadeo P. Giannini	06/27/73	.40	.20	1.65	(4)	1.50	
	Coil Stamps, Perf. 10 Vertically							
1401	6¢ dark blue gray Eisenhower							
	(1393)	08/06/70	.20	.20	.50	(2)	1.00	
a	Untagged (Bureau precanceled)			.20				
b	Imperf., pair		2,000.00		—	(2)		
1402	8¢ deep claret Eisenhower							
	(1394)	05/10/71	.20	.20	.55	(2)	1.00	
a	Imperf., pair		45.00		70.00	(2)		
b	Untagged (Bureau precanceled)			.20				
c	Pair, imperf. between		6,250.00					
1403-04	Not assigned							
	Issues of 1970, Perf. 11							
1405	6¢ Edgar Lee Masters	08/22/70	.20	.20	.50	(4)	1.00	138
a	Tagging omitted		30.00	—				
1406	6¢ Woman Suffrage	08/26/70	.20	.20	.50	(4)	1.00	135
1407	6¢ South Carolina Settlement	09/12/70	.20	.20	.50	(4)	1.00	136
1408	6¢ Stone Mountain Memorial	09/19/70	.20	.20	.50	(4)	1.00	133
1409	6¢ Ft. Snelling	10/17/70	.20	.20	.50	(4)	1.00	135
	Anti-Pollution Issue, Perf. 11 x 10.5							
1410	6¢ Save Our Soil							
	Globe and Wheat Field	10/28/70	.25	.20			1.25	40
1411	6¢ Save Our Cities							
	Globe and City Playground	10/28/70	.25	.20			1.25	40
1412	6¢ Save Our Water							
	Globe and Bluegill Fish	10/28/70	.25	.20			1.25	40
1413	6¢ Save Our Air							
	Globe and Seagull	10/28/70	.25	.20			1.25	40
a	Block of 4, #1410-13		1.10	1.25	2.25	(10)	4.00	

1393 **1393D** **1394** **1396**

1397 **1398** **1399** **1400**

1405 **1406** **1407**

1408 **1409**

1410 **1411**

1412 **1413** **1413a**

1414

1414a

1415　　　　1416

1417　　　　1418　　　1418b

1419

1420

1421　　　1422　　1422a

1423

1424

1425

1426

1427　　　　　　1428

1429　　　　1430　　　　1430a

	Issues of 1970		Un	U	PB	#	FDC	Q(M)
	Christmas Issue, Perf. 10.5 x 11							
1414	6¢ Nativity, by Lorenzo Lotto	11/05/70	.20	.20	1.10	(8)	1.25	639*
a	Precanceled		.20	.20	1.90	(8)	7.50	358
b	Black omitted		550.00					
c	As "a," blue omitted		1,500.00					
d	Type II		.20	.20	2.75	(8)		
e	Type II, precanceled		.25	.20	4.00	(8)		

#1414a-18a were furnished to 68 cities. Unused prices are for copies with gum and used prices are for copies with or without gum but with an additional cancellation.
*Includes #1414a.

			Un	U	PB	#	FDC	Q(M)
	Perf. 11 x 10.5							
1415	6¢ Tin and Cast-iron							
	Locomotive	11/05/70	.30	.20			1.40	122
a	Precanceled		.75	.20				110
b	Black omitted		2,500.00					
1416	6¢ Toy Horse on Wheels	11/05/70	.30	.20			1.40	122
a	Precanceled		.75	.20				110
b	Black omitted		2,500.00					
c	Imperf., pair			4,000.00				
1417	6¢ Mechanical Tricycle	11/05/70	.30	.20			1.40	122
a	Precanceled		.75	.20				110
b	Black omitted		2,500.00					
1418	6¢ Doll Carriage	11/05/70	.30	.20			1.40	122
a	Precanceled		.75	.20				110
b	Block of 4, #1415-18		1.25	1.50	3.00	(8)	5.00	
c	Block of 4, #1415a-18a		3.25	3.25	6.25	(8)	15.00	
d	Black omitted		2,500.00					
	Perf. 11							
1419	6¢ United Nations	11/20/70	.20	.20	.50	(4)	1.25	128
	Pair with full horizontal gutter between		—					
1420	6¢ Landing of the Pilgrims	11/21/70	.20	.20	.50	(4)	1.00	130
a	Orange and yellow omitted		900.00					
	Disabled American Veterans and Servicemen Issue							
1421	6¢ Disabled American							
	Veterans Emblem	11/24/70	.20	.20			2.00	67
1422	6¢ U.S. Servicemen	11/24/70	.20	.20			2.00	67
a	Attached pair, #1421-22		.30	.30	1.00	(4)	3.00	
	Issues of 1971							
1423	6¢ American Wool Industry	01/19/71	.20	.20	.50	(4)	1.00	136
a	Tagging omitted		11.00	—				
1424	6¢ Gen. Douglas MacArthur	01/26/71	.20	.20	.50	(4)	1.25	135
1425	6¢ Blood Donor	03/12/71	.20	.20	.50	(4)	1.10	131
a	Tagging omitted		11.00	—				
	Perf. 11 x 10.5							
1426	8¢ Missouri Statehood	05/08/71	.20	.20	2.00	(12)	1.00	161
	Wildlife Conservation Issue, Perf. 11							
1427	8¢ Trout	06/12/71	.20	.20			1.25	44
1428	8¢ Alligator	06/12/71	.20	.20			1.25	44
1429	8¢ Polar Bear and Cubs	06/12/71	.20	.20			1.25	44
1430	8¢ California Condor	06/12/71	.20	.20			1.25	44
a	Block of 4, #1427-30		.80	.90	.90	(4)	3.00	
b	As "a," light green and dark green omitted from #1427-28		4,500.00					
c	As "a," red omitted from #1427, 1429-30		9,000.00					

1971

	Issues of 1971		Un	U	PB	#	FDC	Q(M)
1431	8¢ Antarctic Treaty	06/23/71	.20	.20	.65	(4)	1.00	139
a	Tagging omitted		9.00					
	American Revolution Bicentennial Issue							
1432	8¢ Bicentennial Commission							
	Emblem	07/04/71	.20	.20	.85	(4)	1.00	138
a	Gray and black omitted		650.00					
b	Gray omitted		1,150.00					
1433	8¢ John Sloan	08/02/71	.20	.20	.70	(4)	1.00	152
a	Tagging omitted		—					
	Space Achievement Decade Issue							
1434	8¢ Earth, Sun and Landing							
	Craft on Moon	08/02/71	.20	.20				88
a	Tagging omitted		30.00				2.00	
1435	8¢ Lunar Rover and							
	Astronauts	08/02/71	.20	.20	.65	(4)		88
a	Tagging omitted		30.00					
b	Pair #1434-1435		.40	.45				
c	As "b", tagging omitted		—					
d	As "b", blue & red omitted		1,500.00					
1436	8¢ Emily Dickinson	08/28/71	.20	.20	.65	(4)	1.00	143
a	Black and olive omitted		800.00					
b	Pale rose omitted		7,500.00					
1437	8¢ San Juan, Puerto Rico	09/12/71	.20	.20	.65	(4)	1.00	149
a	Tagging omitted		9.00					
	Perf. 10.5 x 11							
1438	8¢ Prevent Drug Abuse	10/04/71	.20	.20	1.00	(6)	1.00	139
1439	8¢ CARE	10/27/71	.20	.20	1.25	(8)	1.00	131
a	Black omitted		4,750.00					
b	Tagging omitted		5.00					
	Historic Preservation Issue, Perf. 11							
1440	8¢ Decatur House,							
	Washington, D.C.	10/29/71	.20	.20			1.25	43
1441	8¢ Whaling Ship *Charles W. Morgan*,							
	Mystic, Connecticut	10/29/71	.20	.20			1.25	43
1442	8¢ Cable Car, San Francisco	10/29/71	.20	.20			1.25	43
1443	8¢ San Xavier del Bac Mission,							
	Tucson, Arizona	10/29/71	.20	.20			1.25	43
a	Block of 4, #1440-43		.75	.85	.90	(4)	3.00	
b	As "a," black brown omitted		2,250.00					
c	As "a," ocher omitted		—					
d	As "a," tagging omitted		65.00					
	Christmas Issue, Perf. 10.5 x 11							
1444	8¢ Adoration of the Shepherds,							
	by Giorgione	11/10/71	.20	.20	1.80	(12)	1.10	1,074
a	Gold omitted		550.00					
1445	8¢ Partridge in a Pear Tree	11/10/71	.20	.20	1.80	(12)	1.10	980

1431

1432

1433

1434   **1435**   **1435b**

1436

1437

1438

1439

1440   **1441**

1442   **1443**   **1443a**

1444

1445

1446

1447

1448   1449

1450   1451   1451a

1452

1454

1453

1455

1456   1457

1458   1459   1459a

1460

1461

1462

1463

	Issues of 1972		Un	U	PB	#	FDC	Q(M)
1446	8¢ Sidney Lanier	02/03/72	.20	.20	.65	(4)	1.00	137
a	Tagging omitted		15.00					
	Perf. 10.5 x 11							
1447	8¢ Peace Corps	02/11/72	.20	.20	1.00	(6)	1.00	150
a	Tagging omitted		5.00					
	National Parks Centennial Issue (See also #C84)							
1448	2¢ Ship at Sea	04/05/72	.20	.20				43
1449	2¢ Cape Hatteras Lighthouse	04/05/72	.20	.20				43
1450	2¢ Laughing Gulls on							
	Driftwood	04/05/72	.20	.20				43
1451	2¢ Laughing Gulls and Dune	04/05/72	.20	.20				43
a	Block of 4, #1448-51		.25	.25	.50	(4)	1.50	
b	As "a," black omitted		2,750.00					
1452	6¢ Performance at Wolf Trap Farm,							
	Shouse Pavilion	06/26/72	.20	.20	.55	(4)	1.00	104
a	Tagging omitted		11.00					
1453	8¢ Old Faithful, Yellowstone	03/01/72	.20	.20	.70	(4)	1.00	164
a	Tagging omitted		15.00					
1454	15¢ View of Mount McKinley							
	in Alaska	07/28/72	.30	.20	1.30	(4)	1.00	54

Note: Beginning with this National Parks Centennial issue, the USPS began to offer stamp collectors first day cancellations affixed to 8" x 101/2" souvenir pages. The pages are similar to the stamp announcements that have appeared on Post Office bulletin boards beginning with Scott #1132. See "Souvenir Pages" listed in the back of this book (see Table of Contents)

1455	8¢ Family Planning	03/18/72	.20	.20	.65	(4)	1.00	153
a	Yellow omitted		1,250.00					
b	Dark brown and olive omitted		—					
c	Dark brown omitted		9,500.00					
	American Bicentennial Issue, Perf. 11 x 10.5							
1456	8¢ Glass Blower	07/04/72	.20	.20			1.00	50
1457	8¢ Silversmith	07/04/72	.20	.20			1.00	50
1458	8¢ Wigmaker	07/04/72	.20	.20			1.00	50
1459	8¢ Hatter	07/04/72	.20	.20			1.00	50
a	Block of 4, #1456-59		.65	.75	.80	(4)	2.50	
	Olympic Games Issue, (See also #C85)							
1460	6¢ Bicycling and Olympic							
	Rings	08/17/72	.20	.20	1.25	(10)	1.00	67
	Cylinder flaw (broken red ring)		10.00					
1461	8¢ Bobsledding and							
	Olympic Rings	08/17/72	.20	.20	1.60	(10)	1.00	180
a	Tagging omitted		7.50					
1462	15¢ Running and Olympic							
	Rings	08/17/72	.30	.20	3.00	(10)	1.00	46
1463	8¢ Parent Teachers							
	Association	09/15/72	.20	.20	.65	(4)	1.00	180

	Issues of 1972		Un	U	PB	#	FDC	Q(M)
	Wildlife Conservation Issue, Perf. 11							
1464	8¢ Fur Seals	09/20/72	.20	.20			1.50	50
1465	8¢ Cardinal	09/20/72	.20	.20			1.50	50
1466	8¢ Brown Pelican	09/20/72	.20	.20			1.50	50
1467	8¢ Bighorn Sheep	09/20/72	.20	.20			1.50	50
a	Block of 4, #1464-67		.65	.75	.75	(4)	3.00	
b	As "a," brown omitted		4,000.00					
c	As "a," green and blue omitted		4,750.00					
d	As "a," red & brown omitted		4,000.00					
	Note: With this Wildlife Conservation issue the USPS introduced the "American Commemorative Series" Stamp Panels. Each panel contains a block of four or more mint stamps with text and background illustrations. See pages 493-497 for a complete listing.							
1468	8¢ Mail Order Business	09/27/72	.20	.20	1.75	(12)	1.00	185
	Perf. 10.5 x 11							
1469	8¢ Osteopathic Medicine	10/09/72	.20	.20	1.00	(6)	1.00	162
	American Folklore Issue, Perf. 11							
1470	8¢ Tom Sawyer Whitewashing							
	a Fence, by Norman Rockwell	10/13/72	.20	.20	.65	(4)	1.50	163
a	Horizontal pair, imperf. between		4,500.00					
b	Red and black omitted		1,900.00					
c	Yellow and tan omitted		2,400.00					
	Christmas Issue, Perf. 10.5 x 11							
1471	8¢ Angels from "Mary, Queen of Heaven"							
	by the Master of the							
	St. Lucy Legend	11/09/72	.20	.20	1.75	(12)	1.00	1,003
a	Pink omitted		150.00					
b	Black omitted		4,000.00					
1472	8¢ Santa Claus	11/09/72	.20	.20	1.75	(12)	1.00	1,017
	Perf. 11							
1473	8¢ Pharmacy	11/10/72	.20	.20	.65	(4)	6.50	166
a	Blue and orange omitted		825.00					
b	Blue omitted		2,250.00					
c	Orange omitted		2,250.00					
1474	8¢ Stamp Collecting	11/17/72	.20	.20	.65	(4)	1.25	167
a	Black omitted		600.00					
	Issues of 1973, Perf. 11 x 10.5							
1475	8¢ Love	01/26/73	.20	.20	1.00	(6)	2.50	320
	American Bicentennial Issue, Perf. 11							
1476	8¢ Printer and Patriots Examining							
	Pamphlet	02/16/73	.20	.20	.65	(4)	1.00	166
1477	8¢ Posting a Broadside	04/13/73	.20	.20	.65	(4)	1.00	163
	Pair with full horizontal gutter between		—					
1478	8¢ Postrider	06/22/73	.20	.20	.65	(4)	1.00	159
1479	8¢ Drummer	09/28/73	.20	.20	.65	(4)	1.00	147
	Boston Tea Party							
1480	8¢ British Merchantman	07/04/73	.20	.20			1.00	49
1481	8¢ British Three-Master	07/04/73	.20	.20			1.00	49
1482	8¢ Boats and Ship's Hull	07/04/73	.20	.20			1.00	49
1483	8¢ Boat and Dock	07/04/73	.20	.20			1.00	49
a	Block of 4, #1480-83		.65	.75	.75	(4)	3.00	
b	As "a," blk. (engraved) omitted		1,500.00					
c	As "a," blk. (lithographed) omitted		1,400.00					

1464

1465

1466

1467

1467a

1468

1469

1470

1471

1472

1473

1474

1475

1476

1477

1478

1479

1480

1481

1482

1483

1483a

1973

1484

1485

1486

1487

1488

1489   **1490**   **1491**   **1492**   **1493**

| Nearly 27 billion U.S. stamps are sold yearly to carry your letters to every corner of the world. | Mail is picked up from nearly a third of a million local collection boxes, as well as your mailbox. | More than 87 billion letters and packages are handled yearly—almost 300 million every delivery day. | The People in your Postal Service handle and deliver more than 500 million packages yearly. | Thousands of machines, buildings, and vehicles must be operated and maintained to keep your mail moving. |
| People Serving You | People Serving You | People Serving You | People Serving You | People Serving You |

1494   **1495**   **1496**   **1497**   **1498**

| The skill of sorting mail manually is still vital to delivery of your mail. | Employees use modern, high-speed equipment to sort and process huge volumes of mail in central locations. | Thirteen billion pounds of mail are handled yearly by postal employees as they speed your letters and packages. | Our customers include 54 million urban and 12 million rural families, plus 9 million businesses. | Employees cover 4 million miles each delivery day to bring mail to your home or business. |
| People Serving You | People Serving You | People Serving You | People Serving You | People Serving You |

	Issues of 1973		Un	U	PB	#	FDC	Q(M)
	American Arts Issue, Perf. 11							
1484	8¢ George Gershwin and Scene							
	from "Porgy and Bess"	02/28/73	.20	.20	1.75	(12)	1.00	139
a	Vertical pair, imperf. horizontally		240.00					
1485	8¢ Robinson Jeffers, Man and Children							
	of Carmel with Burro	08/13/73	.20	.20	1.75	(12)	1.00	128
a	Vertical pair, imperf. horizontally		250.00					
1486	8¢ Henry Ossawa Tanner,							
	Palette and Rainbow	09/10/73	.20	.20	1.75	(12)	1.00	146
1487	8¢ Willa Cather, Pioneer Family							
	and Covered Wagon	09/20/73	.20	.20	1.75	(12)	1.00	140
a	Vertical pair, imperf. horizontally		275.00					
1488	8¢ Nicolaus Copernicus	04/23/73	.20	.20	.65	(4)	1.50	159
a	Orange omitted		1,000.00					
b	Black omitted		900.00					
	Postal Service Employees Issue, Perf. 10.5 x 11							
1489	8¢ Stamp Counter	04/30/73	.20	.20			1.00	49
1490	8¢ Mail Collection	04/30/73	.20	.20			1.00	49
1491	8¢ Letter Facing on Conveyor	04/30/73	.20	.20			1.00	49
1492	8¢ Parcel Post Sorting	04/30/73	.20	.20			1.00	49
1493	8¢ Mail Canceling	04/30/73	.20	.20			1.00	49
1494	8¢ Manual Letter Routing	04/30/73	.20	.20			1.00	49
1495	8¢ Electronic Letter Routing	04/30/73	.20	.20			1.00	49
1496	8¢ Loading Mail on Truck	04/30/73	.20	.20			1.00	49
1497	8¢ Mail Carrier	04/30/73	.20	.20			1.00	49
1498	8¢ Rural Mail Delivery	04/30/73	.20	.20			1.00	49
a	Strip of 10, #1489-98		1.75	1.75	3.25	(20)	5.00	

#1489-98 were the first United States postage stamps to have printing on the back.

(See also 1559-62.)

American Culture: *Atlas*

Rockefeller Center is at the heart of midtown Manhattan in New York City. Named for John D. Rockefeller, Jr., whose enormous drive and personal fortune transformed an urban renewal project of the 1930s into an art-deco commercial complex of world renown, this 21-acre "city within a city" is noted for upscale shops, fine restaurants, first-rate theaters, and spectacular art and architecture.

The tallest structure in the complex is the 70-story GE Building (formerly the RCA Building) at 30 Rockefeller Plaza, built from 1932 to 1940. At its main entrance is W*isdom*, with L*ight* and S*ound*, a stunning 3-piece work by sculptor Lee Lawrie (1877–1963). At its base, in the sunken plaza popular with ice skaters each winter, is another work of art: Paul Manship's *Prometheus*, a gilded statue depicting the Titan who in Greek mythology stole fire from heaven and gave it to humankind. Another Titan—Atlas, whose shoulders held up the heavens—stands in front of the 38-story International Building, also in Rockefeller Center. Installed in January 1937, Lee Lawrie's monumental *Atlas* holds an armillary sphere, an old astronomical instrument whose axis points to the North Star. This striking example of art-deco sculpture was featured in the American Culture stamp series. ■

	Issues of 1973		Un	U	PB	#	FDC	Q(M)
	Perf. 11							
1499	8¢ Harry S. Truman	05/08/73	.20	.20	.65	(4)	1.00	157
	Progress in Electronics Issue, (See also #C86)							
1500	6¢ Marconi's Spark							
	Coil and Gap	07/10/73	.20	.20	.55	(4)	1.00	53
1501	8¢ Transistors and Printed							
	Circuit Board	07/10/73	.20	.20	.70	(4)	1.00	160
a	Black omitted		450.00					
b	Tan and lilac omitted		1,250.00					
1502	15¢ Microphone, Speaker, Vacuum							
	Tube, TV Camera Tube	07/10/73	.30	.20	1.30	(4)	1.00	39
a	Black omitted		1,350.00					
1503	8¢ Lyndon B. Johnson	08/27/73	.20	.20	1.90	(12)	1.00	153
a	Horizontal pair, imperf. vertically		350.00					
	Issues of 1973-74, Rural America Issue							
1504	8¢ Angus and Longhorn Cattle,							
	by F.C. Murphy	10/05/73	.20	.20	.65	(4)	1.00	146
a	Green and red brown omitted		950.00					
b	Vertical pair, imperf. between		—					
1505	10¢ Chautauqua Tent and							
	Buggies	08/06/74	.20	.20	.85	(4)	1.00	151
1506	10¢ Wheat Fields and Train	08/16/74	.20	.20	.85	(4)	1.00	141
a	Black and blue omitted		750.00					
	Issues of 1973, Christmas Issue, Perf. 10.5 x 11							
1507	8¢ Small Cowper Madonna,							
	by Raphael	11/07/73	.20	.20	1.75	(12)	1.00	885
	Pair with full vertical gutter between		—					
1508	8¢ Christmas Tree in							
	Needlepoint	11/07/73	.20	.20	1.75	(12)	1.00	940
	Pair with full horizontal gutter between		—					
a	Vertical pair, imperf. between		300.00					
	Issues of 1973-74, Perf. 11 x 10.5							
1509	10¢ 50-Star and							
	13-Star Flags	12/08/73	.20	.20	4.25	(20)	1.00	
a	Horizontal pair, imperf. between		50.00	—				
b	Blue omitted		175.00					
c	Imperf., pair		950.00					
d	Horizontal pair, imperf. vertically		1,000.00					
e	Tagging omitted		9.00					
1510	10¢ Jefferson Memorial	12/14/73	.20	.20	.85	(4)	1.00	
a	Untagged (Bureau precanceled)			.20				
b	Booklet pane of 5 + label		1.65	.55			2.25	
c	Booklet pane of 8		1.65	.70			2.50	
d	Booklet pane of 6	08/05/74	5.25	1.00			3.00	
e	Vertical pair, imperf. horizontally		525.00					
f	Vertical pair, imperf. between		—					
g	Tagging omitted		5.00					

1499

1500

1501

1502

1503

1504

1505

1506

1507

1508

1509

1510

1974

1511

1518

1525

1526

1527

1528

1529

1530   **1531**   **1532**   **1533**

Letters mingle souls Raphael	Universal Postal Union Hokusai	Letters mingle souls Peto	Universal Postal Union Liotard
Donne 10c US	1874-1974 10c US	Donne 10c US	1874-1974 10c US

Letters mingle souls Terborch	Universal Postal Union Chardin	Letters mingle souls Gainsborough	Universal Postal Union Goya
Donne 10c US	1874-1974 10c US	Donne 10c US	1874-1974 10c US

1537a

1534   **1535**   **1536**   **1537**

	Issues of 1973-74		Un	U	PB/LP	#	FDC	Q(M)
1511	10¢ ZIP Code	01/04/74	.20	.20	1.75	(8)	1.00	
	Pair with full horizontal gutter between		—					
a	Yellow omitted		65.00					
1512-17	Not assigned							
	Coil Stamps, Perf. 10 Vertically							
1518	6.3¢ Liberty Bell	10/01/74	.20	.20	.80	(2)	1.00	
a	Untagged (Bureau precanceled)			.20	.80	(2)		
b	Imperf., pair		210.00		550.00	(2)		
c	As "a," imperf., pair			100.00	250.00	(2)		
1519	10¢ red and blue Flags (1509)	12/08/73	.20	.20			1.00	
a	Imperf., pair		37.50					
1520	10¢ blue Jefferson Memorial							
	(1510)	12/14/73	.25	.20	.75	(2)	1.00	
a	Untagged (Bureau precanceled)			.25				
b	Imperf., pair		40.00		70.00	(2)		
1521-24	Not assigned							
	Issues of 1974, Perf. 11							
1525	10¢ Veterans of Foreign Wars	03/11/74	.20	.20	.85	(4)	1.00	149
	Perf. 10.5 x 11							
1526	10¢ Robert Frost	03/26/74	.20	.20	.85	(4)	1.00	145
	Perf. 11							
1527	10¢ Expo '74 World's Fair	04/18/74	.20	.20	2.50	(12)	1.00	135
	Perf. 11 x 10.5							
1528	10¢ Horse Racing	05/04/74	.20	.20	2.50	(12)	2.00	156
a	Blue omitted		900.00					
b	Red omitted		—					
	Perf. 11							
1529	10¢ Skylab	05/14/74	.20	.20	.85	(4)	1.50	164
a	Vertical pair, imperf. between		—					
	Universal Postal Union Issue							
1530	10¢ Michelangelo, from "School							
	of Athens," by Raphael	06/06/74	.20	.20			1.00	24
1531	10¢ "Five Feminine Virtues,"							
	by Hokusai	06/06/74	.20	.20			1.00	24
1532	10¢ "Old Scraps," by							
	John Fredrick Peto	06/06/74	.20	.20			1.00	24
1533	10¢ "The Lovely Reader,"							
	by Jean Etienne Liotard	06/06/74	.20	.20			1.00	24
1534	10¢ "Lady Writing Letter,"							
	by Gerard Terborch	06/06/74	.20	.20			1.00	24
1535	10¢ Inkwell and Quill, from							
	"Boy with a Top," by Jean-Baptiste							
	Simeon Chardin	06/06/74	.20	.20			1.00	24
1536	10¢ Mrs. John Douglas,							
	by Thomas Gainsborough	06/06/74	.20	.20			1.00	24
1537	10¢ Don Antonio Noriega,							
	by Francisco de Goya	06/06/74	.20	.20			1.00	24
a	Block of 8, #1530-37		1.75	1.60	3.50	(16)	4.00	
b	As "a," imperf. vertically		7,500.00					

	Issues of 1974		Un	U	PB	#	FDC	Q(M)
	Mineral Heritage Issue, Perf. 11							
1538	10¢ Petrified Wood	06/13/74	.20	.20			1.00	42
a	Light blue and yellow omitted		—					
1539	10¢ Tourmaline	06/13/74	.20	.20			1.00	42
a	Light blue omitted		—					
b	Black and purple omitted		—					
1540	10¢ Amethyst	06/13/74	.20	.20			1.00	42
a	Light blue and yellow omitted		—					
1541	10¢ Rhodochrosite	06/13/74	.20	.20			1.00	42
a	Block of 4, #1538-41		.80	.90	.90	(4)	2.75	
b	As "a," light blue and							
	yellow omitted		1,900.00					
c	Light blue omitted		—					
d	Black and red omitted		—					
1542	10¢ First Kentucky Settlement-							
	Ft. Harrod	06/15/74	.20	.20	.85	(4)	1.00	156
a	Dull black omitted		850.00					
b	Green, black and blue omitted		3,750.00					
c	Green omitted		—					
d	Green and black omitted		—					
e	Tagging omitted		—					
	American Bicentennial Issue, First Continental Congress							
1543	10¢ Carpenters' Hall	07/04/74	.20	.20			1.00	49
1544	10¢ "We Ask but for Peace,							
	Liberty and Safety"	07/04/74	.20	.20			1.00	49
1545	10¢ "Deriving Their Just Powers							
	from the Consent of							
	the Governed"	07/04/74	.20	.20			1.00	49
1546	10¢ Independence Hall	07/04/74	.20	.20			1.00	49
a	Block of 4, #1543-46		.80	.90	.90	(4)	2.75	
1547	10¢ Energy Conservation	09/23/74	.20	.20	.85	(4)	1.00	149
a	Blue and orange omitted		850.00					
b	Orange and green omitted		600.00					
c	Green omitted		825.00					
	American Folklore Issue							
1548	10¢ Headless Horseman							
	and Ichabod Crane	10/10/74	.20	.20	.85	(4)	2.00	157
1549	10¢ Retarded Children	10/12/74	.20	.20	.85	(4)	1.00	150
a	Tagging omitted		7.50					
	Christmas Issue, Perf. 10.5 x 11							
1550	10¢ Angel from Perussis							
	Altarpiece	10/23/74	.20	.20	2.10	(10)	1.00	835
	Perf. 11 x 10.5							
1551	10¢ "The Road-Winter," by							
	Currier and Ives	10/23/74	.20	.20	2.50	(12)	1.00	883
a	Buff omitted		35.00					
	Precanceled Self-Adhesive, Imperf.							
1552	10¢ Dove Weather Vane atop							
	Mount Vernon	11/15/74	.20	.20	4.25	(20)	1.50	213
	Issues of 1975, American Arts Issue, Perf. 10.5 x 11							
1553	10¢ Benjamin West,							
	Self-Portrait	02/10/75	.20	.20	2.10	(10)	1.00	157
	Perf. 11							
1554	10¢ Paul Laurence Dunbar							
	and Lamp	05/01/75	.20	.20	2.10	(10)	1.00	146
a	Imperf., pair		1,300.00					
1555	10¢ D.W. Griffith and							
	Motion-Picture Camera	05/27/75	.20	.20	.85	(4)	1.00	149
a	Brown omitted		625.00					

1538

1539

1540

1541   1541a

1542

1543   1544

1545   1546   1546a

1547

1548

1549

1550

1551

1552

1553

1554

1555

1975

1556

1557

1558

1559

1560

1561

YOUTHFUL HEROINE
On the dark night of April 26, 1777, 16-year-old Sybil Ludington rode her horse "Star" alone through the Connecticut countryside rallying her father's militia to repel a raid by the British on Danbury.

GALLANT SOLDIER
The conspicuously courageous actions of black foot soldier Salem Poor at the Battle of Bunker Hill on June 17, 1775, earned him citations for his bravery and leadership ability.

FINANCIAL HERO
Businessman and broker Haym Salomon was responsible for raising most of the money needed to finance the American Revolution and later to save the new nation from collapse.

1562

US Bicentennial 10cents

1563

US Bicentennial 10c

1564

FINANCIAL HERO
Businessman and broker Haym Salomon was responsible for raising most of the money needed to finance the American Revolution and later to save the new nation from collapse.

1565   1566   1569

1567   1568   1568a

1570   1570a

Issues of 1975		Un	U	PB	#	FDC	Q(M)
Space Issues, Perf. 11							
1556	10¢ Pioneer 10 Passing						
	Jupiter	02/28/75	.20	.20	.85	(4)	2.00	174
a	Red and yellow omitted	1,400.00					
b	Blue omitted	950.00					
c	Tagging omitted	9.00					
1557	10¢ Mariner 10, Venus						
	and Mercury	04/04/75	.20	.20	.85	(4)	2.00	159
a	Red omitted	450.00					
b	Ultramarine and bister omitted	2,000.00					
c	Tagging omitted	9.00					
1558	10¢ Collective Bargaining	03/13/75	.20	.20	1.75	(8)	1.00	153
	Imperfs. of #1558 exist from printer's waste						
American Bicentennial Issue Perf. 11 x 10.5							
1559	8¢ Sybil Ludington						
	Riding Horse	03/25/75	.20	.20	1.50	(10)	1.00	63
a	Back inscription omitted	225.00					
1560	10¢ Salem Poor Carrying						
	Musket	03/25/75	.20	.20	2.10	(10)	1.00	158
a	Back inscription omitted	225.00					
1561	10¢ Haym Salomon						
	Figuring Accounts	03/25/75	.20	.20	2.10	(10)	1.00	167
a	Back inscription omitted	225.00					
b	Red omitted	250.00					
1562	18¢ Peter Francisco						
	Shouldering Cannon	03/25/75	.35	.20	3.60	(10)	1.00	45
Battle of Lexington & Concord, Perf. 11							
1563	10¢ "Birth of Liberty,"						
	by Henry Sandham	04/19/75	.20	.20	2.50	(12)	1.00	144
a	Vertical pair, imperf. horizontally	425.00					
Battle of Bunker Hill							
1564	10¢ "Battle of Bunker						
	Hill," by John Trumbull	06/17/75	.20	.20	2.50	(12)	1.00	140
Military Uniforms							
1565	10¢ Soldier with Flintlock						
	Musket, Uniform Button	07/04/75	.20	.20			1.00	45
1566	10¢ Sailor with Grappling						
	Hook, First Navy Jack, 1775	07/04/75	.20	.20			1.00	45
1567	10¢ Marine with Musket,						
	Full-Rigged Ship	07/04/75	.20	.20			1.00	45
1568	10¢ Militiaman with						
	Musket, Powder Horn	07/04/75	.20	.20			1.00	45
a	Block of 4, #1565-68		.85	.90	2.50	(12)	2.50	
Apollo Soyuz Space Issue							
1569	10¢ Apollo and Soyuz						
	after Link-up and Earth	07/15/75	.20	.20			3.00	81
	Pair with full horizontal gutter between	—					
1570	10¢ Spacecraft before Link-up,						
	Earth and Project Emblem	07/15/75	.20	.20			3.00	81
a	Attached pair, #1569-70		.45	.40	2.50	(12)	
b	As "a", tagging omitted	30.00					
c	As "a," vertical pair,						
	imperf. horizontally	2,000.00					

	Issues of 1975		Un	U	PB	#	FDC	Q(M)
	Perf. 11 x 10.5							
1571	10¢ International							
	Women's Year	08/26/75	.20	.20	1.30	(6)	1.00	146
	Postal Service Bicentennial Issue							
1572	10¢ Stagecoach and							
	Trailer Truck	09/03/75	.20	.20			1.00	42
1573	10¢ Old and New							
	Locomotives	09/03/75	.20	.20			1.00	42
1574	10¢ Early Mail Plane and Jet	09/03/75	.20	.20			1.00	42
1575	10¢ Satellite for Mailgrams	09/03/75	.20	.20			1.00	42
a	Block of 4, #1572-75		.85	.90	2.50	(12)	1.75	
b	As "a," red "10¢" omitted		9,500.00					
	Perf. 11							
1576	10¢ World Peace Through Law	09/29/75	.20	.20	.85	(4)	1.25	147
a	Tagging omitted		8.00					
	Banking and Commerce Issue							
1577	10¢ Engine Turning, Indian Head							
	Penny and Morgan Silver Dollar	10/06/75	.25	.20			1.00	73
1578	10¢ Seated Liberty Quarter, $20							
	Gold Piece and Engine Turning	10/06/75	.25	.20			1.00	73
a	Attached pair, #1577-78		.50	.40	1.20	(4)	1.25	
b	Brown and blue omitted		2,250.00					
c	As "a," brn., blue and yel. omitted		2,750.00					
	Christmas Issue							
1579	(10¢) Madonna and Child,							
	by Domenico Ghirlandaio	10/14/75	.20	.20	2.50	(12)	1.00	739
a	Imperf., pair		90.00					
	Plate flaw ("d" damaged)		5.00	—				
	Perf. 11.2							
1580	(10¢) Christmas Card,							
	by Louis Prang, 1878	10/14/75	.20	.20	2.50	(12)	1.00	879
a	Imperf., pair		90.00					
c	Perf. 10.9		.25	.20	3.50	(12)		
	Perf. 10.5 x 11.3							
1580B	(10¢) Christmas Card,							
	by Louis Prang, 1878		.65	.20	15.00	(12)		
	Issues of 1977-1981, Americana Issue, Perf. 11 x 10.5 (Designs 18.5 x 22.5mm; #1590-90a, 17.5 x 20mm; see also 1606, 1608, 1610-19, 1622-23, 1625, 1811, 1813, 1816)							
1581	1¢ Inkwell & Quill	12/08/77	.20	.20	.25	(4)	1.00	
a	Untagged (Bureau precanceled)			.20				
d	Tagging omitted		4.50					
1582	2¢ Speaker's Stand	12/08/77	.20	.20	.25	(4)	1.00	
a	Untagged (Bureau precanceled)			.20				
b	Cream paper, dull gum, *1981*		.20	.20	.25	(4)		
c	Tagging omitted		4.50					
1583	Not assigned							
1584	3¢ Early Ballot Box	12/08/77	.20	.20	.30	(4)	1.00	
a	Untagged (Bureau precanceled)			.20				
b	Tagging omitted		7.50					
1585	4¢ Books, Bookmark, Eyeglasses	12/08/77	.20	.20	.40	(4)	1.00	
a	Untagged (Bureau precanceled)			1.25				
1586-89	Not assigned							
	Booklet Stamp							
1590	9¢ Capitol Dome, single (1591)							
	from booklet (1623a)	03/11/77	.45	.20			1.00	
	Booklet Stamp, Perf. 10							
1590A	Single (1591) from booklet (1623c)		22.50	15.00				
	#1590 is on white paper; #1591 is on gray paper.							

1572 **1573**

1571

1574 **1575** **1575a**

1576

1577 **1578** **1578a**

1581 **1582**

1579 **1580**

1584 **1585**

1591

1592

1593

1594

1595

1596

1597

1599

1603

1604

1605

1606

1608

1610

1611

1612

	Issues of 1975-1981		Un	U	PB/LP	#	FDC
	Americana Issue, Perf. 11 x 10.5						
1591	9¢ Capitol Dome	11/24/75	.20	.20	.85	(4)	1.00
a	Untagged (Bureau precanceled)			.20			
b	Tagging omitted		5.00				
1592	10¢ Contemplation of Justice	11/17/77	.20	.20	.90	(4)	1.00
a	Untagged (Bureau precanceled)			.25			
b	Tagging omitted		7.50				
1593	11¢ Printing Press	11/13/75	.20	.20	.90	(4)	1.00
a	Tagging omitted		4.00				
1594	12¢ Torch, Statue of Liberty	04/08/81	.25	.20	1.60	(4)	1.00
a	Tagging omitted		5.00				
1595	13¢ Liberty Bell, single from booklet		.30	.20			1.00
a	Booklet pane of 6	10/31/75	2.25	.75			2.00
b	Booklet pane of 7 + label		2.25	.75			2.75
c	Booklet pane of 8		2.25	1.00			2.50
d	Booklet pane of 5 + label	04/02/76	1.75	.75			2.25
e	Vertical pair, imperf. between		800.00				
	Perf. 11						
1596	13¢ Eagle and Shield	12/01/75	.25	.20	3.25	(12)	1.00
a	Imperf., pair		50.00	—			
b	Yellow omitted		160.00				
d	Line perforated		27.50	—	375.00	(12)	
1597	15¢ Ft. McHenry Flag	06/30/78	.30	.20	1.90	(6)	1.00
a	Imperf., pair		20.00				
b	Gray omitted		600.00				
d	Tagging omitted		3.00				
	Booklet Stamp, Perf. 11 x 10.5						
1598	15¢ Ft. McHenry Flag (1597), single from booklet		.40	.20			1.00
a	Booklet pane of 8	06/30/78	4.25	.80			2.50
1599	16¢ Head, Statue of Liberty	03/31/78	.35	.20	1.90	(4)	1.00
1600-02	Not assigned						
1603	24¢ Old North Church	11/14/75	.50	.20	2.25	(4)	1.00
a	Tagging omitted		7.50				
1604	28¢ Ft. Nisqually	08/11/78	.55	.20	2.40	(4)	1.25
	Dull finish gum		1.10		10.00	(4)	
1605	29¢ Sandy Hook Lighthouse	04/14/78	.60	.20	3.00	(4)	1.25
	Dull finish gum		2.00		15.00	(4)	
1606	30¢ Morris Township School No.2	08/27/79	.55	.20	2.40	(4)	1.25
a	Tagging omitted		15.00				
1607	Not assigned						
	Perf. 11						
1608	50¢ Iron "Betty" Lamp	09/11/79	.85	.20	3.75	(4)	1.50
a	Black omitted		300.00				
b	Vertical pair, imperf. horizontally		1,750.00				
c	Tagging omitted		11.00				
1609	Not assigned						
1610	$1 Rush Lamp and Candle	07/02/79	2.00	.20	8.50	(4)	3.00
a	Brown omitted		250.00				
b	Tan, orange and yellow omitted		350.00				
c	Brown inverted		14,000.00				
d	Tagging omitted		15.00				
1611	$2 Kerosene Table Lamp	11/16/78	3.75	.75	16.00	(4)	5.00
1612	$5 Railroad Conductor's Lantern	08/23/79	8.25	1.75	35.00	(4)	12.50

1975-1979

	Issues of 1975-1981		Un	U	PB/LP	#	FDC
	Coil Stamps, Perf. 10 Vertically						
1613	3.1¢ Six String Guitar	10/25/79	.20	.20	1.50	(2)	1.00
a	Untagged (Bureau precanceled)			.50			
b	Imperf., pair		1,400.00		3,600.00	(2)	
1614	7.7¢ Saxhorns	11/20/76	.20	.20	1.00	(2)	1.00
a	Untagged (Bureau precanceled)			.35			
b	As "a," imperf., pair			1,600.00	4,400.00	(2)	
1615	7.9¢ Drum	04/23/76	.20	.20	.75	(2)	1.00
a	Untagged (Bureau precanceled)			.20			
b	Imperf., pair		600.00				
1615C	8.4¢ Steinway Grand Piano	07/13/78	.20	.20	3.25	(2)	1.00
d	Untagged (Bureau precanceled)			.30			
e	As "d," pair, imperf. between			60.00	125.00	(2)	
f	As "d," imperf., pair			17.50	35.00	(2)	
	Americana Issue, Perf. 10 Vertically (See also #1581-82, 1584-85, 1590-99, 1603-05, 1811, 1813, 1816)						
1616	9¢ slate green Capitol Dome (1591)	03/05/76	.20	.20	1.00	(2)	1.00
a	Imperf., pair		160.00		375.00	(2)	
b	Untagged (Bureau precanceled)			.35			
c	As "b," imperf., pair			700.00	—	(2)	
1617	10¢ purple Contemplation of Justice (1592)	11/04/77	.20	.20	1.10	(2)	1.00
	Dull finish gum			.30	2.75	(2)	
a	Untagged (Bureau precanceled)			.25			
b	Imperf., pair		60.00		125.00	(2)	
1618	13¢ brown Liberty Bell (1595)	11/25/75	.25	.20	.70	(2)	1.00
a	Untagged (Bureau precanceled)			.45			
b	Imperf., pair		25.00		65.00	(2)	
g	Pair, imperf. between		—				
1618C	15¢ Ft. McHenry Flag (1597)	06/30/78	.40	.20			1.00
d	Imperf., pair		25.00				
e	Pair, imperf. between		150.00				
f	Gray omitted		40.00				
i	Tagging omitted		20.00				
1619	16¢ blue Head of Liberty (1599)	03/31/78	.35	.20	1.50	(2)	1.00
a	Huck Press printing (white background with a bluish tinge, fraction of a millimeter smaller)		.50	.20			
1620-21	Not assigned						
	Perf. 11 x 10.75						
1622	13¢ Flag over Independence Hall	11/15/75	.25	.20	5.75	(20)	1.00
a	Horizontal pair, imperf. between		50.00				
b	Imperf., pair		1,100.00				
e	Horizontal pair, imperf. vertically		—				
f	Tagging omitted		4.00				
	Perf. 11.25						
1622C	13¢ Star Flag over Independence Hall		1.00	.25	20.00	(6)	
d	Vertical pair, imperf.		150.00				
	Booklet Stamps, Perf. 11						
1623	13¢ Flag over Capitol, single from booklet (1623a)		.25	.20			1.50
a	Booklet pane of 8, (1 #1590 and 7 #1623)	03/11/77	2.25	1.10			25.00
d	Attached pair, #1590 and 1623		.70	.70			

1613 **1614** **1615** **1615C**

1622

1623a

1629   1630   1631   1631a

1632

1633

1634

1635

1636

1637

1638

1639

1640

1641

1642

1643

1644

1645

1646

1647

Issues of 1975-1977		Un	U	PB	#	FDC	Q(M)
Booklet Stamps, Perf. 10 x 9.75							
1623B 13¢ Single from booklet		.80	.80				
c	Booklet pane of 8,						
	(1 #1590a and 7 #1623b)	29.00	—			12.50	
e	Attached pair, #1590a and 1623b	24.00	22.50				
	#1623, 1623b issued only in booklets. All stamps are imperf. at one side or imperf. at one side and bottom.						
1624	Not assigned						
Coil Stamp, Perf. 10 Vertically							
1625	13¢ Flag over Independence Hall (1622)	11/15/75	.25	.20			1.00	
a	Imperf. pair		25.00				
American Bicentennial Issue, Perf. 11							
1629	13¢ Drummer Boy	01/01/76	.25	.20			1.25	73
1630	13¢ Old Drummer	01/01/76	.25	.20			1.25	73
1631	13¢ Fifer	01/01/76	.25	.20			1.25	73
a	Strip of 3, #1629-31		.75	.65	3.50	(12)	2.00	
b	As "a," imperf.	1,050.00					
c	Imperf., pair, #1631	800.00					
1632	13¢ *Interphil* 76	01/17/76	.20	.20	1.00	(4)	1.00	158
State Flags							
1633	13¢ Delaware	02/23/76	.25	.20			1.50	9
1634	13¢ Pennsylvania	02/23/76	.25	.20			1.50	9
1635	13¢ New Jersey	02/23/76	.25	.20			1.50	9
1636	13¢ Georgia	02/23/76	.25	.20			1.50	9
1637	13¢ Connecticut	02/23/76	.25	.20			1.50	9
1638	13¢ Massachusetts	02/23/76	.25	.20			1.50	9
1639	13¢ Maryland	02/23/76	.25	.20			1.50	9
1640	13¢ South Carolina	02/23/76	.25	.20			1.50	9
1641	13¢ New Hampshire	02/23/76	.25	.20			1.50	9
1642	13¢ Virginia	02/23/76	.25	.20			1.50	9
1643	13¢ New York	02/23/76	.25	.20			1.50	9
1644	13¢ North Carolina	02/23/76	.25	.20			1.50	9
1645	13¢ Rhode Island	02/23/76	.25	.20			1.50	9
1646	13¢ Vermont	02/23/76	.25	.20			1.50	9
1647	13¢ Kentucky	02/23/76	.25	.20			1.50	9

Greetings From Delaware

According to legend, Thomas Jefferson once called Delaware a jewel among states bordering the Atlantic Ocean; hence the nickname "Diamond State." The coastal setting for this geographic gem includes miles of beaches—playgrounds for thousands of summer visitors—and large wildlife areas that provide safe havens for several waterbird species.

People also call Delaware "the First State." In 1787, its legislators gathered at a tavern on the green in Dover, the state capital, and became the first to ratify the Constitution of the United States. Today, legislators still meet beside the green, but they do so in the State House, a graceful Georgian brick dating from 1792.

In the northern tip of Delaware lies the historic Brandywine Valley, a setting for magnificent estates built by wealthy industrialists in the du Pont family. The famed Winterthur Museum, once home to Henry Francis du Pont, boasts extensive gardens and a prized collection of American decorative arts dating from the 1640s to the 1860s. ■

	Issues of 1976		Un	U	FDC	Q(M)
	American Bicentennial Issue (continued), State Flags					
1648	13¢ Tennessee	02/23/76	.25	.20	1.50	9
1649	13¢ Ohio	02/23/76	.25	.20	1.50	9
1650	13¢ Louisiana	02/23/76	.25	.20	1.50	9
1651	13¢ Indiana	02/23/76	.25	.20	1.50	9
1652	13¢ Mississippi	02/23/76	.25	.20	1.50	9
1653	13¢ Illinois	02/23/76	.25	.20	1.50	9
1654	13¢ Alabama	02/23/76	.25	.20	1.50	9
1655	13¢ Maine	02/23/76	.25	.20	1.50	9
1656	13¢ Missouri	02/23/76	.25	.20	1.50	9
1657	13¢ Arkansas	02/23/76	.25	.20	1.50	9
1658	13¢ Michigan	02/23/76	.25	.20	1.50	9
1659	13¢ Florida	02/23/76	.25	.20	1.50	9
1660	13¢ Texas	02/23/76	.25	.20	1.50	9
1661	13¢ Iowa	02/23/76	.25	.20	1.50	9
1662	13¢ Wisconsin	02/23/76	.25	.20	1.50	9
1663	13¢ California	02/23/76	.25	.20	1.50	9
1664	13¢ Minnesota	02/23/76	.25	.20	1.50	9
1665	13¢ Oregon	02/23/76	.25	.20	1.50	9
1666	13¢ Kansas	02/23/76	.25	.20	1.50	9
1667	13¢ West Virginia	02/23/76	.25	.20	1.50	9

Greetings From Alabama

Alabama lies in the heart of the Deep South, at the southern end of the Appalachian Mountains. With its mild climate, long growing season, and fertile soils, the state regularly enjoys good harvests of soybeans and cotton, peanuts and pecans; its very name may derive from the Choctaw words *alba* and *amo*, meaning "plant gatherer." Important minerals also come out of the ground, helping make the state a major manufacturer of steel and other metals.

In the far southwest, where Alabama dips a "toe" into the Gulf of Mexico, tourists come to fish, bask in the sun, and see the World War II-era *USS Alabama* in Mobile. Civil War enthusiasts often visit Mobile Bay, scene of a Union Navy victory in 1864, or head inland to Montgomery, the state capital. There, in 1861, Southern leaders established the Confederate States of America, and President Jefferson Davis took up residence in the first White House of the Confederacy. ■

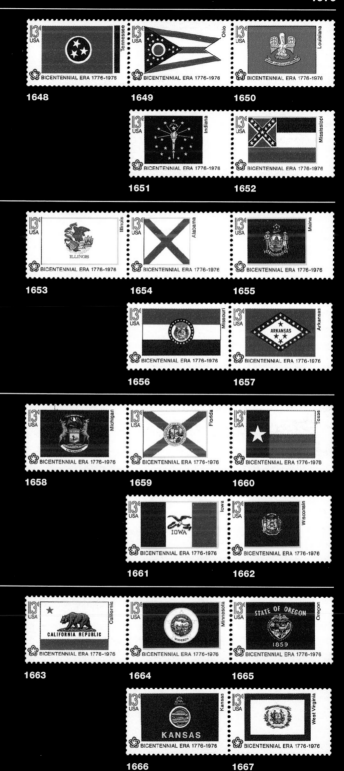

1648   1649   1650

1651   1652

1653   1654   1655

1656   1657

1658   1659   1660

1661   1662

1663   1664   1665

1666   1667

1976

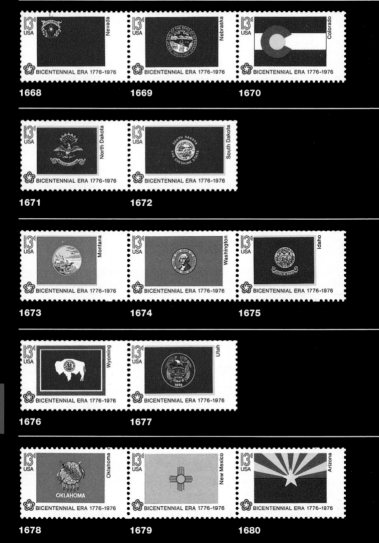

1668   1669   1670

1671   1672

1673   1674   1675

1676   1677

1678   1679   1680

1681   1682

	Issues of 1976		Un	U	FDC	Q(M)
	American Bicentennial Issue (continued), State Flags					
1668	13¢ Nevada	02/23/76	.25	.20	1.50	9
1669	13¢ Nebraska	02/23/76	.25	.20	1.50	9
1670	13¢ Colorado	02/23/76	.25	.20	1.50	9
1671	13¢ North Dakota	02/23/76	.25	.20	1.50	9
1672	13¢ South Dakota	02/23/76	.25	.20	1.50	9
1673	13¢ Montana	02/23/76	.25	.20	1.50	9
1674	13¢ Washington	02/23/76	.25	.20	1.50	9
1675	13¢ Idaho	02/23/76	.25	.20	1.50	9
1676	13¢ Wyoming	02/23/76	.25	.20	1.50	9
1677	13¢ Utah	02/23/76	.25	.20	1.50	9
1678	13¢ Oklahoma	02/23/76	.25	.20	1.50	9
1679	13¢ New Mexico	02/23/76	.25	.20	1.50	9
1680	13¢ Arizona	02/23/76	.25	.20	1.50	9
1681	13¢ Alaska	02/23/76	.25	.20	1.50	9
1682	13¢ Hawaii	02/23/76	.25	.20	1.50	9
a	Pane of 50, #1633-82		15.00	—	27.50	

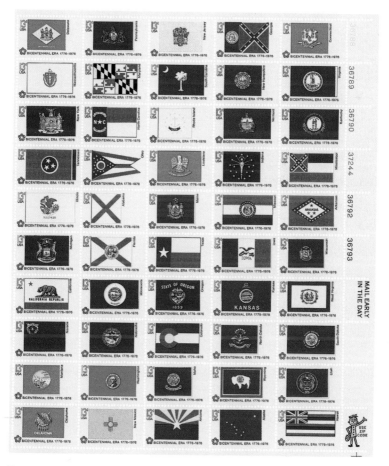

Example of 1682a

	Issues of 1976		Un	U	PB	#	FDC	Q(M)
1683	13¢ Telephone Centennial	03/10/76	.25	.20	1.10	(4)	1.00	158
1684	13¢ Commercial Aviation	03/19/76	.25	.20	2.75	(10)	1.00	156
1685	13¢ Chemistry	04/06/76	.25	.20	3.25	(12)	2.00	158
	Pair with full vertical gutter between		—					
American Bicentennial Issue Souvenir Sheets, 5 stamps each, Perf. 11								
1686	13¢ The Surrender of Lord Cornwallis at Yorktown, by John Trumbull	05/29/76	3.25	—			6.00	2
a	13¢ Two American Officers		.45	.40				2
b	13¢ Gen. Benjamin Lincoln		.45	.40				2
c	13¢ George Washington		.45	.40				2
d	13¢ John Trumbull, Col. David Cobb, General Friedrich von Steuben, Marquis de Lafayette and Thomas Nelson		.45	.40				2
e	13¢ Alexander Hamilton, John Laurens and Walter Stewart		.45	.40				2
f	"USA/13¢" omitted on "b," "c" and "d," imperf.		—	2,250.00				
g	"USA/13¢" omitted on "a" and "e"		450.00	—				
h	Imperf. (untagged)			2,250.00				
i	"USA/13¢" omitted on "b," "c" and "d"		450.00					
j	"USA/13¢" double on "b"		—					
k	"USA/13¢" omitted on "c" and "d"		750.00					
l	"USA/13¢" omitted on "e"		500.00					
m	"USA/13¢" omitted, imperf. (untagged)		—					
n	As "g", imperf., untagged		—					
1687	18¢ The Declaration of Independence, 4 July 1776 at Philadelphia, by John Trumbull	05/29/76	4.25	—			7.50	2
a	18¢ John Adams, Roger Sherman and Robert R. Livingston		.55	.55				2
b	18¢ Thomas Jefferson and Benjamin Franklin		.55	.55				2
c	18¢ Thomas Nelson, Jr., Francis Lewis, John Witherspoon and Samuel Huntington		.55	.55				2
d	18¢ John Hancock and Charles Thomson		.55	.55				2
e	18¢ George Read, John Dickinson and Edward Rutledge		.55	.55				2
f	Design and marginal inscriptions omitted		3,000.00					
g	"USA/18¢" omitted on "a" and "c"		750.00					
h	"USA/18¢" omitted on "b," "d" and "e"		450.00					
i	"USA/18¢" omitted on "d"		500.00	500.00				
j	Black omitted in design		2,000.00					
k	"USA/18¢" omitted, imperf. (untagged)		3,000.00					
m	"USA/18¢" omitted on "b" and "e"		500.00					

1683

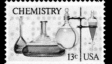

1684

1685

The Surrender of Lord Cornwallis at Yorktown
From a Painting by John Trumbull

1686

The Declaration of Independence, 4 July 1776 at Philadelphia
From a Painting by John Trumbull

1687

Washington Crossing the Delaware
From a Painting by Emanuel Leutze / Eastman Johnson

1688

Washington Reviewing His Ragged Army at Valley Forge
From a Painting by William T. Trego

1689

Issues of 1976		Un	U	FDC	Q(M)
American Bicentennial Issue Souvenir Sheets, 5 stamps each (continued)					
1688	24¢ Washington Crossing the Delaware, by Emanuel Leutze/ Eastman Johnson 05/29/76	5.25	—	8.50	2
a	24¢ Boatmen	.70	.70		2
b	24¢ George Washington	.70	.70		2
c	24¢ Flagbearer	.70	.70		2
d	24¢ Men in Boat	.70	.70		2
e	24¢ Steersman and Men on Shore	.70	.70		2
f	"USA/24¢" omitted, imperf.	3,500.00			
g	"USA/24¢" omitted on "d" and "e"	450.00	450.00		
h	Design and marginal inscriptions omitted	3,500.00			
i	"USA/24¢" omitted on "a," "b" and "c"	500.00	—		
j	Imperf. (untagged)	3,000.00			
k	"USA/24¢" inverted on "d" and "e"	—			
1689	31¢ Washington Reviewing His Ragged Army at Valley Forge, by William T. Trego 05/29/76	6.25	—	9.50	2
a	31¢ Two Officers	.85	.85		2
b	31¢ George Washington	.85	.85		2
c	31¢ Officer and Brown Horse	.85	.85		2
d	31¢ White Horse and Officer	.85	.85		2
e	31¢ Three Soldiers	.85	.85		2
f	"USA/31¢" omitted, imperf.	2,750.00			
g	"USA/31¢" omitted on "a" and "c"	400.00			
h	"USA/31¢" omitted on "b," "d" and "e"	450.00	—		
i	"USA/31¢" omitted on "e"	450.00			
j	Black omitted in design	2,000.00			
k	Imperf. (untagged)		2,250.00		
l	"USA/31¢" omitted on "b" and "d"	—			
m	"USA/31¢" omitted on "a," "c" and "e"	—			
n	As "m," imperf. (untagged)	—			
p	As "h," imperf. (untagged)		2,500.00		
q	As "g," imperf. (untagged)	2,750.00			
r	"USA/31¢" omitted on "d" & "e"	—			
s	As "f", untagged	2,250.00			

	Issues of 1976		Un	U	PB	#	FDC	Q(M)
	American Bicentennial Issue, Perf. 11							
1690	13¢ Bust of Benjamin Franklin,							
	Map of North America, 1776	06/01/76	.25	.20	1.10	(4)	1.00	165
a	Light blue omitted		250.00					
b	Tagging omitted		7.50					
	Declaration of Independence, by John Trumbull							
1691	13¢ Delegates	07/04/76	.30	.20			1.00	41
1692	13¢ Delegates and John Adams	07/04/76	.30	.20			1.00	41
1693	13¢ Roger Sherman, Robert R.							
	Livingston, Thomas Jefferson							
	and Benjamin Franklin	07/04/76	.30	.20			1.00	41
1694	13¢ John Hancock, Charles							
	Thomson, George Read,							
	John Dickinson and							
	Edward Rutledge	07/04/76	.30	.20			1.00	41
a	Strip of 4, #1691-94		1.20	1.10	6.00	(20)	2.00	
	Olympic Games Issue							
1695	13¢ Diver and Olympic Rings	07/16/76	.25	.20			1.00	46
1696	13¢ Skier and Olympic Rings	07/16/76	.25	.20			1.00	46
1697	13¢ Runner and Olympic							
	Rings	07/16/76	.25	.20			1.00	46
1698	13¢ Skater and Olympic							
	Rings	07/16/76	.25	.20			1.00	46
a	Block of 4, #1695-98		1.10	1.10	3.25	(12)	2.00	
b	As "a," imperf.		700.00					
1699	13¢ Clara Maass	08/18/76	.25	.20	3.25	(12)	1.50	131
a	Horizontal pair, imperf. vertically		450.00					
1700	13¢ Adolph S. Ochs	09/18/76	.25	.20	1.10	(4)	1.00	158
	Christmas Issue							
1701	13¢ Nativity, by							
	John Singleton Copley	10/27/76	.25	.20	3.25	(12)	1.00	810
a	Imperf., pair		100.00					
1702	13¢ "Winter Pastime,"							
	by Nathaniel Currier	10/27/76	.25	.20	2.75	(10)	1.00	482*
a	Imperf., pair		100.00					
	*Includes #1703 printing							
1703	13¢ as #1702	10/27/76	.25	.20	6.00	(20)	1.00	
a	Imperf., pair		110.00					
b	Vertical pair, imperf. between		—					
c	Tagging omitted		12.50					

#1702 has overall tagging. Lettering at base is black and usually ½mm below design. As a rule, no "snowflaking" in sky or pond. Pane of 50 has margins on 4 sides with slogans. #1703 has block tagging the size of the printed area. Lettering at base is gray-black and usually ¾mm below design. "Snowflaking" generally in sky and pond. Pane of 50 has margin only at right or left and no slogans.

	Issues of 1977, American Bicentennial Issue							
1704	13¢ Washington, Nassau Hall,							
	Hessian Prisoners and							
	13-star Flag, by							
	Charles Willson Peale	01/03/77	.25	.20	2.75	(10)	1.00	150
a	Horizontal pair, imperf. vertically		550.00					
1705	13¢ Sound Recording	03/23/77	.25	.20	1.10	(4)	1.00	177

1690

1691   1692   1693   1694   1694a

1695   1696

1699

1700

1697   1698   1698a

1701

1702

1703

1704

1705

1977

1706   **1707**

1708   **1709**   **1709a**

1710

1711

1712   **1713**

1714   **1715**   **1715a**

1716

1717   **1718**

1719   **1720**   **1720a**

1721

Issues of 1977		Un	U	PB	#	FDC	Q(M)
American Folk Art Issue, Pueblo Pottery, Perf. 11							
1706 13¢ Zia Pot	04/13/77	.25	.20			1.00	49
1707 13¢ San Ildefonso Pot	04/13/77	.25	.20			1.00	49
1708 13¢ Hopi Pot	04/13/77	.25	.20			1.00	49
1709 13¢ Acoma Pot	04/13/77	.25	.20			1.00	49
a Block of 4, #1706-09		1.00	1.00	2.75	(10)	2.00	
b As "a," imperf. vertically		2,500.00					
1710 13¢ Solo Transatlantic Flight	05/20/77	.25	.20	3.25	(12)	2.00	209
a Imperf. pair		1,050.00					
1711 13¢ Colorado Statehood	05/21/77	.25	.20	3.25	(12)	1.00	192
a Horizontal pair, imperf. between		600.00					
b Horizontal pair, imperf. vertically		900.00					
c Perf. 11.2		.35	.25	20.00	(12)		
Butterfly Issue							
1712 13¢ Swallowtail	06/06/77	.25	.20			1.00	55
1713 13¢ Checkerspot	06/06/77	.25	.20			1.00	55
1714 13¢ Dogface	06/06/77	.25	.20			1.00	55
1715 13¢ Orange-Tip	06/06/77	.25	.20			1.00	55
a Block of 4, #1712-15		1.00	1.00	3.25	(12)	2.00	
b As "a," imperf. horizontally		15,000.00					
American Bicentennial Issue							
1716 13¢ Marquis de Lafayette	06/13/77	.25	.20	1.10	(4)	1.25	160
Skilled Hands for Independence							
1717 13¢ Seamstress	07/04/77	.25	.20			1.00	47
1718 13¢ Blacksmith	07/04/77	.25	.20			1.00	47
1719 13¢ Wheelwright	07/04/77	.25	.20			1.00	47
1720 13¢ Leatherworker	07/04/77	.25	.20			1.00	47
a Block of 4, #1717-20		1.00	1.00	3.25	(12)	2.00	
Perf. 11 x 10.5							
1721 13¢ Peace Bridge	08/04/77	.25	.20	1.10	(4)	1.00	164

Greetings From Colorado

Standing atop Pikes Peak in the late 19th century, writer Katharine Lee Bates gazed in wonder at the "purple mountain majesties" of the Rocky Mountains and at the vast grasslands stretching toward the eastern horizon of Colorado. She would later wax poetic about her visit, writing the words to "America the Beautiful."

Pikes Peak is just one of 54 Colorado peaks with summits over 14,000 feet; hundreds more stand at least 10,000 feet above sea level. Among the so-called "fourteeners" are the Maroon Bells, a striking backdrop to the world-famous ski resort of Aspen.

An outdoor playground every season of the year, Colorado is a magnet for skiers, mountain climbers, backpackers, bicyclists, and campers. Many people just want to wander through any of the 200-plus wildlife areas; explore centuries-old cliff dwellings at Mesa Verde; or perhaps go for a soak in the huge hot-spring pool at Glenwood Springs.

Most Colorado residents live east of the Rockies, especially in or around Denver, the mile-high capital of the state. ■

Issues of 1977			Un	U	PB	#	FDC	Q(M)
American Bicentennial Issue, Perf. 11								
1722	13¢ Herkimer at Oriskany,							
	by Frederick Yohn	08/06/77	.25	.20	2.75	(10)	1.00	156
	Energy Issue							
1723	13¢ Energy Conservation	10/20/77	.25	.20			1.25	79
1724	13¢ Energy Development	10/20/77	.25	.20			1.25	79
a	Attached pair, #1723-24		.50	.50	3.25	(12)		
1725	13¢ First Civil Settlement							
	Alta, California	09/09/77	.25	.20	1.10	(4)	1.00	154
	American Bicentennial Issue							
1726	13¢ Members of Continental							
	Congress in Conference	09/30/77	.25	.20	1.10	(4)	1.00	168
1727	13¢ Talking Pictures	10/06/77	.25	.20	1.10	(4)	1.50	157
	American Bicentennial Issue							
1728	13¢ Surrender of Burgoyne,							
	at Saratoga	10/07/77	.25	.20	2.75	(10)	1.00	154
	Christmas Issue							
1729	13¢ Washington at Valley							
	Forge, by J.C. Leyendecker	10/21/77	.25	.20	5.75	(20)	1.00	882
a	Imperf., pair		75.00					
1730	13¢ Rural Mailbox	10/21/77	.25	.20	2.75	(10)	1.00	922
a	Imperf., pair		300.00					
	Issues of 1978							
1731	13¢ Carl Sandburg	01/06/78	.25	.20	1.10	(4)	1.00	157
	Captain Cook Issue							
1732	13¢ Capt. James Cook							
	Alaska, by Nathaniel Dance	01/20/78	.25	.20			2.00	101
1733	13¢ *Resolution* and *Discovery*							
	Hawaii, by John Webber	01/20/78	.25	.20			2.00	101
a	Vertical pair, imperf. horizontally		—					
b	Attached pair, #1732-33		.50	.50	1.10	(4)		
c	As " b," imperf. between		4,500.00					
1734	13¢ Indian Head Penny	01/11/78	.25	.20	1.25	(4)	1.00	
	Pair with full horizontal gutter between							
a	Horizontal pair, imperf. vertically		300.00					
1735	(15¢) "A" Stamp	05/22/78	.25	.20	1.25	(4)	1.00	
a	Imperf., pair		90.00					
b	Vertical pair, imperf. horizontally		700.00					
c	Perf. 11.2		.25	.20	1.75	(4)		
	Booklet Stamp, Perf. 11 x 10.5							
1736	(15¢) "A" orange Eagle (1735),							
	single from booklet	05/22/78	.25	.20			1.00	
a	Booklet pane of 8	05/22/78	2.25	.90			2.50	
	Roses Booklet Issue, Perf. 10							
1737	15¢ Roses, single from							
	booklet	07/11/78	.25	.20			1.00	
a	Booklet pane of 8	07/11/78	2.25	.90			2.50	
b	As "a," imperf.		—					
c	As "a," tagging omitted		40.00					

#1736-37 issued only in booklets. All stamps are imperf. on one side or on one side and bottom.

1723

1722

1725

1724   **1724a**

1726

1727

1728

1729   **1730**

1732

1731

1733   **1733b**

1734

1735

1737

1738 1739 1740 1741 1742 1742a

1745 1746

1744

1747 1748

1748a

1750

1752

1749

1751 1752a

1753

1754

1755

1756

	Issues of 1980		Un	U	PB/LP	#	FDC	Q(M)
	Windmills Booklet Issue, Perf. 11							
1738	15¢ Virginia, 1720	02/07/80	.30	.20			1.00	
1739	15¢ Rhode Island, 1790	02/07/80	.30	.20			1.00	
1740	15¢ Massachusetts, 1793	02/07/80	.30	.20			1.00	
1741	15¢ Illinois, 1860	02/07/80	.30	.20			1.00	
1742	15¢ Texas, 1890	02/07/80	.30	.20			1.00	
a	Booklet pane of 10, #1738-42		3.50	*3.00*			3.50	
b	Strip of 5, #1730-1742		1.50	1.40				
	#1737-42 issued only in booklets. All stamps are imperf. top or bottom, or top or bottom and right side.							
	Issues of 1978, Coil Stamp, Perf. 10 Vertically							
1743	(15¢) "A" orange Eagle (1735)	05/22/78	.25	.20	.65	(2)	1.00	
a	Imperf., pair		90.00		—	(2)		
	Black Heritage Issue, Perf. 10.5 x 11							
1744	13¢ Harriet Tubman and Cart Carrying Slaves	02/01/78	.25	.20	3.25	(12)	1.50	157
	American Folk Art Issue, Quilts, Perf. 11							
1745	13¢ Basket design, red and orange	03/08/78	.25	.20			1.00	41
1746	13¢ Basket design, red	03/08/78	.25	.20			1.00	41
1747	13¢ Basket design, orange	03/08/78	.25	.20			1.00	41
1748	13¢ Basket design, brown	03/08/78	.25	.20			1.00	41
a	Block of 4, #1745-48		1.00	1.00	3.25	(12)	2.00	
	American Dance Issue							
1749	13¢ Ballet	04/26/78	.25	.20			1.00	39
1750	13¢ Theater	04/26/78	.25	.20			1.00	39
1751	13¢ Folk	04/26/78	.25	.20			1.00	39
1752	13¢ Modern	04/26/78	.25	.20			1.00	39
a	Block of 4, #1749-52		1.00	1.00	3.25	(12)	2.00	
	American Bicentennial Issue, French Alliance							
1753	13¢ King Louis XVI and Benjamin Franklin, by Charles Gabriel Sauvage	05/04/78	.25	.20	1.10	(4)	1.00	103
	Perf. 10.5 x 11							
1754	13¢ Early Cancer Detection	05/18/78	.25	.20	1.10	(4)	1.00	152
	Performing Arts Issue, Perf. 11							
1755	13¢ Jimmie Rodgers with Guitar and Brakeman's Cap, Locomotive	05/24/78	.25	.20	3.25	(12)	1.00	95
1756	15¢ George M. Cohan, "Yankee Doodle Dandy" and Stars	07/03/78	.30	.20	4.00	(12)	1.00	152

1978

	Issues of 1978		Un	U	PB	#	FDC	Q(M)
	CAPEX '78 Souvenir Sheet, Perf. 11							
1757	13¢ Souvenir sheet of 8	06/10/78	2.00	2.00	2.25	(8)	2.75	15
a	13¢ Cardinal		.25	.20				15
b	13¢ Mallard		.25	.20				15
c	13¢ Canada Goose		.25	.20				15
d	13¢ Blue Jay		.25	.20				15
e	13¢ Moose		.25	.20				15
f	13¢ Chipmunk		.25	.20				15
g	13¢ Red Fox		.25	.20				15
h	13¢ Raccoon		.25	.20				15
i	Yellow, green, red, brown and black (litho.) omitted		7,000.00					
1758	15¢ Photography	06/26/78	.30	.20	4.00	(12)	1.50	163
1759	15¢ Viking Missions to Mars	07/20/78	.30	.20	1.35	(4)	2.00	159
	Wildlife Conservation: American Owls Issue							
1760	15¢ Great Gray Owl	08/26/78	.30	.20			1.25	47
1761	15¢ Saw-Whet Owl	08/26/78	.30	.20			1.25	47
1762	15¢ Barred Owl	08/26/78	.30	.20			1.25	47
1763	15¢ Great Horned Owl	08/26/78	.30	.20			1.25	47
a	Block of 4, #1760-63		1.25	1.25	1.40	(4)	2.00	
	Wildlife Conservation: American Trees Issue							
1764	15¢ Giant Sequoia	10/09/78	.30	.20			1.25	42
1765	15¢ White Pine	10/09/78	.30	.20			1.25	42
1766	15¢ White Oak	10/09/78	.30	.20			1.25	42
1767	15¢ Gray Birch	10/09/78	.30	.20			1.25	42
a	Block of 4, #1764-67		1.25	1.25	4.00	(12)	2.00	
b	As "a," imperf. horizontally		15,000.00					

Fort Nisqually

A remote outpost for a vast fur-trading empire, Fort Nisqually in Washington State was the first European settlement on Puget Sound—and the subject of a 1978 Americana stamp issued by the Postal Service. The original fort, which no longer stands, was founded in 1833 by Archibald McDonald of the Hudson's Bay Company of London. In those days, Great Britain and the United States both claimed this part of North America, a region then known as the Oregon Country. Then, a treaty between the two countries in 1846 divided the region along the 49th parallel: The British got land to the north; the U.S. eventually took control of territory to the south, including Fort Nisqually.

The old fort closed for business in 1869, but its memory lives on at Fort Nisqually Historic Site in Point Defiance Park near Tacoma Narrows. There, a reconstructed post includes the original Granary and Factor's House, both listed on the National Register of Historic Places. On display are artifacts of the fur trade and replicas of 19th-century pottery and blankets; volunteers and staff reenact 1850s-era activities such as beadwork, spinning, and blacksmithing. The site also hosts a winter lecture series, holds a summer history camp, and celebrates an old-fashioned Christmas. ■

a   b   c   d

1757   e   f   g   h

1758

1759

1760   **1761**

1762   **1763**   **1763a**

1764   **1765**

1766   **1767**   **1767a**

1768

1769

1770

1771

1775   **1776**

1772

1773

1774

1777   **1778**   **1778a**

1779   **1780**

1781   **1782**   **1782a**

1783   **1784**

1785   **1786**   **1786a**

Issues of 1978		Un	U	PB	#	FDC	Q(M)
Christmas Issues, Perf. 11							
1768 15¢ Madonna and Child with Cherubim, by Andrea della Robbia	10/18/78	.30	.20	4.00	(12)	1.00	963
a Imperf., pair		90.00					
1769 15¢ Child on Hobby Horse and Christmas Trees	10/18/78	.30	.20	4.00	(12)	1.00	917
Pair with full horizontal gutter between		—					
a Imperf., pair		100.00					
b Vertical pair, imperf. horizontally		2,000.00					
Issues of 1979, Perf. 11							
1770 15¢ Robert F. Kennedy	01/12/79	.35	.20	1.75	(4)	2.00	159
Black Heritage Issue							
1771 15¢ Martin Luther King, Jr., and Civil Rights Marchers	01/13/79	.30	.20	4.00	(12)	2.50	166
a Imperf., pair		—					
1772 15¢ International Year of the Child	02/15/79	.30	.20	1.40	(4)	1.00	163
Literary Arts Issue, Perf. 10.5 x 11							
1773 15¢ John Steinbeck, by Philippe Halsman	02/27/79	.30	.20	1.40	(4)	1.25	155
1774 15¢ Albert Einstein	03/04/79	.35	.20	1.75	(4)	4.00	157
Pair with full horizontal gutter between		—					
American Folk Art: Pennsylvania Toleware Issue, Perf. 11							
1775 15¢ Straight-Spout Coffeepot	04/19/79	.30	.20			1.00	44
1776 15¢ Tea Caddy	04/19/79	.30	.20			1.00	44
1777 15¢ Sugar Bowl	04/19/79	.30	.20			1.00	44
1778 15¢ Curved-Spout Coffeepot	04/19/79	.30	.20			1.00	44
a Block of 4, #1775-78		1.25	1.25	3.25	(10)	2.00	
b As "a," imperf. horizontally		4,250.00					
American Architecture Issue							
1779 15¢ Virginia Rotunda, by Thomas Jefferson	06/04/79	.30	.20			1.00	41
1780 15¢ Baltimore Cathedral, by Benjamin Latrobe	06/04/79	.30	.20			1.00	41
1781 15¢ Boston State House, by Charles Bulfinch	06/04/79	.30	.20			1.00	41
1782 15¢ Philadelphia Exchange, by William Strickland	06/04/79	.30	.20			1.00	41
a Block of 4, #1779-82		1.25	1.25	1.45	(4)	2.00	
Endangered Flora Issue							
1783 15¢ Persistent Trillium	06/07/79	.30	.20			1.00	41
1784 15¢ Hawaiian Wild Broadbean	06/07/79	.30	.20			1.00	41
1785 15¢ Contra Costa Wallflower	06/07/79	.30	.20			1.00	41
1786 15¢ Antioch Dunes Evening Primrose	06/07/79	.30	.20			1.00	41
a Block of 4, #1783-86		1.25	1.25	4.00	(12)	2.00	
As "a," full vertical gutter between		—					
b As "a," imperf.		600.00					

	Issues of 1979		Un	UPB	PB	#	FDC	Q(M)
1787	15¢ Seeing Eye Dogs	06/15/79	.30	.20	6.50	(20)	1.00	162
a	Imperf., pair		425.00					
b	Tagging omitted		10.00					
1788	15¢ Special Olympics	08/09/79	.30	.20	3.25	(10)	1.00	166
	American Bicentennial Issue, Perf. 11 x 12							
1789	15¢ John Paul Jones,							
	by Charles Willson Peale	09/23/79	.30	.20	3.25	(10)	1.25	160
c	Vertical pair, imperf. horizontally		175.00					
1789A	Perf. 11		.50	.20	4.00	(10)		
d	Vertical pair,							
	imperf. horizontally		150.00					
1789B	Perf. 12		2,500.00	1,000.00	27,500.00	(10)		
	Numerous varieties of printer's waste of #1789 exist							
	Olympic Summer Games Issue, Perf. 11 (See also #C97)							
1790	10¢ Javelin Thrower	09/05/79	.20	.20	3.00	(12)	1.00	67
1791	15¢ Runner	09/28/79	.30	.20			1.25	47
1792	15¢ Swimmer	09/28/79	.30	.20			1.25	47
1793	15¢ Rowers	09/28/79	.30	.20			1.25	47
1794	15¢ Equestrian Contestant	09/28/79	.30	.20			1.25	47
a	Block of 4, #1791-94		1.25	1.25	4.00	(12)	2.00	
b	As "a," imperf.		1,500.00					
	Issues of 1980, Olympic Winter Games Issue, Perf. 11 x 10.5							
1795	15¢ Speed Skater	02/01/80	.35	.20			1.25	52
1796	15¢ Downhill Skier	02/01/80	.35	.20			1.25	52
1797	15¢ Ski Jumper	02/01/80	.35	.20			1.25	52
1798	15¢ Ice Hockey	02/01/80	.35	.20			1.25	52
a	Perf. 11, #1795-98		1.05	.60				
b	Block of 4, #1795-98		1.50	1.40	4.50	(12)	2.00	
c	Block of 4, #1795a-98a		4.25	3.50	14.00	(12)		
	Issues of 1979, Christmas Issue, Perf. 11							
1799	15¢ Virgin and Child with							
	Cherubim, by Gerard David	10/18/79	.30	.20	4.00	(12)	1.00	874
a	Imperf., pair		90.00					
b	Vertical pair, imperf. horizontally		700.00					
c	pair, imperf. between		2,250.00					
1800	15¢ Santa Claus, Christmas							
	Tree Ornament	10/18/79	.30	.20	4.00	(12)	1.00	932
a	Green and yellow omitted		625.00					
b	Green, yellow and tan omitted		700.00					
	Performing Arts Issue							
1801	15¢ Will Rogers and Rogers as a							
	Cowboy Humorist	11/04/79	.30	.20	4.00	(12)	1.25	161
a	Imperf., pair		225.00					
1802	15¢ Vietnam Veterans	11/11/79	.30	.20	3.25	(10)	4.00	173
	Issues of 1980 (continued), Performing Arts Issue							
1803	15¢ W.C. Fields and							
	Fields as a Juggler	01/29/80	.30	.20	4.00	(12)	1.75	169
	Black Heritage Issue							
1804	15¢ Benjamin Banneker							
	and Banneker as Surveyor	02/15/80	.35	.20	4.50	(12)	1.00	160
a	Horizontal pair, imperf. vertically		800.00					

1787   **1788**   **1789**

1791   **1792**

1793   **1794**

1790   **1794a**

1795   **1796**

1797   **1798**

1798b

1799   **1800**

1801   **1802**   **1803**   **1804**

1805

1807

1809

1813

1806

1808

1810

1816

1818

Frances Perkins
USA **15c**

1821

1822

Emily Bissell
Crusader Against Tuberculosis
USA **15c**

1823

HELEN KELLER
ANNE SULLIVAN

1824

1827

1828

1825

1826

1829

1830

1830a

	Issues of 1980		Un	U	PB/LP	#	FDC	Q(M)
	Letter Writing Issue, Perf. 11							
1805	15¢ Letters Preserve Memories	02/25/80	.30	.20			1.00	39
1806	15¢ purple P.S. Write Soon	02/25/80	.30	.20			1.00	39
1807	15¢ Letters Lift Spirits	02/25/80	.30	.20			1.00	39
1808	15¢ green P.S. Write Soon	02/25/80	.30	.20			1.00	39
1809	15¢ Letters Shape Opinions	02/25/80	.30	.20			1.00	39
1810	15¢ red and blue P.S. Write Soon	02/25/80	.30	.20			1.00	39
a	Vertical Strip of 6, #1805-10		1.85	2.00	11.00	(36)	2.50	
	Issues of 1980-81, Americana Issue, Coil Stamps, Perf. 10 Vertically							
	(See also #1581-82, 1584-85, 1590-99, 1603-06, 1608, 1610-19, 1622-23, 1625)							
1811	1¢ dark blue, greenish Inkwelll							
	and Quill (1581)	03/06/80	.20	.20	.40	(2)	1.00	
a	Imperf., pair		175.00		275.00	(2)		
1812	Not assigned							
1813	3.5¢ Weaver Violins	06/23/80	.20	.20	1.00	(2)	1.00	
a	Untagged (Bureau precanceled)			.20				
b	Imperf., pair		225.00		450.00	(2)		
1814-15	Not assigned							
1816	12¢ red brown, *beige* Torch from							
	Statue of Liberty (1594)	04/08/81	.25	.20	1.50	(2)	1.00	
a	Untagged (Bureau precanceled)			.25				
b	Imperf., pair		200.00		400.00	(2)		
1817	Not assigned							
	Issues of 1981, Perf. 11 x 10.5							
1818	(18¢) "B" Stamp	03/15/81	.35	.20	1.60	(4)	1.25	
	Booklet Stamp, Perf. 10							
1819	(18¢) "B" Stamp (1818),							
	single from booklet	03/15/81	.40	.20			1.00	
a	Booklet pane of 8	03/15/81	3.75	1.75			3.00	
	Coil Stamp, Perf. 10 Vertically							
1820	(18¢) "B" Stamp (1818)	03/15/81	.40	.20	1.60	(2)	1.00	
a	Imperf., pair		100.00		250.00	(2)		
	Issues of 1980, Perf. 10.5 x 11							
1821	15¢ Frances Perkins	04/10/80	.30	.20	1.30	(4)	1.00	164
	Perf. 11							
1822	15¢ Dolley Madison	05/20/80	.30	.20	1.40	(4)	1.00	257
1823	15¢ Emily Bissell	05/31/80	.35	.20	1.75	(4)	1.00	96
a	Vertical pair, imperf. horizontally		400.00					
1824	15¢ Helen Keller/Anne Sullivan	06/27/80	.30	.20	1.30	(4)	1.00	154
1825	15¢ Veterans Administration	07/21/80	.30	.20	1.30	(4)	1.50	160
a	Horizontal pair, imperf. vertically		450.00					
	American Bicentennial Issue							
1826	15¢ General Bernardo de Galvez,							
	Battle of Mobile	07/23/80	.30	.20	1.30	(4)	1.00	104
a	Red, brown and blue omitted		800.00					
b	Bl., brn., red and yel. omitted		1,400.00					
	Coral Reefs Issue							
1827	15¢ Brain Coral, Beaugregory							
	Fish	08/26/80	.30	.20			1.00	51
1828	15¢ Elkhorn Coral, Porkfish	08/26/80	.30	.20			1.00	51
1829	15¢ Chalice Coral, Moorish Idol	08/26/80	.30	.20			1.00	51
1830	15¢ Finger Coral, Sabertooth							
	Blenny	08/26/80	.30	.20			1.00	51
a	Block of 4, #1827-30		1.25	1.10	4.00	(12)	2.00	
b	As "a," imperf.		1,000.00					
c	As "a," imperf. between, vertically		—					
d	As "a," imperf. vertically		3,000.00					

	Issues of 1980		Un	U	PB	#	FDC	Q(M)
1831	15¢ Organized Labor	09/01/80	.30	.20	3.50	(12)	1.00	167
a	Imperf., pair		375.00					
	Literary Arts Issue, Edith Wharton, Perf. 10.5 x 11							
1832	15¢ Edith Wharton Reading							
	Letter	09/05/80	.30	.20	1.30	(4)	1.00	163
	Perf. 11							
1833	15¢ Education	09/12/80	.30	.20	1.90	(6)	1.00	160
a	Horizontal pair, imperf. vertically		240.00					
	American Folk Art Issue, Pacific Northwest Indian Masks							
1834	15¢ Heiltsuk, Bella Bella Tribe	09/25/80	.30	.20			1.00	39
1835	15¢ Chilkat Tlingit Tribe	09/25/80	.30	.20			1.00	39
1836	15¢ Tlingit Tribe	09/25/80	.30	.20			1.00	39
1837	15¢ Bella Coola Tribe	09/25/80	.30	.20			1.00	39
a	Block of 4, #1834-37		1.25	1.25	3.60	(10)	2.00	
	American Architecture Issue							
1838	15¢ Smithsonian Institution,							
	by James Renwick	10/09/80	.30	.20			1.00	39
1839	15¢ Trinity Church, by Henry							
	Hobson Richardson	10/09/80	.30	.20			1.00	39
1840	15¢ Pennsylvania Academy							
	of Fine Arts, by Frank Furness	10/09/80	.30	.20			1.00	39
1841	15¢ Lyndhurst, by Alexander							
	Jefferson Davis	10/09/80	.30	.20			1.00	39
a	Block of 4, #1838-41		1.25	1.25	1.50	(4)	2.00	
b	As "a", red omitted on #1838,1839		400.00					
	Christmas Issue							
1842	15¢ Madonna and Child							
	from Epiphany Window,							
	Washington Cathedral	10/31/80	.30	.20	4.00	(12)	1.00	693
a	Imperf., pair		70.00					
	Pair with full vertical gutter between		—					
1843	15¢ Wreath and Toys	10/31/80	.30	.20	6.50	(20)	1.00	719
a	Imperf., pair		70.00					
b	Buff omitted		25.00					
c	Vertical pair, imperf. horizontally		—					
d	Horizontal pair, imperf. between		4,000.00					

AJ Davis 1803-1892 Lyndhurst Tarrytown NY
Architecture USA 15c

Lyndhurst

From Albany to New York City, the Hudson River flows through a scenic stretch of countryside once home to writer Washington Irving, painter Frederick Church, and generations of Rockefellers, Vanderbilts, Roosevelts, and other rich and famous folks. One of the grandest homes, a Gothic Revival masterpiece now known as Lyndhurst, overlooks the river at Tarrytown and boasts vaulted ceilings, rich furnishings, and a conservatory. Architect Alexander Davis designed it in 1838 for former New York City mayor William Paulding, who called it Knoll.

In the 1860s, Davis enlarged the mansion for new owner George Merritt, a wealthy New York merchant who renamed it "Lyndenhurst" for the property's many linden trees. In 1880, railroad magnate Jay Gould bought the estate and made it his country retreat. He died in 1892, but Lyndhurst remained in his family until 1961, when daughter Anna, Duchess of Talleyrand-Perigord, died and passed the estate to the National Trust for Historic Preservation. ∎

1831

1832

1834   **1835**

1833

1836   1837   1837a

1838   **1839**

1840   1841   1841a

1842

1843

Dorothea Dix
USA 1c

1844

Igor Stravinsky
USA 2c

1845

Henry Clay
USA 3c

1846

Carl Schurz
4c USA

1847

Pearl Buck
USA 5c

1848

Walter Lippmann
6 USA

1849

Abraham Baldwin
USA 7

1850

Henry Knox
USA 8

1851

Sylvanus Thayer
USA 9

1852

Richard Russell
USA 10c

1853

Alden Partridge
USA 11

1854

USA 13c Crazy Horse

1855

Sinclair Lewis
USA 14

1856

Rachel Carson
USA 17c

1857

George Mason
USA 18c

1858

USA 19c
Sequoyah

1859

Ralph Bunche
USA 20c

1860

Thomas H. Gallaudet
USA 20c

1861

Harry S Truman
USA 20c

1862

John J. Audubon
USA 22

1863

	Issues of 1980-85		Un	U	PB	#	FDC
	Great Americans Issue, Perf. 11 (See also #2168-73, 2176-80, 2182-86, 2188, 2190-92, 2194-97)						
1844	1¢ Dorothea Dix	09/23/83	.20	.20	.35	(6)	1.00
a	Imperf., pair		300.00				
b	Vertical pair, imperf. between		3,000.00				
c	Perf. 10.9, small block tagging		.20	.20	.35	(6)	
d	Perf. 10.9, large block tagging		.20	.20	.35	(6)	
e	Vertical pair, imperf. horizontally		—				
	Perf. 11 x 10.5						
1845	2¢ Igor Stravinsky	11/18/82	.20	.20	.35	(4)	1.00
	Vertical pair, full gutter between		—				
1846	3¢ Henry Clay	07/13/83	.20	.20	.55	(4)	1.00
a	Tagging omitted		4.00				
1847	4¢ Carl Schurz	06/03/83	.20	.20	.65	(4)	1.00
a	Tagging omitted		4.00				
1848	5¢ Pearl Buck	06/25/83	.20	.20	.70	(4)	1.00
	Perf. 11						
1849	6¢ Walter Lippman	09/19/85	.20	.20	.85	(6)	1.00
a	Vertical pair, imperf. between		2,250.00				
1850	7¢ Abraham Baldwin	01/25/85	.20	.20	.95	(6)	1.00
1851	8¢ Henry Knox	07/25/85	.20	.20	.85	(4)	1.00
1852	9¢ Sylvanus Thayer	06/07/85	.20	.20	1.30	(6)	1.25
1853	10¢ Richard Russell	05/31/84	.25	.20	2.00	(6)	1.00
a	Large block tagging		.30	.20	2.25	(6)	
b	Vertical pair, imperf. between and at bottom		900.00				
c	Horizontal pair, imperf. between		2,250.00				
1854	11¢ Alden Partridge	02/12/85	.25	.20	1.50	(4)	1.25
a	Tagging omitted		9.00				
	Perf. 11 x 10.5						
1855	13¢ Crazy Horse	01/15/82	.25	.20	2.00	(4)	1.50
a	Tagging omitted		7.50				
	Perf. 11						
1856	14¢ Sinclair Lewis	03/21/85	.30	.20	2.25	(6)	1.00
a	Large block tagging		.30	.20	2.25	(6)	
b	Vertical pair, imperf. horizontally		125.00				
c	Horizontal pair, imperf. between		9.00				
d	Vertical pair, imperf. between		1,500.00				
	Perf. 11 x 10.5						
1857	17¢ Rachel Carson	05/28/81	.35	.20	2.00	(4)	1.00
a	Tagging omitted		10.00				
1858	18¢ George Mason	05/07/81	.35	.20	3.00	(4)	1.00
a	Tagging omitted		7.50				
1859	19¢ Sequoyah	12/27/80	.40	.20	2.75	(4)	1.50
1860	20¢ Ralph Bunche	01/12/82	.40	.20	3.75	(4)	1.25
a	Tagging omitted		7.50				
1861	20¢ Thomas H. Gallaudet	06/10/83	.45	.20	4.00	(4)	1.25
	Perf. 11						
1862	20¢ Harry S. Truman	01/26/84	.40	.20	4.50	(6)	1.25
a	Perf. 11.2, large block tagging, dull gum	.40	.40	.20	3.00	(4)	
b	Perf. 11.2, overall tagging, dull gum		.40	—	3.75	(4)	
c	Perf. 11.2, tagging omitted		8.50				
1863	22¢ John J. Audubon	04/23/85	.55	.20	6.00	(6)	1.25
a	Large block tagging		1.00	.20	8.00	(6)	
b	Perf. 11.2, large block tagging		.55	.20	8.00	(4)	
c	Tagging omitted		7.50				
d	Vertical pair, imperf. horizontally		2,500.00				
e	Vertical pair, imperf. between		—				
f	Horizontal pair, imperf. between		2,500.00				

	Issues of 1981-1985		Un	U	PB/PNC	#	FDC	Q(M)
	Great Americans Issue (continued), Perf. 11							
1864	30¢ Frank C. Laubach	09/02/84	.55	.20	3.50	(6)	1.25	
a	Perf. 11.2, large block tagging		.55	.20	3.25	(4)		
b	Perf. 11.2, overall tagging		1.50	.20	22.50	(4)		
	Perf. 11 x 10.5							
1865	35¢ Charles R. Drew, MD	06/03/81	.70	.20	4.00	(4)	1.25	
1866	37¢ Robert Millikan	01/26/82	.75	.20	3.50	(4)	1.25	
a	Tagging omitted		10.00					
	Perf. 11							
1867	39¢ Grenville Clark	03/20/85	.80	.20	5.50	(6)	1.25	
a	Vertical pair, imperf. horizontally		600.00					
b	Vertical pair, imperf. between		2,000.00					
c	Perf. 10.9, large block tagging		.80	.20	5.50	(6)		
d	Perf. 11.2, large block tagging		.75	.20	5.50	(4)		
1868	40¢ Lillian M. Gilbreth	02/24/84	.80	.20	6.00	(6)	1.25	
a	Perf. 11.2, large block tagging		.80	.20	6.50	(4)		
1869	50¢ Chester W. Nimitz	02/22/85	.95	.20	7.50	(4)	2.00	
a	Perf. 11.2, large block tagging, dull gum		.95	.20	6.25	(4)		
b	Tagging omitted		11.00					
c	Perf. 11.2, tagging omitted, dull gum		8.00					
d	Perf. 11.2, overall tagging, dull gum		1.50	.20	8.50	(4)		
e	Perf. 11.2, prephosphored uncoated paper, shiny gum		.90	.20	5.00	(4)		
1870-73	Not assigned							
1874	15¢ Everett Dirksen	01/04/81	.30	.20	1.40	(4)	1.00	160
	Black Heritage Issue							
1875	15¢ Whitney Moore Young at Desk	01/30/81	.35	.20	1.75	(4)	1.00	160
	Flower Issue							
1876	18¢ Rose	04/23/81	.35	.20			1.00	53
1877	18¢ Camellia	04/23/81	.35	.20			1.00	53
1878	18¢ Dahlia	04/23/81	.35	.20			1.00	53
1879	18¢ Lily	04/23/81	.35	.20			1.00	53
a	Block of 4, #1876-79		1.40	1.25	1.75	(4)	2.50	
	Wildlife Booklet Issue							
1880	18¢ Bighorn Sheep	05/14/81	.55	.20			1.00	
1881	18¢ Puma	05/14/81	.55	.20			1.00	
1882	18¢ Harbor Seal	05/14/81	.55	.20			1.00	
1883	18¢ Buffalo	05/14/81	.55	.20			1.00	
1884	18¢ Brown Bear	05/14/81	.55	.20			1.00	
1885	18¢ Polar Bear	05/14/81	.55	.20			1.00	
1886	18¢ Elk (Wapiti)	05/14/81	.55	.20			1.00	
1887	18¢ Moose	05/14/81	.55	.20			1.00	
1888	18¢ White-Tailed Deer	05/14/81	.55	.20			1.00	
1889	18¢ Pronghorn Antelope	05/14/81	.55	.20			1.00	
a	Booklet pane of 10, #1880-89		8.50	7.00			5.00	
	#1880-89 issued only in booklets. All stamps are imperf. at one side or imperf. at one side and bottom.							
	Flag and Anthem Issue							
1890	18¢ "…for amber waves of grain"	04/24/81	.35	.20	2.25	(6)	1.00	
a	Imperf., pair		125.00					
b	Vertical pair, imperf. horizontally		850.00					
	Coil Stamp, Perf. 10 Vertically							
1891	18¢ "…from sea to shining sea"	04/24/81	.35	.20	4.00	(3)	1.00	
a	Imperf., pair		30.00	—				

Beginning with #1891, all coil stamps except 1947 feature a small plate number at the bottom of the design at varying intervals in a roll, depending on the press used. The basic "plate number coil" (PNC) collecting unit is a strip of three stamps, with the plate number appearing on the middle stamp. PNC values are for the most common plate number.

1864

1865

1866

1867

1868

1869

1876   1877

1874

1875

1878   1879   1879a

1880   1881
1882   1883
1884   1885
1886   1887
1888   1889

1889a

1890

1891

1892

1893

1894

1893a

1897   **1897A**   **1898**   **1898A**

1899   **1900**   **1901**   **1902**

1903   **1904**

	Issues of 1981-82		Un	U	PB/PNC/LP	#	FDC	Q(M)
	Booklet Stamps, Perf. 11							
1892	6¢ USA Circle of Stars,							
	single from booklet (1893a)	04/24/81	.50	.20			1.00	
1893	18¢ "...for purple mountain majesties,"							
	single from booklet (1893a)	04/24/81	.30	.20			1.00	
a	Booklet pane of 8 (2 #1892 & 6 #1893)		3.00	2.25			2.50	
b	As "a," imperf. vertically between		75.00					
c	Se-tenant pair, #1892 and #1893		.90	1.00				
	#1892-93 issued only in booklets. All stamps are imperf. at one side or imperf. at one side and bottom.							
	Flag Over Supreme Court Issue							
1894	20¢ Flag Over Supreme Court	12/17/81	.40	.20	2.75	(6)	1.00	
a	Imperf., pair		35.00					
b	Vertical pair, imperf. horizontally		550.00					
c	Dark blue omitted		85.00					
d	Black omitted		325.00					
e	Perf. 11.2, shiny gum		.35	.20	2.50	(6)		
	Coil Stamp, Perf. 10 Vertically							
1895	20¢ Flag Over Supreme							
	Court (1894)	12/17/81	.40	.20	3.50	(3)	1.00	
a	Narrow block tagging		.40	.20	3.25	(3)		
b	Untagged (Bureau precanceled)		.50	.50	57.50	(3)		
c	Tagging omitted		—					
d	Imperf., pair		10.00					
e	Pair, imperf. between		1,250.00					
f	Black omitted		50.00					
g	Blue omitted		1,500.00					
	Booklet Stamp, Perf. 11 x 10.5							
1896	20¢ Flag over Supreme Court							
	(1894), single from booklet	12/17/81	.40	.20			1.00	
a	Booklet pane of 6	12/17/81	3.00	2.00			6.00	
b	Booklet pane of 10	06/01/82	5.25	3.25			10.00	
	Issues of 1981-84, Transportation Issue, Coil Stamps, Perf. 10 Vertically							
	(See also #2123-36, 2225-26, 2228, 2231, 2252-66, 2452-53A, 2457, 2464, 2468)							
1897	1¢ Omnibus 1880s	08/19/83	.20	.20	.35	(3)	1.00	
b	Imperf., pair		675.00		—	(2)		
1897A	2¢ Locomotive 1870s	05/20/82	.20	.20	.45	(3)	1.50	
e	Imperf., pair		55.00		—	(2)		
1898	3¢ Handcar 1880s	03/25/83	.20	.20	.65	(3)	1.00	
1898A	4¢ Stagecoach 1890s	08/19/82	.20	.20	.95	(3)	1.00	
b	Untagged (Bureau precanceled)		.20	.20	4.75	(3)		
c	As "b," imperf., pair		750.00					
d	Imperf., pair		900.00	—				
1899	5¢ Motorcycle 1913	10/10/83	.20	.20	.80	(3)	1.50	
a	Imperf., pair		2,750.00					
1900	5.2¢ Sleigh 1880s	03/21/83	.20	.20	5.50	(3)	1.00	
a	Untagged (Bureau precanceled)		.20	.20	11.75	(3)		
1901	5.9¢ Bicycle 1870s	02/17/82	.25	.20	6.00	(3)	1.00	
a	Untagged (Bureau precanceled)		.20	.20	27.50	(3)		
b	As "a," imperf., pair		200.00		—	(2)		
1902	7.4¢ Baby Buggy 1880s	04/07/84	.20	.20	7.50	(3)	1.00	
a	Untagged (Bureau precanceled)		.20	.20	4.75	(3)		
1903	9.3¢ Mail Wagon 1880s	12/15/81	.30	.20	6.50	(3)	1.00	
a	Untagged (Bureau precanceled)		.25	.25	2.75	(3)		
b	As "a," imperf., pair		125.00		200.00	(2)		
1904	10.9¢ Hansom Cab 1890s	03/26/82	.30	.20	13.00	(3)	1.00	
a	Untagged (Bureau precanceled)		.30	.25	26.00	(3)		
b	As "a," imperf., pair		150.00			(2)		

	Issues of 1981-84		Un	U	PB	#	FDC	Q(M)
	Transportation Issue (continued)							
1905	11¢ RR Caboose 1890s	02/03/84	.30	.20	3.50	(3)	1.50	
a	Untagged (Bureau precanceled)		.25	.20	3.25	(3)		
1906	17¢ Electric Auto 1917	06/25/81	.35	.20	2.00	(3)	1.00	
a	Untagged (Bureau precanceled)		.35	.35	3.50	(3)		
b	Imperf., pair		165.00		—	(2)		
c	As "a," imperf., pair		650.00		—	(2)		
1907	18¢ Surrey 1890s	05/18/81	.35	.20	2.75	(3)	1.00	
a	Imperf., pair		150.00		—	(2)		
1908	20¢ Fire Pumper 1860s	12/10/81	.35	.20	2.50	(3)	1.50	
a	Imperf., pair		110.00		300.00	(2)		
	Values for plate # coil strips of 3 stamps for #1897-1908 are for the most common plate numbers. Other plate #s and strips of 5 stamps may have higher values.							
	Issue of 1983, Express Mail Booklet Issue, Perf. 10 Vertically							
1909	$9.35 Eagle and Moon, single from booklet	08/12/83	21.00	15.00			45.00	
a	Booklet pane of 3		65.00	—			125.00	
	#1909 issued only in booklets. All stamps are imperf. at top and bottom or imperf. at top, bottom and right side.							
	Issues of 1981, Perf. 10.5 x 11							
1910	18¢ American Red Cross	05/01/81	.35	.20	1.50	(4)	1.00	165
	Perf. 11							
1911	18¢ Savings and Loans	05/08/81	.35	.20	1.50	(4)	1.00	107
	Space Achievement Issue, Perf. 11							
1912	18¢ Exploring the Moon — Moon Walk	05/21/81	.40	.20			1.00	42
1913	18¢ Benefiting Mankind (upper left) Columbia Space Shuttle	05/21/81	.40	.20			1.00	42
1914	18¢ Benefiting Mankind— Space Shuttle Deploying Satellite	05/21/81	.40	.20			1.00	42
1915	18¢ Understanding the Sun— Skylab	05/21/81	.40	.20			1.00	42
1916	18¢ Probing the Planets— Pioneer 11	05/21/81	.40	.20			1.00	42
1917	18¢ Benefiting Mankind— Columbia Space Shuttle Lifting Off	05/21/81	.40	.20			1.00	42
1918	18¢ Benefiting Mankind—Space Shuttle Preparing to Land	05/21/81	.40	.20			1.00	42
1919	18¢ Comprehending the Universe — Telescope	05/21/81	.40	.20			1.00	42
a	Block of 8, #1912-19		3.25	3.00	3.75	(8)	3.00	
b	As "a," imperf.		9,000.00					
1920	18¢ Professional Management	06/18/81	.35	.20	1.50	(4)	1.00	99
	Preservation of Wildlife Habitats Issue							
1921	18¢ Save Wetland Habitats— Great Blue Heron	06/26/81	.35	.20			1.00	45
1922	18¢ Save Grassland Habitats— Badger	06/26/81	.35	.20			1.00	45
1923	18¢ Save Mountain Habitats— Grizzly Bear	06/26/81	.35	.20			1.00	45
1924	18¢ Save Woodland Habitats— Ruffled Grouse	06/26/81	.35	.20			1.00	45
a	Block of 4, #1921-24		1.50	1.25	2.00	(4)	2.50	

1905

1906

1907

1908

1909

1910

1911

1912 **1913** **1914** **1915**

1916 **1917** **1918** **1919** **1919a**

1921

1920

1922

1923

1924

1924a

1981

1925

1926

Alcoholism
You can beat it!
USA 18c

1927

1928   1929

1930   1931

1932

1931a

1933

1934

1935

1936

1937

1938   1938a

Issues of 1981		Un	U	PB	#	FDC	Q(M)
Perf. 11							
1925 18¢ International Year							
of the Disabled	06/29/81	.35	.20	1.50	(4)	1.00	100
a Vertical pair, imperf. horizontally		2,750.00					
1926 18¢ Edna St. Vincent Millay	07/10/81	.35	.20	1.50	(4)	1.00	100
a Black omitted		300.00	—				
1927 18¢ Alcoholism	08/19/81	.40	.20	10.00	(6)	1.50	98
a Imperf., pair		400.00					
b Vertical pair, imperf. horizontally		2,500.00					
American Architecture Issue							
1928 18¢ NYU Library, by							
Sanford White	08/28/81	.40	.20			1.00	42
1929 18¢ Biltmore House, by							
Richard Morris Hunt	08/28/81	.40	.20			1.00	42
1930 18¢ Palace of the Arts,							
by Bernard Maybeck	08/28/81	.40	.20			1.00	42
1931 18¢ National Farmer's Bank,							
by Louis Sullivan	08/28/81	.40	.20			1.00	42
a Block of 4, #1928-31		1.65	1.50	2.10	(4)	2.50	
American Sports Issue, Perf. 10.5 x 11							
1932 18¢ Babe Zaharias Holding							
Trophy	09/22/81	.40	.20	3.00	(4)	7.00	102
1933 18¢ Bobby Jones Teeing off	09/22/81	.40	.20	3.00	(4)	10.00	99
Perf. 11							
1934 18¢ Frederic Remington	10/09/81	.35	.20	1.60	(4)	1.00	101
a Vertical pair, imperf. between		275.00					
b Brown omitted		450.00					
1935 18¢ James Hoban	10/13/81	.35	.20	1.60	(4)	1.00	101
1936 20¢ James Hoban	10/13/81	.35	.20	1.65	(4)	1.00	167
American Bicentennial Issue							
1937 18¢ Battle of Yorktown 1781	10/16/81	.35	.20			1.00	81
1938 18¢ Battle of the Virginia							
Capes 1781	10/16/81	.35	.20			1.00	81
a Attached pair, #1937-38		.90	.75	2.00	(4)	1.50	
b As "a," black omitted		400.00					

Richard Morris Hunt 1828-1895 Biltmore Asheville NC

Architecture USA 18c

Biltmore House

A luxurious 250-room mansion in a naturally beautiful setting, Biltmore House is not only the largest private residence in the country but also a national historic landmark. This French Renaissance chateau is the centerpiece of an 8,000-acre estate in the Blue Ridge Mountains, near Asheville, North Carolina. In the 1890s, it became the home of George Washington Vanderbilt, who had hired friend and architect Richard Morris Hunt to build it on a site then encompassing 125,000 acres. Landscape architect Frederick Law Olmsted, renowned for his work in New York, Washington, D.C., Chicago, and Boston, designed the gardens surrounding this gem of the Gilded Age.

Grandson of wealthy industrialist Cornelius Vanderbilt, George Vanderbilt was an enthusiastic art collector, purchasing thousands of paintings, sculptures, carpets, and items of furniture on his many travels abroad and in the United States. Currently, the Biltmore collection comprises 70,000 items, including works by John Singer Sargent, James McNeill Whistler, and Pierre-Auguste Renoir. Family portraits by Whistler and other notables of the time still gaze from the walls of the 74-foot-long Banquet Hall, where Vanderbilt entertained guests visiting his magnificent estate. ■

	Issues of 1981		Un	U	PB/LP	#	FDC	Q(M)
	Christmas Issue							
1939	20¢ Madonna and Child,							
	by Botticelli	10/28/81	.40	.20	1.75	(4)	1.00	598
a	Imperf., pair		125.00					
b	Vertical pair, imperf. horizontally		1,650.00					
1940	20¢ Felt Bear on Sleigh	10/28/81	.40	.20	1.75	(4)	1.00	793
a	Imperf., pair		275.00					
b	Vertical pair, imperf. horizontally		2,500.00					
1941	20¢ John Hanson	11/05/81	.40	.20	1.75	(4)	1.00	167
	Desert Plants Issue, Perf. 11							
1942	20¢ Barrel Cactus	12/11/81	.35	.20			1.00	48
1943	20¢ Agave	12/11/81	.35	.20			1.00	48
1944	20¢ Beavertail Cactus	12/11/81	.35	.20			1.00	48
1945	20¢ Saguaro	12/11/81	.35	.20			1.00	48
a	Block of 4, #1942-45		1.50	1.25	1.90	(4)	2.50	
b	As "a," deep brown omitted		7,500.00					
c	#1945 vertical pair, imperf.		5,250.00					
	Perf. 11 x 10.5							
1946	(20¢) "C" Stamp	10/11/81	.40	.20	2.00	(4)	1.00	
a	Tagging omitted		9.00					
	Coil Stamp, Perf. 10 Vertically							
1947	(20¢) "C" brown Eagle (1946)	10/11/81	.60	.20	1.50	(2)	1.00	
a	Imperf., pair		1,500.00		—	(2)		
	Booklet Stamp, Perf. 11 x 10.5							
1948	(20¢) "C" brown Eagle (1946),							
	single from booklet	10/11/81	.40	.20			1.00	
a	Booklet pane of 10	10/11/81	4.50	3.00			3.50	
	Issues of 1982, Perf. 11							
1949	20¢ Bighorn Sheep,							
	single from booklet	01/08/82	.55	.20			1.00	
a	Booklet pane of 10		5.50	2.50			6.00	
b	As "a," imperf. between		110.00					
c	Type II		.55	.20				
d	Type II, booklet pane of 10		11.00	—				
e	As #1949, tagging omitted		3.00	—				
f	As "e," booklet pane of 10		30.00					
	#1949 issued only in booklets. All stamps are imperf. at one side or imperf. at one side and bottom.							
1950	20¢ Franklin D. Roosevelt	01/30/82	.40	.20	1.75	(4)	1.00	164
	Perf. 11 x 10.5							
1951	20¢ Love	02/01/82	.40	.20	1.75	(4)	1.00	447
b	Imperf., pair		275.00					
c	Blue omitted		225.00					
d	Yellow omitted		1,000.00					
e	Purple omitted		—					
1951A	Perf. 11.25 x 10.5		.75	.25	3.50	(4)		
	Perf. 11							
1952	20¢ George Washington	02/22/82	.40	.20	1.75	(4)	1.00	181

1939

1940

1941

1942   **1943**   **1945**

1944   **1945a**

1946

1949

1950

1951

1952

Alabama USA 20c — Yellowhammer & Camellia — 1953
Alaska USA 20c — Willow Ptarmigan & Forget-Me-Not — 1954
Arizona USA 20c — Cactus Wren & Saguaro Cactus Blossom — 1955
Arkansas USA 20c — Mockingbird & Apple Blossom — 1956
California USA 20c — California Quail & California Poppy — 1957

Colorado USA 20c — Lark Bunting & Rocky Mountain Columbine — 1958
Connecticut USA 20c — Robin & Mountain Laurel — 1959
Delaware USA 20c — Blue Hen Chicken & Peach Blossom — 1960
Florida USA 20c — Mockingbird & Orange Blossom — 1961
Georgia USA 20c — Brown Thrasher & Cherokee Rose — 1962

Hawaii USA 20c — Hawaiian Goose & Hibiscus — 1963
Idaho USA 20c — Mountain Bluebird & Syringa — 1964
Illinois USA 20c — Cardinal & Violet — 1965
Indiana USA 20c — Cardinal & Peony — 1966
Iowa USA 20c — Eastern Goldfinch & Wild Rose — 1967

Kansas USA 20c — Western Meadowlark & Sunflower — 1968
Kentucky USA 20c — Cardinal & Goldenrod — 1969
Louisiana USA 20c — Brown Pelican & Magnolia — 1970
Maine USA 20c — Chickadee & White Pine Cone and Tassel — 1971
Maryland USA 20c — Baltimore Oriole & Black-Eyed Susan — 1972

Massachusetts USA 20c — Black-Capped Chickadee & Mayflower — 1973
Michigan USA 20c — Robin & Apple Blossom — 1974
Minnesota USA 20c — Common Loon & Showy Lady Slipper — 1975
Mississippi USA 20c — Mockingbird & Magnolia — 1976
Missouri USA 20c — Eastern Bluebird & Red Hawthorn — 1977

	Issues of 1982		Un	U	FDC	Q(M)
	State Birds & Flowers Issue, Perf. 10.5 x 11					
1953	20¢ Alabama: Yellowhammer and Camellia	04/14/82	.50	.25	1.25	13
1954	20¢ Alaska: Willow Ptarmigan and Forget-Me-Not	04/14/82	.50	.25	1.25	13
1955	20¢ Arizona: Cactus Wren and Saguaro Cactus Blossom	04/14/82	.50	.25	1.25	13
1956	20¢ Arkansas: Mockingbird and Apple Blossom	04/14/82	.50	.25	1.25	13
1957	20¢ California: California Quail and California Poppy	04/14/82	.50	.25	1.25	13
1958	20¢ Colorado: Lark Bunting and Rocky Mountain Columbine	04/14/82	.50	.25	1.25	13
1959	20¢ Connecticut: Robin and Mountain Laurel	04/14/82	.50	.25	1.25	13
1960	20¢ Delaware: Blue Hen Chicken and Peach Blossom	04/14/82	.50	.25	1.25	13
1961	20¢ Florida: Mockingbird and Orange Blossom	04/14/82	.50	.25	1.25	13
1962	20¢ Georgia: Brown Thrasher and Cherokee Rose	04/14/82	.50	.25	1.25	13
1963	20¢ Hawaii: Hawaiian Goose and Hibiscus	04/14/82	.50	.25	1.25	13
1964	20¢ Idaho: Mountain Bluebird and Syringa	04/14/82	.50	.25	1.25	13
1965	20¢ Illinois: Cardinal and Violet	04/14/82	.50	.25	1.25	13
1966	20¢ Indiana: Cardinal and Peony	04/14/82	.50	.25	1.25	13
1967	20¢ Iowa: Eastern Goldfinch and Wild Rose	04/14/82	.50	.25	1.25	13
1968	20¢ Kansas: Western Meadowlark and Sunflower	04/14/82	.50	.25	1.25	13
1969	20¢ Kentucky: Cardinal and Goldenrod	04/14/82	.50	.25	1.25	13
1970	20¢ Louisiana: Brown Pelican and Magnolia	04/14/82	.50	.25	1.25	13
1971	20¢ Maine: Chickadee and White Pine Cone and Tassel	04/14/82	.50	.25	1.25	13
1972	20¢ Maryland: Baltimore Oriole and Black-Eyed Susan	04/14/82	.50	.25	1.25	13
1973	20¢ Massachusetts: Black-Capped Chickadee and Mayflower	04/14/82	.50	.25	1.25	13
1974	20¢ Michigan: Robin and Apple Blossom	04/14/82	.50	.25	1.25	13
1975	20¢ Minnesota: Common Loon and Showy Lady Slipper	04/14/82	.50	.25	1.25	13
1976	20¢ Mississippi: Mockingbird and Magnolia	04/14/82	.50	.25	1.25	13
1977	20¢ Missouri: Eastern Bluebird and Red Hawthorn	04/14/82	.50	.25	1.25	13

	Issues of 1982		Un	U	FDC	Q(M)
	State Birds & Flowers Issue (continued)					
1978	20¢ Montana: Western Meadowlark & Bitterroot	04/14/82	.50	.25	1.25	13
1979	20¢ Nebraska: Western Meadowlark & Goldenrod	04/14/82	.50	.25	1.25	13
1980	20¢ Nevada: Mountain Bluebird & Sagebrush	04/14/82	.50	.25	1.25	13
1981	20¢ New Hampshire: Purple Finch & Lilac	04/14/82	.50	.25	1.25	13
1982	20¢ New Jersey: American Goldfinch & Violet	04/14/82	.50	.25	1.25	13
1983	20¢ New Mexico: Roadrunner & Yucca Flower	04/14/82	.50	.25	1.25	13
1984	20¢ New York: Eastern Bluebird & Rose	04/14/82	.50	.25	1.25	13
1985	20¢ North Carolina: Cardinal & Flowering Dogwood	04/14/82	.50	.25	1.25	13
1986	20¢ North Dakota: Western Meadowlark & Wild Prairie Rose	04/14/82	.50	.25	1.25	13
1987	20¢ Ohio: Cardinal & Red Carnation	04/14/82	.50	.25	1.25	13
1988	20¢ Oklahoma: Scissor-tailed Flycatcher & Mistletoe	04/14/82	.50	.25	1.25	13
1989	20¢ Oregon: Western Meadowlark & Oregon Grape	04/14/82	.50	.25	1.25	13
1990	20¢ Pennsylvania: Ruffed Grouse & Mountain Laurel	04/14/82	.50	.25	1.25	13
1991	20¢ Rhode Island: Rhode Island Red & Violet	04/14/82	.50	.25	1.25	13
1992	20¢ South Carolina: Carolina Wren & Carolina Jessamine	04/14/82	.50	.25	1.25	13
1993	20¢ South Dakota: Ring-Necked Pheasant & Pasqueflower	04/14/82	.50	.25	1.25	13
1994	20¢ Tennessee: Mockingbird & Iris	04/14/82	.50	.25	1.25	13
1995	20¢ Texas: Mockingbird & Bluebonnet	04/14/82	.50	.25	1.25	13
1996	20¢ Utah: California Gull & Sego Lily	04/14/82	.50	.25	1.25	13
1997	20¢ Vermont: Hermit Thrush & Red Clover	04/14/82	.50	.25	1.25	13
1998	20¢ Virginia: Cardinal & Flowering Dogwood	04/14/82	.50	.25	1.25	13
1999	20¢ Washington: American Goldfinch & Rhododendron	04/14/82	.50	.25	1.25	13
2000	20¢ West Virginia: Cardinal & Rhododendron Maximum	04/14/82	.50	.25	1.25	13
2001	20¢ Wisconsin: Robin & Wood Violet	04/14/82	.50	.25	1.25	13
2002	20¢ Wyoming: Western Meadowlark & Indian Paintbrush	04/14/82	.50	.25	1.25	13
a	Any single, perf. 11.25 x 11		.55	.30		
b	Pane of 50 (with plate #)		25.00	—	30.00	
c	Pane of 50, perf. 11.25 x 11		27.50	—		
d	Pane of 50, imperf.		27,500.00			

Greetings From New Hampshire

New Hampshire takes its state motto, "Live Free or Die," seriously: In 1774, it was first among the 13 American Colonies to declare independence from England. It was also the first state to hold a constitutional convention, in 1778, and to require the submitting of its constitution to state residents for their approval.

Known as the "Granite State," New Hampshire has extensive outcroppings of that ancient rock in the White Mountains of the north. This region is home to an abundance of wildlife watched over by the Old Man of the Mountains, a 40-foot-high natural rock formation that has become the state's most celebrated landmark. Towering over the other peaks is 6,288-foot Mount Washington; it is the highest summit in the Northeast and one of the world's windiest places.

A heavily forested land of enormous scenic beauty, New Hampshire looks to tourism and forestry as major industries within its economy. ■

Montana USA 20c — *Western Meadowlark & Bitterroot* — 1978
Nebraska USA 20c — *Western Meadowlark & Goldenrod* — 1979
Nevada USA 20c — *Mountain Bluebird & Sagebrush* — 1980
New Hampshire USA 20c — *Purple Finch & Lilac* — 1981
New Jersey USA 20c — *American Goldfinch & Violet* — 1982

New Mexico USA 20c — *Roadrunner & Yucca Flower* — 1983
New York USA 20c — *Eastern Bluebird & Rose* — 1984
North Carolina USA 20c — *Cardinal & Flowering Dogwood* — 1985
North Dakota USA 20c — *Western Meadowlark & Wild Prairie Rose* — 1986
Ohio USA 20c — *Cardinal & Red Carnation* — 1987

Oklahoma USA 20c — *Scissor-tailed Flycatcher & Mistletoe* — 1988
Oregon USA 20c — *Western Meadowlark & Oregon Grape* — 1989
Pennsylvania USA 20c — *Ruffed Grouse & Mountain Laurel* — 1990
Rhode Island USA 20c — *Rhode Island Red & Violet* — 1991
South Carolina USA 20c — *Carolina Wren & Carolina Jasmine* — 1992

South Dakota USA 20c — *Ring-Necked Pheasant & Pasqueflower* — 1993
Tennessee USA 20c — *Mockingbird & Iris* — 1994
Texas USA 20c — *Mockingbird & Bluebonnet* — 1995
Utah USA 20c — *California Gull & Sego Lily* — 1996
Vermont USA 20c — *Hermit Thrush & Red Clover* — 1997

Virginia USA 20c — *Cardinal & Flowering Dogwood* — 1998
Washington USA 20c — *American Goldfinch & Rhododendron* — 1999
West Virginia USA 20c — *Cardinal & Rhododendron Maximum* — 2000
Wisconsin USA 20c — *Robin & Wood Violet* — 2001
Wyoming USA 20c — *Western Meadowlark & Indian Paintbrush* — 2002

1982

2003

2004

2005

2006   **2007**

2008   **2009**   **2009a**

2010

2012

2011

2013

2014

America's
ABC
Libraries
XYZ
USA 20c
Legacies To Mankind

2015

2016

2017

2018

2019   **2020**

2021   **2022**   **2022a**

	Issues of 1982		Un	U	PB/PNC/LP	#	FDC	Q(M)
	Perf. 11							
2003	20¢ USA/The Netherlands	04/20/82	.40	.20	3.50	(6)	1.00	109
a	Imperf., pair		325.00					
2004	20¢ Library of Congress	04/21/82	.40	.20	1.75	(4)	1.00	113
	Coil Stamp, Perf. 10 Vertically							
2005	20¢ Consumer Education	04/27/82	.55	.20	25.00	(3)	1.00	
a	Imperf., pair		100.00		400.00	(2)		
b	Tagging omitted		7.50					

Value for plate no. coil strip of 3 stamps is for most common plate nos. Other plate nos. and strips of 5 stamps may have higher values.

	Issues of 1982		Un	U	PB/PNC/LP	#	FDC	Q(M)
	Knoxville World's Fair Issue, Perf. 11							
2006	20¢ Solar Energy	04/29/82	.40	.20			1.00	31
2007	20¢ Synthetic Fuels	04/29/82	.40	.20			1.00	31
2008	20¢ Breeder Reactor	04/29/82	.40	.20			1.00	31
2009	20¢ Fossil Fuels	04/29/82	.40	.20			1.00	31
a	Block of 4, #2006-09		1.65	1.50	2.00	(4)	2.50	
2010	20¢ Horatio Alger	04/30/82	.40	.20	1.75	(4)	1.00	108
2011	20¢ Aging Together	05/21/82	.40	.20	1.75	(4)	1.00	173
	Performing Arts Issue							
2012	20¢ John, Ethel and Lionel Barrymore	06/08/82	.40	.20	1.75	(4)	1.00	107
2013	20¢ Dr. Mary Walker	06/10/82	.40	.20	1.75	(4)	1.00	109
2014	20¢ International Peace Garden	06/30/82	.40	.20	1.75	(4)	1.00	183
a	Black and green omitted		260.00					
2015	20¢ America's Libraries	07/13/82	.40	.20	1.75	(4)	1.00	169
a	Vertical pair, imperf. horizontally		300.00					
b	Tagging omitted		7.50					
	Black Heritage Issue, Perf. 10.5 x 11							
2016	20¢ Jackie Robinson and Robinson Stealing Home Plate	08/02/82	1.10	.20	5.50	(4)	6.00	164
	Perf. 11							
2017	20¢ Touro Synagogue	08/22/82	.40	.20	11.00	(20)	1.25	110
a	Imperf., pair		2,500.00					
2018	20¢ Wolf Trap Farm Park	09/01/82	.40	.20	1.75	(4)	1.00	111
	American Architecture Issue							
2019	20¢ Fallingwater, by Frank Lloyd Wright	09/30/82	.45	.20			1.00	41
2020	20¢ Illinois Institute of Technology, by Ludwig Mies van der Rohe	09/30/82	.45	.20			1.00	41
2021	20¢ Gropius House, by Walter Gropius	09/30/82	.45	.20			1.00	41
2022	20¢ Dulles Airport by Eero Saarinen	09/30/82	.45	.20			1.00	41
a	Block of 4, #2019-22		2.00	1.60	2.50	(4)	2.50	

	Issues of 1982		Un	U	PB	#	FDC	Q(M)
2023	20¢ St. Francis of Assisi	10/07/82	.40	.20	1.75	(4)	1.00	174
2024	20¢ Ponce de Leon	10/12/82	.40	.20	3.25	(6)	1.00	110
a	Imperf., pair		500.00					
	Christmas Issue							
2025	13¢ Puppy and Kitten	11/03/82	.25	.20	1.40	(4)	1.25	234
a	Imperf., pair		650.00					
2026	20¢ Madonna and Child,							
	by Tiepolo	10/28/82	.40	.20	11.00	(20)	1.00	703
a	Imperf., pair		150.00					
b	Horizontal pair, imperf. vertically		—					
c	Vertical pair, imperf. horizontally		—					
	Seasons Greetings Issue							
2027	20¢ Children Sledding	10/28/82	.50	.20			1.00	197
2028	20¢ Children Building							
	a Snowman	10/28/82	.50	.20			1.00	197
2029	20¢ Children Skating	10/28/82	.50	.20			1.00	197
2030	20¢ Children Trimming a Tree	10/28/82	.50	.20			1.00	197
a	Block of 4, #2027-30		2.25	1.50	2.75	(4)	2.50	
b	As "a," imperf.		2,750.00					
c	As "a," imperf. horizontally		3,250.00					
	Issues of 1983							
2031	20¢ Science & Industry	01/19/83	.40	.20	1.75	(4)	1.00	119
a	Black omitted		1,400.00					
	Balloons Issue							
2032	20¢ Intrepid, 1861	03/31/83	.40	.20			1.00	57
2033	20¢ Hot Air Ballooning							
	(wording lower right)	03/31/83	.40	.20			1.00	57
2034	20¢ Hot Air Ballooning							
	(wording upper left)	03/31/83	.40	.20			1.00	57
2035	20¢ Explorer II, 1935	03/31/83	.40	.20			1.00	57
a	Block of 4, #2032-35		1.65	1.50	1.75	(4)	2.50	
b	As "a," imperf.		4,250.00					
c	As "a," right stamp perf.,							
	otherwise imperf.		4,500.00					
2036	20¢ U.S./Sweden Treaty	03/24/83	.40	.20	1.75	(4)	1.00	118
2037	20¢ Civilian Conservation							
	Corps	04/05/83	.40	.20	1.75	(4)	1.00	114
a	Imperf., pair		2,750.00					
2038	20¢ Joseph Priestley	04/13/83	.40	.20	1.75	(4)	1.00	165
2039	20¢ Voluntarism	04/20/83	.40	.20	3.00	(6)	1.25	120
a	Imperf., pair		800.00					
2040	20¢ Concord-German							
	Immigration, Apr. 29	04/29/83	.40	.20	1.75	(4)	1.00	117

2023

2024

2025

2027   **2028**

2026

2029

2030   **2030a**

2032   **2033**

2031

2034   **2035**   **2035a**

2036

2037

2038

2039

2040

1983

2041

2042

2043

2044

2045

2046

2047

2048   2049

2052

2050   2051   2051a

2053

2055   2056

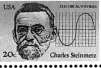

2057   2058   2058a

Issues of 1983		Un	U	PB	#	FDC	Q(M)
2041	20¢ Brooklyn Bridge 05/17/83	.40	.20	1.75	(4)	1.00	182
2042	20¢ Tennessee Valley Authority 05/18/83	.40	.20	11.00	(20)	1.00	114
2043	20¢ Physical Fitness 05/14/83	.40	.20	3.00	(6)	1.00	112
	Black Heritage Issue						
2044	20¢ Scott Joplin Portrait						
	and Joplin Playing the Piano 06/09/83	.40	.20	2.00	(4)	1.00	115
a	Imperf., pair	475.00					
2045	20¢ Medal of Honor 06/07/83	.40	.20	1.75	(4)	4.00	109
a	Red omitted	250.00					
	American Sports Issue, Perf. 10.5 x 11						
2046	20¢ Babe Ruth Hitting						
	a Home Run 07/06/83	1.25	.20	7.00	(4)	5.00	185
	Literary Arts Issue, Perf. 11						
2047	20¢ Nathaniel Hawthorne,						
	by Cephus Giovanni Thompson 07/08/83	.45	.20	2.10	(4)	1.00	111
	Olympic Summer Games Issue (See also #2082-85, C101-12)						
2048	13¢ Discus Thrower 07/28/83	.35	.20			1.25	99
2049	13¢ High Jumper 07/28/83	.35	.20			1.25	99
2050	13¢ Archer 07/28/83	.35	.20			1.25	99
2051	13¢ Boxers 07/28/83	.35	.20			1.25	99
a	Block of 4, #2048-51	1.50	1.25	1.75	(4)	2.50	
	American Bicentennial Issue						
2052	20¢ Signing of Treaty of Paris						
	(John Adams, Benjamin Franklin						
	and John Jay observing David						
	Hartley), by Benjamin West 09/02/83	.40	.20	1.75	(4)	1.00	104
2053	20¢ Civil Service 09/09/83	.40	.20	3.00	(6)	1.00	115
2054	20¢ Metropolitan Opera 09/14/83	.40	.20	1.75	(4)	1.00	113
	American Inventors Issue						
2055	20¢ Charles Steinmetz						
	and Curve on Graph 09/21/83	.45	.20			1.00	48
2056	20¢ Edwin Armstrong and						
	Frequency Modulator 09/21/83	.45	.20			1.00	48
2057	20¢ Nikola Tesla and						
	Induction Motor 09/21/83	.45	.20			1.00	48
2058	20¢ Philo T. Farnsworth and						
	First Television Camera 09/21/83	.45	.20			1.00	48
a	Block of 4, #2055-58	1.80	1.25	2.50	(4)	2.50	
b	As "a," black omitted	350.00					

Brooklyn Bridge

The 3,460-foot-long Brooklyn Bridge was—in the words of ironmaker and future New York City mayor Abram Hewitt—"the crowning glory of an age memorable for great industrial achievements" when it finally spanned the East River in 1883. Designed by John Roebling, it ranked as the longest suspension bridge in the world at the time, and its 276-foot neo-Gothic support towers stood taller than every structure in Manhattan, except for the steeple of the Trinity Church on Wall Street.

For much of the 19th century, crossing the river meant taking crowded ferries and often facing long delays or bad weather. But after the bridge was built, people could walk, bike, ride in wagons or railway cars, and eventually drive automobiles across. It became a vital link in the transportation system and a major influence on both the economy and demographics of the area—especially in Brooklyn, where the population grew from 580,000 to nearly one million between 1883 and 1898. ∎

Issues of 1983		Un	U	PB	#	FDC	Q(M)
Streetcars Issue, Perf. 11							
2059 20¢ First American Streetcar	10/08/83	.45	.20			1.00	52
2060 20¢ Early Electric Streetcar	10/08/83	.45	.20			1.00	52
2061 20¢ "Bobtail" Horsecar	10/08/83	.45	.20			1.00	52
2062 20¢ St. Charles Streetcar	10/08/83	.45	.20			1.00	52
a Block of 4, #2059-62		1.80	1.40	2.50	(4)	2.50	
b As "a," black omitted		425.00					
c As "a," black omitted on #2059, 2061		—					
Christmas Issue							
2063 20¢ Niccolini-Cowper							
Madonna, by Raphael	10/28/83	.40	.20	1.75	(4)	1.00	716
2064 20¢ Santa Claus	10/28/83	.40	.20	3.00	(6)	1.00	849
a Imperf., pair		175.00					
2065 20¢ Martin Luther	11/11/83	.40	.20	1.75	(4)	1.50	165
Issues of 1984							
2066 20¢ 25th Anniversary							
of Alaska Statehood	01/03/84	.40	.20	1.75	(4)	1.00	120
Winter Olympic Games Issue, Perf. 10.5 x 11							
2067 20¢ Ice Dancing	01/06/84	.50	.20			1.00	80
2068 20¢ Downhill Skiing	01/06/84	.50	.20			1.00	80
2069 20¢ Cross-country Skiing	01/06/84	.50	.20			1.00	80
2070 20¢ Hockey	01/06/84	.50	.20			1.00	80
a Block of 4, #2067-70		2.10	1.50	3.00	(4)	2.50	
Perf. 11							
2071 20¢ Federal Deposit							
Insurance Corporation	01/12/84	.40	.20	1.75	(4)	1.25	103

Columbus Landing in Puerto Rico

In 1492, Christopher Columbus left Spain and headed west into the Atlantic Ocean, bound for China. Instead, he found the Americas— unknowingly, of course. On October 12, he made first landfall on a small island, named it San Salvador, and

sailed on in a fruitless search for Asian cities. He arrived back in Spain in March 1493 and began preparations for a second expedition.

A year, a month, and a day after "discovering" San Salvador, Christopher Columbus set foot on Puerto Rico. The Postal Service commemorated the 500th anniversary of this event with a 29-cent stamp issued on November 19, 1993.

In 1493, about 50,000 Arawak Indians inhabited Puerto Rico. Some of them befriended Columbus, pointing out gold nuggets in a river and all but ensuring that the Spanish would be back. Sure enough, 15 years later Ponce de Leon returned to explore more of the island and attempt colonization. ■

2059 **2060**

2061 **2062** **2062a**

2064

2063 **2065**

2067 **2068**

2066 **2071**

2069 **2070** **2070a**

2072

2073

2074

2075

2076   **2077**

2080

2081

2078   **2079**   **2079a**

2082   **2083**

2086

2087

2084   **2085**   **2085a**

Issues of 1984		Un	U	PB	#	FDC	Q(M)
Perf. 11 x 10.5							
2072 20¢ Love	01/31/84	.40	.20	11.50	(20)	1.00	555
a Horizontal pair, imperf. vertically		175.00					
b Tagging omitted		5.00					
Black Heritage Issue, Carter G. Woodson, Perf. 11							
2073 20¢ Carter G. Woodson							
Holding History Book	02/01/84	.40	.20	1.75	(4)	1.00	120
a Horizontal pair, imperf. vertically		1,600.00					
2074 20¢ Soil and Water							
Conservation	02/06/84	.40	.20	1.75	(4)	1.25	107
2075 20¢ 50th Anniversary							
of Credit Union Act	02/10/84	.40	.20	1.75	(4)	1.00	107
Orchids Issue							
2076 20¢ Wild Pink	03/05/84	.50	.20			1.00	77
2077 20¢ Yellow Lady's-Slipper	03/05/84	.50	.20			1.00	77
2078 20¢ Spreading Pogonia	03/05/84	.50	.20			1.00	77
2079 20¢ Pacific Calypso	03/05/84	.50	.20			1.00	77
a Block of 4, #2076-79		2.00	1.50	2.50	(4)	2.50	
2080 20¢ 25th Anniversary							
of Hawaii Statehood	03/12/84	.40	.20	1.70	(4)	1.00	120
2081 20¢ National Archives	04/16/84	.40	.20	1.70	(4)	1.00	108
Olympic Summer Games Issue (See also #2048-52, C101-12)							
2082 20¢ Diving	05/04/84	.55	.20			1.25	78
2083 20¢ Long Jump	05/04/84	.55	.20			1.25	78
2084 20¢ Wrestling	05/04/84	.55	.20			1.25	78
2085 20¢ Kayak	05/04/84	.55	.20			1.25	78
a Block of 4, #2082-85		2.40	1.90	3.50	(4)	2.50	
2086 20¢ Louisiana World							
Exposition	05/11/84	.40	.20	1.75	(4)	1.00	130
2087 20¢ Health Research	05/17/84	.40	.20	1.75	(4)	1.00	120

Greetings From Louisiana

Louisiana lies on the Gulf Coast, where the Mississippi River ends its long journey through the middle of America. Much has changed since the Sieur de La Salle claimed the river's entire watershed for France in 1682, but Louisiana has never forgotten its French heritage.

In New Orleans, the oldest section of the city is called the French Quarter. Here, streets have French names; cafés serve up beignets and café au lait; and Mardi Gras is a major celebration, with elaborate floats rolling through streets jam-packed with partygoers. But the music one might hear here is a New Orleans original known as jazz.

Along the River Road from New Orleans to the state capital at Baton Rouge are several restored plantation houses, reminders of antebellum days when southern aristocracy lived in grand mansions on large cotton plantations. Cotton remains an important part of the Louisiana economy, along with rice, sugarcane, soybeans, seafood, and oil and gas. ■

Issues of 1984		Un	U	PB	#	FDC	Q(M)
Performing Arts Issue, Perf. 11							
2088 20¢ Douglas Fairbanks Portrait							
and Fairbanks in Pirate Role	05/23/84	.40	.20	12.00	(20)	1.00	117
American Sports Issue							
2089 20¢ Jim Thorpe							
on Football Field	05/24/84	.40	.20	2.00	(4)	3.00	116
Performing Arts Issue							
2090 20¢ John McCormack Portrait							
and McCormack in Tenor Role	06/06/84	.40	.20	1.75	(4)	1.00	117
2091 20¢ 25th Anniversary							
of St. Lawrence Seaway	06/26/84	.40	.20	1.75	(4)	1.00	120
2092 20¢ Migratory Bird Hunting							
and Preservation Act	07/02/84	.50	.20	2.50	(4)	1.25	124
a Horizontal pair, imperf. vertically		400.00					
2093 20¢ Roanoke Voyages	07/13/84	.40	.20	1.75	(4)	1.00	120
Pair with full horizontal gutter between		—					
Literary Arts Issue							
2094 20¢ Herman Melville	08/01/84	.40	.20	1.75	(4)	1.25	117
2095 20¢ Horace Moses	08/06/84	.45	.20	3.50	(6)	1.00	117
2096 20¢ Smokey the Bear	08/13/84	.40	.20	2.00	(4)	2.50	96
a Horizontal pair, imperf. between		300.00					
b Vertical pair, imperf. between		250.00					
c Block of 4, imperf. between							
vertically and horizontally		5,500.00					
d Horizontal pair, imperf. vertically		1,750.00					
American Sports Issue							
2097 20¢ Roberto Clemente in Pirates Cap, Puerto							
Rican Flag in Background	08/17/84	1.60	.20	8.00	(4)	9.00	119
a Horizontal pair, imperf. vertically		2,000.00					
American Dogs Issue							
2098 20¢ Beagle and Boston Terrier	09/07/84	.45	.20			1.25	54
2099 20¢ Chesapeake Bay Retriever							
and Cocker Spaniel	09/07/84	.45	.20			1.25	54
2100 20¢ Alaskan Malamute							
and Collie	09/07/84	.45	.20			1.25	54
2101 20¢ Black and Tan Coonhound							
and American Foxhound	09/07/84	.45	.20			1.25	54
a Block of 4, #2098-2101		1.90	1.75	3.00	(4)	3.00	

Saint Lawrence Seaway

In 1959, the United States and Canada completed construction of a complex inland navigation system known as the St. Lawrence Seaway. By doing so, they fulfilled a decades-old dream of allowing deep-draft vessels to travel between the Atlantic Ocean and the Great Lakes.

From Lake Ontario, the St. Lawrence River flows northeastward about 750 miles and empties into the Gulf of St. Lawrence. But before the Seaway opened, a 180-mile stretch of river between the lake and Montreal was a barrier for oceangoing ships: In a series of hazardous rapids, the river drops about 226 feet in elevation. People had built locks and canals to help boats get around the rapids, but these bypasses were never large enough for transoceanic vessels. The Seaway changed all that, replacing them with longer, deeper structures.

Today, the Seaway is a vital link in the Great Lakes-St. Lawrence River system. Each year, thousands of vessels make the 2,340-mile journey from the Atlantic to the western shore of Lake Superior. ■

2088   2089   2090

2091   2092

2093

2094   2095   2096   2097

2098   2099

2100   2101   2101a

2102

2103

2104

2105

2106

2107

2108

2109

2110

2111

2114

2115b

2116

	Issues of 1984		Un	U	PB/PNC	#	FDC	Q(M)
2102	20¢ Crime Prevention	09/26/84	.40	.20	1.75	(4)	1.00	120
2103	20¢ Hispanic Americans	10/31/84	.40	.20	1.75	(4)	1.00	108
a	Vertical pair, imperf. horizontally		2,250.00					
2104	20¢ Family Unity	10/01/84	.40	.20	14.00	(20)	1.00	118
a	Horizontal pair, imperf. vertically		550.00					
b	Tagging omitted		7.50					
2105	20¢ Eleanor Roosevelt	10/11/84	.40	.20	1.75	(4)	1.00	113
2106	20¢ A Nation of Readers	10/16/84	.40	.20	1.75	(4)	1.00	117
	Christmas Issue							
2107	20¢ Madonna and Child,							
	by Fra Filippo Lippi	10/30/84	.40	.20	1.70	(4)	1.00	751
2108	20¢ Santa Claus	10/30/84	.40	.20	1.70	(4)	1.00	786
a	Horizontal pair, imperf. vertically		950.00					
2109	20¢ Vietnam Veterans'							
	Memorial	11/10/84	.40	.20	2.25	(4)	5.00	105
	Issues of 1985, Performing Arts Issue							
2110	22¢ Jerome Kern Portrait and							
	Kern Studying Sheet Music	01/23/85	.40	.20	1.75	(4)	1.00	125
a	Tagging omitted		7.50					
2111	(22¢)"D" Stamp	02/01/85	.55	.20	4.50	(6)	1.00	
a	Imperf., pair		35.00					
b	Vertical pair, imperf. horizontally		1,350.00					
	Coil Stamp, Perf. 10 Vertically							
2112	(22¢)"D" green Eagle (2111)	02/01/85	.60	.20	5.00	(3)	1.00	
a	Imperf., pair		47.50					
b	As "a," tagging omitted		125.00					
	Booklet Stamp, Perf. 11							
2113	(22¢)"D" green Eagle (2111),							
	single from booklet	02/01/85	.80	.20			1.00	
a	Booklet pane of 10	02/01/85	8.50	3.00			7.50	
b	As "a," imperf. between horizontally		—					
	Issues of 1985-87, Flag Over Capitol Issue							
2114	22¢ Flag Over Capitol	03/29/85	.40	.20	1.90	(4)	1.00	
	Pair with full horizontal gutter between		—					
	Coil Stamp, Perf. 10 Vertically							
2115	22¢ Flag Over Capitol (2114)	03/29/85	.40	.20	3.25	(3)	1.00	
a	Narrow block tagging		.40	.20	3.50	(3)	1.00	
b	Inscribed "T" at bottom	05/23/87	.50	.40	3.00	(3)		
c	Black field of stars		—	—				
	#2115b issued for test on prephosphored paper. Paper is whiter and colors are brighter							
	than on 2115.							
d	Tagging omitted		4.50					
e	Imperf., pair		15.00					
	Booklet Stamp, Perf. 10 Horizontally							
2116	22¢ Flag over Capitol,							
	single from booklet		.50	.20			1.00	
a	Booklet pane of 5	03/29/85	2.50	1.25			3.50	
	#2116 issued only in booklets. All stamps are imperf. at both sides or imperf. at both sides							
	and bottom.							

	Issues of 1985		Un	U	PNC	#	FDC
	Seashells Booklet Issue, Perf. 10						
2117	22¢ Frilled Dogwinkle	04/04/85	.40	.20			1.00
2118	22¢ Reticulated Helmet	04/04/85	.40	.20			1.00
2119	22¢ New England Neptune	04/04/85	.40	.20			1.00
2120	22¢ Calico Scallop	04/04/85	.40	.20			1.00
2121	22¢ Lightning Whelk	04/04/85	.40	.20			1.00
a	Booklet pane of 10		4.00	2.50			7.50
b	As "a," violet omitted		800.00				
c	As "a," imperf. between vertically		600.00				
e	Strip of 5, #2117-21		2.00	—			
	Express Mail Booklet Issue, Perf. 10 Vertically						
2122	$10.75 Eagle and Moon,						
	booklet single	04/29/85	19.00	7.50			40.00
a	Booklet pane of 3		60.00	—			95.00
b	Type II		21.00	10.00			
c	As "b," booklet pane of 3		65.00	—			
	#2122 issued only in booklets. All stamps are imperf. at top and bottom or at top, bottom and one side.						
	Issues of 1985-89, Coil Stamps, Transportation Issue (See also #1897-1908, 2225-31, 2252-66, 2451-68)						
2123	3.4¢ School Bus 1920s	06/08/85	.20	.20	.90	(5)	1.00
a	Untagged (Bureau precanceled)		.20	.20	3.75	(5)	
2124	4.9¢ Buckboard 1880s	06/21/85	.20	.20	.90	(5)	1.00
a	Untagged (Bureau precanceled)		.20	.20	1.50	(5)	
2125	5.5¢ Star Route Truck 1910s	11/01/86	.20	.20	1.65	(5)	1.00
a	Untagged (Bureau precanceled)		.20	.20	2.00	(5)	
2126	6¢ Tricycle 1880s	05/06/85	.20	.20	1.80	(5)	1.00
a	Untagged (Bureau precanceled)		.20	.20	1.75	(5)	
b	As "a," imperf., pair		200.00				
2127	7.1¢ Tractor 1920s	02/06/87	.20	.20	2.40	(5)	1.00
a	Untagged (Bureau precanceled "Nonprofit org.")		.20	.20	3.25	(5)	5.00
b	Untagged (Bureau precanceled "Nonprofit 5-Digit ZIP + 4")	05/26/89	.20	.20	1.75	(5)	
2128	8.3¢ Ambulance 1860s	06/21/85	.20	.20	1.50	(5)	1.00
a	Untagged (Bureau precanceled)		.20	.20	1.50	(5)	
2129	8.5¢ Tow Truck 1920s	01/24/87	.20	.20	3.00	(5)	1.25
a	Untagged (Bureau precanceled)		.20	.20	2.75	(5)	
2130	10.1¢ Oil Wagon 1890s	04/18/85	.25	.20	2.50	(5)	1.25
a	Untagged (Bureau precanceled, red)		.25	.25	2.25	(5)	1.25
	Untagged (Bureau precanceled, black)		.25	.25	2.50	(5)	
b	As "a," red precancel, imperf., pair		15.00		100.00	(6)	
	As "a," black precancel, imperf., pair		100.00				
2131	11¢ Stutz Bearcat 1933	06/11/85	.25	.20	1.75	(5)	1.25
2132	12¢ Stanley Steamer 1909	04/02/85	.25	.20	2.50	(5)	1.25
a	Untagged (Bureau precanceled)		.25	.25	2.50	(5)	
b	As "a," type II		.40	.30	19.00	(5)	
	Type II has "Stanley Steamer 1909" .5 mm shorter (17.5 mm) than #2132 (18mm).						
2133	12.5¢ Pushcart 1880s	04/18/85	.25	.20	2.75	(5)	1.25
a	Untagged (Bureau precanceled)		.25	.25	3.00	(5)	
b	As "a," imperf., pair		55.00				
2134	14¢ Iceboat 1880s	03/23/85	.30	.20	2.25	(5)	1.25
a	Imperf., pair		100.00				
b	Type II		.30	.20	3.25	(5)	
2135	17¢ Dog Sled 1920s	08/20/86	.30	.20	3.25	(5)	1.25
a	Imperf., pair		500.00				
2136	25¢ Bread Wagon 1880s	11/22/86	.45	.20	3.75	(5)	1.25
a	Imperf., pair		10.00				
b	Pair, imperf. between		750.00				
c	Tagging omitted		25.00				

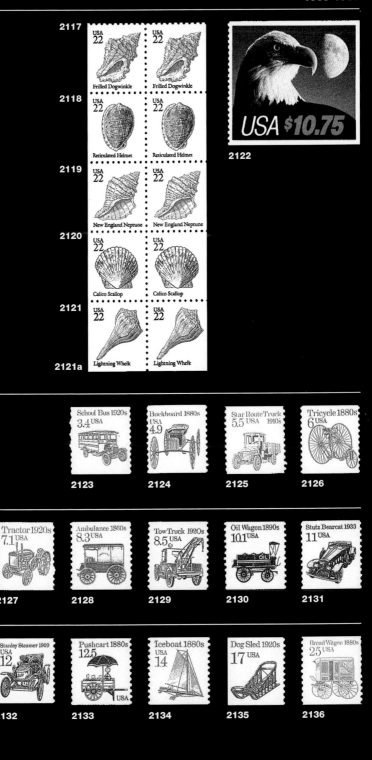

2117 USA 22 Frilled Dogwinkle — Frilled Dogwinkle

2118 USA 22 Reticulated Helmet — Reticulated Helmet

2119 USA 22 New England Neptune — New England Neptune

2120 USA 22 Calico Scallop — Calico Scallop

2121 USA 22 Lightning Whelk — Lightning Whelk

2121a

2122 USA $10.75

2123 School Bus 1920s 3.4 USA

2124 Buckboard 1880s USA 4.9

2125 Star Route Truck 5.5 USA 1910s

2126 Tricycle 1880s 6 USA

2127 Tractor 1920s 7.1 USA

2128 Ambulance 1860s 8.3 USA

2129 TowTruck 1920s 8.5 USA

2130 Oil Wagon 1890s 10.1 USA

2131 Stutz Bearcat 1933 11 USA

2132 Stanley Steamer 1909 USA 12

2133 Pushcart 1880s 12.5 USA

2134 Iceboat 1880s USA 14

2135 Dog Sled 1920s 17 USA

2136 Bread Wagon 1880s 25 USA

2137

2138   2139

2140   **2141**   **2141a**

2142

2143

2144

2145

2146

2147

2149

2150

2152

2153

Issues of 1985		Un	U	PB/PNC	#	FDC	Q(M)
Black Heritage Issue, Perf. 11							
2137 22¢ Mary McLeod Bethune	03/05/85	.40	.20	2.50	(4)	1.00	120
American Folk Art: Duck Decoys Issue							
2138 22¢ Broadbill Decoy	03/22/85	.65	.20			1.00	75
2139 22¢ Mallard Decoy	03/22/85	.65	.20			1.00	75
2140 22¢ Canvasback Decoy	03/22/85	.65	.20			1.00	75
2141 22¢ Redhead Decoy	03/22/85	.65	.20			1.00	75
a Block of 4, #2138-41		4.00	2.25	5.50	(4)	2.75	
2142 22¢ Winter Special Olympics	03/25/85	.40	.20	1.75	(4)	1.00	121
a Vertical pair, imperf. horizontally		600.00					
2143 22¢ Love	04/17/85	.40	.20	1.70	(4)	1.00	730
a Imperf., pair		1,500.00					
2144 22¢ Rural Electrification							
Administration	05/11/85	.45	.20	20.00	(20)	1.00	125
2145 22¢ AMERIPEX '86	05/25/85	.40	.20	1.75	(4)	1.00	203
a Red, black and blue omitted		200.00					
b Red and black omitted		1,250.00					
2146 22¢ Abigail Adams	06/14/85	.40	.20	1.90	(4)	1.00	126
a Imperf., pair		275.00					
2147 22¢ Frederic A. Bartholdi	07/18/85	.40	.20	1.90	(4)	1.00	130
2148 Not assigned							
Coil Stamps, Perf. 10 Vertically							
2149 18¢ George Washington,							
Washington Monument	11/06/85	.35	.20	3.00	(5)	1.25	
a Untagged (Bureau precanceled)		.35	.35	2.75	(5)		
b Imperf., pair		950.00					
c As "a," imperf. pair		800.00					
d Tagging omitted		—	—				
e As "a," tagged (error), dull gum		2.00	1.75	—			
2150 21.1¢ Sealed Envelopes	10/22/85	.40	.20	3.25	(5)	1.25	
a Untagged (Bureau precanceled)		.40	.40	40.00	(5)		
b As "a," tagged (error)		.40	.40	3.25	(5)		
2151 Not assigned							
Perf. 11							
2152 22¢ Korean War Veterans	07/26/85	.40	.20	2.50	(4)	3.00	120
2153 22¢ Social Security Act,							
50th Anniversary	08/14/85	.40	.20	1.90	(4)	1.00	120

Statue of Liberty

"We will not forget that Liberty has here made her home," said President Grover Cleveland at the 1886 dedication ceremony for the Statue of Liberty—a powerful symbol of democracy, freedom, and the friendship between two nations. A gift from the people of France to the people of the United States, the 151-foot-tall statue stands atop a 154-foot pedestal on Liberty Island in New York Harbor. The pedestal itself was made in America, and largely financed through the fund-raising efforts of publisher Joseph Pulitzer; inside it are museum exhibits and an observation deck, from which visitors can gaze out upon the harbor. A 354-step climb to the statue's crown affords an even better view.

French sculptor Frederic Auguste Bartholdi designed the statue, with the engineering assistance of Alexandre Gustave Eiffel—best known for the Eiffel Tower. Together, they produced one of the most widely recognized landmarks in the world. Designated a national monument in 1924, "Liberty" still lifts her lamp beside America's shores. ■

Issues of 1985, Perf. 11		Un	U	PB	#	FDC	Q(M)
2154 22¢ World War I Veterans	08/26/85	.40	.20	2.25	(4)	3.00	120
American Horses Issue							
2155 22¢ Quarter Horse	09/25/85	1.00	.20			1.50	37
2156 22¢ Morgan	09/25/85	1.00	.20			1.50	37
2157 22¢ Saddlebred	09/25/85	1.00	.20			1.50	37
2158 22¢ Appaloosa	09/25/85	1.00	.20			1.50	37
a Block of 4, #2155-58		6.00	4.50	8.50	(4)	3.00	
2159 22¢ Public Education	10/01/85	.45	.20	2.75	(4)	1.00	120
International Youth Year Issue							
2160 22¢ YMCA Youth Camping	10/07/85	.65	.20			1.00	33
2161 22¢ Boy Scouts	10/07/85	.65	.20			2.00	33
2162 22¢ Big Brothers/Big Sisters	10/07/85	.65	.20			1.00	33
2163 22¢ Camp Fire	10/07/85	.65	.20			1.00	33
a Block of 4, #2160-63		3.00	2.25	4.50	(4)	2.50	
2164 22¢ Help End Hunger	10/15/85	.45	.20	2.00	(4)	1.00	120
Christmas Issue							
2165 22¢ Genoa Madonna, by Luca Della Robbia	10/30/85	.40	.20	1.75	(4)	1.00	759
a Imperf., pair		*100.00*					
2166 22¢ Poinsettia Plants	10/30/85	.40	.20	1.70	(4)	1.00	758
a Imperf., pair		*130.00*					

Greetings From Kentucky

In 1775, frontiersman Daniel Boone led westbound settlers through the Cumberland Gap—now part of a national historical park encompassing more than 20,000 acres in Kentucky, Tennessee, and Virginia. Seventeen years later, the land of Kentucky joined the Union as the first state on the west side of the Appalachian Mountains.

Nicknamed the "Bluegrass State" for its well-known grass with the bluish-green stems, Kentucky claims fame on other fronts as well. It holds vast deposits of coal in its hilly eastern region, protects a wealth of gold at Fort Knox, boasts the longest known cave system in the world at Mammoth Cave National Park, and leads the nation in the breeding of Thoroughbreds. Each May, the state plays host to the Kentucky Derby, one of the world's premier horse-racing events. The "run for the roses" has been held at Churchill Downs in Louisville every year since 1875. ■

2154

2155   **2156**

2157   **2158**   **2158a**

2159

2160   **2161**

2162   **2163**   **2163a**

2164

2165

2166

2167

2168

2169

2170

2171

2172

2173

2175

2176

2177

2178

2179

2180

2181

2182

2183

2184

2185

2186

2187

2188

2189

2190

2191

	Issues of 1986		Un	U	PB	#	FDC	Q(M)
2167	22¢ Arkansas Statehood	01/03/86	.40	.20	2.00	(4)	1.00	130
a	Vertical pair, imperf. horizontally		—					
	Issues of 1986-91, Great Americans Issue (See also #1844-69)							
2168	1¢ Margaret Mitchell	06/30/86	.20	.20	.25	(4)	1.50	
a	Tagging omitted		5.00					
2169	2¢ Mary Lyon	02/28/87	.20	.20	.30	(4)	1.00	
a	Untagged		.20	.20	.35	(4)		
2170	3¢ Paul Dudley White, MD	09/15/86	.20	.20	.50	(4)	1.00	
a	Untagged, dull gum		.20	.20	.50	(4)		
2171	4¢ Father Flanagan	07/14/86	.20	.20	.60	(4)	1.00	
a	Grayish violet, untagged		.20	.20	.40	(4)		
b	Deep grayish blue, untagged		.20	.20	.50	(4)		
2172	5¢ Hugo L. Black	02/27/86	.20	.20	.65	(4)	1.00	
a	Tagging omitted		10.00					
2173	5¢ Luis Munoz Marin	02/18/90	.20	.20	.75	(4)	1.25	
a	Untagged		.20	.20	.60	(4)		
2174	Not assigned							
2175	10¢ Red Cloud	08/15/87	.20	.20	.85	(4)	1.75	
a	Overall tagging	1990	.30	.20	10.00	(4)		
b	Tagging omitted		12.50					
c	Prephosphored coated paper (solid tagging)		.30	.20	1.40	(4)		
d	Prephosphored uncoated paper (mottled tagging)		.20	.20	1.25	(4)		
e	Carmine, prephosphored uncoated paper (mottled tagging)		.25	.20	1.25	(4)		
2176	14¢ Julia Ward Howe	02/12/87	.25	.20	1.50	(4)	1.00	
2177	15¢ Buffalo Bill Cody	06/06/88	.30	.20	6.00	(4)	1.75	
a	Overall tagging	1990	.30	—	3.25	(4)		
b	Prephosphored coated paper (solid tagging)		.40	—	3.25	(4)		
c	Tagging omitted		15.00	—				
2178	17¢ Belva Ann Lockwood	06/18/86	.35	.20	2.00	(4)	1.00	
a	Tagging omitted		10.00					
	Perf. 11 x 11.1							
2179	20¢ Virginia Apgar	10/24/94	.40	.20	2.00	(4)	1.50	
a	Orange brown		.40	.20	2.25	(4)		
	Perf. 11							
2180	21¢ Chester Carlson	10/21/88	.40	.20	2.50	(4)	1.25	
2181	23¢ Mary Cassatt	11/04/88	.45	.20	2.50	(4)	1.25	
a	Overall tagging, dull gum		.45	—	5.00	(4)		
b	Prephosphored coated paper (solid tagging)		.60	—	3.25	(4)		
c	Prephosphored uncoated paper (mottled tagging)		.50	.20	3.25	(4)		
d	Tagging omitted		7.50					
2182	25¢ Jack London	01/11/86	.45	.20	2.75	(4)	1.50	
a	Booklet pane of 10	05/03/88	4.50	3.75			6.00	
b	Tagging omitted	1990	—					
2183	28¢ Sitting Bull	09/28/89	.50	.20	2.50	(4)	1.50	
2184	29¢ Earl Warren	03/09/92	.55	.20	2.50	(4)	1.25	
	Perf. 11.5 x 11							
2185	29¢ Thomas Jefferson	04/13/93	.50	.20	2.50	(4)	1.25	
2186	35¢ Dennis Chavez	04/03/91	.65	.20	3.25	(4)	1.25	
2187	40¢ Claire Lee Chennault	09/06/90	.70	.20	3.75	(4)	2.00	
a	Prephosphored coated paper (solid tagging)		.75	.35	4.25	(4)		
b	Prephosphored uncoated paper (mottled tagging)		.75	.20	7.50	(4)		
2188	45¢ Harvey Cushing, MD	06/17/88	.85	.20	3.75	(4)	1.25	
a	Overall tagging	1990	1.65	.20	11.00	(4)		
b	Tagging omitted		15.00					
2189	52¢ Hubert H. Humphrey	06/03/91	1.10	.20	7.50	(4)	1.40	
a	Prephosphored uncoated paper (mottled tagging)		1.10	—	5.50	(4)		
2190	56¢ John Harvard	09/03/86	1.10	.20	6.00	(4)	2.50	
2191	65¢ H.H. 'Hap' Arnold	11/05/88	1.20	.20	5.00	(4)	2.50	

1986-1992

	Issues of 1986-1992		Un	U	PB	#	FDC	Q(M)
	Perf. 11							
2192	75¢ Wendell Willkie	02/16/92	1.30	.20	5.50	(4)	2.75	
a	Prephosphored uncoated paper (mottled tagging)	1.30	—		5.50	(4)		
2193	$1 Bernard Revel	09/23/86	2.50	.50	14.00	(4)	3.50	
2194	$1 Johns Hopkins	06/07/89	1.75	.50	7.00	(4)	3.50	
b	Overall tagging	1990	1.75	.50	7.00	(4)		
c	Tagging omitted		*10.00*					
d	Dark blue, prephosphored coated paper							
	(solid tagging)		1.75	.50	7.00	(4)		
e	Blue, prephosphored uncoated paper							
	(mottled tagging)		2.00	.60	8.00	(4)		
f	Blue, prephosphored coated paper							
	(grainy solid tagging)		1.75	.50	7.00	(4)		
2195	$2 William Jennings Bryan	03/19/86	3.50	.50	15.00	(4)	5.50	
a	Tagging omitted		*45.00*					
2196	$5 Bret Harte	08/25/87	8.00	1.00	32.50	(4)	20.00	
a	Tagging omitted		—					
b	Prephosphored paper (solid tagging)		8.00	—	32.50	(4)		
	Booklet Stamp, Perf. 10							
2197	25¢ Jack London (2182), single from booklet.	45	.45	.20		1.25		
a	Booklet pane of 6	05/03/88	3.00	2.25			4.00	
b	Tagging omitted		*4.50*					
c	As "b," booklet pane of 6		*60.00*					
	United States — Sweden Stamp Collecting Booklet Issue, Perf. 10 Vertically							
2198	22¢ Handstamped Cover	01/23/86	.45	.20			1.00	17
2199	22¢ Boy Examining							
	Stamp Collection	01/23/86	.45	.20			1.00	17
2200	22¢ #836 Under Magnifying							
	Glass	01/23/86	.45	.20			1.00	17
2201	22¢ 1986 Presidents							
	Miniature Sheet	01/23/86	.45	.20			1.00	17
a	Booklet pane of 4, #2198-2201		2.00	*1.75*			4.00	17
b	As "a," black omitted							
	on #2198, 2201		65.00	—				
c	As "a," blue omitted							
	on #2198-2200		*2,500.00*					
d	As "a," buff omitted		—					
	#2198-2201 issued only in booklets. All stamps are imperf. at top and bottom or imperf. at top, bottom and right side.							
	Perf. 11							
2202	22¢ Love	01/30/86	.40	.20	1.75	(4)	1.50	949
	Black Heritage Issue							
2203	22¢ Sojourner Truth							
	and Truth Lecturing	02/04/86	.40	.20	1.75	(4)	2.00	130
2204	22¢ Republic of Texas,							
	150th Anniversary	03/02/86	.40	.20	1.75	(4)	1.50	137
a	Horizontal pair, imperf. vertically		*1,100.00*					
b	Dark red omitted		*2,750.00*					
c	Dark blue omitted		*8,500.00*					
	Fish Booklet Issue, Perf. 10 Horizontally							
2205	22¢ Muskellunge	03/21/86	.50	.20			1.25	44
2206	22¢ Atlantic Cod	03/21/86	.50	.20			1.25	44
2207	22¢ Largemouth Bass	03/21/86	.50	.20			1.25	44
2208	22¢ Bluefin Tuna	03/21/86	.50	.20			1.25	44
2209	22¢ Catfish	03/21/86	.50	.20			1.25	44
a	Booklet pane of 5, #2205-09		4.50	*2.75*			3.50	44
	#2205-09 issued only in booklets. All stamps are imperf. at sides or imperf. at sides and bottom.							

2192   2193   2194   2195   2196

2198   2199   2200   2201   2201a

2202

2203

2205

2206

2207

2208

2204

2209

2209a

255

2210

2211

2216a

2216b

2216c

2216d

2216e

2216f

2216g

2216h

2216i

2217a

2217b

2217c

2217d

2217e

2217f

2217g

2217h

2217i

Issues of 1986		Un	U	PB	#	FDC	Q(M)
Perf. 11							
2210 22¢ Public Hospitals	04/11/86	.40	.20	1.75	(4)	1.00	130
a Vertical pair, imperf. horizontally		325.00					
b Horizontal pair, imperf. vertically		1,350.00					
Performing Arts Issue							
2211 22¢ Duke Ellington							
and Piano Keys	04/29/86	.40	.20	1.90	(4)	1.75	130
a Vertical pair, imperf. horizontally		1,000.00					
2212-15 Not assigned							
AMERIPEX '86 Issue, Presidents Miniature Sheets							
2216 Sheet of 9	05/22/86	4.25	—			4.00	6
a 22¢ George Washington		.45	.25			1.50	
b 22¢ John Adams		.45	.25			1.50	
c 22¢ Thomas Jefferson		.45	.25			1.50	
d 22¢ James Madison		.45	.25			1.50	
e 22¢ James Monroe		.45	.25			1.50	
f 22¢ John Quincy Adams		.45	.25			1.50	
g 22¢ Andrew Jackson		.45	.25			1.50	
h 22¢ Martin Van Buren		.45	.25			1.50	
i 22¢ William H. Harrison		.45	.25			1.50	
j Blue omitted		3,500.00					
k Black inscription omitted		2,000.00					
l Imperf.		10,500.00					
2217 Sheet of 9	05/22/86	4.25	—			4.00	6
a 22¢ John Tyler		.45	.25			1.50	
b 22¢ James Polk		.45	.25			1.50	
c 22¢ Zachary Taylor		.45	.25			1.50	
d 22¢ Millard Fillmore		.45	.25			1.50	
e 22¢ Franklin Pierce		.45	.25			1.50	
f 22¢ James Buchanan		.45	.25			1.50	
g 22¢ Abraham Lincoln		.45	.25			1.50	
h 22¢ Andrew Johnson		.45	.25			1.50	
i 22¢ Ulysses S. Grant		.45	.25			1.50	

Presidents of
the United States: I

AMERIPEX 86
International
Stamp Show
Chicago, Illinois
May 22-June 1, 1986

#2216

Presidents of
the United States: II

AMERIPEX 86
International
Stamp Show
Chicago, Illinois
May 22-June 1, 1986

#2217

1986

	Issues of 1986		Un	U	FDC	Q(M)
	AMERIPEX '86 Issue (continued), Presidents Miniature Sheets					
2218	Sheet of 9	05/22/86	4.25	—	4.00	6
a	22¢ Rutherford B. Hayes		.45	.25	1.50	
b	22¢ James A. Garfield		.45	.25	1.50	
c	22¢ Chester A. Arthur		.45	.25	1.50	
d	22¢ Grover Cleveland		.45	.25	1.50	
e	22¢ Benjamin Harrison		.45	.25	1.50	
f	22¢ William McKinley		.45	.25	1.50	
g	22¢ Theodore Roosevelt		.45	.25	1.50	
h	22¢ William H. Taft		.45	.25	1.50	
i	22¢ Woodrow Wilson		.45	.25	1.50	
j	Brown omitted		—			
k	Black inscription omitted		*2,9000.00*			
2219	Sheet of 9	05/22/86	4.25	—	4.00	6
a	22¢ Warren G. Harding		.45	.25	1.50	
b	22¢ Calvin Coolidge		.45	.25	1.50	
c	22¢ Herbert Hoover		.45	.25	1.50	
d	22¢ Franklin D. Roosevelt		.45	.25	1.50	
e	22¢ White House		.45	.25	1.50	
f	22¢ Harry S. Truman		.45	.25	1.50	
g	22¢ Dwight D. Eisenhower		.45	.25	1.50	
h	22¢ John F. Kennedy		.45	.25	2.50	
i	22¢ Lyndon B. Johnson		.45	.25	1.50	
j	Blackish blue inscription omitted		—			
k	Tagging omitted		—			

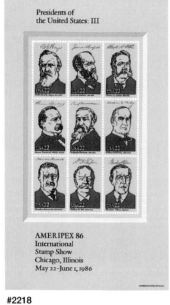

#2218

#2219

USA 22

Rutherford B. Hayes 1877-1881

2218a

USA 22

James A. Garfield 1880-1881

2218b

USA 22

Chester A. Arthur 1881-1885

2218c

USA 22

Grover Cleveland 1885-89, 1893-97

2218d

USA 22

Benjamin Harrison 1889-1893

2218e

USA 22

William McKinley 1897-1901

2218f

USA 22

Theodore Roosevelt 1901-1909

2218g

USA 22

William H. Taft 1909-1913

2218h

USA 22

Woodrow Wilson 1913-1921

2218i

USA 22

Warren G. Harding 1921-1923

2219a

USA 22

Calvin Coolidge 1923-1929

2219b

USA 22

Herbert C. Hoover 1929-1933

2219c

USA 22

Franklin D. Roosevelt 1933-1945

2219d

USA 22

The White House

2219e

USA 22

Harry S. Truman 1945-1953

2219f

USA 22

Dwight D. Eisenhower 1953-1961

2219g

USA 22

John F. Kennedy 1961-1963

2219h

USA 22

Lyndon B. Johnson 1963-1969

2219i

2220 2221

Elisha Kent Kane

Adolphus W. Greely

Vilhjalmur Stefansson

Robert E. Peary, Matthew Henson

2222 2223 2223a

2224

Omnibus 1880s

2225

Locomotive 1870s

2226

2235 2236

Navajo Art USA 22

Navajo Art USA 22

Navajo Art USA 22

Navajo Art USA 22

2237 2238 2238a

T.S. Eliot

22 USA

2239

2240 2241

Wood Carving: Highlander Figure

Wood Carving: Ship Figurehead

Folk Art USA 22

Folk Art USA 22

Wood Carving: Nautical Figure

Wood Carving: Cigar-Store Figure

Folk Art USA 22

Folk Art USA 22

2242 2243 2243a

CHRISTMAS 22
Perugino, National Gallery

2244

GREETINGS

2245

1837-1987
Michigan Statehood

2246

Pan American Games Indianapolis 1987

2247

LOVE

USA 22

2248

Jean Baptiste
Pointe Du Sable 22

Black Heritage USA

2249

	Issues of 1986		Un	U	PB/PNC	#	FDC	Q(M)
	Arctic Explorers Issue, Perf. 11							
2220	22¢ Elisha Kent Kane	05/28/86	.65	.20			1.00	33
2221	22¢ Adolphus W. Greely	05/28/86	.65	.20			1.00	33
2222	22¢ Vilhjalmur Stefansson	05/28/86	.65	.20			1.00	33
2223	22¢ Robt. Peary, Matt. Henson	05/28/86	.65	.20			1.00	33
a	Block of 4, #2220-23		2.75	2.25	4.50	(4)	2.50	
b	As "a," black omitted		9,500.00					
2224	22¢ Statue of Liberty	07/04/86	.40	.20	2.25	(4)	2.00	221
	Issues of 1986-1987, Reengraved Transportation Issue, Coil Stamps, Perf. 10 Vertically							
	(See also #1897-1908, 2123-36, 2252-66, 2452-53A, 2457, 2464, 2468)							
2225	1¢ Omnibus	11/26/86	.20	.20	.60	(5)	1.00	
a	Prephosphored uncoated paper (mottled tagging)		.20	.20	13.00	(5)		
b	Untagged, dull gum		.20	.20	.75	(5)		
c	Imperf., pair		2,000.00					
2226	2¢ Locomotive	03/06/87	.20	.20	.75	(5)	1.50	
a	Untagged, dull gum		.20	.20	.65	(5)		
2227, 2229-30, 2232-34 Not assigned								
2228	4¢ Stagecoach (1898A)	08/86	.20	.20	1.25	(5)		
a	Overall tagging		.70	.20	11.00	(5)		
b	Imperf., pair		300.00					
2231	8.3¢ Ambulance (2128)							
	(Bureau precanceled)	08/29/86	.20	.20	5.00	(5)		

On #2228, "Stagecoach 1890s" is 17mm long; on #1898A, it is 19.5mm long. On #2231, "Ambulance 1860s" is 18mm long; on #2128, it is 18.5mm long.

	American Folk Art: Navajo Art Issue, Perf. 11							
2235	22¢ Navajo Art, four "+" marks horizontally through middle	09/04/86	.50	.20			1.00	60
2236	22¢ Navajo Art, vertical diamond pattern	09/04/86	.50	.20			1.00	60
2237	22¢ Navajo Art, horizontal diamond pattern	09/04/86	.50	.20			1.00	60
2238	22¢ Navajo Art, jagged line horizontally through middle	09/04/86	.50	.20			1.00	60
a	Block of 4, #2235-38		2.50	2.00	4.00	(4)	2.50	
b	As "a," black omitted		350.00					
	Literary Arts Issue							
2239	22¢ T.S. Eliot	09/26/86	.40	.20	1.90	(4)	1.00	132
	American Folk Art: Wood Carved Figurines Issue							
2240	22¢ Highlander Figure	10/01/86	.40	.20			1.00	60
2241	22¢ Ship Figurehead	10/01/86	.40	.20			1.00	60
2242	22¢ Nautical Figure	10/01/86	.40	.20			1.00	60
2243	22¢ Cigar Store Figure	10/01/86	.40	.20			1.00	60
a	Block of 4, #2240-43		1.75	1.75	3.00	(4)	2.50	
b	As "a," imperf. vertically		1,500.00					
	Christmas Issue							
2244	22¢ Madonna and Child	10/24/86	.40	.20	2.00	(4)	1.00	690
2245	22¢ Village Scene	10/24/86	.40	.20	1.90	(4)	1.00	882
	Issues of 1987							
2246	22¢ Michigan Statehood	01/26/87	.40	.20	1.90	(4)	1.00	167
	Pair with full vertical gutter between							
2247	22¢ Pan American Games	01/29/87	.40	.20	1.90	(4)	1.00	167
a	Silver omitted		1,500.00					
	Perf. 11.5 x 11							
2248	22¢ Love	01/30/87	.40	.20	1.90	(4)	1.25	842
	Black Heritage Issue, Perf. 11							
2249	22¢ Jean Baptiste Point Du Sable and Chicago Settlement	02/20/87	.40	.20	1.90	(4)	1.00	143
a	Tagging omitted		10.00					

Issues of 1987-1988		Un	U	PNC	#	FDC	Q(M)
Performing Arts Issue							
2250 22¢ Enrico Caruso as the Duke							
of Mantua in Rigoletti	02/27/87	.40	.20	1.90	(4)	1.00	130
a Black (engr.) omitted		5,000.00					
2251 22¢ Girl Scouts	03/12/87	.40	.20	1.90	(4)	2.50	150
a All litho colors omitted		2,500.00					
Coil Stamps, Transportation Issue, Perf. 10 Vertically							
(See also #1897-1908, 2123-36, 2225-31, 2451-68)							
2252 3¢ Conestoga Wagon 1800s	02/29/88	.20	.20	1.00	(5)	1.00	
a Untagged, dull gum		.20	.20	1.25	(5)		
2253 5¢ Milk Wagon 1900s	09/25/87	.20	.20	.90	(5)	1.00	
2254 5.3¢ Elevator 1900s,							
Bureau precanceled	09/16/88	.20	.20	1.50	(5)	1.25	
2255 7.6¢ Carreta 1770s,							
Bureau precanceled	08/30/88	.20	.20	2.40	(5)	1.25	
2256 8.4¢ Wheel Chair 1920s,							
Bureau precanceled	08/12/88	.20	.20	2.25	(5)	1.25	
a Imperf., pair		700.00					
2257 10¢ Canal Boat 1880s	04/11/87	.20	.20	2.75	(5)	1.00	
a Overall tagging, dull gum		.20	.20	5.00	(5)		
b Prephosphored uncoated paper		.20	.20	3.75	(5)		
d Tagging omitted		20.00					
2258 13¢ Patrol Wagon 1880s,							
Bureau precanceled	10/29/88	.25	.25	3.50	(5)	1.50	
2259 13.2¢ Coal Car 1870s,							
Bureau precanceled	07/19/88	.25	.25	2.75	(5)	1.50	
a Imperf., pair		100.00					
2260 15¢ Tugboat 1900s	07/12/88	.25	.20	2.25	(5)	1.25	
a Overall tagging		.25	.20	3.25	(5)		
b Tagging omitted		3.75					
c Imperf., pair		800.00					
2261 16.7¢ Popcorn Wagon 1902,							
Bureau precanceled	07/07/88	.30	.30	3.25	(5)	1.25	
a Imperf., pair		225.00					
2262 17.5¢ Racing Car 1911	09/25/87	.30	.20	3.50	(5)	1.00	
a Untagged (Bureau precanceled)		.35	.30	3.75	(5)		
b Imperf., pair		2,250.00					
2263 20¢ Cable Car 1880s	10/28/88	.35	.20	3.50	(5)	1.50	
a Imperf., pair		75.00					
b Overall tagging		.35	.20	7.50	(5)		
2264 20.5¢ Fire Engine 1920s,							
Bureau precanceled	09/28/88	.40	.40	4.50	(5)	2.00	
2265 21¢ Railroad Mail Car 1920s,							
Bureau precanceled	08/16/88	.40	.40	3.75	(5)	1.50	
a Imperf., pair		65.00					
2266 24.1¢ Tandem Bicycle 1890s,							
Bureau precanceled	10/26/88	.45	.45	4.00	(5)	1.75	
Issues of 1987, Special Occasions Booklet Issue, Perf. 10							
2267 22¢ Congratulations!	04/20/87	.60	.20			1.00	1,222
2268 22¢ Get Well!	04/20/87	.75	.20			1.00	611
2269 22¢ Thank you!	04/20/87	.75	.20			1.00	611
2270 22¢ Love You, Dad!	04/20/87	.75	.20			1.00	611
2271 22¢ Best Wishes!	04/20/87	.75	.20			1.00	611
2272 22¢ Happy Birthday!	04/20/87	.60	.20			1.00	1,222
2273 22¢ Love You, Mother!	04/20/87	1.00	.20			1.00	611
2274 22¢ Keep In Touch!	04/20/87	.75	.20			1.00	611
a Booklet pane of 10, #2268-71, 2273-74							
and 2 each of #2267, 2272		8.00	5.00			5.00	611

#2267-74 issued only in booklets. All stamps are imperf. at one or two sides or imperf. at sides and bottom.

Enrico Caruso 22USA

2250

GIRL SCOUTS USA 22

2251

Conestoga Wagon 1800s
3 USA

2252

Milk Wagon 1900s
5 USA

2253

Elevator 1900s
5.3 USA
Nonprofit Carrier Route Sort

2254

Carreta 1770s
7.6 USA
Nonprofit

2255

Wheel Chair 1920s
8.4 USA
Nonprofit

2256

Canal Boat 1880s
10 USA

2257

Patrol Wagon 1880s
USA 13 Presorted First-Class

2258

Coal Car 1870s
13.2 USA Bulk Rate

2259

Tugboat 1900s
USA 15

2260

Popcorn Wagon 1902
16.7 USA Bulk Rate

2261

Racing Car 1911
USA 17.5

2262

Cable Car 1880s
USA 20

2263

Fire Engine 1900s
20.5 USA ZIP+4 Presort

2264

Railroad Mail Car 1920s Presorted First-Class
21 USA

2265

Tandem Bicycle 1890s
24.1 USA ZIP+4

2266

2267
Congratulations! USA 22

2268
Get Well!
USA 22

2269
Thank You!

2270
Love You, Dad! USA 22

2271
Best Wishes! USA 22

2272
Happy Birthday! USA 22

2273
Love You, Mother! USA 22

2274
Keep In Touch! USA 22

2272
Happy Birthday! USA 22

2267
Congratulations! USA 22

2274a

2275

2276

2277

2278

2279

2280

2281

2283

2283c

2282a

2285b

2284   **2285**

	Issues of 1987		Un	U	PB/PNC	#	FDC	Q(M)
2275	22¢ United Way	04/28/87	.40	.20	1.90	(4)	1.00	157
2276	22¢ Flag with Fireworks	05/09/87	.40	.20	1.90	(4)	1.00	
a	Booklet pane of 20	11/30/87	8.50				8.00	
	Issues of 1988-89 (All issued in 1988 except #2280 on prephosphored paper)							
2277	(25¢) "E" Stamp	03/22/88	.45	.20	2.00	(4)	1.25	
2278	25¢ Flag with Clouds	05/06/88	.45	.20	1.90	(4)	1.25	
	Pair with full vertical gutter between		—					
	Coil Stamps, Perf. 10 Vertically							
2279	(25¢) "E" Earth	03/22/88	.45	.20	3.00	(5)	1.25	
a	Imperf., pair		90.00	—				
2280	25¢ Flag over Yosemite	05/20/88	.45	.20	3.75	(5)	1.25	
a	Prephosphored paper	02/14/89	.45	.20	3.75	(5)	1.25	
b	Imperf., pair, large block tagging		35.00					
c	Imperf., pair, prephosphored paper		15.00					
d	Tagging omitted		5.00					
e	Black trees		100.00	—				
f	Pair, imperf. between		800.00					
2281	25¢ Honeybee	09/02/88	.45	.20	3.00	(3)	1.25	
a	Imperf., pair		50.00					
b	Black (engr.) omitted		60.00					
c	Black (litho) omitted		450.00					
d	Pair, imperf. between		1,000.00					
e	Yellow (litho) omitted		1,250.00					
	Booklet Stamp, Perf. 10							
2282	(25¢) "E" Earth (#2277), single from booklet		.50	.20			1.25	
a	Booklet pane of 10	03/22/88	6.50	3.50			6.00	
	Pheasant Booklet Issue, Perf. 11							
2283	25¢ Pheasant, single from booklet		.50	.20			1.25	
a	Booklet pane of 10	04/29/88	6.00	3.50			6.00	
b	Single, red removed from sky		6.25	.20				
c	As "b," booklet pane of 10		67.50	—				
d	As "a," imperf. horizontally between		2,250.00					
	#2283 issued only in booklets. All stamps have one or two imperf. edges. Imperf. and part perf. pairs and panes exist from printer's waste.							
	Owl and Grosbeak Booklet Issue, Perf. 10							
2284	25¢ Grosbeak, single from booklet		.50	.20			1.25	
2285	25¢ Owl, single from booklet		.50	.20			1.25	
b	Booklet pane of 10, 5 each of #2284, 2285	05/28/88	5.00	3.50			6.00	
d	Pair, #2284, 2285		1.10	.25				
e	As "d," tagging omitted		12.50					
	#2284 and 2285 issued only in booklets. All stamps are imperf. at one side or imperf. at one side and bottom.							
2285A	25¢ Flag with Clouds (#2278), single from booklet		.50	.20			1.25	
c	Booklet pane of 6	07/05/88	3.00	2.00			4.00	

	Issues of 1987		Un	U	FDC	Q(M)
	American Wildlife Issue, Perf. 11					
2286	22¢ Barn Swallow	06/13/87	.85	.20	1.50	13
2287	22¢ Monarch Butterfly	06/13/87	.85	.20	1.50	13
2288	22¢ Bighorn Sheep	06/13/87	.85	.20	1.50	13
2289	22¢ Broad-tailed Hummingbird	06/13/87	.85	.20	1.50	13
2290	22¢ Cottontail	06/13/87	.85	.20	1.50	13
2291	22¢ Osprey	06/13/87	.85	.20	1.50	13
2292	22¢ Mountain Lion	06/13/87	.85	.20	1.50	13
2293	22¢ Luna Moth	06/13/87	.85	.20	1.50	12
2294	22¢ Mule Deer	06/13/87	.85	.20	1.50	13
2295	22¢ Gray Squirrel	06/13/87	.85	.20	1.50	13
2296	22¢ Armadillo	06/13/87	.85	.20	1.50	13
2297	22¢ Eastern Chipmunk	06/13/87	.85	.20	1.50	13
2298	22¢ Moose	06/13/87	.85	.20	1.50	13
2299	22¢ Black Bear	06/13/87	.85	.20	1.50	13
2300	22¢ Tiger Swallowtail	06/13/87	.85	.20	1.50	13
2301	22¢ Bobwhite	06/13/87	.85	.20	1.50	13
2302	22¢ Ringtail	06/13/87	.85	.20	1.50	13
2303	22¢ Red-winged Blackbird	06/13/87	.85	.20	1.50	13
2304	22¢ American Lobster	06/13/87	.85	.20	1.50	13
2305	22¢ Black-tailed Jack Rabbit	06/13/87	.85	.20	1.50	13
2306	22¢ Scarlet Tanager	06/13/87	.85	.20	1.50	13
2307	22¢ Woodchuck	06/13/87	.85	.20	1.50	13
2308	22¢ Roseate Spoonbill	06/13/87	.85	.20	1.50	13
2309	22¢ Bald Eagle	06/13/87	.85	.20	1.50	13
2310	22¢ Alaskan Brown Bear	06/13/87	.85	.20	1.50	13

Wolf Trap Farm Park

Early in the 17th century, the wilderness around present-day Vienna, Virginia, was the domain of large numbers of wolves. Then, colonists arrived in the area and set traps or used guns to kill all the wolves; a small local stream, Wolf Trap Run, is a reminder of those times.

Land along this stream changed hands several times before Catherine Filene Shouse, in 1930, began buying up parcels that would become her beloved Wolf Trap Farm. In 1966, Mrs. Shouse gave one hundred acres of this "cherished piece of property" to the United States government, along with funds to build an indoor-outdoor theater—the Filene Center; her gift was followed 15 years later by more land and money, this time for an indoor theater to be called the Barns of Wolf Trap. Today, the not-for-profit Wolf Trap Foundation raises funds to support and develop education and performing arts programs; it also manages ticket sales, marketing, and publicity for its programs. The National Park Service maintains the buildings and grounds at Wolf Trap Farm Park—America's National Park for the Performing Arts. ■

2286 2287 2288 2289 2290

2291 2292 2293 2294 2295

2296 2297 2298 2299 2300

2301 2302 2303 2304 2305

2306 2307 2308 2309 2310

2311 — *Iiwi* — 22 USA
2312 — *Badger* — 22 USA
2313 — *Pronghorn* — 22 USA
2314 — *River Otter* — 22 USA
2315 — *Ladybug* — 22 USA

2316 — *Beaver* — 22 USA
2317 — *White-tailed Deer* — 22 USA
2318 — *Blue Jay* — 22 USA
2319 — *Pika* — 22 USA
2320 — *Bison* — 22 USA

2321 — *Snowy Egret* — 22 USA
2322 — *Gray Wolf* — 22 USA
2323 — *Mountain Goat* — 22 USA
2324 — *Deer Mouse* — 22 USA
2325 — *Black-tailed Prairie Dog* — 22 USA

2326 — *Box Turtle* — 22 USA
2327 — *Wolverine* — 22 USA
2328 — *American Elk* — 22 USA
2329 — *California Sea Lion* — 22 USA
2330 — *Mockingbird* — 22 USA

2331 — *Raccoon* — 22 USA
2332 — *Bobcat* — 22 USA
2333 — *Black-footed Ferret* — 22 USA
2334 — *Canada Goose* — 22 USA
2335 — *Red Fox* — 22 USA

	Issues of 1987		Un	U	FDC	Q(M)
	American Wildlife Issue (continued), Perf. 11					
2311	22¢ Iiwi	06/13/87	.85	.20	1.50	13
2312	22¢ Badger	06/13/87	.85	.20	1.50	13
2313	22¢ Pronghorn	06/13/87	.85	.20	1.50	13
2314	22¢ River Otter	06/13/87	.85	.20	1.50	13
2315	22¢ Ladybug	06/13/87	.85	.20	1.50	13
2316	22¢ Beaver	06/13/87	.85	.20	1.50	13
2317	22¢ White-tailed Deer	06/13/87	.85	.20	1.50	13
2318	22¢ Blue Jay	06/13/87	.85	.20	1.50	13
2319	22¢ Pika	06/13/87	.85	.20	1.50	13
2320	22¢ Bison	06/13/87	.85	.20	1.50	13
2321	22¢ Snowy Egret	06/13/87	.85	.20	1.50	13
2322	22¢ Gray Wolf	06/13/87	.85	.20	1.50	13
2323	22¢ Mountain Goat	06/13/87	.85	.20	1.50	13
2324	22¢ Deer Mouse	06/13/87	.85	.20	1.50	13
2325	22¢ Black-tailed Prairie Dog	06/13/87	.85	.20	1.50	13
2326	22¢ Box Turtle	06/13/87	.85	.20	1.50	13
2327	22¢ Wolverine	06/13/87	.85	.20	1.50	13
2328	22¢ American Elk	06/13/87	.85	.20	1.50	13
2329	22¢ California Sea Lion	06/13/87	.85	.20	1.50	13
2330	22¢ Mockingbird	06/13/87	.85	.20	1.50	13
2331	22¢ Raccoon	06/13/87	.85	.20	1.50	13
2332	22¢ Bobcat	06/13/87	.85	.20	1.50	13
2333	22¢ Black-footed Ferret	06/13/87	.85	.20	1.50	13
2334	22¢ Canada Goose	06/13/87	.85	.20	1.50	13
2335	22¢ Red Fox	06/13/87	.85	.20	1.50	13
a	Pane of 50, #2286-2335		47.50		50.00	

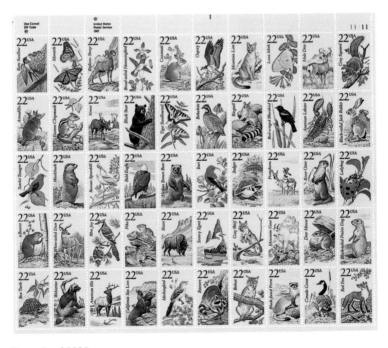

Example of 2335a

Issues of 1987-1990		Un	U	PB	#	FDC	Q(M)
Ratification of the Constitution Issue, Perf. 11							
2336	22¢ Delaware	07/04/87	.60	.20	2.75	(4)	1.25	168
2337	22¢ Pennsylvania	08/26/87	.60	.20	2.75	(4)	1.25	187
2338	22¢ New Jersey	09/11/87	.60	.20	2.75	(4)	1.25	184
a	Black omitted		6,000.00					
2339	22¢ Georgia	01/06/88	.60	.20	2.75	(4)	1.25	169
2340	22¢ Connecticut	01/09/88	.60	.20	2.75	(4)	1.25	155
2341	22¢ Massachusetts	02/06/88	.60	.20	2.75	(4)	1.25	102
2342	22¢ Maryland	02/15/88	.60	.20	2.75	(4)	1.25	103
2343	25¢ South Carolina	05/23/88	.60	.20	2.75	(4)	1.25	162
2344	25¢ New Hampshire	06/21/88	.60	.20	2.75	(4)	1.25	153
2345	25¢ Virginia	06/25/88	.60	.20	2.75	(4)	1.25	160
2346	25¢ New York	07/26/88	.60	.20	2.75	(4)	1.25	183
2347	25¢ North Carolina	08/22/89	.60	.20	2.75	(4)	1.25	
2348	25¢ Rhode Island	05/29/90	.60	.20	2.75	(4)	1.25	164
2349	22¢ Friendship with Morocco	07/18/87	.40	.20	1.75	(4)	1.00	157
a	Black omitted		275.00					
Literary Arts Issue							
2350	22¢ William Faulkner	08/03/87	.40	.20	1.75	(4)	1.00	156
American Folk Art: Lace Making Issue							
2351	22¢ Squash Blossoms	08/14/87	.45	.20			1.00	41
2352	22¢ Floral Piece	08/14/87	.45	.20			1.00	41
2353	22¢ Floral Piece	08/14/87	.45	.20			1.00	41
2354	22¢ Dogwood Blossoms	08/14/87	.45	.20			1.00	41
a	Block of 4, #2351-54		1.90	1.90	3.25	(4)	2.75	
b	As "a," white omitted		950.00					

Greetings From Connecticut

Known as "the Constitution State," Connecticut is said to have created America's first written constitution in the 1600s. It also boasts other important "firsts": The nation's first public school opened here, and the country's longest continuously published newspaper, *The Hartford Courant*, still hits the newsstands every day. Connecticut takes pride in its cultural legacy and in its New England heritage. In quiet corners, sometimes just a stone's throw from industrial and commercial centers, are small farms amid rolling hills; quaint towns with neat village greens and high-steepled churches; and trim little seaports steeped in history.

Tucked away near the southeast coast is Mystic Seaport, a reconstructed 19th-century port with a working shipyard, historic vessels, and maritime artifacts. Nearby is the old shipbuilding center of Groton, from which privateers sailed out to prey on British ships during the Revolutionary War; this old shipbuilding center is now home to the *USS Nautilus* and Submarine Force Museum. ■

Dec 7, 1787 USA
Delaware 22
2336

Dec 12, 1787
Pennsylvania
2337

Dec 18, 1787 USA
New Jersey 22
2338

22 USA
January 2, 1788
Georgia
2339

22 USA
January 9, 1788
Connecticut
2340

22 USA
Feb 6, 1788
Massachusetts
2341

April 28, 1788 USA
Maryland 22
2342

25 USA
May 23, 1788
South Carolina
2343

25 USA
June 21, 1788
New Hampshire
2344

June 25, 1788 USA
Virginia 25
2345

July 26, 1788 USA
New York 25
2346

25 USA
November 21, 1789
North Carolina
2347

25 USA
May 29, 1790
Rhode Island
2348

2351   **2352**

Friendship
with Morocco
1787-1987
USA 22
2349

William Faulkner
USA 22
2350

Lacemaking USA 22
Lacemaking USA 22
Lacemaking USA 22
Lacemaking USA 22

2353   **2354**   **2354a**

2355

2356

2357

2358

2359

2359a

2360

2361

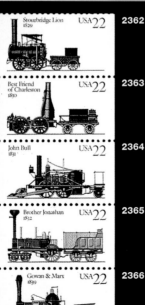

2362

2363

2364

2365

2366

2366a

2367

2368

	Issues of 1987		Un	U	PB	#	FDC	Q(M)
	Drafting of the Constitution Booklet Issue, Perf. 10 Horizontally							
2355	22¢ "The Bicentennial..."	08/28/87	.55	.20			1.25	122
2356	22¢ "We the people..."	08/28/87	.55	.20			1.25	122
2357	22¢ "Establish justice..."	08/28/87	.55	.20			1.25	122
2358	22¢ "And secure..."	08/28/87	.55	.20			1.25	122
2359	22¢ "Do ordain..."	08/28/87	.55	.20			1.25	122
a	Booklet pane of 5, #2355-59		2.75	2.25			4.00	122
	#2355-59 issued only in booklets. All stamps are imperf. at sides or imperf. at sides and bottom.							
	Signing of the Constitution Issue, Perf. 11							
2360	22¢ Constitution and Signer's Hand-Holding Quill Pen	09/17/87	.45	.20	2.25	(4)	1.00	169
2361	22¢ Certified Public Accountants	09/21/87	1.90	.20	8.00	(4)	4.00	163
a	Black omitted		725.00					
	Locomotives Booklet Issue, Perf. 10 Horizontally							
2362	22¢ Stourbridge Lion, 1829	10/01/87	.55	.20			1.50	143
2363	22¢ Best Friend of Charleston, 1830	10/01/87	.55	.20			1.50	143
2364	22¢ John Bull, 1831	10/01/87	.55	.20			1.50	143
2365	22¢ Brother Jonathan, 1832	10/01/87	.55	.20			1.50	143
a	Red omitted		—					
2366	22¢ Gowan & Marx, 1839	10/01/87	.55	.20			1.50	143
a	Booklet pane of 5, #2362-66		2.75	2.50			4.50	143
	#2362-66 issued only in booklets. All stamps are imperf. at sides or imperf. at sides and bottom.							
	Christmas Issue, Perf. 11							
2367	22¢ Madonna and Child, by Moroni	10/23/87	.40	.20	2.00	(4)	1.00	529
2368	22¢ Christmas Ornaments	10/23/87	.40	.20	1.75	(4)	1.00	978
	Pair with full vertical gutter between		—					

Library of Congress

Founded in 1800, the Library of Congress in Washington, D.C., recently marked its 200th anniversary, and the Postal Service helped celebrate the milestone with a commemorative stamp featuring the interior dome of the Main Reading Room in the Thomas Jefferson Building. This magnificent building near the United States Capitol opened in 1897, providing a new home for a growing collection of books and papers that had been tucked away in the Capitol for decades. More than 110 million publications, maps, recordings, and other items now reside here and in two massive 20th-century structures: the John Adams and James Madison Memorial Buildings.

In the words of James H. Billington, Librarian of Congress, the library is now the "world's largest and most accessible repository of recorded knowledge." It not only meets the research needs of members of Congress and their staffs but also makes its vast holdings available to every other person in the country. ∎

	Issues of 1988		Un	U	PB	#	FDC	Q(M)
	Winter Olympic Games Issue, Perf. 11							
2369	22¢ Skier and Olympic Rings	01/10/88	.40	.20	1.75	(4)	1.00	159
2370	22¢ Australia Bicentennial	01/10/88	.40	.20	1.75	(4)	1.00	146
	Black Heritage Issue							
2371	22¢ James Weldon Johnson and Music from "Lift Ev'ry Voice and Sing"	02/02/88	.40	.20	1.75	(4)	1.25	97
	American Cats Issue							
2372	22¢ Siamese and Exotic Shorthair	02/05/88	.45	.20			2.00	40
2373	22¢ Abyssinian and Himalayan	02/05/88	.45	.20			2.00	40
2374	22¢ Maine Coon and Burmese	02/05/88	.45	.20			2.00	40
2375	22¢ American Shorthair and Persian	02/05/88	.45	.20			2.00	40
a	Block of 4, #2372-75		1.90	1.90	3.75	(4)	4.50	
	American Sports Issue							
2376	22¢ Knute Rockne Holding Football on Field	03/09/88	.40	.20	2.25	(4)	4.00	97
2377	25¢ Francis Ouimet and Ouimet Hitting Fairway Shot	06/13/88	.45	.20	2.50	(4)	4.50	153
2378	25¢ Love	07/04/88	.45	.20	1.90	(4)	1.50	841
a	Imperf., pair		3,000.00					
2379	45¢ Love	08/08/88	.65	.20	3.25	(4)	1.75	180
	Summer Olympic Games Issue							
2380	25¢ Gymnast on Rings	08/19/88	.45	.20	1.90	(4)	1.25	157

New York Public Library Lion

A masterpiece in white marble, the Beaux Art main building of the New York Public Library in Manhattan fronts Fifth Avenue between 40th and 42nd Streets, site of the old Croton Reservoir. The structure was dedicated on May 23, 1911, fulfilling a wish of one-time governor Samuel J. Tilden (1814-1886), who had bequeathed much of his estate to "establish and maintain a free library and reading room in the city of New York." Today, its holdings are part of a system comprising four research centers and 82 branch libraries; all told, the New York Public Library holds more materials than any other public library in the United States.

Guarding the main entrance of the main building are the library's "mascots," two male lions carved by Edward Clark Potter (1857–1923). The pair were originally known as Leo Astor and Leo Lenox, after important library benefactors John Jacob Astor and James Lenox, and later came to be called Lord Astor and Lady Lenox. Then, in the 1930s, Mayor Fiorello La Guardia named them Patience and Fortitude, reminding New Yorkers of the qualities they would need to get through the Great Depression. The lion known as Patience was featured on a nondenominated, presorted standard stamp issued in 2000. ■

2370

2369

2371

2372   **2373**

2374   **2375**   **2375a**

2378

2376   **2377**   **2379**

2380

2381 1928 Locomobile

2382 1929 Pierce-Arrow

2383 1931 Cord

2384 1932 Packard

2385 1935 Duesenberg

2385a

2390 2391

2392 2393 2393a

2386 Nathaniel Palmer

2387 Lt. Charles Wilkes

2388 Richard E. Byrd

2389 Lincoln Ellsworth

2389a

Issues of 1988		Un	U	PB	#	FDC	Q(M)
Classic Cars Booklet Issue, Perf. 10 Horizontally							
2381 25¢ 1928 Locomobile	08/25/88	.50	.20			1.25	127
2382 25¢ 1929 Pierce-Arrow	08/25/88	.50	.20			1.25	127
2383 25¢ 1931 Cord	08/25/88	.50	.20			1.25	127
2384 25¢ 1932 Packard	08/25/88	.50	.20			1.25	127
2385 25¢ 1935 Duesenberg	08/25/88	.50	.20			1.25	127
a Booklet pane of 5, #2381-85		5.00	2.25			4.00	127
#2381-85 issued only in booklets. All stamps are imperf. at sides or imperf. at sides and bottom.							
Antarctic Explorers Issue, Perf. 11							
2386 25¢ Nathaniel Palmer	09/14/88	.65	.20			1.25	41
2387 25¢ Lt. Charles Wilkes	09/14/88	.65	.20			1.25	41
2388 25¢ Richard E. Byrd	09/14/88	.65	.20			1.25	41
2389 25¢ Lincoln Ellsworth	09/14/88	.65	.20			1.25	41
a Block of 4, #2386-89		2.75	2.00	4.50	(4)	3.00	
b As "a," black omitted		1,500.00					
c As "a," imperf. horizontally		3,000.00					
American Folk Art Issue, Carousel Animals							
2390 25¢ Deer	10/01/88	.65	.20			2.00	76
2391 25¢ Horse	10/01/88	.65	.20			2.00	76
2392 25¢ Camel	10/01/88	.65	.20			2.00	76
2393 25¢ Goat	10/01/88	.65	.20			2.00	76
a Block of 4, #2390-93		3.00	2.00	4.00	(4)	4.00	

Old North Church

"One if by land, two if by sea." Those words and the Old North Church of Boston, Massachusetts, appear on a 1975 postage stamp commemorating a pivotal moment in American history. On the night of April 18, 1775, two lanterns blazed from the church's 191-foot steeple— a signal from sexton Robert Newman that British troops were sailing up the Charles River—and soon after, Paul Revere made his famous ride to spread the alarm. The British were coming! The next day, colonial militia engaged British Regulars on Lexington Green, about ten miles northwest of Boston, and ignited the Revolutionary War.

The Old North Church—officially known as Christ Church in the City of Boston—sits atop Copp's Hill near the waterfront at the city's north end. Built in 1723, it is the oldest church in Boston and a fixture on the Freedom Trail walking route that winds through the city. Inside the church are box pews, chandeliers, bells, an organ, and a clock, all dating from the 18th century. There is also a life-like bust of George Washington, who assumed command of the Continental armies in July 1775 and forced the British out of Boston early the next year. ■

	Issues of 1988		Un	U	PB	#	FDC	Q(M)
2394	$8.75 Express Mail	10/04/88	13.50	8.00	54.00	(4)	25.00	
	Special Occasions Booklet Issue							
2395	25¢ Happy Birthday	10/22/88	.50	.20			1.25	120
2396	25¢ Best Wishes	10/22/88	.50	.20			1.25	120
a	Booklet pane of 6, 3 #2395 and							
	3 #2396 with gutter between		3.50	3.25			4.00	
2397	25¢ Thinking of You	10/22/88	.50	.20			1.25	120
2398	25¢ Love You	10/22/88	.50	.20			1.25	120
a	Booklet pane of 6, 3 #2397 and							
	3 #2398 with gutter between		3.50	3.25			4.00	
b	As "a," imperf. horizontally		—					
	#2395-98a issued only in booklets. All stamps are imperf. on one side or on one side and top or bottom.							
	Christmas Issue							
2399	25¢ Madonna and Child,							
	by Botticelli	10/20/88	.45	.20	1.90	(4)	1.25	844
a	Gold omitted		30.00					
2400	25¢ One-Horse Open							
	Sleigh and Village Scene	10/20/88	.45	.20	1.90	(4)	1.25	1,038
	Pair with full vertical gutter between		—					

Greetings From Indiana

Crisscrossed by several interstate high-ways, Indiana calls itself "the crossroads of America." Four of the roads meet like spokes on a wheel at Indianapolis, the state capital and site of the Indy 500 auto race held every Memorial Day weekend.

Besides automobiles, heavy river, lake, and rail traffic also moves through or around Indiana. In the north, the state borders Lake Michigan, while in the south, the Ohio River affords access to the Mississippi and its ports. With such an excellent transportation network, it's not surprising that Indiana farmers—whose land makes up much of the state—annually export more than one billion dollars' worth of agricultural goods.

Much history has been made and preserved near the Ohio River. Angel Mounds State Historic Site, for example, contains earthworks raised by an ancient mound-building culture. The Lincoln Boyhood National Memorial includes a farm where young Abraham Lincoln lived, and Corydon preserves Indiana's first state capitol building and other early 19th-century structures. ■

2394

2395   2396   2396a

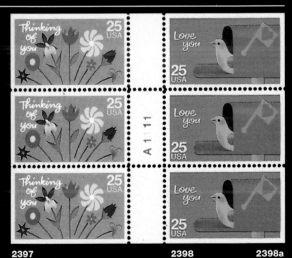

2397   2398   2398a

2400

2401

2402

2403

2404

2405

2406

2407

2408

2409

2409a

2410

2411

2412

2413

2414

2415

2416

2417

2418

	Issues of 1989		Un	U	PB	#	FD	Q(M)
2401	25¢ Montana Statehood	01/15/89	.45	.20	2.00	(4)	1.25	165
	Black Heritage Issue							
2402	25¢ A. Philip Randolph, Pullman							
	Porters and Railroad Cars	02/03/89	.45	.20	2.00	(4)	1.25	152
2403	25¢ North Dakota Statehood	02/21/89	.45	.20	1.90	(4)	1.25	163
2404	25¢ Washington Statehood	02/22/89	.45	.20	2.00	(4)	1.25	265
	Steamboats Booklet Issue, Perf. 10 Horizontally							
2405	25¢ Experiment 1788-90	03/03/89	.45	.20			1.25	159
2406	25¢ Phoenix 1809	03/03/89	.45	.20			1.25	159
2407	25¢ New Orleans 1812	03/03/89	.45	.20			1.25	159
2408	25¢ Washington 1816	03/03/89	.45	.20			1.25	159
2409	25¢ Walk in the Water 1818	03/03/89	.45	.20			1.25	159
a	Booklet pane of 5, #2405-09		2.25	1.75			4.00	159
	#2405-09 issued only in booklets. All stamps are imperf. at sides or imperf. at sides and bottom.							
	Perf. 11							
2410	25¢ World Stamp Expo '89	03/16/89	.45	.20	1.90	(4)	1.25	164
	Performing Arts Issue							
2411	25¢ Arturo Toscanini							
	Conducting with Baton	03/25/89	.45	.20	2.00	(4)	1.25	152
	Issues of 1989-90, Constitution Bicentennial Issue							
2412	25¢ U.S. House of							
	Representatives	04/04/89	.50	.20	2.25	(4)	1.25	139
2413	25¢ U.S. Senate	04/06/89	.50	.20	2.25	(4)	1.25	138
2414	25¢ Executive Branch, George							
	Washington	04/16/89	.50	.20	2.25	(4)	1.25	139
2415	25¢ Supreme Court, Chief Justice							
	John Marshall	02/02/90	.50	.20	2.25	(4)	1.25	151
	Issues of 1989							
2416	25¢ South Dakota							
	Statehood	05/03/89	.45	.20	1.90	(4)	1.25	165
	American Sports Issue							
2417	25¢ Lou Gehrig,							
	Gehrig Swinging Bat	06/10/89	.50	.20	3.00	(4)	4.00	263
	Literary Arts Issue							
2418	25¢ Ernest Hemingway, African							
	Landscape in Background	07/17/89	.45	.20	2.00	(4)	1.25	192

Greetings From Washington

Washington achieved statehood in 1889, adding its dramatic landscapes to the nation's treasure chest of natural splendors. From west to east, Washington is a patchwork of wild Pacific beaches, ancient rain forests, towering mountains, scenic islands and valleys, massive snowcapped volcanoes, and vast tablelands piled high with prehistoric lava flows.

The state's most important waterway is the Columbia River, which tumbles down from the Canadian Rockies and cuts south and west through central Washington. Several dams along its route make water available to the state's drier eastern areas and help generate vast amounts of hydroelectric power. Largest of the dams is Grand Coulee, a gargantuan concrete marvel 550 feet high and a mile across. The Columbia turns west at the Oregon border, rolls through a spectacular gorge of its own making, and eventually empties into the Pacific. In November 1805, explorers Lewis and Clark camped near the river's mouth after blazing a trail across the continent. ■

1989

	Issues of 1989		Un	U	PB	#	FDC	Q(M)
	Priority Mail Issue, Perf. 11 x 11.5							
2419	$2.40 Moon Landing	07/20/89	4.00	2.00	17.50	(4)	7.50	
a	Black (engr.) omitted		2,500.00					
b	Imperf., pair		750.00					
c	Black (litho.) omitted		4,500.00					
	Perf. 11							
2420	25¢ Letter Carriers	08/30/89	.45	.20	1.90	(4)	1.25	188
	Constitution Bicentennial Issue							
2421	25¢ Bill of Rights	09/25/89	.45	.20	3.00	(4)	1.25	192
a	Black omitted		325.00					
	Prehistoric Animals Issue							
2422	25¢ Tyrannosaurus	10/01/89	.65	.20			1.50	102
2423	25¢ Pteranodon	10/01/89	.65	.20			1.50	102
2424	25¢ Stegosaurus	10/01/89	.65	.20			1.50	102
2425	25¢ Brontosaurus	10/01/89	.65	.20			1.50	102
a	Block of 4, #2422-25		3.00	2.00	3.50	(4)	3.00	
b	As "a," black omitted		750.00					
	America/PUAS Issue (See also #C121)							
2426	25¢ Southwest Carved Figure (A.D. 1150-1350), Emblem of the Postal Union of the Americas	10/12/89	.45	.20	2.00	(4)	1.25	137
	Christmas Issue, Perf. 11.5							
2427	25¢ Madonna and Child, by Caracci	10/19/89	.45	.20	2.00	(4)	1.25	913
a	Booklet pane of 10		4.75	3.50			6.00	
b	Red (litho.) omitted		850.00					
	Perf. 11							
2428	25¢ Sleigh Full of Presents	10/19/89	.45	.20	1.90	(4)	1.25	900
a	Vertical pair, imperf. horizontally		2,000.00					
	Booklet Stamp Issue, Perf. 11.5 on 2 or 3 sides							
2429	25¢ Single from booklet pane (#2428)	10/19/89	.45	.20			1.25	399
a	Booklet pane of 10		4.75	3.50			6.00	40
b	As "a," imperf. horiz. between		—					
c	Vertical pair, imperf. horizontally		—					
d	As "a," red omitted		—					
e	Imperf., pair		—					
	In #2429, runners on sleigh are twice as thick as in 2428; bow on package at rear of sleigh is same color as package; board running underneath sleigh is pink.							
2430	Not assigned							
	Self-Adhesive, Die-Cut							
2431	25¢ Eagle and Shield	11/10/89	.50	.20			1.25	75
a	Booklet pane of 18		11.00					
b	Vertical pair, no die-cutting between		850.00					
2432	Not assigned							

2420

2421

2419

2423

2425

2426

2425a

27

28

31

▶ ▶ ▶ ▶ Peel this strip and Fold here ◀ ◀ ◀ ◀

▶ ▶ ▶ ▶ Peel this strip and Fold here ◀ ◀ ◀ ◀

WORLD STAMP EXPO '89.

The classic 1869 U.S. Abraham Lincoln stamp is reborn in these four larger versions commemorating World Stamp Expo '89, held in Washington, D.C. during the 20th Universal Postal Congress of the UPU. These stamps show the issued colors and three of the trial proof color combinations.

2439

2433

2434

2435

2436

2437

2437a

20th Universal Postal Congress

A review of historical methods of delivering the mail in the United States is the theme of these four stamps issued in commemoration of the convening of the 20th Universal Postal Congress in Washington, D.C. from November 13 through December 15, 1989. The United States, as host nation to the Congress for the first time in ninety-two years, welcomed more than 1,000 delegates from most of the member nations of the Universal Postal Union to the major international event.

Issues of 1989		Un	U	PB	#	FDC	Q(M)
	World Stamp Expo '89 Issue Souvenir Sheet, Imperf.						
2433	Reproduction of #122, 90¢ Lincoln,						
	and three essays of #122 11/17/89	14.00	9.00			7.00	2
a-d	Single stamp from sheet	2.00	1.75				
	20th UPU Congress Issues, Classic Mail Transportation, Perf. 11						
	(See also #C122-25)						
2434	25¢ Stagecoach 11/19/89	.45	.20			1.25	41
2435	25¢ Paddlewheel Steamer 11/19/89	.45	.20			1.25	41
2436	25¢ Biplane 11/19/89	.45	.20			1.25	41
2437	25¢ Depot-Hack Type						
	Automobile 11/19/89	.45	.20			1.25	41
a	Block of 4, #2434-37	2.00	1.00	3.75	(4)	3.00	
b	As "a," dark blue omitted	700.00					
	Souvenir Sheet, Imperf. (See also #C126)						
2438	Designs of #2434-37 11/28/89	4.00	1.75			2.00	2
a-d	Single stamp from sheet	.65	.25				
	Issues of 1990, Perf. 11						
2439	25¢ Idaho Statehood 01/06/90	.45	.20	2.00	(4)	1.25	173
	Perf. 12.5 x 13						
2440	25¢ Love 01/18/90	.45	.20	2.00	(4)	1.25	886
a	Imperf., pair	800.00					
	Booklet Stamp, Perf. 11.5						
2441	25¢ Love, single from booklet 01/18/90	.45	.20			1.25	995
a	Booklet pane of 10 01/18/90	4.75	3.50			6.00	
b	As "a," bright pink omitted	1,900.00					
c	As "b," single stamp	180.00					
	Black Heritage Issue, Perf. 11						
2442	25¢ Ida B. Wells,						
	Marchers in Background 02/01/90	.45	.20	2.00	(4)	1.25	153
	Beach Umbrella Booklet Issue, Perf. 11.5 x 11						
2443	15¢ Beach Umbrella,						
	single from booklet 02/03/90	.30	.20			1.25	
a	Booklet pane of 10 02/03/90	3.00	2.00			4.25	
b	As "a," blue omitted	1,750.00					
c	As #2443, blue omitted	170.00					

#2443 issued only in booklets. All stamps are imperf. at one side or imperf. at one side and bottom.

Greetings From Idaho

One of the most mountainous states in the West, rugged Idaho encompasses the Bitterroot Range and the Clearwater, Sawtooth, and Salmon River Mountains. Long, fast-moving rivers rush through the state, giving Idaho more than 3,000 miles of white water and making it a favorite destination for rafting and kayaking.

After cutting westward across southern Idaho, the Snake River makes a sharp turn to the north and slices through Hells Canyon, even deeper than the Grand Canyon. Numerous cascades lie along the Snake's path, including spectacular Shoshone Falls. The Salmon, or "River of No Return," and the lovely Clearwater make east-to-west crossings farther north.

Most residents live in the south, where economic mainstays include potatoes, commercial trout, cattle, and sheep. But outdoor sports and other activities are popular throughout Idaho. Besides rafting and kayaking, these include skiing, golfing, biking, rock climbing, fishing, and hiking. ∎

	Issues of 1990		Un	U	PB	#	FDC	Q(M)
	Perf 11							
2444	25¢ Wyoming Statehood	02/23/90	.45	.20	2.00	(4)	1.25	169
a	Black (engr.) omitted		2,500.00	—				
	Classic Films Issue							
2445	25¢ The Wizard of Oz	03/23/90	1.00	.20			2.50	44
2446	25¢ Gone With the Wind	03/23/90	1.00	.20			2.50	44
2447	25¢ Beau Geste	03/23/90	1.00	.20			2.50	44
2448	25¢ Stagecoach	03/23/90	1.00	.20			2.50	44
a	Block of 4, #2445-48		4.50	3.50	6.00	(4)	5.00	
	Literary Arts Issue							
2449	25¢ Marianne Moore	04/18/90	.45	.20	2.00	(4)	1.25	150
2450	Not assigned							
	Issues of 1990-95, Transportation Issue, Coil Stamps, Perf. 9.8 Vertically							
2451	4¢ Steam Carriage 1866	01/25/91	.20	.20	1.25	(5)	1.25	
a	Imperf., pair		700.00					
b	Untagged		.20	.20	1.25	(5)		
2452	5¢ Circus Wagon 1900s,							
	intaglio printing	08/31/91	.20	.20	1.25	(5)	1.50	
a	Untagged, dull gum		.20	.20	1.75	(5)		
c	Imperf., pair		900.00					
2452B	5¢ Circus Wagon							
	(2452), gravure printing	12/08/92	.20	.20	1.75	(5)	1.50	
f	Printed with luminescent ink		.20	.20	2.25	(5)		
2452D	5¢ Circus Wagon							
	(2452), gravure printing	03/20/95	.20	.20	1.60	(5)	2.00	
e	Imperf., pair		—					
g	Printed with luminescent ink		.20	.20	2.00	(5)		
2453	5¢ Canoe 1800s, precanceled,							
	intaglio printing	05/25/91	.20	.20	1.50	(5)	1.25	
a	Imperf., pair		350.00					
2454	5¢ Canoe 1800s,							
	precanceled, gravure printing	10/22/91	.20	.20	1.60	(5)	1.25	
2455-56	Not assigned							
2457	10¢ Tractor Trailer, Bureau							
	precanceled, intaglio printing	05/25/91	.20	.20	2.25	(5)	1.25	
a	Imperf., pair		350.00					
2458	10¢ Tractor Trailer, Bureau							
	precanceled, gravure printing	05/25/94	.20	.20	2.50	(5)	1.25	
2459-62	Not assigned							
2463	20¢ Cog Railway Car 1870s	06/09/95	.40	.20	4.25	(5)	1.50	
a	Imperf., pair		150.00					
2464	23¢ Lunch Wagon 1890s	04/12/91	.45	.20	3.75	(5)	1.25	
a	Prephosphored uncoated paper		.45	.20	4.50	(5)		
b	Imperf., pair		175.00					
2465	Not assigned							
2466	32¢ Ferryboat 1900s	06/02/95	.60	.20	5.75	(5)	1.50	
a	Imperf., pair		—					
b	Bright blue, prephosphored							
	uncoated paper		6.00	4.50	120.00	(5)		
2467	Not assigned							
2468	$1 Seaplane 1914	04/20/90	1.75	.50	11.00	(5)	2.50	
a	Imperf., pair		2,500.00	—				
b	Prephosphored uncoated paper		1.75	.50	10.00	(5)		
c	Prephosphored coated paper		1.75	.50	10.00	(5)		
2469	Not assigned							

2444

2445

2446

2447

2448

2448a

2449

2451

2452

2452D

2453

2454

2457

2463

2464

2466

2468

2474a

2470　　**2471**　　**2472**　　**2473**　　**2474**

2475

2476　　**2477**　　**2478**

2479　　**2480**　　**2481**　　**2482**

2483　　**2484**　　**2485**

	Issues of 1990-1995		Un	U	PB	#	FDC	Q(M)
	Lighthouses Booklet Issue, Perf. 10 Vertically							
2470	25¢ Admiralty Head, WA	04/26/90	1.00	.20			1.75	147
2471	25¢ Cape Hatteras, NC	04/26/90	1.00	.20			1.75	147
2472	25¢ West Quoddy Head, ME	04/26/90	1.00	.20			1.75	147
2473	25¢ American Shoals, FL	04/26/90	1.00	.20			1.75	147
2474	25¢ Sandy Hook, NJ	04/26/90	1.00	.20			1.75	147
a	Booklet pane of 5, #2470-74		5.50	2.00			4.50	147
b	As "a," white (USA 25) omitted		80.00					
	Self-Adhesive Issue, Die-Cut							
2475	25¢ Flag, single from pane	05/18/90	.50	.25			1.25	36
a	Pane of 12	05/18/90	6.00					
	Flora and Fauna Issues, Perf. 11							
2476	1¢ American Kestrel	06/22/91	.20	.20	.20	(4)	1.25	
2477	1¢ American Kestrel	05/10/95	.20	.20	.20	(4)	1.25	
2478	3¢ Eastern Bluebird	06/22/91	.20	.20	.30	(4)	1.25	
	Perf. 11.5 x 11							
2479	19¢ Fawn	03/11/91	.35	.20	1.75	(4)	1.25	
a	Tagging omitted		10.00					
b	Red omitted		850.00					
2480	30¢ Cardinal	06/22/91	.50	.20	2.25	(4)	1.25	
	Perf. 11							
2481	45¢ Pumpkinseed Sunfish	12/02/92	.80	.20	3.90	(4)	1.75	
a	Black omitted		525.00	—				
2482	$2 Bobcat	06/01/90	3.00	1.25	12.00	(4)	5.00	
a	Black omitted		300.00					
b	Tagging omitted		15.00					
	Perf. 10.9 x 9.8							
2483	20¢ Blue Jay	06/15/95	.50	.20			1.50	
a	Booklet pane of 10		5.25	2.25				
	Wood Duck Booklet Issue, Perf. 10							
2484	29¢ Black and multicolored	04/12/91	.50	.20			1.25	
a	Booklet pane of 10		5.50	3.75			5.00	
b	As "a," horizontal imperf. between		—					
c	Prephosphored coated paper		.40	.20				
d	As "c," booklet pane of 10		5.50	3.75				
	Perf. 11							
2485	29¢ Red and multicolored	04/12/91	.50	.20			1.25	
a	Booklet pane of 10		5.50	4.00			5.00	
b	Vertical pair, imperf. between		275.00					
c	As "b," booklet pane of 10		1,500.00					

#2484-85a issued only in bklts. All stamps are imperf. top or bottom, or top or bottom and right edge.

	Issues of 1993-1995		Un	U	PB	#	FDC	Q(M)
	Perf. 10 x 11 on 2 or 3 sides							
2486	29¢ African Violet	10/08/93	.50	.20			1.25	
a	Booklet pane of 10		5.50	*4.00*			4.50	
2487	32¢ Peach	07/08/95	.60	.20			1.50	
2488	32¢ Pear	07/08/95	.60	.20			1.50	
a	Booklet pane, 5 each #2487-88		6.00	*4.25*			7.50	
b	Pair, #2487-88		1.25	.30				
	Issues of 1993, Self-Adhesive, Die-Cut							
2489	29¢ Red Squirrel	06/25/93	.50	.20			1.25	
a	Booklet pane of 18		10.00					
2490	29¢ Red Rose	08/19/93	.50	.20			1.25	
a	Booklet pane of 18		10.00					
2491	29¢ Pine Cone	11/05/93	.50	.20			1.25	
a	Booklet pane of 18		11.00					
b	Horizontal pair, no die cutting between		—					
c	Coil with plate #B1		—	4.00	7.00	(5)		
	Serpentine Die-Cut 11.3 x 11.7 on 2, 3 or 4 sides							
2492	32¢ Pink Rose	06/02/95	.60	.20			1.40	
a	Booklet pane of 20 plus label		12.00					
b	Booklet pane of 15 plus label		8.75					
c	Horizontal pair, no die cutting between		—					
d	As "a," 2 stamps and parts of 7 others printed on backing liner		—					
e	Booklet pane of 14		21.00					
f	Booklet pane of 16		21.00					
g	Coil with plate #S111		—	3.25	6.50	(5)		
h	Vertical pair, no die cutting between		—					
2493	32¢ Peach	07/08/95	.60	.20			1.25	
2494	32¢ Pear	07/08/95	.60	.20			1.25	
a	Booklet pane, 10 each #2493-2494		12.50					
b	Pair, #2493-2494		1.20					
	Coil Stamps, Serpentine Die Cut Vert.							
2495	32¢ Peach	07/08/95	.60	.20			1.25	
2495A	32¢ Pear	07/08/95	.60	.20			1.25	
b	Pair #2495-2495A		1.20		6.75	(5)		
	Issues of 1990, Olympians Issue, Perf. 11							
2496	25¢ Jesse Owens	07/06/90	.60	.20			1.25	36
2497	25¢ Ray Ewry	07/06/90	.60	.20			1.25	36
2498	25¢ Hazel Wightman	07/06/90	.60	.20			1.25	36
2499	25¢ Eddie Eagan	07/06/90	.60	.20			1.25	36
2500	25¢ Helene Madison	07/06/90	.60	.20			1.25	36
a	Strip of 5, #2496-2500		3.25	2.50	8.00	(10)	3.00	7
	Indian Headdresses Booklet Issue, Perf. 11 on 2 or 3 sides							
2501	25¢ Assiniboine Headdress	08/17/90	.80	.20			1.25	124
2502	25¢ Cheyenne Headdress	08/17/90	.80	.20			1.25	124
2503	25¢ Comanche Headdress	08/17/90	.80	.20			1.25	124
2504	25¢ Flathead Headdress	08/17/90	.80	.20			1.25	124
2505	25¢ Shoshone Headdress	08/17/90	.80	.20			1.25	124
a	Booklet pane of 10, 2 each of #2501-05		8.50	*3.50*			6.00	62
b	As "a," black omitted		*3,250.00*					
c	Strip of 5		2.75	1.00				
d	As "a," horizontal imperf. between		—					
	#2501-05 issued only in booklets. All stamps imperf. top or bottom, or top or bottom and right edge.							

2486

2487 **2488**

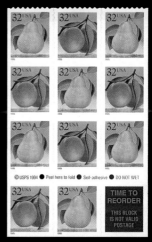

2487-2488a

2489 **2490** **2491** **2492**

2496 **2497** **2498** **2499** **2500** **2500a**

2501 **2502** **2503** **2504** **2505** **2505a**

1990-1991

2506   **2507**   **2507a**

2508   **2509**

2510   **2511**   **2511a**

2512   **2513**   **2514**   **2515**

2517   **2519**   **2520**   **2521**

2522   **2523**   **2523A**

	Issues of 1990		Un	U	PB	#	FDC	Q(M)
	Micronesia/Marshall Islands Issue, Perf. 11							
2506	25¢ Canoe and Flag of the Federated States of Micronesia	09/28/90	.45	.20			1.25	76
2507	25¢ Stick Chart, Canoe and Flag of the Marshall Islands	09/28/90	.45	.20			1.25	76
a	Pair, #2506-07		.90	.60	2.25	(4)	2.00	61
b	As "a," black omitted		3,000.00					
	Creatures of the Sea Issue							
2508	25¢ Killer Whales	10/03/90	.45	.20			1.25	70
2509	25¢ Northern Sea Lions	10/03/90	.45	.20			1.25	70
2510	25¢ Sea Otter	10/03/90	.45	.20			1.25	70
2511	25¢ Common Dolphin	10/03/90	.45	.20			1.25	70
a	Block of 4, #2508-11		1.90	1.75	2.50	(4)	3.00	70
b	As "a," black omitted		750.00					
	America/PUAS Issue, (See also #C127) 1990-1991							
2512	25¢ Grand Canyon	10/12/90	.45	.20	2.00	(4)	1.25	151
2513	25¢ Dwight D. Eisenhower	10/13/90	.60	.20	3.00	(4)	1.25	143
a	Imperf., pair		2,250.00					
	Christmas Issue, Perf. 11.5							
2514	25¢ Madonna and Child, by Antonello	10/18/90	.45	.20	2.00	(4)	1.25	500
a	Booklet pane of 10		5.00	3.25			6.00	23
	Perf. 11							
2515	25¢ Christmas Tree	10/18/90	.45	.20	2.00	(4)	1.25	599
a	Vertical pair, imperf. horizontally		1,100.00					
	Booklet Stamp, Perf. 11.5 x 11 on 2 or 3 sides							
2516	Single (2515) from booklet pane	10/18/90	.45	.20			1.25	
a	Booklet pane of 10	10/18/90	5.00	3.25			6.00	32
	Issues of 1991, Perf. 13							
2517	(29¢) "F" Stamp	01/22/91	.50	.20	2.50	(4)	1.25	
a	Imperf., pair		750.00					
b	Horizontal pair, imperf. vertically		1,250.00					
	Coil Stamp, Perf. 10 Vertically							
2518	(29¢) "F" Tulip (2517)	01/22/91	.50	.20	3.50	(5)	1.25	
a	Imperf., pair		42.50					
	Booklet Stamps, Perf. 11 on 2 or 3 sides							
2519	(29¢) "F", single from booklet		.50	.20			1.25	
a	Booklet pane of 10	01/22/91	6.50	4.50			7.25	
2520	(29¢) "F", single from booklet		.50	.20			1.25	
a	Booklet pane of 10	01/22/91	18.00	4.50			8.00	
	#2519 has bull's-eye perforations that measure approximately 11.2. #2520 has less-pronounced black lines in the leaf, which is a much brighter green than on #2519.							
	Perf. 11							
2521	(4¢) Makeup Rate	01/22/91	.20	.20	.40	(4)	1.25	
a	Vertical pair, imperf. horizontally		110.00					
	Self-Adhesive, Die-Cut, Imperf.							
2522	(29¢) F Flag, single from pane		.55	.25			1.25	
a	Pane of 12	01/22/91	7.00					
	Coil Stamps, Perf. 10 Vertically							
2523	29¢ Flag Over Mt. Rushmore, intaglio printing	03/29/91	.50	.20	4.25	(5)	1.25	
b	Imperf., pair		25.00					
c	Blue, red and brown		5.00	—	180.00	(5)		
d	Prephosphored coated paper		5.00	—	650.00	(5)		
2523A	29¢ Flag Over Mt. Rushmore, gravure printing	07/04/91	.50	.20	4.25	(5)	1.25	

	Issues of 1991		Un	U	PB	#	FDC	Q(M)
	Perf. 11							
2524	29¢ Tulip	04/05/91	.50	.20	2.25	(4)	1.25	
2524A	Perf. 13		.75	.20	4.50	(4)		
	Coil Stamps, Roulette 10 Vertically							
2525	29¢ Tulip	08/16/91	.50	.20	4.75	(5)	1.25	
	Issues of 1992, Perf. 10 Vertically							
2526	29¢ Tulip	03/03/92	.50	.20	4.75	(5)	1.25	
	Issues of 1991, Booklet Stamp, Perf. 11 on 2 or 3 sides							
2527	29¢ Tulip (2524), single from bklt.		.50	.20			1.25	
a	Booklet pane of 10	04/05/91	5.50	3.50			5.00	
b	As "a," vertically imperf. between		1,500.00					
c	Horizontal pair, imperf. vertically		300.00					
d	As "a," imperf. horizontally		2,750.00					
	Flag With Olympic Rings Booklet Issue, Perf. 11							
2528	29¢ U.S. Flag, Olympic Rings,							
	single from booklet	04/21/91	.50	.20			1.25	
a	Booklet pane of 10	04/21/91	5.25	3.50			5.00	
	Issues of 1991-94, Perf. 10 Vertically							
2529	19¢ Fishing Boat	08/08/91	.35	.20	3.50	(5)	1.40	
a	New printing, Type II	1993	.35	.20	3.75	(5)		
b	As "a," untagged		1.00	.40	7.75	(5)		
	Perf. 9.8							
2529C	19¢ Fishing Boat	06/25/94	.50	.20	7.75	(5)	1.40	
	Type II stamps have finer dot pattern, smoother edges along type. #2529C has only one loop of rope tying up the boat.							
	Issue of 1991, Ballooning Booklet Issue, Perf. 10							
2530	19¢ Overhead View of Balloon,							
	single from booklet	05/17/91	.35	.20			1.25	
a	Booklet pane of 10	05/17/91	3.50	2.75			5.00	
	#2530 was issued only in booklets. All stamps are imperf. on one side or on one side and bottom.							
	Perf. 11							
2531	29¢ Flags on Parade	05/30/91	.50	.20	2.40	(4)	1.25	
	Self-Adhesive, Die-Cut, Imperf.							
2531A	29¢ Liberty Torch, single							
	stamp from pane	06/25/91	.55	.25			1.25	
b	Pane of 18	06/25/91	10.50					
	Perf. 11							
2532	50¢ Founding of Switzerland	02/22/91	1.00	.25	5.00	(4)	1.40	100
a	Vertical pair, imperf. horizontally		2,250.00					
2533	29¢ Vermont Statehood	03/01/91	.55	.20	2.75	(4)	1.50	0.1
2534	29¢ Savings Bonds	04/30/91	.50	.20	2.50	(4)	1.25	151
	Perf. 12.5 x 13							
2535	29¢ Love	05/09/91	.50	.20	2.50	(4)	1.25	631
2535A	Perf. 11		.70	.20	4.00	(4)		
	Booklet Stamp, Perf. 11 on 2 or 3 sides							
2536	29¢ (2535), single from booklet		.50	.20			1.25	
a	Booklet pane of 10	05/09/91	5.25	3.50			5.00	
	Perf. 11							
2537	52¢ Love	05/09/91	.90	.20	4.50	(4)	1.40	200

2524   **2525**   **2526**

2528
2529   **2529C**

2531

2530

2531A

2532

2533   **2534**

2535

2537

2538

2539

2540

2541

2542

2543

2544

2545

2546

2547

2548

2549

2549a

Issues of 1991		Un	U	PB	#	FDC	Q(M)
Literary Arts Issue, Perf. 11							
2538 29¢ William Saroyan	05/22/91	.50	.20	2.50	(4)	1.50	161
Issues of 1991–93, Perf. 11							
2539 $1 USPS Logo/Olympic Rings	09/29/91	1.75	.50	8.00	(4)	2.25	
2540 $2.90 Priority Mail	07/07/91	5.00	2.50	20.00	(4)	4.50	
2541 $9.95 Domestic Express Mail	06/16/91	15.00	7.50	60.00	(4)	12.50	
2542 $14 International Express Mail	08/31/91	22.50	10.00	90.00	(4)	19.00	
a Red omitted		*1,500.00*					
Perf 11 x 10.5							
2543 $2.90 Space Vehicle	06/03/93	5.00	2.25	22.50	(4)	6.00	
Perf. 11.2							
2544 $3 Space Shuttle *Challenger*	06/22/95	5.25	2.25	21.00	(4)	7.00	
Express Mail Rate, Perf. 11							
2544A $10.75 Space Shuttle *Endeavour*	08/04/95	17.50	7.50	70.00	(4)	15.00	
Issues of 1991, Fishing Flies Booklet Issue, Perf. 11 Horizontally							
2545 29¢ Royal Wulff	05/31/91	1.00	.20			1.25	149
2546 29¢ Jock Scott	05/31/91	1.00	.20			1.25	149
2547 29¢ Apte Tarpon Fly	05/31/91	1.00	.20			1.25	149
2548 29¢ Lefty's Deceiver	05/31/91	1.00	.20			1.25	149
2549 29¢ Muddler Minnow	05/31/91	1.00	.20			1.25	149
a Booklet pane of 5, #2545-49		5.50	*2.50*			3.00	149

#2545-49 were issued only in booklets. All stamps are imperf. at sides or imperf. at sides and bottom.

Greetings From Texas

Texans and tourists often say, "It's like a whole other country"; in fact, the "Lone Star State" once was a separate country. In 1836, Texas won its freedom from Mexico when Gen. Sam Houston led his forces to victory in the Battle of San Jacinto, just six weeks after the fall of the Alamo. General Houston, a former Tennessee governor and United States congressman, became the first president of the new republic. A red, white, and blue banner with a lone star served as the republic's official flag and remained as such after Texas joined the Union in 1845.

As a state, Texas grew rich on cattle, cotton, and oil, and its cities sprouted skyscrapers as they developed into leaders of industry, banking, and commerce. But outside the city limits, Texans have long enjoyed wide-open spaces where nature spreads carpets of wildflowers every spring and an amazing number of birds and other wildlife continue to make their homes. ■

Issues of 1991		Un	U	PB	#	FDC	Q(M)
Performing Arts Issue, Perf. 11							
2550	29¢ Cole Porter at Piano,						
	Sheet Music 06/08/91	.50	.20	2.50	(4)	1.25	150
a	Vertical pair, imperf. horizontally	650.00					
2551	29¢ Operations Desert Shield/						
	Desert Storm 07/02/91	.50	.20	2.50	(4)	2.50	200
a	Vertical pair, imperf. horizontally	2,000.00					
Booklet Stamp, Perf. 11 on 1 or 2 sides							
2552	29¢ Operations Desert Shield/Desert						
	Storm (2551), single from booklet 07/02/91	.50	.20			2.50	200
a	Booklet pane of 5 07/02/91	2.75	2.25			4.50	40
Summer Olympic Games Issue, Perf. 11							
2553	29¢ Pole Vaulter 07/12/91	.50	.20			1.25	34
2554	29¢ Discus Thrower 07/12/91	.50	.20			1.25	34
2555	29¢ Women Sprinters 07/12/91	.50	.20			1.25	34
2556	29¢ Javelin Thrower 07/12/91	.50	.20			1.25	34
2557	29¢ Women Hurdlers 07/12/91	.50	.20			1.25	34
a	Strip of 5, #2553-57	2.75	2.25	7.50	(10)	3.00	34
2558	29¢ Numismatics 08/13/91	.50	.20	2.50	(4)	1.25	150
World War II Issue, 1941: A World at War, Miniature Sheet							
2559	Sheet of 10 and central label 09/03/91	5.25	4.50			7.00	15
a	29¢ Burma Road	.50	.30			1.50	15
b	29¢ America's First Peacetime Draft	.50	.30			1.50	15
c	29¢ Lend-Lease Act	.50	.30			1.50	15
d	29¢ Atlantic Charter	.50	.30			1.50	15
e	29¢ Arsenal of Democracy	.50	.30			1.50	15
f	29¢ Destroyer Reuben James	.50	.30			1.50	15
g	29¢ Civil Defense	.50	.30			1.50	15
h	29¢ Liberty Ship	.50	.30			1.50	15
i	29¢ Pearl Harbor	.50	.30			1.50	15
j	29¢ U.S. Declaration of War	.50	.30			1.50	15
k	29¢ Black omitted	10,000.00					

Greetings From Hawaii

Hawaii, "the Aloha State," lies in the Pacific Ocean more than 2,000 miles southwest of California. It is the nation's southernmost state, blessed with a tropical climate, sandy beaches, lush rain forests, tropical flowers, pineapples and sugarcane, and a host of marine animals.

Born under the sea millions of years ago, the Hawaiian Islands are actually the tops of enormous volcanoes rising more than 30,000 feet from the ocean floor. On the Big Island of Hawaii, red-hot lava frequently flows from Kilauea, one of the world's most active volcanoes, while on Oahu, tourists in Honolulu regularly flow toward Waikiki Beach and the extinct Diamond Head volcano, two of the most famous places on the planet.

Honolulu is also the setting for the Iolani Palace, once occupied by Hawaiian royalty but now a museum. Just west of town is Pearl Harbor, where the USS Arizona Memorial honors those who lost their lives in the deadly attack of December 7, 1941. ■

2550

2551

2553 2554 2555 2556 2557 2557a

2558

a b c d e

f g h i j 2559

2560

2561

2562 **2563** **2564** **2565** **2566** **2566a**

2567

2568 **2569** **2570** **2571** **2572**

2573 **2574** **2575** **2576** **2577** **2577a**

	Issues of 1991		Un	U	PB	#	FDC	Q(M)
2560	29¢ Basketball	08/28/91	.50	.20	2.50	(4)	2.00	150
2561	29¢ District of Columbia	09/07/91	.50	.20	2.50	(4)	1.25	149
a	Black omitted		125.00					
	Comedians Booklet Issue, Perf. 11 on 2 or 3 sides							
2562	29¢ Stan Laurel and Oliver Hardy	08/29/91	.50	.20			1.50	140
2563	29¢ Edgar Bergen and							
	Dummy Charlie McCarthy	08/29/91	.50	.20			1.50	140
2564	29¢ Jack Benny	08/29/91	.50	.20			1.50	140
2565	29¢ Fanny Brice	08/29/91	.50	.20			1.50	140
2566	29¢ Bud Abbott and Lou Costello	08/29/91	.50	.20			1.50	140
a	Booklet pane of 10,							
	2 each of #2562-66		5.50	3.50			6.00	70
b	As "a," scarlet and bright violet omitted		700.00					
c	Strip of 5		2.50	—				
	#2562-66 issued only in booklets. All stamps are imperf. at top or bottom, or at top or bottom and right side.							
	Black Heritage Issue, Perf. 11							
2567	29¢ Jan Matzeliger and							
	Shoe-Lasting Machine Diagram	09/15/91	.50	.20	2.50	(4)	1.75	149
a	Horizontal pair, imperf. vertically		1,500.00					
b	Vertical pair, imperf. horizontally		1,500.00					
c	Imperf., pair		1,250.00					
	Space Exploration Booklet Issue, Perf. 11 on 2 or 3 sides							
2568	29¢ Mercury, Mariner 10	10/01/91	.85	.20			1.25	33
2569	29¢ Venus, Mariner 2	10/01/91	.85	.20			1.25	33
2570	29¢ Earth, Landsat	10/01/91	.85	.20			1.25	33
2571	29¢ Moon, Lunar Orbiter	10/01/91	.85	.20			1.25	33
2572	29¢ Mars, Viking Orbiter	10/01/91	.85	.20			1.25	33
2573	29¢ Jupiter, Pioneer 11	10/01/91	.85	.20			1.25	33
2574	29¢ Saturn, Voyager 2	10/01/91	.85	.20			1.25	33
2575	29¢ Uranus, Voyager 2	10/01/91	.85	.20			1.25	33
2576	29¢ Neptune, Voyager 2	10/01/91	.85	.20			1.25	33
2577	29¢ Pluto	10/01/91	.85	.20			1.25	33
a	Booklet pane of 10, #2568-77		9.00	3.50			5.00	33
	#2568-77 issued only in booklets. All stamps are imperf. at top or bottom, or at top or bottom and right side.							

Greetings From Florida

In "the Sunshine State" of Florida, palmetto palms rustle near seemingly endless beaches, orange blossoms scent the air, and citrus fruits grow in abundance. The southernmost state in the mainland United States enjoys a mild climate, and people as well as plants make the most of it. Tourism is a major industry.

Every year, millions of tourists pour into Florida, looking for fun in the sun. They come for the beautiful beaches, the magic of Walt Disney World, or perhaps the incredible sight of a space shuttle lifting off from the Kennedy Space Center.

The first known visitor from Europe was Spanish explorer Juan Ponce de León, who stepped ashore in April of 1513 and gave Florida its name, honoring the springtime celebration of *Pascua florida*, meaning "feast of flowers." In those days, the local residents were Native Americans whose ancestors had arrived in the region thousands of years before. Today, three-quarters of all residents once lived outside the state. ∎

1991-1995

Issues of 1991-1995		Un	U	PB	#	FDC	Q(M)
Christmas Issue, Perf. 11							
2578	29¢ Madonna and Child,						
	by Antoniazzo Romano 10/17/91	.50	.20	2.50	(4)	1.25	401
a	Booklet pane of 10	5.50	3.25				30
b	As "a," single, red and black omitted	3,500.00					
2579	29¢ Santa Claus in Chimney 10/17/91	.50	.20	2.50	(4)	1.25	900
a	Horizontal pair, imperf. vertically	325.00					
b	Vertical pair, imperf. horizontally	525.00					
Booklet Stamps, Perf. 11 on 2 or 3 sides							
2580	29¢ Santa Claus (2579),						
	Type I, single from booklet 10/17/91	1.75	.20			1.25	
2581	29¢ Santa Claus (2579),						
	Type II, single from booklet 10/17/91	1.75	.20			1.25	
a	Pair, #2580, 2581 10/17/91	3.50	.25				28
b	Booklet pane, 2 each	7.50	1.25			2.50	
The extreme left brick in top row of chimney is missing from Type II, #2581.							
2582	29¢ Santa Claus Checking						
	List, single from booklet 10/17/91	.50	.20			1.25	
a	Booklet pane of 4 10/17/91	2.00	1.25			2.50	28
2583	29¢ Santa Claus with Present						
	Under Tree, single from booklet 10/17/91	.50	.20			1.25	
a	Booklet pane of 4 10/17/91	2.00	1.25			2.50	28
2584	29¢ Santa Claus at Fireplace,						
	single from booklet 10/17/91	.50	.20			1.25	
a	Booklet pane of 4 10/17/91	2.00	1.25			2.50	28
2585	29¢ Santa Claus and Sleigh,						
	single from booklet 10/17/91	.50	.20			1.25	
a	Booklet pane of 4 10/17/91	2.00	1.25			2.50	28
#2582-85 issued only in booklets. All stamps are imperf. at top or bottom, or at top or bottom and right side.							
Perf. 11.2							
2587	32¢ James K. Polk 11/02/95	.60	.20	3.00	(4)	1.50	
Issues of 1994, Perf. 11.5							
2590	$1 Victory at Saratoga 05/05/94	1.90	.50	7.60	(4)	3.00	
2592	$5 Washington and Jackson 08/19/94	8.00	2.50	40.00	(4)	9.00	

2578

2579

2580   2581   2581a

2582   2583

2584   2585

2587

2590   2592

2593

2594

2595

2596

2597

2598

2599

2602

2603

2604

2605

2606

2607

2608

2609

	Issues of 1991-1994		Un	U	PB	#	FDC	Q(M)
	Perf. 10							
2593	29¢ Pledge of Allegiance	09/08/92	.50	.20			1.25	
a	Booklet of 10		5.25	4.25			5.00	
	Perf. 11 x 10							
2593B	Pledge of Allegiance, shiny gum		1.00	.50				
c	Booklet pane of 10, shiny gum		10.00	6.00				
	Issue of 1993, Perf. 11 x 10							
2594	29¢ Pledge of Allegiance	04/08/93	.50	.20				
a	Booklet of 10		5.25	4.25				
b	Imperf., pair		900.00					
	Issues of 1992, Self-Adhesive Booklet and Coil Stamps							
2595	29¢ Eagle and Shield							
	(brown lettering)	09/25/92	.50	.25			1.50	
a	Pane of 17 + label		13.00					
b	Pair, no die-cutting		225.00					
c	Brown omitted		475.00					
d	As "a," no die-cutting		1,800.00					
2596	29¢ Eagle and Shield							
	(green lettering)	09/25/92	.50	.25			1.50	
a	Pane of 17 + label		12.00					
2597	29¢ Eagle and Shield							
	(red lettering)	09/25/92	.50	.25			1.50	
a	Pane of 17 + label		10.00					
	Issues of 1994, Self-Adhesive, Die-Cut							
2598	29¢ Eagle	02/04/94	.50	.20			1.25	
a	Booklet pane of 18		10.00					
b	Coil		—	3.50	8.25	(5)		
2599	29¢ Statue of Liberty	06/24/94	.50	.20			1.25	
a	Booklet pane of 18		10.00					
b	Coil		—	3.75	8.50	(5)		
	Issues of 1991-1993, Perf. 10 Vertically							
2602	10¢ Eagle and Shield							
	(inscribed "Bulk Rate USA")	12/13/91	.20	.20	2.50	(5)	1.25	
2603	10¢ Eagle and Shield							
	(inscribed "USA Bulk Rate")	05/29/93	.20	.20	3.00	(5)	1.25	
a	Imperf., pair		30.00					
b	Tagged (error), shiny gum		2.00	1.50	13.50	(5)		
2604	10¢ Eagle and Shield (metallic,							
	inscribed "USA Bulk Rate")	05/29/93	.20	.20	3.00	(5)	1.25	
2605	23¢ Flag, Presorted First-Class	09/27/91	.40	.40	3.50	(5)	1.25	
	Issues of 1992, Perf. 11							
2606	23¢ USA	07/21/92	.40	.40	4.00	(5)	1.25	
2607	23¢ USA (Bureau)							
	(In #2607, "23" is 7mm long)	10/09/92	.40	.40	4.00	(5)	1.25	
a	Tagged (error), shiny gum		5.00	4.50	115.00	(5)		
c	Imperf., pair		100.00					
2608	23¢ USA (violet)	05/14/93	.40	.40	4.25	(5)	1.25	
2609	29¢ Flag Over White House	04/23/92	.50	.20	4.50	(5)	1.25	
a	Imperf., pair		20.00					
b	Pair, imperf. between		100.00					

	Issues of 1992		Un	U	PB	#	FDC	Q(M)
	Winter Olympic Games Issue							
2611	29¢ Hockey	01/11/92	.50	.20			1.25	32
2612	29¢ Figure Skating	01/11/92	.50	.20			1.25	32
2613	29¢ Speed Skating	01/11/92	.50	.20			1.25	32
2614	29¢ Skiing	01/11/92	.50	.20			1.25	32
2615	29¢ Bobsledding	01/11/92	.50	.20			1.25	32
a	Strip of 5, #2611-15		2.75	2.25	6.50	(10)	3.00	
2616	29¢ World Columbian							
	Stamp Expo	01/24/92	.50	.20	2.50	(4)	1.25	149
a	Tagging omitted		8.50					
	Black Heritage Issue							
2617	29¢ W.E.B. DuBois	01/31/92	.50	.20	2.50	(4)	1.25	150
2618	29¢ Love	02/06/92	.50	.20	2.50	(4)	1.25	835
a	Horizontal pair, imperf. vertically		800.00					
2619	29¢ Olympic Baseball	04/03/92	.50	.20	2.75	(4)	2.00	160
	First Voyage of Christopher Columbus Issue, Perf. 11 x 10.5							
2620	29¢ Seeking Queen Isabella's							
	Support	04/24/92	.50	.20			1.25	40
2621	29¢ Crossing The Atlantic	04/24/92	.50	.20			1.25	40
2622	29¢ Approaching Land	04/24/92	.50	.20			1.25	40
2623	29¢ Coming Ashore	04/24/92	.50	.20			1.25	40
a	Block of 4, #2620-23		2.00	1.90	2.50	(4)	2.75	

Niagara Falls

Among the most famous waterfalls in the world, Niagara Falls lies on the Niagara River, between Lakes Ontario and Erie. The United States-Canadian border divides this spectacular natural feature into the 1,100-foot-wide, 167-foot-high American Falls and the 2,500-foot-wide, 158-foot-high Canadian, or Horseshoe, Falls. Around 12,000 years ago, runoff from an Ice Age glacier began cutting the falls about seven miles north of where they are now, and their present location and incredible beauty are testaments to the erosive force of water flowing over rocks.

For hundreds, perhaps thousands, of years, people have come to the Niagara Falls area, drawn not only by the beauty and power of the water but also by the location. During the War of 1812, this frontier region was the setting for several engagements between American and British forces, including the bloody battle of Lundy's Lane. After the war, water-driven mills and the arrival of the railroad transformed the area into a manufacturing center. The 19th century also brought painters and poets, whose evocative works caused thousands of tourists to want to see the falls for themselves. Over the years, daredevils have washed over the falls in barrels or other contrivances, and some have walked across on tightropes; celebrities have come to see and be seen; and newlyweds have sought romantic bliss here. All the while, the falls have kept working their magic, continuing to migrate southward about one foot every ten years. ■

2611   2612   2613   2614   2615   2615a

2616

2617   2618   2619

2620   2621

2622   2623   2623a

2624

2625

2626

2627

2628

2629

Issues of 1992		Un	U	PB	#	FDC	Q(M)
The Voyages of Columbus Souvenir Sheets, Perf. 10.5							
2624 First Sighting of Land,							
sheet of 3	05/22/92	1.75	—			2.10	2
a 1¢ deep blue		.20	.20			1.25	
b 4¢ ultramarine		.20	.20			1.25	
c $1 salmon		1.65	1.00			2.00	
2625 Claiming a New World,							
sheet of 3	05/22/92	6.75	—			8.00	2
a 2¢ brown violet		.20	.20			1.25	
b 3¢ green		.20	.20			1.25	
c $4 crimson lake		6.50	4.00			8.00	
2626 Seeking Royal Support,							
sheet of 3	05/22/92	1.40	—			1.75	2
a 5¢ chocolate		.20	.20			1.25	
b 30¢ orange brown		.50	.30			1.25	
c 50¢ slate blue		.80	.50			1.50	
2627 Royal Favor Restored,							
sheet of 3	05/22/92	5.25	—			6.25	2
a 6¢ purple		.20	.20			1.25	
b 8¢ magenta		.20	.20			1.25	
c $3 yellow green		4.75	3.00			6.00	
2628 Reporting Discoveries,							
sheet of 3	05/22/92	3.75	—			4.50	2
a 10¢ black brown		.20	.20			1.25	
b 15¢ dark green		.25	.20			1.25	
c $2 brown red		3.25	2.00			4.00	
2629 $5 Christopher Columbus,							
sheet of 1	05/22/92	8.50	—			10.00	2
a $5 black		8.00	5.00				

National Archives

The National Archives and Records Administration (NARA) preserves and protects the essential documents and records of the United States. These include such treasures as the Charters of Freedom—the Declaration of Independence, the Constitution, and the Bill of Rights—which are encased in special glass and displayed in the Rotunda of the National Archives Building in Washington, D.C. Every year, almost a million people visit the building to view these and other historically important or legally significant materials.

NARA maintains more than 30 additional facilities around the country to help manage millions of federal records, posters, still pictures, maps, charts, and aerial photographs, as well as thousands of video and sound recordings and reels of motion picture film. These items document the rights of U.S. citizens, actions taken by government officials, and our experiences as a nation; NARA not only preserves them but also strives to make them readily available to public servants and private citizens alike. ■

	Issues of 1992		Un	U	PB	#	FDC	Q(M)
	Perf. 11							
2630	29¢ New York Stock Exchange							
	Bicentennial	05/17/92	.50	.20	2.50	(4)	1.75	148
	Space Adventures Issue							
2631	29¢ Cosmonaut, US Space							
	Shuttle	05/29/92	.50	.20			1.50	37
2632	29¢ Astronaut, Russian							
	Space Station	05/29/92	.50	.20			1.50	37
2633	29¢ Sputnik, Vostok, Apollo							
	Command and Lunar Modules	05/29/92	.50	.20			1.50	37
2634	29¢ Soyuz, Mercury and							
	Gemini Spacecraft	05/29/92	.50	.20			1.50	37
a	Block of 4, #2631-34		2.00	1.75	2.50	(4)	2.75	
2635	29¢ Alaska Highway, 50th							
	Anniversary	05/30/92	.50	.20	2.50	(4)	1.25	147
a	Black (engr.) omitted		500.00					
2636	29¢ Kentucky Statehood							
	Bicentennial	06/01/92	.50	.20	2.50	(4)	1.25	160
	Summer Olympic Games Issue							
2637	29¢ Soccer	06/11/92	.50	.20			1.25	32
2638	29¢ Gymnastics	06/11/92	.50	.20			1.25	32
2639	29¢ Volleyball	06/11/92	.50	.20			1.25	32
2640	29¢ Boxing	06/11/92	.50	.20			1.25	32
2641	29¢ Swimming	06/11/92	.50	.20			1.25	32
a	Strip of 5, #2637-41		2.50	2.25	5.50	(10)	3.00	
	Hummingbirds Issue							
2642	29¢ Ruby-Throated	06/15/92	.50	.20			1.25	88
2643	29¢ Broad-Billed	06/15/92	.50	.20			1.25	88
2644	29¢ Costa's	06/15/92	.50	.20			1.25	88
2645	29¢ Rufous	06/15/92	.50	.20			1.25	88
2646	29¢ Calliope	06/15/92	.50	.20			1.25	88
a	Booklet pane of 5, #2642-46		2.75	2.25			3.00	

Alaska Highway

In 1992, the Postal Service issued a 29-cent stamp celebrating the 50th anniversary of the Alaska Highway, a triumph of road construction dating from World War II. Thousands of United States Army troops and U.S. and Canadian civilians labored from March to November 1942 to build an overland route for moving military materiel to Alaska.

Heading northwest out of Dawson Creek in the Canadian province of British Columbia, the Alaska Highway reaches into the Yukon Territory and then winds toward the Alaskan border. From there, it rolls on to Delta Junction, about a hundred miles south of Fairbanks, Alaska.

At first the road was largely a cleared trail stretching through 1,500 miles of untamed wilderness. Later it was paved, widened to two lanes, and re-routed where necessary to make it more suitable for commercial traffic and for vacationers seeking adventure on the open road. It has become one of the most important routes in North America. ■

2631

2632

2630

2633

2634

2634a

2636

2635

2637   2638   2639   2640   2641   2641a

2642   2643   2644   2645   2646   2646a

Indian Paintbrush — 2647

Fragrant Water Lily — 2648

Meadow Beauty — 2649

Jack-in-the-Pulpit — 2650

California Poppy — 2651

Large-flowered Trillium — 2652

Tickseed — 2653

Shooting Star — 2654

Stream Violet — 2655

Bluets — 2656

Herb Robert — 2657

Marsh Marigold — 2658

Sweet White Violet — 2659

Claret Cup Cactus — 2660

White Mountain Avens — 2661

Sessile Bellwort — 2662

Blue Flag — 2663

Harlequin Lupine — 2664

Twinflower — 2665

Common Sunflower — 2666

Sego Lily — 2667

Virginia Bluebells — 2668

Ohi'a Lehua — 2669

Rosebud Orchid — 2670

Showy Evening Primrose — 2671

Issues of 1992			Un	U	FDC	Q(M)
Wildflowers Issue, Perf. 11						
2647	29¢ Indian Paintbrush	07/24/92	.50	.20	1.25	11
2648	29¢ Fragrant Water Lily	07/24/92	.50	.20	1.25	11
2649	29¢ Meadow Beauty	07/24/92	.50	.20	1.25	11
2650	29¢ Jack-in-the-Pulpit	07/24/92	.50	.20	1.25	11
2651	29¢ California Poppy	07/24/92	.50	.20	1.25	11
2652	29¢ Large-Flowered Trillium	07/24/92	.50	.20	1.25	11
2653	29¢ Tickseed	07/24/92	.50	.20	1.25	11
2654	29¢ Shooting Star	07/24/92	.50	.20	1.25	11
2655	29¢ Stream Violet	07/24/92	.50	.20	1.25	11
2656	29¢ Bluets	07/24/92	.50	.20	1.25	11
2657	29¢ Herb Robert	07/24/92	.50	.20	1.25	11
2658	29¢ Marsh Marigold	07/24/92	.50	.20	1.25	11
2659	29¢ Sweet White Violet	07/24/92	.50	.20	1.25	11
2660	29¢ Claret Cup Cactus	07/24/92	.50	.20	1.25	11
2661	29¢ White Mountain Avens	07/24/92	.50	.20	1.25	11
2662	29¢ Sessile Bellwort	07/24/92	.50	.20	1.25	11
2663	29¢ Blue Flag	07/24/92	.50	.20	1.25	11
2664	29¢ Harlequin Lupine	07/24/92	.50	.20	1.25	11
2665	29¢ Twinflower	07/24/92	.50	.20	1.25	11
2666	29¢ Common Sunflower	07/24/92	.50	.20	1.25	11
2667	29¢ Sego Lily	07/24/92	.50	.20	1.25	11
2668	29¢ Virginia Bluebells	07/24/92	.50	.20	1.25	11
2669	29¢ Ohi'a Lehua	07/24/92	.50	.20	1.25	11
2670	29¢ Rosebud Orchid	07/24/92	.50	.20	1.25	11
2671	29¢ Showy Evening Primrose	07/24/92	.50	.20	1.25	11

Greetings From South Carolina

Near and dear to the people of South Carolina is the palmetto. This familiar coastal plant is the state tree and source of the state nickname; its likeness appears on automobile license plates, the state flag, and the state seal, serving as a reminder of the palmetto-log fort that held off a British attack in the Revolutionary War. That battle occurred on Sullivan's Island, just north of the first place to be fired on during the Civil War: Fort Sumter, at the entrance to Charleston Harbor.

Charleston was founded in the late 1600s and quickly became a busy port. Today, its harbor front boasts beautifully restored old homes where 18th-century merchants and sea captains once dwelled quite comfortably, and where gardens grow lush and magnolia trees still blossom in the warm, low-country air.

The Blue Ridge Mountains rise in the state's northwest corner, a scenic region presided over by 3,560-foot Sassafras Mountain, highest peak in South Carolina. ■

	Issues of 1992		Un	U	FDC	Q(M)
	Wildflowers Issue (continued)					
2672	29¢ Fringed Gentian	07/24/92	.50	.20	1.25	11
2673	29¢ Yellow Lady's Slipper	07/24/92	.50	.20	1.25	11
2674	29¢ Passionflower	07/24/92	.50	.20	1.25	11
2675	29¢ Bunchberry	07/24/92	.50	.20	1.25	11
2676	29¢ Pasqueflower	07/24/92	.50	.20	1.25	11
2677	29¢ Round-Lobed Hepatica	07/24/92	.50	.20	1.25	11
2678	29¢ Wild Columbine	07/24/92	.50	.20	1.25	11
2679	29¢ Fireweed	07/24/92	.50	.20	1.25	11
2680	29¢ Indian Pond Lily	07/24/92	.50	.20	1.25	11
2681	29¢ Turk's Cap Lily	07/24/92	.50	.20	1.25	11
2682	29¢ Dutchman's Breeches	07/24/92	.50	.20	1.25	11
2683	29¢ Trumpet Honeysuckle	07/24/92	.50	.20	1.25	11
2684	29¢ Jacob's Ladder	07/24/92	.50	.20	1.25	11
2685	29¢ Plains Prickly Pear	07/24/92	.50	.20	1.25	11
2686	29¢ Moss Campion	07/24/92	.50	.20	1.25	11
2687	29¢ Bearberry	07/24/92	.50	.20	1.25	11
2688	29¢ Mexican Hat	07/24/92	.50	.20	1.25	11
2689	29¢ Harebell	07/24/92	.50	.20	1.25	11
2690	29¢ Desert Five Spot	07/24/92	.50	.20	1.25	11
2691	29¢ Smooth Solomon's Seal	07/24/92	.50	.20	1.25	11
2692	29¢ Red Maids	07/24/92	.50	.20	1.25	11
2693	29¢ Yellow Skunk Cabbage	07/24/92	.50	.20	1.25	11
2694	29¢ Rue Anemone	07/24/92	.50	.20	1.25	11
2695	29¢ Standing Cypress	07/24/92	.50	.20	1.25	11
2696	29¢ Wild Flax	07/24/92	.50	.20	1.25	11
a	Pane of 50, #2647-96		25.00	—	30.00	11

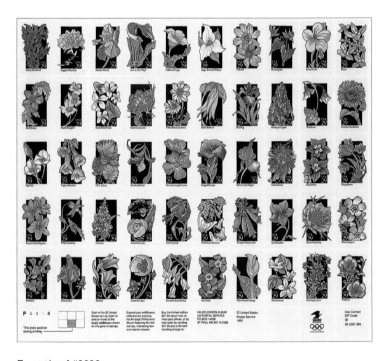

Example of #2696a

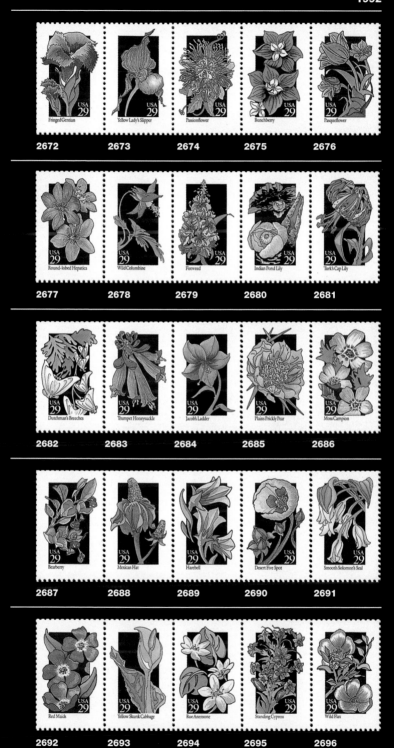

Fringed Gentian | USA 29
2672

Yellow Lady's Slipper | USA 29
2673

Passionflower | USA 29
2674

Bunchberry | USA 29
2675

Pasqueflower | USA 29
2676

Round-lobed Hepatica | USA 29
2677

Wild Columbine | USA 29
2678

Fireweed | USA 29
2679

Indian Pond Lily | USA 29
2680

Turk's Cap Lily | USA 29
2681

Dutchman's Breeches | USA 29
2682

Trumpet Honeysuckle | USA 29
2683

Jacob's Ladder | USA 29
2684

Plains Prickly Pear | USA 29
2685

Moss Campion | USA 29
2686

Bearberry | USA 29
2687

Mexican Hat | USA 29
2688

Harebell | USA 29
2689

Desert Five Spot | USA 29
2690

Smooth Solomon's Seal | USA 29
2691

Red Maids | USA 29
2692

Yellow Skunk Cabbage | USA 29
2693

Rue Anemone | USA 29
2694

Standing Cypress | USA 29
2695

Wild Flax | USA 29
2696

1992

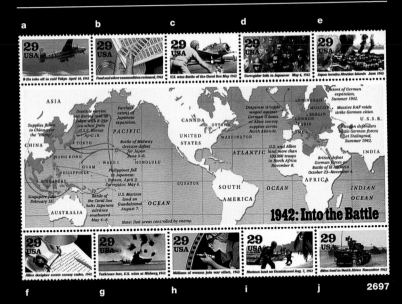

a — 29 USA — B-25s take off to raid Tokyo April 18, 1942
b — 29 USA — Food and other commodities rationed, 1942
c — 29 USA — U.S. wins Battle of the Coral Sea May 1942
d — 29 USA — Corregidor falls to Japanese May 6, 1942
e — 29 USA — Japan invades Aleutian Islands June 1942

1942: Into the Battle

f — 29 USA — Allies decipher secret enemy codes, 1942
g — 29 USA — Yorktown lost, U.S. wins at Midway, 1942
h — 29 USA — Millions of women join war effort, 1942
i — 29 USA — Marines land on Guadalcanal Aug. 7, 1942
j — 29 USA — Allies land in North Africa November 1942

2697

2698

Dorothy Parker
American Writer 1893–1967

2699

Theodore von Kármán
Aerospace Scientist
USA 29

2700 2701

Minerals USA 29 — Azurite
Minerals USA 29 — Copper
Minerals USA 29 — Variscite
Minerals USA 29 — Wulfenite

2702 2703 2703a

Explorer of California 1542
29 USA
Juan Rodriguez CABRILLO

2704

	Issues of 1992		Un	U	PB	#	FDC	Q(M)
	World War II Issue, 1942: Into the Battle, Miniature Sheet, Perf. 11							
2697	Sheet of 10 and central label	08/17/92	5.25	4.50			7.00	12
a	29¢ B-25s Take Off to Raid Tokyo		.50	.30			1.50	12
b	29¢ Food and Other Commodities Rationed		.50	.30			1.50	12
c	29¢ U.S. Wins Battle of the Coral Sea		.50	.30			1.50	12
d	29¢ Corregidor Falls to Japanese		.50	.30			1.50	12
e	29¢ Japan Invades Aleutian Islands		.50	.30			1.50	12
f	29¢ Allies Decipher Secret Enemy Codes		.50	.30			1.50	12
g	29¢ *Yorktown* Lost		.50	.30			1.50	12
h	29¢ Millions of Women Join War Effort		.50	.30			1.50	12
i	29¢ Marines Land on Guadalcanal		.50	.30			1.50	12
j	29¢ Allies Land in North Africa		.50	.30			1.50	12
	Literary Arts Issue							
2698	29¢ Dorothy Parker	08/22/92	.50	.20	2.50	(4)	1.25	105
2699	29¢ Dr. Theodore von Karman	08/31/92	.50	.20	2.50	(4)	1.25	143
	Minerals Issue							
2700	29¢ Azurite	09/17/92	.50	.20			1.25	37
2701	29¢ Copper	09/17/92	.50	.20			1.25	37
2702	29¢ Variscite	09/17/92	.50	.20			1.25	37
2703	29¢ Wulfenite	09/17/92	.50	.20			1.25	37
a	Block of 4, #2700-03		2.00	1.75	2.50	(4)	2.75	
b	As "a," silver (litho.) omitted		8,500.00					
2704	29¢ Juan Rodriguez Cabrillo	09/28/92	.50	.20	2.50	(4)	1.25	85
a	Black (engr.) omitted		4,000.00					

California Statehood

California celebrated 150 years of statehood in 2000, and the Postal Service marked the occasion with a stamp depicting the ruggedly beautiful Big Sur coastline south of Monterey. The state has many more natural treasures, as well as a wealth of historical sites preserved in scores of parks scattered across the landscape.

For countless generations, California's sole inhabitants were Native American groups. Then, in the 16th century, Spain claimed the land. This European power lost it early in the 19th century to Mexico, which in turn gave it up to the United States following the Mexican-American War. In 1848, not long after California became a U.S. territory, gold was discovered at Sutter's Mill northeast of Sacramento. The population soared as thousands of gold seekers—the forty-niners—poured in, and on September 9, 1850, California became the 31st state in the Union. ■

Issues of 1992			Un	U	PB	#	FDC	Q(M)
Wild Animals Issue, Perf. 11 Horizontally								
2705	29¢ Giraffe	10/01/92	.50	.20			1.25	80
2706	29¢ Giant Panda	10/01/92	.50	.20			1.25	80
2707	29¢ Flamingo	10/01/92	.50	.20			1.25	80
2708	29¢ King Penguins	10/01/92	.50	.20			1.25	80
2709	29¢ White Bengal Tiger	10/01/92	.50	.20			1.25	80
a	Booklet pane of 5, #2705-09		2.50	*2.00*			3.25	
b	As "a," imperf.		*3,000.00*					
Christmas Issue, Perf. 11.5 x 11								
2710	29¢ Madonna and Child by Giovanni Bellini	10/22/92	.50	.20	2.50	(4)	1.25	300
a	Booklet pane of 10		5.25	*3.50*			7.25	349
2711	29¢ Horse and Rider	10/22/92	.50	.20			1.25	125
2712	29¢ Toy Train	10/22/92	.50	.20			1.25	125
2713	29¢ Toy Steamer	10/22/92	.50	.20			1.25	125
2714	29¢ Toy Ship	10/22/92	.50	.20			1.25	125
a	Block of 4, #2711-14		2.00	1.10	2.50	(4)	2.75	
Perf. 11								
2715	29¢ Horse and Rider	10/22/92	.85	.20			1.25	102
2716	29¢ Toy Train	10/22/92	.85	.20			1.25	102
2717	29¢ Toy Steamer	10/22/92	.85	.20			1.25	102
2718	29¢ Toy Ship	10/22/92	.85	.20			1.25	102
a	Booklet pane of 4, #2715-18		3.50	*1.25*			2.75	
2719	29¢ Toy Train (self-adhesive)	10/22/92	.60	.20			1.25	22
a	Booklet pane of 18		11.00					
Lunar New Year Issue								
2720	29¢ Year of the Rooster	12/30/92	.50	.20	2.00	(4)	2.00	

District of Columbia Bicentennial

Pennsylvania Avenue, circa 1903

USA 29

District of Columbia

In July 1790, the United States Congress—then located in Philadelphia, Pennsylvania, along with the rest of the U.S. government—authorized President George Washington to select a permanent site for the new federal government. Washington announced his choice the following January: a marshy, wooded area about 16 miles up the Potomac River from his Virginia estate. Over the next several months, surveyors marked boundary lines, and architect-engineer Pierre L'Enfant drew up city plans. Secretary of State Thomas Jefferson helped select names for the new city and territory: Washington, for the President, and Columbia, for Christopher Columbus. By 1800, the federal government was in place and more than 3,000 people were in residence.

Since then, the District of Columbia has grown into a national and international center of political power, education, culture, and tourism. Millions come every year to tour the museums, monuments, memorials, and ever popular National Zoo. But beyond the federal enclave and tourist attractions is a rich mosaic of neighborhoods, where Washingtonians enjoy a small-town atmosphere within the bounds of a major city. ■

2705

Giraffe

2706

Giant Panda

2707

Flamingo

2708

King Penguins

2709

White Bengal Tiger

2709a

2710

2711   2712

2713   2714   2714a

2715   2716

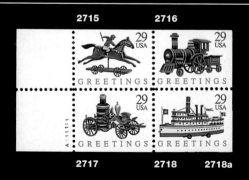

A 111111

2717   2718   2718a

GREETINGS

2719

2720

1993

2721

2722

2723

2724 2725 2726 2727 2728

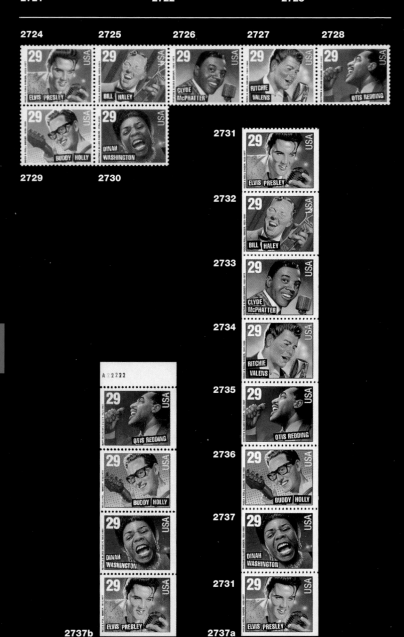

2729 2730

2731

2732

2733

2734

2735

2736

2737

2731

2737b 2737a

	Issues of 1993		Un	U	PB	#	FDC	Q(M)
	Legends of American Music Series, Perf. 11							
2721	29¢ Elvis Presley	01/08/93	.50	.20	2.50	(4)	1.75	517
	Perf. 10							
2722	29¢ *Oklahoma!*	03/30/93	.50	.20	2.50	(4)	1.25	150
2723	29¢ Hank Williams	06/09/93	.50	.20	2.50	(4)	1.25	152
	Perf. 11.2 x 11.5							
2723A	29¢ Hank Williams		22.50	9.00	140.00	(4)	1.25	
	Legends of American Music Series, Rock & Roll/Rhythm & Blues Issue, Perf. 10							
2724	29¢ Elvis Presley	06/16/93	.60	.20			1.25	14
2725	29¢ Bill Haley	06/16/93	.60	.20			1.25	14
2726	29¢ Clyde McPhatter	06/16/93	.60	.20			1.25	14
2727	29¢ Ritchie Valens	06/16/93	.60	.20			1.25	14
2728	29¢ Otis Redding	06/16/93	.60	.20			1.25	14
2729	29¢ Buddy Holly	06/16/93	.60	.20			1.25	14
2730	29¢ Dinah Washington	06/16/93	.60	.20			1.25	14
a	Vertical strip of 7, #2724-30		4.25		8.00	(10)	5.00	
	Perf. 11 Horizontally							
2731	29¢ Elvis Presley	06/16/93	.50	.20			1.25	99
2732	29¢ Bill Haley (2725)	06/16/93	.50	.20			1.25	33
2733	29¢ Clyde McPhatter (2726)	06/16/93	.50	.20			1.25	33
2734	29¢ Ritchie Valens (2727)	06/16/93	.50	.20			1.25	33
2735	29¢ Otis Redding	06/16/93	.50	.20			1.25	66
2736	29¢ Buddy Holly	06/16/93	.50	.20			1.25	66
2737	29¢ Dinah Washington	06/16/93	.50	.20			1.25	66
a	Booklet pane, 2 #2731, 1 each #2732-37		4.25	2.25			5.25	
b	Booklet pane of 4, #2731, 2735-37		2.25	1.50			2.75	
2738-40	Not assigned							

Greetings From Ohio

Eight United States Presidents were born or raised in Ohio. Two astronauts also grew up here: John Glenn, first American to orbit Earth, was born in the state, and so was Neil Armstrong, first man on the moon.

Long before the United States was born, an ancient mound-building culture flourished in Ohio. The Serpent Mound State Memorial in Adams County preserves a thousand-year-old, quarter-mile-long snake-shaped effigy; it is the largest such feature in the country.

The state preserves artifacts and memorabilia from American culture, too, at such places as the Pro Football Hall of Fame in Canton, the Rock and Roll Hall of Fame and Museum in Cleveland, and the Motorcycle Hall of Fame in Pickerington. Several museums have transportation themes, and these include the U.S. Air Force Museum in Dayton, the Bicycle Museum of America in New Bremen, the Neil Armstrong Air & Space Museum in Wapakoneta, and the National Road/Zane Grey Museum at Norwich. ■

1993

	Issues of 1993		Un	U	PB	#	FDC	Q(M)
	Space Fantasy Issue, Perf. 11 Vertically on 1 or 2 sides							
2741	29¢ multicolored	01/25/93	.50	.20			1.25	140
2742	29¢ multicolored	01/25/93	.50	.20			1.25	140
2743	29¢ multicolored	01/25/93	.50	.20			1.25	140
2744	29¢ multicolored	01/25/93	.50	.20			1.25	140
2745	29¢ multicolored	01/25/93	.50	.20			1.25	140
a	Booklet pane of 5, #2741-45		2.50	2.25			3.25	
	Black Heritage Issue							
2746	29¢ Percy Lavon Julian	01/29/93	.50	.20	2.50	(4)	1.25	105
2747	29¢ Oregon Trail	02/12/93	.50	.20	2.50	(4)	1.25	110
a	Tagging omitted		20.00					
2748	29¢ World University Games	02/25/93	.50	.20	2.50	(4)	1.25	110
2749	29¢ Grace Kelly	03/25/93	.50	.20	2.50	(4)	2.00	173
	Circus Issue, Perf. 11							
2750	29¢ Clown	04/06/93	.55	.20			1.50	66
2751	29¢ Ringmaster	04/06/93	.55	.20			1.50	66
2752	29¢ Trapeze Artist	04/06/93	.55	.20			1.50	66
2753	29¢ Elephant	04/06/93	.55	.20			1.50	66
a	Block of 4, #2750-53		2.25	1.75	4.50	(6)	3.00	
2754	29¢ Cherokee Strip	04/17/93	.50	.20	2.00	(4)	1.25	110
2755	29¢ Dean Acheson	04/21/93	.50	.20	2.50	(4)	1.25	116
	Sporting Horses Issue, Perf. 11 x 11.5							
2756	29¢ Steeplechase	05/01/93	.50	.20			1.75	40
2757	29¢ Thoroughbred Racing	05/01/93	.50	.20			1.75	40
2758	29¢ Harness Racing	05/01/93	.50	.20			1.75	40
2759	29¢ Polo	05/01/93	.50	.20			1.75	40
a	Block of 4, #2756-59		2.00	1.75	2.50	(4)	3.50	

Greetings From Oregon

In the mid-1800s, wagon trains rattled along the Oregon Trail, carrying thousands of pioneers to new lands and new lives in the Pacific Northwest. Their deep wheel ruts still mark some of the wide-open landscapes of eastern Oregon.

Most settlers chose to put down roots in the verdant Willamette Valley, tucked between the Cascade Mountains in the east and the Coast Range in the west. Today, the majority of Oregon's population continues to reside here, enjoying the valley's bountiful harvests of fruits, vegetables, nuts, herbs, and flowers, as well as a thriving wine industry.

To the north, the Columbia River tumbles down from Washington, veers sharply west, and slices through the mountains before emptying into the Pacific. Visible from the river's spectacular gorge is the snow-covered summit of Mount Hood, highest peak in the state.

Among Oregon's other natural treasures are tall waterfalls, towering redwoods, splendid Pacific beaches, and abundant wildlife, including a national treasure known as the bald eagle. ■

2741   2742   2743   2744   2745   2745a

2746

2747

2748

2749

2750   2751

2752   2753

2753a

2754

2755

2756   2757

2758   2759

2759a

2760   2761   2762   2763   2764   2764a

2765

2766

2767

2768

2769

2770

2770a

	Issues of 1993		Un	U	PB	#	FDC	Q(M)
	Garden Flowers Issue, Perf. 11 Vertically							
2760	29¢ Hyacinth	05/15/93	.50	.20			1.75	200
2761	29¢ Daffodil	05/15/93	.50	.20			1.75	200
2762	29¢ Tulip	05/15/93	.50	.20			1.75	200
2763	29¢ Iris	05/15/93	.50	.20			1.75	200
2764	29¢ Lilac	05/15/93	.50	.20			1.75	200
a	Booklet pane of 5, #2760-64		2.50	2.00			4.00	
b	As "a," black omitted		250.00					
c	As "a," imperf.		2,500.00					
	World War II Issue, 1943: Turning The Tide, Miniature Sheet, Perf. 11							
2765	Sheet of 10 and central label	05/31/93	5.25	4.50			7.00	
a	29¢ Allied Forces Battle German U-boats		.50	.30			1.50	12
b	29¢ Military Medics Treat the Wounded.		.50	.30			1.50	12
c	29¢ Sicily Attacked by Allied Forces		.50	.30			1.50	12
d	29¢ B-24s Hit Ploesti Refineries		.50	.30			1.50	12
e	29¢ V-Mail Delivers Letters from Home.		50	.30			1.50	12
f	29¢ Italy Invaded by Allies		.50	.30			1.50	12
g	29¢ Bonds and Stamps Help War Effort		.50	.30			1.50	12
h	29¢ "Willie and Joe" Keep Spirits High.		50	.30			1.50	12
i	29¢ Gold Stars Mark World War II Losses		.50	.30			1.50	12
j	29¢ Marines Assault Tarawa		.50	.30			1.50	12
2766	29¢ Joe Louis	06/22/93	.50	.20	2.50	(4)	1.75	160
	Legends of American Music Series, Broadway Musicals Issue, Perf. 11 Horizontally							
2767	29¢ *Show Boat*	07/14/93	.50	.20			1.25	129
2768	29¢ *Porgy & Bess*	07/14/93	.50	.20			1.25	129
2769	29¢ *Oklahoma!*	07/14/93	.50	.20			1.25	129
2770	29¢ *My Fair Lady*	07/14/93	.50	.20			1.25	129
a	Booklet pane of 4, #2767-70		2.50	2.00			3.25	

Longleaf Pine Forest

Vast numbers of longleaf pines once covered the coastal plain from southern Virginia to eastern Texas, but settlers and the timber industry reduced the great forests to scattered woodlands. Still, today's smaller tracts support an amazing variety of plants and animals. How is this possible?

In these woods, fire spreads quickly because of the resin-rich pine needles that accumulate on the ground. The trees themselves tolerate fire fairly well, having evolved adaptations that include thick, protective bark. When fire moves through a forest, it releases nutrients from dead vegetation, clears the ground for seedlings to take root, and weeds out less fire-resistant trees and shrubs that block sunlight and compete for space.

After a burn, plants such as wiregrass produce abundant seeds, and surviving wildflowers bloom in profusion—a boon to birds, insects, and other wildlife. More than 300 kinds of animals protect themselves from fires and predators by taking shelter in burrows dug by gopher tortoises, the so-called innkeepers of the forest. ■

	Issues of 1993		Un	U	PB	#	FDC	Q(M)
	Legends of American Music Series, Country & Western Issue, Perf. 10							
2771	29¢ Hank Williams (2775)	09/25/93	.55	.20			1.25	25
2772	29¢ Patsy Cline (2777)	09/25/93	.55	.20			1.25	25
2773	29¢ The Carter Family (2776)	09/25/93	.55	.20			1.25	25
2774	29¢ Bob Wills (2778)	09/25/93	.55	.20			1.25	25
a	Block or horiz. strip of 4, #2771-74		2.20	1.75	3.00	(4)	2.75	
	Booklet Stamps, Perf. 11 Horizontally							
2775	29¢ Hank Williams	09/25/93	.50	.20			1.25	170
2776	29¢ The Carter Family	09/25/93	.50	.20			1.25	170
2777	29¢ Patsy Cline	09/25/93	.50	.20			1.25	170
2778	29¢ Bob Wills	09/25/93	.50	.20			1.25	170
a	Booklet pane of 4, #2775-78		2.50	2.00			2.75	
	National Postal Museum Issue, Perf. 11							
2779	Independence Hall, Benjamin Franklin, Printing Press, Colonial Post Rider	07/30/93	.50	.20			1.25	38
2780	Pony Express Rider, Civil War Soldier, Concord Stagecoach	07/30/93	.50	.20			1.25	38
2781	Biplane, Charles Lindbergh, Railway Mail Car, 1931 Model A Ford Mail Truck	07/30/93	.50	.20			1.25	38
2782	California Gold Rush Miner's Letter, Barcode and Circular Date Stamp	07/30/93	.50	.20			1.25	38
a	Block or strip of 4, #2779-82		2.00	1.75	2.00	(4)	2.75	
c	As "a," imperf.	3,500.00						
	American Sign Language Issue, Perf. 11.5							
2783	29¢ Recognizing Deafness	09/20/93	.50	.20			1.25	42
2784	29¢ American Sign Language	09/20/93	.50	.20			1.25	42
a	Pair, #2783-84		1.00	.65	2.00	(4)	2.00	
	Classic Books Issues, Perf. 11							
2785	29¢ Rebecca of Sunnybrook Farm	10/23/93	.50	.20			1.25	38
2786	29¢ Little House on the Prairie	10/23/93	.50	.20			1.25	38
2787	29¢ The Adventures of Huckleberry Finn	10/23/93	.50	.20			1.25	38
2788	29¢ Little Women	10/23/93	.50	.20			1.25	38
a	Block or horiz. strip of 4, #2785-88		2.00	1.75	4.75	(4)	2.75	
b	As "a," imperf.	3,000.00						

Greetings From Tennessee

Tennessee occupies a special place in the hearts of American music fans. This is where composer W. C. Handy, writing songs at his Beale Street address in Memphis, became "Father of the Blues"; where singer Elvis Presley, recording in the Memphis studios of Sun Records, assumed the title of "King of Rock and Roll"; and where the stars of Nashville's Grand Ole Opry made the state capital the country-and-western capital of the world.

Tennessee is also honored for the accomplishments of its many heroes, including Sequoyah, inventor of the Cherokee alphabet; frontiersman Davy Crockett; Adm. David Farragut of the Union Navy; Lt. Gen. Nathan Bedford Forrest of the Confederate Army; and Sgt. Alvin C. York of World War I fame.

Today, vacationers come from all over the United States and from abroad to visit not only the music shrines and historic sites but also the natural wonders of Tennessee—particularly the fabled peaks in Great Smoky Mountains National Park, one of the country's most popular parks. ■

2771 2772

2773 2774 2774a

2775

2776

2777

2778

2778a

2779 2780

2781 2782 2782a

2783 2784 2784a

2785 2786

2787 2788 2788a

2789

2790

2791 2792

2793 2794 2794a

2795 2796

2797 2798 2798c

2799 2800

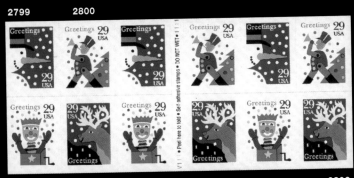

2801 2802 2802a

2803

2804

2805

2806 2806a

	Issues of 1993		Un	U	PB	#	FDC	Q(M)
	Christmas Issue, Perf. 11							
2789	29¢ Madonna and Child	10/21/93	.50	.20	2.50	(4)	1.25	500
	Booklet Stamps, Perf. 11.5 x 11 on 2 or 3 sides							
2790	29¢ Madonna and Child (2789)	10/21/93	.50	.20			1.25	500
a	Booklet pane of 4		2.25	1.75			2.50	
	Perf. 11.5							
2791	29¢ Jack-in-the-Box	10/21/93	.50	.20			1.25	250
2792	29¢ Red-Nosed Reindeer	10/21/93	.50	.20			1.25	250
2793	29¢ Snowman	10/21/93	.50	.20			1.25	250
2794	29¢ Toy Soldier	10/21/93	.50	.20			1.25	250
a	Block or strip of 4, #2791-94		2.00	1.75	3.75	(4)	2.75	
	Booklet Stamps, Perf. 11 x 10 on 2 or 3 sides							
2795	29¢ Toy Soldier (2794)	10/21/93	.85	.20			1.25	200
2796	29¢ Snowman (2793)	10/21/93	.85	.20			1.25	200
2797	29¢ Red-Nosed Reindeer (2792)	10/21/93	.85	.20			1.25	200
2798	29¢ Jack-in-the-Box (2791)	10/21/93	.85	.20			1.25	200
a	Booklet pane, 3 each #2795-96, 2 each #2797-98		8.50	4.00			6.50	
b	Booklet pane, 3 each #2797-98, 2 each #2795-96		8.50	4.00			6.50	
c	Block of 4		3.40	1.75				
	Self-Adhesive, Die-Cut							
2799	29¢ Snowman	10/28/93	.50	.20			1.25	120
a	Coil with plate		—	3.50	6.00	(5)		
2800	29¢ Toy Soldier	10/28/93	.50	.20			1.25	120
2801	29¢ Jack-in-the-Box	10/28/93	.50	.20			1.25	120
2802	29¢ Red-Nosed Reindeer	10/28/93	.50	.20			1.25	120
a	Booklet pane, 3 each #2799-2802		7.00					
b	Block of 4		2.00					
2803	29¢ Snowman	10/28/93	.50	.20			1.25	18
a	Booklet pane of 18		10.00					
	Perf. 11							
2804	29¢ Northern Mariana Islands	11/04/93	.50	.20	2.00	(4)	1.25	88
2805	29¢ Columbus Landing in Puerto Rico	11/19/93	.50	.20	2.50	(4)	1.25	105
2806	29¢ AIDS Awareness	12/01/93	.50	.20	2.50	(4)	1.25	100
a	Booklet version		.50	.20			1.25	250
b	Booklet pane of 5		2.50	2.00			3.25	

1994

Issues of 1994			Un	U	PB	#	FDC	Q(M)
Winter Olympic Games Issue, Perf. 11.2								
2807	29¢ Slalom	01/06/94	.50	.20			1.25	36
2808	29¢ Luge	01/06/94	.50	.20			1.25	36
2809	29¢ Ice Dancing	01/06/94	.50	.20			1.25	36
2810	29¢ Cross-Country Skiing	01/06/94	.50	.20			1.25	36
2811	29¢ Ice Hockey	01/06/94	.50	.20			1.25	36
a	Strip of 5, #2807-11		2.50	2.25	5.00	(10)	3.00	36
2812	29¢ Edward R. Murrow	01/21/94	.50	.20	2.50	(4)	1.25	151
2813	29¢ Love Sunrise	01/27/94	.50	.20	8.00	(5)	1.25	358
a	Booklet of 18 (self-adhesive)		11.00					
b	Coil with plate		—	3.50				
Perf. 10.9 x 11.1								
2814	29¢ Love Stamp	02/14/94	.50	.20			1.25	830
a	Booklet pane of 10		5.50	3.50			6.50	
Perf. 11.1								
2814C	29¢ Love Stamp	06/11/94	.50	.20	2.50	(4)	1.25	300
Perf. 11.2								
2815	52¢ Love Birds	02/14/94	1.00	.20	5.00	(4)	1.40	175
Black Heritage Issue								
2816	29¢ Dr. Allison Davis	02/01/94	.50	.20	2.00	(4)	1.25	156
Lunar New Year Issue								
2817	29¢ Year of the Dog	02/05/94	.55	.20	2.20	(4)	1.75	105
Perf. 11.5 x 11.2								
2818	29¢ Buffalo Soldiers	04/22/94	.50	.20	2.00	(4)	1.50	186
Stars of the Silent Screen Issue, Perf. 11.2								
2819	29¢ Rudolph Valentino	04/27/94	.50	.20			1.50	19
2820	29¢ Clara Bow	04/27/94	.50	.20			1.50	19
2821	29¢ Charlie Chaplin	04/27/94	.50	.20			1.50	19
2822	29¢ Lon Chaney	04/27/94	.50	.20			1.50	19
2823	29¢ John Gilbert	04/27/94	.50	.20			1.50	19
2824	29¢ Zasu Pitts	04/27/94	.50	.20			1.50	19
2825	29¢ Harold Lloyd	04/27/94	.50	.20			1.50	19
2826	29¢ Keystone Cops	04/27/94	.50	.20			1.50	19
2827	29¢ Theda Bara	04/27/94	.50	.20			1.50	19
2828	29¢ Buster Keaton	04/27/94	.50	.20			1.50	19
a	Block of 10 #2819-2828		5.00	4.00	6.00	(10)	6.50	19
b	As "a," black (litho.) omitted		—					
c	As "a," black, red &							
	bright violet (litho.) omitted		—					

Greetings From South Dakota

In South Dakota, prairie dogs still scamper about their prairie home, while the deer, antelope, elk, and bison continue roaming the range in places such as Custer State Park. Named for the Army officer who met defeat at the Battle of the Little Bighorn, Custer is one of several parks, monuments, and historical sites in the southwest corner of the state.

The southwest is known as the Black Hills region, spiritual homeland for the Sioux, who now make up only about 7 percent of the state population. The hills also hold the Homestake Mine, largest gold mine in North America, as well as Mount Rushmore National Memorial, Wind Cave National Park, Jewel Cave National Monument, and historic Deadwood, whose streets were walked in the 1870s by the likes of Wild Bill Hickok and Calamity Jane. To the east lie the barren but beautiful Badlands, and farther east, beyond the Missouri River, stretch gently rolling farmlands thick with corn and other crops. ■

2807 2808 2809 2810 2811 2811a

2812 2813 2814 2814C

2815 2816 2817 2818

2819 2820 2821 2822 2823

2824 2825 2826 2827 2828 2828a

2829 2830 2831 2832 2833 2833a

2834 2835 2836

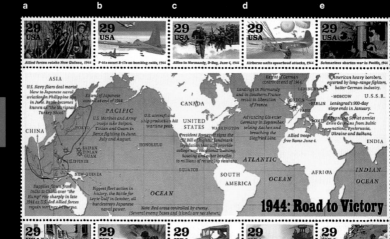

2838

	Issues of 1994		Un	U	PB	#	FDC	Q(M)
	Garden Flowers Booklet Issue, Perf. 10.9 Vertically							
2829	29¢ Lily	04/28/94	.50	.20			1.25	166
2830	29¢ Zinnia	04/28/94	.50	.20			1.25	166
2831	29¢ Gladiola	04/28/94	.50	.20			1.25	166
2832	29¢ Marigold	04/28/94	.50	.20			1.25	166
2833	29¢ Rose	04/28/94	.50	.20			1.25	166
a	Booklet pane of 5, #2829-2833		2.50				3.25	
b	As "a," imperf.		2,250.00					
c	As "a," black (engr.) omitted		300.00					
	1994 World Cup Soccer Championships Issue, Perf. 11.1							
2834	29¢ Soccer Player	05/26/94	.50	.20	2.00	(4)	1.25	201
2835	40¢ Soccer Player	05/26/94	.80	.20	3.20	(4)	1.40	300
2836	50¢ Soccer Player	05/26/94	1.00	.20	4.00	(4)	1.40	269
2837	Souvenir Sheet of 3,							
	#2834-2836	05/26/94	2.50	2.00			2.50	60
a	29¢ Soccer Player							
b	40¢ Soccer Player							
c	50¢ Soccer Player							
	World War II Issue, 1944: Road to Victory Miniature, Sheet, Perf. 10.9							
2838	Sheet of 10 and central label	06/06/94	6.00	4.50			7.00	12
a	29¢ Allies Retake New Guinea		.60	.30			1.50	12
b	29¢ Bombing Raids		.60	.30			1.50	12
c	29¢ Allies in Normandy, D-Day		.60	.30			1.50	12
d	29¢ Airborne Units		.60	.30			1.50	12
e	29¢ Submarines Shorten War		.60	.30			1.50	12
f	29¢ Allies Free Rome, Paris		.60	.30			1.50	12
g	29¢ Troops Clear Siapan Bunkers		.60	.30			1.50	12
h	29¢ Red Ball Express		.60	.30			1.50	12
i	29¢ Battle for Leyte Gulf		.60	.30			1.50	12
j	29¢ Battle of the Bulge		.60	.30			1.50	12

Example of #2837

	Issues of 1994		Un	U	PB	#	FDC	Q(M)
	Norman Rockwell Issue, Perf. 10.9 x 11.1							
2839	29¢ Rockwell Self-Portrait	07/01/94	.50	.20	2.50	(4)	1.25	209
2840	Four Freedoms souvenir sheet	07/01/94	4.00	2.75			3.50	20
a	50¢ Freedom from Want		1.00	.65			1.50	20
b	50¢ Freedom from Fear		1.00	.65			1.50	20
c	50¢ Freedom of Speech		1.00	.65			1.50	20
d	50¢ Freedom of Worship		1.00	.65			1.50	20
	First Moon Landing Issue, Perf. 11.2 x 11.1							
2841	29¢ sheet of 12	07/20/94	7.50	—			6.50	13
a	Single stamp		.60	.60			1.50	155
	Perf. 10.7 x 11.1							
2842	$9.95 Moon Landing	07/20/94	17.50	7.50	70.00	(4)	15.00	101
	Locomotives Issue, Perf. 11 Horizontally							
2843	29¢ Hudson's General	07/28/94	.50	.20			1.25	159
2844	29¢ McQueen's Jupiter	07/28/94	.50	.20			1.25	159
2845	29¢ Eddy's No. 242	07/28/94	.50	.20			1.25	159
2846	29¢ Ely's No. 10	07/28/94	.50	.20			1.25	159
2847	29¢ Buchanan's No. 999	07/28/94	.50	.20			1.25	159
a	Booklet pane of 5, #2843-2847		2.50	2.00			3.25	159
	Perf. 11.1 x 11							
2848	29¢ George Meany	08/16/94	.50	.20	2.50	(4)	1.25	151
	Legends of American Music Series, Popular Singers Issue, Perf. 10.1 x 10.2							
2849	29¢ Al Jolson	09/01/94	.60	.20			1.25	35
2850	29¢ Bing Crosby	09/01/94	.60	.20			1.25	35
2851	29¢ Ethel Waters	09/01/94	.60	.20			1.25	35
2852	29¢ Nat "King" Cole	09/01/94	.60	.20			1.25	35
2853	29¢ Ethel Merman	09/01/94	.60	.20			1.25	35
a	Vert. strip of 5, #2849-2853		3.00	2.00			3.25	

Greetings From Massachusetts

From colonial days to the present, Massachusetts has been at the forefront of American history, education, arts, and industry. History books tell of Plymouth colonists, Lexington and Concord patriots, and revered statesmen and educators. Libraries hold the great literary works of numerous native sons and daughters, among them Henry David Thoreau, who made Walden Pond famous around the world.

The nation's first university, Harvard, was founded in 1636, and today it is one of several noted institutions of higher learning in the state, including the Massachusetts Institute of Technology. Both are located in Cambridge, just across the Charles River from Boston. Largest city in the state, Boston features numerous colonial-era attractions, as well as the John F. Kennedy Library and Museum, the New England Aquarium, and Fenway Park, one of the oldest baseball parks in the country.

In the southeastern part of the state, the Cape Cod peninsula curls around the bay of the same name. Here are cranberry bogs and the sandy beaches of the 27,000-acre Cape Cod National Seashore. ■

2839

a   b

Norman Rockwell

From our doughboys in WWI to our astronauts striding across the moon, Norman Rockwell's artwork has captured America's traditional values along with the characteristic optimism of its people. Rockwell loved people, and people loved him. He was an enormously skilled technician and, according to several new reassessments, a true artist. He had a genius for capturing the emotional content of the commonplace.

1894 1894

c   d

2840

2841a

First Moon Landing, 1969

2842

2843

2844

2845

2846

2847

2847a

2848

2849

2850

2851

2852

2853

2853a

1994

2854 2855 2856 2857 2858

2859 2860 2861

2862

2863 2864

2865 2866

2866a

2867 2868 2868a

	Issues of 1994		Un	U	PB	#	FDC	Q(M)
	Legends of American Music Series, Jazz and Blues Singers Issue, Perf. 11 x 10.8							
2854	29¢ Bessie Smith	09/17/94	.60	.20			1.25	25
2855	29¢ Muddy Waters	09/17/94	.60	.20			1.25	25
2856	29¢ Billie Holiday	09/17/94	.60	.20			1.25	25
2857	29¢ Robert Johnson	09/17/94	.60	.20			1.25	20
2858	29¢ Jimmy Rushing	09/17/94	.60	.20			1.25	20
2859	29¢ "Ma" Rainey	09/17/94	.60	.20			1.25	20
2860	29¢ Mildred Bailey	09/17/94	.60	.20			1.25	20
2861	29¢ Howlin' Wolf	09/17/94	.60	.20			1.25	20
a	Block of 9, #2854-2861							
	+ 1 additional stamp		5.50	4.50	8.00	(10)	6.00	
	Literary Arts Issue, Perf. 11							
2862	29¢ James Thurber	09/10/94	.50	.20	2.50	(4)	1.25	151
	Wonders of the Sea Issue, Perf. 11 x 10.9							
2863	29¢ Diver, Motorboat	10/03/94	.50	.20			1.25	56
2864	29¢ Diver, Ship	10/03/94	.50	.20			1.25	56
2865	29¢ Diver, Ship's Wheel	10/03/94	.50	.20			1.25	56
2866	29¢ Diver, Coral	10/03/94	.50	.20			1.25	56
a	Block of 4, #2963-2966		2.00	1.50	2.00	(4)	2.75	56
b	As "a" imperf.		1,750.00					
	Cranes Issue, Perf. 10.8 x 11							
2867	29¢ Black-Necked Crane	10/09/94	.50	.20			1.25	78
2868	29¢ Whooping Crane	10/09/94	.50	.20			1.25	78
a	Pair, #2867-2868		1.00	.65	2.00	(4)	2.00	78
b	Black and magenta (engr.) omitted		2,000.00					

Greetings From Rhode Island

"Hope" is Rhode Island's motto. While this state is the smallest one in the nation, it is also a place of big dreams—and dreams come true.

In 1636, Puritan minister Roger Williams, exiled from Massachusetts for protesting the failure of other Puritan leaders to practice religious tolerance, founded a settlement in the wilderness at the head of Narragansett Bay. He called it Providence. In time, this community became a major seaport, the state capital, a manufacturing center, and one of the largest cities in New England.

Religious exiles established a haven at Newport in 1639. Perched on a large island at the entrance to Narrangansett Bay, Newport grew into a fashionable resort for rich 18th- and 19th-century merchants and industrialists. Families such as the Astors, Belmonts, and Vanderbilts spent summers here, entertaining friends in grand mansions built atop a stretch of oceanside cliffs. Today, people flock to Newport for its annual yacht races, jazz festivals, and the International Lawn Tennis Hall of Fame. ■

	Issues of 1994		Un	U	PB	#	FDC	Q(M)
	Legends of the West Issue, Perf. 10.1 x 10							
2869	Sheet of 20	10/18/94	12.00	—			14.00	20
a	29¢ Home on the Range		.60	.20			1.75	20
b	29¢ Buffalo Bill Cody		.60	.20			1.75	20
c	29¢ Jim Bridger		.60	.20			1.75	20
d	29¢ Annie Oakley		.60	.20			1.75	20
e	29¢ Native American Culture		.60	.20			1.75	20
f	29¢ Chief Joseph		.60	.20			1.75	20
g	29¢ Bill Pickett		.60	.20			1.75	20
h	29¢ Bat Masterson		.60	.20			1.75	20
i	29¢ John C. Fremont		.60	.20			1.75	20
j	29¢ Wyatt Earp		.60	.20			1.75	20
k	29¢ Nellie Cashman		.60	.20			1.75	20
l	29¢ Charles Goodnight		.60	.20			1.75	20
m	29¢ Geronimo		.60	.20			1.75	20
n	29¢ Kit Carson		.60	.20			1.75	20
o	29¢ Wild Bill Hickok		.60	.20			1.75	20
p	29¢ Western Wildlife		.60	.20			1.75	20
q	29¢ Jim Beckwourth		.60	.20			1.75	20
r	29¢ Bill Tilghman		.60	.20			1.75	20
s	29¢ Sacagawea		.60	.20			1.75	20
t	29¢ Overland Mail		.60	.20			1.75	20
2870	29¢ Sheet of 20 (recalled)	10/18/94	190.00	—				0.1

Greetings From Wyoming

Nicknamed the "Equality State," Wyoming has long adhered to its motto of "Equal Rights." It was first to grant women the right to vote, first to appoint a woman justice of the peace, and first to elect a female governor.

People also know Wyoming as a land of natural wonders. The spectacular peaks of the Teton Range, named by early French fur traders, stand a sheer 7,000 feet above the Jackson Hole valley. Stretching to the southeast is the immense Bridger-Teton National Forest, named for celebrated mountain man Jim Bridger.

Yellowstone National Park lies in the state's northwest corner. In 1872, this amazing realm of mountains, lakes, waterfalls, and breathtaking geothermal features became the world's first national park. It has also been designated a World Heritage site and an international biosphere reserve. Across the state, looming above the high plains in Wyoming's northeast corner, is the volcanic mass of Devils Tower, the country's first national monument. ■

2869

a	b	c	d	e
f	g	h	i	j
k	l	m	n	o
p	q	r	s	t

1994

2871

2872

2873

2874

2875

2876

2877

2878

Issues of 1994			Un	U	PB	#	FDC	Q(M)
	Christmas Issue, Perf. 11.1							
2871	29¢ Madonna and Child	10/20/94	.50	.20	2.50	(4)	1.25	
2871A	Perf. 9.8 x 10.8		.60	.20			1.25	
b	As "a," booklet pane of 10		6.25	3.50				50
c	As "a," Imperf.		—					
2872	29¢ Stocking	10/20/94	.50	.20	2.50	(4)	1.25	603
a	Booklet pane of 20		10.50	3.00				30
	Self-Adhesive							
2873	29¢ Santa Claus	10/20/94	.50	.20	7.75	(5)	1.25	240
a	Booklet pane of 12		6.25					20
2874	29¢ Cardinal in Snow	10/20/94	.50	.20			1.25	36
a	Booklet pane of 18		9.50					2
	Bureau of Engraving and Printing Issue, Perf.11							
2875	$2.00 Sheet of 4	11/03/94	15.00	—			12.00	5
a	Single stamp		3.00	1.25				20
	Lunar New Year Issue, Perf. 11.2 x 11.1							
2876	29¢ Year of the Boar	12/30/94	.55	.20	2.25	(4)	1.50	80
	Untagged, Perf. 11 x 10.8							
2877	(3¢) Dove Make-Up Rate	12/13/94	.20	.20	.30	(4)	1.25	
a	Imperf., pair		200.00					
	Perf. 10.8 x 10.9							
2878	(3¢) Dove Make-Up Rate	12/13/94	.20	.20	.30	(4)	1.25	

Oregon Trail

The Oregon National Historic Trail starts in Independence, Missouri, and runs for more than 2,000 miles through Kansas, Nebraska, Wyoming, Idaho, and Oregon. In the 19th century, hundreds of thousands of missionaries, settlers, traders, and fortune seekers made their way west along this route and on  parallel or connecting trails, a journey lasting about five months. Large-scale migration along what was first known as "The Oregon Road" and later the Oregon Trail began in 1843, and in 1993, the U.S. Postal Service marked the 150th anniversary of this event by issuing a 29-cent commemorative stamp.

Today, deep ruts left by countless wagon wheels are preserved in such places as Rock Creek Station State Historic Park near Fairbury, Nebraska, and in Massacre Rocks State Park, near American Falls, Idaho. Among the most notable natural landmarks along the old route are Chimney Rock and Scotts Bluff in western Nebraska, and Independence Rock in central Wyoming. ■

	Issues of 1994-1997		Un	U	PB	#	FDC	Q(M)
	Tagged, Perf. 11.2 x 11.1							
2879	(20¢) Old Glory Postcard Rate	12/13/94	.40	.20	5.00	(4)	1.25	
	Perf. 11 x 10.9							
2880	(20¢) Old Glory Postcard Rate	12/13/94	.50	.20	9.00	(4)	1.25	
	Perf. 11.2 x 11.1							
2881	(32¢) "G" Old Glory	12/13/94	.75	.20	70.00	(4)	1.25	
a	Booklet pane of 10		6.00	3.75			7.50	
	Perf. 11 x 10.9							
2882	(32¢) "G" Old Glory	12/13/94	.60	.20	3.00	(4)	1.25	
	Booklet Stamps, Perf. 10 x 9.9 on 2 or 3 sides							
2883	(32¢) "G" Old Glory	12/13/94	.60	.20			1.25	
a	Booklet pane of 10		6.25	3.75			7.50	
	Perf. 10.9							
2884	(32¢) "G" Old Glory	12/13/94	.60	.20			1.25	
a	Booklet pane of 10		6.00	3.75			7.50	
	Perf. 11 x 10.9							
2885	(32¢) "G" Old Glory	12/13/94	.65	.20			1.25	
a	Booklet pane of 10		6.50	3.75			7.50	
	Self-Adhesive, Die-Cut							
2886	(32¢) "G" Old Glory	12/13/94	.60	.20	7.75	(5)	1.25	
a	Booklet pane of 18		11.50					
b	Coil with plate		—	3.25				
2887	(32¢) "G" Old Glory	12/13/94	.60	.20			1.25	
a	Booklet pane of 18		11.50					
	Coil Stamps, Perf. 9.8 Vertically							
2888	(25¢) Old Glory First-Class Presort	12/13/94	.50	.50	4.50	(5)	1.25	
2889	(32¢) Black "G"	12/13/94	.60	.20	8.50	(5)	1.25	
a	Imperf., pair		300.00					
2890	(32¢) Blue "G"	12/13/94	.60	.20	5.00	(5)	1.25	
2891	(32¢) Red "G"	12/13/94	.60	.20	5.00	(5)	1.25	
	Rouletted							
2892	(32¢) Red "G"	12/13/94	.60	.20	5.25	(5)	1.25	
	Issue of 1995, Perf. 9.8 Vertically							
2893	(5¢) Green	01/12/95	.20	.20	2.00	(5)		
	Perf. 10.4							
2897	32¢ Flag Over Porch	05/19/95	.60	.20	3.00	(4)	1.25	
	Coil Stamps, Perf. 9.8 Vertically							
2902	(5¢) Butte	03/10/95	.20	.20	1.50	(5)	1.25	
a	Imperf., pair		750.00					
	Self-Adhesive, Serpentine Die-Cut 11.5 Vertically							
2902B	(5¢) Butte	06/15/96	.20	.20	1.75	(5)	1.25	550
	Perf. 9.8 Vertically							
2903	(5¢) Mountain, purple and multi	03/16/96	.20	.20	1.60	(5)	1.25	150
a	Tagged (error)		4.00	3.50	85.00	(5)		
2904	(5¢) Mountain, blue and multi	03/16/96	.20	.20	2.00	(5)	1.25	150
c	Imperf., pair		500.00					
	Self-Adhesive, Serpentine Die-Cut 11.2							
2904A	(5¢) Mountain, purple and multi	06/15/96	.20	.20	1.60	(5)	1.25	
	Self-Adhesive, Serpentine Die-Cut 9.8 Vertically							
2904B	(5¢) Mountain, purple and multi	01/24/97	.20	.20	1.75	(5)	1.25	148
c	Tagged (error)		4.00	3.50	85.00	(5)		
	Perf. 9.8 Vertically							
2905	(10¢) Automobile	03/10/95	.20	.20	2.50	(5)	1.25	
	Self-Adhesive, Serpentine Die-Cut 11.5 Vertically							
2906	(10¢) Automobile	06/15/96	.20	.20	2.75	(5)	1.25	450
2907	(10¢) Eagle and Shield	05/21/96	.20	.20	2.25	(5)	1.25	450

2879

2880

2881

2882

2883

2884

2885

2886

2887

2888

2889

2890

2891

2892

2893

2897

2902

2903

2904

2905

2906

2907

For details and illustrations of the new 2002 issues, see pages 20-35.

2908

2909

2910

2911

2912

2913

2914

2915

2916

2919

2920

2921

2933

2934

2935

2936

2938

2940

2941

	Issues of 1995-1999		Un	U	PB	#	FDC	Q(M)
	Perf. 9.8 Vertically							
2908	(15¢) Auto Tail Fin, bureau printing	03/17/95	.30	.30	3.00	(5)	1.25	
2909	(15¢) Auto Tail Fin, private printing	03/17/95	.30	.30	3.00	(5)	1.25	
	Self-Adhesive, Serpentine Die-Cut 11.5 Vertically							
2910	(15¢) Auto Tail Fin	06/15/96	.30	.30	3.00	(5)	1.25	
	Perf. 9.8 Vertically							
2911	(25¢) Juke Box, bureau printing	03/17/95	.50	.50	4.25	(5)	1.25	
2912	(25¢) Juke Box, private printing	03/17/95	.50	.50	3.50	(5)	1.25	
	Self-Adhesive, Serpentine Die-Cut 11.5 Vertically							
2912A	(25¢) Juke Box	06/15/96	.50	.50	4.00	(5)	1.25	550
	Self-Adhesive, Serpentine Die-Cut 9.8 Vertically							
2912B	(25¢) Juke Box	01/24/97	.50	.50	4.00	(5)	1.25	20
	Perf. 9.8 Vertically							
2913	32¢ Flag Over Porch	05/19/95	.60	.20	5.25	(5)	1.25	
a	Imperf., pair		60.00					
2914	32¢ Flag Over Porch	05/19/95	.60	.20	4.50	(3)	1.25	
	Self-Adhesive, Serpentine Die-Cut 8.7 Vertically							
2915	32¢ Flag Over Porch	04/18/95	.60	.30	6.75	(5)	1.25	
	Self-Adhesive, Serpentine Die-Cut Perf. 9.8 Vertically							
2915A	32¢ Flag Over Porch	05/21/96	.60	.20	5.25	(5)	1.25	
	Self-Adhesive, Serpentine Die-Cut 11.5 Vertically							
2915B	32¢ Flag Over Porch	06/15/96	.60	.20	5.25	(5)	1.25	
	Self-Adhesive, Serpentine Die-Cut 10.9 Vertically							
2915C	32¢ Flag Over Porch	06/21/96	.60	.20	12.50	(5)	1.25	
	Self-Adhesive, Serpentine Die-Cut 9.8 Vertically							
2915D	32¢ Flag Over Porch	01/24/97	.60	.20	6.00	(5)	1.25	300
	Booklet Stamps, Perf. 10.8 x 9.8 on 2 or 3 adjacent sides							
2916	32¢ Flag Over Porch	05/19/95	.60	.20			1.25	
a	Booklet pane of 10		6.00	3.25			7.50	
b	As "a," imperf.		—					
	Self-Adhesive, Die-Cut							
2919	32¢ Flag Over Field	03/17/95	.60	.20			1.25	
a	Booklet pane of 18		11.00					
	Self-Adhesive, Serpentine Die-Cut 8.7 on 2, 3 or 4 adjacent sides							
2920	32¢ Flag Over Porch	04/18/95	.60	.20			1.25	
a	Booklet pane of 20 + label		12.00					
b	Small date		4.00	.20				
c	As "b," booklet pane of 20 + label		110.00					
f	As #2920, pane of 15 + label		9.00					
h	As #2920, booklet pane of 15		35.00					
	Self-Adhesive, Serpentine Die-Cut 11.3 on 3 sides							
2920D	32¢ Flag Over Porch	01/20/96	.70	.25				789
e	Booklet pane of 10		7.50					
	Self-Adhesive, Serpentine Die-Cut Perf. 9.8 on 2 or 3 sides							
2921	32¢ Flag Over Porch	05/21/96	.75	.20			1.25	7,344
a	Booklet pane of 10		7.50					
b	As #2921, dated red "1997"		.75	.20				
c	As "a," dated red "1997"		7.50					
d	Booklet pane of 5 + label		3.75					
	Great Americans Issue, Perf. 11.2							
2933	32¢ Milton S. Hershey	09/13/95	.60	.20	3.00	(4)	1.25	
2934	32¢ Cal Farley	04/26/96	.60	.20	3.00	(4)	1.25	150
2935	32¢ Henry R. Luce	04/03/98	.60	.20	2.40	(4)	1.25	
2936	32¢ Lila and DeWitt Wallace	07/16/98	.60	.20	2.40	(4)	1.25	
2938	46¢ Ruth Benedict	10/20/95	.90	.20	4.50	(4)	1.40	
2940	55¢ Alice Hamilton, MD	07/11/95	1.10	.20	5.50	(4)	1.40	
	Self-Adhesive, Serpentine Die-Cut 11.7 x 11.5							
2941	55¢ Justin S. Morrill	07/17/99	1.10	.20	4.40	(4)	1.40	

1995-1998

	Issues of 1995-1998		Un	U	PB	#	FDC
	Self-Adhesive, Serpentine Die-Cut 11.7 x 11.5						
2942	77¢ Mary Breckenridge	11/09/98	1.50	.20	6.00	(4)	1.75
	Perf. 11.2						
2943	78¢ Alice Paul	08/18/95	1.60	.20	7.50	(4)	1.75
a	78¢ dull violet		1.60	.20	7.50	(4)	
b	78¢ pale violet		1.75	.30	12.00	(4)	
	Love Issue, Perf. 11.2						
2948	(32¢) Love, Cherub from						
	Sistine Madonna, by Raphael	02/01/95	.60	.20	3.00	(4)	1.25
	Self-Adhesive, Die-Cut						
2949	(32¢) Love, Cherub from						
	Sistine Madonna, by Raphael	02/01/95	.60	.20			1.25
a	Booklet pane of 20 + label		12.00				
b	As "a," red (engr.) omitted		450.00				
	Perf. 11.1						
2950	32¢ Florida Statehood,						
	150th Anniversary	03/03/95	.60	.20	2.40	(4)	1.25
	Kids Care Earth Day Issue, Perf. 11.1 x 11						
2951	32¢ Earth Clean-Up	04/20/95	.60	.20			1.25
2952	32¢ Solar Energy	04/20/95	.60	.20			1.25
2953	32¢ Tree Planting	04/20/95	.60	.20			1.25
2954	32¢ Beach Clean-Up	04/20/95	.60	.20			1.25
a	Block of 4, #2951-54		2.40	1.75	2.40	(4)	2.75
	Perf. 11.2						
2955	32¢ Richard Nixon	04/26/95	.60	.20	3.00	(4)	1.25
a	Red (engr.) omitted		1,400.00				
	Black Heritage Issue						
2956	32¢ Bessie Coleman	04/27/95	.60	.20	3.00	(4)	1.25
	Love Issue						
2957	32¢ Love, Cherub from						
	Sistine Madonna, by Raphael	05/12/95	.60	.20	3.00	(4)	1.25
2958	55¢ Love, Cherub from						
	Sistine Madonna, by Raphael	05/12/95	1.10	.20	5.50	(4)	1.40
	Booklet Stamps, Perf. 9.8 x 10.8						
2959	32¢ Love, Cherub from						
	Sistine Madonna, by Raphael	05/12/95	.60	.20			1.25
a	Booklet pane of 10		6.00	3.25			7.50
	Self-Adhesive, Die-Cut						
2960	55¢ Love, Cherub from						
	Sistine Madonna, by Raphael	05/12/95	1.10	.20			1.40
a	Booklet pane of 20 + label		22.50				
	Recreational Sports Issue, Perf. 11.2						
2961	32¢ Volleyball	05/20/95	.60	.20			1.50
2962	32¢ Softball	05/20/95	.60	.20			1.50
2963	32¢ Bowling	05/20/95	.60	.20			1.50
2964	32¢ Tennis	05/20/95	.60	.20			1.50
2965	32¢ Golf	05/20/95	.60	.20			1.50
a	Vertical strip of 5, #2961-65		3.00	2.00	6.00	(10)	3.25
b	As "a," imperf.						
c	As "a," yellow omitted		2,500.00				
d	As "a," yellow, blue and						
	magenta omitted		2,500.00				
2966	32¢ Prisoners of War						
	and Missing in Action	05/29/95	.60	.20	2.40	(4)	2.50
	Pane of 20		12.00	—			

2942

2943

2948

2950

2951

2953

2952

2954

2955

2954a

2956

2958

2961

2962

2963

2965

2964

2965a

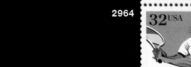

2966

LEGENDS of HOLLYWOOD

Marilyn Monroe

Few other actresses personified the phrase "Hollywood movie star" as did Marilyn Monroe (1926–1962). Classically beautiful, Marilyn set the motion picture standard for glamour and sensuality in film favorites such as *Some Like It Hot, Gentlemen Prefer Blondes, Bus Stop,* and *The Seven Year Itch.*

2967

2968

2969

2970

2971

2972

2973 **2973a**

Issues of 1995		Un	U	PB	#	FDC
Legends of Hollywood Issue, Perf. 11.1						
2967	32¢ Marilyn Monroe	06/01/95	.60	.20	5.00	(4)	2.50
a	Imperf., pair		600.00				
	Perf. 11.2						
2968	32¢ Texas Statehood	06/16/95	.60	.20	2.40	(4)	1.75
Great Lakes Lighthouses Issue, Perf. 11.2 Vertically						
2969	32¢ Split Rock, Lake Superior	06/17/95	.60	.20			1.75
2970	32¢ St. Joseph, Lake Michigan	06/17/95	.60	.20			1.75
2971	32¢ Spectacle Reef, Lake Huron	06/17/95	.60	.20			1.75
2972	32¢ Marblehead, Lake Erie	06/17/95	.60	.20			1.75
2973	32¢ Thirty Mile Point, Lake Ontario	06/17/95	.60	.20			1.75
a	Booklet pane of 5, #2969-73		3.00	2.75			5.00

Cape Hatteras

Cape Hatteras, North Carolina, occupies a special place in maritime history. For centuries, the infamous shallows near this Hatteras Island promontory claimed many storm-tossed ships, bringing them to ruin in the so-called Graveyard of the Atlantic.

In 1803, a lighthouse was built to help mariners avoid these hazardous waters. A newer structure replaced it in 1870, but by 1987 the encroaching sea had crept to within 160 feet. Though ships no longer needed the light—they relied on modern navigational aids—the imminent loss of the historic landmark was inconceivable.

In 1999, the National Park Service moved the lighthouse to a new site 1,600 feet from the ocean. At the subsequent re-dedication ceremonys on May 5, 2001, Francis Peltier, Superintendent of the Outer Banks National Park Service Group, recalled its "magnificent heritage, exemplified by the keepers…. Their commitment and concern for the safety of others represents some of the best of the American character." ■

	Issues of 1995		Un	U	PB	#	FDC
2974	32¢ United Nations,						
	50th Anniversary	06/26/95	.60	.20	2.40	(4)	1.25
	Civil War Issue, Perf. 10.1						
2975	Sheet of 20	06/29/95	12.00	—			13.00
a	32¢ *Monitor and Virginia*		.60	.20			1.50
b	32¢ Robert E. Lee		.60	.20			1.50
c	32¢ Clara Barton		.60	.20			1.50
d	32¢ Ulysses S. Grant		.60	.20			1.50
e	32¢ Battle of Shiloh		.60	.20			1.50
f	32¢ Jefferson Davis		.60	.20			1.50
g	32¢ David Farragut		.60	.20			1.50
h	32¢ Frederick Douglass		.60	.20			1.50
i	32¢ Raphael Semmes		.60	.20			1.50
j	32¢ Abraham Lincoln		.60	.20			1.50
k	32¢ Harriet Tubman		.60	.20			1.50
l	32¢ Stand Watie		.60	.20			1.50
m	32¢ Joseph E. Johnston		.60	.20			1.50
n	32¢ Winfield Hancock		.60	.20			1.50
o	32¢ Mary Chesnut		.60	.20			1.50
p	32¢ Battle of Chancellorsville		.60	.20			1.50
q	32¢ William T. Sherman		.60	.20			1.50
r	32¢ Phoebe Pember		.60	.20			1.50
s	32¢ "Stonewall" Jackson		.60	.20			1.50
t	32¢ Battle of Gettysburg		.60	.20			1.50

Civil War: Gettysburg

From July 1 to July 3, 1863, the largest and bloodiest battle of the Civil War raged in and around the little town of Gettysburg, Pennsylvania. This epic struggle ended in a victory for the North, but the toll was staggering: More than 23,000 of the 83,000 troops commanded by Union Gen. George G. Meade were killed, wounded, or captured, while some 28,000 of the 75,000 soldiers led by Confederate Gen. Robert E. Lee suffered a similar fate.

In 1895, the United States Congress approved legislation establishing Gettysburg National Military Park. Today, this park preserves nearly 6,000 acres as a memorial to the thousands who faced each other along Seminary Ridge and Cemetery Ridge; fought along the narrow roads and in the Peach Orchard, Wheatfield, and "Devil's Den"; and witnessed firsthand the march forever known as Pickett's Charge. More than 3,500 of these men were laid to rest at the Soldiers' National Cemetery, which President Abraham Lincoln helped dedicate on November 19, 1863. ■

2974

2975   a   b   c   d   e

2976   2977

2980

2978   2979   2979a

a   b   c   d   e

1945: Victory at Last

f   g   h   i   j   2981

Issues of 1995		Un	U	PB	#	FDC
Carousel Horse Issue, Perf. 11						
2976	32¢ Golden Horse with Roses 07/21/95	.60	.20			1.25
2977	32¢ Black Horse with Gold Bridle 07/21/95	.60	.20			1.25
2978	32¢ Horse with Armor 07/21/95	.60	.20			1.25
2979	32¢ Brown Horse with					
	Green Bridle 07/21/95	.60	.20			1.25
a	Block of 4, #2976-79	2.40	1.75	2.40	(4)	3.25
Perf. 11.1 x 11						
2980	32¢ Women's Suffrage 08/26/95	.60	.20	3.00	(4)	1.25
a	Black (engr.) omitted	425.00				
World War II Issue, 1945: Victory at Last, Miniature Sheet, Perf. 11.1						
2981	Block of 10 and central label 09/02/95	6.00	4.50			7.00
a	32¢ Marines Raise					
	Flag on Iwo Jima	.60	.30			1.50
b	32¢ Fierce Fighting Frees Manila					
	by March 3, 1945	.60	.30			1.50
c	32¢ Soldiers Advancing: Okinawa,					
	the Last Big Battle	.60	.30			1.50
d	32¢ Destroyed Bridge: U.S. and					
	Soviets Link Up at Elbe River	.60	.30			1.50
e	32¢ Allies Liberate Holocaust					
	Survivors	.60	.30			1.50
f	32¢ Germany Surrenders at Reims	.60	.30			1.50
g	32¢ Refugees: By 1945, World War II					
	Has Uprooted Millions	.60	.30			1.50
h	32¢ Truman Announces Japan's					
	Surrender	.60	.30			1.50
i	32¢ Sailor Kissing Nurse: News of					
	Victory Hits Home	.60	.30			1.50
j	32¢ Hometowns Honor Their					
	Returning Veterans	.60	.30			1.50

Greetings From Virginia

Some of the most significant events in our nation's history have unfolded on Virginia soil. At Jamestown in 1607, colonists founded America's first permanent English settlement, and in 1619, the country's first public assembly convened there. The Revolutionary War came to an end when the British surrendered at Yorktown in 1781. After turning Virginia into a bloody battleground, the Civil War ended at Appomattox in 1865.

Four of the first five Presidents were born in Virginia. The first, George Washington, carved his initials into Natural Bridge, a spectacular 215-foot-high limestone arch later owned by the third, Thomas Jefferson. Washington also left a legacy at Mount Vernon, his beautiful estate overlooking the Potomac near Alexandria.

After nearly 400 years, the state remains in the forefront of our national government and defense: Northern Virginia lies across the Potomac from Washington, D.C., and is home to many federal offices, while in the south, Norfolk serves as home base for the U.S. Navy's Atlantic fleet. ■

1995

	Issues of 1995		Un	U	PB	#	FDC	Q(M)
	Legends of American Music Series, Jazz Musicians Issue, Perf. 11.1 x 11							
2982	32¢ Louis Armstrong, white denomination	09/01/95	.80	.20	3.20	(4)	1.25	
2983	32¢ Coleman Hawkins	09/16/95	.80	.20			1.25	
2984	32¢ Louis Armstrong, black denomination	09/16/95	.80	.20			1.25	
2985	32¢ James P. Johnson	09/16/95	.80	.20			1.25	
2986	32¢ Jelly Roll Morton	09/16/95	.80	.20			1.25	
2987	32¢ Charlie Parker	09/16/95	.80	.20			1.25	
2988	32¢ Eubie Blake	09/16/95	.80	.20			1.25	
2989	32¢ Charles Mingus	09/16/95	.80	.20			1.25	
2990	32¢ Thelonious Monk	09/16/95	.80	.20			1.25	
2991	32¢ John Coltrane	09/16/95	.80	.20			1.25	
2992	32¢ Erroll Garner	09/16/95	.80	.20			1.25	
a	Vertical block of 10, #2983-92		8.00	—	8.00	(10)	6.50	
	Pane of 20		16.00	—				
	Garden Flowers Issue, Perf. 10.9 Vertically							
2993	32¢ Aster	09/19/95	.60	.20			1.25	800
2994	32¢ Chrysanthemum	09/19/95	.60	.20			1.25	800
2995	32¢ Dahlia	09/19/95	.60	.20			1.25	800
2996	32¢ Hydrangea	09/19/95	.60	.20			1.25	800
2997	32¢ Rudbeckia	09/19/95	.60	.20			1.25	800
a	Booklet pane of 5, #2993-97		3.00	2.25			4.00	
	Perf. 11.1							
2998	60¢ Eddie Rickenbacker, Aviator	09/25/95	1.25	.25	6.25	(4)	1.50	
a	Large date, 2000		1.25	.25	6.25	(4)		
2999	32¢ Republic of Palau	09/29/95	.60	.20	3.00	(4)	1.25	

Greetings From Missouri

More than 250 years ago, French settlers in the Mississippi Valley founded what is now the oldest community in Missouri: Ste. Genevieve. Even now, long after Americans began streaming into the area in the early 19th century, the French heritage is still evident in the town's architecture, street names, family names, and celebrations.

For thousands of 19th-century pioneers, the gateway to the west lay farther upriver, at St. Louis. From there they made a short trip to St. Charles and traveled along the Missouri River to the Independence and Kansas City area, where they picked up the Santa Fe, Oregon, and California Trails. The 630-foot Gateway Arch, completed at St. Louis in 1965, commemorates the city's historic role as a portal to the West. St. Louis has other claims to fame, including those of a musical nature: Ragtime composer Scott Joplin, for one, lived here in the early 1900s.

Farther north along the Mississippi is the town of Hannibal, best known as the boyhood home of Mark Twain. ■

2982

2983

2984

2985

2986

2987

2988

2989

2990

2991

2992

2992a

2993 2994 2995 2996 2997 2997a

2998

2999

COMIC STRIP CLASSICS

3000	a	b	c	d
	e	f	g	h
	i	j	k	l
	m	n	o	p
	q	r	s	t

3001

3002

Issues of 1995		Un	U	PB	#	FDC
Comic Strip Classics Issue, Perf. 10						
3000 Pane of 20	10/01/95	12.00	—			13.00
a 32¢ The Yellow Kid		.60	.20			1.75
b 32¢ Katzenjammer Kids		.60	.20			1.75
c 32¢ Little Nemo in Slumberland		.60	.20			1.75
d 32¢ Bringing Up Father		.60	.20			1.75
e 32¢ Krazy Kat		.60	.20			1.75
f 32¢ Rube Goldberg's Inventions		.60	.20			1.75
g 32¢ Toonerville Folks		.60	.20			1.75
h 32¢ Gasoline Alley		.60	.20			1.75
i 32¢ Barney Google		.60	.20			1.75
j 32¢ Little Orphan Annie		.60	.20			1.75
k 32¢ Popeye		.60	.20			1.75
l 32¢ Blondie		.60	.20			1.75
m 32¢ Dick Tracy		.60	.20			1.75
n 32¢ Alley Oop		.60	.20			1.75
o 32¢ Nancy		.60	.20			1.75
p 32¢ Flash Gordon		.60	.20			1.75
q 32¢ Li'l Abner		.60	.20			1.75
r 32¢ Terry and the Pirates		.60	.20			1.75
s 32¢ Prince Valiant		.60	.20			1.75
t 32¢ Brenda Starr, Reporter		.60	.20			1.75
Perf 10.9						
3001 32¢ U.S. Naval Academy, 150th Anniversary	10/10/95	.60	.20	2.40	(4)	1.25
Literary Arts Issue, Perf 11.1						
3002 32¢ Tennessee Williams	10/13/95	.60	.20	2.40	(4)	1.25

United States Naval Academy

The "healthy and secluded" site of Annapolis, Maryland, was just what Secretary of the Navy George Bancroft was looking for in the 1840s. Located on the Severn River, near the Chesapeake Bay, this small seaport held fewer of "the temptations and distractions that necessarily connect with a large and populous city"—such as Philadelphia, New York, or Boston—and it would therefore prove quite suitable as a place for the teaching and training of midshipmen. It was here, on October 10, 1845, that the Navy established the United States Naval Academy.

Today, the Academy still dominates the north side of Annapolis, but just a few blocks to the southwest is the seat of the Maryland government. Dating from 1780, the State House is the oldest state capitol building still in use; it also served as the U.S. Capitol for a short time after the Revolutionary War. Several other 18th-century structures remain, all within easy walking distance of the city's lively waterfront. ∎

	Issues of 1995		Un	U	PB	#	FDC
	Christmas Issue, Perf. 11.2						
3003	32¢ Madonna and Child,						
	by Giotto di Bondone	10/19/95	.60	.20	3.00	(4)	1.25
c	Black (engr., denom.) omitted		250.00				
	Booklet Stamp, Perf. 9.8 x 10.9						
3003A	32¢ Madonna and Child	10/19/95	.65	.20			1.25
b	Booklet pane of 10		6.50	4.00			7.25
3004	32¢ Santa Claus Entering Chimney	09/30/95	.60	.20			1.25
3005	32¢ Child Holding Jumping Jack	09/30/95	.60	.20			1.25
3006	32¢ Child Holding Tree	09/30/95	.60	.20			1.25
3007	32¢ Santa Claus Working on Sled	09/30/95	.60	.20			1.25
a	Block of 4, #3004-07		2.40	1.25	3.00	(4)	3.25
b	Booklet pane of 10, 3 each #3004-05,						
	2 each 3006-07		6.00	4.00			7.25
c	Booklet pane of 10, 2 each #3004-05,						
	3 each 3006-07		6.00	4.00			7.25
d	As "a," imperf.		700.00				
	Self-Adhesive, Serpentine Die-Cut						
3008	32¢ Santa Claus Working on Sled	09/30/95	.60	.20			1.25
3009	32¢ Child Holding Jumping Jack	09/30/95	.60	.20			1.25
3010	32¢ Santa Claus Entering Chimney	09/30/95	.60	.20			1.25
3011	32¢ Child Holding Tree	09/30/95	.60	.20			1.25
a	Booklet pane of 20, 5 each						
	#3008-11 + label		12.00				
3012	32¢ Midnight Angel	10/19/95	.60	.20			1.25
a	Booklet pane of 20 + label		12.00				
	Self-Adhesive, Die-Cut						
3013	32¢ Children Sledding	10/19/95	.60	.20			1.25
a	Booklet pane of 18		11.00				
	Self-Adhesive Coil Stamps, Serpentine Die-Cut Vertically						
3014	32¢ Santa Claus Working on Sled	09/30/95	.60	.30			1.25
3015	32¢ Child Holding Jumping Jack	09/30/95	.60	.30			1.25
3016	32¢ Santa Claus Entering Chimney	09/30/95	.60	.30			1.25
3017	32¢ Child Holding Tree	09/30/95	.60	.30			1.25
a	Strip of 4, #3014-17		2.40		7.50	(8)	3.25
3018	32¢ Midnight Angel	10/19/95	.60	.30	7.00	(5)	1.25

Greetings From Illinois

Illinois "the Prairie State" also calls itself the "Land of Lincoln." Its favorite son, Abraham Lincoln, became the 16th President of the United States, and his old residence in Springfield, the capital city, continues to draw Lincoln admirers and Civil War buffs from around the world. Illinois was also home to Union General Ulysses S. Grant, who became the 18th U.S. President; his house in Galena, near the Mississippi River, has been preserved as well.

Sprawling along the southwestern shore of Lake Michigan is Chicago, one of the most populous cities in the nation and a major center for commerce, shipping, and transportation. The quarter-mile-high Sears Tower, tallest building on the continent, dominates all the other downtown skyscrapers, and O'Hare Airport ranks as one of the country's busiest airports.

Out in the countryside, farmers have made Illinois an important agricultural state, growing large crops of soybeans and grains, and raising hogs and cattle on the level landscapes of the midwestern prairie. ■

3003

3004

3005

3006

3007

3007a

3008   3009   3010   3011   3011a

3012   3013

3019

3020

3021

3022

3023

3023a

3024

3025   3026   3027   3028   3029 3029a

3030   3032   3033   3036   3044

3048   3049   3050   3052

	Issues of 1995-1999		Un	U	PB	#	FDC	Q(M)
	Antique Automobiles Issue							
3019	32¢ 1893 Duryea	11/03/95	.60	.20			1.25	
3020	32¢ 1894 Haynes	11/03/95	.60	.20			1.25	
3021	32¢ 1898 Columbia	11/03/95	.60	.20			1.25	
3022	32¢ 1899 Winton	11/03/95	.60	.20			1.25	
3023	32¢ 1901 White	11/03/95	.60	.20			1.25	
a	Vertical or horizontal strip of 5, #3019-23		3.00	2.00			3.25	
3024	32¢ Utah Statehood	01/04/96	.60	.20	3.00	(4)	1.25	
	Issues of 1996, Garden Flowers Issue, Perf 10.9 Vertically							
3025	32¢ Crocus	01/19/96	.60	.20			1.25	
3026	32¢ Winter Aconite	01/19/96	.60	.20			1.25	
3027	32¢ Pansy	01/19/96	.60	.20			1.25	
3028	32¢ Snowdrop	01/19/96	.60	.20			1.25	
3029	32¢ Anemone	01/19/96	.60	.20			1.25	
a	Booklet pane of 5, #3025-3029		3.00	2.25			4.00	
	Love Issue, Serpentine Die-Cut Perf. 11.3							
3030	32¢ Love Cherub from Sistine							
	Madonna, by Raphael	01/20/96	.60	.20			1.25	
a	Booklet pane of 20 + label		12.00					
b	Booklet pane of 15 + label		9.00					
	Flora and Fauna Issue, Self-Adhesive, Serpentine Die-Cut 10.5							
3031	1¢ American Kestrel	11/19/99	.20	.20	.25		1.25	120
	Perf. 11							
3032	2¢ Red-Headed Woodpecker	02/02/96	.20	.20	.25	(4)	1.25	311
3033	3¢ Eastern Bluebird	04/03/96	.20	.20	.25	(4)	1.25	317
	Self-Adhesive, Serpentine Die-Cut 11.5 x 11.25							
3036	$1 Red Fox	08/14/98	2.00	.50	8.00	(4)		
	Coil Stamps, Perf. 9.75 Vertically							
3044	1¢ American Kestrel	01/20/96	.20	.20	.75	(5)	1.25	
a	Large date		.20	.20	1.00	(5)		
3045	2¢ Red-Headed Woodpecker	06/22/99	.20	.20	.75	(5)	1.25	100
	Booklet Stamps, Self-Adhesive, Serpentine Die-Cut 10.5 x 10.75 on 3 sides							
3048	20¢ Blue Jay	08/02/96	.40	.20			1.25	491
a	Booklet pane of 10		4.00					
b	Booklet pane of 4		1.60					
c	Booklet pane of 6		2.40					
	Serpentine Die-Cut 11.25 x 11.75 on 2, 3 or 4 sides							
3049	32¢ Yellow Rose	10/24/96	.60	.20			1.25	2,900
a	Booklet pane of 20 and label		12.00					
b	Booklet pane of 4	12/96	2.75					
c	Booklet pane of 5	12/96	3.20					
d	Booklet pane of 6	12/96	3.60					
	Serpentine Die-Cut 11.25 on 2 or 3 sides							
3050	20¢ Ring-neck Pheasant	07/31/98	.40	.20			1.25	
a	Booklet pane of 10		4.00					
	Serpentine Die-Cut 10.5 x 11 on 3 sides							
3051	20¢ Ring-neck Pheasant	07/99	.60	.20				634
a	Serpentine Die-Cut 10.5 on 3 Sides		1.30	.20				
b	Booklet pane of 5, 4 #3051, 1 #3051a							
	turned sideways at top		3.75					
c	Booklet pane of 5, 4 #3051, 1 #3051a							
	turned sideways at bottom		3.75					
	Serpentine Die-Cut 11.5 x 11.25 on 2, 3 or 4 sides							
3052	33¢ Coral Pink Rose	08/13/99	.65	.20			1.25	1,000
a	Booklet pane of 4		2.60					
b	Booklet pane of 5 + label		3.25					
c	Booklet pane of 6		3.90					
d	Booklet pane of 20		13.00					

	Issues of 1996-2000		Un	U	PB	#	FDC	Q(M)
	Serpentine Die Cut 10.75 x 10.5 on 2 or 3 Sides							
3052E	33¢ Coral Pink Rose	04/07/00	.65	.20			1.25	
f	Booklet pane of 20		13.00					
	Coil Stamps, Serpentine Die-Cut 11.5 Vertically							
3053	20¢ Blue Jay	08/02/96	.40	.20	4.50	(5)	1.25	330
	Coil Stamps, Self-Adhesive, Serpentine Die-Cut 9.75 Vertically							
3054	32¢ Yellow Rose	08/01/97	.60	.20	6.00	(5)	1.25	
a	Imperf., pair		90.00					
3055	20¢ Ring-necked Pheasant	07/31/98	.40	.20	3.75	(5)	1.25	
	Black Heritage Issue, Perf. 11.1							
3058	32¢ Ernest E. Just	02/01/96	.60	.20	2.40	(4)	1.25	92
3059	32¢ Smithsonian Institution	02/07/96	.60	.20	2.40	(4)	1.25	115
	Lunar New Year Issue							
3060	32¢ Year of the Rat	02/08/96	.60	.20	3.00	(4)	1.50	93
	Pioneers of Communication Issue, Perf. 11.1 x 11							
3061	32¢ Eadweard Muybridge	02/22/96	.60	.20			1.25	96
3062	32¢ Ottmar Mergenthaler	02/22/96	.60	.20			1.25	96
3063	32¢ Frederic E. Ives	02/22/96	.60	.20			1.25	96
3064	32¢ William Dickson	02/22/96	.60	.20			1.25	96
a	Block or strip of 4, #3061-3064		2.40	1.75	2.40	(4)	3.25	
	Perf. 11.1							
3065	32¢ Fulbright Scholarships	02/28/96	.60	.20	3.00	(4)	1.25	130
	Pioneers of Aviation Issue							
3066	50¢ Jacqueline Cochran	03/09/96	1.00	.20	5.00	(4)	1.40	314
a	Black omitted		60.00					
3067	32¢ Marathon	04/11/96	.60	.20	2.40	(4)	1.25	209

Smithsonian Institution

The Smithsonian Institution of Washington, D.C., began as an idea in the mind of James Smithson (1765-1829), a British man of letters who bequeathed more than £100,000 to the United States "to found at Washington…an establishment for the increase and diffusion of knowledge…."

In 1846, Smithson's wish became reality when President James Polk signed an act of Congress establishing the institution.

Today, the Smithsonian comprises 16 museums and galleries, as well as the National Zoological Park and several research stations. Nine facilities, including the immensely popular National Air and Space Museum, stand along the National Mall. Five others—such as the National Postal Museum—are located elsewhere in Washington, and two are in New York City.

The oldest Smithsonian building is the Norman-style Castle designed by architect James Renwick (1818-1895) and completed in 1855; its image appeared on an American Architecture issue in 1980 and on commemorative stamps celebrating the centennial and sesquicentennial of the institution in 1946 and 1996. ■

3059

3060

3058

3063

3064

3061

3062

3064a

3066

3065

3067

1996

Atlanta 1996
CENTENNIAL OLYMPIC GAMES

CLASSIC
COLLECTIONS

.32
x 20
$6.40

PLATE
POSITION

© 1996
United
States
Postal
Service

3068

	a	b	c	d	e
	f	g	h	i	j
	k	l	m	n	o
	p	q	r	s	t

3069

3070

3072   3073   3074   3075   3076   3076a

	Issues of 1996		Un	U	PB	#	FDC	Q(M)
	Summer Olympic Games Issue, Perf. 11.1							
3068	Pane of 20	05/02/96	12.00	—			13.00	324
a	32¢ Decathlon		.60	.20			1.25	
b	32¢ Canoeing		.60	.20			1.25	
c	32¢ Women's running		.60	.20			1.25	
d	32¢ Women's diving		.60	.20			1.25	
e	32¢ Cycling		.60	.20			1.25	
f	32¢ Freestyle wrestling		.60	.20			1.25	
g	32¢ Women's gymnastic		.60	.20			1.25	
h	32¢ Women's sailboarding		.60	.20			1.25	
i	32¢ Shot put		.60	.20			1.25	
j	32¢ Women's soccer		.60	.20			1.25	
k	32¢ Beach volleyball		.60	.20			1.25	
l	32¢ Rowing		.60	.20			1.25	
m	32¢ Sprinting		.60	.20			1.25	
n	32¢ Women's swimming		.60	.20			1.25	
o	32¢ Women's softball		.60	.20			1.25	
p	32¢ Hurdles		.60	.20			1.25	
q	32¢ Swimming		.60	.20			1.25	
r	32¢ Gymnastics		.60	.20			1.25	
s	32¢ Equestrian		.60	.20			1.25	
t	32¢ Basketball		.60	.20			1.25	
	Perf. 11.6 x 11.4							
3069	32¢ Georgia O'Keeffe	05/23/96	.65	.20	2.75	(4)	1.25	156
a	Imperf., pair		200.00					
	Perf. 11.1							
3070	32¢ Tennessee Statehood	05/31/96	.60	.20	3.00	(4)	1.25	100
	Self-Adhesive, Serpentine Die-Cut 9.9 x 10.8							
3071	32¢ Tennessee Statehood	05/31/96	.60	.30			1.25	60
a	Booklet pane of 20		12.00					
	American Indian Dances Issue, Perf. 11.1							
3072	32¢ Fancy Dance	06/07/96	.60	.20			1.25	139
3073	32¢ Butterfly Dance	06/07/96	.60	.20			1.25	139
3074	32¢ Traditional Dance	06/07/96	.60	.20			1.25	139
3075	32¢ Raven Dance	06/07/96	.60	.20			1.25	139
3076	32¢ Hoop Dance	06/07/96	.60	.20			1.25	139
a	Strip of 5, #3072-3076		3.00	1.75	6.00	(10)	3.50	139

Greetings From Georgia

Larger than any other state east of the Mississippi River, Georgia stretches from the Appalachians in the northwest to the Atlantic Ocean in the southeast. Atlanta, the capital city, began as a railroad terminus in 1837 and served as a Confederate supply center during the Civil War—until Union General William T. Sherman set it afire on his devastating march to the sea. Afterward, the city rose boldly from the ashes to become a major commercial, financial, and transportation center in the 20th century.

Several architectural treasures from the antebellum period still stand in Georgia, especially in Savannah, which was spared Sherman's torch. Founded by British General James Oglethorpe in 1733, this historic city was Georgia's first settlement.

Georgia is widely celebrated for its peaches, its peanuts, and the Okefenokee—an enormous freshwater swamp reaching into Florida. The name derives from Indian words describing large areas of unstable peat deposits and means "land of trembling earth." ■

1996

	Issues of 1996		Un	U	PB	#	FDC	Q(M)
	Prehistoric Animals Issue, Perf. 11.1 x 11							
3077	32¢ Eohippus	06/08/96	.60	.20			1.50	150
3078	32¢ Woolly Mammoth	06/08/96	.60	.20			1.50	150
3079	32¢ Mastodon	06/08/96	.60	.20			1.50	150
3080	32¢ Saber-tooth Cat	06/08/96	.60	.20			1.50	150
a	Block or strip of 4, #3077-3080		2.40	1.50	2.40	(4)	3.25	150
	Pane of 20		12.00	—				
	Perf. 11.1							
3081	32¢ Breast Cancer Awareness	06/15/96	.60	.20	2.40	(4)	1.25	96
	Legends of Hollywood Issue, Perf. 11.1							
3082	32¢ James Dean	06/24/96	.60	.20	2.75	(4)	1.75	300
	Pane of 20		14.00	—				
a	Imperf., pair		350.00					
	Folks Heroes Issue, Perf. 11.1 x 11							
3083	32¢ Mighty Casey	07/11/96	.60	.20			1.25	113
3084	32¢ Paul Bunyan	07/11/96	.60	.20			1.25	113
3085	32¢ John Henry	07/11/96	.60	.20			1.25	113
3086	32¢ Pecos Bill	07/11/96	.60	.20			1.25	113
a	Block or strip of 4, #3083-3086		2.40	1.50	2.40	(4)	3.25	
	Centennial Olympic Games Issue, Perf. 11.1							
3087	32¢ Centennial Olympic Games	07/11/96	.65	.20	3.75	(4)	1.25	134
	Pane of 20		17.50	—				
3088	32¢ Iowa Statehood	08/01/96	.60	.20	3.00	(4)	1.25	103
	Booklet Stamp, Self-Adhesive, Serpentine Die-Cut 11.6 x 11.4							
3089	32¢ Iowa Statehood	08/01/96	.60	.30			1.25	60
a	Booklet pane of 20		12.00					
	Perf. 11.2 x 11							
3090	32¢ Rural Free Delivery	08/07/96	.60	.20	2.40	(4)	1.25	134

Greetings From Iowa

Located between the Mississippi and Missouri Rivers, Iowa occupies a transition zone where eastern forestlands give way to vast croplands of corn and alfalfa. These, in turn, give way to boundless western prairies dotted here and there with wild roses.

More than worthy of a painter's brush, the gently rolling landscapes of Iowa appear in several works by artist Grant Wood, who was born here in 1892 and later taught at the University of Iowa. He is perhaps best known for *American Gothic*.

Several scenic routes showcase the beauty and bounty of Iowa. Near the Mississippi, the Great River Road meanders past high bluffs and through old river towns and woodlands. Another route winds along the Iowa River, passing through such historic villages as the Amana Colonies, which were settled by a German religious group in the mid-1800s. In the far west, a scenic byway threads through miles and miles of windblown soil deposits known as loess; only the loess hills of China reach such dramatic heights. ■

3077 Eohippus
3078 Woolly mammoth
3079 Mastodon
3080 Saber-tooth cat

3080a

3081

3082

3083
3086

3085
3084

3086a

3087

3088

3090

3091

3092

3093

3094

3095

3095a

3096

3097

3098

3099

3099a

3100

3101

3102

3103

3103a

3104

Issues of 1996		Un	U	PB	#	FDC	Q(M)
Riverboats Issue, Serpentine Die-Cut 11 x 11.1							
3091	32¢ Robert E. Lee	08/22/96	.60	.20			1.25	160
3092	32¢ Sylvan Dell	08/22/96	.60	.20			1.25	160
3093	32¢ Far West	08/22/96	.60	.20			1.25	160
3094	32¢ Rebecca Everingham	08/22/96	.60	.20			1.25	160
3095	32¢ Bailey Gatzert	08/22/96	.60	.20			1.25	160
a	Vertical strip of 5, #3091-3095		3.00		6.00	(10)	3.50	
b	Strip of 5, #3091-3095 with special die-cutting		75.00	50.00	140.00	(10)		
Legends of American Music Series, Big Band Leaders Issue, Perf. 11.1 x 11							
3096	32¢ Count Basie	09/11/96	.60	.20			1.25	92
3097	32¢ Tommy and Jimmy Dorsey	09/11/96	.60	.20			1.25	92
3098	32¢ Glenn Miller	09/11/96	.60	.20			1.25	92
3099	32¢ Benny Goodman	09/11/96	.60	.20			1.25	92
a	Block or strip of 4, #3096-3099		2.40	1.50	2.40	(4)	3.25	
Legends of American Music Series, Songwriters Issue							
3100	32¢ Harold Arlen	09/11/96	.60	.20			1.25	92
3101	32¢ Johnny Mercer	09/11/96	.60	.20			1.25	92
3102	32¢ Dorothy Fields	09/11/96	.60	.20			1.25	92
3103	32¢ Hoagy Carmichael	09/11/96	.60	.20			1.25	92
a	Block or strip of 4, #3100-3103		2.40	1.50	2.40	(4)	3.25	
Literary Arts Issue, Perf. 11.1							
3104	23¢ F. Scott Fitzgerald	09/11/96	.45	.20	2.25	(4)	1.25	300

Palace of Fine Arts

In 1915, San Francisco welcomed the world to the Panama-Pacific International Exposition—a grand celebration of the 1914 opening of the Panama Canal and a splendid way of showing that the city had recovered from the devastating earthquake of 1906. Visitors soon found themselves dazzled by one complex in particular: the Palace of Fine Arts designed by Bernard

Maybeck, an architect widely recognized for extraordinary ability, individuality, and a great sense of drama. For his theme, Maybeck had chosen to evoke the haunting character of Roman ruins—perfect examples of "the mortality of grandeur and the vanity of human wishes."

The building complex includes the Colonnade, atop which stand statues of weeping women carved by sculptor Ulric Ellerhusen; an exhibition hall; a pond with swans; and the classic Beaux Arts Rotunda, rich in detail and highly ornamented. The Rotunda is the central feature on one of the four architecture stamps issued by the Postal Service in 1981.

In 1962, the Palace of Fine Arts underwent a much-needed restoration. Today, the complex continues to be a popular venue for concerts, lectures, film festivals, dance events, and weddings; it also houses the Exploratorium, a hands-on science museum. ■

	Issues of 1996		Un	U	PB	#	FDC	Q(M)
	Endangered Species Issue, Perf. 11.1 x 11							
3105	Pane of 15	10/02/96	9.00	—			7.50	224
a	32¢ Black-footed ferret		.60	.20			1.25	
b	32¢ Thick-billed parrot		.60	.20			1.25	
c	32¢ Hawaiian monk seal		.60	.20			1.25	
d	32¢ American crocodile		.60	.20			1.25	
e	32¢ Ocelot		.60	.20			1.25	
f	32¢ Schaus swallowtail butterfly		.60	.20			1.25	
g	32¢ Wyoming toad		.60	.20			1.25	
h	32¢ Brown pelican		.60	.20			1.25	
i	32¢ California condor		.60	.20			1.25	
j	32¢ Gilatrout		.60	.20			1.25	
k	32¢ San Francisco garter snake		.60	.20			1.25	
l	32¢ Woodland caribou		.60	.20			1.25	
m	32¢ Florida panther		.60	.20			1.25	
n	32¢ Piping plover		.60	.20			1.25	
o	32¢ Florida manatee		.60	.20			1.25	
	Perf. 10.9 x 11.1							
3106	32¢ Computer Technology	10/08/96	.60	.20	3.00	(4)	1.25	94
	Christmas Issue, Perf. 11.1 x 11.2							
3107	32¢ Madonna and Child							
	by Paolo de Matteis	10/08/96	.60	.20	3.00	(4)	1.25	848
	Perf. 11.3							
3108	32¢ Family at Fireplace	10/08/96	.60	.20			1.25	226
3109	32¢ Decorating Tree	10/08/96	.60	.20			1.25	226
3110	32¢ Dreaming of Santa Claus	10/08/96	.60	.20			1.25	226
3111	32¢ Holiday Shopping	10/08/96	.60	.20			1.25	226
a	Block or strip of 4, #3108-3111		2.40	1.50	3.00	(4)	3.25	
	Self-Adhesive Booklet Stamps, Serpentine Die-Cut 10 on 2, 3 or 4 sides							
3112	32¢ Madonna and Child							
	by Paolo de Matteis	10/08/96	.60	.20			1.25	244
a	Booklet pane of 20 + label		12.00					
b	No die-cutting, pair		75.00					
3113	32¢ Family at Fireplace	10/08/96	.60	.20			1.25	1,805
3114	32¢ Decorating Tree	10/08/96	.60	.20			1.25	1,805
3115	32¢ Dreaming of Santa Claus	10/08/96	.60	.20			1.25	1,805
3116	32¢ Holiday Shopping	10/08/96	.60	.20			1.25	1,805
a	Booklet pane, 5 ea #3113-3116		12.00				3.25	
	Die-Cut							
3117	32¢ Skaters	10/08/96	.60	.20			1.25	495
a	Booklet pane of 18		11.00					
	Self-Adhesive, Serpentine Die-Cut 11.1							
3118	32¢ Hanukkah	10/22/96	.60	.20	2.40	(4)	1.25	104
	Cycling Issue, Perf. 11 x 11.1							
3119	32¢ Souvenier sheet of 2	11/01/96	2.00	2.00			2.50	
a	50¢ orange		1.00	1.00			1.50	
b	50¢ blue and green		1.00	1.00			1.50	

3105

a b c

d e f

g h i

j k l

m n o

3106

3107

3108   3111

3111a

3109   3110

3117

3118

3119a

3119b

3120

3121

3122

3123

3124

3125

3126

3127

3130

3131

3132

3133

3134

3135

	Issues of 1997		Un	U	PB	#	FDC	Q(M)
	Lunar New Year Issue, Perf. 11.2							
3120	32¢ Year of the Ox	01/05/97	.60	.20	2.40	(4)	1.50	106
	Black Heritage Issue, Serpentine Die-Cut 11.4							
3121	32¢ Brig. Gen. Benjamin							
	O. Davis Sr.	01/28/97	.60	.20	2.40	(4)	1.25	112
	Self-Adhesive Booklet Stamps, Serpentine Die-Cut 11 on 2, 3 or 4 sides							
3122	32¢ Statue of Liberty,							
	Type of 1994	02/01/97	.60	.20			1.25	2,855
a	Booklet panel of 20 + label		12.00					
b	Booklet pane of 4		2.50					
c	Booklet pane of 5 + label		3.20					
d	Booklet pane of 6		3.60					
	Self-Adhesive, Serpentine Die-Cut 11.5 x 11.8 on 2, 3 or 4 sides							
3122E	32¢ Statue of Liberty		1.10	.20				
f	Booklet pane of 20 + label		35.00					
g	Booklet pane of 6		7.00					
	Self-Adhesive, Serpentine Die-Cut 11.8 x 11.6 on 2, 3 or 4 sides							
3123	32¢ Love Swans	02/04/97	.60	.20			1.25	1,660
a	Booklet pane of 20 + label		12.00					
b	No die-cutting, pair		250.00					
	Serpentine Die-Cut 11.6 x 11.8 on 2, 3 or 4 sides							
3124	55¢ Love Swans	02/04/97	1.00	.20			1.50	814
a	Booklet pane of 20 + label		21.00					
	Self-Adhesive, Serpentine Die-Cut 11.6 x 11.7							
3125	32¢ Helping Children Learn	02/18/97	.60	.20	2.40	(4)	1.25	122
	Merian Botanical Print Issues, Self-Adhesive,							
	Serpentine Die-Cut 10.9 x 10.2 on 2, 3 or 4 sides							
3126	32¢ Citron, Roth, Larvae,							
	Pupa, Beetle	03/03/97	.60	.20			1.25	2,048
3127	32¢ Flowering Pineapple,							
	Cockroaches	03/03/97	.60	.20			1.25	2,048
a	Booklet pane, 10 each #3126-3127 + label		12.00					
b	Pair, #3126-3127		1.20					
	Serpentine Die-Cut 11.2 x 10.8 on 2 or 3 sides							
3128	32¢ Citron, Roth, Larvae,							
	Pupa, Beetle	03/03/97	.60	.20			1.25	30
b	Booklet pane, 2 each #3128-3129		3.00					
3129	32¢ Flowering Pineapple,							
	Cockroaches	03/03/97	.60	.20			1.25	30
b	Booklet pane of 5,							
	2 each #3128-29, 1 #3129a		3.00					
c	Pair, #3128-3129		1.20					
	Pacific 97 Issues, Perf. 11.2							
3130	32¢ Sailing Ship	03/13/97	.60	.20			1.25	130
3131	32¢ Stagecoach	03/13/97	.60	.20			1.25	130
a	Pair #3130-31		1.25	.30	2.50	(4)	1.75	
	Coil Stamps, Self-Adhesive, Imperf.							
3132	25¢ Juke Box	03/14/97	.50	.50	4.75	(5)	1.25	24
	Coil Stamps, Serpentine Die-Cut 9.9 Vertically							
3133	32¢ Flag Over Porch	03/14/97	.60	.20	7.50	(5)	1.25	1
	Literary Arts Issue, Perf. 11.1							
3134	32¢ Thornton Wilder	04/17/97	.60	.20	2.40	(4)	1.25	98
3135	32¢ Raoul Wallenberg	04/24/97	.60	.20	2.40	(4)	1.50	96

	Issues of 1997		Un	U	FDC	Q(M)
	The World of Dinosaurs Issue, Perf. 11 x 11.1					
3136	Sheet of 15	05/01/97	9.00	—	7.50	219
a	32¢ Ceratosaurus		.60	.20	1.25	
b	32¢ Camptosaurus		.60	.20	1.25	
c	32¢ Camarasaurus		.60	.20	1.25	
d	32¢ Brachiosaurus		.60	.20	1.25	
e	32¢ Goniopholis		.60	.20	1.25	
f	32¢ Stegosaurus		.60	.20	1.25	
g	32¢ Allosaurus		.60	.20	1.25	
h	32¢ Opisthias		.60	.20	1.25	
i	32¢ Edmontonia		.60	.20	1.25	
j	32¢ Einiosaurus		.60	.20	1.25	
k	32¢ Daspletosaurus		.60	.20	1.25	
l	32¢ Palaeosaniwa		.60	.20	1.25	
m	32¢ Corythosaurus		.60	.20	1.25	
n	32¢ Ornithominus		.60	.20	1.25	
o	32¢ Parasaurolophus		.60	.20	1.25	
	Looney Tunes Issue, Self-Adhesive, Serpentine Die-Cut 11					
3137	Bugs Bunny Pane of 10	05/22/97	6.00			265
a	32¢ single		.60	.20	1.75	
b	Booklet pane of 9		5.40			
c	Booklet pane of 1		.60			
	Die-cutting on #3137b does not extend through the backing paper.					
3138	Pane of 10	05/22/97	*125.00*			
a	32¢ single		*2.00*			
b	Booklet pane of 9		—			
c	Booklet pane of 1, imperf.		—			
	Die-cutting on #3138b extends through the backing paper.					

Greetings From Montana

Wide-open grasslands and immense fields of wheat stretch across eastern Montana, while in the Rocky Mountain west, the state lives up to its Spanish name, meaning "mountainous." Montana also lives up to its "Treasure State" nickname, for within its 147,046 square miles lies a wealth of silver, gold, coal, and copper. At the Museum of the Rockies in Bozeman, visitors can learn about Montana's mineral riches—and see interesting exhibits on dinosaurs, too.

Scenic treasures can be found all over the state. In the northwest, Glacier National Park protects a million spectacular acres of glaciated landscape. In central Montana, some of the 1.1 million acres in Charles M. Russell National Wildlife Refuge look just as they did when Lewis and Clark traveled through in 1805. And in the south, the walls of Bighorn Canyon soar a thousand feet above the canyon floor. It was not far from here that Lt. Col. George A. Custer met defeat at the hands of the Lakota Sioux and other tribes in 1876. ∎

3136 a b c d f g

e h

i j k m n o

l

3137

3139

3140

3141

Issues of 1997		Un	U	PB	#	FDC	Q(M)
Pacific 97 Issues, Perf. 10.5 x 10.4							
3139 Benjamin Franklin Pane of 12	05/29/97	12.00	—			12.00	56
a 50¢ single		1.00	.50			2.00	
3140 George Washington Pane of 12	05/30/97	14.50	—			14.50	56
a 60¢ single		1.20	.60			2.50	
The Marshall Plan, 50th Anniversary Issue, Perf. 11.1							
3141 32¢ The Marshall Plan	06/04/97	.60	.20	2.40	(4)	1.25	45

Peace Bridge

The 5,800-foot-long Peace Bridge between Buffalo, New York, and Fort Erie, Ontario reaches across the Niagara River and ties two nations together. It is a symbol of the peaceful relations enjoyed for more than a hundred years by the United States and Canada—a no- or  low-hassle gateway for international travelers and a relatively free-flowing conduit for commercial goods. In 1977, the Postal Service issued the Peace Bridge stamp, pairing the bridge with a dove of peace on the 50th anniversary of its opening to traffic.

Because the bridge plays such a major role in international trade and travel, the Buffalo and Fort Erie Public Bridge Authority has undertaken a capital expansion program to enlarge the present bridge, build an adjacent bridge, and make the processing of commercial vehicles even smoother. These steps are all in keeping with the goals of the 1993 North American Free Trade Agreement, committing the United States, Canada, and Mexico to easing the flow of people and goods across their borders. ■

1997

	Issues of 1997		Un	U	PB	#	FDC	Q(M)
	Classic American Aircraft Issue, Perf. 10.1							
3142	Pane of 20	07/19/97	12.00	—			15.00	161
a	32¢ Mustang		.60	.20			1.50	
b	32¢ Model B		.60	.20			1.50	
c	32¢ Cub		.60	.20			1.50	
d	32¢ Vega		.60	.20			1.50	
e	32¢ Alpha		.60	.20			1.50	
f	32¢ B-10		.60	.20			1.50	
g	32¢ Corsair		.60	.20			1.50	
h	32¢ Stratojet		.60	.20			1.50	
i	32¢ Gee Bee		.60	.20			1.50	
j	32¢ Staggerwing		.60	.20			1.50	
k	32¢ Flying Fortress		.60	.20			1.50	
l	32¢ Stearman		.60	.20			1.50	
m	32¢ Constellation		.60	.20			1.50	
n	32¢ Lightning		.60	.20			1.50	
o	32¢ Peashooter		.60	.20			1.50	
p	32¢ Tri-Motor		.60	.20			1.50	
q	32¢ DC-3		.60	.20			1.50	
r	32¢ 314 Clipper		.60	.20			1.50	
s	32¢ Jenny		.60	.20			1.50	
t	32¢ Wildcat		.60	.20			1.50	
	Legendary Football Coaches Issue, Perf. 11.2							
3143	32¢ Bear Bryant	07/25/97	.60	.20			1.50	90
3144	32¢ Pop Warner	07/25/97	.60	.20			1.50	90
3145	32¢ Vince Lombardi	07/25/97	.60	.20			1.50	90
3146	32¢ George Halas	07/25/97	.60	.20			1.50	90
a	Block or strip of 4, #3143-3146		2.40	—	2.40	(4)	4.00	

Greetings From Utah

"This is the right place," said Mormon leader Brigham Young when he and his followers arrived at Salt Lake Valley in 1847. In this isolated area of the Great Basin, the Latter-day Saints would build new homes, found new towns, and live free from religious persecution. In 1849, they established a provisional state named Deseret, their word for the honeybee—symbol for hard work and the inspiration for the nickname "Beehive State."

Actual statehood was finally achieved in 1896, but the Deseret name was changed to Utah in honor of the Ute people who once ranged all over the region. Salt Lake City, site of the Mormon Tabernacle, remained the state capital; in 2002, the city welcomed the world to the Winter Olympics.

In southern and eastern Utah, several spectacular national parks and scores of state parks protect a wide array of scenic landscapes and multitudes of wildlife. There are red-rock pinnacles, multicolored cliffs, graceful sandstone arches, and vistas as far as the eye can see. ■

3142

a	b	c	d
e	f	g	h
i	j	k	l
m	n	o	p
q	r	s	t

3145   3146   3143   3144   3146a

3147

3148

3149

3150

CLASSIC
American Dolls

PLATE
POSITION
P11111

32
x15
$4.80

© 1996 U

"Alabama Baby" and Martha Chase   "The Columbian Doll"   Johnny Gruelle's "Raggedy Ann"   Martha Chase   "American Child"
"Baby Coos"   Plains Indian   Izannah Walker   "Babyland Rag"   "Scootles"
Ludwig Greiner   "Betsy McCall"   Percy Crosby's "Skippy"   "Maggie Mix-up"   Albert Schoenhut

The above names include doll makers, designers, trade names and common names.

3151   **a**   **b**   **c**   **d**   **e**

     f   **g**   **h**   **i**   **j**

	Issues of 1997		Un	U	PB	#	FDC	Q(M)
	Legendary Football Coaches Issue, Perf. 11							
3147	32¢ Vince Lombardi	08/05/97	.60	.30	2.40	(4)	1.50	20
3148	32¢ Bear Bryant	08/07/97	.60	.30	2.40	(4)	1.50	20
3149	32¢ Pop Warner	08/08/97	.60	.30	2.40	(4)	1.50	10
3150	32¢ George Halas	08/16/97	.60	.30	2.40	(4)	1.50	10
	Classic American Dolls Issue, Perf. 10.9 x 11.1							
3151	Pane of 15	07/28/97	9.00	—			8.00	105
a	32¢ "Alabama Baby," and doll by Martha Chase		.60	.20			1.50	
b	32¢ "Columbian Doll"		.60	.20			1.50	
c	32¢ Johnny Gruelle's "Raggedy Ann"		.60	.20			1.50	
d	32¢ Doll by Martha Chase		.60	.20			1.50	
e	32¢ "American Child"		.60	.20			1.50	
f	32¢ "Baby Coos"		.60	.20			1.50	
g	32¢ Plains Indian		.60	.20			1.50	
h	32¢ Doll by Izannah Walker		.60	.20			1.50	
i	32¢ "Babyland Rag"		.60	.20			1.50	
j	32¢ "Scootles"		.60	.20			1.50	
k	32¢ Doll by Ludwig Greiner		.60	.20			1.50	
l	32¢ "Betsy McCall"		.60	.20			1.50	
m	32¢ Percy Crosby's "Skippy"		.60	.20			1.50	
n	32¢ "Maggie Mix-up"		.60	.20			1.50	
o	32¢ Dolls by Albert Schoenhut		.60	.20			1.50	

Greetings From West Virginia

West Virginia, the "Mountain State," boasts a higher average elevation—1,500 feet— than any other state east of the Mississippi River. This rugged Appalachian region belonged to Virginia until that state voted to secede during the Civil War. The action spurred the pro-Union, independent-minded residents of the northwest to part ways with the rest of Virginia and set up their own state, which President Abraham Lincoln gladly welcomed into the Union in 1863.

Today, West Virginia is heavily industrialized; even so, much of the countryside remains unspoiled and inviting. Its lush woodlands are havens for black bears and a variety of other wildlife, and its nearly 2,000 miles of streams hold trout, bass, and other fish sought by countless anglers who regularly try to catch them. River runners come here, too, drawn by spectacular stretches of rapids that have made West Virginia the "whitewater capital of the East." Hiking, biking, rock climbing, spelunking, skiing, and birdwatching are also popular activities. ■

Issues of 1997			Un	U	PB	#	FDC	Q(M)
Legends of Hollywood Issue, Perf. 11.1								
3152	32¢ Humphrey Bogart	07/31/97	.60	.20	2.50	(4)	1.25	195
3153	32¢ "The Stars and Stripes							
	Forever"	08/21/97	.60	.20	3.00	(4)	1.25	323
Legends of American Music Series, Opera Singers Issue, Perf. 11								
3154	32¢ Lily Pons	09/10/97	.65	.20			1.25	86
3155	32¢ Richard Tucker	09/10/97	.65	.20			1.25	86
3156	32¢ Lawrence Tibbett	09/10/97	.65	.20			1.25	86
3157	32¢ Rosa Ponselle	09/10/97	.65	.20			1.25	86
a	Block or strip of 4, #3154-3157		2.60	—	2.60	(4)	3.25	

Sonoran Desert

Named for the Mexican state of Sonora, the 118,000-square-mile Sonoran Desert reaches from northwestern Mexico into southeastern California and southwestern Arizona. In this region, temperatures often climb above 110 degrees in summer and sometimes slip below the freezing mark in winter; even so, many flora and fauna cope very well in the tropical to subtropical climate. The creosote bush, brittlebush, and teddy bear cholla, for example, thrive in some parts of the desert, surviving on the moisture they receive during occasional rainy periods. The saguaro, or giant cactus, is another successful member of the plant community. It serves as a home for Gila woodpeckers, which peck out holes to build their nests, and for opportunistic birds that move in when the woodpecker families eventually move out.

Among the other desert creatures are shy but poisonous Gila monsters, banded geckos, western diamondback rattlesnakes, and desert tortoises, all of which appear on the 1999 Sonoran Desert stamp pane—first in the Nature of America series. ■

LEGENDS OF HOLLYWOOD

Over the course of a career spanning
a quarter of a century and 75 films,
Humphrey Bogart rose to legendary status
as one of America's most beloved 'tough guys'.
Renowned for his roles in *The Maltese Falcon* (1941)
and *Casablanca* (1943), he won the Academy Award
for Best Actor in *The African Queen* (1951).
"Bogie" became an international
cult figure in the 1960s.

3152

3153

3154   3155

3156   3157

3157a

3158   3159   3160   3161

3162   3163   3164   3165   3165a

3167

3166

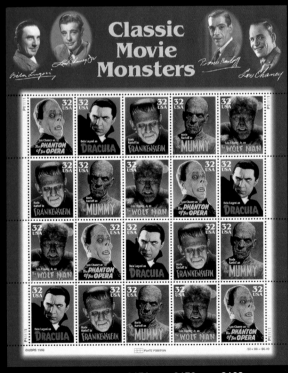

3169   3170   3171   3172   3168

Issues of 1997			Un	U	PB	#	FDC	Q(M)
Legends of American Music Series, Classical Composers & Conductors Issue, Perf. 11								
3158	32¢ Leopold Stokowski	09/12/97	.65	.20			1.25	86
3159	32¢ Arthur Fiedler	09/12/97	.65	.20			1.25	86
3160	32¢ George Szell	09/12/97	.65	.20			1.25	86
3161	32¢ Eugene Ormandy	09/12/97	.65	.20			1.25	86
3162	32¢ Samuel Barber	09/12/97	.65	.20			1.25	86
3163	32¢ Ferde Grofé	09/12/97	.65	.20			1.25	86
3164	32¢ Charles Ives	09/12/97	.65	.20			1.25	86
3165	32¢ Louis Moreau Gottschalk	09/12/97	.65	.20			1.25	86
a	Block of 8, #3158-3165		5.25	—	8.00	(8)	5.25	
	Perf. 11.2							
3166	32¢ Padre Félix Varela	09/15/97	.60	.20	2.40	(4)	1.25	2,855
Department of the Air Force, 50th Anniversary Issue, Perf. 11.2 x 11.1								
3167	32¢ Thunderbirds Aerial Demonstration Squadron	09/18/97	.60	.20	2.40	(4)	1.25	45
Classic Movie Monsters Issue, Perf. 10.2								
3168	32¢ Lon Chaney as the Phantom of the Opera	09/30/97	.60	.20			1.25	145
3169	32¢ Bela Lugosi as Dracula	09/30/97	.60	.20			1.25	145
3170	32¢ Boris Karloff as Frankenstein's Monster	09/30/97	.60	.20			1.25	145
3171	32¢ Boris Karloff as the Mummy	09/30/97	.60	.20			1.25	145
3172	32¢ Lon Chaney, Jr. as the Wolf Man	09/30/97	.60	.20			1.25	145
a	Strip of 5, #3168-3172		3.00	—	6.00	(10)	3.75	

Beginning with No. 3167, a hidden 3-D design can be seen on some stamps when they are viewed with a special viewer sold by the post office.

Arkansas River Navigation

Rising near Leadville, Colorado, and flowing across Kansas, northeastern Oklahoma, and Arkansas, before emptying into the Mississippi River, the 1,450-mile long Arkansas River ranks as the longest tributary in the Mississippi-Missouri system.

Two hundred years ago, Frenchmen traded with native peoples living along the waterway, exchanging goods for furs, skins, and other items. Today, commercial traffic on the Arkansas River annually carries millions of tons of soybeans, wheat, petroleum products, iron and steel, sand and rock, fertilizer, and so much more.

In 1946, Congress authorized the building of the McClellan-Kerr Arkansas River Navigation System (MKARNS) from the Mississippi River to the port of Catoosa, Oklahoma, and by the end of 1970, 17 locks and dams had been constructed not only to permit navigation by barges and other large vessels but also to control flood waters and generate hydropower. The MKARNS offers recreational opportunities as well, including fishing, non-commercial boating, and areas for picnicking, camping, and hiking. President Richard M. Nixon and other dignitaries dedicated the system on June 5, 1971. ∎

Issues of 1997-1998		Un	U	PB	#	FDC	Q(M)
Self-Adhesive, Serpentine Die-Cut 11.4							
3173 32¢ First Supersonic Flight, 50th Anniversary	10/14/97	.60	.20	2.40	(4)	1.25	173
Perf. 11.1							
3174 32¢ Women in Military Service	10/18/97	.60	.20	2.40	(4)	1.25	
Self-Adhesive, Serpentine Die-Cut 11							
3175 32¢ Kwanzaa	10/22/97	.60	.20	3.00	(4)	1.25	133
Holiday Traditional Issue, Self-Adhesive Booklet Stamps, Serpentine Die-Cut 9.9 on 2, 3 or 4 sides							
3176 32¢ Madonna and Child by Sano di Pietro	10/09/97	.60	.20			1.25	883
a Booklet pane of 20 + label		12.00					
Holiday Contemporary Issue, Self-Adhesive Booklet Stamps, Serpentine Die-Cut 11.2 x 11.8 on 2, 3 or 4 sides							
3177 32¢ American Holly	10/30/97	.60	.20			1.25	180
a Booklet pane of 20 + label		12.00					
b Booklet pane of 4		2.50					
c Booklet pane of 5 + label		3.00					
d Booklet pane of 6		3.75					
Mars Pathfinder, Perf. 11 x 11.1							
3178 $3 Mars Rover Sojourner	12/10/97	6.00	3.00			6.00	15
a $3, single stamp		5.50	2.75				
Lunar New Year Issue, Perf. 11.2							
3179 32¢ Year of the Tiger	01/05/98	.60	.20	2.40	(4)	1.25	

Stone Mountain Memorial

Three heroic figures of the Confederate States of America ride into glory at the Stone Mountain Memorial northwest of Atlanta, Georgia: President Jefferson Davis, commanding general Robert E. Lee, and the hero of Bull Run, Stonewall Jackson. Carved into the gray granite wall of a massive dome-shaped mountain, they stand 90 feet tall and stretch 190 feet across the rock face.

A Confederate memorial on Stone Mountain was the dream of the United Daughters of the Confederacy—and a major challenge for three sculptors. Gutzon Borglum began the work in 1923 but quit in 1925; he later carved Mount Rushmore. In 1925, Augustus Lukeman took on the job, but he stopped after his contract expired in 1928 and the property owners reclaimed their land. The state of Georgia bought Stone Mountain in 1958, made it a state park, and asked Walter Hancock to finish the sculpture. Finally, in May 1970, a formal dedication was held, followed in September of that year by the issuance of the Stone Mountain Memorial commemorative stamp. ■

3173

3174

3175

3176

3177

3178

3180

3181

3182   a   b   c   d   e

f   g   h

i   j

k   l   m   n   o

	Issues of 1998		Un	U	PB	#	FDC	Q(M)
	Winter Sports Issue, Perf. 11.2							
3180	32¢ Winter Sports-Skiing	1/2/98	.60	.20	2.40	(4)	1.25	80
	Black Heritage Issue, Self-Adhesive, Serpentine Die-Cut 11.6 x 11.3							
3181	32¢ Madam C. J. Walker	1/28/98	.60	.20	2.40	(4)	1.25	45
	Celebrate The Century® Issue, Perf. 11.5							
3182	Pane of 15, 1900-1909	2/3/98	9.00	—			7.50	188
a	32¢ Model T Ford		.60	.30			1.25	
b	32¢ Theodore Roosevelt		.60	.30			1.25	
c	32¢ Motion picture, "The Great Train Robbery"		.60	.30			1.25	
d	32¢ Crayola Crayons introduced, 1903		.60	.30			1.25	
e	32¢ St. Louis World's Fair, 1904		.60	.30			1.25	
f	32¢ Design used on Hunt's Remedy stamp (#RS56), Pure Food & Drug Act, 1906		.60	.30			1.25	
g	32¢ Wright Brothers first flight, Kitty Hawk, 1903		.60	.30			1.25	
h	32¢ Boxing match shown in painting "Stag at Sharkey's," by George Bellows of the Ash Can School		.60	.30			1.25	
i	32¢ Immigrants arrive		.60	.30			1.25	
j	32¢ John Muir, preservationist		.60	.30			1.25	
k	32¢ "Teddy" Bear created		.60	.30			1.25	
l	32¢ W.E.B. Du Bois, social activist		.60	.30			1.25	
m	32¢ Gibson Girl		.60	.30			1.25	
n	32¢ First baseball World Series, 1903		.60	.30			1.25	
o	32¢ Robie House, Chicago, designed by Frank Lloyd Wright		.60	.30			1.25	

Greetings From North Carolina

In 1903, Orville Wright took off from the Outer Banks of North Carolina in "Flyer 1" and made the world's first successful flight of a motor-powered aircraft. That historic event unfolded not far from Roanoke Island, where Sir Walter Raleigh's expedition made landfall in 1585 and established the first English colony in North America. Neither the flight nor the settlement lasted very long, but each ushered in a new era in American history.

Today, tourists flock to the sandy beaches, and lighthouses show the way for mariners off the North Carolina coast. At the other end of the state, the Blue Ridge Mountains also draw crowds every year. This region is known for hot springs, misty waterfalls, black bears, and 6,684-foot Mount Mitchell, the highest point east of the Mississippi River. Western North Carolina is also home to the Eastern Band of Cherokee.

Between the Blue Ridge and the Outer Banks lie large cities, high-tech research centers, a host of textile manufacturers and furniture-makers, and farms growing acres of tobacco. ■

Issues of 1998			Un	U	FDC	Q(M)
Celebrate The Century® Issue, Perf. 11.5						
3183	Pane of 15, 1910-1919	02/03/98	9.00	—	7.50	188
a	32¢ Charlie Chaplin as the Little Tramp		.60	.30	1.25	
b	32¢ Federal Reserve System created, 1913		.60	.30	1.25	
c	32¢ George Washington Carver		.60	.30	1.25	
d	32¢ Avant-garde art introduced at Armory Show, 1913		.60	.30	1.25	
e	32¢ First transcontinental telephone line, 1914		.60	.30	1.25	
f	32¢ Panama Canal opens, 1914		.60	.30	1.25	
g	32¢ Jim Thorpe wins decathlon at Stockholm Olympics, 1912		.60	.30	1.25	
h	32¢ Grand Canyon National Park, 1919		.60	.30	1.25	
i	32¢ U.S. enters World War I		.60	.30	1.25	
j	32¢ Boy Scouts started in 1910, Girl Scouts formed in 1912		.60	.30	1.25	
k	32¢ Woodrow Wilson		.60	.30	1.25	
l	32¢ First crossword puzzle published, 1913		.60	.30	1.25	
m	32¢ Jack Dempsey wins heavyweight title, 1919		.60	.30	1.25	
n	32¢ Construction toys		.60	.30	1.25	
o	32¢ Child labor reform		.60	.30	1.25	

Grand Canyon

Celebrated as an American treasure and a World Heritage site, Grand Canyon National Park encompasses more than a million acres in northwestern Arizona. It is a place of great natural beauty, with spectacular features, colorful landscapes, deep chasms, and sweeping vistas along 277 miles of the Colorado River. At its deepest point, the Grand Canyon drops 6,000 vertical feet from rim to river; at its widest, it measures 18 miles from rim to rim.

Millions of years ago, the Colorado flowed out of the Rocky Mountains and began cutting down through the layers of an enormous plateau. Rain, snowmelt, and wind further shaped the rocks exposed by the river. Today, the Grand Canyon is of great geological significance: Its multilayered, multihued walls reveal a thick sequence of progressively older rocks that record hundreds of millions of years of Earth's history. Every year, scientists and five million other visitors come to view this natural wonder of the world. ■

1998

TECHNOLOGY • ENTERTAINMENT • SCIENCE

1910s
CELEBRATE THE CENTURY™

America Looks Beyond its Borders

Halley's comet lit up the sky to begin the decade. American workers began moving from farms to factories. The Ford Motor Co. refined the automobile assembly line. Traffic lights and white lane dividers became part of the American landscape. Scientific and technological achievements changed society. In 1911, in New York, fingerprint evidence alone was used for the first time in the United States to arrest a burglar. Jim Thorpe was an international sports star, but Tarzan was an even more popular hero.

The accidental sinking of the luxury liner Titanic shocked the nation, but it was the sinking of another ship, the Lusitania, that upset society, leading to U.S. involvement in World War I. Two million American soldiers fought in Europe and more than 116,500 lost their lives. Americans saw the light as the decade ended: Daylight saving time was instituted in 1918.

New words: camouflage, electronics, troublemaker

3183   a   b   c

1920s

CELEBRATE THE CENTURY™

The Roaring Twenties

Two Constitutional amendments went into effect in 1920, turning the nation upside down. The 18th Amendment prohibited the manufacture and sale of alcoholic beverages, and the 19th gave women the right to vote. Prohibition backfired, leading to widespread disrespect for the law. A federal highway system was organized and the number of automobiles nearly tripled. Spreading electrification spawned the golden age of radio.

The Roaring Twenties, as the decade came to be known, was an age of thrill seekers and heroes. In 1926 Gertrude Ederle swam the English Channel faster than any man had. The following year Charles Lindbergh flew nonstop across the Atlantic alone and Babe Ruth hit 60 home runs.

The first feature-length film with talking parts, The Jazz Singer, appeared in 1927 and the first Academy Awards were presented in 1929. The prosperous times ended with the stock market crash of Thursday, October 24, 1929.

New words: motel, robot, fan mail, teenage.

3184   a   b   c   d   e

Issues of 1998		Un	U	FDC	Q(M)
Celebrate The Century® Issue, Perf. 11.5					
3184 Pane of 15, 1920-1929	05/28/98	9.00	—	7.50	188
a 32¢ Babe Ruth		.60	.30	1.25	
b 32¢ The Gatsby style		.60	.30	1.25	
c 32¢ Prohibition enforced		.60	.30	1.25	
d 32¢ Electric toy trains		.60	.30	1.25	
e 32¢ Nineteenth Amendment (woman voting)		.60	.30	1.25	
f 32¢ Emily Post's Etiquette		.60	.30	1.25	
g 32¢ Margaret Mead, anthropologist		.60	.30	1.25	
h 32¢ Flappers do the Charleston		.60	.30	1.25	
i 32¢ Radio entertains America		.60	.30	1.25	
j 32¢ Art Deco style (Chrysler Building)		.60	.30	1.25	
k 32¢ Jazz flourishes		.60	.30	1.25	
l 32¢ Four Horsemen of Notre Dame		.60	.30	1.25	
m 32¢ Lindbergh flies the Atlantic		.60	.30	1.25	
n 32¢ American realism (The Automat, by Edward Hopper)		.60	.30	1.25	
o 32¢ Stock Market crash, 1929		.60	.30	1.25	

Greetings From New York

From Long Island in the south to the Thousand Islands in the north, the "Empire State" of New York boasts a world of natural wonders and man-made splendors.

The state's most developed island must be Manhattan, the skyscraper-filled heart of New York City. Block after block of high-rise engineering and architectural marvels, such as the Empire State and Chrysler Buildings, stand beside world-class museums, theaters, concert halls, restaurants, hotels, and shops.

To the north lie the Catskill Mountains—a popular resort area and source of inspiration for several 19th-century writers and artists—and the Hudson River Valley, where history mingles with charm in centuries-old towns, inns, and estates. The six million acres of Adirondack Park, in the northeast, make this the largest state park outside of Alaska.

New York also includes the lovely Finger Lakes region, spectacular Niagara Falls, and the little village of Cooperstown, home to the National Baseball Hall of Fame. ■

Issues of 1998			Un	U	FDC	Q(M)
Celebrate The Century Issue®, Perf. 11.5						
3185	Pane of 15, 1930-1939	09/10/98	9.00	—	7.50	188
a	32¢ Franklin D. Roosevelt		.60	.30	1.25	
b	32¢ The Empire State Building		.60	.30	1.25	
c	32¢ First Issue of Life Magazine, 1936		.60	.30	1.25	
d	32¢ Eleanor Roosevelt		.60	.30	1.25	
e	32¢ FDR's New Deal		.60	.30	1.25	
f	32¢ Superman arrives, 1938		.60	.30	1.25	
g	32¢ Household conveniences		.60	.30	1.25	
h	32¢ "Snow White and the Seven Dwarfs," 1937		.60	.30	1.25	
i	32¢ "Gone with the Wind," 1936		.60	.30	1.25	
j	32¢ Jesse Owens		.60	.30	1.25	
k	32¢ Streamline design		.60	.30	1.25	
l	32¢ Golden Gate Bridge		.60	.30	1.25	
m	32¢ America survives the Depression		.60	.30	1.25	
n	32¢ Bobby Jones wins golf Grand Slam, 1938		.60	.30	1.25	
o	32¢ The Monopoly Game		.60	.30	1.25	

Golden Gate Bridge

California's Golden Gate Bridge stands at the entrance to San Francisco Bay, spanning the mile-wide strait for which it was named. Most historians give John C. Frémont (1813-1890) credit for naming the strait back in the 1840s; the famous explorer and U.S. Army officer is said to have called it Chrysopylae, or Golden Gate, because it resembled the Golden Horn at Istanbul, Turkey.

For decades, people dreamed of bridging the Golden Gate, and in the 1930s, engineer Joseph Strauss (1870-1938) actually did it. After more than four years of construction in the face of strong winds, powerful tides, and other hazards, the San Francisco landmark—painted orange vermilion to make it compatible with the natural setting—opened to traffic in May 1937. Since then, over 1.6 vehicles have driven across the spectacular structure.

The Golden Gate's 4,200-foot-long central span, supported by 3-foot-wide cables attached to twin towers, made it the longest suspension bridge in the world until New York built the Verrazano-Narrows Bridge in 1964. ■

1930s
CELEBRATE THE CENTURY™

Depression, Dust Bowl, and a New Deal

By 1933 the average wage was 60 percent less than in 1929 and unemployment had skyrocketed to 25 percent. Dust storms forced many farmers to give up their land.

Americans escaped harsh realities by playing Monopoly, reading the adventures of "Buck Rogers" and "Flash Gordon," and listening to Hoagy Carmichael's "Stardust." Popular films included *King Kong* and *It Happened One Night*. For the first time, African-American athletes became national idols. Joe Louis in boxing and Jesse Owens in track and field.

Prohibition was repealed in 1933. President Franklin Roosevelt fought the Great Depression with his New Deal programs. The "Star-Spangled Banner" was chosen as the national anthem. The Empire State Building rose above the Manhattan skyline and the Golden Gate Bridge spanned the San Francisco Bay. Back on the ground, the parking meter made its first appearance in 1935.

As the decade closed, many Americans were anxious about the growing war in Europe.

New words: all-star, oops, pizza, racism

3185   a   b   c   d   e

TECHNOLOGY • ENTERTAINMENT • SCIENCE

POLITICAL FIGURES

HISTORICAL EVENTS

SPORTS

ART

LIFESTYLE

1940s
CELEBRATE THE CENTURY™

World War II Transforms America

After the bombing of Pearl Harbor, on December 7, 1941, the United States entered World War II. More than 16 million American men and women served in the military while millions of housewives worked to help keep the economy running. The U.S. emerged from the war as the world's most powerful nation. Americans, after surviving years of depression and war, eagerly started families. A surge in the 1946 birthrate began the postwar baby boom.

Movie fans enjoyed the films of Bing Crosby and Betty Grable. Commercial television was launched, and Milton Berle and Ed Sullivan became household names. Jackie Robinson broke the color barrier in Major League Baseball. For the first time people played with Slinkys and Silly Putty. Nylon stockings were the rage for women, while teenagers sported socks with loafers or saddle shoes and rolled-up blue jeans. The jitterbug was popularized by music from live bands and jukeboxes. New words: hot rod, pinup, bikini, self-employed

3186   a   b   c

Issues of 1999			Un	U	FDC	Q(M)
Celebrate The Century®, Perf. 11.5						
3186	Pane of 15, 1940-1949	02/18/99	9.75		7.50	12.5
a	33¢ World War II		.65	.30	1.25	
b	33¢ Antibiotics save lives		.65	.30	1.25	
c	33¢ Jackie Robinson		.65	.30	1.25	
d	33¢ Harry S. Truman		.65	.30	1.25	
e	33¢ Women support war effort		.65	.30	1.25	
f	33¢ TV entertains America		.65	.30	1.25	
g	33¢ Jitterbug sweeps nation		.65	.30	1.25	
h	33¢ Jackson Pollock, Abstract Expressionism		.65	.30	1.25	
i	33¢ GI Bill, 1944		.65	.30	1.25	
j	33¢ The Big Band Sound		.65	.30	1.25	
k	33¢ International style of architecture		.65	.30	1.25	
l	33¢ Postwar baby boom		.65	.30	1.25	
m	33¢ Slinky, 1945		.65	.30	1.25	
n	33¢ "A Streetcar Named Desire", 1947		.65	.30	1.25	
o	33¢ Orson Welles' "Citizen Kane"		.65	.30	1.25	

Touro Synagogue

Dedicated in December 1763, the Touro Synagogue at 85 Touro Street in Newport, Rhode Island, is the oldest synagogue in the United States. It is also one of the finest efforts by renowned architect Peter Harrison, who designed it in the style of earlier Amsterdam and London buildings, using bricks he imported from England. Inside the synagogue, 12 Ionic columns representing the 12 tribes of ancient Israel hold up the women's gallery, and five enormous brass candelabra hang from the ceiling. At the east end of the sanctuary, resting beneath a painting of the Ten Commandments by Newport artist Benjamin Howland, is the Holy Ark containing the oldest Torah in North America. When members of the congregation face the Ark, they also face Jerusalem.

Among the historical treasures at the synagogue—now a national historic site—is a letter written by George Washington in 1790, assuring the Touro congregation that the United States would "give to bigotry no sanction, to persecution no assistance." ■

Issues of 1999		Un	U	FDC	Q(M)
Celebrate The Century®, Perf. 11.5					
3187 Pane of 15, 1950-1959	05/26/99	9.75	—	7.50	12.5
a	33¢ Polio vaccine developed	.65	.30	1.25	
b	33¢ Teen fashions	.65	.30	1.25	
c	33¢ The "Shot Heard 'Round the World"	.65	.30	1.25	
d	33¢ U.S. launches satellites	.65	.30	1.25	
e	33¢ Korean War	.65	.30	1.25	
f	33¢ Desegregating public schools	.65	.30	1.25	
g	33¢ Tail fins, chrome	.65	.30	1.25	
h	33¢ Dr. Seuss' "The Cat in the Hat"	.65	.30	1.25	
i	33¢ Drive-in movies	.65	.30	1.25	
j	33¢ World Series rivals	.65	.30	1.25	
k	33¢ Rocky Marciano, undefeated boxer	.65	.30	1.25	
l	33¢ "I Love Lucy"	.65	.30	1.25	
m	33¢ Rock 'n Roll	.65	.30	1.25	
n	33¢ Stock car racing	.65	.30	1.25	
o	33¢ Movies go 3-D	.65	.30	1.25	

Greetings From Michigan

The Michigan state motto—"If you seek a pleasant peninsula, look about you"—not only extends an invitation to visitors but may also remind residents of why they or their forebears moved here in the first place. Surrounded by four of the five Great Lakes, Michigan actually comprises two major peninsulas. Pictured Rocks National Lakeshore and many inland lakes, streams, and forests make the Upper Peninsula a popular vacationland for hikers and canoeists. The Lower Peninsula, shaped like an upraised mitten, also boasts its share of "water wonderlands," as well as thousands of farms and orchards where cherries, apples, peaches, and pears grow in abundance.

The state's largest city, Detroit, was founded as a trading post in 1701. Little more than two centuries later, Michigan-born Henry Ford introduced the nation's first assembly line, transforming the city into the automobile-manufacturing capital of the world. ■

• TECHNOLOGY • ENTERTAINMENT • SCIENCE •

1950s
CELEBRATE THE CENTURY™

Family Fun, Suburbia, and Nuclear Threats

The 1950s were, for the most part, years of peace and prosperity. Millions of families moved to the suburbs. Americans liked Dwight D. Eisenhower, their kindly war-hero President.

Television became popular; *I Love Lucy* and *Gunsmoke* were hits. Teenagers chose their own fashions and music. Elvis Presley thrilled young people and shocked their elders.

The decade also had a serious side. The Korean War took more than 50,000 American lives. The first hydrogen bomb was detonated. In 1954 the U.S. Supreme Court declared racial segregation in public schools unconstitutional, and in 1955, in Montgomery, Alabama, Rosa Parks refused to give up her bus seat to a white man. But in 1957 President Eisenhower had to use the Arkansas National Guard and paratroopers to enforce integration at a Little Rock high school.

In January 1959 Alaska was admitted as the 49th state, and in August Hawaii became the 50th state.

New words: brainwashing, ballpoint, high-rise, centerfold

HISTORICAL EVENTS • SPORTS

POLITICAL FIGURES • LIFE STYLE

3187   a   b   c   d   e

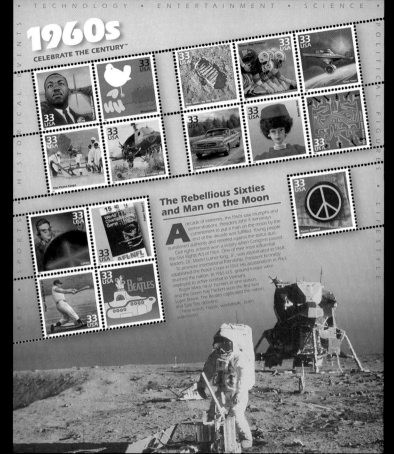

TECHNOLOGY • ENTERTAINMENT • SCIENCE •

1960s
CELEBRATE THE CENTURY™

The Rebellious Sixties
and Man on the Moon

A decade of extremes, the 1960s saw triumphs and demonstrations. President John F. Kennedy's commitment to put a man on the moon by the end of the decade was fulfilled. Young people questioned authority and rebelled against the status quo. Civil rights activists won a victory when Congress passed the Civil Rights Act of 1964. One of their most influential leaders, Dr. Martin Luther King, Jr., was assassinated in 1968.

To promote international friendship, President Kennedy established the Peace Corps in 1961. His assassination in 1963 stunned the nation. In 1965 U.S. ground troops were deployed to active combat in Vietnam.

Roger Maris hit 61 homers in one season, and the Green Bay Packers won the first two Super Bowls. The Beatles captivated the nation, and Star Trek debuted.

New words: hippie, workaholic, team, skateboard.

Issues of 1999		Un	U	FDC	Q(M)
Celebrate The Century®, Perf. 11.5					
3188 Pane of 15, 1960-1969	09/17/99	9.75	—	7.50	8
a 33¢ "I have a dream"		.65	.30	1.25	
b 33¢ Woodstock		.65	.30	1.25	
c 33¢ Man walks on the moon		.65	.30	1.25	
d 33¢ Green Bay Packers		.65	.30	1.25	
e 33¢ Star Trek		.65	.30	1.25	
f 33¢ The Peace Corps		.65	.30	1.25	
g 33¢ The Vietnam War		.65	.30	1.25	
h 33¢ Ford Mustang		.65	.30	1.25	
i 33¢ Barbie Doll		.65	.30	1.25	
j 33¢ The integrated circuit		.65	.30	1.25	
k 33¢ Lasers		.65	.30	1.25	
l 33¢ Super Bowl I		.65	.30	1.25	
m 33¢ Peace Symbol		.65	.30	1.25	
n 33¢ Roger Maris, 61 in '61		.65	.30	1.25	
o 33¢ The Beatles		.65	.30	1.25	

Ryman Auditorium

Once home to the Grand Ole Opry, Ryman Auditorium of Nashville, Tennessee, is a cultural center within a cultural center. Its setting is a vibrant state capital noted, in part, for several institutions of higher learning and a thriving recording industry. Often called the "Athens of the South," Nashville even has a full-size replica of the Parthenon.

Ryman Auditorium, Nashville, Tennessee

Riverboat captain Tom Ryman built the auditorium in the late 19th century, intending it to be a tabernacle and revival house, but by 1901 his Union Gospel Tabernacle was offering performances by professional musicians and actors as a way to pay the bills. Over the next several years, audiences thrilled to such greats as opera singer Enrico Caruso, dancers Isadora Duncan and Anna Pavlova, actress Sarah Bernhardt, and "the march king" John Philip Sousa.

The Grand Ole Opry took the stage in the 1940s and stayed for more than 30 years, with fans pouring in to hear country music stars such as Tammy Wynette, Hank Williams, and Roy Acuff. The Opry moved out in 1974 and became the centerpiece of a theme park complex known as Opryland USA. Still, the Ryman survived. It underwent a careful restoration in 1994 and once again hosts many of the top musicians and singers in the country. ∎

	Issues of 1999		Un	U	FDC	Q(M)
	Celebrate The Century®, Perf. 11.5					
3189	Pane of 15, 1970-1979	11/18/99	9.75	—	7.50	6
a	33¢ Earth Day celebrated		.65	.30	1.25	
b	33¢ TV series "All in the Family"		.65	.30	1.25	
c	33¢ "Sesame Street"		.65	.30	1.25	
d	33¢ Disco music		.65	.30	1.25	
e	33¢ Steelers win four Super Bowls		.65	.30	1.25	
f	33¢ U.S. celebrates 200th birthday		.65	.30	1.25	
g	33¢ Secretariat wins the Triple Crown		.65	.30	1.25	
h	33¢ VCRs transform entertainment		.65	.30	1.25	
i	33¢ Pioneer 10		.65	.30	1.25	
j	33¢ Women's Rights Movement		.65	.30	1.25	
k	33¢ 1970s fashions		.65	.30	1.25	
l	33¢ "Monday Night Football"		.65	.30	1.25	
m	33¢ America smiles		.65	.30	1.25	
n	33¢ Jumbo jet		.65	.30	1.25	
o	33¢ Medical imaging		.65	.30	1.25	

Sandy Hook Lighthouse

In 1761, shipwrecks on the Sandy Hook Peninsula of New Jersey, about 15 miles south of Manhattan, threatened New York City merchants with financial ruin. The shop owners lobbied for help, and in May of that year the Colony of New York passed a measure to raise money for "purchasing so much of Sandy-Hook as shall be necessary, and thereon to erect a proper Light House." On June 11, 1764, an octagonal, 103-foot-tall tower with "48 oil blazes" first cast its light into the night.

During the Revolutionary War, New Yorkers struggled with the British Navy for control of the lighthouse, even using a couple of cannon to shut it down. Then, in 1787, they faced a challenge from New Jersey over ownership, after which the federal government stepped in to accept title and jurisdiction.

Now part of the Gateway National Recreation Area, Sandy Hook is still in operation and nearly 240 years old, making it the country's oldest original lighthouse. ■

TECHNOLOGY • ENTERTAINMENT • SCIENCE •

1970s
CELEBRATE THE CENTURY™

Bicentennial, Watergate, and Earth Day

In the 1970s, the U.S. celebrated its 200-year history and made a commitment to protect the environment. The 26th Amendment lowered the voting age to 18 for all elections. Gender-based discrimination was prohibited, and a woman's right to have an abortion was defined. As a result of the Watergate scandal, Richard Nixon became the first U.S. President to resign from office.

Jumbo jets doubled airplane passenger capacity, and the first national speed limit, 55 mph, was instituted to conserve energy during an oil embargo. Fiber optics advanced telephone calls became a reality. Ultrasound, CAT scans, and MRIs revolutionized medical imaging.

Sesame Street educated children, Monday Night Football entertained sports fans, and All in the Family introduced its audience to a new kind of TV series. Viewers taped TV shows with VCRs, and some Americans caught disco fever.

New words: Junk food, slam dunk, miniseries

3189   a   b   c

TECHNOLOGY • ENTERTAINMENT • SCIENCE •

1980s
CELEBRATE THE CENTURY®

Space Shuttle Launched, Berlin Wall Falls

The space shuttle Columbia, the first reusable spacecraft, was originally launched April 12, 1981. Sandra Day O'Connor became the first female justice on the U.S. Supreme Court, and Sally Ride became the first American woman in space. The Iran-Contra hearings made headlines. Several events signaled the easing of international tensions. In December 1987 President Ronald Reagan and Soviet leader Mikhail Gorbachev signed a nuclear arms reduction treaty. The fall of the Berlin Wall in November 1989 presaged the end of the Cold War. The Vietnam Veterans Memorial was dedicated November 13, 1982. A new national holiday, Martin Luther King Day, was first celebrated in January 1986.

The growth of cable television, video games, and compact discs had a major impact on home entertainment. Dallas and The Cosby Show topped TV ratings. Hip-hop culture and music videos gained popularity.

New Words: yuppie, infomercial, biodiversity.

3190   a   b   c   d   e

	CTC Issues of 2000		Un	U	FDC	Q(M)
	Celebrate The Century®, Perf. 11.6					
3190	Pane of 15, 1980-1989	01/12/00	9.75	—	7.50	6
a	33¢ Space Shuttle Program		.65	.30	1.25	
b	33¢ "Cats", Broadway show		.65	.30	1.25	
c	33¢ San Fransico 49ers		.65	.30	1.25	
d	33¢ Hostages Come Home		.65	.30	1.25	
e	33¢ Figure Skating		.65	.30	1.25	
f	33¢ Cable TV		.65	.30	1.25	
g	33¢ Vietnam Veterans Memorial		.65	.30	1.25	
h	33¢ Compact Discs		.65	.30	1.25	
i	33¢ Cabbage Patch Kids		.65	.30	1.25	
j	33¢ "The Cosby Show"		.65	.30	1.25	
k	33¢ Fall of the Berlin Wall		.65	.30	1.25	
l	33¢ Video Games		.65	.30	1.25	
m	33¢ "E.T. The Extra-Terrestrial"		.65	.30	1.25	
n	33¢ Personal Computers		.65	.30	1.25	
o	33¢ Hip-Hop Culture		.65	.30	1.25	

Vietnam Veterans Memorial USA 20c

Vietnam Veterans Memorial

The "wall that heals." That's what many people call the wall of names at the Vietnam Veterans Memorial on the National Mall in Washington, D.C. Designed by architect Maya Lin and dedicated on November 13, 1982, this monument to the men and women lost during the Vietnam conflict honors all who served during the war; it is also a place of pilgrimage for veterans and other visitors from across the country and around the world. Cut into the earth, the memorial consists of an enormous wedge whose polished, black-granite wings stretch 246.75 feet from their 10.1-foot-high intersection point to their 8-inch-high ends. One tapered end points to the Lincoln Memorial, the other to the Washington Monument. Etched in the black granite are the names of more than 58,000 dead and missing.

The wall of names was featured on the 20-cent Vietnam Veterans Memorial stamp issued in 1984. That same year, Fredrick Hart's *Three Servicemen* statue was added near the wall, and in 1993 the Vietnam Women's Memorial by Glenna Goodacre completed the site. ∎

2000

	CTC Issues of 2000		Un	U	FDC	Q(M)
	Celebrate The Century®, Perf. 11.6					
3191	Pane of 15, 1990-1999	05/02/00	9.75	—	7.50	5.5
a	33¢ New Baseball Records		.65	.30	1.25	
b	33¢ Gulf War		.65	.30	1.25	
c	33¢ "Seinfeld", television series		.65	.30	1.25	
d	33¢ Extreme Sports		.65	.30	1.25	
e	33¢ Improving Education		.65	.30	1.25	
f	33¢ Computer Art and Graphics		.65	.30	1.25	
g	33¢ Recovering Species		.65	.30	1.25	
h	33¢ Return to Space		.65	.30	1.25	
i	33¢ Special Olympics		.65	.30	1.25	
j	33¢ Virtual Reality		.65	.30	1.25	
k	33¢ "Jurassic Park"		.65	.30	1.25	
l	33¢ "Titanic"		.65	.30	1.25	
m	33¢ Sports Utility Vehicle		.65	.30	1.25	
n	33¢ World Wide Web		.65	.30	1.25	
o	33¢ Cellular Phones		.65	.30	1.25	

Mount McKinley

With an elevation of 20,320 feet, Mount McKinley towers over every other peak in North America. It also features one of Earth's sharpest vertical rises, thrusting more than three miles into the air from 2,000-foot-high lowlands in Alaska's Denali National Park and Preserve. Named in honor of former President William McKinley, this immense mountain has long borne other names as well, including Denali, an Athabascan word meaning "the high one."

For much of the time, a thick mantle of clouds covers McKinley. Even so, people come from far and wide every summer, pouring into Denali National Park and hoping that the mountain will reveal itself. But this park is more than just a mountain: Within its bounds are six million acres of stunning natural beauty and an amazing diversity of wildlife. Grizzly bears, Dall's sheep, moose, caribou, and wolves move quietly through the wilderness as eagles soar silently above. ∎

• TECHNOLOGY • ENTERTAINMENT • SCIENCE •

1990s

CELEBRATE THE CENTURY®

In Final Decade, Cold War Ends, Economy Booms

The Soviet Union collapsed, effectively ending the Cold War. Troops were deployed by the United States in the Persian Gulf, in Somalia, and in the Balkans. In 1992—often called the Year of the Woman— a record number of women were elected to political office. American astronauts joined Russian cosmonauts on the Mir space station, and Mars Pathfinder and Mars Global Surveyor sent back extraordinary images of the red planet. A grouping of planets resembling our solar system was found by astronomers. The World Wide Web and e-mail revolutionized communications. Millions of Americans bought cellular phones as service expanded. In Washington, D.C., the Holocaust Museum drew huge crowds, while in Los Angeles, the Getty Center's architecture got rave reviews. Moviegoers flocked to see Titanic and Jurassic Park. Extreme sports, such as snowboarding and BMX biking, attracted young people, and the U.S. women's softball, soccer, and basketball teams proved themselves the best in the world. New words: e-commerce, Web site, Y2K.

HISTORICAL EVENTS • SPORTS

POLITICAL FIGURES • LIFE

3191   a   b   c

3192

3193   3194   3195   3196   3197   3197a

3198   3199   3200   3201   3202   3202a

3203

3204b

Issues of 1998		Un	U	PB	#	FDC	Q(M)
Perf. 11.2 x 11							
3192 32¢ "Remember the Maine"							
Spanish-American War	02/15/98	.60	.20	2.40	(4)	1.25	30
Flowering Trees Issue, Die-Cut, Perf. 11.3							
3193 32¢ Southern Magnolia	03/19/98	.60	.20			1.25	
3194 32¢ Blue Paloverde	03/19/98	.60	.20			1.25	
3195 32¢ Yellow Poplar	03/19/98	.60	.20			1.25	
3196 32¢ Prairie Crab Apple	03/19/98	.60	.20			1.25	
3197 32¢ Pacific Dogwood	03/19/98	.60	.20			1.25	
a Strip of 5, #3193-3197	03/19/98	3.00		6.00	(10)	3.75	250
Alexander Calder Issue, Perf. 10.2							
3198 32¢ Black Cascade	03/25/98	.60	.20			1.25	
3199 32¢ Untitled	03/25/98	.60	.20			1.25	
3200 32¢ Rearing Stallion	03/25/98	.60	.20			1.25	
3201 32¢ Portrait of a Young Man	03/25/98	.60	.20			1.25	
3202 32¢ Un Effet du Japonais	03/25/98	.60	.20			1.25	
a Strip of 5, #3198-3202	03/25/98	3.00	—	6.00	(10)	3.75	80
Holiday Celebrations Issue, Self-Adhesive, Serpentine Die-Cut 11.7 x 10.9							
3203 32¢ Cinco de Mayo	04/16/98	.60	.20	2.40	(4)	1.25	85
Looney Tunes Issue, Self-Adhesive, Serpentine Die-Cut 11.1							
3204 Sylvester & Tweety Pane of 10	04/27/98	6.00					300
a 32¢ single		.60	.20			1.50	
b Booklet pane of 9, #3204a		5.40					
c Booklet pane of 1, #3204a		.60					

Fort McHenry

On September 7, 1997, as part of its Historic Preservation series, the Postal Service issued a postal card to honor Fort McHenry, "birthplace of the national anthem." This star-shaped fort in Baltimore, Maryland, dates from the late 18th-century and is best known for what happened there during the War of 1812.

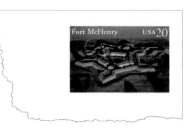

On this site in September 1814, American forces endured relentless bombardment by the powerful British fleet. But Fort McHenry did not fall, and in the early morning hours of September 14, the invaders withdrew. Watching from a ship in Baltimore Harbor was Francis Scott Key, a Washington lawyer who had recently negotiated with the British for the release of physician William Beanes, captured a few days earlier. Moved by what he saw—the raising of an enormous U.S. flag over the fort—Key dashed off a poem and called it "Defence of Fort M'Henry"; the *Baltimore Patriot* published this stirring work just a few days later. In time, the poem was set to the music of John Stafford Smith's "To Anacreon in Heaven" and called "The Star-Spangled Banner"; in 1931, it became the national anthem of the United States.

Fort McHenry was made a national park in 1925, then redesignated a national monument and historic shrine in 1939—a unique honor within the National Park system. ■

Issues of 1998		Un	U	PB	#	FDC	Q(M)
Self-Adhesive, Serpentine Die-Cut 10.8 x 10.9							
3206	32¢ Wisconsin Statehood 05/29/98	.60	.30	2.40	(4)	1.25	16
American Scenes Issue, Coil Stamps, Perf. 10 Vertically							
3207	5¢ Wetlands (Nonprofit) 06/05/98	.20	.20	1.65	(5)	1.25	
Coil Stamps, Self-Adhesive, Serpentine Die-Cut 9.7 Vertically							
3207A	5¢ Wetlands (Nonprofit) 12/04/98	.20	.20	1.65	(5)	1.25	650
American Culture Issue, Coil Stamps, Perf. 10 Vertically							
3208	25¢ Diner 06/05/98	.50	.50	4.00	(5)	1.25	400
Coil Stamps, Self-Adhesive, Serpentine Die-Cut 9.7 Vertically							
3208A	25¢ Diner 09/30/98	.50	.50	4.00	(5)	1.25	
1898 Trans-Mississippi Reissue, Perf. 12 x 12.4							
3209	Pane of 9 06/18/98	7.75	5.00			6.50	19.8
a	1¢ Marquette on the Mississippi	.20	.20			1.25	
b	2¢ Mississippi River Bridge	.20	.20			1.25	
c	4¢ Indian Hunting Buffalo	.20	.20			1.25	
d	5¢ Fremont on the Rocky Mountains	.20	.20			1.25	
e	8¢ Troops Guarding Train	.20	.20			1.25	
f	10¢ Hardships of Emigration	.20	.20			1.25	
g	50¢ Western Mining Prospector	1.00	.60			1.50	
h	$1 Western Cattle in Storm	2.00	1.25			2.00	
i	$2 Farm in the West	4.00	2.50			4.00	
3210	Pane of 9 #3209h, single 06/18/98	18.00	—			15.00	
	Perf. 11.2						
3211	32¢ Berlin Airlift 06/26/98	.60	.20	2.40	(4)	1.25	30

Greetings From Wisconsin

Two Great Lakes and three large rivers border Wisconsin, the nation's 30th state. Other rivers and more than 14,000 lakes add to the state's enormous water resources and are magnets for vacationers. The land itself is mostly rolling plains with, among other things, 15 million acres of forests, thousands and thousands of farms, a large Indian reservation, numerous parks, 43 automobile racetracks, and 36 downhill ski areas.

About half of all the farms specialize in raising, grazing, and milking more than a million dairy cows, which can supply 86 million people with cheese, 68 million people with butter, and 42 million people with milk—for a year. When it comes to cheese, Wisconsin produces more of it, and in more varieties, than any other state in the nation. Small wonder people call Wisconsin "America's Dairyland."

The state's largest city, Milwaukee, has a title of its own: It's known as the "Beer Capital of the United States." ∎

3206

3207A

3208A

1998 Bi-Color Re-Issue of the 1898 Trans-Mississippi Stamp Designs

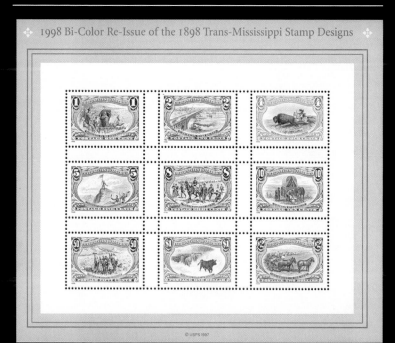

3209

a	b	c
d	e	f
g	h	i

3210

3211

3212   3213

3214   3215   3215a

3219   3218

3216   3217   3219a

3220   3221

3222   3223

3224   3225   3225a

	Issues of 1998		Un	U	PB	#	FDC	Q(M)
	Legends of American Music Series, Folk Musicians, Perf. 10.1 x 10.2							
3212	32¢ Huddie "Leadbelly"							
	Ledbetter	06/26/98	.60	.20			1.25	
3213	32¢ Woody Guthrie	06/26/98	.60	.20			1.25	
3214	32¢ Sonny Terry	06/26/98	.60	.20			1.25	
3215	32¢ Josh White	6/26/98	.60	.20			1.25	
a	Block or strip of 4, #3212-3215	06/26/98	2.40	—	2.40	(4)	3.25	45
	Legends of American Music Series, Gospel Singers Issue, Perf. 10.1 x 10.3							
3216	32¢ Mahalia Jackson	07/15/98	.60	.20			1.25	
3217	32¢ Roberta Martin	07/15/98	.60	.20			1.25	
3218	32¢ Clara Ward	07/15/98	.60	.20			1.25	
3219	32¢ Sister Rosetta Tharpe	07/15/98	.60	.20			1.25	
a	Block or strip of 4, #3216-3219	07/15/98	2.40	—	2.40	(4)	3.25	45
	Perf. 11.2							
3220	32¢ Spanish Settlement of							
	the Southwest	07/11/98	.60	.20	2.40	(4)	1.25	46
	Literary Arts Series							
3221	32¢ Stephen Vincent Benét	07/22/98	.60	.20	2.40	(4)	1.25	
	Tropical Birds Issue							
3222	32¢ Antillean Euphonia	07/29/98	.60	.20			1.25	
3223	32¢ Green-throated Carib	07/29/98	.60	.20			1.25	
3224	32¢ Crested Honeycreeper	07/29/98	.60	.20			1.25	
3225	32¢ Cardinal Honeyeater	07/29/98	.60	.20			1.25	
a	Block of 4, #3222-3225		2.40	—	2.40	(4)	3.25	70

Greetings From New Mexico

Cactus flowers brighten New Mexico's deserts and bloom beside the adobe walls of its ancient pueblos. Shimmering in the sun at White Sands National Monument is the world's largest field of gypsum dunes, while sprawling below the ground at Carlsbad Caverns National Park is one of Earth's most enormous

natural underground chambers—aglow with artificial light. In winter, snow caps towering peaks along the Continental Divide and dusts the deep valley of the Rio Grande.

People have long dwelled in this "Land of Enchantment." Scientists have found stone points fashioned thousands of years ago near Folsom, and in Chaco Canyon they have excavated multistoried structures at an archaeological site dating from A.D. 900. Some of New Mexico's ancient sites are still occupied, including Taos Pueblo, where adobe buildings date from A.D 1000. In the early 1500s, the Spanish entered the region; around 1609, they established a seat of government at Santa Fe—now the oldest capital in the United States and a major tourist center. ∎

	Issues of 1998		Un	U	PB	#	FDC	Q(M)
	Legends of Hollywood Issue, Perf. 11.1							
3226	32¢ Alfred Hitchcock	08/03/98	.60	.20	2.40	(4)	1.50	65
	Self-Adhesive, Serpentine Die-Cut 11.7							
3227	32¢ Organ & Tissue Donation	08/05/98	.60	.20	2.40	(4)	1.25	25
	Coil Stamp, Self-Adhesive, Serpentine Die-Cut 9.8 Vertically							
3228	(10¢) Green Bicycle	08/14/98	.20	.20	2.75	(5)	1.25	
	Coil Stamp, Perf. 9.9 Vertically							
3229	(10¢) Green Bicycle	08/14/98	.20	.20	2.50	(5)	1.25	
	Bright Eyes Issue, Self-Adhesive, Serpentine Die-Cut 9.9							
3230	32¢ Dog	08/20/98	.60	.20			1.50	
3231	32¢ Goldfish	08/20/98	.60	.20			1.50	
3232	32¢ Cat	08/20/98	.60	.20			1.50	
3233	32¢ Parakeet	08/20/98	.60	.20			1.50	
3234	32¢ Hamster	08/20/98	.60	.20			1.50	
a	Strip of 5, #3230-3234	08/20/98	3.00		6.00	(8)	3.25	180
	Perf. 11.1							
3235	32¢ Klondike Gold Rush	08/21/98	.60	.20	2.40	(4)	1.25	28

Klondike Gold Rush

In August 1896, Skookum Jim Mason, Tagish Charlie, and George Washington Carmack got lucky: They found gold lying in the gravel of Rabbit Creek (they renamed it Bonanza Creek), a tributary of the Klondike River in what is now the Yukon Territory of Canada. The big news was slow getting out of this remote region, but by the summer of 1897, the rush was definitely on. A hundred thousand would-be millionaires stampeded north over the next year from ports such as Seattle, Washington, and San Francisco, California. Steamships took them to southeastern Alaska, where they debarked at either Skagway or Dyea, gateways to the White Pass and Chilkoot Trails over the Coast Mountains; however, by the time most of the stampeders struggled over the mountains and raced down the rivers to the Klondike gold fields, they were too late. The best sites had already been staked.

The Skagway–White Pass Trail is now part of the Klondike Gold Rush National Historical Park, and the Chilkoot Trail is included in the Klondike Gold Rush International Historical Park. The centennial of the gold rush itself was commemorated with a 32-cent stamp issued by the Postal Service on August 21, 1998. ■

3226

3227

3228

3230

3231

3232

3233

3234

3234a

3235

FOUR CENTURIES OF
American Art

John Foster (1648–1681) 32 USA | The Freake Limner (Pre-c. 1674) 32 USA | Ammi Phillips (1788–1865) 32 USA | Rembrandt Peale (1778–1860) 32 USA | John James Audubon (1785–1851) 32 USA

George Caleb Bingham (1811–1879) 32 USA | Asher B. Durand (1796–1886) 32 USA | Joshua Johnson (active 1796–1824) 32 USA | William M. Harnett (1848–1892) 32 USA | Winslow Homer (1836–1910) 32 USA

George Catlin (1796–1872) 32 USA | Thomas Moran (1837–1926) 32 USA | Albert Bierstadt (1830–1902) 32 USA | Frederic Edwin Church (1826–1900) 32 USA | Mary Cassatt (1845–1926) 32 USA

Edward Hopper (1882–1967) 32 USA | Grant Wood (1891–1942) 32 USA | Charles Sheeler (1883–1965) 32 USA | Franz Kline (1910–1962) 32 USA | Mark Rothko (1903–1970) 32 USA

3236   a   b   c   d   e

f   g   h   i   j

k   l   m   n   o

p   q   r   s   t

	Issues of 1998		Un	U	PB	#	FDC	Q(M)
	Four Centuries of American Art Issue, Perf. 10.2							
3236	Pane of 20	08/27/98	12.00	—			10.00	80
a	32¢ "Portrait of Richard Mather," by John Foster		.60	.20			1.25	
b	32¢ "Mrs. Elizabeth Freake and Baby Mary," by The Freake Limner		.60	.20			1.25	
c	32¢ "Girl in Red Dress with Cat and Dog," by Ammi Phillips		.60	.20			1.25	
d	32¢ "Rubens Peale with a Geranium," by Rembrandt Peale		.60	.20			1.25	
e	32¢ "Long-billed Curlew, Numenius Longrostris," by John James Audubon		.60	.20			1.25	
f	32¢ "Boatmen on the Missouri," by George Caleb Bingham		.60	.20			1.25	
g	32¢ "Kindred Spirits," by Asher B. Durand		.60	.20			1.25	
h	32¢ "The Westwood Children," by Joshua Johnson		.60	.20			1.25	
i	32¢ "Music and Literature," by William Harnett		.60	.20			1.25	
j	32¢ "The Fog Warning," by Winslow Homer		.60	.20			1.25	
k	32¢ "The White Cloud, Head Chief of the Iowas," by George Catlin		.60	.20			1.25	
l	32¢ "Cliffs of Green River," by Thomas Moran		.60	.20			1.25	
m	32¢ "The Last of the Buffalo," by Alfred Bierstadt		.60	.20			1.25	
n	32¢ "Niagara," by Frederic Edwin Church		.60	.20			1.25	
o	32¢ "Breakfast in Bed," by Mary Cassatt		.60	.20			1.25	
p	32¢ "Nighthawks," by Edward Hopper		.60	.20			1.25	
q	32¢ "American Gothic," by Grant Wood		.60	.20			1.25	
r	32¢ "Two Against the White," by Charles Sheeler		.60	.20			1.25	
s	32¢ "Mahoning," by Franz Kline		.60	.20			1.25	
t	32¢ "No. 12" by Mark Rothko		.60	.20			1.25	
	Perf. 10.9 x 11.1							
3237	32¢ Ballet	09/16/98	.60	.20	2.40	(4)	1.25	130

1998

	Issues of 1998		Un	U	PB	#	FDC	Q(M)
	Space Discovery Issue, Perf. 11.1							
3238	32¢ Multicolored	10/01/98	.60	.20			1.25	
3239	32¢ Multicolored	10/01/98	.60	.20			1.25	
3240	32¢ Multicolored	10/01/98	.60	.20			1.25	
3241	32¢ Multicolored	10/01/98	.60	.20			1.25	
3242	32¢ Multicolored	10/01/98	.60	.20			1.25	
a	Strip of 5, #3238-3242		3.00	—			3.75	
	Self-Adhesive, Serpentine Die-Cut 11.1							
3243	32¢ Philanthropy, Giving and Sharing	10/07/98	.60	.20			1.25	50
	Holiday Traditional, Booklet Stamps, Self-Adhesive, Serpentine Die-Cut 10.1 x 9.9 on 2, 3 or 4 sides							
3244	32¢ The Madonna and Child by Hans Memling	10/15/98	.60	.20			1.25	925.2
a	Booklet pane of 20 + label		12.00					
	Holiday Contemporary, Booklet Stamps, Self-Adhesive, Serpentine Die-Cut 11.3 x 11.6 on 2 or 3 sides							
3245	32¢ Evergreen Wreath	10/15/98	.75	.20			1.25	
3246	32¢ Victorian Wreath	10/15/98	.75	.20			1.25	
3247	32¢ Chili Pepper Wreath	10/15/98	.75	.20			1.25	
3248	32¢ Tropical Wreath	10/15/98	.75	.20			1.25	
a	Booklet pane of 4, #3245-3248		4.00				3.25	
b	Booklet pane of 5, #3245, #3246, 3248, 2 #3247 and label		5.00					
c	Booklet pane of 6, #3247-3248, 2 each #3245-3246		6.00					
	Serpentine Die-Cut 11.4 x 11.6 on 2, 3 or 4 sides							
3249	32¢ Evergreen Wreath	10/15/98	.60	.20			1.25	
3250	32¢ Victorian Wreath	10/15/98	.60	.20			1.25	
3251	32¢ Chili Pepper Wreath	10/15/98	.60	.20			1.25	
3252	32¢ Tropical Wreath	10/15/98	.60	.20			1.25	
a	Block of 4, #3249-3252		2.40		2.40	(4)	3.25	
b	Booklet pane, 5 each #3249-3252		12.00					
	Perf. 11.2							
3257	(1¢) Make-Up Rate Weathervane	11/09/98	.20	.20	.25	(4)	1.25	
3258	(1¢) Make-Up Rate Weathervane	11/09/98	.20	.20	.25	(4)	1.25	
	#3257 is 18mm high, has thin letters, white USA, and black 1998.							
	#3258 is 17mm high, has thick letters, pale blue USA, and blue 1998.							
	Self-Adhesive, Serpentine Die-Cut 10.8							
3259	22¢ Uncle Sam	11/09/98	.45	.20	2.25	(4)	1.25	
	Perf. 11.2							
3260	(33¢) H-Series	11/09/98	.65	.20	2.60	(4)	1.25	

3238   3239   3240   3241   3242 3242a

3243

CHRISTMAS

3244

3245   3246

3247   3248

                                   3248a

3258

3259

3260

3261

3262

B1

	Issues of 1998		Un	U	PB	#	FDC	Q(M)
	Self-Adhesive, Serpentine Die-Cut 11.5							
3261	$3.20 Space Shuttle Landing	11/09/98	6.00	3.00	24.00	(4)	6.50	245
	Self-Adhesive, Serpentine Die-Cut 11.5							
3262	$11.75 Express Mail	11/19/98	22.50	11.50	90.00	(4)	25.00	21
	Coil Stamps, Self-Adhesive, Serpentine Die-Cut 9.9 Vertically							
3263	22¢ Uncle Sam	11/09/98	.45	.20	3.50	(5)	1.25	
	Perf. 9.8 Vertically							
3264	33¢ Unce Sam's Hat	11/09/98	.65	.20	5.00	(5)	1.25	
	Self-Adhesive, Serpentine Die-Cut 9.9 Vertically							
3265	33¢ H-Series	11/09/98	.65	.20	5.00	(5)	1.25	
	Serpentine Die-Cut 9.9 Vertically							
3266	33¢ Uncle Sam's Hat	11/09/98	.65	.20	4.75	(5)	1.25	
	Booklet Stamps, Self-Adhesive, Serpentine Die-Cut 9.9 on 2 or 3 sides							
3267	33¢ H-Series	11/09/98	.65	.20			1.25	
a	Booklet pane of 10		6.50					
	Serpentine Die-Cut 11.2 x 11.1 on 2, 3 or 4 sides							
3268	33¢ Uncle Sam's Hat	11/09/98	.65	.20			1.25	
a	Booklet pane of 10		6.50					
b	Serpentine die-cut II		.65	.20				
c	As "b", booklet pane of 20 + label		13.00					
	Die-Cut 8 on 2, 3 or 4 sides							
3269	33¢ Uncle Sam's Hat	11/09/98	.65	.20			1.25	
a	Booklet pane of 18		12.00					
	Coil Stamps, Perf. 9.8 Vertically							
3270	10¢ Eagle with Shield	12/14/98	.20	.20	2.75	(5)	1.25	
	Self-Adhesive, Serpentine Die-Cut 9.9 Vertically							
3271	10¢ Eagle with Shield	12/14/98	.20	.20	2.75	(5)	1.25	
a	Large date		.20	.20	4.25	(5)		
b	Tagged (error)		1.25	1.10				
	Semi-postal Stamp, Self-Adhesive, Serpentine Die-Cut 11							
B1	32¢ + 8¢ Breast Cancer							
	Research	07/29/98	.80	.60	3.25	(4)		200

Nine-Mile Prairie

Nine-Mile Prairie—named for its location nine miles north and west of downtown Lincoln, Nebraska—preserves 230 acres of tallgrass prairie "as a living tribute to our pioneer forebears and as a legacy for future generations." Remarkably, 210 of these acres somehow escaped the sod-busting plows of 19th-century settlers.

In the 1920s, Professor John W. Weaver and students from the University of Nebraska began plant ecology studies here, and over the ensuing years others took up the work, making Nine-Mile Prairie the longest-studied natural area in the state. About 350 plant species have since been identified, and they are all part of a grassland ecosystem that supports scores of bird species, as well as several kinds of mammals, insects, and reptiles.

Today, the University of Nebraska Foundation owns the land and leases it to the University of Nebraska-Lincoln for a dollar a year. In 2001, the Postal Service chose Nine-Mile Prairie as the subject of an international postcard-rate stamp. ■

1999

	Issues of 1999		Un	U	PB	#	FDC	Q(M)
	Lunar New Year Issue, Perf. 11.2							
3272	33¢ Year of the Rabbit	01/05/99	.65	.20	2.60	(4)	1.25	51
	Black Heritage Issue, Self-Adhesive, Serpentine Die-Cut 11.4							
3273	33¢ Malcolm X	01/20/99	.65	.20	2.60	(4)	1.25	100
	Booklet Stamp, Self-Adhesive, Die-Cut							
3274	33¢ Love	01/28/99	.65	.20			1.25	1,500
a	Booklet pane of 20		13.00					
3275	55¢ Love	01/20/99	1.10	.20	4.40	(4)	2.00	300
	Serpentine Die-Cut 11.4							
3276	33¢ Hospice Care	02/09/99	.65	.20	2.60	(4)	1.25	100
	Perf. 11.2							
3277	33¢ City Flag	02/25/99	.65	.20	2.60	(4)	1.25	200
	Self-Adhesive, Serpentine Die-Cut 11.1 on 2, 3 or 4 sides							
3278	33¢ City Flag	02/25/99	.65	.20	2.60	(4)	1.25	
a	Booklet pane of 4		2.60					
b	Booklet pane of 5 + label		3.25					
c	Booklet pane of 6		3.90					
d	Booklet pane of 10		6.50					
e	Booklet pane of 20 + label		13.00					
	Booklet Stamps, Serpentine Die-Cut 11.5 x 11.75 on 2, 3 or 4 sides							
3278F	33¢ City Flag		.65	.20				
g	Booklet pane of 20 + label		13.00					
	Self-Adhesive, Serpentine Die-Cut 9.8 on 2 or 3 sides							
3279	33¢ City Flag	02/25/99	.65	.20			1.25	
a	Booklet pane of 10		6.50					
	Coil Stamps, Perf. 9.9 Vertically							
3280	33¢ City Flag	02/25/99	.65	.20	5.00	(5)	1.25	
	Self-Adhesive, Serpentine Die-Cut 9.8 Vertically							
3281	33¢ City Flag	02/25/99	.65	.20	5.00	(5)	1.25	
3282	33¢ City Flag	02/25/99	.65	.20	5.00	(5)	1.25	
	Rounded corners.							
	Booklet Stamp, Self-Adhesive, Serpentine Die-Cut 7.9 on 2, 3 or 4 sides							
3283	33¢ Flag and Chalkboard	03/13/99	.65	.20			1.25	306
a	Booklet pane of 18		12.00					
	Perf. 11.2							
3286	33¢ Irish Immigration	02/26/99	.65	.20	2.60	(4)	1.25	40.4
3287	33¢ Alfred Lunt & Lynn Fontanne	03/02/99	.65	.20	2.60	(4)	1.25	42.5

3272

3273

3274

3275

3276

3277

3278

3279

3280

3286

3287

3288 3289 3290 3291 3292 3292a

ARCTIC ANIMALS

.33 x 15 = $4.95

PANE POSITION B 111111

© USPS 1998

	Issues of 1999		Un	U	PB	#	FDC	Q(M)
	Arctic Animals Issue, Perf. 11							
3288	33¢ Arctic Hare	03/12/99	.65	.20			1.50	15.3
3289	33¢ Arctic Fox	03/12/99	.65	.20			1.50	15.3
3290	33¢ Snowy Owl	03/12/99	.65	.20			1.50	15.3
3291	33¢ Polar Bear	03/12/99	.65	.20			1.50	15.3
3292	33¢ Gray Wolf	03/12/99	.65	.20			1.50	15.3
a	Strip of 5, #3288-3292		3.25				3.75	

Greetings From Alaska

Alaska is an enormous land blessed with a wealth of natural wonders, resources, and beauty. Encompassing more than half a million square miles, "the Last Frontier" is the largest state in the nation. More than 13 million acres of that land lie in Wrangell-St. Elias National Park, largest national park in the country; just a couple of hundred miles to the northwest, crowning Denali National Park and Preserve, is 20,320-foot Mount McKinley, the highest peak in North America.

Roaming the spectacular landscapes and fishing the salmon-streaked rivers are the largest brown bears in the world. Some weigh 1,700 pounds and stand more than nine feet tall on their hind feet. In the far north, giant polar bears haunt the Arctic shores as vast herds of caribou range across a coastal plain warmed by the midnight sun of summer.

Thousands of years ago, nomadic hunters walked across a land bridge from Asia, probably following large, migrating herds. Today, people still come to find the animals and other marvels of Alaska—and to gaze upon them in wonder. ■

1999-2000

Issues of 1999-2000			Un	U	PB	#	FDC	Q(M
Sonoran Desert Issue, Self-Adhesive, Serpentine Die-Cut Perf. 11.2								
3293	Pane of 10	04/06/99	6.50				6.75	10.3
a	33¢ Cactus Wren, brittlebush,							
	teddy bear cholla		.65	.20			1.25	
b	33¢ Desert tortoise		.65	.20			1.25	
c	33¢ White-winged dove		.65	.20			1.25	
d	33¢ Gambel quail		.65	.20			1.25	
e	33¢ Saguaro cactus		.65	.20			1.25	
f	33¢ Desert mule deer		.65	.20			1.25	
g	33¢ Desert cottontail, hedgehog cactus		.65	.20			1.25	
h	33¢ Gila monster		.65	.20			1.25	
i	33¢ Western diamondback rattlesnake,							
	cactus mouse		.65	.20			1.25	
j	33¢ Gila woodpecker		.65	.20			1.25	
Fruit Berries Issue, Self-Adhesive, Serpentine Die-Cut 11.25 x 11.75 on 2,3 or 4 sides,								
Serpentine Die-Cut 11.5 x 11.75 on 2 or 3 sides (3294a-3297a)								
3294	33¢ Blueberries	04/10/99	.65	.20			1.25	
a	Dated "2000"	03/15/00	.65	.20			1.25	
3295	33¢ Raspberries	04/10/99	.65	.20			1.25	
a	Dated "2000"	03/15/00	.65	.20			1.25	
3296	33¢ Strawberries	04/10/99	.65	.20			1.25	
a	Dated "2000"	03/15/00	.65	.20			1.25	
3297	33¢ Blackberries	04/10/99	.65	.20			1.25	
a	Dated "2000"	03/15/00	.65	.20			1.25	
b	Booklet pane, 5 each #3294-3297 + label		13.00	—			3.25	
c	Block of 4, #3294-3297		2.60					
d	Booklet pane, 5 #3297e		13.00					
e	Block of 4, #3294a-3297a		2.60					
Serpentine Die-Cut 9.5 x 10 on 2 or 3 sides								
3298	33¢ Blueberries	04/10/99	.65	.20			1.25	
3299	33¢ Raspberries	04/10/99	.65	.20			1.25	
3300	33¢ Strawberries	04/10/99	.65	.20			1.25	
3301	33¢ Blackberries	04/10/99	.65	.20			1.25	
a	Booklet pane of 4							
	#3298-#3301		2.60				3.25	
b	Booklet pane of 5							
	#3298, #3299, #3301							
	2 #3300 + label		3.25					
c	Booklet pane of 6							
	#3300, #3301,							
	2 #3298, #3299		4.00					
d	Block of 4, #3298-#3301		2.60					
Coil Stamps, Serpentine Die-Cut 8.5 Vertically								
3302	33¢ Blueberries	04/10/99	.65	.20			1.25	
3303	33¢ Raspberries	04/10/99	.65	.20			1.25	
3304	33¢ Strawberries	04/10/99	.65	.20			1.25	
3305	33¢ Blackberries	04/10/99	.65	.20			1.25	
a	Strip of 4		2.60				3.25	

SONORAN DESERT

FIRST IN A SERIES

N A T U R E   O F   A M E R I C A

3293

e

c   f   j

a   b   d   g   h

i

3294   3296

3295   3297

3297c

3305a

3306a

3308

3309

3310   **3311**

3312   **3313**   **3313a**

3314

3315

3316

3317   **3318**   **3319**   **3320**   **3320a**

Issues of 1999		Un	U	PB	#	FDC	Q(M)
Looney Tunes Issue, Self-Adhesive, Serpentine Die-Cut 11.1							
3306	Pane of 10	04/16/99	6.50				
a	33¢ Daffy Duck		.65	.20			1.25	427
b	Booklet pane of 9 #3306a		5.85				
c	Booklet pane of 1 #3306a		.65				
3307	Pane of 10		*6.50*				
a	33¢ Single		*.65*				
Literary Arts Issue, Perf. 11.2							
3308	33¢ Ayn Rand	04/22/99	.65	.20	2.60	(4)	2.00	42.5
Self-Adhesive, Serpentine Die-Cut 11.6 x 11.3							
3309	33¢ Cinco De Mayo	04/27/99	.65	.20	2.60	(4)	1.25	113
Tropical Flowers Issue, Self-Adhesive, Serpentine Die-Cut 10.9 on 2 or 3 sides							
3310	33¢ Bird of Paradise	05/01/99	.65	.20			1.25	
3311	33¢ Royal Poinciana	05/01/99	.65	.20			1.25	
3312	33¢ Gloriosa Lily	05/01/99	.65	.20			1.25	
3313	33¢ Chinese Hibiscus	05/01/99	.65	.20			1.25	
a	Block of 4 #3310-3313		2.60				3.25	
b	Booklet pane of 5 #3313a		13.00				
Self-Adhesive, Perf. 11.5							
3314	33¢ John & William Bartram	05/18/99	.65	.20	2.60	(4)	1.25	145
Self-Adhesive, Perf. 11							
3315	33¢ Prostate Cancer Awareness	05/28/99	.65	.20	2.60	(4)	1.25	78
Perf. 11.25							
3316	33¢ California Gold Rush 1849	06/18/99	.65	.20	2.60	(4)	1.25	89
Aquarium Fish Issue, Self-Adhesive, Serpentine Die-Cut 11.5							
3317	33¢ Yellow fish, red fish, cleaner shrimp	06/24/99	.65	.20			1.25	39
3318	33¢ Fish, thermometer	06/24/99	.65	.20			1.25	39
3319	33¢ Red fish, blue & yellow fish	06/24/99	.65	.20			1.25	39
3320	33¢ Fish, heater/aerator	06/24/99	.65	.20			1.25	39
a	Strip of 4, #3317-3320		2.60		5.20	(8)	3.50	

California Gold Rush

In 1848, carpenter James Marshall was building Sutter's Mill in the foothills of the Sierra Nevada, about 35 miles northeast of Sacramento, when he happened to spy golden flakes glimmering in the tailrace. It was a pivotal moment in the history of California, then a U.S. territory. Marshall's find would not only change his life but also launch the human stampede known as the California Gold Rush.

As word got out over the next year, mining camps packed with gold seekers—the aptly named forty-niners—sprang up overnight. Each new discovery drew thousands more fortune hunters, all of whom needed food, shelter, and supplies. The population was growing, business was booming, and local leaders were clamoring for statehood, which came in 1850.

By the end of the 1850s, miners had found nearly 600 million dollars worth of gold. But not everyone got rich, and of those who did, not everyone hung on to their fortunes. Sadly, James Marshall ended his days in poverty. ∎

	Issues of 1999		Un	U	PB	#	FDC	Q(M)
	Extreme Sports Issue, Self-Adhesive, Serpentine Die-Cut 11							
3321	33¢ Skateboarding	06/25/99	.65	.20			1.25	38
3322	33¢ BMX Biking	06/25/99	.65	.20			1.25	38
3323	33¢ Snowboarding	06/25/99	.65	.20			1.25	38
3324	33¢ Inline Skating	06/15/99	.65	.20			1.25	38
a	Block of 4, #3321-3324		2.60		2.60	(4)	3.50	
	American Glass Issue, Perf. 11							
3325	33¢ Free-Blown Glass	06/29/99	.65	.20			1.25	29
3326	33¢ Mold-Blown Glass	06/29/99	.65	.20			1.25	29
3327	33¢ Pressed Glass	06/29/99	.65	.20			1.25	29
3328	33¢ Art Glass	06/29/99	.65	.20			1.25	29
a	Strip or block of 4, #3325-3328		2.60	—			3.50	
	Legends of Hollywood Issue, Perf. 11							
3329	33¢ James Cagney	07/22/99	.65	.20	2.60	(4)	1.25	75.5
	Pioneers of Aviation Issue, Self-Adhesive, Serpentine Die-Cut 9.75 x 10							
3330	55¢ Gen. William "Billy" L. Mitchell	07/30/99	1.10	.20	4.40	(4)	1.25	101
	Self-Adhesive, Serpentine Die-Cut 11							
3331	33¢ Honoring Those Who Served	08/16/99	.65	.20	2.60	(4)	1.25	102
	Perf. 11							
3332	45¢ Universal Postal Union	08/25/99	.90	.20	3.60	(4)	1.40	43
	ALL ABOARD! Twentieth Century Trains Issue, Perf. 11							
3333	33¢ Daylight	08/26/99	.65	.20			1.25	24
3334	33¢ Congressional	08/26/99	.65	.20			1.25	24
3335	33¢ 20th Century Limited	08/26/99	.65	.20			1.25	24
3336	33¢ Hiawatha	08/26/99	.65	.20			1.25	24
3337	33¢ Super Chief	08/26/99	.65	.20			1.25	24
a	Strip of 5, #3333-3337		3.25	—			3.75	

Greetings From Pennsylvania

Nicknamed the "Keystone State," Pennsylvania occupied the central position among the original 13 Colonies, with six to the south and six more to the north and east. This was an ideal meeting place for the Continental Congress, which gathered at Philadelphia's Independence Hall in 1776 and on July 4 adopted the Declaration of Independence. The ringing of the Liberty Bell called citizens together for the first public reading of the revered document. After the Revolutionary War, Philadelphia served as the capital of the United States from 1790 to 1800.

During the Civil War, Pennsylvania played an essential role in preserving the nation it had helped create. Its shipbuilders, railroads, iron and steel industry, farms, and soldiers proved vital to the war effort. And in July 1863, the Union Army stopped Robert E. Lee's Confederates at the little town of Gettysburg, a turning point of the war. Later, at the dedication of a cemetery on the site, President Abraham Lincoln delivered his memorable Gettysburg Address. ■

3321 **3322**

3325 **3326**

3323 **3324** **3324a**

3327 **3328** **3328a**

3329

3330

3333

3334

3335

3336

3331

3337

3332

3337a

3338

3339
3340
3341
3342
3343
3344
3344a

3345
3346
3347
3348
3349
3350
3350a

	Issues of 1999		Un	U	PB	#	FDC	Q(M)
	Perf. 11							
3338	33¢ Frederick Law Olmstead	09/13/99	.65	.20	2.60	(4)	1.25	42.5
	Legends of American Music Series, Hollywood Composers Issue							
3339	33¢ Max Steiner	09/16/99	.65	.20			1.25	
3340	33¢ Dimitri Tiomkin	09/16/99	.65	.20			1.25	
3341	33¢ Bernard Herrmann	09/16/99	.65	.20			1.25	
3342	33¢ Franz Waxman	09/16/99	.65	.20			1.25	
3343	33¢ Alfred Newman	09/16/99	.65	.20			1.25	
3344	33¢ Erich Wolfgang Korngold	09/16/99	.65	.20			1.25	
a	Block of 6, #3339-3344		3.90		3.90	(6)	3.75	
	Legends of American Music Series, Broadway Songwriters Issue							
3345	33¢ Ira & George Gershwin	09/21/99	.65	.20			1.25	
3346	33¢ Lerner & Loewe	09/21/99	.65	.20			1.25	
3347	33¢ Lorenz Hart	09/21/99	.65	.20			1.25	
3348	33¢ Rodgers & Hammerstein	09/21/99	.65	.20			1.25	
3349	33¢ Meredith Willson	09/21/99	.65	.20			1.25	
3350	33¢ Frank Loesser	09/21/99	.65	.20			1.25	
a	Block of 6, #3345-3350		3.90	—	3.90	(6)	3.75	

United States Military Academy

About 50 miles north of New York City, a high promontory on the west bank of the Hudson River affords breathtaking views of the surrounding area. Known as West Point, it was considered one of the most strategically important sites during the Revolutionary War. General George

Washington ordered fortifications built atop it, and to keep out British ships, his men stretched a 150-ton chain across the river below. If the British had ever captured West Point, they could have controlled shipping on the Hudson and easily divided the new United States. Thanks to Washington, they never did.

West Point has served as a military post since the days of the Revolution, and in 1802 it became the spectacular setting for an educational institution as well. That year, President Thomas Jefferson signed into law an act establishing the United States Military Academy. For two hundred years, the academy has shaped the minds of some of the greatest military leaders and engineers in the country. ∎

	Issues of 1999		Un	U	PB	#	FDC	Q(M
	Insects & Spiders Issue, Perf. 11							
3351	Pane of 20	10/01/99	13.00	—			10.00	4.23
a	Black widow		.65	.20			1.25	
b	Elderberry longhorn		.65	.20			1.25	
c	Lady beetle		.65	.20			1.25	
d	Yellow garden spider		.65	.20			1.25	
e	Dogbane beetle		.65	.20			1.25	
f	Flower Fly		.65	.20			1.25	
g	Assassin bug		.65	.20			1.25	
h	Ebony jewelwing		.65	.20			1.25	
i	Velvet ant		.65	.20			1.25	
j	Monarch caterpillar		.65	.20			1.25	
k	Monarch butterfly		.65	.20			1.25	
l	Eastern Hercules beetle		.65	.20			1.25	
m	Bombardier beetle		.65	.20			1.25	
n	Dung beetle		.65	.20			1.25	
o	Spotted water beetle		.65	.20			1.25	
p	True katydid		.65	.20			1.25	
q	Spinybacked spider		.65	.20			1.25	
r	Periodical cicada		.65	.20			1.25	
s	Scorpionfly		.65	.20			1.25	
t	Jumping spider		.65	.20			1.25	

Great Lakes Lighthouses

More than 220 lighthouses stand sentinel along the shores of America's Great Lakes. For generations of mariners, these beacons of hope have beamed paths of light through fog, storms, and the darkness of night, and in 1995 the Postal Service honored them with stamps depicting lighthouses from all five lakes.

Funds to build Minnesota's Split Rock Lighthouse, on Lake Superior's north shore, were approved in 1907 after a single violent storm damaged 29 ships. Michigan's St. Joseph Lighthouse aids ships navigating the changeable waters along the southeast shore of Lake Michigan; this structure replicates a lighthouse built in 1832.

Until Spectacle Reef Lighthouse was up and running in 1874, treacherous eyeglass-shaped rocks east of the Mackinac Straits claimed vessels on Lake Huron. Lake Erie's Marblehead Lighthouse, the oldest light still in operation, has guided sailors since 1822, while Thirty Mile Point Lighthouse, on the south shore of Lake Ontario, began warning ships of dangerous shoals in 1875. ■

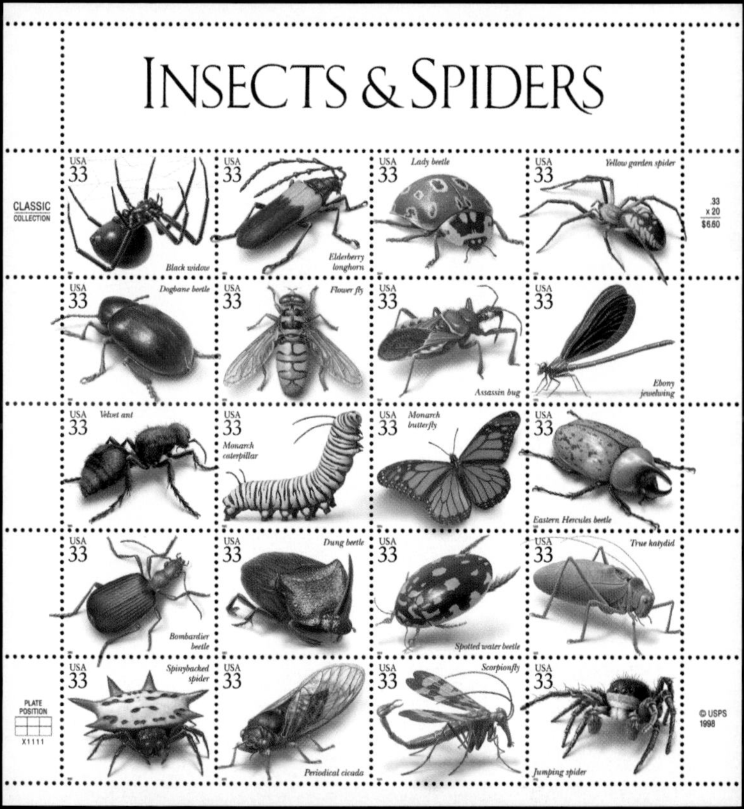

INSECTS & SPIDERS

CLASSIC
COLLECTION

33
x 20
$6.60

USA 33 — Black widow
USA 33 — Elderberry longhorn
USA 33 — Lady beetle
USA 33 — Yellow garden spider

USA 33 — Dogbane beetle
USA 33 — Flower fly
USA 33 — Assassin bug
USA 33 — Ebony jewelwing

USA 33 — Velvet ant
USA 33 — Monarch caterpillar
USA 33 — Monarch butterfly
USA 33 — Eastern Hercules beetle

USA 33 — Bombardier beetle
USA 33 — Dung beetle
USA 33 — Spotted water beetle
USA 33 — True katydid

PLATE POSITION
X1111
USA 33 — Spinybacked spider
USA 33 — Periodical cicada
USA 33 — Scorpionfly
USA 33 — Jumping spider

© USPS 1998

3351   a   b   c   d

e   f   g   h

i   j   k   l

3352

3353

3354

3355

3356　**3357**

3359　　**3358**

3359a

3368

	Issues of 1999		Un	U	PB	#	FDC	Q(M)
	Self-Adhesive, Serpentine Die-Cut 11							
3352	33¢ Hanukkah	10/08/99	.65	.20	2.60	(4)	1.25	65
	Coil Stamp, Perf. 9.75							
3353	22¢ Uncle Sam	10/08/99	.45	.20	3.50	(5)	1.25	150
	Perf. 11.25							
3354	33¢ NATO 50th Anniversary	10/13/99	.65	.20	2.60	(4)	1.25	44.6
	Holiday Traditional, Issue, Self-Adhesive Booklet Stamps, Serpentine Die-Cut 11.25 on 2 or 3 sides							
3355	33¢ Madonna and child by							
	Bartolomeo Vivarini	10/20/99	.65	.15			1.25	1,556
a	Booklet pane of 20		13.00					
	Holiday Contemporary Issue, Self-Adhesive, Serpentine Die-Cut 11.25							
3356	33¢ Red Deer	10/20/99	.65	.20			1.25	
3357	33¢ Blue Deer	10/20/99	.65	.20			1.25	
3358	33¢ Purple Deer	10/20/99	.65	.20			1.25	
3359	33¢ Green Deer	10/20/99	.65	.20			1.25	
a	Block or strip, #3356-3359		2.60		2.60	(4)	3.25	
	Booklet Stamps, Serpentine Die-Cut 11.25 on 2, 3 or 4 sides							
3360	33¢ Red Deer	10/20/99	.65	.20			1.25	
3361	33¢ Blue Deer	10/20/99	.65	.20			1.25	
3362	33¢ Purple Deer	10/20/99	.65	.20			1.25	
3363	33¢ Green Deer	10/20/99	.65	.20			1.25	
a	Booklet pane of 20		13.00				3.25	
	Booklet Stamps, Serpentine Die-Cut 11.5 x 11.25 on 2 or 3 sides							
3364	33¢ Red Deer	10/20/99	.65	.20			1.25	
3365	33¢ Blue Deer	10/20/99	.65	.20			1.25	
3366	33¢ Purple Deer	10/20/99	.65	.20			1.25	
3367	33¢ Green Deer	10/20/99	.65	.20			1.25	
a	Booklet pane of 4		2.60				3.25	
b	Block pane of 5, #3364, #3366, #3367							
	2 #3365 + label		3.25					
c	Block pane of 6, #3365, #3367,							
	2 #3364, #3366		4.00					
	Self-Adhesive, Serpentine Die-Cut 11							
3368	33¢ Kwanzaa	10/29/99	.65	.20	2.60	(4)	1.25	95

Greetings From North Dakota

Several unforgettable figures in American history spent time in North Dakota. In 1805, explorers Lewis and Clark met Sacagawea at a Mandan village. In 1876, George Armstrong Custer rode west from Fort Abraham Lincoln for his fateful encounter with Sitting Bull; in 1881, the Sioux chief surrendered at Fort Buford, now a state historic site. Soldiers brought Chief Joseph of the Nez Perce to the same fort after his capture in 1877. And in the 1880s, Theodore Roosevelt, a New Yorker, came west and raised cattle on Elkhorn Ranch.

North Dakota also boasts memorable terrain, which includes the fertile Red River Valley, prairie potholes and other wetlands favored by nesting waterfowl, and the rugged Badlands. The state features a bit of geographic trivia, too—the geographical center of North America lies near the town of Rugby—and helps celebrate international harmony with the 2,300-acre International Peace Garden stretching along the border with Canada. ■

Issues of 1999-2000		Un	U	PB	#	FDC	Q(M)
Self-Adhesive, Serpentine Die-Cut 11.25							
3369	33¢ Year 2000	12/27/99	.65	.20	2.75	(4)	1.25	124
Lunar New Year Issue, Perf. 11.25							
3370	33¢ Year of the Dragon	01/06/00	.65	.20	2.60	(4)	1.25	106
Black Heritage Issue, Serpentine Die-Cut 11.5 x 11.25							
3371	33¢ Patricia Harris	01/27/00	.65	.20	2.60	(4)	1.25	150
U.S. Navy Submarines Issue, Perf. 11							
3372	33¢ Los Angeles Class	03/27/00	.65	.20	2.60	(4)	1.25	65.15
3373	22¢ S Class	03/27/00	.45	.20			1.25	3
3374	33¢ Los Angeles Class	03/27/00	.65	.30			1.25	3
3375	55¢ Ohio Class	03/27/00	1.10	.50			1.50	3
3376	60¢ USS Holland	03/27/00	1.25	.55			1.50	3
3377	$3.20 Gato Class	03/27/00	6.50	3.00			6.00	3
a	Booklet Pane of 5, #3373-3377		10.00					

Pacific Coast Rain Forest

The lush rain forest of the Pacific Northwest is one of the largest remaining temperate rain forests on Earth, stretching from the well-watered coast of northern California to the misty shores of the Gulf of Alaska. Here, in a relatively narrow band paralleling the coast, the average annual precipitation ranges from 80 inches to as much as 160 inches. In summer, dense fog creeps silently through the forest, but when winter arrives, intense storms often come ashore, unleashing heavy rain and high winds.

Towering over the forest are giant, centuries-old Sitka spruce; they and numerous other tree species are part of a canopy protecting an understory of shrubs, mosses, ferns, and herbs. Many species of mammals and birds dwell among the luxuriant plantlife, and these include the Roosevelt elk, Douglas' squirrel, harlequin duck, and northern spotted owl. Cutthroat trout, the tailed frog, and other fish and amphibian species live in streams and rivers flowing through the forest. Twenty-six members of the plant and animal species that inhabit this extraordinary ecosystem are pictured on the 2000 Pacific Coast Rain Forest stamp pane—the second issuance in the Postal Service's Nature of America series. ■

3369

3370

3371

3372

3376 **3373**

3377

3374 **3375**

3377a

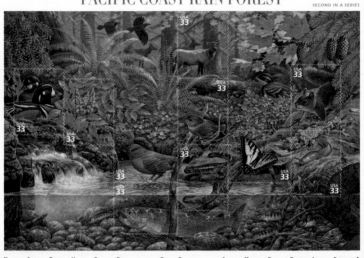

PACIFIC COAST RAIN FOREST

SECOND IN A SERIES

NATURE OF AMERICA

3378

a   b

c

d

e

f

g   h

i

j

3379   3380   3381   3382   3383   3383a

Issues of 2000		Un	U	PB	#	FDC	Q(M)
Pacific Coast Rain Forest Issue, Self-Adhesive, Serpentine Die-Cut 11.25 x 11.5							
3378 Pane of 10	03/29/00	6.50				6.75	10
a 33¢ Harlequin duck		.65	.20			1.25	10
b 33¢ Dwarf oregongrape,							
snail eating ground beetle		.65	.20			1.25	10
c 33¢ American dipper, horizontal		.65	.20			1.25	10
d 33¢ Cutthroat trout, horizontal		.65	.20			1.25	10
e 33¢ Roosevelt elk		.65	.20			1.25	10
f 33¢ Winter wren		.65	.20			1.25	10
g 33¢ Pacific giant salamander,							
Rough-skinned newt		.65	.20			1.25	10
h 33¢ Western tiger swallowtail, horizontal		.65	.20			1.25	10
i 33¢ Douglass squirrel, foliose lichen		.65	.20			1.25	10
j 33¢ Foliose lichen, banana slug		.65	.20			1.25	10
Louise Nevelson Issue, Perf. 11 x 11.25							
3379 33¢ Silent Music I	04/06/00	.65	.20	6.50	(10)	1.25	11
3380 33¢ Royal Tide I	04/06/00	.65	.20	6.50	(10)	1.25	11
3381 33¢ Black Chord	04/06/00	.65	.20	6.50	(10)	1.25	11
3382 33¢ Nightsphere-Light	04/06/00	.65	.20	6.50	(10)	1.25	11
3383 33¢ Dawn's Wedding Chapel I	04/06/00	.65	.20	6.50	(10)	1.25	11
a Strip of 5, #3379-3383		3.25				3.25	

Cliff Palace, Mesa Verde

Mesa Verde National Park, in southwestern Colorado, preserves thousands of archaeological sites and artifacts associated with the Ancestral Puebloans, an agricultural people who lived there until about seven centuries ago. In the A.D. 500s, these ancient farmers were raising crops and digging pit houses atop Mesa Verde; a couple of centuries later, they were constructing pole-and-adobe homes clustered together into compact villages known as pueblos.

By the year 1000, the Puebloans had mastered stone masonry, and around A.D. 1200, they were building multistoried homes in large alcoves beneath the cliffs of the mesa. The most spectacular structure from that period is the 217-room Cliff Palace, largest known cliff dwelling in North America.

Mesa Verde National Park became the first cultural park in the National Park System when it was established in 1906. It is also a World Cultural Heritage site, having received that designation from UNESCO in 1978. ■

	Issues of 2000		Un	U	PB	#	FDC	Q(M)
	Edwin Powell Hubble/Telescope, Perf. 11							
3384	33¢ Eagle Nebula	04/10/00	.65	.20	6.50	(10)	1.25	21.07
3385	33¢ Ring Nebula	04/10/00	.65	.20	6.50	(10)	1.25	21.07
3386	33¢ Lagoon Nebula	04/10/00	.65	.20	6.50	(10)	1.25	21.07
3387	33¢ Egg Nebula	04/10/00	.65	.20	6.50	(10)	1.25	21.07
3388	33¢ Galaxy NGC 1316	04/10/00	.65	.20	6.50	(10)	1.25	21.07
a	Strip of 5, #3384-3388		3.25				3.25	
3389	33¢ American Samoa	04/17/00	.65	.20	2.60	(4)	1.25	16
3390	33¢ Library of Congress	04/24/00	.65	.20	2.60	(4)	1.25	55
	Looney Tunes Issue, Self-Adhesive, Serpentine Die-Cut 11							
3391	Pane of 10	04/26/00	6.50					
a	33¢ Road Runner & Wile E. Coyote		.65	.20			1.25	300
3392	Pane of 10		6.50					
	Distinguished Soldiers Issue, Perf. 11							
3393	33¢ Maj. Gen. John L. Hines	08/16/00	.65	.20	2.60	(4)	1.25	13.75
3394	33¢ Gen. Omar N. Bradley	08/16/00	.65	.20	2.60	(4)	1.25	13.75
3395	33¢ Sgt. Alvin C. York	08/16/00	.65	.20	2.60	(4)	1.25	13.75
3396	33¢ Second Lt. Audie L. Murphy	08/16/00	.65	.20	2.60	(4)	1.25	13.75
a	Block Strip of 4, #3393-3396		2.60				3.25	
	Perf. 11							
3397	33¢ Summer Sports	05/05/00	.65	.20	2.60	(4)	1.25	90.6

American Samoa

Warm tropical seas lap the five volcanic islands and two coral atolls making up American Samoa, the southernmost territory of the United States. This island group lies in the heart of Polynesia, at the center of a triangle formed by Hawaii, Tahiti, and New Zealand.

In Samoa, rugged highlands cloaked with rain forests characterize the interiors of the volcanic isles, so most people choose to live in villages along the coast. The capital, Pago Pago, hugs the shores of a deep inlet on the main island of Tutuila and is a popular port of call for cruise ships in the South Pacific.

In 1900, Samoan chiefs ceded Tutuila and Aunuu Islands to the United States. The other islands and atolls became part of American Samoa in 1904 and 1925. On the hundredth anniversary of the U.S.-American Samoa political affiliation, the Postal Service issued a stamp depicting a traditional double canoe riding the seas beneath Sunuitao Peak on Ofu Island. ■

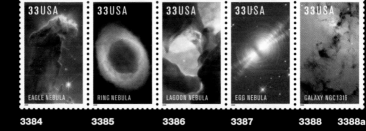

| 3384 | 3385 | 3386 | 3387 | 3388 | 3388a |

3389

3390

3391a

3393  3394

3395  3396

3396a

3397

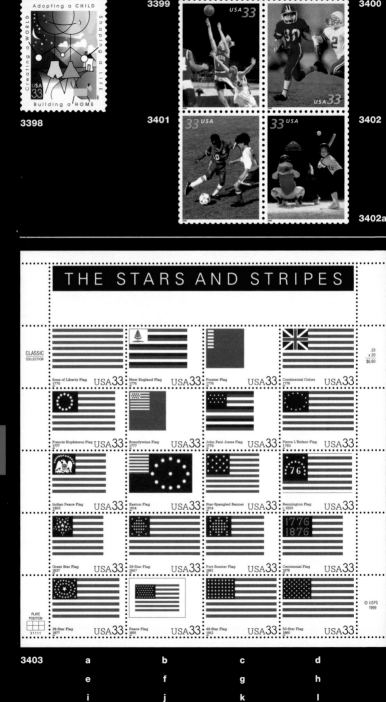

	Issues of 2000		Un	U	PB	#	FDC	Q(M)
	Self-Adhesive, Serpentine Die-Cut 11.5							
3398	33¢ Adoption	05/10/00	.65	.20	2.60	(4)	1.25	200
	Youth Team Sports Issue, Self-Adhesive, Serpentine Die-Cut 11.5							
3399	33¢ Basketball	05/27/00	.65	.20	2.60	(4)	1.25	22
3400	33¢ Football	05/27/00	.65	.20	2.60	(4)	1.25	22
3401	33¢ Soccer	05/27/00	.65	.20	2.60	(4)	1.25	22
3402	33¢ Baseball	05/27/00	.65	.20	2.60	(4)	1.25	22
a	Block strip of 4, #3399-3402		2.60				3.25	
	The Stars and Stripes Issue, Perf. 10.5 x 11							
3403	Pane of 20	06/14/00	13.00				10.00	
a	33¢ Sons of Liberty Flag, 1775		.65	.30			1.25	80
b	33¢ New England Flag, 1775		.65	.30			1.25	80
c	33¢ Forster Flag, 1775		.65	.30			1.25	80
d	33¢ Continental Colors, 1776		.65	.30			1.25	80
e	33¢ Francis Hopkinson Flag, 1777		.65	.30			1.25	80
f	33¢ Brandywine Flag, 1777		.65	.30			1.25	80
g	33¢ John Paul Jones Flag, 1779		.65	.30			1.25	80
h	33¢ Pierre L'Enfant Flag, 1783		.65	.30			1.25	80
i	33¢ Indian Peace Flag, 1803		.65	.30			1.25	80
j	33¢ Easton Flag, 1814		.65	.30			1.25	80
k	33¢ Star-Spangled Banner, 1814		.65	.30			1.25	80
l	33¢ Bennington Flag, c. 1820		.65	.30			1.25	80
m	33¢ Great Star Flag, 1837		.65	.30			1.25	80
n	33¢ 29-Star Flag, 1847		.65	.30			1.25	80
o	33¢ Fort Sumter Flag, 1861		.65	.30			1.25	80
p	33¢ Centennial Flag, 1876		.65	.30			1.25	80
q	33¢ 38-Star Flag, 1877		.65	.30			1.25	80
r	33¢ Peace Flag, 1891		.65	.30			1.25	80
s	33¢ 48-Star Flag, 1912		.65	.30			1.25	80
t	33¢ 50-Star Flag, 1960		.65	.30			1.25	80

El Capitan, Yosemite

A spectacular realm of high waterfalls, towering cliffs, and giant sequoias, Yosemite National Park lies in the Sierra Nevada range of central California. Among the many splendors in the 748,000-acre park is El Capitan—a gigantic block of granite believed to be the largest exposed monolith in the world. From the floor of the Yosemite Valley, the sheer walls of this massive peak rise 3,593 vertical feet.

The sheer face of El Capitan exerts a powerful pull on photographers and painters, who try to capture its image in just the right light, and on rock climbers, who come from around the world to challenge it. Every year, from spring to fall, bold climbers can be seen carefully inching their way from the base to the summit.

The Postal Service put El Capitan's image on a National Parks issue of 1934, on the Trans-Mississippi Philatelic Exposition Souvenir Sheet of 1934, and on a Yosemite issue of 1935. ■

	Issues of 2000		Un	U	PB	#	FDC	Q(M)
	Fruit Berries Issue, Self-Adhesive, Serpentine Die-Cut 8.5 Horizontally							
3404	33¢ Blueberries	06/16/00	.65	.20			1.25	82.5
3405	33¢ Strawberries	06/16/00	.65	.20			1.25	82.5
3406	33¢ Blackberries	06/16/00	.65	.20			1.25	82.5
3407	33¢ Raspberries	06/16/00	.65	.20			1.25	82.5
a	Strip of 4, #3404-3407			2.60			3.25	
	Legends of Baseball Issue, Self-Adhesive, Serpentine Die-Cut 11.25							
3408	Pane of 20	07/06/00	13.00				10.00	
a	33¢ Jackie Robinson		.65	.20			1.25	11.25
b	33¢ Eddie Collins		.65	.20			1.25	11.25
c	33¢ Christy Mathewson		.65	.20			1.25	11.25
d	33¢ Ty Cobb		.65	.20			1.25	11.25
e	33¢ George Sisler		.65	.20			1.25	11.25
f	33¢ Rogers Hornsby		.65	.20			1.25	11.25
g	33¢ Mickey Cochrane		.65	.20			1.25	11.25
h	33¢ Babe Ruth		.65	.20			1.25	11.25
i	33¢ Walter Johnson		.65	.20			1.25	11.25
j	33¢ Roberto Clemente		.65	.20			1.25	11.25
k	33¢ Lefty Grove		.65	.20			1.25	11.25
l	33¢ Tris Speaker		.65	.20			1.25	11.25
m	33¢ Cy Young		.65	.20			1.25	11.25
n	33¢ Jimmie Foxx		.65	.20			1.25	11.25
o	33¢ Pie Traynor		.65	.20			1.25	11.25
p	33¢ Satchel Paige		.65	.20			1.25	11.25
q	33¢ Honus Wagner		.65	.20			1.25	11.25
r	33¢ Josh Gibson		.65	.20			1.25	11.25
s	33¢ Dizzy Dean		.65	.20			1.25	11.25
t	33¢ Lou Gehrig		.65	.20			1.25	11.25

Legendary Playing Fields

Just mention the names of baseball parks, and fans think not only of the teams who play there but of the cities where they stand: Tiger Stadium calls to mind the Detroit Tigers; Fenway Park, the Boston Red Sox; Yankee Stadium, the New York Yankees, of course.

On the north side of Chicago, Illinois, a huge sign at the corner of Addison and Clark Streets identifies Wrigley Field as the home of the Chicago Cubs. For generations of fans, "Wrigleyville" has meant narrow streets, corner taverns, a red-brick fire station, hot dog and ice cream vendors, and brownstone apartments with rooftop views of the ballpark. The stadium itself is pure Americana—a painting of a bygone era seemingly come to life.

Gone but not forgotten, old Comiskey Park at 35th Street and Shields Avenue was once home to the Chicago White Sox. This imposing "Baseball Palace of the World" stood for 80 years on the city's south side, where fans had to be tough to face the often-chill winds blowing in from Lake Michigan. In 1991, the new Comiskey Park opened across the street from where the old landmark had stood, continuing the long tradition of baseball in this part of town. ■

3404	3405	3406	3407 3407a

Legends of Baseball

ALL-CENTURY TEAM 2000

CLASSIC
COLLECTION

.33
x 20
$6.60

USA 33 JACKIE ROBINSON	USA 33 EDDIE COLLINS	USA 33 CHRISTY MATHEWSON	USA 33 TY COBB	USA 33 GEORGE SISLER
USA 33 ROGERS HORNSBY	USA 33 MICKEY COCHRANE	USA 33 BABE RUTH	USA 33 WALTER JOHNSON	USA 33 ROBERTO CLEMENTE
USA 33 LEFTY GROVE	USA 33 TRIS SPEAKER	USA 33 CY YOUNG	USA 33 JIMMIE FOXX	USA 33 PIE TRAYNOR
USA 33 SATCHEL PAIGE	USA 33 HONUS WAGNER	USA 33 JOSH GIBSON	USA 33 DIZZY DEAN	USA 33 LOU GEHRIG

© USPS
2000

PLATE
POSITION

X1111

3408	a	b	c	d	e

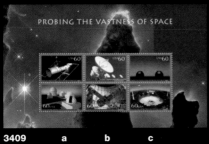

3409 a b c

     d e f

3410 a   3411 a b

  e   b

    d c

3412

3413

Issues of 2000		Un	U	PB	#	FDC	Q(M)
Space Issue, Perf. 10.5 x 11							
3409 Probing the Vastness of Space	07/10/00	7.50	—			6.00	1.695
a	60¢ Hubble Space Telescope	1.25	.60			1.50	
b	60¢ Radio interferometer very large array, New Mexico	1.25	.60			1.50	
c	60¢ Optical and infrared telescopes, Keck Observatory, Hawaii	1.25	.60			1.50	
d	60¢ Optical telescopes Cerro Tololo Observatory, Chile	1.25	.60			1.50	
e	60¢ Optical telescope, Mount Wilson Observatory, California	1.25	.60			1.50	
f	60¢ Radio telescope, Arecibo Observatory, Puerto Rico	1.25	.60			1.50	
Perf. 10.75							
3410 Exploring the Solar System	07/11/00	10.00	—			9.00	1.695
a	$1 Sun and corona	2.00	1.00			2.00	
b	$1 Cross-section of sun	2.00	1.00			2.00	
c	$1 Sun and earth	2.00	1.00			2.00	
d	$1 Sun and solar flare	2.00	1.00			2.00	
e	$1 Sun and clouds	2.00	1.00			2.00	
Hologram, Perf. 10.5, 10.75 (#3412)							
3411 Escaping the Gravity of Earth	07/09/00	12.50	—			9.50	1.695
a	$3.20 Space Shuttle and Space Station	6.25	3.00			3.75	
b	$3.20 Astronauts working in space	6.25	3.00			3.75	
3412 $11.75 Space Achievement and Exploration	07/07/00	22.50	11.50			17.50	1.695
3413 $11.75 Landing on the Moon	07/08/00	22.50	11.50			17.50	1.695
Uncut sheet of 5 panes #3409-3412 (not shown)		75.00					

The Erie Canal

Seventy-five percent of New Yorkers live along a corridor formed by the Hudson River and the old Erie Canal, a strong indication of how historically important these waterways have been to the development of the Empire State.

When the Erie Canal opened in 1825, this 4-foot-deep, 40-foot-wide marvel of engineering stretched 363 miles from a point north of Albany, on the Hudson River, west to Buffalo, on Lake Erie. It quickly proved popular with shippers and travelers. Thousands of boats used it each year, and within five years tolls exceeded a million dollars annually—a boon to the economy. Cities along the route experienced phenomenal growth: Albany's population jumped 400 percent in only 25 years.

In the early 20th century, the waterway was made part of the New York Barge Canal system, whose commercial usefulness diminished with the advent of interstate highways. Its waters are now mostly playgrounds for pleasure boaters, and old towpaths are trails for hikers, bicyclists, and cross-country skiers. ■

Issues of 2000-2001		Un	U	PB	#	FDC	Q(M)
Stampin' The Future™ Issue, Self-Adhesive, Serpentine Die-Cut 11.25							
3414	33¢ By Zachary Canter	07/13/00	.65	.20	5.25	(8)	1.25	25
3415	33¢ By Sarah Lipsey	07/13/00	.65	.20	5.25	(8)	1.25	25
3416	33¢ By Morgan Hill	07/13/00	.65	.20	5.25	(8)	1.25	25
3417	33¢ By Ashley Young	07/13/00	.65	.20	5.25	(8)	1.25	25
a	Horizontal Strip of 4, #3414-3417		2.60		5.25	(8)	3.25	
	Perf. 11							
3420	10¢ Joseph W. Stillwell	08/24/00	.20	.20	.80	(4)	1.25	100
3426	33¢ Claude Pepper	09/07/00	.65	.20	2.60	(4)	1.25	56
	Self-Adhesive, Serpentine Die-Cut 11							
3431	76¢ Hattie Caraway	02/21/01	1.50	.20	6.00	(4)	1.75	108
3438	33¢ California Statehood	09/08/00	.65	.20	2.60	(4)	1.25	53
	Deep Sea Creatures Issue, Perf. 10 x 10.25							
3439	33¢ Fanfin Angelfish	10/02/00	.65	.20			1.25	17
3440	33¢ Sea Cucumber	10/02/00	.65	.20			1.25	17
3441	33¢ Fangtooth	10/02/00	.65	.20			1.25	17
3442	33¢ Amphipod	10/02/00	.65	.20			1.25	17
3443	33¢ Medusa	10/02/00	.65	.20			1.25	17
a	Vertical Strip 5, #3439-3443		3.25	—			3.75	

Greetings From California

Golden in more ways than one, "the Golden State" of California basks in sunshine, Hollywood glitz, and past and present glories. Enormous fortunes have been made here, not just in gold but also in oil, land, winemaking, films, and high technology, and the hope of riches to come still fuels the dreams of millions of newcomers every year. More people now live in California than in any other state.

In the north, San Franciscans celebrate their fabled fog as much as Los Angelenos and San Diegans revel in their golden sun. The fog creeps past the Golden Gate Bridge, then over Alcatraz, Treasure, and Yerba Buena Islands to the Bay Bridge, which ties San Francisco to Oakland and the east-bay region.

Beyond the great cities lie many natural treasures, including Earth's tallest tree, at Humboldt Redwoods State Park; the largest living thing, the General Sherman Tree in Sequoia National Park; and the oldest living things, bristlecone pines in Inyo National Forest. ■

3414

3415

3416

3417

3417a

3420

3426

3431

3438

FANFIN ANGLERFISH

3439

SEA CUCUMBER

3440

FANGTOOTH

3441

AMPHIPOD

3442

MEDUSA

3443

3443a

3444

3445

3446

3447

3448

3451

3454   3455

3456   3457   3457a

	Issues of 2000		Un	U	PB	#	FDC	Q(M)
	Literary Arts Issue, Perf. 11							
3444	33¢ Thomas Wolfe	10/03/00	.65	.20	2.60	(4)	1.25	53
	Serpentine Die-Cut 11.25							
3445	33¢ White House	10/18/00	.65	.20	2.60	(4)	1.25	125
	Legends of Hollywood Issue, Perf. 11							
3446	33¢ Edward G. Robinson	10/24/00	.65	.20	2.60	(4)	1.25	52
	Serpentine Die-Cut 11.5 Vertically							
3447	(10¢) The New York Public Library	11/09/00	.20	.20			1.25	100
	Perf. 11.25							
3448	(34¢) Flag Over Farm	12/15/00	.65	.20	2.60	(4)	1.25	25
	Self-Adhesive, Serpentine Die-Cut 11.25							
3449	(34¢) Flag Over Farm	12/15/00	.65	.20	2.60	(4)	1.25	200
	Booklet Stamps, Self-Adhesive, Serpentine Die-Cut 8 on 2, 3 or 4 sides							
3450	(34¢) Flag Over Farm	12/15/00	.65	.20			1.25	
a	Booklet Pane of 18							300
	Booklet Stamps, Self-Adhesive, Serpentine Die-Cut 11 on 2, 3 or 4 sides							
3451	34¢ Statue of Liberty	12/15/00	.65	.20	2.60	(4)	1.25	1.5
	Coil Stamps, Perf. 9.75 Vertically							
3452	34¢ Statue of Liberty	12/15/00	.65	.20	5.00	(5)	1.25	200
	Serpentine Die-Cut 10 Vertically							
3453	34¢ Statue of Liberty	12/15/00	.65	.20	5.00	(5)	1.25	
	Booklet Stamps, Self-Adhesive, Serpentine Die-Cut 10.25 x 10.75 on 2 or 3 sides							
3454	(34¢) Purple Flower	12/15/00	.65	.20			1.25	375
3455	(34¢) Tan Flower	12/15/00	.65	.20			1.25	375
3456	(34¢) Green Flower	12/15/00	.65	.20			1.25	375
3457	(34¢) Red Flower	12/15/00	.65	.20			1.25	375
a	Block of 4		2.60				3.25	
b	Booklet pane of 4		2.60					
c	Booklet pane of 6		3.90					
d	Booklet pane of 6		3.90					
e	Booklet pane of 20		13.00					
	Booklet Stamps, Self-Adhesive, Serpentine Die-Cut 11.5 x 11.75 on 2 or 3 sides							
3458	34¢ Purple Flower	12/15/00	.65	.20			1.25	125
3459	34¢ Tan Flower	12/15/00	.65	.20			1.25	125
3460	34¢ Green Flower	12/15/00	.65	.20			1.25	125
3461	34¢ Red Flower	12/15/00	.65	.20			1.25	125
a	Block of 4		2.60					
b	Booklet pane of 20, 2 each #3461a		13.00					
c	Booklet pane of 20, 3 each #3461a		13.00					
	Coil Stamps, Serpentine Die-Cut 8.5 Vertically							
3462	34¢ Green Flower	12/15/00	.65	.20			1.25	125
3463	34¢ Red Flower	12/15/00	.65	.20			1.25	125
3464	34¢ Tan Flower	12/15/00	.65	.20			1.25	125
3465	34¢ Purple Flower	12/15/00	.65	.20			1.25	125
a	Strip of 4		2.60		5.00	(5)	3.25	

	Issues of 2001		Un	U	PB	#	FDC	Q(M)
	Coil Stamp, Self-Adhesive, Serpentine Die-Cut 9.75							
3466	34¢ Statue of Liberty	01/07/01	.65	.20	5.00	(5)	1.25	240
	Tagged, Self-Adhesive, Serpentine Die-Cut 11							
3468	21¢ Buffalo	02/22/01	.40	.20	1.60	(4)	1.25	25
	Tagged, Serpentine Die-Cut, Perf. 11.25							
3469	34¢ Flag Over Farm	02/07/01	.65	.20	2.60	(4)	1.25	200
	Self-Adhesive, Serpentine Die-Cut 11.25							
3470	34¢ Flag Over Farm	03/06/01	.65	.20	2.60	(4)	1.25	204
	Self-Adhesive, Serpentine Die-Cut 10.75							
3471	55¢ Art Deco Eagle	02/22/01	1.10	.20	4.40	(4)	1.50	100
	Self-Adhesive, Serpentine Die-Cut 11.25 x 11.5							
3472	$3.50 U. S. Capitol	01/29/01	7.00	3.50	28.00	(4)	6.25	125
	Self-Adhesive, Serpentine Die-Cut 11.25 x 11.5							
3473	$12.25 Washington Monument	01/29/01	22.50	10.00	90.00	(4)	14.00	35
	Coil Stamp, Self-Adhesive, Serpentine Die-Cut 8.5 Vertically							
3475	21¢ Buffalo	02/22/01	.40	.20	3.50	(5)	1.25	680
	Self-Adhesive, Perf. 9.75 Vertically							
3476	34¢ Statue of Liberty	02/07/01	.65	.20	5.00	(5)	1.25	379.8
	Self-Adhesive, Serpentine Die-Cut 9.75 Vertically							
3477	34¢ Statue of Liberty	02/07/01	.65	.20	5.00	(5)	1.25	281

The White House

The White House, at 1600 Pennsylvania Avenue, Washington, D.C., has been home to U.S. Presidents and their families ever since John and Abigail Adams moved into the mansion in 1800. One of the most recognizable buildings in the world, the White House stands as a symbol of the American Presidency and of the nation itself.

In the 1790s, architect James Hoban (c.1762-1831) designed and supervised construction of the "President's House"—the name preferred by George Washington, whose term of office ended before the house was ready for occupancy. Later, Hoban helped rebuild the mansion after British troops torched it during the War of 1812.

Through the years, the appearance of the White House has evolved to reflect the fashions of the times and the styles of our leaders and their families. It has been featured on numerous postage stamps, including a 2000 issue commemorating its 200th year as the home of America's First Family. ■

3466

3468

3470

3471

3472

3473

3478  3479

3480 3481

3482

3481a

3492a

3491 3492

3497

3499

3500

3501

	Issues of 2001		Un	U	PB	#	FDC	Q(M)
	Coil Stamps, Self-Adhesive, Serpentine Die-Cut 8.5 Vertically							
3478	34¢ Green Flower	02/07/01	.65	.20			3.25	200
3479	34¢ Red Flower	02/07/01	.65	.20			3.25	200
3480	34¢ Tan Flower	02/07/01	.65	.20			3.25	200
3481	34¢ Purple Flower	02/07/01	.65	.20			3.25	200
a	Strip of 4, #3478-3481		2.60		5.00	(5)	1.25	
	Booklet Stamps, Self-Adhesive, Serpentine Die-Cut 11.25 on 3 sides							
3482	20¢ George Washington	02/22/01	.40	.20			1.25	20.5
a	Booklet pane of 10		4.00					
b	Booklet pane of 4		1.60					
c	Booklet pane of 6		2.40					
	Self-Adhesive, Serpentine Die-Cut 10.5 x 11.25 on 3 sides							
3483	20¢ George Washington	02/22/01	.40	.20			1.25	
a	Booklet pane of 4		*5.00*					
b	Booklet pane of 6		*8.00*					
c	Booklet pane of 10		*10.00*					
d	Booklet pane of 4		*5.00*					
e	Booklet pane of 6		*8.00*					
f	Booklet pane of 10		*10.00*					
	Self-Adhesive, Serpentine Die-Cut 11 on 2, 3 or 4 sides							
3485	34¢ Statue of Liberty	02/07/01	.65	.20			1.25	
a	Booklet pane of 10		6.50					
b	Booklet pane of 20		13.00					
c	Booklet pane of 4		2.60					
d	Booklet pane of 6		3.90					
	Self-Adhesive, Serpentine Die-Cut 10.25 x 10.75 on 2 or 3 sides							
3487	34¢ Purple Flower	02/07/01	.65	.20			3.25	
3488	34¢ Tan Flower	02/07/01	.65	.20			3.25	
3489	34¢ Green Flower	02/07/01	.65	.20			3.25	
3490	34¢ Red Flower	02/07/01	.65	.20			3.25	
	Block of 4, #3487-3490		2.60				1.25	
	Self-Adhesive, Serpentine Die-Cut 11.25 on 2, 3 or 4 sides							
3491	34¢ Apple	03/06/01	.65	.20			2.25	3
3492	34¢ Orange	03/06/01	.65	.20			2.25	3
a	Pair, #3491-3492		1.30				1.25	
b	Booklet pane of 20, #3491-3492		13.00					
	Booklet Stamps, Self-Adhesive, Serpentine Die-Cut 11.5 x 10.75 on 2 or 3 sides							
3493	34¢ Apple	05/01	.65	.20				101
3494	34¢ Orange	05/01	.65	.20				101
a	Pair, #3493-3494		1.30		2.60	(4)		
b	Booklet pane of 2, #3493-3494		2.60					
	Self-Adhesive, Serpentine Die-Cut 11.75, on 2, 3 or 4 sides							
3496	34¢ Rose and Love Letter	01/19/01	.65	.20			1.25	
a	Booklet pane of 20		13.00					
	Self-Adhesive, Serpentine Die-Cut 11.25							
3497	34¢ Rose and Love Letter	02/14/01	.65	.20			1.25	1.50
a	Booklet pane of 20		13.00					
	Self-Adhesive, Serpentine Die-Cut 11.5 x 10.75 on 2 or 3 sides							
3498	34¢ Rose and Love Letter	02/14/01	.65	.20			1.25	81
a	Booklet pane of 4		2.60					
b	Booklet pane of 6		3.90					
3499	55¢ Rose and Love Letter	02/14/01	1.10	.20	4.50	(4)	1.50	
	Lunar New Year Issue, Self-Adhesive, Serpentine Die-Cut, Perf. 11.25							
3500	34¢ Year of the Snake	01/20/01	.65	.20	2.60	(4)	1.25	55
	Black Heritage Issue, Self-Adhesive, Serpentine Die-Cut 11.5 x 11.25							
3501	34¢ Roy Wilkins	01/24/01	.65	.20	2.60	(4)	1.25	200

	Issues of 2001		Un	U	PB	#	FDC	Q(M)
	American Illustrators Issue, Self-Adhesive, Serpentine Die-Cut 11.25							
3502	Pane of 20	02/01/01	13.00				9.50	
a	34¢ James Montgomery Flagg			.65	.30		1.25	144.8
b	34¢ Maxfield Parrish			.65	.30		1.25	144.8
c	34¢ J. C. Leyendecker			.65	.30		1.25	144.8
d	34¢ Robert Fawcett			.65	.30		1.25	144.8
e	34¢ Coles Phillips			.65	.30		1.25	144.8
f	34¢ Al Parker			.65	.30		1.25	144.8
g	34¢ A. B. Frost			.65	.30		1.25	144.8
h	34¢ Howard Pyle			.65	.30		1.25	144.8
i	34¢ Rose O'Neill			.65	.30		1.25	144.8
j	34¢ Dean Cornwell			.65	.30		1.25	144.8
k	34¢ Edwin Austin Abbey			.65	.30		1.25	144.8
l	34¢ Jessie Willcox Smith			.65	.30		1.25	144.8
m	34¢ Neysa McMein			.65	.30		1.25	144.8
n	34¢ Jon Whitcomb			.65	.30		1.25	144.8
o	34¢ Harvey Dunn			.65	.30		1.25	144.8
p	34¢ Frederic Remington			.65	.30		1.25	144.8
q	34¢ Rockwell Kent			.65	.30		1.25	144.8
r	34¢ N. C. Wyeth			.65	.30		1.25	144.8
s	34¢ Norman Rockwell			.65	.30		1.25	144.8
t	34¢ John Held, Jr.			.65	.30		1.25	144.8

Old Faithful, Yellowstone National Park

Every hour or so, a fountain of water explodes from the ground at Yellowstone National Park and climbs 90 to 180 feet into the air. This is Old Faithful, perhaps the most famous geyser on the planet. It is, however, not the only geyser in the park. Yellowstone encompasses a world of geothermal wonders, including more than 300 geysers among the 10,000 hot springs, bubbling mud pots, and seething fumaroles dotting the park's 2.2 million acres.

Straddling the borders of Wyoming, Montana, and Idaho, Yellowstone was established by the U.S. Congress in 1872 and is the world's oldest national park. Much of it occupies a caldera created by a gigantic volcanic eruption some 600,000 years ago; hence the thousands of geothermal features. Other wonders include high waterfalls, alpine lakes and meadows, the Grand Canyon of the Yellowstone, and rare wildlife such as gray wolves, grizzly bears, bison, and bald eagles. ∎

AMERICAN ILLUSTRATORS

CLASSIC COLLECTION

34 x 20 $6.80

© 2000 USPS

PLATE POSITION

X1111

3502   a   b   c   d   e

f   g   h   i   j

k   l   m   n   o

3503

3504

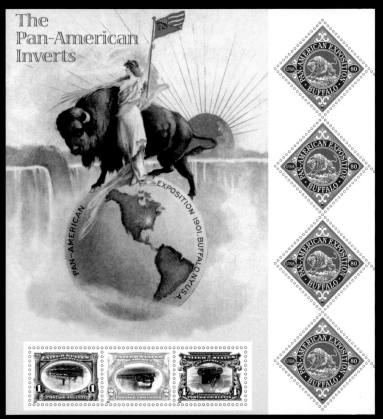

3505   a   b   c   d

	Issues of 2001		Un	U	PB	#	FDC	Q(M)
	Self-Adhesive, Serpentine Die-Cut 11.25							
3503	34¢ Diabetes Awareness	03/16/01	.65	.20	2.60	(4)	1.25	100
	Tagged, Perf. 11							
3504	34¢ The Nobel Prize	03/22/01	.65	.20	2.60	(4)	1.25	35
	The Pan-American Inverts Issue, Tagged, Perf. 12							
3505	34¢ Pane of 7	03/29/01	6.75	—			6.00	11.18
a	1¢ green			.20	.20		1.25	
b	2¢ carmine			.20	.20		1.25	
c	4¢ deep red brown			.20	.20		1.25	
d	80¢ red & blue			1.60	.35		1.75	

Redwood Library and Athenæum

"Having nothing in view but the good of mankind" was the guiding principle for Abraham Redwood and his associates when they established the Redwood Library and Athenæum at Newport, Rhode Island, in 1747. A wealthy, well-educated Quaker, Redwood donated £500 for "a collection of useful Books suitable for a Public Library." The founders housed the collection, purchased in England in 1749, in a Palladian-style structure designed by Peter Harrison; with its classical portico, the library is regarded as one of the most architecturally significant public buildings of that era.

In continuous use ever since it opened in 1750, the Redwood Library and Athenæum is the country's oldest lending library. Its holdings now total more than 155,000 volumes, including almost 90 percent of the approximately 750 titles in the original collection. Among the volumes are pattern books of 18th-century furniture, a notable collection of works on Newport, and a Venetian Bible dating from the 1480s. ■

	Issues of 2001		Un	U	PB	#	FDC	Q(M)
	Great Plains Prairie Issue, Self-Adhesive, Serpentine Die-Cut 10							
3506	Pane of 10	04/19/01	7.00				7.00	89.6
a	34¢ Pronghorns, Canada geese		.65	.20				
b	34¢ Burrowing owls, American buffalo		.65	.20				
c	34¢ American buffalo, Black-tailed prairie dogs, wild alfalfa		.65	.20				
d	34¢ Black-tailed prairie dog, American buffalo		.65	.20				
e	34¢ Painted lady butterfly, American buffalo, prairie coneflowers, prairie wild roses		.65	.20				
f	34¢ Western meadowlark, camel cricket, prairie coneflowers, prairie wild roses		.65	.20				
g	34¢ Badger, harvester ants		.65	.20				
h	34¢ Eastern short-horned lizard, plains pocket gopher		.65	.20				
i	34¢ Plains spadefoot, dung beetle, prairie wild roses		.65	.20				
j	34¢ Two-stripped grasshopper, Ord's kangaroo rat		.65	.20				
	Peanuts Comic Strip Issue, Self-Adhesive, Serpentine Die-Cut 11.25 x 11.5							
3507	34¢ Snoopy	05/17/01	.65	.20	2.60	(4)	1.25	125
	Self-Adhesive, Serpentine Die-Cut 11.25 x 11.5							
3508	34¢ Honoring Veterans	05/23/01	.65	.20	2.60	(4)	1.25	200
	Self-Adhesive, Serpentine Die-Cut, Perf. 11.25							
3509	34¢ Frida Kahlo	06/21/01	.65	.20	2.60	(4)	1.25	55

Crater Lake, Oregon

A lake more than 1,900 feet deep fills the gigantic crater of an ancient volcano in the Cascades of western Oregon. Its name, fittingly, is Crater Lake, and its volcanic setting is Mount Mazama, scene of a cataclysmic eruption about 7,700 years ago.

Try to imagine an eruption 42 times greater than the one at Mount Saint Helens in 1980. If you can, you'll have some idea of what happened when Mount Mazama exploded: The summit ripped away, leaving a gaping 3,000-foot-deep hole. Over the centuries, rain and snow fell into the hole and slowly created what is now the deepest lake in the United States.

Since 1902, the lake and the volcano have formed the centerpiece of 183,000-acre Crater Lake National Park. Climbing Mazama's slopes are forests of red fir, mountain hemlock, and ponderosa pine, while clinging to its rim are twisted whitebark pines—and scenic overlooks where visitors gaze in wonder at Crater Lake's unbelievably blue waters. ■

GREAT PLAINS PRAIRIE

THIRD IN A SERIES

N A T U R E   O F   A M E R I C A

3506   a   b   c   d   e   f

       g   h   i   j

3507

3508

3509

3510

Ebbets Field, Brooklyn
USA 34

3511

Tiger Stadium, Detroit
USA 34

3512

USA 34
Crosley Field, Cincinnati

3513

Yankee Stadium, New York City
USA 34

3514

USA 34
Polo Grounds, New York City

3515

USA 34
Forbes Field, Pittsburgh

3516

Fenway Park, Boston
USA 34

3517

USA 34
Comiskey Park, Chicago

3518

Shibe Park, Philadelphia
USA 34

3519

Wrigley Field, Chicago
USA 34

3519a

	Issues of 2001		Un	U	PB	#	FDC	Q(M)
	Baseball's Legendary Playing Fields, Self-Adhesive, Serpentine Die-Cut, Perf. 11.25							
3510	34¢ Ebbets Field, Brooklyn	06/27/01	.65	.20			1.25	125
3511	34¢ Tiger Stadium, Detroit	06/27/01	.65	.20			1.25	125
3512	34¢ Crosley Field, Cincinnati	06/27/01	.65	.20			1.25	125
3513	34¢ Yankee Stadium, New York City	06/27/01	.65	.20			1.25	125
3514	34¢ Polo Grounds, New York City	06/27/01	.65	.20			1.25	125
3515	34¢ Forbes Field, Pittsburgh	06/27/01	.65	.20			1.25	125
3516	34¢ Fenway Park, Boston	06/27/01	.65	.20			1.25	125
3517	34¢ Comiskey Park, Chicago	06/27/01	.65	.20			1.25	125
3518	34¢ Shibe Park, Philadelphia	06/27/01	.65	.20			1.25	125
3519	34¢ Wrigley Field, Chicago	06/27/01	.65	.20			1.25	125
a	Block of 10, #3510-3519		6.50		6.50	(10)	6.50	

Great Smoky Mountains

The Cherokee knew the high, hazy peaks of North Carolina and Tennessee as Shaconage, or "place of blue smoke." The ancient name stuck, evolving into the Smoky Mountains and then becoming the Great Smoky Mountains when Congress and President Franklin Roosevelt made the region a national park in 1934.

Up close, the Smokies appear amazingly green. They are cloaked in lush vegetation that UNESCO says includes "perhaps the best example of undisturbed hardwood forest in the United States." About 130 tree species and 1,500 kinds of flowering plants grow in the national park. Roaming its woodlands are exotic wild hogs, black bears, foxes, bobcats, and 27 salamander species; about 200 species of birds are found here.

Generations of Cherokee as well as Scotch-Irish and other settlers hunted, farmed, and raised their families on these lands. Their legacy has not been forgotten: Great Smoky Mountain National Park is also a World Heritage site, protecting a wealth of structures and cultural items from the 19th and early 20th centuries. ■

	Issues of 2001		Un	U	PB	#	FDC	Q(M)
	Self-Adhesive, Serpentine Die-Cut 8.5 Vertically							
3520	10¢ *Atlas* Statue	06/29/01	.20	.20	2.75	(5)	1.25	400
	Self-Adhesive, Serpentine Die-Cut, Perf. 11.25							
3521	34¢ Leonard Bernstein	07/10/01	.65	.20	2.60	(4)	1.25	55
	Coil Stamp, Self-Adhesive, Serpentine Die-Cut 11.5 Vertically							
3522	15¢ Woody Wagon	08/03/01	.30	.20	3.25	(5)	1.25	160
	Legends of Hollywood Issue, Self-Adhesive Serpentine Die-Cut 11							
3523	34¢ Lucille Ball	08/06/01	.65	.20	2.60	(4)	1.25	110

Trinity Church, Boston

Renowned American architect Henry Hobson Richardson (1838-1886) designed Boston's celebrated Trinity Church on Copley Square. Dedicated in 1877, this superb example of a Romanesque-revival style known as Richardsonian-Romanesque stands on the site of an earlier church ravaged by the Great Boston Fire of 1872.  For more than a century, many architects have ranked Trinity Church among the ten greatest buildings in the United States. The Postal Service honored it in the American Architecture issue of 1980.

Among Trinity's treasures are stained-glass windows designed by American landscape painter John LaFarge and by English artists William Morris and Edward Burne-Jones. LaFarge's talents are also on display in the lovely murals adorning the church's interior. Serving as an apprentice on the mural project was Augustus Saint-Gaudens, who would become one of the foremost American sculptors of the 19th century; Saint-Gaudens later carved the statue of Bishop Phillips Brooks that stands outside Trinity's north transcept. ■

3520

3521

3522

3523

3524

3525

3526

3527

3527a

3528

3529

3530

3531

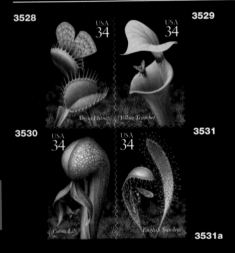

3531a

	Issues of 2001		Un	U	PB	#	FDC	Q(M)
	American Treasures Issue: Amish Quilts, Self-Adhesive, Serpentine Die-Cut 11.25 x 11.5							
3524	34¢ Diamond in the Square	08/09/01	.65	.20			1.25	96
3525	34¢ Lone Star	08/09/01	.65	.20			1.25	96
3526	34¢ Sunshine and Shadow	08/09/01	.65	.20			1.25	96
3527	34¢ Double Ninepatch	08/09/01	.65	.20			1.25	96
a	Block or strip of 4 #3524-3527		2.60		2.60	(4)	3.25	
	Carnivorous Plants Issue, Self-Adhesive, Serpentine Die-Cut 11.5							
3528	34¢ Venus Flytrap	08/23/01	.65	.20				98.6
3529	34¢ Yellow Trumpet	08/23/01	.65	.20				98.6
3530	34¢ Cobra Lily	08/23/01	.65	.20				98.6
3531	34¢ English Sundew	08/23/01	.65	.20				98.6
a	Block or strip of 4 #3528-3531		2.60		2.60	(4)		

Tropical Birds

Only one state in the Union lies south of the Tropic of Cancer: Hawaii. This remote chain of volcanic islands rises from the floor of the north-central Pacific Ocean about 2,400 miles southwest of San Francisco, California.

When Polynesians began settling here nearly 2,000 years ago, they found a variety of landscapes, from tropical shores to snow-covered peaks, from great barren stretches of hardened lava to deeply forested hillsides. In the green paradise of the rain forests they encountered multitudes of birds, including the crested honey-creeper, named for the gray, white, or gold crest on its head and for the way it moves while feeding. This beautiful native bird now lives only in the woodlands hugging the windward slopes of Maui's Haleakala volcano; it creeps among the colorful blossoms of flowering trees and sips nectar through its hook-shaped beak.

In 1998, the Postal Service issued a booklet of stamps featuring the honeycreeper and three tropical birds from American Samoa and the West Indies. ■

Issues of 2001		Un	U	PB	#	FDC	Q(M)
Holiday Celebration Issue, Self-Adhesive, Serpentine Die-Cut 11.25							
3532	34¢ EID	09/01/01	.65	.20	2.60	(4)		75
Self-Adhesive, Serpentine Die-Cut 11.25							
3533	34¢ Enrico Fermi	09/29/01	.65	.20				30
Looney Tunes Issue, Self-Adhesive, Serpentine Die-Cut 11.1							
3534	Pane of 10	10/01/01						
a	34¢ Porky Pig "That's all Folks!"		.65	.20			—	275
Holiday Traditional Issue, Self-Adhesive Booklet Stamps, Serpentine Die-Cut 11.25 on 2 or 3 sides							
3536	34¢ Madonna and Child by Lorenzo Costa	10/10/01	.65	.20			1.25	800
a	Pane of 20							
Holiday Contemporary Issue, Self-Adhesive, Serpentine Die-Cut 11.25							
3537	34¢ Santa wearing tan hood	10/10/01	.65	.20			—	81
3538	34¢ Santa wearing blue hat	10/10/01	.65	.20			—	81
3539	34¢ Santa wearing red hat	10/10/01	.65	.20			—	81
3540	34¢ Santa wearing gold hood	10/10/01	.65	.20			—	81
a	Block of 4 #3537-3540							

Riverboats

Planes, trains, and automobiles now take travelers swiftly and comfortably across the vast plains, high mountains, and deep valleys of America. But in the early to middle decades of the 19th century such technological marvels were unavailable and, for most people, probably unimaginable. This was still an era of horses, wagons, and boats, with the steam-driven riverboat praised as the transportation wonder of the age.

In 1807, Robert Fulton made his first steamboat run on the Hudson River, and by the middle of the century, the country's vast network of waterways had become an "interstate highway system" for riverboats. In 1850 alone, the Mississippi River port of St. Louis, Missouri, welcomed nearly 3,000 steam-powered vessels to its waterfront. Perhaps the most famous arrival came in 1870, when the Robt. E. Lee raced the Natchez from New Orleans to St. Louis and won with a record time of 18 hours, 14 minutes. In 1996, the Postal Service honored the Robt. E. Lee and four other legends of America's waterways with five beautifully illustrated commemorative stamps. ■

3532

3533

3534a

3536

3537

3538

3539

3540

3540a

3545

3546

3547

3548

3549

	Issues of 2001		Un	U	PB	#	FDC	Q(M)
	Self-Adhesive, Serpentine Die-Cut 11.25							
3545	34¢ James Madison	10/18/01	.65	.20				70
	Holiday Celebrations Issue, Self-Adhesive, Serpentine Die-Cut 11.25							
3546	34¢ We Give Thanks	10/19/01	.65	.20				
	Self-Adhesive, Serpentine Die-Cut 11.25							
3547	34¢ Hanukkah	10/21/01	.65	.20	2.60	(4)	1.25	40
3548	34¢ Kwanzaa	10/21/01	.65	.20	2.60	(4)	1.25	40
3549	34¢ United We Stand	10/24/01	.65	.20				70
	Coil Stamp							
3550	34¢ United We Stand	10/24/01	.65	.20				
3551	57¢ Rose and Love Letter	11/19/01	1.10	.20				

Endangered Species

From the Everglades of Florida to the shores of California, a vast array of wildlife still roams the nation's wild lands and waterways. Some creatures maintain footholds in or near residential areas, finding ways to coexist with the country's ever growing human population, while others find refuge in out-of-the-way places.

In south Florida, for example, panthers pad silently through swamplands and forests, and American crocodiles lurk in the murky waters of some swamps and estuaries. Secluded coastal areas and quiet coves and rivers hide gentle manatees as they float near the surface and feed on aquatic plants. Just off the state's southern tip, four-to-five-inch-long Schaus swallowtail butterflies ride ocean breezes over the upper Florida Keys.

On the opposite side of the country, brown pelicans build nests on islands off the coast of southern California, while in the northern part of the state, colorful four-foot-long garter snakes glide through isolated wetlands and grasslands around San Francisco Bay.

In 1996, the Postal Service issued a pane of 15 stamps designed to promote awareness of these animals and other endangered wildlife throughout the United States. ■

A New Name . . .

A New Design . . .

A New Subscription Series Program . . .

Introducing American Commemorative Collectibles—an easy and affordable way to acquire all of your stamp collectibles!

Choose any or all of the official U.S. Postal Service American Commemorative Collectibles to enhance your collection.

American Commemorative Panels

Obtain photo or steel engravings, mint condition stamps and subject related text presented on a beautifully designed page. Only $6.00* each, depending on the value of the stamps.

American Commemorative Collection

An easy and uniform way to collect and learn about commemorative issues. Just mount the stamps on the specially designed sheet and place them in a three ring binder. Just $3.25* each, depending on the value of the stamps.

American Commemorative Cancellations

Get first day cancellations and stamp(s) that have been affixed to colorful, specially tinted sheets to enhance your display. About $2.00* each, depending on the value of the stamps.

First Day of Issue Ceremony Programs

Receive detailed information about each first day of issue ceremony held for all new stamps and stationery issuances. Collect these valuable programs for only $4.95 each.

Order Now.

Establish your American Commemorative Collectibles account(s). To order or for more information call **1 800 STAMP-24**. Customers may order online by visiting The Postal Store at **www.usps.com**

Prices subject to change without notice.

American Commemorative Panels

American Commemorative Collection

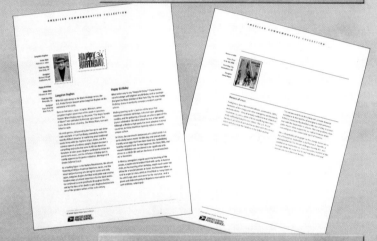

American Commemorative Cancellations

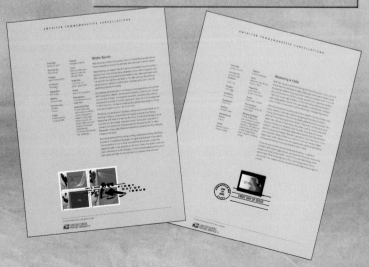

Airmail Stamps

1918-1938

C1

C2

C3

C3a

C4

C5

C6

C7

C10

C11

C12

C13

C14

C15

C18

C20

C21

C23

	Issues of 1918		Un	U	PB	#	FDC	Q(M)
	Perf. 11							
	For prepayment of postage on all mailable matter sent by airmail. All unwatermarked.							
C1	6¢ Curtiss Jenny	12/10/18	70.00	30.00	750.00	(6)	*32,500.00*	3
	Double transfer		90.00	45.00				
C2	16¢ Curtiss Jenny	07/11/18	90.00	35.00	1,075.00	(6)	*32,500.00*	4
C3	24¢ Curtiss Jenny	05/13/18	90.00	35.00	425.00	(4)	*27,500.00*	2
a	Center Inverted		*170,000.00*		*1,200,000.00*	(4)		0.0001
	Issues of 1923							
C4	8¢ Airplane Radiator and							
	Wooden Propeller	08/15/23	25.00	14.00	240.00	(6)	450.00	6
C5	16¢ Air Service Emblem	08/17/23	90.00	30.00	1,700.00	(6)	650.00	5
C6	24¢ De Havilland Biplane	08/21/23	100.00	30.00	2,250.00	(6)	850.00	5
	Issues of 1926-27							
C7	10¢ Map of U.S. and							
	Two Mail Planes	02/13/26	2.80	.35	35.00	(6)	60.00	42
	Double transfer		5.75	1.10				
C8	15¢ olive brown (C7)	09/18/26	3.25	2.50	37.50	(6)	75.00	16
C9	20¢ yellow green (C7)	01/25/27	8.50	2.00	85.00	(6)	100.00	18
	Issue of 1927-28							
C10	10¢ Lindbergh's							
	"Spirit of St. Louis"	06/18/27	7.75	2.50	95.00	(6)	25.00	20
a	Booklet pane of 3	05/26/28	75.00	*65.00*			825.00	
	Issue of 1928							
C11	5¢ Beacon on Rocky							
	Mountains	07/25/28	5.25	.75	175.00	(8)	50.00	107
	Recut frame line at left		6.75	1.25				
a	Vertical pair, imperf. between		*5,500.00*					
	Issues of 1930							
C12	5¢ Winged Globe	02/10/30	11.00	.50	140.00	(6)	12.00	98
a	Horizontal pair, imperf. between		*4,500.00*					
	Graf Zeppelin Issue							
C13	65¢ Zeppelin over							
	Atlantic Ocean	04/19/30	250.00	160.00	2,300.00	(6)	1,250.00	0.09
C14	$1.30 Zeppelin							
	Between Continents	04/19/30	500.00	375.00	5,750.00	(6)	1,100.00	0.07
C15	$2.60 Zeppelin							
	Passing Globe	04/19/30	800.00	575.00	8,250.00	(6)	1,250.00	0.06
	Issues of 1931-32, Perf. 10.5 x 11							
C16	5¢ violet (C12)	08/19/31	5.50	.60	75.00	(4)	175.00	57
C17	8¢ olive bister (C12)	09/26/32	2.40	.40	27.50	(4)	15.00	77
	Issue of 1933, Century of Progress Issue, Perf. 11							
C18	50¢ Zeppelin, Federal Building							
	at Chicago Exposition and							
	Hangar at Friedrichshafen	10/02/33	75.00	70.00	575.00	(6)	200.00	0.3
	Beginning with #C19, unused values are for never-hinged stamps.							
	Issue of 1934, Perf. 10.5 x 11							
C19	6¢ dull orange (C12)	06/30/34	3.50	.25	22.50	(4)	*175.00*	302
	Issues of 1935-37, Trans-Pacific Issue, Perf. 11							
C20	25¢ "China Clipper"							
	over the Pacific	11/22/35	1.40	1.00	20.00	(6)	40.00	10
C21	20¢ "China Clipper"							
	over the Pacific	02/15/37	11.00	1.75	100.00	(6)	45.00	13
C22	50¢ carmine (C21)	02/15/37	10.00	5.00	100.00	(6)	50.00	9
	Issue of 1938							
C23	6¢ Eagle Holding Shield,							
	Olive Branch and Arrows	05/14/38	.50	.20	7.50	(4)	15.00	350
	6¢ ultramarine and carmine		*150.00*	300.00	*1,500.00*	(4)		
a	Vertical pair, imperf. horizontally		*350.00*					
b	Horizontal pair, imperf. vertically		*12,500.00*		*37,500.00*	(4)		

	Issue of 1939		Un	U	PB/LP	#	FDC	Q(M)
	Transatlantic Issue, Perf. 11							
C24	30¢ Winged Globe	05/16/39	10.50	1.50	130.00	(6)	47.50	20
	Issues of 1941-44, Perf. 11 x 10.5							
C25	6¢ Twin-Motor Transport Plane	06/25/41	.20	.20	.65	(4)	2.50	4,477
a	Booklet pane of 3	03/18/43	5.00	1.50			25.00	
	Singles of #C25a are imperf. at sides or imperf. at sides and bottom.							
b	Horizontal pair, imperf. between		2,250.00					
C26	8¢ olive green (C25)	03/21/44	.20	.20	1.10	(4)	3.75	1,745
C27	10¢ violet (C25)	08/15/41	1.25	.20	6.00	(4)	8.00	67
C28	15¢ brn. carmine (C25)	08/19/41	2.75	.35	11.50	(4)	10.00	78
C29	20¢ bright green (C25)	08/27/41	2.25	.30	10.00	(4)	12.50	42
C30	30¢ blue (C25)	09/25/41	2.50	.35	11.00	(4)	20.00	60
C31	50¢ orange (C25)	10/29/41	11.00	3.00	55.00	(4)	40.00	11
	Issue of 1946							
C32	5¢ DC-4 Skymaster	09/25/46	.20	.20	.45	(4)	2.00	865
	Issues of 1947, Perf. 10.5 x 11							
C33	5¢ DC-4 Skymaster	03/26/47	.20	.20	.50	(4)	2.00	972
	Perf. 11 x 10.5							
C34	10¢ Pan American Union Bldg., Washington, D.C. and Martin 2-0-2	08/30/47	.25	.20	1.10	(4)	2.00	208
a	Dry printing		.40	.20	1.75	(4)		
C35	15¢ Statue of Liberty, N.Y. Skyline and Lockheed Constellation	08/20/47	.35	.20	1.50	(4)	2.00	756
a	Horizontal pair, imperf. between		2,250.00					
b	Dry printing		.55	.20	2.50	(4)		
C36	25¢ San Francisco-Oakland Bay Bridge and Boeing Stratocruiser	07/30/47	.85	.20	3.50	(4)	2.50	133
a	Dry printing		1.00	.20	4.25	(4)		
	Issues of 1948, Coil Stamp, Perf. 10 Horizontally							
C37	5¢ carmine (C33)	01/15/48	1.00	.80	10.00	(2)	1.75	33
	Perf. 11 x 10.5							
C38	5¢ New York City	07/31/48	.20	.20	3.75	(4)	1.75	38
	Issues of 1949, Perf. 10.5 x 11							
C39	6¢ carmine (C33)	01/18/49	.20	.20	.50	(4)	1.50	5,070
a	Booklet pane of 6	11/18/49	10.00	5.00				
b	Dry printing		.50	.20	2.25	(4)		
c	As "a," dry printing		15.00	—				
	Perf. 11 x 10.5							
C40	6¢ Alexandria, Virginia	05/11/49	.20	.20	.50	(4)	1.50	75
	Coil Stamp, Perf. 10 Horizontally							
C41	6¢ carmine (C33)	08/25/49	3.25	.20	15.00	(2)	1.25	260
	Universal Postal Union Issue, Perf. 11 x 10.5							
C42	10¢ Post Office Dept. Bldg.	11/18/49	.20	.20	1.40	(4)	1.75	21
C43	15¢ Globe and Doves Carrying Messages	10/07/49	.30	.25	1.25	(4)	2.50	37
C44	25¢ Boeing Stratocruiser and Globe	11/30/49	.50	.40	5.75	(4)	3.50	16
C45	6¢ Wright Brothers	12/17/49	.20	.20	.65	(4)	3.00	80
	Issue of 1952							
C46	80¢ Diamond Head, Honolulu, Hawaii	03/26/52	5.00	1.25	22.50	(4)	17.50	19
	Issue of 1953							
C47	6¢ Powered Flight	05/29/53	.20	.20	.55	(4)	1.50	78
	Issue of 1954							
C48	4¢ Eagle in Flight	09/03/54	.20	.20	1.40	(4)	1.00	50

C24

C25

C32   C33

C34   C35   C36

C38   C40

C42   C43

C44   C45

C46   C47   C48

C49

C51

C53

C54

C55

C56

C57

C58

C59

C61

C62

C63

C64

C66

C67

C68

C69

C70

C71

	Issue of 1957		Un	U	PB/LP	#	FDC	Q(M)
	Perf. 11 x 10.5							
C49	6¢ Air Force	08/01/57	.20	.20	.75	(4)	1.75	63
	Issues of 1958							
C50	5¢ rose red (C48)	07/31/58	.20	.20	1.40	(4)	1.00	72
	Perf. 10.5 x 11							
C51	7¢ Jet Airliner	07/31/58	.20	.20	.60	(4)	1.00	1,327
a	Booklet pane of 6		13.00	7.00			9.00	221
	Coil Stamp, Perf. 10 Horizontally							
C52	7¢ blue (C51)	07/31/58	2.25	.20	15.00	(2)	1.00	157
	Issues of 1959, Perf. 11 x 10.5							
C53	7¢ Alaska Statehood	01/03/59	.20	.20	.60	(4)	1.00	90
	Perf. 11							
C54	7¢ Balloon Jupiter	08/17/59	.20	.20	.60	(4)	1.10	79
	Perf. 11 x 10.5							
C55	7¢ Hawaii Statehood	08/21/59	.20	.20	.60	(4)	1.00	85
	Perf. 11							
C56	10¢ Pan American Games	08/27/59	.25	.25	1.25	(4)	1.00	39
	Issues of 1959-66							
C57	10¢ Liberty Bell	06/10/60	1.25	.70	5.50	(4)	1.25	40
C58	15¢ Statue of Liberty	11/20/59	.35	.20	1.50	(4)	1.25	98
C59	25¢ Abraham Lincoln	04/22/60	.50	.20	2.00	(4)	1.75	
a	Tagged	12/29/66	.60	.30	2.50	(4)	15.00	
	Issues of 1960, Perf. 10.5 x 11							
C60	7¢ carmine (C61)	08/12/60	.20	.20	.60	(4)	1.00	1,289
	Pair with full horizontal gutter between							
a	Booklet pane of 6	08/19/60	16.00	8.00			9.50	
b	Vertical pair, imperf. between		5,500.00					
	Coil Stamp, Perf. 10 Horizontally							
C61	7¢ Jet Airliner	10//22/60	4.25	.25	37.50	(2)	1.00	87
	Issues of 1961-67, Perf. 11							
C62	13¢ Liberty Bell	06/28/61	.40	.20	1.65	(4)	1.00	
a	Tagged	02/15/67	.75	.50	5.00	(4)	10.00	
C63	15¢ Statue of Liberty	01/13/61	.30	.20	1.25	(4)	1.00	
a	Tagged	01/11/67	.35	.20	1.50	(4)	15.00	
b	As "a," horiz. pair, imperf. vertically		15,000.00					
	#C63 has a gutter between the two parts of the design; C58 does not.							
	Issues of 1962-65, Perf. 10.5 x 11							
C64	8¢ Jetliner over Capitol	12/05/62	.20	.20	.65	(4)	1.00	
a	Tagged	08/01/63	.20	.20	.65	(4)	4.50	
b	Bklt. pane of 5 + label		7.00	3.00			3.50	
c	As "b," tagged	1964	2.00	.75				
	Coil Stamp, Perf. 10 Horizontally							
C65	8¢ carmine (C64)	12/05/62	.40	.20	3.75	(2)	1.00	
a	Tagged	01/14/65	.35	.20	1.50	(2)	—	
	Issue of 1963, Perf. 11							
C66	15¢ Montgomery Blair	05/03/63	.60	.55	2.60	(4)	1.10	42
	Issues of 1963-67, Perf. 11 x 10.5							
C67	6¢ Bald Eagle	07/12/63	.20	.20	1.80	(4)	1.00	
a	Tagged	02/15/67	4.00	3.00	55.00	(4)	15.00	
	Issue of 1963, Perf. 11							
C68	8¢ Amelia Earhart	07/24/63	.20	.20	1.00	(4)	2.50	64
	Issue of 1964							
C69	8¢ Robert H. Goddard	10/05/64	.40	.20	1.75	(4)	2.50	62
	Issues of 1967							
C70	8¢ Alaska Purchase	03/30/67	.25	.20	1.40	(4)	1.00	56
C71	20¢ "Columbia Jays,"							
	by Audubon, (See also #1241)	04/26/67	.80	.20	3.50	(4)	2.00	165
a	Tagging omitted		10.00					

1968-1976

	Issues of 1968		Un		PB/LP	#	FDC	Q(M)
	Unwmk., Perf. 11 x 10.5							
C72	10¢ 50-Star Runway	01/05/68	.20	.20	.90	(4)	1.00	
b	Booklet pane of 8		2.00	.75			3.50	
c	Booklet pane of 5 + label	01/06/68	3.75	.75			125.00	
	Coil Stamp, Perf. 10 Vertically							
C73	10¢ carmine (C72)	01/05/68	.30	.20	1.70	(2)	1.00	
a	Imperf., pair		600.00		900.00	(2)		
	Perf. 11							
C74	10¢ U.S. Air Mail Service	05/15/68	.25	.20	2.00	(4)	1.50	
b	Tagging omitted		7.50					
C75	20¢ USA and Jet	11/22/68	.35	.20	1.75	(4)	1.10	
a	Tagging omitted		10.00					
	Issue of 1969							
C76	10¢ Moon Landing	09/09/69	.25	.20	1.10	(4)	5.00	152
a	Rose red omitted		500.00	—				
	Issues of 1971-73, Perf. 10.5 x 11							
C77	9¢ Delta Wing Plane	05/15/71	.20	.20	.90	(4)	1.00	
	Perf. 11 x 10.5							
C78	11¢ Silhouette of Jet	05/07/71	.20	.20	.90	(4)	1.00	
a	Booklet pane of 4 + 2 labels		1.25	.75			1.75	
b	Untagged (Bureau precanceled)			.30				
c	Tagging omitted (not Bureau precanceled)		7.50					
C79	13¢ Winged Airmail Envelope	11/16/73	.25	.20	1.10	(4)	1.00	
a	Booklet pane of 5 + label	12/27/73	1.50	.75			1.75	
b	Untagged (Bureau precanceled)			.30				
	Perf. 11							
C80	17¢ Statue of Liberty	07/13/71	.35	.20	1.60	(4)	1.00	
a	Tagging omitted		10.00	—				
C81	21¢ USA and Jet	05/21/71	.40	.20	2.00	(4)	1.00	
a	Tagging omitted		10.00					
	Coil Stamps, Perf. 10 Vertically							
C82	11¢ carmine (C78)	05/07/71	.25	.20	.80	(2)	1.00	
a	Imperf., pair		300.00		450.00	(2)		
C83	13¢ carmine (C79)	12/27/73	.30	.20	1.10	(2)	1.00	
a	Imperf., pair		75.00		150.00	(2)		
	Issues of 1972, National Parks Centennial Issue, Perf. 11 (See also #1448-54)							
C84	11¢ Kii Statue and Temple at City							
	of Refuge Historical National Park,							
	Honaunau, Hawaii	05/03/72	.20	.20	.90	(4)	1.00	78
a	Blue and green omitted		800.00					
	Olympic Games Issue, Perf. 11 x 10.5 (See also #1460-62)							
C85	11¢ Skiers and Olympic Rings	08/17/72	.20	.20	2.50	(10)	1.00	96
	Issues of 1973, Progress in Electronics Issue, Perf. 11 (See also #1500-02)							
C86	11¢ DeForest Audions	07/10/73	.20	.20	.95	(4)	1.00	59
a	Vermilion and green omitted		1,400.00					
b	Tagging omitted		20.00					
	Issues of 1974							
C87	18¢ Statue of Liberty	01/11/74	.35	.25	1.50	(4)	1.00	
a	Tagging omitted		17.50					
C88	26¢ Mount Rushmore							
	National Memorial	01/02/74	.50	.20	2.25	(4)	1.25	
a	Tagging omitted		17.50					
	Issues of 1976							
C89	25¢ Plane and Globes	01/02/76	.50	.20	2.25	(4)	1.25	
C90	31¢ Plane, Globes and Flag	01/02/76	.60	.20	2.60	(4)	1.25	
a	Tagging omitted		10.00					

C72

C74

C75

C76

C77

C78

C79

C80

C81

C84

C85

C86

C87

C88

C89

C90

C91   C93   C95

C97

C98

C92   C92a   C94   C94a   C96   C96a

C99   C100

C101   C102   C105   C106

C107   C108   C108b

C103   C104   C104a

C109   C110

C111   C112   C112a

	Issues of 1978		Un	U	PB	#	FDC	Q(M)
	Aviation Pioneers Issue, Perf. 11 (See also #C93-96)							
C91	31¢ Wright Brothers, Flyer A	09/23/78	.65	.30			3.00	157
C92	31¢ Wright Brothers, Flyer A							
	and Shed	09/23/78	.65	.30			3.00	157
a	Vert. pair, #C91-92		1.30	1.10	3.00	(4)	4.00	
b	As "a," ultramarine and black omitted		800.00					
c	As "a," black omitted		—					
d	As "a," black, yellow, magenta,							
	blue and brown omitted		2,250.00					
	Issues of 1979, Aviation Pioneers Issue							
C93	21¢ Octave Chanute and Biplane							
	Hang-Glider	03/29/79	.70	.30			3.00	29
C94	21¢ Biplane Hang-Glider							
	and Chanute	03/29/79	.70	.30			3.00	29
a	Attached pair, #C93-94		1.40	1.10	3.25	(4)	4.00	
b	As "a," ultramarine and black omitted		4,500.00					
	Aviation Pioneers Issue (See also #C99-100)							
C95	25¢ Wiley Post and							
	"Winnie Mae"	11/20/79	1.10	.35			3.00	32
C96	25¢ NR-105-W, Post in							
	Pressurized Suit and Portrait	11/20/79	1.10	.35			3.00	32
a	Vert. pair, #C95-96		2.25	1.25	6.00	(4)	4.00	
	Olympic Summer Games Issue (See also #1790-94)							
C97	31¢ High Jumper	11/01/79	.70	.30	9.50	(12)	1.25	47
	Issues of 1980-82							
C98	40¢ Philip Mazzei	10/13/80	.80	.20	10.00	(12)	1.40	81
b	Imperf., pair		3,250.00					
d	Tagging omitted		10.00					
	Perf. 10.5 x 11.25							
C98A	40¢ Philip Mazzei	1982	6.50	1.50	110.00	(12)		
	Issues of 1980, Aviation Pioneers Issue, Perf. 11							
C99	28¢ Blanche Stuart Scott							
	and Biplane	12/30/80	.60	.20	8.50	(12)	1.25	20
C100	35¢ Glen Curtiss							
	and "Pusher" Biplane	12/30/80	.65	.20	9.00	(12)	1.25	23
	Issues of 1983, Olympic Summer Games Issue (See also #2048-51 and 2082-85)							
C101	28¢ Gymnast	06/17/83	1.00	.30			1.50	43
C102	28¢ Hurdler	06/17/83	1.00	.30			1.50	43
C103	28¢ Basketball Player	06/17/83	1.00	.30			1.50	43
C104	28¢ Soccer Player	06/17/83	1.00	.30			1.50	43
a	Block of 4, #C101-04		4.50	2.00	6.00	(4)	3.75	
	Olympic Summer Games Issue, Perf. 11.2 Bullseye (See also #2048-51 and 2082-85)							
C105	40¢ Shotputter	04/08/83	.90	.40			1.75	67
a	Perf. 11 line		1.00	.45				
C106	40¢ Gymnast	04/08/83	.90	.40			1.75	67
a	Perf. 11 line		1.00	.45				
C107	40¢ Swimmer	04/08/83	.90	.40			1.75	67
a	Perf. 11 line		1.00	.45				
C108	40¢ Weightlifter	04/08/83	.90	.40			1.75	67
a	Perf. 11 line		1.00	.45			5.00	
b	Block of 4, #C105-#C108		4.25	2.50	5.00	(4)		
c	Block of 4, #C105a-#C108a		5.00	—	7.50	(4)		
d	Block of 4, imperf.		1,250.00					
	Olympic Summer Games Issue, Perf. 11 (See also #2048-51 and 2082-85)							
C109	35¢ Fencer	11/04/83	.90	.50			1.50	43
C110	35¢ Bicyclist	11/04/83	.90	.50			1.50	43
C111	35¢ Volleyball Players	11/04/83	.90	.50			1.50	43
C112	35¢ Pole Vaulter	11/04/83	.90	.50			1.50	43
a	Block of 4, #C109-12		4.00	3.00	7.00	(4)	4.50	

Issues of 1985		Un	U	PB	#	FDC	Q(M)
Aviation Pioneers Issues, Perf. 11							
C113	33¢ Alfred Verville						
	and Airplane Diagram	02/13/85	.65	.20	3.25	(4)	1.25	168
a	Imperf., pair		850.00				
C114	39¢ Lawrence and						
	Elmer Sperry	02/13/85	.80	.25	3.75	(4)	1.40	168
a	Imperf., pair		1,400.00				
C115	44¢ Transpacific Airmail	02/15/85	.85	.25	4.00	(4)	1.50	209
a	Imperf., pair		900.00				
C116	44¢ Junipero Serra	08/22/85	1.00	.30	8.50	(4)	1.50	164
a	Imperf., pair		1,500.00				
Issues of 1988							
C117	44¢ New Sweden	03/29/88	1.00	.25	6.75	(4)	1.40	137
Aviation Pioneers Issues (See also #C128-29)							
C118	45¢ Samuel P. Langley	05/14/88	.90	.20	4.25	(4)	1.40	406
a	Overall tagging		3.00	.50	30.00	(4)		
C119	36¢ Igor Sikorsky	06/23/88	.70	.20	3.25	(4)	3.00	179
Issues of 1989, Perf. 11.5 x 11							
C120	45¢ French Revolution	07/14/89	.95	.20	4.75	(4)	1.40	38
America/PUAS Issue, Perf. 11 (See also #2426)							
C121	45¢ Southeast Carved Wood Figure,						
	Key Marco Cat (A.D. 700-1450),						
	Emblem of the Postal Union of the						
	Americas and Spain	10/12/89	.90	.20	5.25	(4)	1.40	39
20th UPU Congress Issue (See also #2434-38)							
C122	45¢ Hypersonic Airliner	11/27/89	1.00	.40			1.40	27
C123	45¢ Air-Cushion Vehicle	11/27/89	1.00	.40			1.40	27
C124	45¢ Surface Rover	11/27/89	1.00	.40			1.40	27
C125	45¢ Shuttle	11/27/89	1.00	.40			1.40	27
a	Block of 4, #C122-25		4.25	3.00	5.50	(4)	5.00	
b	As "a," light blue omitted		800.00				

Glacier National Park

On May 11, 1910, President William Howard Taft signed a bill transforming more than a million acres of Montana wilderness into Glacier National Park. This wonderland of glaciers, icy lakes, and jagged peaks became a park largely through the efforts of George Bird Grinnell (1849-1938), an explorer, naturalist, and writer who also helped found the National Audubon Society.

Within its spectacular landscapes, Glacier National Park shelters more than 60 mammal species, including bighorn sheep, mountain goats, elk, moose, black bears, grizzlies, mule deer, beavers, marmots, and river otters. Among its 270 kinds of birds are ospreys, golden eagles, and bald eagles.

Although Glacier's acres stop at the U.S.-Canadian border, the natural wonders do not: Beyond the boundary line, Canada's Waterton Lakes National Park preserves 130,000 scenic acres. In 1932, the two parks were designated Waterton-Glacier International Peace Park to celebrate the long friendship between the U.S. and Canada. They became a biosphere reserve in 1976 and a World Heritage site in 1995. ■

C113

C114

C115

C116

C117

C118

C119

C120

C121

C122 **C123**

C124 **C125**

C125a

20th Universal Postal Congress

A glimpse at several potential mail delivery methods of the future is the theme of these four stamps issued by the U.S. in commemoration of the convening of the 20th Universal Postal Congress in Washington, D.C. from November 13 through December 14, 1989. The United States, as host nation to the Congress for the first time in ninety-two years, welcomed more than 1,000 delegates from most of the member nations of the Universal Postal Union to the major international event.

©USPS 1989

C126

C127

C128

C129

C130

C131

C133

C134

C135

C136

C137

C138

CE1

CE2

	Issues of 1989		Un	U	PB	#	FDC	Q(M)
	20th UPU Congress Issue Souvenir Sheet, Imperf.							
C126	Designs of #C122-25	11/24/89	4.75	3.75			3.00	2
a-d	Single stamp from sheet		1.00	.50				
	Issue of 1990, America/PUAS Issue, Perf. 11 (See also #2512)							
C127	45¢ Tropical Coast	10/12/90	.90	.20	6.75	(4)	1.40	39
	Issues of 1991, Aviation Pioneers Issues							
C128	50¢ Harriet Quimby							
	and Early Plane	04/27/91	1.00	.25	5.50	(4)	1.40	
a	Vertical pair, imperf. horizontally		2,000.00					
b	Perf. 11.2	04/27/91	1.10	.25	6.00	(4)		
C129	40¢ William T. Piper							
	and Piper Cub Airplane	05/17/91	.80	.20	4.00	(4)	1.25	
C130	50¢ Antarctic Treaty	06/21/91	1.00	.25	5.00	(4)	1.40	113
	Issues of 1991-93, America/PUAS Issue							
C131	50¢ Eskimo and Bering							
	Land Bridge	10/12/91	1.00	.25	5.25	(4)	1.40	15
	Perf. 11.2							
C132	40¢ William T. Piper	1993	1.20	.20	15.00	(4)		
	Issues of 1999, Self-Adhesive, Perf. 11							
C133	48¢ Niagara Falls	05/12/99	.95	.20	4.00	(4)	1.40	
	Self-Adhesive, Serpentine Die-Cut 11							
C134	40¢ RioGrande	07/30/99	.80	.60	3.20	(4)	1.50	
	Issue of 2000, Serpentine Die-Cut 11.25 x 11.5							
C135	60¢ Grand Canyon	01/20/2000	1.25	.25	5.00	(4)	1.50	100
	Issues of 2001, Self-Adhesive, Serpentine Die-Cut 11.25 x 11.5							
C136	70¢ Nine-Mile Prairie	03/06/01	1.40	.30	5.60	(4)	1.60	
	Self-Adhesive, Tagged, Serpentine Die-Cut 11							
C137	80¢ Mount McKinley	04/17/01	1.60	.35	6.40	(4)	1.75	
	Self-Adhesive, Serpentine Die-Cut 11.25 x 11.5							
C138	60¢ Acadia National Park	05/30/01	1.25	.25	5.00	(4)	1.25	
	Airmail Special Delivery Stamps							
	Issues of 1934, Perf. 11							
CE1	16¢ Great Seal of the							
	United States	08/30/34	.60	.65	17.50	(6)	25.00	
	For imperforate variety see #77							
	Issue of 1936							
CE2	16¢ red and blue	02/10/36	.40	.25	6.50	(4)	17.50	
a	Horizontal pair, imperf. vertically		4,000.00					

O3   O7   O11   O14   O16

O18   O25   O34   O37   O44

O47   O52   O57   O74   O76

O87   O91   O121   O124   O125

O126   O127   O129A   O139   O140

O143   O146A   O151   O152   O153

Issues of 1873		Un	U
Thin, Hard Paper, Perf. 12, Unwmkd.			

Official Stamps

The franking privilege having been abolished as of July 1, 1873, these stamps were provided for each of the departments of government for the prepayment on official matter. These stamps were supplanted on May 1, 1879, by penalty envelopes and on July 5, 1884, were declared obsolete.

	Department of		
	Agriculture Issue: Yellow		
O1	1¢ Franklin	170.00	150.00
	Ribbed paper	180.00	150.00
O2	2¢ Jackson	135.00	60.00
O3	3¢ Washington	120.00	12.00
	Double transfer	—	—
O4	6¢ Lincoln	135.00	50.00
O5	10¢ Jefferson	270.00	175.00
	10¢ golden yellow	285.00	180.00
	10¢ olive yellow	310.00	185.00
O6	12¢ Clay	360.00	225.00
	12¢ golden yellow	380.00	230.00
O7	15¢ Webster	300.00	200.00
	15¢ olive yellow	340.00	220.00
O8	24¢ Scott	300.00	180.00
	24¢ golden yellow	325.00	190.00
O9	30¢ Hamilton	390.00	235.00
	30¢ olive yellow	425.00	250.00
	Executive Dept. Issue: Carmine		
O10	1¢ Franklin	650.00	400.00
O11	2¢ Jackson	425.00	200.00
O12	3¢ Washington	475.00	160.00
O13	6¢ Lincoln	725.00	475.00
O14	10¢ Jefferson	700.00	550.00
	Dept. of the Interior Issue: Vermilion		
O15	1¢ Franklin	37.50	8.00
	Ribbed paper	42.50	9.50
O16	2¢ Jackson	32.50	9.00
O17	3¢ Washington	50.00	5.00
O18	6¢ Lincoln	37.50	5.00
O19	10¢ Jefferson	37.50	15.00
O20	12¢ Clay	52.50	7.75
O21	15¢ Webster	90.00	17.00
	Double transfer		
	of left side	150.00	25.00
O22	24¢ Scott	65.00	14.00
O23	30¢ Hamilton	90.00	14.00
O24	90¢ Perry	200.00	37.50
	Dept. of Justice Issue: Purple		
O25	1¢ Franklin	120.00	85.00
O26	2¢ Jackson	210.00	85.00
O27	3¢ Washington	210.00	20.00
O28	6¢ Lincoln	190.00	30.00

Issues of 1873		Un	U
	Dept. of Justice Issue: Purple		
	(continued)		
O29	10¢ Jefferson	225.00	70.00
	Double transfer	—	—
O30	12¢ Clay	170.00	45.00
O31	15¢ Webster	325.00	150.00
O32	24¢ Scott	875.00	325.00
O33	30¢ Hamilton	700.00	250.00
	Double transfer at top	750.00	175.00
O34	90¢ Perry	1,050.00	500.00
	Navy Dept. Issue: Ultramarine		
O35	1¢ Franklin	80.00	40.00
a	1¢ dull blue	90.00	42.50
O36	2¢ Jackson	65.00	17.00
a	2¢ dull blue	75.00	15.00
	2¢ gray blue	70.00	15.00
O37	3¢ Washington	62.50	9.00
a	3¢ dull blue	72.50	11.00
O38	6¢ Lincoln	62.50	14.00
a	6¢ dull blue	72.50	14.50
	Vertical line through		
	"N" of "NAVY"	125.00	25.00
O39	7¢ Stanton	425.00	175.00
a	7¢ dull blue	450.00	175.00
O40	10¢ Jefferson	85.00	30.00
a	10¢ dull blue	90.00	30.00
	Plate scratch	*175.00*	—
O41	12¢ Clay	100.00	30.00
	Double transfer		
	of left side	260.00	175.00
O42	15¢ Webster	180.00	57.50
O43	24¢ Scott	200.00	65.00
a	24¢ dull blue	200.00	—
O44	30¢ Hamilton	150.00	35.00
O45	90¢ Perry	725.00	225.00
a	Double impression		*3,750.00*
	Post Office Dept. Issue: Black		
O47	1¢ Figure of Value	14.00	7.50
O48	2¢ Figure of Value	17.50	7.00
a	Double impression	325.00	300.00
O49	3¢ Figure of Value	5.50	1.00
	Cracked plate	—	—
O50	6¢ Figure of Value	17.50	6.00
	Vertical ribbed paper	—	11.00
O51	10¢ Figure of Value	75.00	40.00
O52	12¢ Figure of Value	37.50	8.25
O53	15¢ Figure of Value	50.00	14.00
	Double transfer	—	—
O54	24¢ Figure of Value	65.00	17.00
O55	30¢ Figure of Value	65.00	17.00
O56	90¢ Figure of Value	95.00	14.00

1873-1879

Issues of 1873	Un	U
Dept. of State Issue: Green, Perf. 12		
O57 1¢ Franklin	120.00	55.00
O58 2¢ Jackson	225.00	75.00
O59 3¢ Washington	90.00	17.00
Double paper	—	—
O60 6¢ Lincoln	85.00	22.00
O61 7¢ Stanton	170.00	50.00
Ribbed paper	190.00	55.00
O62 10¢ Jefferson	130.00	40.00
Short transfer	165.00	52.50
O63 12¢ Clay	210.00	90.00
O64 15¢ Webster	220.00	65.00
O65 24¢ Scott	450.00	180.00
O66 30¢ Hamilton	425.00	140.00
O67 90¢ Perry	800.00	275.00
O68 $2 Seward	900.00	750.00
O69 $5 Seward	6,000.00	3,500.00
O70 $10 Seward	4,000.00	2,500.00
O71 $20 Seward	3,250.00	1,800.00
Treasury Dept. Issue: Brown		
O72 1¢ Franklin	40.00	5.00
Double transfer	47.50	6.25
O73 2¢ Jackson	50.00	5.00
Double transfer	—	8.50
Cracked plate	67.50	—
O74 3¢ Washington	35.00	1.25
Shaded circle outside right frame line	—	—
O75 6¢ Lincoln	45.00	2.50
Dirty plate	45.00	4.00
O76 7¢ Stanton	95.00	25.00
O77 10¢ Jefferson	95.00	7.75
O78 12¢ Clay	95.00	6.00
O79 15¢ Webster	90.00	7.75
O80 24¢ Scott	450.00	70.00
O81 30¢ Hamilton	150.00	9.00
Short transfer top right	190.00	20.00
O82 90¢ Perry	160.00	10.00
War Dept. Issue: Rose		
O83 1¢ Franklin	145.00	8.50
O84 2¢ Jackson	130.00	9.50
Ribbed paper	140.00	11.50
O85 3¢ Washington	135.00	2.75
O86 6¢ Lincoln	450.00	6.00
O87 7¢ Stanton	130.00	72.50
O88 10¢ Jefferson	45.00	15.00

Issues of 1873	Un	U
War Dept. Issue (continued): Rose		
O89 12¢ Clay	170.00	10.00
Ribbed paper	185.00	10.50
O90 15¢ Webster	40.00	11.00
Ribbed paper	45.00	14.00
O91 24¢ Scott	40.00	6.75
O92 30¢ Hamilton	42.50	6.75
O93 90¢ Perry	95.00	40.00
Issues of 1879, Soft, Porous Paper		
Dept. of Agriculture: Yellow		
O94 1¢ Franklin, issued without gum	3,250.00	
O95 3¢ Washington	300.00	65.00
Dept. of the Interior Issue: Vermilion		
O96 1¢ Franklin	250.00	220.00
O97 2¢ Jackson	4.25	1.25
O98 3¢ Washington	3.75	1.00
O99 6¢ Lincoln	5.50	5.50
O100 10¢ Jefferson	70.00	60.00
O101 12¢ Clay	130.00	90.00
O102 15¢ Webster	325.00	225.00
Double transfer	375.00	—
O103 24¢ Scott	*3,250.00*	—
O104-05 Not assigned		
Dept. of Justice Issue: Bluish Purple		
O106 3¢ Washington	100.00	65.00
O107 6¢ Lincoln	225.00	175.00
Post Office Dept. Issue: Black		
O108 3¢ Figure of Value	16.00	5.00
Treasury Dept. Issue: Brown		
O109 3¢ Washington	47.50	6.75
O110 6¢ Lincoln	90.00	35.00
O111 10¢ Jefferson	160.00	50.00
O112 30¢ Hamilton	1,300.00	275.00
O113 90¢ Perry	2,100.00	275.00
War Dept. Issue: Rose Red		
O114 1¢ Franklin	3.75	2.75
O115 2¢ Jackson	5.25	3.25
O116 3¢ Washington	5.25	1.20
b Double impression	*750.00*	
Double transfer	8.75	4.75
O117 6¢ Lincoln	4.75	1.00
O118 10¢ Jefferson	40.00	37.50
O119 12¢ Clay	32.50	10.00
O120 30¢ Hamilton	85.00	67.50

Issues of 1910-1985	Un	U
Perf. 12		

Official Postal Savings Mail

These stamps were used to prepay postage on official correspondence of the Postal Savings Division of the Post Office Department. Discontinued Sept. 23, 1914.

		Un	U
O121	2¢ Postal Savings	15.00	1.50
	Double transfer	20.00	2.50
O122	50¢ dark green	145.00	40.00
O123	$1 ultramarine	135.00	11.00
Wmkd. (190)			
O124	1¢ dark violet	8.00	1.50
O125	2¢ Postal Savings (O121)	47.50	5.50
O126	10¢ carmine	18.00	1.60

Penalty Mail Stamps

Stamps for use by government departments were reinstituted in 1983. Now known as Penalty Mail stamps, they help provide a better accounting of actual mail costs for official departments and agencies, etc.

Beginning with #O127, unused values are for never-hinged stamps.

Issues of 1983-1985, Unwmkd., Perf. 11 x 10.5, O129A is Perf. 11			
O127	1¢, Jan. 12, 1983	.20	.20
O128	4¢, Jan. 12, 1983	.20	.25
O129	13¢, Jan. 12, 1983	.45	.75
O129A	14¢, May 15, 1985	.45	.50
O130	17¢, Jan. 12, 1983	.60	.40

Issues of 1983-2001	Un	U
Perf. 11 x 10.5		
O131, O134, O137, O142 Not assigned		
O132 $1, Jan. 12, 1983	2.00	1.00
O133 $5, Jan. 12, 1983	9.00	9.00
Coil Stamps, Perf. 10 Vertically		
O135 20¢, Jan. 12, 1983	1.75	*2.00*
a Imperf. pair	*2,000.00*	
O136 22¢, May 15, 1985	.80	*2.00*
Perf. 11		
O138 "D" postcard rate		
(14¢) Feb. 4, 1985	5.25	*5.00*
Coil Stamps, Perf. 10 Vertically		
O138A 15¢, June 11, 1988	.45	.50
O138B 20¢, May 19, 1988	.45	.30
O139 "D" (22¢), Feb. 4, 1985	5.25	*3.00*
O140 "E" (25¢), Mar. 22, 1988	.75	*2.00*
O141 25¢, June 11, 1988	.65	.50
Perf. 11		
O143 1¢, July 5, 1989	.20	.20
Perf. 10		
O144 "F" (29¢), Jan. 22, 1991	.75	.50
O145 29¢, May 24, 1991	.65	.30
Perf. 11		
O146 4¢, Apr. 6, 1991	.20	*.30*
O146A 10¢, Oct. 19, 1993	.25	*.30*
O147 19¢, May 24, 1991	.40	*.50*
O148 23¢, May 24, 1991	.45	.30
O151 $1, Sept., 1993	2.00	.75
O152 (32¢), Dec. 13, 1994	.65	—
O153 32¢, May 9, 1995	.65	.30
O154 1¢, May 9, 1995	.20	.20
O155 20¢, May 9, 1995	.45	.30
O156 23¢, May 9, 1995	.50	.30
O157 33¢, Oct. 8, 1999	.65	—
O158 34¢, Feb. 27, 2001	.65	.30

Variable Rate Coil Stamps

These are coil postage stamps printed without denominations. The denomination is imprinted by the dispensing equipment called a Postage and Mailing Center (PMC). Denominations can be set between 1¢ and $99.99. In 1993, the minimum denomination was adjusted to 19¢ (the postcard rate at the time).

Date of Issue:
August 20, 1992
Printing: Intaglio

Date of Issue:
February 19, 1994
Printing: Gravure

Date of Issue:
January 26, 1996
Printing: Gravure

Stamped Envelopes

1853-1886

U9   **U14**   **U19**   **U36**

U45   **U46**   **U62**   **U64**

U84   **U85**   **U97**

U103   **U113**   **U142**

Issues of 1853-1865	Un	U

Represented below is only a partial listing of stamped envelopes. At least one example is listed for most die types; most die types exist on several colors of envelope paper. Values are for cut squares; prices for entire envelopes are higher. Color in italic is the color of the envelope paper; when no color is specified, envelope paper is white. "W" with catalog number indicates wrapper instead of envelope.

		Un	U
U1	3¢ red Washington (top label 13mm wide), *buff*	325.00	30.00
U4	3¢ red Washington (top label 15mm wide) *buff*	310.00	25.00
U5	3¢ red (label has octagonal ends)	5,500.00	450.00
U7	3¢ red (label 20mm wide)	1,500.00	90.00
U9	3¢ red (label 14½mm)	35.00	3.50
U12	6¢ red Washington, *buff*	150.00	65.00
U14	6¢ green Washington, *buff*	200.00	85.00
U15	10¢ green Washington (label 15½mm wide)	450.00	85.00
U17	10¢ green (label 20mm)	325.00	125.00
a	10¢ pale green	325.00	100.00
U19	1¢ blue Franklin (period after "POSTAGE"), *buff*	37.50	15.00
U23	1¢ blue (bust touches inner frame line), *orange*	600.00	350.00
U24	1¢ blue (no period after "POSTAGE"), *buff*	300.00	125.00
U27	3¢ red, no label, *buff*	26.00	13.00
U28	3¢ + 1¢ (U12 and U9)	375.00	240.00
U30	6¢ red Wash., no label	2,750.00	1,250.00
U33	10¢ green, no label, *buff*	1,500.00	250.00
U34	3¢ pink Washington (outline lettering)	26.00	5.75
U36	3¢ pink, blue (letter sheet)	80.00	50.00
U39	6¢ pink Washington, *buff*	70.00	62.50
U40	10¢ yellow green Wash.	37.50	30.00
U42	12¢ red, brn. Wash., *buff*	210.00	160.00
U44	24¢ Washington, *buff*	240.00	200.00
U45	40¢ blk., red Wash., *buff*	375.00	350.00
U46	2¢ black Jackson ("U.S. POSTAGE" downstroke, tail of "2" unite near point)	42.50	20.00
U49	2¢ black ("POSTAGE" downstroke and tail of "2" touch but do not merge), *orange*	1,400.00	
U50	2¢ blk. Jack. ("U.S. POST." stamp 24-25mm wide), *buff*	16.00	9.00
W51	2¢ blk. Jack. ("U.S. POST." stamp 24-25mm wide), *buff*	325.00	160.00
U54	2¢ blk. Jack. ("U.S. POST." stp. 25½-26½mm), *buff*	15.00	9.00
W55	2¢ blk. Jack. ("U.S. POST." stp. 25½-26½mm), *buff*	90.00	57.50
U58	3¢ pink Washington (solid lettering)	8.00	1.60
U60	3¢ brown Washington	50.00	30.00
U62	6¢ pink Washington	77.50	29.00

Issues of 1863-1886	Un	U
U64	6¢ purple Washington	55.00	26.00
U66	9¢ lemon Washington, *buff*	425.00	250.00
U67	9¢ orange Washington, *buff*	125.00	90.00
U68	12¢ brn. Wash., *buff*	325.00	250.00
U69	12¢ red brown Wash., *buff*	125.00	55.00
U70	18¢ red Washington, *buff*	95.00	95.00
U71	24¢ bl. Washington, *buff*	100.00	95.00
U72	30¢ green Washington, *buff*	125.00	75.00
U73	40¢ rose Washington, *buff*	125.00	250.00
U75	1¢ blue Franklin (bust points to end of "N" of "ONE"), *amber*	32.50	27.50
U78	2¢ brown Jackson (bust narrow at back; small, thick numerals)	40.00	16.00
U84	3¢ grn. Washington ("ponytail" projects below bust), *cream*	10.00	4.25
U85	6¢ dark red Lincoln (neck very long at back)	25.00	16.00
a	6¢ vermilion	25.00	16.00
U88	7¢ verm. Stanton (figures 7 normal), *amber*	50.00	*190.00*
U89	10¢ olive blk. Jefferson	850.00	750.00
U92	10¢ brown Jefferson, *amber*	85.00	50.00
U93	12¢ plum Clay (chin prominent)	100.00	82.50
U97	15¢ red orange Webster (has side whiskers), *amber*	210.00	300.00
U99	24¢ purple Scott (locks of hair project, top of head)	140.00	140.00
U103	30¢ black Hamilton (back of bust very narrow), *amber*	250.00	500.00
U105	90¢ carmine Perry (front of bust very narrow, pointed)	150.00	350.00
U113	1¢ lt. blue Frank. (lower part of bust points to end of "E" in "ONE")	1.75	1.00
a	1¢ dark blue	8.50	7.50
U114	1¢ lt. blue (lower part of bust points to end of "E" in "Postage"), *amber*	4.25	4.00
U122	2¢ brown Jackson (bust narrow at back; numerals thin)	110.00	40.00
U128	2¢ brown Jackson (numerals in long ovals)	45.00	32.50
U132	2¢ brown, die 3 (left numeral touches oval)	70.00	27.50
U134	2¢ brown Jackson (similar to U128-31 but "O" of "TWO" has center netted instead of plain)	1,250.00	150.00
U139	2¢ brown (bust broad; numerals short, thick)	50.00	35.00
U142	2¢ verm. Jackson (U139)	7.00	3.00

1874-1893

		Un	U
U149	2¢ verm. Jackson (similar to U139-48 but circles around ovals much heavier)	55.00	30.00
W155	2¢ verm. Jackson (like U149 but middle stroke of "N" as thin as verticals), *manila*	22.50	9.50
U156	2¢ verm. Jackson (bottom of bust cut almost semi-circularly)	1,300.00	150.00
U159	3¢ grn. Wash. (thin letters, long numerals)	26.00	6.75
U163	3¢ grn. Wash. (thick letters, "ponytail" does not project below bust)	1.40	.30
U169	3¢ grn. (top of head egg-shaped; "ponytail" knot projects as point), *amber*	260.00	110.00
U172	5¢ Taylor, die 1 (numerals have thick, curved tops)	12.00	8.00
U177	5¢ blue, die 2 (numerals have long, thin tops)	9.00	6.75
U183	6¢ red Lincoln (neck short at back), *cream*	40.00	13.00
U186	7¢ verm. Stanton (figures turned up at ends), *amber*	125.00	62.50
U187	10¢ brown Jefferson (very large head)	37.50	20.00
U190	10¢ choc. Jeff. (knot of "ponytail" stands out) *amb.*	8.00	7.00
U195	12¢ plum Clay (chin receding)	450.00	100.00
U198	15¢ orange Webster (no side whiskers)	47.50	37.50
U201	24¢ purple Scott (hair does not project)	175.00	150.00
U204	30¢ blk. Hamilton (back of bust rather broad)	62.50	27.50
U212	90¢ carm. Perry (front of bust broad, sloping), *amber*	225.00	300.00
U218	3¢ red Post Rider, Train (1 line under "POSTAGE")	50.00	25.00
U225	5¢ brown Garfield, *blue*	70.00	35.00
U228	2¢ red Washington, *amber*	4.75	2.75
U234	2¢ red, four wavy lines in oval (wavy lines fine, clear), *fawn*	5.75	4.75
U236	2¢ red (wavy lines thick, blurred)	10.00	4.00
U240	2¢ red Washington (3½ links over left "2")	85.00	42.50
U244	2¢ red Wash. (2 links below right "2"), *amber*	275.00	75.00
U249	2¢ red Washington (round "O" in "TWO"), *fawn*	1,100.00	400.00
U250	4¢ green Jackson, die 1 (left numeral 2¾mm wide)	3.75	3.50

		Un	U
U256	4¢ green, die 2 (left numeral 3¼mm wide)	8.00	5.00
U259	4¢, die 2, amber *manila*	14.00	7.50
U262	2¢ brn. Wash. (U234), *blue*	16.00	10.00
U267	2¢ brn. Wash. (U236)	17.50	6.25
U270	2¢ brown Washington (2 links below right "2")	100.00	40.00
U274	2¢ brown Wash. (round "O" in "TWO"), *amber*	250.00	85.00
U277	2¢ brn. Washington (extremity of bust below "ponytail" forms point)	.50	.20
U288	2¢ brn. Wash. (extremity of bust is rounded)	300.00	42.50
U294	1¢ blue Franklin, no wavy lines	.55	.20
U302	1¢ dark blue, *manila*	27.50	10.00
U307	2¢ grn. Washington ("G" of "POSTAGE" has no bar), *oriental buff*	80.00	30.00
U314	2¢ green ("G" has bar, ear indicated by 1 heavy line), *blue*	.65	.30
U320	2¢ green (like U314 but ear indicated by 2 curved lines), *oriental buff*	160.00	40.00
U327	4¢ carmine Jackson, *blue*	5.50	4.00
U331	5¢ blue Grant (space between beard and collar), *amber*	5.25	2.25
U335	5¢ blue (collar touches beard), *amber*	12.00	5.50
U340	30¢ red brown Hamilton (U204), *manila*	50.00	45.00
U344	90¢ pur. Perry (U212), *oriental buff*	85.00	*85.00*
U348	1¢ Columbus and Liberty	2.25	1.10
U351	10¢ slate brown	35.00	30.00
U355	1¢ grn. Frank. (U294), bl.	13.50	7.50
U358	2¢ carm. Washington bust points to first notch of inner oval)	3.00	1.75
U362	2¢ carmine (bust points to middle of second notch of inner oval, "ponytail")	.35	.20
U368	2¢ carm. (same as U362 but hair flowing; no ribbon "ponytail"), *amber*	9.00	6.75
U371	4¢ brown Lincoln (bust pointed, undraped)	19.00	11.00
U374	4¢ brown (head larger; inner oval has no notches)	14.00	8.00
U377	5¢ blue Grant (like U331, U335 but smaller)	12.50	9.50

W155

U159

U172

U190

U204

U218

U250

U294

U314

U348

U351

U358

U368

U374

U377

U379

U386

U390

U393

U398

U400

U406

U416

U429

U447

U468

W485

U522

U523

U524

Issues of 1899-1906	Un	U
U379 1¢ green Franklin, horizontal oval	.70	.20
U386 2¢ carm. Wash. (1 short, 2 long vertical lines at right of "CENTS"), *amber*	1.90	.20
U390 4¢ chocolate Grant	22.50	11.00
U393 5¢ blue Lincoln	20.00	12.50
U398 2¢ carm. Washington, recut die (lines at end of "TWO CENTS" all short), *blue*	3.50	.90
U400 1¢ grn. Frank., oval, die 1 (wide "D" in "UNITED")	.30	.20
U401a 1¢ grn. Frank., die 2 (narrow "D"), *amber*	1.75	.70
U402b 1¢, grn. die 3 (wide "S" in "STATES"), *oriental buff*	11.00	1.50
U403c 1¢, die 4 (sharp angle at back of bust, "N," "E" of "ONE" are parallel), *blue*	7.50	1.25
U406 2¢ brn. red Wash., die 1 (oval "O" in "TWO" and "C" in "CENTS")	.80	.20
U407a 2¢, die 2 (like die 1, but hair recut in 2 distinct locks, top of head), *amb.*	225.00	45.00
U408b 2¢, die 3 (round "O" in "TWO" and "C" in "CENTS," coarse letters), *or. buff*	6.50	2.50
U411c 2¢ carmine, die 4 (like die 3 but lettering, hair lines fine, clear)	.40	.20
U412d 2¢ carmine Wash., die 5 (all S's wide), *amber*	.60	.35
U413e 2¢ carm., die 6 (like die 1 but front of bust narrow), *oriental buff*	.55	.35
U414f 2¢ carm., die 7 (like die 6 but upper corner of front of bust cut away), *blue*	30.00	19.00
g 2¢ carm., die 8 (like die 7 but lower stroke of "S" in "CENTS" straight line; hair as in die 2), *blue*	30.00	19.00
U416 4¢ blk. Wash., die 2 ("F" is 1¾mm from left "4")	4.00	2.25
a 4¢, die 1 ("F" is 1mm from left "4")	4.50	3.00
U420 1¢ grn. Frank., round, die 1 ("UNITED" nearer inner circle than outer circle)	.20	.20
U421a 1¢, die 2 (large "U"; "NT" closely spaced), *amber*	425.00	175.00
U423a 1¢ grn. die 3 (knob of hair at back of neck; large "NT" widely spaced), *blue*	.75	.45
b 1¢, die 4 ("UNITED" nearer outer circle than inner)	1.25	.65
c 1¢, die 5 (narrow, oval "C")	.80	.35

Issues of 1907-19 32	Un	U
U429 2¢ carmine Washington, die 1 (letters broad, numerals vertical, "E" closer than "N" to inner circle)	.20	.20
a 2¢, die 2 (like die 1 but "U" far from left circle), *amber*	12.50	6.00
b 2¢, die 3 (like die 2 but inner circles very thin)	40.00	25.00
U430b 2¢, die 4 (like die 1 but "C" very close to left circle), *amber*	45.00	20.00
c 2¢, die 5 (small head, 8¾mm from tip of nose to back of neck; "TS" of "CENTS" close at bottom)	1.10	.35
U431d 2¢, die 6 (like die 6 but "TS" of "CENTS" far apart at bottom; left numeral slopes right), *oriental buff*	3.00	2.00
e 2¢, die 7 (large head, both numerals slope right, T's have short top strokes)	2.75	1.75
U432h 2¢, die 8 (like die 7 but all T's have long top strokes), *blue*	.60	.25
i 2¢, die 9 (narrow, oval "C")	.90	.30
U436 3¢ dk. violet Washington, die 1 (as 2¢)	.55	.20
U440 4¢ black Washington	1.50	.60
U447 2¢ on 3¢ dark violet, rose surcharge	7.75	6.50
U458 Same as U447, black surcharge, bars 2mm apart	.50	.35
U468 Same as U458, bars 1½mm apart	.70	.45
U481 1½¢ brown Washington, die 1 (as U429)	.20	.20
W485 1½¢ brown, *manila*	.80	.20
U490 1½¢ on 1¢ grn. Franklin, black surcharge	5.00	3.50
U499 1½¢ on 1¢, *manila*	12.50	6.00
U510 1½¢ on 1¢ grn., outline numeral in surcharge	2.40	1.25
U522 2¢ carmine Liberty Bell	1.10	.50
a 2¢, center bar of "E" of "Postage" same length as top bar	7.00	3.75
U523 1¢ ol. grn. Mount Vernon	1.00	.80
U524 1½¢ choc. Mount Vernon	2.00	1.50

Issues of 1916-1962	Un	U
U525 2¢ carmine Mount Vernon	.40	.20
a 2¢, die 2 "S" of		
"POSTAGE" raised	70.00	16.00
U526 3¢ violet Mount Vernon	2.00	.35
U527 4¢ black Mount Vernon	18.00	16.00
U528 5¢ dark blue Mount Vernon	4.00	3.50
U529 6¢ orange Washington	5.50	4.00
U530 6¢ orange Wash., *amber*	11.00	8.00
U531 6¢ or. Washington, *blue*	11.00	10.00
U532 1¢ green Franklin	5.00	1.75
U533 2¢ carmine Wash. (oval)	.75	.25
U534 3¢ dk. violet Washington, die 4		
(short N in UNITED, thin		
crossbar in A of STATES)	.40	.20
U535 1½¢ brown Washington	5.00	3.50
U536 4¢ red violet Franklin	.80	.20
U537 2¢ + 2¢ Wash. (U429)	3.25	1.50
U538 2¢ + 2¢ Washington (U533)	.75	.20
U539 3¢ + 1¢ purple, die 1		
(4½mm tall, thick "3")	15.00	11.00
U540 3¢ + 1¢ purple, die 3		
(4mm tall, thin "3")	.50	.20
a Die 2 (4½mm tall,		
thin "3" in medium		
circle), entire	—	—
U541 1¼¢ turquoise Franklin	.75	.50
a Die 2 ("4" 3½mm		
high), precanceled		1.50
U542 2½¢ dull blue Washington	.85	.50
U543 4¢ brn. Pony Express Rider	.60	.30
U544 5¢ dark blue Lincoln	.85	.20
c With albino impression		
of 4¢ U536)	60.00	—
U545 4¢ + 1¢, type 1 (U536)	1.40	.50
U546 5¢ New York World's Fair	.60	.40
U547 1¼¢ brown Liberty Bell		.20
U548 1⁴⁄₁₀¢ brown Liberty Bell		.20
U548A 1⁹⁄₁₀¢ orange Liberty Bell		.20
U549 4¢ blue Old Ironsides	.75	.20
U550 5¢ purple Eagle	.75	.20
a Tagged	1.25	.20
U551 6¢ green Statue of Liberty	.70	.20
U552 4¢ + 2¢ brt. bl. (U549)	3.75	2.00
U553 5¢ + 1¢ brt. pur. (U550)	3.50	2.50
U554 6¢ lt. blue Herman Melville	.50	.20
U555 6¢ Youth Conference	.75	.20
U556 1⁷⁄₁₀¢ lilac Liberty Bell		.20
U557 8¢ ultramarine Eagle	.40	.20
U561 6¢ + (2¢) lt. grn.	1.00	.30
U562 6¢ + (2¢) lt. blue	2.00	1.60
U563 8¢ rose red Bowling	.70	.20
U564 8¢ Aging Conference	.50	.20
U565 8¢ Transpo '72	.50	.20
U566 8¢ + 2¢ brt. ultra.	.40	.20
U567 10¢ emerald Liberty Bell	.40	.20
U568 1⁹⁄₁₀¢ Volunteer Yourself		.20

Issues of 1962-1978	Un	U
U569 10¢ Tennis Centenary	.65	.20
U571 10¢ Compass Rose	.30	.20
a Brown "10¢/USA"		
omitted, entire	125.00	
U572 13¢ Quilt Pattern	.35	.20
U573 13¢ Sheaf of Wheat	.35	.20
U574 13¢ Mortar and Pestle	.35	.20
U575 13¢ Tools	.35	.20
U576 13¢ Liberty Tree	.30	.20
U577 2¢ red Nonprofit		.20
U578 2.1¢ yel. green Nonprofit		.20
U579 2.7¢ green Nonprofit		.20
U580 15¢ orange Eagle, A	.40	.20
U581 15¢ red Uncle Sam	.40	.20
U582 13¢ emerald Centennial	.35	.20
U583 13¢ Golf	.65	.20
U584 13¢ Energy Conservation	.40	.20
d Blk, red omitted, ent.	425.00	
U585 13¢ Energy Development	.40	.20
U586 15¢ on 16¢ blue USA	.35	.20
U587 15¢ Auto Racing	.35	.20
a Black omitted, entire	120.00	
U588 15¢ on 13¢ (U576)	.35	.20
U589 3.1¢ ultramarine nonprofit		.20
U590 3.5¢ purple Violins		.20
U591 5.9¢ Auth Nonprofit Org		.20
U592 18¢ violet Eagle, B	.45	.20
U593 18¢ dark blue Star	.45	.20
U594 20¢ brown Eagle, C	.45	.20
U595 15¢ Veterinary Medicine	.50	.20
U596 15¢ Summer Oly. Games	.60	.20
a Red, grn. omitted, ent.	225.00	
U597 15¢ Highwheeler Bicycle	.40	.20
a Blue "15¢ USA"		
omitted, entire	100.00	
U598 15¢ America's Cup	.40	.20
U599 Brown 15¢ Honeybee	.35	.20
a Brown "15¢ USA"		
omitted, entire	125.00	
U600 18¢ Blind Veterans	.45	.20
U601 20¢ Capitol Dome	.45	.20
U602 20¢ Great Seal of U.S.	.45	.20
U603 20¢ Purple Heart	.65	.20
U604 5.2¢ Auth Nonprofit Org		.20
U605 20¢ Paralyzed Veterans	.45	.20
U606 20¢ Small Business	.50	.20
U607 22¢ Eagle, D	.55	.20
U608 22¢ Bison	.55	.20
U609 6¢ *USS Constitution*		.20
U610 8.5¢ *Mayflower*		.20
U611 25¢ Stars	.60	.20
U612 8.4¢ *US Frigate Constellation*		.20
U613 25¢ Snowflake	.60	.25
U614 25¢ USA, Stars (Philatelic Mail)	.50	.25

U530

U531

U541

U543

U569

U542

U587

U576

U581

U601

U609

U610

U611

U614

U616

U617

U631

U632

U634

U635

U636

Issues of 1989-1992	Un	U
U615 25¢ Stars (lined paper)	.50	.25
U616 25¢ Love	.50	.25
U617 25¢ Space hologram	.60	.30
U618 25¢ Football hologram	.60	.25
U619 29¢ Star	.60	.30
U620 11.1¢ Birds		.20
U621 29¢ Love	.60	.30
U622 29¢ Magazine Industry	.60	.30
U623 29¢ Star and Bars	.60	.30
U624 29¢ Country Geese	.60	.60
U625 29¢ Space Shuttle	.60	.25
U626 29¢ Western Americana	.60	.30
U627 29¢ Protect the Environment	.60	.30
U628 19.8¢ Bulk Rate precanceled		.40

Issues of 1992-1995	Un	U
U629 29¢ Disabled Americans	.60	.30
U630 29¢ Kitten	.60	.30
U631 29¢ Football	.60	.30
U632 32¢ Liberty Bell	.65	.30
U633 32¢ Old Glory	.65	.30
U634 32¢ Old Glory	.65	.30
U635 5¢ Nonprofit		.20
U636 10¢ Graphic Eagle		.20
U637 32¢ Spiral Heart	.65	.30

Greetings From Arizona

The rugged landscapes of Arizona include vast deserts, high mountains, sweeping plateaus, and a famous canyon and valley that have become familiar symbols of the American Southwest.

Cutting through the state's northwest corner, the Grand Canyon measures as much as 18 miles across from rim to rim, making it the largest canyon on any continent. In the northeast, overlapping the Utah border, Monument Valley features monument-like buttes rising a thousand feet from a sandy plain. This spectacular setting has appeared in many Western films, television episodes, and car commercials. It lies within the Navajo Reservation, home to one of the largest Native American groups in the United States. The reservation also includes the Painted Desert, a region of heavily eroded rock surfaces whose colorful hues deepen or fade as the sun moves across the sky.

Much of southern Arizona is desert land inhabited by a diverse collection of animals and plants. Perhaps the most unique desert native is the saguaro cactus; this 60-foot giant grows nowhere else but Mexico. ■

1995-1999

Issues of 1995-1999	Un	U
U639 32¢ Space Shuttle	.65	.35
U640 32¢ Save Our Environment	.60	.30
U641 32¢ 1996 Paralympic Games	.60	.30
U642 33¢ Flag (yellow, red, blue)	.65	.30

Issues of 1999		Un	U
U643 33¢ Flag (blue & red)		.65	.30
U644 33¢ Victorian Love		.65	.30
U645 33¢ Lincoln		.65	.30
Issues of 2001			
U646 34¢ Federal Eagle	01/07/01	.65	.30
U647 34¢ lovebirds	01/14/01	.65	.30
U648 34¢ Federal Eagle	02/20/01	.65	.30

ALL ABOARD! Twentieth Century Trains

Sleek passenger trains were all the rage in the 1930s and '40s, giving Americans fast yet elegant alternatives to planes and automobiles. Known as streamliners, these speedsters possessed both brawn and beauty, with powerful engines clad in classy art deco exteriors. In 1999, the Postal Service featured some of the era's most popular trains on five new stamps.

Gleaming engines and passenger cars on the Congressional route between Washington and New York dazzled riders with red-white-and-blue interiors and etched glass. Onboard the Twentieth Century Limited, passengers enjoyed fine dining and impeccable service between New York and Chicago. In Chicago, travelers bound for St. Paul, Minnesota, could hop aboard swift, smooth-riding Hiawatha trains and make the 410-mile trip in 6 hours, 30 minutes.

For Hollywood stars traveling between Chicago and Los Angeles, the Super Chief waited to whisk them away in style. In California, passengers lauded the Daylight route linking Los Angeles and San Francisco, praising it for luxurious dining and spectacular views of the coast. ■

U639

U640

U641

U642

U643

U644

U645

U646

U647

U648

Airmail Envelopes and Aerogrammes

1929-1973

UC1

UC3

UC7

UC8

UC14

UC21

UC25

UC26

UC30

UC39

UC46

	Issues of 1929-1945	Un	U
UC1	5¢ blue Airplane, die 1		
	(vertical rudder is not		
	semicircular)	3.50	2.00
	1933 wmk., entire	750.00	750.00
	1937 wmk., entire	—	2,500.00
	Bicolored border		
	omitted, entire	1,300.00	
UC2	5¢ blue, die 2 (vertical		
	rudder is semicircular)	11.00	5.00
	1929 wmk., entire	—	1,500.00
	1933 wmk., entire	650.00	—
UC3	6¢ orange Airplane, die 2a		
	("6" is 6½mm wide)	1.45	.40
a	With #U436a added		
	impression	4,000.00	
UC4	6¢ orange, die 2b		
	("6" is 6mm wide)	2.75	2.00
UC5	6¢ orange, die 2c		
	("6" is 5mm wide)	.75	.30
UC6	6¢ orange, die 3 (vertical≤		
	rudder leans forward)	1.00	.35
a	6¢ orange, *blue*,		
	entire	3,500.00	2,400.00
UC7	8¢ olive green Airplane	13.00	3.50
UC8	6¢ on 2¢ carm.		
	Washington (U429)	1.25	.65
a	6¢ on 1¢ green		
	(U420)	1,750.00	
c	6¢ on 3¢ purple		
	(U437a)	3,000.00	
UC9	6¢ on 2¢ Wash. (U525)	75.00	40.00
	Issues of 1946-1956		
UC10	5¢ on 6¢ orange (UC3)	2.75	1.50
a	Double surcharge	60.00	
UC11	5¢ on 6¢ orange (UC4)	9.00	5.50
UC13	5¢ on 6¢ orange (UC6)	.80	.60
a	Double surcharge	60.00	
UC14	5¢ carm. DC-4, die 1		
	(end of wing on right		
	is smooth curve)	.75	.20
UC16	10¢ red, DC-4		
	2-line back inscription,		
	entire, *pale blue*	7.50	6.00
a	"Air Letter" on face,		
	4-line back inscription	16.00	14.00
	Die-cutting reversed	275.00	
b	10¢ chocolate	450.00	
c	"Air Letter" and		
	"Aerogramme" on face	45.00	12.50
d	3-line back inscription	8.00	8.00

	Issues of 1946-1956	Un	U
UC17	5¢ Postage Centenary	.40	.25
UC18	6¢ carm. Airplane (UC14),		
	type I (6's lean right)	.35	.20
a	Type II (6's upright)	.75	.25
UC20	6¢ on 5¢ (UC15)	.80	.50
a	6¢ on 6¢ carmine,		
	entire	1,500.00	
b	Double surcharge	500.00	—
UC21	6¢ on 5¢ (UC14)	27.50	17.50
UC22	6¢ on 5¢ (UC14)	3.50	2.50
a	Double surcharge	200.00	
UC23	6¢ on 5¢ (UC17)	1,250.00	
UC25	6¢ red Eagle	.75	.50
	Issues of 1958-1973		
UC26	7¢ blue (UC14)	.65	.50
UC27	6¢ + 1¢ orange (UC3)	275.00	225.00
UC28	6¢ + 1¢ orange (UC4)	75.00	75.00
UC29	6¢ + 1¢ orange (UC5)	45.00	50.00
UC30	6¢ + 1¢ (UC5)	1.00	.50
UC32	10¢ Jet Airliner, back		
	inscription in 2 lines	6.00	5.00
a	Type 1, entire	10.00	5.00
UC33	7¢ blue Jet Silhouette	.60	.25
UC34	7¢ carmine (UC33)	.60	.25
UC35	11¢ Jet, Globe, entire	2.75	2.25
a	Red omitted	875.00	
	Die-cutting reversed	35.00	
UC36	8¢ red Jet Airliner	.55	.20
UC37	8¢ red Jet in Triangle	.35	.20
a	Tagged	3.50	.30
UC39	13¢ John Kennedy, entire	3.00	2.75
a	Red omitted	500.00	
UC40	10¢ Jet in Triangle	.50	.20
UC41	8¢ + 2¢ (UC37)	.65	.20
UC42	13¢ Human Rights, entire	8.00	4.00
	Die-cutting reversed	75.00	
UC43	11¢ Jet in Circle	.50	.20
UC44	15¢ gray, red, white		
	and blue Birds in Flight	1.50	1.10
UC45	10¢ + (1¢) (UC40)	1.50	.20
UC46	15¢ red, white, bl.	.75	.40

Issues of 1973-1983		Un	U
UC47	13¢ red Bird in Flight	.30	.20
UC48	18¢ USA, entire	.90	.30
UC50	22¢ red and bl. USA, entire	.90	.40
UC51	22¢ blue USA, entire	.70	.25
	Die-cutting reversed	25.00	
UC52	22¢ Summer Olympic		
	Games	1.50	.25
UC53	30¢ blue, red, brn. Tour		
	the United States, entire	.65	.30
a	Red "30" omitted	*70.00*	
UC54	30¢ *yellow, magenta, blue*		
	and *black* (UC53), entire	.65	.30
	Die-cutting reversed	20.00	
UC55	30¢ Made in USA, entire	.65	.30
UC56	30¢ World Communications		
	Year, entire	.65	.30
	Die-cutting reversed	25.00	

Issues of 1983-1999		Un	U
UC57	30¢ Olympic Games, entire	.65	.30
UC58	36¢ Landsat, entire	.70	.35
UC59	36¢ Tourism Week, entire	.70	.35
UC60	36¢ Mark Twain/		
	Halley's Comet, entire	.70	.35
UC61	39¢ Envelope	.80	.40
UC62	39¢ Montgomery Blair	.80	.40
UC63	45¢ Eagle, entire, *blue*	.90	.45
a	White paper	.90	.45
UC64	50¢ Thaddeus Lowe,		
	Balloonist	1.00	.50
UC65	60¢ Voyageurs Nat'l Park,		
	Minnesota	1.25	.65

Greetings From Minnesota

Minnesota is the northernmost state in the lower 48, thanks to a nub of land cutting into Canada just north of Lake of the Woods. This body of water is just one of more than 10,000 lakes dotting the countryside. Another, Lake Itasca, gives rise to the Mississippi, longest river in the United States. Surrounding Minnesota's lakes are millions of acres of forest that provide a rich habitat for moose, black bears, timber wolves, beavers, and foxes. The lakes themselves hold northern pike, walleye, muskie, bass, trout, and sunfish.

The northeast corner of the state touches Lake Superior, largest and westernmost of the five Great Lakes; from the port of Duluth, cargo vessels carry iron ore, agricultural products, timber, and industrial goods all the way to the Atlantic and beyond.

The Minnesota "twins"—St. Paul, the state capital, and Minneapolis, the largest city—sit on either side of the Mississippi River in the southeast. Both are thriving centers of business, technology, transportation, and culture. ∎

UC48

UC52

UC53

UC56

UC57

UC59

UC63

UC64

UO1

UO16

UO20

UO73

UO84

UO88

UO89

UO90

Issues of 1873-1875	Un	U
Official Envelopes		
Post Office Department		
Numeral 9½mm high		
UO1 2¢ black, *lemon*	19.00	9.00
Numeral 10½mm high		
UO5 2¢ black, *lemon*	8.00	4.00
UO9 3¢ black, *amber*	80.00	35.00
Postal Service		
UO16 blue, *amber*	150.00	30.00
War Department		
UO20 3¢ dk. red Washington	60.00	40.00
UO26 12¢ dark red Clay	125.00	50.00
UO39 10¢ vermilion Jefferson	275.00	
UO48 2¢ red Jackson, *amber*	29.00	14.00
UO55 3¢ red Washington, *fawn*	4.50	2.75

Issues of 1983-2001	Un	
Penalty Mail Envelopes		
UO73 20¢ blue Great Seal	1.25	*30.00*
UO74 22¢ (seal embossed)	.90	*10.00*
UO75 22¢ (seal typographed)	1.00	*20.00*
UO76 "E" (25¢) Great Seal	1.10	*20.00*
UO77 25¢ black, blue Great Seal (seal embossed)	.80	*15.00*
UO78 25¢ (seal typographed)	.90	*25.00*
UO79 45¢ (stars illegible)	1.25	—
UO80 65¢ (stars illegible)	1.75	—
UO81 45¢ (stars clear)	1.25	—
UO82 65¢ (stars clear)	1.60	—
UO83 "F" (29¢) Great Seal	1.10	*20.00*
UO84 29¢ black, blue, entire	.75	*10.00*
UO88 32¢ Official Mail	.80	*10.00*
UO89 33¢ Official Mail	.70	*10.00*
UO90 34¢ Official Mail	.85	—

The Great River Road

Meandering from north to south through the heartland of America, the Great River Road has been called the country's "greatest undiscovered scenic drive." It is actually made up of several roads that run along either side of the Mississippi River from Minnesota to Louisiana. The route dates from 1938, when a network of local, state, and federal roads received this designation as part of an effort to show off the ten states that border the Mississippi.

Marked by green pilot wheel signs, the Great River Road rolls past steep cliffs, old farms, pleasant meadows, and cypress swamps. It enters quaint towns, where restaurants may serve up catfish specials or buffalo burgers, and passes through large cities with more cosmopolitan tastes. Now and then the river itself appears beyond a levee or through the trees, and giant barges or the *Delta Queen* riverboat might be spied cutting through the storied waters of the Big Muddy. ∎

1873-1968

UX5   UX6   UX11   UX14

UX16   UX18   UX25   UX27

UX28   UX37   UX43

UX44   UX45   UX46   UX48

Issues of 1873-1917	Un	U

Represented below is only a partial listing of postal cards. Values are for entire cards. Color in italic is color of card. Cards preprinted with written address or message usually sell for much less.

		Un	U
UX1	1¢ brown Liberty, wmkd. (90 x 60mm)	325.00	17.50
UX3	1¢ brown Liberty, wmkd. (53 x 36mm)	75.00	2.50
UX4	1¢ blk. Liberty, wmkd., USPOD in monogram	2,250.00	325.00
UX5	1¢ blk. Liberty, unwmkd.	65.00	.40
UX6	2¢ blue Liberty, *buff*	25.00	17.50
a	2¢ dark blue, *buff*	32.50	22.50
UX7	1¢ (UX5), inscribed "Nothing But The Address"	60.00	.35
a	23 teeth below "One Cent"	950.00	30.00
b	Printed on both sides	800.00	400.00
UX8	1¢ brown Jefferson, large "one-cent" wreath	47.50	1.25
c	1¢ chocolate	92.50	12.50
UX9	1¢ blk. Jefferson, *buff*	20.00	.55
a	1¢ blk., *dark buff*	22.50	1.25
UX10	1¢ black Grant	35.00	1.40
UX11	1¢ blue Grant	14.00	2.50
UX12	1¢ black Jefferson, wreath smaller than UX14	37.50	.60
UX13	2¢ blue Liberty, *cream*	175.00	75.00
UX14	1¢ Jefferson	27.50	.40
UX15	1¢ black John Adams	42.50	15.00
UX16	2¢ black Liberty	11.00	11.00
UX17	1¢ black McKinley	7,000.00	
UX18	1¢ black McKinley, facing left	12.50	.30
UX19	1¢ black McKinley, triangles in top corners	40.00	.50
UX20	1¢ (UX19), correspondence space at left	52.50	4.00
UX21	1¢ blue McKinley, shaded background	95.00	8.50
a	1¢ bronze blue, *bluish*	200.00	17.50
UX22	1¢ blue McKinley, white background	14.00	.30
UX23	1¢ red Lincoln, solid background	8.50	5.50
UX24	1¢ red McKinley	9.00	.30
UX25	2¢ red Grant	1.50	12.50
UX26	1¢ green Lincoln, solid background	11.00	6.00
UX27	1¢ Jefferson, *buff*	.25	.25
a	1¢ green, *cream*	3.50	.60
UX27C	1¢ green Jefferson, *gray,* die I	4,000.00	175.00
UX28	1¢ green Lincoln, *cream*	.60	.30
a	1¢ green, *buff*	1.50	.60
UX29	2¢ red Jefferson, *buff*	40.00	2.00
a	2¢ lake, *cream*	47.50	2.50
c	2¢ vermilion, *buff*	925.00	75.00

Issues of 1918-1968	Un	U

		Un	U
UX30	2¢ red Jefferson, *cream*	27.50	1.50
	Surcharged in one line by canceling machine.		
UX31	1¢ on 2¢ red Jefferson	5,000.00	4,500.00
	Surcharged in two lines by canceling machine.		
UX32	1¢ on 2¢ red Jeff., *buff*	50.00	12.50
a	1¢ on 2¢ vermilion	150.00	60.00
b	Double surcharge	150.00	100.00
UX33	1¢ on 2¢ red Jefferson, *cream*	12.00	1.90
a	Inverted surcharge	55.00	100.00
b	Double surcharge	55.00	35.00
d	Triple surcharge	350.00	
	Surcharged in two lines by press printing.		
UX34	1¢ on 2¢ red (UX29)	500.00	47.50
UX35	1¢ on 2¢ red Jefferson, *cream*	200.00	32.50
UX36	1¢ on 2¢ red (UX25)		50,000.00
UX37	3¢ red McKinley, *buff*	4.50	10.00
UX38	2¢ carmine rose Franklin	.35	.25
a	Double impression	250.00	
	Surcharged by canceling machine in light green.		
UX39	2¢ on 1¢ green Jefferson, *buff*	.50	.35
b	Double surcharge	19.00	21.00
UX40	2¢ on 1¢ green (UX28)	.65	.45
	Surcharged typographically in dark green.		
UX41	2¢ on 1¢ green Jefferson, *buff*	4.50	1.75
a	Inverted surcharge lower left	77.50	125.00
UX42	2¢ on 1¢ green (UX29)	5.00	2.50
b	Surcharged on back	160.00	
UX43	2¢ carmine Lincoln	.30	*1.00*
UX44	2¢ FIPEX	.25	*1.00*
b	Dk. vio. blue omitted	475.00	250.00
UX45	4¢ Statue of Liberty	1.50	*50.00*
UX46	3¢ purple Statue of Liberty	.50	.20
a	"N GOD WE TRUST"	12.50	22.50
UX47	2¢ + 1¢ carmine rose Franklin	190.00	300.00
UX48	4¢ red violet Lincoln	.50	.20
UX49	7¢ World Vacationland	3.75	*40.00*
UX50	4¢ U.S. Customs	.50	*1.00*
a	Blue omitted	625.00	
UX51	4¢ Social Security	.40	*1.00*
b	Blue omitted	700.00	650.00
UX52	4¢ blue & red Coast Guard	.30	*1.00*
UX53	4¢ Bureau of the Census	.30	*1.00*
UX54	8¢ blue & red (UX49)	4.25	*40.00*
UX55	5¢ emerald Lincoln	.30	.50
UX56	5¢ Women Marines	.35	*1.00*

1970-1990

	Issues of 1970-1983	Un	U
UX57	5¢ Weather Services	.30	1.00
a	Yellow, black omitted	1,400.00	850.00
b	Blue omitted	900.00	
c	Black omitted	1,400.00	800.00
UX58	6¢ brown Paul Revere	.30	1.00
a	Double impression	300.00	
UX59	10¢ blue & red (UX49)	4.25	40.00
UX60	6¢ America's Hospitals	.30	1.00
a	Blue, yellow omitted	1,150.00	
UX61	6¢ USF *Constellation*	.85	6.00
a	Address side blank	300.00	
UX62	6¢ black Monument Valley	.40	6.00
UX63	6¢ Gloucester, MA	.40	6.00
UX64	6¢ blue John Hanson	.25	1.00
UX65	6¢ magenta Liberty	.25	1.00
UX66	8¢ orange Samuel Adams	.25	1.00
UX67	12¢ Visit USA/ Ship's Figurehead	.35	35.00
UX68	7¢ Charles Thomson	.30	7.50
UX69	9¢ John Witherspoon	.25	1.00
UX70	9¢ blue Caesar Rodney	.25	1.00
UX71	9¢ Federal Court House	.25	1.00
UX72	9¢ green Nathan Hale	.25	1.00
UX73	10¢ Cincinnati Music Hall	.30	1.00
UX74	10¢ John Hancock	.30	1.00
UX75	10¢ John Hancock	.30	.20
UX76	14¢ Coast Guard Eagle	.40	20.00
UX77	10¢ Molly Pitcher	.30	1.50
UX78	10¢ George Rogers Clark	.30	1.50
UX79	10¢ Casimir Pulaski	.30	1.50
UX80	10¢ Olympic Sprinter	.60	1.50
UX81	10¢ Iolani Palace	.30	1.50
UX82	14¢ Olympic Games	.60	15.00
UX83	10¢ Salt Lake Temple	.25	1.50
UX84	10¢ Landing of Rochambeau	.25	1.50
UX85	10¢ Battle of Kings Mtn.	.25	1.50
UX86	19¢ Drake's Golden Hinde	.65	25.00
UX87	10¢ Battle of Cowpens	.25	15.00
UX88	12¢ violet Eagle, nondenominated	.30	.60
UX89	12¢ lt. bl. Isaiah Thomas	.30	.50
UX90	12¢ Nathanael Greene	.30	10.00
UX91	12¢ Lewis and Clark	.30	20.00
UX92	13¢ buff Robert Morris	.30	.50
UX93	13¢ buff Robert Morris	.30	.50
UX94	13¢ "Swamp Fox" Francis Marion	.30	1.00
UX95	13¢ LaSalle Claims Louisiana	.30	1.00
UX96	13¢ Academy of Music	.30	1.00
UX97	13¢ Old Post Office, St. Louis, Missouri	.30	1.00
UX100	13¢ Olympic Yachting	.30	1.00

	Issues of 1984-1990	Un	U
UX101	13¢ *Ark* and *Dove*, Maryland	.30	1.00
UX102	13¢ Olympic Torch	.30	1.00
UX103	13¢ Frederic Baraga	.30	1.00
UX104	13¢ Dominguez Adobe	.30	1.00
UX105	14¢ Charles Carroll	.30	.50
UX106	14¢ green Charles Carroll	.45	.25
UX107	25¢ Clipper *Flying Cloud*	.70	10.00
UX108	14¢ brt. grn. George Wythe	.30	.50
UX109	14¢ Settlement of Connecticut	.30	1.00
UX110	14¢ Stamp Collecting	.30	1.00
UX111	14¢ Francis Vigo	.30	1.00
UX112	14¢ Settling of Rhode Island	.30	1.10
UX113	14¢ Wisconsin Territory	.30	.75
UX114	14¢ National Guard	.30	1.10
UX115	14¢ Self-Scouring Plow	.30	1.10
UX116	14¢ Constitutional Convention	.30	.50
UX117	14¢ Stars and Stripes	.30	.50
UX118	14¢ Take Pride in America	.30	1.10
UX119	14¢ Timberline Lodge	.30	1.10
UX120	15¢ Bison and Prairie	.30	.50
UX121	15¢ Blair House	.30	.60
UX122	28¢ *Yorkshire*	.60	7.00
UX123	15¢ Iowa Territory	.30	.60
UX124	15¢ Ohio, Northwest Terr.	.30	.60
UX125	15¢ Hearst Castle	.30	.50
UX126	15¢ The Federalist Papers	.30	.60
UX127	15¢ Hawk and Desert	.30	.60
UX128	15¢ Healy Hall	.30	.60
UX129	15¢ Blue Heron and Marsh	.30	.60
UX130	15¢ Settling of Oklahoma	.30	.60
UX131	21¢ Geese and Mountains	.40	5.00
UX132	15¢ Seagull and Seashore	.30	.60
UX133	15¢ Deer and Waterfall	.30	.60
UX134	15¢ Hull House, Chicago	.30	.60
UX135	15¢ Ind. Hall, Philadelphia	.30	.60
UX136	15¢ Inner Harbor, Baltimore	.30	.60
UX137	15¢ Bridge, New York	.30	.60
UX138	15¢ Capitol, Washington	.30	.60
	#UX139-42 issued in sheets of 4 plus 2 inscribed labels, rouletted 9½ on 2 or 3 sides.		
UX139	15¢ (UX135)	3.25	2.50
UX140	15¢ The White House	3.25	2.50
UX141	15¢ (UX137)	3.25	2.50
UX142	15¢ (UX138)	3.25	2.50
a	Sheet of 4, #UX139-42	13.00	
UX143	15¢ The White House	1.00	1.75
UX144	15¢ Jefferson Memorial	1.00	1.75
UX145	15¢ Papermaking	.30	.30
UX146	15¢ World Literacy Year	.30	.60

UX70

UX79

UX81

UX83

UX94

UX109

UX112

UX113

UX115

UX116

UX118

UX119

UX131

UX143

UX144

UX143 (picture side)

UX144 (picture side)

1994-1998

UX174

UX175

UX176

UX177

UX198

UX199

UX219A

UX220

UX241

UX262

UX263

UX280

UX282

UX283

UX290

UX292

UX298

Issues of 1990-1993	Un	U
UX147 15¢ George Caleb Bingham	1.00	1.50
UX148 15¢ Isaac Royall House	.30	.60
UX150 15¢ Stanford University	.30	.50
UX151 15¢ Constitution Hall	1.00	1.50
UX152 15¢ Chicago Orchestra Hall	.30	.60
UX153 19¢ Flag	.40	.50
UX154 19¢ Carnegie Hall	.40	.60
UX155 19¢ Old Red, UT-Galveston	.40	.60
UX156 19¢ Bill of Rights	.40	.60
UX157 19¢ Notre Dame	.40	.60
UX158 30¢ Niagara Falls	.75	2.50
UX159 19¢ The Old Mill	.40	.60
UX160 19¢ Wadsworth Atheneum	.40	.60
UX161 19¢ Cobb Hall	.40	.60
UX162 19¢ Waller Hall	.40	.60
UX163 19¢ America's Cup	1.00	2.00
UX164 19¢ Columbia River Gorge	.40	.60
UX165 19¢ Ellis Island	.40	.60
UX166 19¢ National Cathedral	.40	.60
UX167 19¢ Wren Building	.40	.60
UX168 19¢ Holocaust Memorial	1.00	2.25
UX169 19¢ Fort Recovery	.40	.60
UX170 19¢ Playmakers Theatre	.40	.60
UX171 19¢ O'Kane Hall	.40	.60

Issues of 1993-1998	Un	U
UX172 19¢ Beecher Hall	.40	.60
UX173 19¢ Massachusetts Hall	.40	.60
UX174 19¢ Lincoln's Home	.40	.60
UX175 19¢ Wittenberg University	.40	.60
UX176 19¢ Canyon de Chelly	.40	.60
UX177 19¢ St. Louis Union Station	.40	.60
UX198 20¢ Red Barn	.40	.60
UX199 20¢ Old Glory	.60	.40
UX219A 50¢ Soaring Eagle	1.00	2.50
UX220 20¢ American Clipper Ships	.40	.60
UX241 20¢ Winter Scene	.40	.40
UX262 20¢ St. John's College	.40	.40
UX263 20¢ Princeton University	.40	.40
UX280 20¢ City College of New York	.40	.40
UX281 20¢ Bugs Bunny	1.20	1.75
UX282 20¢ Pacific 97 Golden Gate Bridge in Daylight	.40	.60
UX283 50¢ Pacific 97 Golden Gate Bridge at Sunset	1.00	1.00
UX284 20¢ Fort McHenry	.40	.40
UX290 20¢ University of Mississippi	.40	.40
UX291 20¢ Sylvester & Tweety	1.20	1.75
UX292 20¢ Girard College	.40	.40
UX298 20¢ Northeastern University	.40	.40

Canyon de Chelly National Monument

Canyon de Chelly National Monument, established in April 1931, encompasses 84,000 acres in northeastern Arizona. The name "de Chelly" is a Spanish version of a Navajo word meaning "rock canyon." Indeed, the place is noted for

eye-catching red-rock formations and 200-million-year-old sandstone deposits slashed by deep gorges and ravines. But perhaps the most important aspect of the canyon—at least to historians and archaeologists—is its rich cultural heritage.

An archaeological sanctuary, this national monument preserves and protects Native American ruins dating from A.D. 350. There are early pit houses and cliff dwellings built by Ancestral Puebloans who lived here for about a thousand years and then left during a 13th-century drought. The Hopi, a later Puebloan group, also occupied sites in the canyon. Around 1700, the Navajo arrived, and among the canyon's numerous rock drawings are their pictographs showing Spanish troops in the area. As Spanish, Mexican, and American colonists settled the region in turn, Canyon de Chelly became a major Navajo stronghold. ∎

	Issues of 1998-2001	Un	U
UX299	20¢ Brandeis University	.40	.40
UX301	20¢ University of		
	Wisconsin-Madison	.40	.40
UX302	20¢ Washington and		
	Lee University	.40	.40
UX303	20¢ Redwood Library		
	& Athenæum	.40	.40
UX305	20¢ Mount Vernon	.40	.40
UX306	20¢ Block Island Lighthouse	.40	.40
UX312	20¢ University of Utah	.40	.40
UX313	20¢ Ryman Auditorium	.40	.40
UX316	20¢ Middlebury College	.40	.40
UX361	20¢ Yale University		
	Stamped Card	.40	.40
UX362	20¢ University of South		
	Carolina Stamped Card	.40	.40
UX363	20¢ Northwestern		
	University Stamped Card	.40	.40
UX364	20¢ University of Portland		
	Stamped Card	.40	.40

	Issues of 1949-1966	Un	U
	Airmail Postal Cards		
UXC1	4¢ orange Eagle	.50	.75
UXC2	5¢ red Eagle (C48)	1.75	.75
UXC3	5¢ UXC2 redrawn "Air		
	Mail-Postal Card" omitted	6.50	2.00
UXC4	6¢ red Eagle	1.10	2.50
UXC5	11¢ Visit The USA	.60	20.00

Mount Vernon

Pleasantly situated on a bluff over-looking the Potomac River, the 18th-century Virginia estate of Mount Vernon was home to our nation's first president, George Washington, and his wife, Martha, for more than 40 years.

Washington inherited Mount Vernon from his half-brother Lawrence in 1752. Over the years, he expanded the estate from 2,100 to 8,000 acres and replaced his brother's simple farmhouse with the 20-room mansion that stands on the site. The Postal Service featured the familiar red-roofed structure on stamps issued in 1936 and 1952 and on a stamped card for 1998. Throughout his extraordinary professional life as a military officer and political leader, Washington returned home each time his duty was done and eagerly resumed the lifestyle of a gentleman farmer.

Today, the mansion, serpentine walkways, rolling lawns, and gardens designed by Washington himself still look much as they did when the former President died at Mount Vernon in 1799. ■

UX299

UX301

UX302

UX303

UX305

UX306

UX312

UX313

UX316

UX361

UX362

UX363

UX364

UXC1

UXC2

UXC4

1926-2001

UXC6

UXC7

UXC8

UXC9

UXC10

UXC11

UXC12

UXC13

UXC19

UXC20

UXC23

UXC25

UXC27

UXC28

UY12

UY41

UY43

	Issues of 1967-2001	Un	U
UXC6	6¢ Virgin Islands	.75	7.50
a	Red, yellow omitted	1,700.00	
UXC7	6¢ Boy Scout		
	World Jamboree	.75	7.50
UXC8	13¢ blue & red (UXC5)	1.50	10.00
UXC9	8¢ Stylized Eagle	.75	2.50
UXC10	9¢ red & blue (UXC5)	.50	1.25
UXC11	15¢ Travel Service	1.75	25.00
UXC12	9¢ black Grand Canyon	.75	30.00
UXC13	15¢ black Niagara Falls	.75	40.00
UXC14	11¢ Stylized Eagle	1.00	10.00
UXC15	18¢ Eagle Weather Vane	1.00	10.00
UXC16	21¢ Angel Weather Vane	.80	10.00
UXC17	21¢ Curtiss Jenny	1.00	8.50
UXC18	21¢ Olympic Gymnast	1.25	12.50
UXC19	28¢ First Transpacific Flight	1.00	7.50
UXC20	28¢ Gliders	1.00	7.50
UXC21	28¢ Olympic Speed Skater	1.00	7.50
UXC22	33¢ China Clipper	1.00	6.50
UXC23	33¢ AMERIPEX '86	1.00	6.50
UXC24	36¢ DC-3	.85	5.00
UXC25	40¢ Yankee Clipper	.90	5.00
UXC27	55¢ Mt. Rainier	1.25	5.00
UXC28	70¢ Badlands		
	Stamped Card	1.40	1.40

	Issues of 1892-2001	Un	U
	Paid Reply Postal Cards		
	Prices are: Un=unsevered,		
	U=severed card.		
UY1	1¢ + 1¢ black Grant	35.00	9.00
UY6	1¢ + 1¢ green G. and M.		
	Washington, double		
	frame line around		
	instructions	150.00	25.00
UY7	1¢ + 1¢ green G. and M.		
	Washington, single		
	frame line	1.25	.50
UY12	3¢ + 3¢ red McKinley	9.00	25.00
UY18	4¢ + 4¢ Lincoln	3.00	2.50
UY23	6¢ + 6¢ John Adams	.90	2.00
UY31	"A" (12¢ + 12¢) Eagle	.75	2.00
UY39	15¢ + 15¢ Bison and Prairie	.75	1.00
UY40	19¢ + 19¢ Flag	.75	1.00
UY41	20¢ Red Barn	.80	1.25
UY43	21¢ White Barn	.85	1.25
	Issues of 1913-95		
	Official Mail Postal Cards		
UZ1	1¢ black Numeral	500.00	250.00
UZ2	13¢ blue Great Seal	.75	65.00
UZ3	14¢ blue Great Seal	.75	65.00
UZ4	15¢ blue Great Seal	.75	65.00
UZ5	19¢ blue Great Seal	.70	65.00
UZ6	20¢ Official Mail	.60	65.00

Mount Rainier

Highest and third most massive volcano in the Cascade Range, Mount Rainier rises 14,410 feet from a 100-square-mile base in western Washington. It got its name in 1792, when British explorer George Vancouver arrived in Puget Sound and gazed in wonder at the huge mountain.

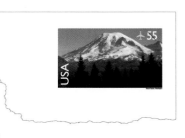

He named it for Peter Rainier, a Rear Admiral in the Royal Navy and a British hero of the Revolutionary War.

In 1870, Hazard Stevens and Philemon Van Trump made the first well-documented ascent of Mount Rainier. Naturalist John Muir climbed the peak in 1888 and then said it was best appreciated from below. Muir and others spoke out for protecting the mountain, which supports four distinct life zones and is drained by five major rivers and their tributaries.

In 1899, President McKinley signed an act of Congress establishing Mount Rainer National Park "for the benefit and enjoyment of the people; and… for the preservation from injury or spoliation of all timber, mineral deposits, natural curiosities, or wonders within said park." ∎

American Commemorative Cancellations

Collect Every **First Day Issue**

- Features stamps issued each year
- Complete with First Day cancellation and informative text
- A convenient, affordable way to collect

The U.S. Postal Service's American Commemorative Cancellations program is your ticket to the year's stamp issues. It's a great way to collect and learn about the stamps and stamp subjects honored during the year.

Fun and Attractive
American Commemorative Cancellations are issued for most stamps—definitives and commemoratives, self-adhesive stamps, coil stamps and booklet panes. Each American Commemorative Cancellations page includes the featured stamp(s), postmarked with a First Day of Issue cancellation, mounted on an 8" x 10½"page. Information on relevant philatelic specifications and a lively narrative about the stamp's subject are included.

Affordable Collectibles
American Commemorative Cancellations are printed in a limited quantity each year. The cost is approximately $2.00 per page. (If the face value of the stamp[s] exceeds $2.00, the price will reflect the face value.)

Money-Back Guarantee
Just return your American Commemorative Cancellations page within 30 days for a full refund.

To order or for more information call **1 800 STAMP-24**. Customers may order online by visiting the Postal Service's Web site at **www.usps.com** and clicking on the Postal Store.

Source Code: #3907

American Commemorative Cancellations

The Postal Service offers American Commemorative Cancellations for new stamps. The series began with a page for the Yellowstone Park Centennial stamp issued March 1, 1972. The pages feature one or more stamps tied by the first day cancel, along with technical data and information on the subject of the issue. More than just collectors' items, American Commemorative Cancellations make wonderful show and conversation pieces. These pages are issued in limited editions. Number in parentheses ( ) indicates the number of stamps on page if there are more than one.

The identifying numbers used below are based on the Postal Service's numbering system for American Commemorative Cancellations; therefore, they do not follow the Scott numbering system.

	1972	
72-00	Family Planning	500.00
72-01	Yellowstone Park	80.00
72-01a	Yellowstone Park with DC cancel	—
72-02	2¢ Cape Hatteras	65.00
72-03	14¢ Fiorello LaGuardia	65.00
72-04	11¢ City of Refuge Park	70.00
72-05	6¢ Wolf Trap Farm Park	22.50
72-06	Colonial Craftsmen (4)	12.50
72-07	15¢ Mount McKinley	17.50
72-08	6¢-15¢ Olympic Games (4)	9.00
72-08E	Olympic Games with broken red circle on 6¢ stamp	—
72-09	PTA	4.50
72-10	Wildlife Conservation (4)	6.00
72-11	Mail Order	4.50
72-12	Osteopathic Medicine	4.50
72-13	Tom Sawyer	5.00
72-14	7¢ Benjamin Franklin	6.25
72-15	Christmas (2)	6.00
72-16	Pharmacy	7.00
72-17	Stamp Collecting	5.00
	1973	
73-01	$1 Eugene O'Neill	55.00
73-01E	$1 Eugene O'Neill picture perf. error	—
73-02	Love	5.50
73-03	Pamphleteer	4.25
73-04	George Gershwin	4.50
73-05	Broadside	5.00
73-06	Copernicus	4.25
73-07	Postal Employees	5.00
73-08	Harry S. Truman	3.75
73-09	Post Rider	4.50
73-10	21¢ Amadeo Gianninni	3.50
73-11	Boston Tea Party (4)	4.75

73-12	6¢-15¢ Electronics (4)	5.75
73-13	Robinson Jeffers	3.50
73-14	Lyndon B. Johnson	2.75
73-15	Henry O. Tanner	4.50
73-16	Willa Cather	2.75
73-17	Colonial Drummer	3.50
73-18	Angus Cattle	3.00
73-19	Christmas (2)	5.75
73-20	13¢ Winged Envelope airmail	2.00
73-21	10¢ Crossed Flags	2.50
73-22	10¢ Jefferson Memorial	2.50
73-23	13¢ Winged Envelope airmail coil (2)	2.50
	1974	
74-01	26¢ Mount Rushmore airmail	4.00
74-02	ZIP Code	3.25
74-02E	ZIP Code with date error 4/4/74	—
74-03	18¢ Statue of Liberty airmail	4.50
74-04	18¢ Elizabeth Blackwell	2.00
74-05	VFW	2.50
74-06	Robert Frost	2.50
74-07	Expo '74	2.50
74-08	Horse Racing	3.25
74-09	Skylab	4.50
74-10	UPU (8)	4.75
74-11	Mineral Heritage (4)	4.75
74-12	Fort Harrod	2.50
74-13	Continental Congress (4)	3.50
74-14	Chautauqua	1.90
74-15	Kansas Wheat	1.90
74-16	Energy Conservation	1.50
74-17	6.3¢ Liberty Bell coil (2)	2.50
74-18	Sleepy Hollow	2.50
74-19	Retarded Children	2.00
74-20	Christmas (3)	4.25
	1975	
75-01	Benjamin West	2.25
75-02	Pioneer/Jupiter	5.00
75-03	Collective Bargaining	2.25
75-04	8¢ Sybil Ludington	2.25
75-05	Salem Poor	2.50
75-06	Haym Salomon	2.25

75-07	18¢ Peter Francisco	2.75
75-08	Mariner 10	4.25
75-09	Lexington & Concord	2.50
75-10	Paul Dunbar	3.00
75-11	D.W. Griffith	2.50
75-12	Bunker Hill	2.50
75-13	Military Uniforms (4)	5.00
75-14	Apollo Soyuz (2)	5.00
75-15	International Women's Year	2.00
75-16	Postal Service Bicentennial (4)	3.00
75-17	World Peace Through Law	2.00
75-18	Banking & Commerce (2)	2.00
75-19	Christmas (2)	3.00
75-20	3¢ Francis Parkman	2.50
75-21	11¢ Freedom of the Press	1.75
75-22	24¢ Old North Church	1.90
75-23	Flag over Independence Hall (2)	2.00
75-24	9¢ Freedom to Assemble (2)	2.00
75-25	Liberty Bell coil (2)	2.00
75-26	Eagle & Shield	2.50
	1976	
76-01	Spirit of '76 (3)	3.25
76-01E	Spirit of '76 with cancellation error Jan. 2, 1976 (3)	—
76-02	25¢ and 31¢ Plane and Globes airmails (2)	2.25
76-03	Interphil '76	2.50
76-04	State Flags, DE to VA (10)	5.50
76-05	State Flags, NY to MS (10)	5.50
76-06	State Flags, IL to WI (10)	5.50
76-07	State Flags, CA to SD (10)	5.50
76-08	State Flags, MT to HI (10)	5.50
76-09	9¢ Freedom to Assemble coil (2)	1.75

No.	Description	Price
76-10	Telephone Centennial	1.75
76-11	Commercial Aviation	1.75
76-12	Chemistry	1.75
76-13	7.9¢ Drum coil (2)	1.90
76-14	Benjamin Franklin	1.75
76-15	Bicentennial souvenir sheet	8.00
76-15E	13¢ Bicentennial souvenir sheet with perforation and numerical errors	7.00
76-16	18¢ Bicentennial souvenir sheet	7.00
76-17	24¢ Bicentennial souvenir sheet	7.00
76-18	31¢ Bicentennial souvenir sheet	7.00
76-19	Declaration of Independence (4)	3.50
76-20	Olympics (4)	3.75
76-21	Clara Maass	1.75
76-22	Adolph S. Ochs	1.75
76-23	Christmas (3)	2.25
76-24	7.7¢ Saxhorns coil (2)	1.75
1977		
77-01	Washington at Princeton	1.75
77-02	Flag over Capitol booklet pane (9¢ and 13¢) Perf. 10 (8)	2.00
77-03	Sound Recording	1.75
77-04	Pueblo Pottery (4)	2.50
77-05	Lindbergh Flight	2.25
77-06	Colorado Centennial	1.90
77-07	Butterflies (4)	2.00
77-08	Lafayette	1.50
77-09	Skilled Hands (4)	2.25
77-10	Peace Bridge	1.60
77-11	Battle of Oriskany	1.60
77-12	Alta, CA, First Civil Settlement	1.60
77-13	Articles of Confederation	1.60
77-14	Talking Pictures	2.00
77-15	Surrender at Saratoga	2.50
77-16	Energy (2)	1.60
77-17	Christmas, Mailbox and Christmas, Valley Forge, Omaha cancel (2)	2.00
77-18	Same, Valley Forge cancel	—
77-19	10¢ Petition for Redress coil (2)	2.25
77-20	10¢ Petition for Redress sheet (2)	2.25
77-21	1¢-4¢ Americana (5)	2.00
1978		
78-01	Carl Sandburg	2.00
78-02	Indian Head Penny	2.00
78-03	Captain Cook, Anchorage cancel (2)	2.00
78-04	Captain Cook, Honolulu cancel (2)	2.00
78-05	Harriet Tubman	3.00
78-06	American Quilts (4)	2.50
78-07	16¢ Statue of Liberty sheet and coil (2)	1.90
78-08	29¢ Sandy Hook Lighthouse	1.90
78-09	American Dance (4)	2.50
78-10	French Alliance	1.90
78-11	Early Cancer Detection	2.50
78-12	"A" (15¢) sheet and coil (2)	3.75
78-13	Jimmie Rodgers	3.00
78-14	CAPEX '78 (8)	5.50
78-15	Oliver Wendell Holmes coil	1.90
78-16	Photography	1.90
78-17	Fort McHenry Flag sheet and coil (2)	1.90
78-18	George M. Cohan	1.60
78-19	Rose booklet single	2.00
78-20	8.4¢ Piano coil (2)	2.00
78-21	Viking Missions	3.75
78-22	28¢ Remote Outpost	2.00
78-23	American Owls (4)	2.50
78-24	31¢ Wright Brothers airmails (2)	2.50
78-25	American Trees (4)	2.75
78-26	Christmas, Madonna	2.00
78-27	Christmas, Hobby Horse	2.00
78-28	$2 Kerosene Lamp	4.50
1979		
79-01	Robert F. Kennedy	2.00
79-02	Martin Luther King, Jr.	3.50
79-03	International Year of the Child	1.75
79-04	John Steinbeck	1.90
79-05	Albert Einstein	3.00
79-06	21¢ Octave Chanute airmails (2)	2.50
79-07	Pennsylvania Toleware (4)	2.50
79-08	American Architecture (4)	2.25
79-09	Endangered Flora (4)	2.50
79-10	Seeing Eye Dogs	1.90
79-11	Candle & Holder	3.75
79-12	Special Olympics	1.90
79-13	$5 Lantern	9.00
79-14	30¢ Schoolhouse	2.75
79-15	10¢ Summer Olympics (2)	2.50
79-16	50¢ Whale Oil Lamp	3.00
79-17	John Paul Jones	2.00
79-18	Summer Olympics (4)	3.75
79-19	Christmas, Madonna	2.50
79-20	Christmas, Santa Claus	2.50
79-21	3.1¢ Guitar coil (2)	3.50
79-22	31¢ Summer Olympics airmail	3.00
79-23	Will Rogers	1.90
79-24	Vietnam Veterans	1.90
79-25	25¢ Wiley Post airmails (2)	3.00
1980		
80-01	W.C. Fields	2.00
80-02	Winter Olympics (4)	3.00
80-03	Windmills booklet pane (10)	4.00
80-04	Benjamin Banneker	2.50
80-05	Letter Writing (6)	2.00
80-06	1¢ Ability to Write (2)	1.60
80-07	Frances Perkins	1.50
80-08	Dolley Madison	2.50
80-09	Emily Bissell	1.90
80-10	3.5¢ Violins coil (2)	2.50
80-11	Helen Keller/ Anne Sullivan	1.90
80-12	Veterans Administration	1.50
80-13	General Bernardo de Galvez	1.75
80-14	Coral Reefs (4)	1.90
80-15	Organized Labor	2.25
80-16	Edith Wharton	2.25
80-17	Education	2.25
80-18	Indian Masks (4)	2.25
80-19	American Architecture (4)	1.90
80-20	40¢ Philip Mazzei airmail	2.00
80-21	Christmas, Madonna	2.25
80-22	Christmas, Antique Toys	2.50
80-23	Sequoyah	1.50
80-24	28¢ Blanche Scott airmail	1.60
80-25	35¢ Glenn Curtiss airmail	1.60
1981		
81-01	Everett Dirksen	1.50
81-02	Whitney M. Young	3.00
81-03	"B" (18¢) sheet and coil (3)	2.00
81-04	"B" (18¢) booklet pane (8)	2.00
81-05	12¢ Freedom of Conscience sheet and coil (3)	1.90
81-06	Flowers block (4)	2.00
81-07	Flag and Anthem sheet and coil (3)	2.00
81-08	Flag and Anthem booklet pane (8 - 6¢ and 18¢)	2.00
81-09	American Red Cross	1.50
81-10	George Mason	1.50
81-11	Savings & Loans	1.50
81-12	Wildlife booklet pane (10)	3.50
81-13	Surrey coil (2)	2.75
81-14	Space Achievement (8)	6.75
81-15	17¢ Rachel Carson (2)	1.75
81-16	35¢ Charles Drew, MD	2.00
81-17	Professional Management	1.40
81-18	17¢ Electric Auto coil (2)	2.50
81-19	Wildlife Habitat (4)	2.00
81-20	International Year of the Disabled	1.50
81-21	Edna St. Vincent Millay	1.50
81-22	Alcoholism	2.25
81-23	American Architecture (4)	2.50
81-24	Babe Zaharias	5.00
81-25	Bobby Jones	5.50
81-26	Frederic Remington	1.75
81-27	"C" (20¢) sheet and coil (3)	3.00
81-28	"C" (18¢) booklet pane (10)	3.00
81-29	18¢ and 20¢ Hoban (2)	1.60
81-30	Yorktown/ Virginia Capes (2)	2.00
81-31	Christmas, Madonna	2.00
81-32	Christmas, Bear on Sleigh	2.00
81-33	John Hanson	1.40
81-34	Fire Pumper coil (2)	4.00
81-35	Desert Plants (4)	2.25

81-36	9.3¢ Mail Wagon coil (3)	3.25
81-37	Flag over Supreme Court sheet and coil (3)	3.00
81-38	Flag over Supreme Court booklet pane (6)	2.75

1982

82-01	Sheep booklet pane (10)	3.00
82-02	Ralph Bunche	4.00
82-03	13¢ Crazy Horse (2)	1.75
82-04	37¢ Robert Millikan	1.50
82-05	Franklin D. Roosevelt	1.50
82-06	Love	1.50
82-07	5.9¢ Bicycle coil (4)	5.00
82-08	George Washington	2.25
82-09	10.9¢ Hansom Cab coil (2)	3.50
82-10	Birds & Flowers, AL-GE (10)	7.00
82-11	Birds & Flowers, HI-MD (10)	7.00
82-12	Birds & Flowers, MA-NJ (10)	7.00
82-13	Birds & Flowers, NM-SC (10)	7.00
82-14	Birds & Flowers, SD-WY (10)	7.00
82-15	USA/Netherlands	1.50
82-16	Library of Congress	1.40
82-17	Consumer Education coil (2)	2.50
82-18	Knoxville World's Fair (4)	1.75
82-19	Horatio Alger	1.25
82-20	2¢ Locomotive coil (2)	2.50
82-21	Aging Together	1.25
82-22	The Barrymores	2.50
82-23	Mary Walker	1.25
82-24	Peace Garden	1.25
82-25	America's Libraries	1.25
82-26	Jackie Robinson	12.50
82-27	4¢ Stagecoach coil (3)	3.50

82-28	Touro Synagogue	1.75
82-29	Wolf Trap Farm Park	1.40
82-30	American Architecture (4)	1.75
82-31	Francis of Assisi	1.40
82-32	Ponce de Leon	1.40
82-33	13¢ Kitten & Puppy (2)	2.00
82-34	Christmas, Madonna	2.50
82-35	Christmas, Seasons Greetings (4)	2.50
82-36	2¢ Igor Stravinsky (2)	2.00

1983

83-01	1¢, 4¢, 13¢ Penalty Mail (5)	2.50
83-02	17¢ Penalty Mail (4)	2.25
83-03	Penalty Mail coil (2)	3.25
83-04	$1 Penalty Mail	4.00
83-05	$5 Penalty Mail	9.50
83-06	Science & Industry	1.75
83-07	5.2¢ Antique Sleigh coil (4)	4.75
83-08	Sweden/USA Treaty	1.75
83-09	3¢ Handcar coil (3)	3.25
83-10	Balloons (4)	1.90
83-11	Civilian Conservation Corps	1.25
83-12	40¢ Olympics airmails (4)	2.75
83-13	Joseph Priestley	1.60
83-14	Volunteerism	1.25
83-15	Concord/German Immigration	1.50
83-16	Physical Fitness	1.75
83-17	Brooklyn Bridge	2.00
83-18	TVA	1.75
83-19	4¢ Carl Schurz (5)	1.50
83-20	Medal of Honor	3.25
83-21	Scott Joplin	3.25
83-22	Thomas H. Gallaudet	1.75
83-23	28¢ Olympics (4)	2.75
83-24	5¢ Pearl S. Buck (4)	1.50

83-25	Babe Ruth	10.00
83-26	Nathaniel Hawthorne	1.60
83-27	3¢ Henry Clay (7)	1.50
83-28	13¢ Olympics (4)	3.00
83-29	$9.35 Eagle booklet single	90.00
83-30	$9.35 Eagle booklet pane (3)	125.00
83-31	1¢ Omnibus coil (3)	2.50
83-32	Treaty of Paris	1.25
83-33	Civil Service	1.25
83-34	Metropolitan Opera	1.90
83-35	Inventors (4)	2.00
83-36	1¢ Dorothea Dix (3)	1.50
83-37	Streetcars (4)	2.25
83-38	5¢ Motorcycle coil (4)	4.25
83-39	Christmas, Madonna	2.00
83-40	Christmas, Santa Claus	2.00
83-41	35¢ Olympics airmails (4)	3.00
83-42	Martin Luther	2.50
83-43	Flag over Supreme Court booklet pane (10)	3.00

1984

84-01	Alaska Statehood	2.00
84-02	Winter Olympics (4)	2.25
84-03	FDIC	1.75
84-04	Harry S. Truman	1.50
84-05	Love	1.60
84-06	Carter G. Woodson	2.25
84-07	11¢ RR Caboose coil (2)	3.25
84-08	Soil & Water Conservation	1.25
84-09	Credit Union Act	1.60
84-10	40¢ Lillian M. Gilbreth	1.50
84-11	Orchids (4)	2.25
84-12	Hawaii Statehood	1.60
84-13	7.4¢ Baby Buggy coil (3)	3.50
84-14	National Archives	1.25

No.	Description	Price
84-15	20¢ Summer Olympics (4)	3.00
84-16	New Orleans World's Fair	1.25
84-17	Health Research	1.25
84-18	Douglas Fairbanks	2.25
84-19	Jim Thorpe	7.00
84-20	10¢ Richard Russell (2)	1.50
84-21	John McCormack	2.25
84-22	St. Lawrence Seaway	1.25
84-23	Migratory Bird Hunting and Conservation Stamp Act	3.00
84-24	Roanoke Voyages	1.25
84-25	Herman Melville	1.40
84-26	Horace Moses	1.25
84-27	Smokey Bear	4.75
84-28	Roberto Clemente	11.00
84-29	30¢ Frank C. Laubach	1.75
84-30	Dogs (4)	2.25
84-31	Crime Prevention	1.50
84-32	Family Unity	2.25
84-33	Eleanor Roosevelt	2.50
84-34	Nation of Readers	2.00
84-35	Christmas, Madonna	2.00
84-36	Christmas, Santa Claus	2.00
84-37	Hispanic Americans	1.25
84-38	Vietnam Veterans Memorial	3.25
1985		
85-01	Jerome Kern	2.25
85-02	7¢ Abraham Baldwin (3)	1.75
85-03	"D" (22¢) sheet and coil (3)	2.25
85-04	"D" (22¢) booklet pane (10)	3.00
85-05	"D" (22¢) Penalty Mail sheet and coil (3)	1.60
85-06	11¢ Alden Partridge (2)	1.50
85-07	33¢ Alfred Verville airmail	1.25
85-08	39¢ Lawrence & Elmer Sperry airmail	1.40
85-09	44¢ Transpacific airmail	1.40
85-10	50¢ Chester Nimitz	1.50
85-11	Mary McLeod Bethune	3.00
85-12	39¢ Grenville Clark	1.50
85-13	14¢ Sinclair Lewis (2)	1.50
85-14	Duck Decoys (4)	2.25
85-15	14¢ Iceboat coil (2)	3.50
85-16	Winter Special Olympics	1.25
85-17	Flag over Capitol sheet and coil (3)	2.25
85-18	Flag over Capitol booklet pane (5)	2.50
85-19	12¢ Stanley Steamer coil (2)	3.50
85-20	Seashells booklet pane (10)	3.50
85-21	Love	2.25
85-22	10.1¢ Oil Wagon coil (3)	2.75
85-23	12.5¢ Pushcart coil (2)	3.00
85-24	John J. Audubon	1.90
85-25	$10.75 Eagle booklet single	30.00
85-26	$10.75 Eagle booklet pane (3)	65.00
85-27	6¢ Tricycle coil (4)	3.00
85-28	Rural Electrification Administration	1.60
85-29	14¢ and 22¢ Penalty Mail sheet and coil (4)	2.00
85-30	AMERIPEX '86	1.50
85-31	9¢ Sylvanus Thayer (3)	1.75
85-32	3.4¢ School Bus coil (7)	3.50
85-33	11¢ Stutz Bearcat coil (2)	3.25
85-34	Abigail Adams	1.25
85-35	4.9¢ Buckboard coil (5)	3.50
85-36	8.3¢ Ambulance coil (3)	3.50
85-37	Frederic Bartholdi	2.25
85-38	8¢ Henry Knox (3)	1.75
85-39	Korean War Veterans	2.50
85-40	Social Security Act	1.50
85-41	44¢ Father Junipero Serra airmail	1.50
85-42	World War I Veterans	2.00
85-43	6¢ Walter Lippmann (4)	1.75
85-44	Horses (4)	3.25
85-45	Public Education	1.75
85-46	International Youth Year (4)	2.75
85-47	Help End Hunger	1.60
85-48	21.1¢ Letters coil (2)	2.75
85-49	Christmas, Madonna	1.75
85-50	Christmas, Poinsettias	2.50
85-51	18¢ Washington/ Washington Monument coil (2)	2.75
1986		
86-01	Arkansas Statehood	1.75
86-02	25¢ Jack London	2.50
86-03	Stamp Collecting booklet pane (4)	3.00
86-04	Love	2.00
86-05	Sojourner Truth	2.50
86-06	5¢ Hugo L. Black (5)	2.50
86-07	Republic of Texas (2)	1.75
86-08	$2 William Jennings Bryan	3.50
86-09	Fish booklet pane (5)	3.50
86-10	Public Hospitals	1.50
86-11	Duke Ellington	3.25
86-12	Presidents, Washington-Harrison (9)	3.75
86-13	Presidents, Tyler-Grant (9)	3.75
86-14	Presidents, Hayes-Wilson (9)	3.75
86-15	Presidents, Harding-Johnson (9)	3.75
86-16	Polar Explorers (4)	3.00
86-17	17¢ Belva Ann Lockwood (2)	1.50
86-18	1¢ Margaret Mitchell (3)	1.90
86-19	Statue of Liberty	2.75
86-20	4¢ Father Flanagan (3)	1.60
86-21	17¢ Dog Sled coil (2)	2.75
86-22	56¢ John Harvard	2.00
86-23	Navajo Blankets (4)	2.75
86-24	3¢ Paul Dudley White, MD (8)	1.75
86-25	$1 Bernard Revel	2.00
86-26	T.S. Eliot	1.50
86-27	Wood-Carved Figurines (4)	3.00
86-28	Christmas, Madonna	2.25
86-29	Christmas, Village Scene	2.25
86-30	5.5¢ Star Route Truck coil (4)	3.00
86-31	25¢ Bread Wagon coil	3.00
1987		
87-01	8.5¢ Tow Truck coil (5)	2.50
87-02	Michigan Statehood	2.50
87-03	Pan American Games	2.50
87-04	Love	2.25
87-05	7.1¢ Tractor coil (5)	2.50
87-06	14¢ Julia Ward Howe (2)	1.50
87-07	Jean Baptiste Pointe Du Sable	4.00
87-08	Enrico Caruso	2.25
87-09	2¢ Mary Lyon (3)	1.75
87-10	Reengraved 2¢ Locomotive coil (6)	2.25
87-11	Girl Scouts	3.50
87-12	10¢ Canal Boat coil (5)	2.00
87-13	Special Occasions booklet pane (10)	3.75
87-14	United Way	1.50
87-15	Flag over Fireworks	1.75
87-16	Flag over Capitol coil, prephosphored paper (2)	2.25
87-17	Wildlife, Swallow-Squirrel (10)	4.50
87-18	Wildlife, Armadillo-Rabbit (10)	4.50
87-19	Wildlife, Tanager-Ladybug (10)	4.50
87-20	Wildlife, Beaver-Prairie Dog (10)	4.50
87-21	Wildlife, Turtle-Fox (10)	4.50
87-22	Delaware Statehood	2.00
87-23	U.S./Morocco Friendship	1.50
87-24	William Faulkner	1.50
87-25	Lacemaking (4)	4.00
87-26	10¢ Red Cloud (3)	2.00
87-27	$5 Bret Harte	8.00
87-28	Pennsylvania Statehood	2.00
87-29	Drafting of the Constitution booklet pane (5)	2.50
87-30	New Jersey Statehood	2.00
87-31	Signing of Constitution	2.00
87-32	Certified Public Accountants	3.25
87-33	5¢ Milk Wagon and 17.5¢ Racing Car coils (4)	3.00
87-34	Locomotives booklet pane (5)	6.75
87-35	Christmas, Madonna	1.75
87-36	Christmas, Ornaments	1.75
87-37	Flag with Fireworks booklet-pair	2.25
1988		
88-01	Georgia Statehood	2.00
88-02	Connecticut Statehood	2.00
88-03	Winter Olympics	1.75
88-04	Australia Bicentennial	2.00
88-05	James Weldon Johnson	2.75
88-06	Cats (4)	4.00
88-07	Massachusetts Statehood	2.25

No.	Description	Value
88-08	Maryland Statehood	2.25
88-09	3¢ Conestoga Wagon coil (8)	2.50
88-10	Knute Rockne	5.00
88-11	"E" (25¢) Earth sheet and coil (3)	2.75
88-12	"E" (25¢) Earth booklet pane (10)	3.50
88-13	"E" (25¢) Penalty Mail coil (2)	2.25
88-14	44¢ New Sweden airmail	2.00
88-15	Pheasant booklet pane (10)	3.75
88-16	Jack London booklet pane (6)	2.50
88-17	Jack London booklet pane (10)	4.25
88-18	Flag with Clouds	1.60
88-19	45¢ Samuel Langley airmail	2.00
88-19A	20¢ Penalty Mail coil (2)	2.25
88-20	Flag over Yosemite coil (2)	2.25
88-21	South Carolina Statehood	2.00
88-22	Owl & Grosbeak booklet pane (10)	3.50
88-23	15¢ Buffalo Bill Cody (2)	1.90
88-24	15¢ and 25¢ Penalty Mail coils (4)	2.75
88-25	Francis Ouimet	6.00
88-26	45¢ Harvey Cushing, MD	1.60
88-27	New Hampshire Statehood	2.00
88-28	36¢ Igor Sikorsky airmail	2.25
88-29	Virginia Statehood	2.00
88-30	10.1¢ Oil Wagon coil, precancel (3)	2.75
88-31	Love	2.00
88-32	Flag with Clouds booklet pane (6)	3.00
88-33	16.7¢ Popcorn Wagon coil (2)	2.75
88-34	15¢ Tugboat coil (2)	2.75
88-35	13.2¢ Coal Car coil (2)	3.00
88-36	New York Statehood	2.25
88-37	45¢ Love	2.00
88-38	8.4¢ Wheelchair coil (3)	2.50
88-39	21¢ Railroad Mail Car coil (2)	3.00
88-40	Summer Olympics	2.00
88-41	Classic Cars booklet pane (5)	4.00
88-42	7.6¢ Carreta coil (4)	2.25
88-43	Honeybee coil (2)	3.25
88-44	Antarctic Explorers (4)	2.75
88-45	5.3¢ Elevator coil (5)	2.25
88-46	20.5¢ Fire Engine coil (2)	3.50
88-47	Carousel Animals (4)	3.25
88-48	$8.75 Eagle	17.50
88-49	Christmas, Madonna	1.75
88-50	Christmas, Snow Scene	1.75
88-51	21¢ Chester Carlson	1.50
88-52	Special Occasions booklet pane (6), Love You, Thinking of You	9.25
88-53	Special Occasions booklet pane (6), Happy Birthday, Best Wishes	14.00
88-54	24.1¢ Tandem Bicycle coil (2)	2.50
88-55	20¢ Cable Car coil (2)	2.75
88-56	13¢ Patrol Wagon coil (2)	2.75
88-57	23¢ Mary Cassatt	1.90
88-58	65¢ H.H. "Hap" Arnold	2.00

1989

No.	Description	Value
89-01	Montana Statehood	2.00
89-02	A. Philip Randolph	3.25
89-03	Flag over Yosemite coil, prephosphored paper (2)	2.25
89-04	North Dakota Statehood	1.90
89-05	Washington Statehood	1.90
89-06	Steamboats booklet pane (5)	3.50
89-07	World Stamp Expo '89	1.50
89-08	Arturo Toscanini	2.00
89-09	U.S. House of Representatives	1.50
89-10	U.S. Senate	1.50
89-11	Executive Branch	1.50
89-12	South Dakota Statehood	1.50
89-13	7.1¢ Tractor coil, precancel (4)	2.75
89-14	$1 Johns Hopkins	2.50
89-15	Lou Gehrig	8.00
89-16	1¢ Penalty Mail	2.25
89-17	45¢ French Revolution airmail	2.25
89-18	Ernest Hemingway	2.50
89-19	$2.40 Moon Landing	12.50
89-20	North Carolina Statehood	2.25
89-21	Letter Carriers	2.00
89-22	28¢ Sitting Bull	1.75
89-23	Drafting of the Bill of Rights	1.50
89-24	Prehistoric Animals (4)	6.50
89-25	25¢ and 45¢ PUAS-America (2)	2.50
89-26	Christmas, Madonna	5.00
89-27	Christmas, Antique Sleigh	5.00
89-28	Eagle and Shield, self-adhesive	2.00
89-29	World Stamp Expo '89 souvenir sheet	7.00
89-30	Classic Mail Transportation (4)	2.75
89-31	Future Mail Transportation souvenir sheet	4.50
89-32	45¢ Future Mail Transportation airmails (4)	4.50
89-33	Classic Mail Transportation souvenir sheet	5.00

1990

No.	Description	Value
90-01	Idaho Statehood	1.50
90-02	Love sheet and booklet pane (10)	3.50
90-03	Ida B. Wells	3.00
90-04	U.S. Supreme Court	1.50
90-05	15¢ Beach Umbrella booklet pane (10)	3.25
90-06	5¢ Luis Munoz Marin (5)	2.00
90-07	Wyoming Statehood	2.25
90-08	Classic Films (4)	5.00
90-09	Marianne Moore	1.50
90-10	$1 Seaplane coil (2)	5.75
90-11	Lighthouses booklet pane (5)	5.00
90-12	Plastic Flag stamp	3.25
90-13	Rhode Island Statehood	2.25
90-14	$2 Bobcat	4.00
90-15	Olympians (5)	4.75
90-16	Indian Headdresses booklet pane (10)	5.50
90-17	5¢ Circus Wagon coil (5)	3.25
90-18	40¢ Claire Lee Chennault	3.25
90-19	Federated States of Micronesia/Marshall Islands (2)	2.25
90-20	Creatures of the Sea (4)	4.75
90-21	25¢ and 45¢ PUAS/America (2)	2.25
90-22	Dwight D. Eisenhower	2.50
90-23	Christmas, Madonna, sheet and booklet pane (11)	5.00
90-24	Christmas, Yule Tree, sheet and booklet pane (11)	5.00

1991

No.	Description	Value
91-01	"F" (29¢) Flower sheet and coil (3)	2.75
91-02	"F" (29¢) Flower booklet panes (20)	9.00
91-03	4¢ Makeup	2.25
91-04	"F" (29¢) ATM booklet single	2.75
91-05	"F" (29¢) Penalty Mail coil (2)	2.50
91-06	4¢ Steam Carriage coil (7)	2.50
91-07	50¢ Switzerland	2.75
91-08	Vermont Statehood	2.75
91-09	19¢ Fawn (2)	2.25
91-10	Flag over Mount Rushmore coil (2)	2.75
91-11	35¢ Dennis Chavez	3.25
91-12	Flower sheet and booklet pane (10)	9.00
91-13	4¢ Penalty Mail (8)	2.25
91-14	Wood Duck booklet panes (10)	11.00
91-15	23¢ Lunch Wagon coil (2)	2.25
91-16	Flag with Olympic Rings booklet pane (10)	5.50
91-17	50¢ Harriet Quimby	2.75
91-18	Savings Bond	2.25
91-19	Love sheet and booklet pane, 52¢ Love (12)	7.50
91-20	19¢ Balloon booklet pane (10)	4.50
91-21	40¢ William Piper airmail	2.75
91-22	William Saroyan	2.75
91-23	Penalty Mail coil and 19¢ and 23¢ sheet (4)	3.50
91-24	5¢ Canoe and 10¢ Tractor Trailer coils (4)	2.50
91-25	Flags on Parade	2.50
91-26	Fishing Flies booklet pane (5)	5.25

No.	Description	Price
91-27	52¢ Hubert H. Humphrey	2.00
91-28	Cole Porter	2.25
91-29	50¢ Antarctic Treaty airmail	3.00
91-30	1¢ Kestrel, 3¢ Bluebird and 30¢ Cardinal (3)	2.25
91-31	Torch ATM booklet single	2.50
91-32	Desert Shield/ Desert Storm sheet and booklet pane (11)	5.00
91-33	Flag over Mount Rushmore coil, gravure printing (darker, 3)	2.75
91-34	Summer Olympics (5)	5.00
91-35	Flower coil, slit perforations (3)	2.75
91-36	Numismatics	2.50
91-37	Basketball	5.75
91-38 through 91-47 are unassigned		
91-48	19¢ Fishing Boat coil (3)	2.50
91-49	Comedians booklet pane (10)	5.00
91-50	World War II miniature sheet (10)	6.50
91-51	District of Columbia	2.50
91-52	Jan Matzeliger	4.50
91-53	$1 USPS/ Olympic Logo	3.00
91-54	Space Exploration booklet pane (10)	6.75
91-55	50¢ PUASP/America airmail	2.75
91-56	Christmas, Madonna sheet and booklet pane (10)	8.50
91-57	Christmas, Santa Claus sheet and booklet pane (11)	12.50
91-58	5¢ Canoe coil, gravure printing (red, 6)	3.00
91-59	29¢ Eagle and Shield, self-adhesive (3)	3.50
91-60	23¢ Flag presort	2.75
91-61	$9.95 Express Mail	22.50
91-62	$2.90 Priority Mail	7.50
91-63	$14.00 Express Mail International	30.00
1992		
92-01	Winter Olympic Games (5)	4.25
92-02	World Columbian Stamp Expo '92	2.50
92-03	W.E.B. DuBois	4.75
92-04	Love	2.50
92-05	75¢ Wendell Willkie	2.25
92-06	29¢ Flower coil, round perforations (2)	2.50
92-07	Earl Warren	3.25
92-08	Olympic Baseball	12.50
92-09	Flag over White House, coil (2)	2.50
92-10	First Voyage of Christopher Columbus (4)	4.25
92-11	New York Stock Exchange	2.50
92-12	Columbian-Columbus	9.00
92-13	Columbian-Seeking Royal Support (3)	9.00
92-14	Columbian-First Sighting of Land (3)	9.00
92-15	Columbian-Claiming New World (3)	9.00
92-16	Columbian-Reporting Discoveries (3)	9.00
92-17	Columbian-Royal Favor Restored (3)	9.00
92-18	Space Adventures (4)	4.75
92-19	Alaska Highway	2.50
92-20	Kentucky Statehood	2.50
92-21	Summer Olympic Games (5)	4.00
92-22	Hummingbirds booklet pane (5)	5.00
92-22A	23¢ Presort (3)	3.25
92-23	Wildflowers (10)	6.50
92-24	Wildflowers (10)	6.50
92-25	Wildflowers (10)	6.50
92-26	Wildflowers (10)	6.50
92-27	Wildflowers (10)	6.50
92-28	World War II miniature sheet (10)	6.00
92-29	29¢ Variable Rate	2.75
92-30	Dorothy Parker	2.75
92-31	Theodore von Karman	4.00
92-32	Pledge of Allegiance (10)	7.00
92-33	Minerals (4)	4.00
92-34	Eagle and Shield (3)	4.75
92-35	Juan Rodriguez Cabrillo	2.50
92-36	Wild Animals booklet pane (5)	5.00
92-37	23¢ Presort (3)	3.50
92-38	Christmas Contemporary, sheet and booklet pane (8)	7.50
92-39	Christmas Traditional, sheet and booklet pane (11)	6.50
92-40	Pumpkinseed Sunfish	3.25
92-41	Circus Wagon	2.75
92-42	Year of the Rooster	7.75
1993		
93-01	Elvis	10.00
93-02	Space Fantasy (5)	6.00
93-03	Percy Lavon Julian	4.00
93-04	Oregon Trail	2.75
93-05	World University Games	2.75
93-06	Grace Kelly	4.75
93-07	Oklahoma!	2.75
93-08	Circus	4.50
93-09	Thomas Jefferson	3.25
93-10	Cherokee Strip	3.50
93-11	Dean Acheson	3.00
93-12	Sporting Horses	5.50
93-13	USA Coil	3.50
93-14	Garden Flowers, booklet pane (5)	4.25
93-15	Eagle and Shield, coil	4.00
93-16	World War II miniature sheet (10)	5.50
93-17	Futuristic Space Shuttle	6.00
93-18	Hank Williams, sheet	5.00
93-19	Rock & Roll/Rhythm & Blues, sheet single, booklet pane (8)	10.00
93-20	Joe Louis	7.50
93-21	Red Squirrel	3.25
93-22	Broadway Musicals, booklet pane (4)	5.25
93-23	National Postal Museum, strip (4)	3.75
93-24	Rose	3.00
93-25	American Sign Language, pair	3.50
93-26	Country & Western Music, sheet and booklet pane (4)	9.25
93-27	African Violets, booklet pane (10)	4.75
93-28	10¢ Official Mail	2.75
93-29	Contemporary Christmas, booklet pane (10), sheet and self-adhesive stamps	8.50
93-30	Traditional Christmas, sheet, booklet pane (4)	5.50
93-31	Classic Books, strip (4)	4.00
93-32	Mariana Islands	3.25
93-33	Pine Cone	3.00
93-34	Columbus' Landing in Puerto Rico	4.00
93-35	AIDS Awareness	6.00
1994		
94-01	Winter Olympics	5.50
94-02	Edward R. Murrow	3.25
94-03	Love, self-adhesive	3.50
94-04	Dr. Allison Davis	5.25
94-05	29¢ Eagle, self-adhesive	3.50
94-06	Year of the Dog	5.25
94-07	Love, booklet pane (10), single sheet stamp	7.00
94-08	Postage and Mailing Center	5.00
94-09	Buffalo Soldiers	6.50
94-10	Silent Screen Stars	6.75
94-11	Garden Flowers, booklet pane (5)	7.00
94-12	Victory at Saratoga	5.50
94-13	10¢ Tractor Trailer gravure printing	5.00
94-14	World Cup Soccer	7.00
94-15	World Cup Soccer souvenir sheet	7.50
94-16	World War II miniature sheet (10)	5.50
94-17	Love, sheet stamp	4.00
94-18	Statue of Liberty	3.50
94-19	Fishing Boat, reissue	4.25
94-20	Norman Rockwell	9.00
94-21	$9.95 and 29¢ Moon Landing	15.00
94-22	Locomotives (5)	7.00
94-23	George Meany	4.25
94-24	$5.00 Washington/ Jackson	10.00
94-25	Popular Singers (5)	7.50
94-26	James Thurber	5.25
94-27	Jazz Singers/Blues Singers (10)	11.50
94-28	Wonders of the Sea (4)	5.75
94-29	Chinese/Joint Issue (2)	8.00
94-30	Holiday Traditional (10)	10.00
94-31	Holiday Contemporary (4)	8.00
94-32	Holiday, self-adhesive	8.50
94-33	20¢ Virginia Apgar	5.00
94-34	BEP Centennial	15.00
94-35	Year of the Boar	7.50
94-G1	G1 (4) Rate Change	10.00
94-G2	G2 (6) Rate Change	10.00
94-G3	G3 (5) Rate Change	10.00
94-G4	G4 (2) Rate Change	10.00
94-36	Legends of West	12.00
1995		
95-01	Love (2)	10.00
95-02	Florida State	9.00
95-03	Butte (7)	10.00
95-04	Automobile (4)	9.00
95-05	Flag Over Field, self-adhesive	10.00
95-06	Juke Box (2+2)	10.00
95-07	Tail Fin (2+2)	10.00
95-08	Circus Wagon (7)	6.00

No.	Item	Price
95-09	Kids Care (4)	10.00
95-10	Richard Nixon	10.00
95-11	Bessie Coleman	10.00
95-12	Official Mail	10.00
95-13	Kestrel with cent sign	8.00
95-14	Love 1 oz. and 2 oz.	10.00
95-15	Flag Over Porch	10.00
95-16	Recreational Sports (5)	12.00
95-17	POW & MIA	10.00
95-18	Marilyn Monroe	12.00
95-19	Pink Rose	7.00
95-20	Ferry Boat (3)	8.00
95-21	Cog Railway Car (3)	8.00
95-22	Blue Jay (10)	6.00
95-23	Texas Statehood	10.00
95-24	Great Lake Lighthouses (5)	10.00
95-25	Challenger Shuttle	12.00
95-26	United Nations	10.00
95-27	Civil War (front and back)	16.00
95-28	Two Fruits	8.00
95-29	Alice Hamilton	10.00
95-30	Carousel Horses	12.00
95-31	Endeavor Shuttle	24.00
95-32	Alice Paul	10.00
95-33	Women's Suffrage	10.00
95-34	Louis Armstrong	10.00
95-35	World War II	10.00
95-36	Milton Hershey	8.00
95-37	Jazz Musicians	14.00
95-38	Fall Garden Flowers (5)	12.00
95-39	Eddie Rickenbacker (airmail)	10.00
95-40	Republic of Palau	10.00
95-41	Holiday Contemporary/ Santa (4)	12.50
95-42	American Comic Strips	20.00
95-43	Naval Academy	10.00
95-44	Tennessee Williams	10.00
95-45	Holiday Children Sledding	10.00
95-46	Holiday Traditional sheet and booklet pane (10)	12.50
95-47	Holiday Midnight Angel	10.00
95-48	Ruth Bendict	10.00
95-49	James K. Polk	9.00
95-50	Antique Automobiles, strip (5)	14.00
1996		
96-01	Utah Statehood	10.00
96-02	Garden Flowers	12.50
96-03	Love/Kestrel	16.00
96-04	Postage and Mailing Center (3)	5.00
96-05	Ernest E. Just	10.00
96-06	Woodpecker	12.00
96-07	Smithsonian Institution	10.00
96-08	Year of the Rat	10.00
96-09	Pioneers of Communication	14.00
96-10	Fulbright Scholarships	10.00
96-11	Jacqueline Cochran	10.00
96-12	Mountain	10.00
96-13	Bluebird	6.00
96-14	Marathon	6.00
96-15	Flag over Porch/ Eagle & Shield	6.50
96-16	Cal Farley	5.00
96-17	Classic Olympic Collection	8.00
96-18	Georgia O'Keefe Art	6.00
96-19	Tennessee	6.00
96-20	American Indian Dances	9.00
96-21	Prehistoric Animals	9.00
96-22	Breast Cancer Awareness	6.00
96-23	Flag over Porch/ Juke Box/Butte/Tail Fin Automobile/Mountain	9.00
96-24	James Dean	6.00
96-25	Folk Heroes	9.00
96-26	Olympic/Discus	6.00
96-27	Iowa	6.00
96-28	Blue Jay	6.00
96-29	Rural Free Delivery	6.00
96-30	Riverboats	9.00
96-31	Big Band Leaders	9.00
96-32	Songwriters	9.00
96-33	F. Scott Fitzgerald	6.00
96-34	Endangered Species	15.00
96-35	Computer Technology	6.00
96-36	Family Scenes	7.50
96-37	Skaters	6.00
96-38	Hanukkah	6.00
96-39	Madonna and Child	7.50
96-40	Yellow Rose	7.00
96-41	Cycling	10.00
1997		
97-01	Year of the Ox	6.00
97-02	Flag Over Porch/ Juke Box/Mountain	8.00
97-03	Benjamin O. Davis Sr.	6.00
97-04	Statue of Liberty	6.00
97-05	Love Swans	6.00
97-06	Helping Children Learn	6.00
97-07	Merian Botanical Plants	7.50
97-08	Pacific 97 - Stagecoach and Ship	7.50
97-09	Linerless Flag Over Porch/Juke Box	8.00
97-10	Thornton Wilder	6.00
97-11	Raoul Wallenberg	6.00
97-12	Dinosaurs	12.50
97-13	Pacific '97 - Franklin	15.00
97-14	Pacific '97 - Washington	15.00
97-15	Bugs Bunny	6.00
97-16	The Marshall Plan	6.00
97-17	Humphrey Bogart	6.00
97-18	Classic Aircraft	15.00
97-19	Classic American Dolls	15.00
97-20	Football Coaches	7.50
97-20A	George Halas	6.00
97-20B	Vince Lombardi	6.00
97-20C	Pop Warner	6.00
97-20D	Bear Bryant	6.00
97-21	Yellow Rose	7.00
97-22	"Stars and Stripes Forever"	6.00
97-23	Padre Félix Varela	6.00
97-24	Composers and Conductors	10.00
97-25	Opera Singers	10.00
97-26	Air Force	8.00
97-27	Movie Monsters	10.00
97-28	Supersonic Flight	8.00
97-29	Women in Military	6.00
97-30	Kwanzaa	7.50
97-31	Holiday Traditional, Madonna and Child	7.50
97-32	Holly	7.50
97-33	Mars Pathfinder	12.00
1998		
98-01	Year of the Tiger	6.00
98-02	Winter Sports	6.00
98-03	Madam C. J. Walker	6.00
98-03A	Celebrate The Century® 1900s	10.00
98-03B	Celebrate The Century® 1910s	10.00
98-04	Spanish American War	6.00
98-05	Flowering Trees	8.00
98-06	Alexander Calder	8.00
98-07	Henry R. Luce	6.00
98-08	Cinco De Mayo	6.00
98-09	Sylvester & Tweety	6.00
98-09A	Celebrate The Century® 1920s	10.00
98-10	Wisconsin	6.00
98-11	Trans-Mississippi Reissue of 1898	10.00
98-12	Trans-Mississippi (single stamp)	6.00
98-13	Folk Singers	8.00
98-14	Berlin Airlift	6.00
98-15	Diner/Wetlands coil	6.00
98-16	Spanish Settlement of the Southwest	6.00
98-17	Gospel Singers	8.00
98-18	The Wallaces	6.00
98-19	Stephen Vincent Benet	6.00
98-20	Tropical Birds	8.00
98-21	Breast Cancer Research (semi-postal)	6.00
98-22	Ring-Neck Pheasant	7.00
98-23	Alfred Hitchcock	6.00
98-24	Organ Donations	6.00
98-24A	Red Fox	7.50
98-24B	Green Bicycle coil	6.00
98-25	Bright Eyes	7.50
98-26	Klondike Gold Rush	6.00
98-26A	Celebrate The Century® 1930s	10.00
98-27	American Art	10.00
98-28	Ballet	6.00
98-28A	Diner coil	6.00
98-29	Space Fantasy	7.50
98-30	Philanthropy	6.00
98-31	Holiday Traditional	6.00
98-32	Holiday Contemporary	7.50
98-33	Hat Rate Change "H" Series/Makeup Rate	10.00
98-34	Uncle Sam — Rate Change	6.00
98-35	Hat Rate Change "H" Series	10.00
98-36	Hat Rate Change "H" Series	10.00
98-37	Mary Breckinridge	6.00
98-38	Space Shuttle Landing	10.00
98-39	Shuttle Piggyback	20.00
98-40	Wetlands non-denominated nonprofit coil and Eagle & Shield non-denominated presort coil	10.00
1999		
99-01	Year of the Hare	6.00
99-02	Malcolm X	6.00
99-03	33¢ Victorian — Love	6.00
99-04	55¢ Victorian — Love	6.00
99-05	Hospice Care	6.00
99-06	Celebrate The Century® 1940s	10.00
99-07	City Flag	8.00
99-08	Irish Immigration	6.00
99-09	Alfred Lunt and Lynn Fontanne	6.00
99-10	Arctic Animals	8.00
99-10A	Classroom Flag	6.00
99-11	Nature of America Sonoran Desert	10.00
99-11A	Fruit Berries	7.50
99-12	Daffy Duck	6.00
99-13	Ayn Rand	6.00
99-14	Cinco de Mayo	6.00

99-15	Tropical Flowers	7.50
99-16	Niagara Falls	7.50
99-17	John and William Bartram	6.00
99-18	Celebrate The Century® 1950s	10.00
99-19	Prostate Cancer	6.00
99-20	California Gold Rush	6.00
99-20A	Woodpecker Stamp	—
99-21	Aquarium Fish	7.50
99-22	Xtreme Sports	7.50
99-23	American Glass	7.50
99-24	Justin Morrill	6.00
99-25	James Cagney	6.00
99-26	Billy Mitchell	6.00
99-27	Rio Grande	6.00
99-28	Pink Coral Rose	7.00
99-29	Honoring Those Who Served	6.00
99-29A	UPU	6.00
99-30	All Aboard!	7.50
99-31	Frederick Law Olmsted	6.00
99-32	Hollywood Composers	7.50
99-33	Celebrate The Century® 1960s	10.00
99-34	Broadway Songwriters	7.50
99-35	Insects and Spiders	10.00
99-36	Hanukkah	6.00
99-37	Official Mail	6.00
99-38	Uncle Sam	6.00
99-39	Nato	6.00
99-40	Holiday Traditional, Bartolomeo Vivarini	6.00
99-41	Holiday Contemporary, Deer	7.50
99-42	Kwanzaa	6.00
99-43	Celebrate The Century® 1970s	10.00
99-44	Kestrel	7.00
Note:	9945–9949	unassigned
99-50	Year 2000	6.00
	2000	
00-01	Year of the Dragon	6.00
00-02	Celebrate The Century® 1980s	10.00
00-03	Grand Canyon	7.50
00-04	Patricia Roberts Harris	6.00
00-05	Fruit Berries	7.50

00-06	U.S. Navy Submarine – Los Angeles Class	6.00
00-07	Pacific Coast Rain Forest	10.00
00-08	Louise Nevelson	7.50
00-09	Coral Pink Rose	—
00-10	Edwin Powell Hubble	7.50
00-11	American Samoa	6.00
00-12	Library of Congress	6.00
00-13	Wile E. Coyote/ Road Runner	6.00
00-14	Celebrate The Century® 1990s	10.00
00-15	Summer Sports	6.00
00-16	Adoption	6.00
00-17	Youth Team Sports	7.50
00-18	Distinguished Soldiers	—
00-19	The Stars and Stripes	10.00
00-20	Legends of Baseball	10.00
00-21	Stampin' The Future™	7.50
00-22	Joseph Stilwell	6.00
00-23	Claude Pepper	6.00
00-24	California Statehood	6.00
00-25	Edward G. Robinson	6.00
00-26	Deep Sea Creatures	7.50
00-27	Thomas Wolfe	6.00
00-28	White House	6.00
00-29	New York Public Library Lion Presort	6.00
	2001	
0101	Farm Flag (1 oz.)	—
0102	Statute of Liberty	NDN
0103	Flowers	—
0104	Statute of Liberty	—
0105	Love Letters (1 oz.)	—
0106	Year of the Snake	—
0107	Roy Wilkins	—
0108	Washington Monument	—
0109	U.S. Capitol	—
0110	American Illustrators (front & back)	—
0111	Farm Flag (1 oz.)	—
0112	Statute of Liberty	—
0113	Flowers	—
0114	Love Letters (1 oz. & 2 oz.)	—
0115	Hattie Caraway (3 oz.)	—
0116	Bison (2 oz.)	—
0117	George Washington	—
0118	Art Deco Eagle (2 oz.)	—
0119	Official Mail	—
0120	Apple and Orange	—

0121	Nine-Mile Prairie	—
0122	Farm Flag (1 oz.)	—
0123	Diabetes Awareness	—
0124	The Nobel Prize	—
0125	The Pan-American Inverts (front and back)	—
0126	Mt. McKinley (Int'l PC)	—
0127	Great Plains Prairie (front and back)	—
0128	Peanuts	—
0129	Honoring Veterans	—
0130	Acadia National Park	—
0131	Frida Kahlo	—
0132	Baseball's Legendary Playing Fields (front and back)	—
0133	Atlas Statue	—
0134	Leonard Bernstein	—
0135	Woody Wagon	—
0136	Lucille Ball	—
0137	The Amish Quilts	—
0138	Carnivorous Plants	—
0139	Holiday Celebration–Eid	—
0140	Dr. Enrico Fermi	—
0141	Bison (2 oz.)	—
0142	George Washington	—
0143	Art Deco Eagle (2 oz.)	—
0144	"That's All Folks!"	—
0145	Holiday Traditional: Lorenza Costa– Virgin and Child	—
0146	Holiday Contemporary: Santas	—
0147	Holiday Celebration: Thanksgiving	—
0148	James Madison	—
0149	Kwanzaa	—
0150	Hanukkah	—
0151	Farm Flag (1 oz.)	—
0152	Love Letters (2 oz.)	—
0153	United We Stand	—

Note: Numbers and prices may be changed without notice due to additional USPS stamp issues and/or different information that may become available on older issues.

American Commemorative Panels

The Postal Service offers American Commemorative Panels for each
new commemorative stamp and special Holiday and Love stamp issued.
The series began in 1972 with the Wildlife Commemorative Panel.
The panels feature mint stamps complemented by fine reproductions of
steel line engravings and the stories behind the commemorated subjects.

The identifying numbers used below are based on the Postal Service's
numbering system for American Commemorative Panels; therefore, they
do not follow the Scott numbering system.

1972

1	Wildlife	5.00
2	Mail Order	4.75
3	Osteopathic Medicine	5.75
4	Tom Sawyer	4.50
5	Pharmacy	6.00
6	Christmas, Angels	8.00
7	Christmas, Santa Claus	8.00
7E	Same with error date (1882)	—
8	Stamp Collecting	5.50

1973

9	Love	6.75
10	Pamphleteers	5.50
11	George Gershwin	6.00
12	Posting a Broadside	5.50
13	Copernicus	5.50
14	Postal People	5.25
15	Harry S. Truman	6.50
16	Post Rider	5.00
17	Boston Tea Party	15.00
18	Electronics	5.50
19	Robinson Jeffers	4.75
20	Lyndon B. Johnson	5.00
21	Henry O. Tanner	5.50
22	Willa Cather	5.00
23	Drummer	8.25
24	Angus Cattle	5.50
25	Christmas, Madonna	7.75
26	Christmas Tree, Needlepoint	7.75

1974

27	VFW	5.25
28	Robert Frost	5.25
29	Expo '74	6.00
30	Horse Racing	7.00
31	Skylab	7.50
32	Universal Postal Union	6.00
33	Mineral Heritage	5.00
34	First Kentucky Settlement	5.25

35	Continental Congress	7.00
35A	Same with corrected logo	—
36	Chautauqua	5.75
37	Kansas Wheat	5.75
38	Energy Conservation	5.25
39	Sleepy Hollow	5.75
40	Retarded Children	5.00
41	Christmas, Currier & Ives	8.00
42	Christmas, Angel Altarpiece	8.00

1975

43	Benjamin West	5.50
44	Pioneer	8.50
45	Collective Bargaining	5.25
46	Contributors to the Cause	5.50
47	Mariner 10	6.50
48	Lexington & Concord	5.50
49	Paul Laurence Dunbar	6.00
50	D.W. Griffith	5.75
51	Bunker Hill	5.75
52	Military Uniforms	5.00
53	Apollo Soyuz	8.25
54	World Peace Through Law	5.00
54A	Same with August 15, 1975 date	—
55	Women's Year	5.75
56	Postal Service Bicentennial	6.00
57	Banking and Commerce	6.25
58	Early Christmas, Card	7.00
59	Christmas, Madonna	7.00

1976

60	Spirit of '76	8.00
61	Interphil 76	7.00
62	State Flags	15.00

63	Telephone	6.75
64	Commercial Aviation	9.25
65	Chemistry	7.00
66	Benjamin Franklin	7.00
67	Declaration of Independence	7.50
68	12th Winter Olympics	7.50
69	Clara Maass	7.00
70	Adolph S. Ochs	7.50
70A	Same with charter logo	—
71	Christmas, Winter Pastime	8.00
71A	Same with charter logo	—
72	Christmas, Nativity	8.75
72A	Same with charter logo	—

1977

73	Washington at Princeton	9.00
73A	Same with charter logo	—
74	Sound Recording	16.00
74A	Same with charter logo	—
75	Pueblo Art	45.00
75A	Same with charter logo	—
76	Solo Transatlantic Lindbergh Flight	50.00
77	Colorado Statehood	12.00
78	Butterflies	12.00
79	Lafayette	11.00
80	Skilled Hands	12.00
81	Peace Bridge	11.00
82	Battle of Oriskany	12.00
83	Alta, CA, Civil Settlement	12.00
84	Articles of Confederation	15.00
85	Talking Pictures	13.50
86	Surrender at Saratoga	15.00
87	Energy	12.00

#	Item	Price
88	Christmas, Valley Forge	14.00
89	Christmas, Mailbox	25.00

1978

#	Item	Price
90	Carl Sandburg	7.00
91	Captain Cook	14.00
92	Harriet Tubman	8.50
93	Quilts	15.00
94	Dance	10.00
95	French Alliance	10.00
96	Early Cancer Detection	8.25
97	Jimmie Rodgers	11.00
98	Photography	8.00
99	George M. Cohan	12.50
100	Viking Missions	26.00
101	Owls	26.00
102	Trees	26.00
103	Christmas, Madonna	10.50
104	Christmas, Hobby Horse	10.50

1979

#	Item	Price
105	Robert F. Kennedy	7.25
106	Martin Luther King, Jr.	7.50
107	International Year of the Child	6.75
108	John Steinbeck	6.75
109	Albert Einstein	7.25
110	Pennsylvania Toleware	6.75
111	Architecture	6.50
112	Endangered Flora	8.00
113	Seeing Eye Dogs	8.00
114	Special Olympics	8.00
115	John Paul Jones	8.25
116	15¢ Olympics	9.50
117	Christmas, Madonna	9.50
118	Christmas, Santa Claus	9.50
119	Will Rogers	7.00
120	Vietnam Veterans	9.50
121	10¢, 31¢ Olympics	9.00

1980

#	Item	Price
122	W.C. Fields	7.50
123	Winter Olympics	7.50
124	Benjamin Banneker	8.50
125	Frances Perkins	6.00
126	Emily Bissell	6.00
127	Helen Keller/ Anne Sullivan	6.00
128	Veterans Administration	6.00
129	General Bernardo de Galvez	6.00
130	Coral Reefs	8.00
131	Organized Labor	6.00
132	Edith Wharton	5.50
133	Education	6.00
134	Indian Masks	7.50
135	Architecture	6.75
136	Christmas, Epiphany Window	8.00
137	Christmas, Toys	8.00

1981

#	Item	Price
138	Everett Dirksen	7.00
139	Whitney Moore Young	7.00
140	Flowers	7.50
141	Red Cross	7.00
142	Savings & Loans	6.75
143	Space Achievement	10.00
144	Professional Management	6.75
145	Wildlife Habitats	9.00
146	Int'l. Year of Disabled Persons	6.25
147	Edna St. Vincent Millay	6.25
148	Architecture	6.50
149	Babe Zaharias/ Bobby Jones	20.00
150	James Hoban	6.75
151	Frederic Remington	6.75
152	Battle of Yorktown/ Virginia Capes	6.75
153	Christmas, Madonna	8.00
154	Christmas, Bear and Sleigh	8.00
155	John Hanson	6.50
156	U.S. Desert Plants	8.00

1982

#	Item	Price
157	Roosevelt	8.25
158	Love	10.00
159	George Washington	9.50
160	State Birds & Flowers	17.00
161	U.S./ Netherlands	10.00
162	Library of Congress	10.50
163	Knoxville World's Fair	9.00
164	Horatio Alger	8.75
165	Aging Together	10.00
166	The Barrymores	12.00
167	Dr. Mary Walker	9.00
168	Peace Garden	10.00
169	America's Libraries	9.00
170	Jackie Robinson	24.00
171	Touro Synagogue	10.50
172	Architecture	12.00
173	Wolf Trap Farm Park	10.00
174	Francis of Assisi	11.00
175	Ponce de Leon	11.00
176	Christmas, Madonna	14.00
177	Christmas, Season's Greetings	14.00
178	Kitten & Puppy	14.00

1983

#	Item	Price
179	Science and Industry	5.25
180	Sweden/ USA Treaty	5.75
181	Balloons	6.00
182	Civilian Conservation Corps	5.25
183	40¢ Olympics	6.50
184	Joseph Priestley	5.25
185	Voluntarism	5.25
186	Concord/German Immigration	5.25
187	Physical Fitness	5.75
188	Brooklyn Bridge	6.00
189	TVA	5.25
190	Medal of Honor	6.50
191	Scott Joplin	7.50
192	28¢ Olympics	6.50
193	Babe Ruth	17.50
194	Nathaniel Hawthorne	5.25
195	13¢ Olympics	8.00
196	Treaty of Paris	5.50
197	Civil Service	5.00
198	Metropolitan Opera	6.50
199	Inventors	6.75
200	Streetcars	7.50
201	Christmas, Madonna	8.00
202	Christmas, Santa Claus	8.00
203	35¢ Olympics	8.00
204	Martin Luther	7.00

1984

#	Item	Price
205	Alaska Statehood	4.50
206	Winter Olympics	5.00
207	FDIC	4.75
208	Love	4.00
209	Carter G. Woodson	6.75
210	Soil and Water Conservation	4.75
211	Credit Union Act	4.75
212	Orchids	6.00
213	Hawaii Statehood	6.25
214	National Archives	4.50
215	20¢ Olympics	5.50
216	Louisiana World Exposition	5.00
217	Health Research	4.75
218	Douglas Fairbanks	4.75
219	Jim Thorpe	8.25
220	John McCormack	4.75
221	St. Lawrence Seaway	6.25
222	Preserving Wetlands	7.50
223	Roanoke Voyages	4.75
224	Herman Melville	4.75
225	Horace Moses	4.75
226	Smokey Bear	10.00
227	Roberto Clemente	20.00
228	Dogs	6.25
229	Crime Prevention	5.25
230	Family Unity	4.75
231	Christmas, Madonna	6.75
232	Christmas, Santa Claus	6.75
233	Eleanor Roosevelt	7.50
234	Nation of Readers	4.75
235	Hispanic Americans	4.50
236	Vietnam Veterans Memorial	8.25

1985

237	Jerome Kern	5.75
238	Mary McLeod Bethune	5.75
239	Duck Decoys	7.25
240	Winter Special Olympics	5.00
241	Love	5.00
242	Rural Electrification Administration	5.00
243	AMERIPEX '86	6.75
244	Abigail Adams	4.75
245	Frederic Auguste Bartholdi	6.50
246	Korean War Veterans	5.50
247	Social Security Act	5.00
248	World War I Veterans	5.00
249	Horses	9.00
250	Public Education	4.50
251	Youth	6.75
252	Help End Hunger	5.00
253	Christmas, Madonna	7.00
254	Christmas, Poinsettias	7.00

1986

255	Arkansas Statehood	5.25
256	Stamp Collecting Booklet	6.75
257	Love	6.00
258	Sojourner Truth	7.50
259	Republic of Texas	6.25
260	Fish Booklet	6.75
261	Public Hospitals	4.75
262	Duke Ellington	7.50
263	U.S. Presidents' Sheet #1	6.25
264	U.S. Presidents' Sheet #2	6.25
265	U.S. Presidents' Sheet #3	6.25
266	U.S. Presidents' Sheet #4	6.25
267	Polar Explorers	6.75
268	Statue of Liberty	7.50
269	Navajo Blankets	7.50
270	T.S. Eliot	6.25
271	Wood-Carved Figurines	6.75
272	Christmas, Madonna	5.75
273	Christmas, Village Scene	5.75

1987

274	Michigan Statehood	5.75
275	Pan American Games	3.50
276	Love	7.00
277	Jean Baptiste Pointe Du Sable	5.00
278	Enrico Caruso	5.50
279	Girl Scouts	4.00
280	Special Occasions Booklet	6.00

281	United Way	4.75
282	#1 American Wildlife	6.50
283	#2 American Wildlife	6.50
284	#3 American Wildlife	6.50
285	#4 American Wildlife	6.50
286	#5 American Wildlife	6.50
287	Delaware Statehood	5.75
288	Morocco/U.S. Diplomatic Relations	4.75
289	William Faulkner	4.75
290	Lacemaking	5.50
291	Pennsylvania Statehood	5.25
292	Constitution Booklet	5.00
293	New Jersey Statehood	5.25
294	Signing of the Constitution	4.75
295	Certified Public Accountants	10.00
296	Locomotives Booklet	5.75
297	Christmas, Madonna	6.25
298	Christmas, Ornaments	5.75

1988

299	Georgia Statehood	5.25
300	Connecticut Statehood	5.25
301	Winter Olympics	6.25
302	Australia	5.75
303	James Weldon Johnson	5.00
304	Cats	6.50
305	Massachusetts Statehood	5.25
306	Maryland Statehood	5.25
307	Knute Rockne	9.00
308	New Sweden	5.75
309	South Carolina Statehood	5.00
310	Francis Ouimet	14.00
311	New Hampshire Statehood	5.25
312	Virginia Statehood	5.25
313	Love	7.00
314	New York Statehood	6.25
315	Summer Olympics	6.25
316	Classic Cars Booklet	6.75
317	Antarctic Explorers	6.25
318	Carousel Animals	6.75
319	Christmas, Madonna, Sleigh	6.75
320	Special Occasions Booklet	6.75

1989

321	Montana Statehood	6.25
322	A. Philip Randolph	8.75
323	North Dakota Statehood	6.25
324	Washington Statehood	6.25
325	Steamboats Booklet	7.50
326	World Stamp Expo '89	5.50
327	Arturo Toscanini	6.25
328	U.S. House of Representatives	7.25
329	U.S. Senate	7.25
330	Executive Branch	7.25
331	South Dakota Statehood	6.25
332	Lou Gehrig	20.00
333	French Revolution	7.50
334	Ernest Hemingway	7.25
335	North Carolina Statehood	6.25
336	Letter Carriers	7.25
337	Drafting of the Bill of Rights	7.25
338	Prehistoric Animals	13.50
339	25¢ and 45¢ America/PUAS	7.25
340	Christmas, Traditional and Contemporary	8.50
341	Classic Mail Transportation	7.25
342	Future Mail Transportation	8.00

1990

343	Idaho Statehood	7.25
344	Love	7.25
345	Ida B. Wells	11.00
346	U.S. Supreme Court	7.25
347	Wyoming Statehood	6.25
348	Classic Films	11.50
349	Marianne Moore	6.25
350	Lighthouses Booklet	10.00
351	Rhode Island Statehood	5.50
352	Olympians	8.50
353	Indian Headdresses Booklet	10.00
354	Micronesia/ Marshall Islands	7.00
355	25¢ and 45¢ America/PUAS	7.50
356	Eisenhower	8.25
357	Creatures of the Sea	11.50
358	Christmas, Traditional and Contemporary	8.50

1991

359	Switzerland	8.75
360	Vermont Statehood	7.25
361	Savings Bonds	6.25
362	29¢ and 52¢ Love	8.00
363	Saroyan	6.50
364	Fishing Flies Booklet	10.00
365	Cole Porter	6.00
366	Antarctic Treaty	8.00
367	Desert Shield/ Desert Storm	20.00
368	Summer Olympics	7.00
369	Numismatics	6.50
370	Basketball	12.50
371	World War II Miniature Sheet	12.00
372	Comedians Booklet	9.50
373	District of Columbia	7.00
374	Jan Matzeliger	7.50
375	Space Exploration Booklet	11.50
376	America/PUAS	8.00
377	Christmas, Traditional and Contemporary	9.50

1992

378	Winter Olympics	7.50
379	World Columbian Stamp Expo '92	8.75
380	W.E.B. Du Bois	10.00
381	Love	8.75
382	Olympic Baseball	25.00
383	Columbus' First Voyage	10.00
384	Space Adventures	10.00
385	New York Stock Exchange	11.00
386	Alaska Highway	8.00
387	Kentucky Statehood	6.50
388	Summer Olympics	8.00
389	Hummingbirds Booklet	10.00
390	World War II Miniature Sheet	10.00
391	Dorothy Parker	6.50
392	Theodore von Karman	9.00
393	Minerals	9.50
394	Juan Rodriguez Cabrillo	9.00
395	Wild Animals Booklet	10.00
396	Christmas, Traditional and Contemporary	9.25
397	Columbus Souvenir Sheets	40.00
398	Columbus Souvenir Sheets	40.00
399	Columbus Souvenir Sheets	40.00
400	Wildflowers #1	20.00
401	Wildflowers #2	20.00
402	Wildflowers #3	20.00
403	Wildflowers #4	20.00
404	Wildflowers #5	20.00
405	Happy New Year	15.00

1993

406	Elvis	20.00
407	Space Fantasy	11.00
408	Percy Julian	10.00
409	Oregon Trail	9.00
410	World Univ. Games	9.00
411	Grace Kelly	13.00
412	Oklahoma!	8.50
413	Circus	9.00
414	Cherokee Strip	8.50
415	Dean Acheson	10.50
416	Sport Horses	10.00
417	Garden Flowers	8.50
418	World War II	12.00
419	Hank Williams	15.00
420	Rock & Roll/R&B	20.00
421	Joe Louis	20.00
422	Broadway Musicals	11.00
423	National Postal Museum	9.00
424	Deaf Communication	9.00
425	Country Western	15.00
426	Christmas, Traditional	10.00
427	Youth Classics	10.00
428	Mariana Islands	9.00
429	Columbus Landing In Puerto Rico	10.50
430	AIDS Awareness	10.00

1994

431	Winter Olympics	12.00
432	Edward R. Murrow	9.00
433	Dr. Allison Davis	10.00
434	Year of the Dog	14.00
435	Love	9.50
436	Buffalo Soldiers	13.00
437	Silent ScreenStars	14.00
438	Garden Flowers	11.00
439	World Cup Soccer	12.50
440	World War II	15.00
441	Norman Rockwell	13.00
442	Moon Landing	16.00
443	Locomotives	12.00
444	George Meany	8.00
445	Popular Singers	12.50
446	James Thurber	8.00
447	Jazz/Blues	15.00
448	Wonders of the Sea	11.00
449	Birds (Cranes)	11.00
450	Christmas, Madonna	8.00
451	Christmas, Stocking	8.00
452	Year of the Boar	13.00

1995

453	Florida Statehood	10.00
454	Bessie Coleman	15.00
455	Kids Care!	10.00
456	Richard Nixon	15.00
457	Love	15.00
458	Recreational Sports	15.00
459	POW & MIA	12.50
460	Marilyn Monroe	20.00
461	Texas Statehood	12.50
462	Great Lakes Lighthouses	14.00
463	United Nations	11.00
464	Carousel Horses	15.00
465	Jazz Musicians	17.50
466	Women's Suffrage	11.00
467	Louis Armstrong	15.00
468	World War II	15.00
469	Fall Garden Flowers	11.00
470	Republic of Palau	11.00
471	Christmas, Contemporary	15.00
472	Naval Academy	15.00
473	Tennessee Williams	12.50
474	Christmas, Traditional	15.00
475	James K. Polk	12.50
476	Antique Automobiles	17.50

1996

477	Utah Statehood	10.00
478	Winter Garden Flowers	10.00
479	Ernest E. Just	12.50
480	Smithsonian Institution	10.00
481	Year of the Rat	17.50
482	Pioneers of Communication	14.00
483	Fulbright Scholarships	10.00
484	Olympics	30.00
485	Marathon	15.00
486	Georgia O'Keefe	10.00
487	Tennessee Statehood	10.00
488	James Dean	17.50
489	Prehistoric Animals	17.50
490	Breast Cancer Awareness	11.00
491	American Indian Dances	17.50
492	Folk Heroes	17.50
493	Centennial Games (Discus)	12.50
494	Iowa Statehood	10.00
495	Rural Free Delivery	10.00
496	Riverboats	17.50
497	Big Band Leaders	17.50
498	Songwriters	17.50
499	Endangered Species	30.00
500	Family Scenes (4 designs)	15.00
501	Hanukkah	12.50
502	Madonna and Child	15.00
503	Cycling	15.00
503A	F. Scott Fitzgerald	15.00
503B	Computer Technology	15.00

1997

504	Year of the Ox	15.00
505	Benjamin O. Davis	14.00
506	Love	12.50
507	Helping Children Learn	11.00
508	Pacific 97 Triangle Stamps	17.50
509	Thornton Wilder	12.00
510	Raoul Wallenberg	12.00
511	Dinosaurs	20.00
512	Bugs Bunny	16.00
513	Pacific 97 Franklin	40.00
514	Pacific 97 Washington	40.00
515	The Marshall Plan	11.00
516	Classic Aircraft	30.00
517	Football Coaches	17.50
518	Dolls	18.00
519	Humphrey Bogart	15.00
520	Stars and Stripes	14.00
521	Opera Singers	15.00
522	Composers and Conductors	15.00
523	Padre Varela	14.00
524	Air Force	13.50
525	Movie Monsters	17.50
526	Supersonic Flight	15.00
527	Women in the Military	14.00
528	Holiday Kwanzaa	15.00
529	Holiday, Traditional	20.00
530	Holiday Holly	22.50

1998

531	Year of the Tiger	13.50
532	Winter Sports	14.00
533	Madam C.J. Walker	14.00
533A	Celebrate The Century® 1900s	22.50
533B	Celebrate The Century® 1910s	22.50
534	Spanish American War	14.00
535	Flowering Trees	16.00
536	Alexander Calder	16.00
537	Cinco de Mayo	14.00
538	Sylvester & Tweety	15.00
538A	Celebrate The Century® 1920s	22.50
539	Wisconsin Statehood	14.00
540	Trans-Mississippi	20.00
541	Folk Singers	14.00
542	Berlin Airlift	14.00
543	Spanish Settlement of the Southwest	14.00
544	Gospel Singers	14.00
545	Stephen Vincent Benet	15.00
546	Tropical Birds	15.00
546A	Breast Cancer Research	15.00
547	Alfred Hitchcock	15.00
548	Organ Donations	15.00
549	Bright Eyes	16.00

550	Klondike Gold Rush	15.00
551	American Art	20.00
551A	Celebrate The Century® 1930s	22.50
552	Ballet	15.00
553	Space Discovery	15.00
554	Philanthropy	15.00
555	Holiday, Traditional	18.00
556	Holiday, Contemporary	15.00

1999

557	Year of the Hare	15.00
558	Malcolm X	15.00
559	33¢ Victorian - Love	20.00
560	55¢ Victorian - Love	15.00
561	Hospice Care	15.00
562	Celebrate The Century® 1940s	22.50
563	Irish Immigration	15.00
564	Alfred Lunt and Lynn Fontanne	15.00
565	Arctic Animals	15.00
566	Nature of America Sonoran Desert	22.50
567	Daffy Duck	22.50
568	Ayn Rand	15.00
569	Cinco de Mayo	15.00
570	John and William Bartram	15.00
571	Celebrate The Century® 1950s	22.50
572	Prostate Cancer	15.00
573	California Gold Rush	15.00
574	Aquarium Fish	15.00
575	Xtreme Sports	15.00
576	American Glass	16.00
577	James Cagney	15.00
578	Honoring Those Who Served	15.00
579	All Aboard!	16.00
580	Frederick Law Olmsted	15.00
581	Hollywood Composers	16.00
582	Celebrate The Century® 1960s	22.50
583	Broadway Songwriters	16.00
584	Insects and Spiders	22.50
585	Hanukkah	15.00
586	Nato	15.00
587	Holiday Traditional, Bartolomeo Vivarini	15.00
588	Holiday Contemporary, Deer	15.00
589	Kwanzaa	15.00
590	Celebrate The Century® 1970s	22.50
591	Year 2000	16.00

2000

592	Year of the Dragon	15.00
593	Celebrate The Century® 1980s	22.50
594	Patricia Roberts Harris	15.00
595	U.S. Navy Submarines – Los Angeles Class	10.00
596	Pacific Coast Rain Forest	25.00
597	Louise Nevelson	10.00
598	Edwin Powell Hubble	10.00
599	American Samoa	10.00
600	Library of Congress	10.00
601	Wile E. Coyote/ Road Runner	10.00
602	Celebrate The Century® 1990s	22.50
603	Summer Sports	10.00
604	Adoption	10.00
605	Youth Team Sports	10.00
606	Distinguished Soldiers	10.00
607	The Stars and Stripes	25.00
608	Legends of Baseball	25.00
609	Stampin' The Future™	10.00
610	Edward G. Robinson	10.00
611	California Statehood	10.00
612	Deep Sea Creatures	10.00
613	Thomas Wolfe	10.00
614	The White House	10.00

2001

615	Love Letters
616	Lunar New Year— Year of the Snake
617	Roy Wilkins
618	American Illustrators
619	Love Letters (1 oz)
620	Love Letters (2 oz)
621	Nine-Mile Prairie
622	Diabetes Awareness
623	The Nobel Prize
624	Mt. McKinley
625	The Pan-American Inverts
626	Great Plains Prairie
627	Peanuts
628	Honoring Veterans
629	Frida Kahlo
630	Baseball's Legendary Playing Fields
631	Leonard Bernstein
632	Lucille Ball
633	The Amish Quilts
634	Carnivorous Plants
635	Holiday Celebration: EID
636	Dr. Enrico Fermi
637	That's All Folks!
638	Holiday Traditional: Lorenzo Costa's Virgin and Child
639	Holiday Contemporary: Santas
640	James Madison
641	Holiday Celebration: Thanksgiving
642	Kwanzas
643	Hanukkah
644	Love Letters

Glossary

Accessories
The tools used by stamp collectors, such as tongs, hinges, etc.

Aerophilately
Stamp collecting that focuses on stamps or postage relating to airmail.

Airmail
Mail which has been transported by air, as distinct from "surface" mail. Most long-distance mail is now transported by air; in the U.S., the distinction (and premium) for domestic airmail ceased in the late 1970s, and for foreign mail in the mid-1990s (now generically called "international rate").

Album
A book designed to hold stamps and covers.

Approvals
Stamps sent by a dealer to a collector for examination. Approvals must either be bought or returned to the dealer within a specified time.

Auction
A sale at which philatelic material is sold to the highest bidder.

Block
An unseparated group of stamps, at least two stamps high and two stamps wide.

Bogus
A completely fictitious, worthless "stamp," created only for sale to collectors. Bogus stamps include labels for nonexistent values added to regularly issued sets, issues for nations without postal systems, etc.

Booklet Pane
A small sheet of stamps specially cut to be sold in booklets.

Bourse
A marketplace, such as a stamp exhibition, where stamps are bought, sold or exchanged.

Cachet (ka-shay')
A design on an envelope describing an event. Cachets appear on first day of issue, first flight and stamp exhibition covers, etc.

Cancellation
A mark placed on a stamp by a postal authority to show that it has been used.

Centering
The position of the design on a postage stamp. On perfectly centered stamps the design is exactly in the middle.

Cinderella
Any stamp-like label without an official postal value.

Classic
An early stamp issue. Most people consider these to be rare stamps, but classic stamps aren't necessarily rare.

Coils
Stamps issued in rolls (one stamp wide) for use in dispensers or vending machines.

Commemoratives
Stamps that honor anniversaries, important people, special events or aspects of national culture.

Compound Perforations
Different gauge perforations on different (normally adjacent) sides of a single stamp.

Condition
Condition is the most important characteristic in determining the value of a stamp. It refers to the state of a stamp regarding such details as centering, color and gum.

Cover
An envelope that has been sent through the mail.

Cracked Plate
A term used to describe stamps which show evidence that the plate from which they were printed was cracked.

Definitives
Regular issues of postage stamps, usually sold over long periods of time.

Denomination
The postage value appearing on a stamp, such as 5 cents.

Die Cut
Scoring of self-adhesive stamps that allows stamp separation from liner.

Directory Markings
Postal markings that indicate a failed delivery attempt, stating reasons such as "No Such Number" or "Address Unknown."

Double Transfer
The condition on a printing plate that shows evidence of a duplication of all or part of the design.

Duplicates
Extra copies of stamps that can be sold or traded. Duplicates should be examined carefully for color and perforation variations.

Entire
An intact piece of postal stationery, in contrast to a cut-out of the printed design.

Error
A stamp with some-thing incorrect in its design or manufacture.

Exploded (booklet)
A stamp booklet that has been separated into its various components for display.

Face Value
The monetary value or denomination of a stamp.

Fake
A genuine stamp that has been altered in some way to make it more attractive to collectors. It may be repaired, reperfed or regummed to resemble a more valuable variety.

First Day Cover (FDC)
An envelope with a new stamp and cancellation showing the date the stamp was issued.

Foreign Entry
When original transfers are erased incompletely from a plate, they can appear with new transfers of a different design which are subsequently entered on the plate.

Franks
Marking on the face of a cover, indicating it is to be carried free of postage. Franks may be written, hand-stamped, imprinted or represented by special adhesives. Such free franking is usually limited to official correspondence, such as the President's mail.

Freak
An abnormal variety of stamps occurring because of paper fold, over-inking, perforation shift, etc., as opposed to a continually appearing variety or a major error.

Grill
A pattern of small, square pyramids in parallel rows impressed or embossed on the stamp to break paper fibers, allowing cancellation ink to soak in and preventing washing and reuse.

Gum
The coating of glue on the back of an unused stamp.

Hinges
Small strips of gummed material used by collectors to affix stamps to album pages.

Imperforate
Indicates stamps without perforations or separating holes. They usually are separated by scissors and collected in pairs.

Label
Any stamp-like adhesive that is not a postage stamp.

Laid Paper
When held to the light, the paper shows alternate light and dark crossed lines.

Line Pairs (LP)
Most coil stamp rolls prior to 1981 freature a line of ink (known as a "joint line") printed between two stamps at various intervals, caused by the joining of two or more curved plates around the printing cylinder.

Liner
The backing paper for self-adhesive stamps.

Linerless Coil
Self-adhesive roll of coil stamps without a liner.

Miniature Sheet
A single stamp or block of stamps with a margin on all sides bearing some special wording or design.

On Paper
Stamps "on paper" are those that still have portions of the original envelope or wrapper stuck to them.

Overprint
Additional printing on a stamp that was not part of the original design.

Packet
A presorted unit of all different stamps. One of the most common and economical ways to begin a collection.

Pane
A full "sheet" of stamps as sold by a Post Office. Four panes typically make up the original sheet of stamps as printed.

Par Avion
French for mail transported "by air."

Perforations
Lines of small holes or cuts between rows of stamps that make them easy to separate.

Philately
The collection and study of postage stamps and other postal materials.

Pictorials
Stamps with a picture of some sort, other than portraits or static designs such as coats of arms.

Plate Block (PB) (or Plate Number Block)
A block of stamps with the margin attached that bears the plate number used in printing that sheet.

Plate Number Coils (PNC)
For most coil stamp rolls beginning with #1891, a small plate number appears at varying intervals in the roll in the design of the stamp.

Postage Due
A stamp issued to collect unpaid postage.

Postal Stationery
Envelopes, postal cards and aerogrammes with stamp designs printed or embossed on them.

Postal Cards
See "stamped cards."

Postcards
Commercially-produced mailable cards, but without imprinted postage (postage must be affixed).

Postmark
A mark put on envelopes or other mailing pieces showing the date and location of the post office where it was mailed.

Precancels
Cancellations applied to stamps before the stamps were affixed to mail.

Presort Stamp
A discounted stamp used by qualified mailers who presort mail.

Registered Mail
First-Class mail with a numbered receipt, including a valuation of the registered item. This guarantees customers will get their money back if an item is lost in the mail.

Reissue
An official reprinting of a stamp that was no longer being printed.

Replicas
Reproductions of stamps sold during the early days of collecting. Usually printed in one color on a sheet containing a number of different designs. Replicas were never intended to deceive either the post office or the collector.

Reprint
A stamp printed from the original plate after the issue is no longer valid for postage. Official reprints are sometimes made for presentation purposes, official collections, etc., and are often distinguished in some way from the "real" ones.

Revenue Stamps
Stamps not valid for postal use but issued for collecting taxes.

Ribbed Paper
Paper which shows fine parallel ridges on one or both sides of a stamp.

Rouletting
The piercing of the paper between stamps to facilitate their separation. No paper is actually removed from the sheet, as is the case in the punching method used in most perforating. Instead, rouletting often gives the appearance of a series of dashes.

Se-tenant
An attached pair, strip or block of stamps that differ in design, value or surcharge.

Secret Marks
Many stamps have included tiny reference points in their designs to foil attempts at counterfeiting and to differentiate issues.

Self-Adhesive Stamp
A stamp with a pressure sensitive adhesive.

Selvage
The unprinted paper around panes of stamps, sometimes called the margin.

Series

A number of individual stamps or sets of stamps having a common purpose or theme, issued over an extended period of time (generally a year or more), including all variations of design and/or denomination.

Set

A group of stamps with a common design or theme issued at one time for a common purpose or over a limited perid of time (generally less than a year).

Souvenir Sheet

A small sheet of stamps with a commemorative inscription of some sort.

Special Issues

Stamps which supplement definitives, while meeting specific needs and having a more commemorative appearance. These include Christmas, Love, Holiday Celebration, airmail, international rate, Express Mail and Priority Mail stamps.

Speculative

A stamp or issue released primarily for sale to collectors, rather than to meet any legitimate postal need.

Stamped Cards

The current term for postal cards, which are mailable cards with postage imprinted directly on them.

Stamped Envelopes

Mailable envelopes with postage embossed and/or imprinted on them.

Strip

Three or more unseparated stamps in a row.

Surcharge

An overprint that changes the denomination of a stamp from its original face value.

Sweatbox

A closed box with a grill over which stuck-together unused stamps are placed. A wet, sponge-like material under the grill creates humidity so the stamps can be separated without removing the gum.

Tagging

The marking of stamps with a phosphor or similar coating (which may be in lines, bars, letters, overall design area or entire stamp surface), done by many countries for use with automatic mail-handling equipment. When a stamp is issued both with and without this marking, catalogs will often note varieties as "tagged" or "untagged."

Thematic

A stamp collection that relates to a specific theme and is arranged to present a logical story and progression.

Tied On

Indicates a stamp whose postmark touches the envelope.

Tongs

A tool, used to handle stamps, that resembles a tweezers with rounded or flattened tips.

Topicals

Indicates a group of stamps with the same theme—space travel, for example.

Unhinged

A stamp without hinge marks, but not necessarily with original gum.

Unused

The condition of a stamp that has no cancellation or other sign of use.

Used

The condition of a stamp that has been canceled.

Variety

A stamp which varies in some way from its standard or original form. Varieties can include missing colors or perforations, constant plate flaws, changes in ink or paper, differences in printing method or in format, such as booklet and coil "varieties" of the same stamp.

Want List

A list of philatelic material needed by a collector.

Watermark

A design pressed into stamp paper during its manufacture. Water Activated Gum Water soluable adhesives such as sugar based starches on back of unused stamps.

Water Activated Gum

Water soluable adhesives such as sugar based starches on back of unused stamps.

Wove Paper

A uniform paper which, when held to the light, shows no light or dark figures.

Organizations

Please enclose a stamped, self-addressed envelope when writing to these organizations.

American Air Mail Society

Rudy Roy
P.O. Box 5367
Virginia Beach, VA 23471-0367
(p) 757/499-5234
AAMSinformation@aol.com
http://ourworld.compuserve.com/homepages/aams/

Specializes in all phases of aerophilately. Membership services include Advance Bulletin Service, Auction Service, free want ads, Sales Department, monthly journal, discounts on Society publications, translation service.

American First Day Cover Society

Douglas Kelsey
Executive Director
P.O. Box 65960
Tucson, AZ 85728-5960
(p) 520/321-0880
520/321-0879
AFDCS@aol.com
http://www.afdcs.org

A full-service, not-for-profit, noncommercial society devoted exclusively to First Day Covers and First Day Cover collecting. Publishes 90-page magazine, First Day, eight times a year. Offers information on 300 current cachet producers, expertizing, foreign covers, translation service, color slide programs and archives covering First Day Covers.

American Ceremony Program Society

John E. Peterson
ACPS Secretary/Treasurer
6987 Coleshill Drive
San Diego, CA 92119-1953
jkpete@pacbell.net
www.webacps.org

The American Ceremony Program Society (ACPS) is a place to learn about First Day and Supplemental (Second Day or later) stamp Ceremonies and Ceremony Programs. The Society publishes a journal, The Ceremonial, which is available online, can be sent to members in a hard copy format at $2.50 per issue. The Society dues are $5 a year.

American Philatelic Society

Robert E. Lamb
Executive Director
P.O. Box 8000
State College, PA
16803-8000
(p) 814/237-3803
(f) 814/237-6128
flsente@stamps.org
http://www.stamps.org

A full complement of services and resources for stamp collectors. Annual membership offers: library services, educational seminars and correspondence courses, expertizing service, estate advisory service, translation service, a stamp theft committee that functions as a clearinghouse for philatelic crime information, on-line intramember sales service and a monthly journal, The American Philatelist, sent to all members. Membership 53,000 worldwide.

American Society for Philatelic Pages and Panels

Gerald Blankenship
P.O. Box 475
Crosby, TX 77532-0475
(p) 281/324-2709
gblank1941@aol.com

Focuses on souvenir pages and commemorative panels. Free ads, member auction, publishes a quarterly journal sent to all members with reports on new issues, varieties, errors, oddities and discoveries.

American Stamp Dealers Association

Joseph B. Savarese
3 School St., Suite 205
Glen Cove, NY 11542-2548
(p) 516/759-7000
(f) 516/759-7014
asdashows@erols.com
http://www.asdaonline.com

Association of dealers engaged in every facet of philately, with 6 regional chapters nationwide. Sponsors national and local shows. Will send you a complete listing of dealers in your area or collecting specialty. A #10 SASE must accompany your request.

American Topical Association

Paul E. Tyler
Executive Director
P.O. Box 50820
Albuquerque, NM 87181-0820
(p) 505/323-8595
(f) 505/323-8795
ATAStamps@juno.com
http://home.prcn.org/~pauld/ata

A service organization concentrating on the specialty of topical stamp collecting. Offers handbooks and checklists on specific topics; exhibition awards; Topical Time, a bimonthly publication dealing with topical interest areas; a slide loan service, and information, translation and sales services.

Ebony Society of Philatelic Events and Reflections

Sanford L. Byrd
P.O. Box 8888
Corpus Christi, TX
78468-8888
(f) 361/980-8675
esper@stx.rr.com
http://slsabyrd.com

Junior Philatelists of America

Jennifer Arnold
Executive Secretary
P.O. Box 2625
Albany, OR 97321-0643
Exec.sec@jpastamps.org
http://www.jpastamps.org/

Member services include: pen pals, philatelic library, stamp identification, contests, study groups, and other services to young collectors. Members receive a bimonthly newsletter, The Philatelic Observer. Adult supporting membership and gift memberships are available. The JPA also publishes various brochures on stamp collecting.

Mailer's Postmark Permit Club
Charles F. Myers
Central Office
P.O. Box 003
Portland, TN 37148-0003
(p) 615/325-9748
(f) 615/451-7930
cfmyers@mindspring.com

Publishes bimonthly newsletter, Permit Patter, which covers all aspects of mailer's precancel postmarks, as well as a catalog and two checklists. Also available, a 10-page step by step brochure "How to obtain a Mailer's Postmark Permit...a basic guide."

Plate Number Coil Collectors Club
Don Eastman
Secretary PNC^3
24 Bemis Street
Berlin, NH 03570-3304
www.pnc3.org

The Plate Number Coil Collectors Club (PNC^3) is an organization that studies the plate numbers and plate varieties of United States coil stamps issued since 1981. The PNC^3 publishes a monthly newsletter, Coil Line. The website discusses plate number coils and PNC^3 at length.

Postal History Society
Kalman V. Illyefalvi
8207 Daren Court
Pikesville, MD 21208-2211
(p) 410/653-0665
kalphyl@juno.com

Devoted to the study of various aspects of the development of the mails and local, national and international postal systems; UPU treaties; and means of transporting mail.

The Souvenir Card Collectors Society, Inc.
Dana M. Marr
P.O. Box 4155
Tulsa, OK 74159-0155
(p) 918/664-6724
DMARR5569@aol.com

Provides member auctions, a quarterly journal and access to limited-edition souvenir cards.

United Postal Stationery Society
UPSS Central Office
Cora Collins
Executive Director
P.O. Box 1792
Norfolk, VA 23501-1792
poststat@juno.com
www.upss.org

Universal Ship Cancellation Society
David Kent
P.O. Box 127
New Britain, CT 06050-0127
(p) 860/667-1400
kentdave@aol.com
http://www.uscs.org

Specializes in naval ship postmarks.

United States Postal Service Stamp Services
475 L'Enfant Plaza SW
Washington, D.C.
20260-2437

United States Stamp Society
Executive Secretary
P.O. Box 6634
Katy, TX 77491-6634
http://www.usstamps.org

An association of collectors to promote the study of all postage and revenue stamps and stamped paper of the United States and U.S.-administered areas produced by the Bureau of Engraving and Printing and other contract printers.

Expertisers

American Philatelic Expertizing Service (APEX)
Mercer Bristow
Director of Expertizing
P.O. Box 8000
State College, PA
16803-8000
Ambristo@stamps.org

Krystal Harter
Expertizing Coordinator
P.O. Box 8000
State College, PA
16803-8000
Krharter@stamps.org
(p) 814/237-3803
(f) 814/237-6128
http://www.stamps.org

A joint project of the American Philatelic Society and the American Stamp Dealers' Association, APEX utilizes the high-tech equipment and outstanding reference collection at APS head-quarters in conjunction with the nation's best philatelic scholars to pass judgement on the identification, authenticity and condition of stamps from all countries. APEX certificates are accepted by all legitimate auction firms, dealers and collectors.

Philatelic Foundation
Attention: Chairman
501 Fifth Ave. Rm. 1901
New York, NY 10017-6102
(p) 212/867-3699

A nonprofit organization known for its excellent expertization service. The Foundation's broad resources, including extensive reference collections, 5,000-volume library and Expert Committee, provide collectors with comprehensive consumer protection. Slide and cassette programs are available on such subjects as the Pony Express, classic U.S. stamps, Confederate Postal History and collecting basics for beginners. Book series include expertizing case histories in Opinions, Foundation seminar subjects in "textbooks" and specialized U.S. subjects in monographs.

Professional Stamp Experts, Inc.
P.O. Box 6170
Newport Beach, CA 92658
(p) 877/782-6788
http://www.collectors.com/pse

A for-profit organization comprised of more than 70 of the leading philatelic experts in the U.S. in the identification and authentication of all U.S. and British Commonwealth postage stamps, covers, revenues, etc. The PSE's expansive resources include a 2,500-volume reference library plus postage stamp reference collection for direct comparison, examination and authentication. PSE issues a Certificate of Authenticity on each submission it receives. These expert opinions are accepted by all legitimate auction firms, dealers and collectors. All submissions are fully insured once reviewed by PSE until items are returned to the original submitter.

Periodicals

The following publications will send you a free copy of their magazine or newspaper upon request.

Global Stamp News
P.O. Box 97
Sidney, OH 45365-0097
(p) 937/492-3183
global@bright.net

America's largest-circulation monthly stamp magazine featuring U.S. and foreign issues.

Linn's Stamp News
P.O. Box 29
Sidney, OH 45365-0097
(p) 937/498-7273
(f) 937/498-0876
(f) 937/498-0814 (outside US)
linns@linns.com
www.linns.com

Linn's Stamps News, the world's largest weekly stamp newspaper, contains breaking news stories of major importance to stamp collectors, features on a variety of stamp-collecting topics, the monthly U.S. Stamp Market Index, Stamp Market Tips and much more. A sample copy of the weekly newspaper is available upon request.

Mekeel's & Stamps Magazine-fa
John Dunn
34 Franklin St. #200-D
Nashua, NH 03064
stampnews@aol.com
http://www.stampnews.com

World's oldest stamp weekly, for intermediate and advanced collectors.

Stamp Collector
Wayne Youngblood
Publisher, Stamps Dept.
700 E. State St.
Iola, WI 54990-0001
(p) 715/445-2214
youngbloodw@krause.com

For beginning and advanced collectors of all ages.

Stamp Wholesaler
Wayne Youngblood
Publisher, Stamps Dept.
700 E. State St.
Iola, WI 54990-0001
(p) 715/445-2214
youngbloodw@krause.com

For dealers of all levels and those interested in the stamp business. (Published monthly as part of Stamp Collector.)

USA Philatelic
Information Fulfillment
Dept. 6270
U.S. Postal Service
P.O. Box 219014
Kansas City, MO 64121-9014
(p) 1 800 STAMP-24

U.S. Stamp News-fb
John Dunn
34 Franklin St. #200-D
Nashua, NH 03064
stampnews@aol.com
http://www.stampnews.com

Monthly magazine for all collectors of U.S. stamps, covers and postal history.

Museums, Libraries and Displays

Please contact the institutions before visiting to confirm hours and any entry fees.

American Philatelic Research Library
Robert E. Lamb
P.O. Box 8000
State College, PA 16803-8000
(p) 814/237-3803
(f) 814/237-6128
gini@stamps.org
http://www.stamps.org

Founded in 1968; now the largest philatelic library in the U.S. Currently receives more than 400 worldwide periodical titles and houses extensive collections of bound journals, books, auction catalogs and dealer pricelists. Directly serves members of the APS and APRL (library members also receive the quarterly Philatelic Literature Review*). The public may purchase photocopies directly or borrow materials through the national interlibrary loan system.*

The Collectors Club
Irene Bromberg
Executive Secretary
22 E. 35th Street
New York, NY
10016-3806
(p) 212/683-0559
(f) 212/481-1269
collectorsclub@nac.net
http://www.collectorsclub.org

Bimonthly journal, publication of various reference works, one of the most extensive reference libraries in the world, reading and study rooms. Regular meetings on the first and third Wednesdays of each month at 6:30 p.m., except July and August.

Friends of the Western Philatelic Library
P.O. Box 2219
Sunnyvale, CA 94087-2219
(p) 408/733-0336
http://www.fwpl.org/

National Postal Museum
Smithsonian Institution
Washington, D.C. 20560-0570
(p) 202/633-9360
http://www.si.edu/postal/
Hours:
7 days 10:00 a.m.-5:30 p.m., except 12/25

Located in the Old City Post Office building at 2 Massachusetts Avenue, NE, near Union Station, the National Postal Museum houses more than 16 million items for exhibition and study purposes. Collections research may be conducted separately or jointly with library materials. Call the museum and its library (202/633-9370) separately to schedule an appointment.

The Postal History Foundation
Betsy Towle
P.O. Box 40725
Tucson, AZ 85717-0725
(p) 520/623-6652
(f) 520/623-6652
phf3@mindspring.com
Hours:
M-F 8:00 a.m.-3:00 p.m.

Regular services include a library, USPS contract post office, philatelic sales, archives, artifacts and collections and a Youth Department.

San Diego County Philatelic Library

Al Kish, Library Manager
7403C Princess View Drive
San Diego, CA 92120
(p) 619/229-8813
Hours:
M & T & Th 6:30 p.m.-
9:30 p.m. and Sat noon-3 p.m.
Other hours available by
appointment. Pleaes call for
confirmation of hours.

Spellman Museum of Stamps and Postal History

Executive Director
235 Wellesley Street
Weston, MA 02193-1538
(p) 781/768-8367
(f) 781/768-7332
info@spellman.org
www.spellman.org
Hours: Th-Sun 12 noon-
5 p.m. (closed holidays)
Adults: $5; students/seniors:
$3; members, visitors to the
Museum Store and Post
office, and children 16 and
under: free.

*Located on the campus of
Regis College. America's
first fully accredited
museum devoted to the
display, collection and
preservation of stamps and
postal history. The three
galleries' exhibitions feature
international rarities, United
States, and worldwide collections. Philatelic research
library and family activity
center open with admission.
Museum Store and Post
Office has collectibles, collecting supplies, and U.S.
postage stamps.*

Western Philatelic Library

P.O. Box 2219
Sunnyvale, CA 94087-2219
(p) 408/733-0336
stulev@ix.netcom.com
http://www.pbbooks.com/w
pl.htm
http://www.fwpl.org

Wineburgh Philatelic Research Library

Erik D. Carlson, Ph.D.
McDermott Library
University of Texas at
Dallas
P.O. Box 830643
Mailstation: MC33
Richardson, TX 75083-0643
(p) 972/883-2570
http://www.utdallas.edu/libr
ary/special/wprl.html
Hours:
M-T 9:00 a.m.–6:00 p.m.;
F 9:00 a.m.-5:00 p.m.

Exchange Service

Stamp Master

Charles Bergeron
P.O. Box 17
Putnam Hall, FL 32185-0017
Cbergero@bellsouth.net

*An "electronic connection"
for philatelists via modem
and computer to
display/review members'
stamp inventories for trading purposes, etc.*

Literature

ArtCraft First Day Cover Price List

Washington Press
2 Vreeland Road
Florham Park, NJ 07932-1501
(p) 973/966-0001
info@washpress.com
http://www.washpress.com

*Includes Presidential
Inaugural covers.*

Basic Philately

Wayne Youngblood
Publisher, Stamps Dept.
700 E. State St.
Iola, WI 54990-0001
(p) 715/445-2214
youngbloodw@krause.com

Brookman's 1st Edition Black Heritage First Day Cachet Cover Catalog

Arlene Dunn
Brookman/Barrett &
Worthen
10 Chestnut Drive
Bedford, NH 03110-5566
(p) 603/472-5575
(f) 603/472-8795

*Illustrated 176-page perfect
bound book.*

Brookman's 2nd Edition Price Guide for Disney Stamps

Arlene Dunn
Brookman/Barrett &
Worthen
10 Chestnut Drive
Bedford, NH 03110-5566
(p) 603/472-5575
(f) 603/472-8795

*Illustrated 256-page perfect
bound book.*

2002 Brookman Price Guide of U.S., U.N. and Canada Stamps and Postal Collectibles

Arlene Dunn
Brookman/Barrett &
Worthen
10 Chestnut Drive
Bedford, NH 03110-5566
(p) 603/472-5575
(f) 603/472-8795

Illustrated 384-page catalog.

Commemorative Cancellation Catalog

Paul Brenner
General Image, Inc.
P.O. Box 335
Maplewood, NJ 07040-0335
Postmark1@earthlink.net
http://home.earthlink.net/
~postmark1
(How-to-do-it is excellent
for beginners)

*Catalog covering all picto-
rial cancellations used in the
U.S. during 1988-1989 is
available. Please send self-
addressed, stamped envelope
for prices and description.
Weekly newsletter is available which also provides
descriptive information on
U.S. pictorial postmarks. A
sample newsletter is available at no charge if you send
a SASE and specifically ask
for a copy.*

Compilation of U.S. Souvenir Cards

Dana M. Marr
P.O. Box 4155
Tulsa, OK 74159-4155
(p) 918/664-6724
DMARR5569@aol.com

Durland Plate Number Catalog

United States Stamp Society
Executive Secretary
P.O. Box 6334
Katy, TX 77491-6634
http://www.stamps.org

Fleetwood's Standard First Day Cover Catalog

Fleetwood
Unicover Corporation
1 Unicover Center
Cheyenne, WY 82008-0001
(p) 307/771-3000
(p) 800/443-4225
http://www.unicover.com

The Hammarskjold Invert
Washington Press
2 Vreeland Road
Florham Park, NJ 07932-1501
(p) 973/966-0001
info@washpress.com
http://www.washpress.com

Tells the story of the Dag Hammarskjold error/invert. FREE for #10 SASE.

Linn's U.S. Stamp Yearbook
P.O. Box 29
Sidney, OH 45365-0097
(p) 937/498-0802
(f) 800/572-6885 (US only)
(f) 937/498-0807 (outside US)
linns@linns.com
www.linns.com

A series of books providing facts and annual figures on every collectible variety of U.S. stamps, postal stationery and souvenir cards issued since 1983.

Linn's World Stamp Almanac
P.O. Box 29
Sidney, OH 45365-0097
(p) 937/498-0802
(f) 800/572-6885 (US only)
(f) 937/498-0807 (outside US)
linns@linns.com
www.linns.com

This book makes accessible to collectors, researchers and dealers a vast storehouse of facts and figures that has never before been available in one place. It is the most useful single reference source a collector can own.

19th Century Envelopes Catalog
UPSS Central Office
Cora Collins
Executive Director
P.O. Box 1792
Norfolk, VA 23501-1792
poststat@juno.com
www.upss.org

Precancel Stamp Society Catalogs
Dick Laetsch
108 Ashwamp Road
Scarborough, ME 04070
(p) 207/883-2505
precancel@aol.com
www.precanceledstamps.com

Scott Specialized Catalogue of U.S. Stamps and Covers
P.O. Box 828
Sidney, OH 45365-0828
(p) 937/498-0802
(p) 800/572-6885
(f) 937/498-0807
ssm@scottonline.com
http://www.scottonline.com

Scott Stamp Monthly
P.O. Box 828
Sidney, OH 45365-0828
(p) 937/498-0802
(p) 800/572-6885
(f) 937/498-0807
ssm@scottonline.com
http://www.scottonline.com

Scott Standard Postage Stamp Catalogue
P.O. Box 828
Sidney, OH 45365-0828
(p) 937/498-0802
(p) 800/572-6885
(f) 973/498-0807
ssm@scottonline.com
http://www.scottonline.com

Stamp Collecting Made Easy
P.O. Box 29
Sidney, OH 45365-0097
(p) 937/498-0802
(p) 800/572-6885 (US only)
(f) 937/498-0807 (outside US)

An illustrated, easy-to-read, 96-page booklet for beginning collectors.

The 24¢ 1918 Air Mail Invert
Washington Press
2 Vreeland Road
Florham Park, NJ 07932-1501
(p) 973/966-0001
info@washpress.com
http://www.washpress.com

Tells all there is to know about this famous stamp. FREE for #10 SASE.

20th Century Envelopes Catalog
UPSS Central Office
Cora Collins
Executive Director
P.O. Box 1792
Norfolk, VA 23501-1792
poststat@juno.com
www.upss.org

U.S. Postal Card Catalog
UPSS Central Office
Cora Collins
Executive Director
P.O. Box 1792
Norfolk, VA 23501-1792
poststat@juno.com
www.upss.org

The U.S. Transportation Coils
Washington Press
2 Vreeland Road
Florham Park, NJ 07932-1501
(p) 973/966-0001
info@washpress.com
http://www.washpress.com

FREE for #10 SASE.

International Agents

Japan Philatelic Agency
PO Box 96 Toshima
Tokyo 170-8668
JAPAN

Max Stern
234 Flinders Street
Box 997 H
GPO Melbourne 3001
AUSTRALIA

Harry Allen
PO Box 5
Watford Herts WD2 5SW
UNITED KINGDOM

Nordfrim
DK 5450 Otterup
DENMARK

DeRosa S.P.A.
Via Privata Maria Teresa 11
I-20123 Milan
ITALY

Hermann Sieger GMBH
Venusberg 32-34
D73545 Lorch Wurttemberg
GERMANY

Alberto Bolaffi
Via Cavour 17
10123 Torino
ITALY

International House of Stamps
98/2 Soi Tonson
Langsuan Rd
Lumpinee, Pathumwan
Bangkok 10330
THAILAND

Philatelic Centers

In addition to the more than 20,000 postal facilities authorized to sell philatelic products, the Postal Service also maintains Philatelic Centers located in major population centers. These Philatelic Centers have been established to serve stamp collectors and make it convenient for them to acquire an extensive range of current postage stamps, postal stationery and philatelic products issued by the Postal Service.

Centers are located at Main Post Offices with a ZIP + 4 of 9998 unless otherwise indicated. For questions about a Philatelic Center near you, call 800-275-8777.

Please note that Philatelic Centers in this listing include offices that may have only one philatelic window or limited hours dedicated to philatelic services.

Alabama
351 24th St. N
Birmingham, AL
35203-9816

Decatur Mowu
400 Well Street NE
Decatur, AL
35602-9998

379 N. Oates St.
Dothan, AL
36302-9998

Downtown Station
615 Clinton Ave. W
Huntsville, AL
35801-

250 St. Joseph St.
Mobile, AL
36601-9998

6701 Winton Blount Blvd.
Montgomery, AL
36124-9998

Alaska
315 Barnette St.
Fairbanks, AK
99701-9998

320 W. 5th Ave.
Suite 348
Anchorage, AK
99501-

Arizona
2400 N. Postal Blvd.
Flagstaff, AZ
86004-9998

Osborne Station
3905 N. Seventh Ave.
Phoenix, AZ
85013-9998

General Mail Facility
4949 E. Van Buren St.
Phoenix, AZ
85026-9998

1501 S. Cherrybell St.
Tucson, AZ
85726-9998

Arkansas
600 E. Capitol Ave.
Little Rock, AR
72202-

California
1180 W. Ball Rd.
Anaheim, CA
92812-2730

3400 Pegasus Dr.
Bakersfield, CA
93380-

18122 Carmenita Rd.
Cerritos, CA
90703-6330

2121 Meridian Park Blvd.
Concord, CA
94520-5708

2020 Fifth St.
Davis, CA
95616-9998

8111 Firestone Blvd.
Downey, CA
90241-9998

401 W. Lexington Ave.
El Cajon, CA
92020-4415

Cutten Station
3901 Walnut Dr.
Eureka, CA
95501-9991

1900 E St.
Fresno, CA
93706-

313 E. Broadway
Glendale, CA
91205-1010

300 N. Long Beach Blvd.
Long Beach, CA
90802-2427

900 N. Alameda St.
Los Angeles, CA
90012-2904

Village Station
11000 W. Wilshire Blvd.
Los Angeles, CA
90024-9998

Airport Station
9029 Airport Blvd.
Los Angeles, CA
90045-9998

715 Kearney Ave.
Modesto, CA
95350-9998

Napa Station
1625 Trancas St.
Napa, CA
94558-

Civic Center Annex
201 13th St.
Oakland, CA
94612-3921

281 E. Colorado Blvd.
Pasadena, CA
91101-1903

4300 Black Ave.
Pleasanton, CA
94566-6103

2323 Churn Creek Rd.
Redding, CA
96049-9998

1201 N. Catalina
Redondo Beach, CA
90277-9998

1900 W Redleandes
San Bernadino, CA
92403-

2535 Midway Dr.
San Diego, CA
92111-3223

180 Steuart St.
San Francisco, CA
94105-1239

1750 Meridian Ave.
San Jose, CA
95125-

40 Bellum Blvd.
San Rafael, CA
94901-

12935 Alcosta Blvd.
San Ramon, CA
94583-

Spurgeon Station
615 Bush St.
Santa Ana, CA
92701-4103

836 Anacapa St.
Santa Barbara, CA
93102-

201 E. Battles Rd.
Santa Maria, CA
93454-7203

730 Second St.
Santa Rosa, CA
95402-

15701 Sherman Way
Van Nuys, CA
91409-

396 S. California Ave.
West Covina, CA
91793-9000

Colorado

16890 E. Alameda Pkwy.
Aurora, CO
80017-

1905 15th St.
Boulder, CO
80302-

201 E. Pikes Peak Ave.
Rm. 205
Colorado Springs, CO
80903-1933

951 20th St.
Denver, CO
80202-2500

7500 E. 53rd Place
Denver, CO
80217-

222 W. Eighth St.
Durango, CO
81301-

301 E. Broadwalk Dr.
Fort Collins, CO
80528-

241 N. Fourth St.
Grand Junction, CO
81501-

9609 S. University Blvd.
Littleton, CO
80124-1927

201 Coffman St.
Longmont, CO
80501-

Connecticut

141 Weston St.
Hartford, CT
06101-9000

11 Silver St.
Middletown, CT
06457-

50 Brewery St.
New Haven, CT
06511-

26 Catoonah St.
Ridgefield, CT
06877-

135 Grand St.
Waterbury, CT
06701-9991

Delaware

55 The Plaza
Dover, DE
19901-9998

Wilmington P&DC
147 Quigley Blvd.
New Castle, DE
19720-9696

Rodney Square Station
1101 N. King St.
Wilmington, DE
19801-

District of Columbia

Pavillion Postique
1100 Penn. Ave. NW
Washington, DC
20004-2501

14th & Constitution
Ave. NW
Washington, DC 20560-

Postal Square
2 Mass. Ave. NE
Washington, DC
20002-9997

Florida

321 Montgomery Rd.
Altamonte Springs, FL
32714-9998

Bradenton MOWU
824 Manatee Ave.
W. Bradenton, FL
34205-

Brooksville MOWU
19101 Cortez Blvd.
Brooksville, FL
34601-

336 E. New York Ave.
Deland, FL
32724-9998

1900 W. Oakland Pk.
Blvd.
Fort Lauderdale, FL
33310-0116

Renaissance Contract
Postal Unit
8695 College Pkwy
Ste. 131
Fort Myers, FL
33919-4892

5000 W. Midway Rd.
Fort Pierce, FL 34981-

1801 Polk St.
Hollywood, FL
33022-0079

210 N. Missouri Ave.
Lakeland, FL
33815-9998

Leesburg Station
1201 S. 14th St.
Leesburg, FL
34748-9998

Longwood Wekiva
Station
920 Wekiva Springs Rd.
Longwood, FL
32779-9998

2200 NW 72nd Ave.
Miami, FL
33152-9617

1200 Goodlette Rd. N
Naples, FL
34102-5254

1335 Kingsley Ave.
Orange Park, FL
32073-4507

46 E. Robinson St.
Orlando, FL
32801-9998

518 N. Ridgewood Dr.
Sebring, FL
33870-9998

St. Petersburg MOWU
3135 First Ave. N
St. Petersburg, FL
33730-9998

Tampa Airport MOWU
Postal Store
5201 W. Spruce St.
Tampa, FL
33630-

1538 Harrison Ave.
Titusville, FL
32780-9998

3200 Summit Blvd.
W. Palm Beach, FL
33406-

Georgia

1072 W. Peachtree St.
NW
Atlanta, GA
30309-

41 Marietta St.
Atlanta, GA
30301-9998

Perimeter Branch
4707 Ashford
Dunwoody Rd.
Atlanta, GA
31146-

3470 McClure Bridge
Rd.
Duluth, GA
30136-

364 Green St. NE
Gainesville, GA
30501-

451 College St.
Macon, GA
31213-9812

257 Lawrence St. NE
Marietta, GA
30060-

2 N. Farm St., Rm 14
Savannah, GA
31402-

Hawaii

335 Merchant St.
Honolulu, HI
96813-

Idaho

770 S. 13th St.
Boise, ID
83708-

220 E. Fifth St.
Moscow, ID
83843-2964

730 E. Clark St.
Pocatello, ID
83201-

Illinois

909 W. Euclid Ave.
Arlington Heights, IL
60004-

525 N. Broadway
Aurora, IL
60507-9998

Moraine Valley Station
7401 W. 100th Place
Bridgeview, IL
60455-9998

1301 E. Main St.
Carbondale, IL
62901-9998

Loop Station
211 S. Clark St.
Chicago, IL
60604-9998

433 W. Harrison St. 2nd
Fl.
Chicago, IL
60607-9208

1000 E. Oakton St.
Des Plaines, IL
60018-

1101 Davis St.
Evanston, IL
60201-

2350 Madison Ave.
Granite City, IL
62040-

2000 McDonough St.
Joliet, IL
60436-9998

1750 W. Ogden Ave.
Naperville, IL
60540-9998

123 Indianwood Blvd.
Park Forest, IL
60466-9998

N. University Station
6310 N. University St.
Peoria, IL
61614-3454

401 William St.
River Forest, IL
60305-1900

5225 Harrison Ave.
Rockford, IL
61125-

1956 Second Ave.
Rock Island, IL
61201-9700

450 W. Schaumburg Rd.
Schaumburg, IL
60194-

2105 E. Cook St.
Springfield, IL
62703-

326 N. Genesee St.
Waukegan, IL
60085-

Indiana

North Park Branch
4490 First Ave.
Evansville, IN
47710-

1501 S. Clinton St.
Fort Wayne, IN
46802-

3450 State Rd. 26 E
Lafayette, IN
47901-9998

424 S. Michigan St.
South Bend, IN
46624-9998

Iowa

615 Sixth Ave. SE
Cedar Rapids, IA
52401-

1165 Second Ave.
Des Moines, IA
50318-9707

214 Jackson St.
Sioux City, IA
51101-9998

Kansas

6029 Broadmoor St.
Shawnee Mission, KS
66202-9998

424 S. Kansas Ave.
Topeka, KS
66603-

330 W. Second St. N
Wichita, KS
67202-

Kentucky

1088 Nandino Blvd.
Lexington, KY
40511-

St. Mathews Station
4600 Shelbyville Rd.
Louisville, KY
40207-

Louisiana

3401 Government St.
Alexandria, LA
71302-9996

750 Florida St.
Baton Rouge, LA
70821-9998

1105 Moss St.
Lafayette, LA
70501-

172 East Telephone Rd.
Lake Charles, LA
70611-9998

921 Moss St.
Lake Charles, LA
70601-9998

3301 17th St.
Metairie, LA
70002-9998

1701 Shannon St.
Monroe, LA
71201-

8940 Mansfield Rd.
Shreveport, LA
71108-9998

701 Loyola Ave.
New Orleans, LA
70113-

1925 E. 70 St.
Shreveport, LA
71105-9998

Maine

40 Western Ave.
Augusta, ME
04330-

125 Forest Ave.
Portland, ME
04101-

Maryland

1 Church Cir.
Annapolis, MD
21401-

900 E. Fayette St.
Baltimore, MD
21233-9998

215 Park St.
Cumberland, MD
21502-9998

201 E. Patrick St.
Fredrick, MD
21701-9998

6411 Baltimore Ave.
Riverdale, MD
20737-

816 E Salisbury Pky.
Salisbury, MD
21801-9998

Massachusetts

McCormack Office
90 Devonshire St.
Boston, MA
02109-9998

120 Commercial St.
Brockton, MA
02402-9997

5 Bedford St.
Burlington, MA
01803-9996

2 Government Center
Fall River, MA
02722-

881 Main St.
Fitchburg, MA
01420-

431 Common St.
Lawrence, MA
01842-9998

155 Father Morissette
Blvd.
Lowell, MA
01854-

695 Pleasant St.
New Bedford, MA
02740-

212 Fenn St.
Pittsfield, MA
01201-9998

2 Margin St.
Salem, MA
01270-

1883 Main St.
Springfield, MA
01101-9998

178 Ave. A
Turner Falls, MA
01376-

4 E. Central St.
Worcester, MA
01613-9998

Michigan

2075 W. Stadium Blvd.
Ann Arbor, MI
48106-

90 S. McCamly St.
Battle Creek, MI
49016-

26200 Ford Rd.
Dearborn Hgts., MI
48127-

1401 W. Fort St.
Detroit, MI
48233-

250 E. Boulevard Dr.
Flint, MI
48502-9998

225 Michigan NW
Grand Rapids, MI
49599-9818

113 W. Michigan Ave.
Jackson, MI
49201-

1121 Miller Rd.
Kalamazoo, MI
49001-9995

General Mail Facility
4800 Collins Rd.
Lansing, MI
48924-

2900 Rodd St.
Midland, MI
48640-

735 W. Huron St.
Pontiac, MI
48343-9997

1300 Military St.
Port Huron, MI
48061-9998

30550 Gratiot St.
Roseville, MI
48066-9998

200 W. Second St.
Royal Oak, MI
48068-6800

1233 S. Washington St.
Saginaw, MI
48605-2510

6300 Wayne Rd.
Westland, MI
48185-3169

Minnesota

2800 W. Michigan
Duluth, MN
55806-1742

1445 Valley High Dr.
Rochester, MN
55901-

100 S. First St.
Minneapolis, MN
55401-2037

Mississippi

401 E. South St.
Jackson, MS
39205-5200

Missouri

401 S. Washington St.
Chillicothe, MO
64601-9998

2300 Bernadette Dr.
Columbia, MO
65203-4607

315 W. Pershing Rd.
Kansas City, MO
64108-9998

Northwest Plaza Station
500 Northwest Plaza
St. Ann, MO
63074-2209

201 S. Eighth St.
St. Joseph, MO
64501-9998

Clayton Branch
7750 Maryland Ave.
St. Louis, MO
63105-9998

500 W. Chestnut
Expwy.
Springfield, MO
65801-9998

Montana

841 S. 26th St.
Billings, MT
59101-

215 First Ave. N.
Stop 1
Great Falls, MT
59401-9911

1100 Kent Ave.
Missoula, MT
59801-9998

Nebraska

204 W. South Front St.
Grand Island, NE
68801-9998

700 R St.
Lincoln, NE
68501-9998

300 E. Third St.
North Platte, NE
69101-9998

1124 Pacific St.
Omaha, NE
68108-9630

Nevada

1001 E. Sunset Rd.
Rm 1053
Las Vegas, NV
89199-0001

2000 Vassar St.
Reno, NV
89510-9998

New Hampshire

112 E. Broadway
North Salem, NH
03073-9998

New Jersey

1701 Atlantic Ave.
Atlantic City, NJ
08401-9998

421 Beningo Blvd.
Bellmawr, NJ
08031-2520

25 Veterans Plaza
Bergenfield, NJ
07621-9998

3 Miln St.
Cranford, NJ
07016-9998

21 Kilmore Rd.
Edison, NJ
08899-9706

229 Main St.
Fort Lee, NJ
07024-

65 Hazlet Ave.
Hazlet, NJ
07730-9998

5 Wannamaker
Municipal Complex
Island Heights, NJ
08732-9998

69 Montgomery St.
Jersey City, NJ
07303-9998

160 Maplewood Ave.
Maplewood, NJ
07040-9998

Morristown/Convent
Station
1 Convent Rd.
Morristown, NJ
07961-9999

Nutley Branch
372 Franklin Ave.
Nutley, NJ
07110-9998

171 Broad St.
Red Bank, NJ
07701-9998

680 US Highway Rt. 130
Trenton, NJ
08650-9998

150 Pompton Plains
Cross Rd.
Wayne, NJ
07470-9998

155 Clinton Rd.
W. Caldwell, NJ
07006-

35 N. Broad St.
Woodbury, NJ
08096-9998

411 Greenwood Ave.
Wyckoff, NJ
07481-9998

New Mexico

1135 Broadway SE
Albuquerque, NM
87101-

200 E. Las Cruces Ave.
Las Cruces, NM
88001-9994

415 N. Pennsylvania Ave.
Roswell, NM
88201-9998

New York

50001 Colonie Ctr. Mall
Albany, NY
12205-

Empire State Plaza
Albany, NY
12220-

1620 Grand Ave. N
Baldwin, NY
11510-1807

345 Hicksville Rd.
Bethpage, NY
11714-3401

115 Henry St.
Binghamton, NY
13902-

Bronx General PO
558 Grand Concourse
Bronx, NY
10451-

271 Cadman Plaza
Brooklyn, NY
11201-

1200 William St.
Buffalo, NY
14240-8500

124 Grove Ave.
Cedarhurst, NY
11516-2315

960 460 Baron
DeHirsch Rd.
Crompond, NY
10517-9998

297 Larkfield Rd.
East Northport, NY
11731-2417

Downtown Station
55 Clemens Center Pkwy.
Elmira, NY
14902-3091

41-65 Main St.
Flushing, NY
11355-9998

Roosevelt Field Mall
630 Old Country Rd.
Unit 507
Garden City, NY
11530-3500

16 Hudson Ave.
Glen Falls, NY
12801-4356

77 Old Glenham Rd.
Glenham, NY
12527-9998

185 W. John St.
Hicksville, NY
11801-9998

445 Furrows Rd.
Holbrook, NY
11741-2720

55 Gerard St.
Huntington, NY
11743-6978

888 E. Hericho Turnpike
Huntingon Station, NY
11746-7505

8840 164th St.
Jamaica, NY
11431-9998

300 E. Third St.
Jamestown, NY
14701-5552

65 E. Hoffman Ave.
Lindenhurst, NY
11747-5005

Church St. Station
90 Church St.
New York, NY
10007-9998

441 Eighth Apve.
New York, NY
10001-9291

Rockefeller Center
610 Fifth Ave.
New York, NY
10020-9991

909 Third Ave.
New York, NY
10022-

352 Main St.
Oneonta, NY
13820-

33 S. Main St.
Pearl River, NY
10965-2456

10 Miller St.
Plattsburgh, NY
12901-1820

55 Mansion St.
Poughkeepsie, NY
12601-9998

1335 Jefferson Rd.
Rochester, NY
14692-9205

29 Jay St.
Schenectady, NY
12305-1912

25 Route 111
Smithtown, NY
11787-3712

2845 Richmond Ave.
Staten Island, NY
10314-9997

40 Queens St.
Syosset, NY
11791-3006

5640 E. Taft Rd.
Syracuse, NY
13220-9800

108 Main St.
Warwick, NY
10990-1370

100 Fisher Ave.
White Plains, NY
10602-1907

79-81 Main St.
Yonkers, NY
10701-2740

North Carolina

West Asheville Station
1302 Patton Ave.
Asheville, NC
28806-2604

Starmount Finance Unit
6241 S. Blvd.
Charlotte, NC
28224-9798

Four Seasons Station
301 Four Seasons Town
Ctr.
Greensboro, NC
27427-

311 New Bern Ave.
Raleigh, NC
27601-1442

North Dakota

220 E. Rosser Ave.
Bismarck, ND
58501-9998

675 Second Ave. N
Fargo, ND
58102-4701

Ohio

675 Wolf Ledges Pky.
Akron, OH
44309-

4420 Dressler Rd. NW
Canton, OH
44718-

525 Vine St. (Skywalk)
Cincinnati, OH
45202-3905

2400 Orange Ave.
Cleveland, OH
44101-

6316 Nicholas Dr.
Columbus, OH
43235-9998

1111 E. Fifth St.
Rm. 212A
Dayton, OH
45401-9712

345 E. Bridge St.
Elyria, OH
44035-

200 N. Diamond St.
Mansfield, OH
44901-9998

150 N. Third St.
Steubenville, OH
43952-9998

435 S. St. Clair St.
Toledo, OH
43601-0101

201 High St. NE
Warren OH
44481-9998

99 S. Walnut St.
Youngstown, OH
44501-9713

Oklahoma

115 W. Broadway
Enid, OK
73701-9998

525 E. Okmulgee St.
Muskogee, OK
74401-9998

129 W. Gray
Norman, OK
73069-9998

Postique
320 SW Fifth Ave.
Oklahoma City, OK
73125-9100

333 W. Fourth St.
Tulsa, OK
74103-9612

Oregon

520 Willamette St.
Eugene, OR
97401-2627

715 NW Hoyt St.
Portland, OR
97208-9998

Pennsylvania

442 W. Hamilton St.
Allentown, PA
18101-1611

535 Wood St.
Bethlehem, PA
18616-

115 Boylston St.
Bradford, PA
16701-9998

44 N. Brady St.
Du Bois, PA
15801-9998

1314 Griswold Plaza
Erie, PA
16501-1730

1025 Valley Forge Rd.
Fairview Village, PA
19409-

238 S. Pennsylvania
Greensburg, PA
15601-9998

1425 Crooked Hill Rd.
Harrisburg, PA
17107-9714

111 Franklin St.
Johnstown, PA
15901-

Downtown Station
48-50 W. Chestnut St.
Lancaster, PA
17603-9998

980 Wheeler Way
Langhorne, PA
19047-

17 S. Commerce Way
Lehigh Valley, PA
18002-9999

435 S. Cascade St.
New Castle, PA
16108-9998

501 11th St.
New Kensington, PA
15068-

Grant Street Station
700 Grant St., Ste. B
Pittsburgh, PA
15219-9998

William Penn Annex
Station
900 Market St.
Philadelphia, PA
19107-

Gus Yatron Facility
2100 N. 13th St.
Reading PA
19612-9998

Southeastern Window
Unit
1000 W. Valley Rd.
Southeastern, PA
19399-9998

237 S. Fraser St.
State College, PA
16801-9998

701 Ann St.
Stroudsburg, PA
18360-2016

300 S. Main St.
Wilkes Barre, PA
18701-

Center City Finance
Station
621 Hepburn St.
Williamsport, PA
17703-

200 S. George St.
York, PA
17405-9998

Puerto Rico

585 Ave. Fed.
Roosevelt, Ste. 180
San Juan, PR
00936-9711

Rhode Island

320 Thames St.
Newport, RI
02840-

40 Montgomery St.
Pawtucket, RI
02860-

24 Corliss St.
Providence, RI
02904-9713

South Carolina

7075 Cross County Rd.
Charleston, SC
29423-

1601 Assembly St.
Columbia, SC
29201-9713

600 W. Washington St.
Greenville, SC
29602-9918

South Dakota

320 S. Second Ave.
Sioux Falls, SD
57104-9998

Tennessee

General Mail Facility
6050 Shallowford Rd.
Chattanooga, TN
37421-9998

200 Martin Luther
King Jr. Dr.
Jackson, TN
38301-9998

530 E. Main St.
Johnson City, TN
37601-9998

General Mail Facility
1237 E. Weisgarber Rd.
Knoxville, TN
37950-9998

Colonial Station
4695 Southern Ave.
Memphis, TN
38124-4809

Crosstown Station
1520 Union Ave.
Memphis, TN
38104-9997

Broadway Station
901 Broadway
Nashville, TN
37203-9998

Texas

341 Pine St.
Abilene, TX
79604-9999

2301 S. Ross
Amarillo, TX
79120-9604

300 E. South St.
Arlington, TX
76004-9998

510 Guadolupe St.
Austin, TX
78701-

5815 Walden
Beaumont, TX
77707-9998

2121 E. Wm. J. Bryan Pky.
Bryan, TX
77801-

2130 Harvey Mitchell
Pky S.
College State, TX
77840-9998

809 Nueces Bay Blvd.
Corpus Christi, TX
78469-

400 N. Ervay St.
Dallas, TX
75201-

Olla Podrida Post Office
12215 Coit Rd.
Dallas, TX
75251-

101 E. McKinney St.
Denton, TX
76201-9998

8401 Boeing Dr.
El Paso, TX
79910-

251 W. Lancaster Ave.
Fort Worth, TX
76102-9998

401 Franklin Ave.
Houston, TX
77201-9901

Copper Mountain
Station
3100 S. W.S. Young Dr.
Killeen, TX
76542-9998

620 E. Pecan
McAllen, TX
78501-9995

100 E. Wall St.
Midland, TX
79701-

433 Belle Grove Dr.
Richardson, TX
75080-9998

1 N. Abe
San Angelo, TX
76902-

Downtown Station
615 E. Houston
San Antonio, TX
78205-

10410 Perrin Beitel Rd.
San Antonio, TX
78284-

1411 Wunsche Loop Dr.
Spring, TX
77373-9998

430 W. State Hwy. 6
Waco, TX
76702-

202 E. Erwin St.
Tyler, TX
75702-

1000 Lamar St.
Wichita Falls, TX
76307-9998

Utah

3680 Pacific Ave.
Ogden, UT
84401-9998

95 W. 1st St.
Prove, UT
84601-9998

1760 W. 2100 S.
Salt Lake City, UT
84199-

Vermont

204 Main St.
Brattleboro, VT
05301-9998

11 Elmwood Ave.
Burlington, VT
05401-9998

195 Sykes Mountain
Ave.
White River Junction, VT
05001-

Virginia

111 Sixth St.
Bristol, VA
24201-9998

1155 Seminole Tr.
Charlottesville, VA
22906-9996

1425 Battlefield Blvd.
N. Chesapeake, VA
23320-9998

700 Main St.
Danville, VA
24542-9998

3300 Odd Fellows Rd.
Lynchburg, VA
24506-9998

Merrifield Branch
8409 Lee Highway
Merrifield, VA
22116-9998

Denigh Station
14104 Warwick Blvd.
Newport News, VA
23608-

600 Church St.
Norfolk, VA
23501-

Thomas Corner
190 Janaf Shopping Ctr.
Norfolk, VA
23502-9998

29 Franklin St.
Petersburg, VA
23804-

933 Broad St.
Portsmouth, VA
23707-

901 First St.
Radford, VA
24141

1801 Brook Rd.
Richmond, VA
23232-9998

419 Rutherford Ave. NE.
Roanoke, VA
24022-9998

501 Viking Dr.
Virginia Beach, VA
23451-

1430 N. Augusta
Staunton, VA
24401-2401

425 N. Boundary St.
Williamsburg, VA
23187-

Washington

11 Third St. NW
Auburn, WA
98002-9998

1171 Bellevue Way NE
Bellevue, WA
98008-9998

315 Prospect St.
Bellingham, WA
98225-9998

3500 W. Court
Pasco, WA
99301-9998

424 E. First St.
Port Angeles, WA
98362-9998

301 Union St.
Seattle, WA
98101-9998

904 N. Riverside Ave.
Spokane, WA
99201-

1102 A St.
Tacoma, WA
98402-9998

205 W. Washington Ave.
Yakima, WA
98903-9998

West Virginia

3010 E. Cumberland Rd.
Bluefield, WV
24701-9998

1057 Charleston Town
Center
Charleston, WV
25357-

200 Cava Dr.
Clarksburg, WV
26301-9998

500 W. Pike St.
Clarksburg, WV
26301-9995

1000 Virginia Ave. W
Huntington, WV
25704-9996

1355 Old Courthouse Sq.
Martinsburg, WV
25401-9998

Wisconsin

126 N. Barstow St.
Eau Claire, WI
54703-3572

425 State St.
La Crosse, WI
54601-3346

3902 Milwaukee St.
Madison, WI
53714-7333

345 W. St. Paul Ave.
Milwaukee, WI
53203-3096

1025 W. 20th Ave.
Oshkosh, WI
54902-9998

235 Forrest St.
Wausau, WI
54403-

Wyoming

2120 Capitol Ave.
Cheyenne, WY
82001-9996

Index

The Numbers listed next to the stamp description are the Scott numbers, and the numbers in the parentheses are the numbers of the pages on which the stamps are listed.

M

S